DINOSAURS

THE MOST COMPLETE, UP-TO-DATE ENCYCLOPEDIA
FOR DINOSAUR LOVERS OF ALL AGES

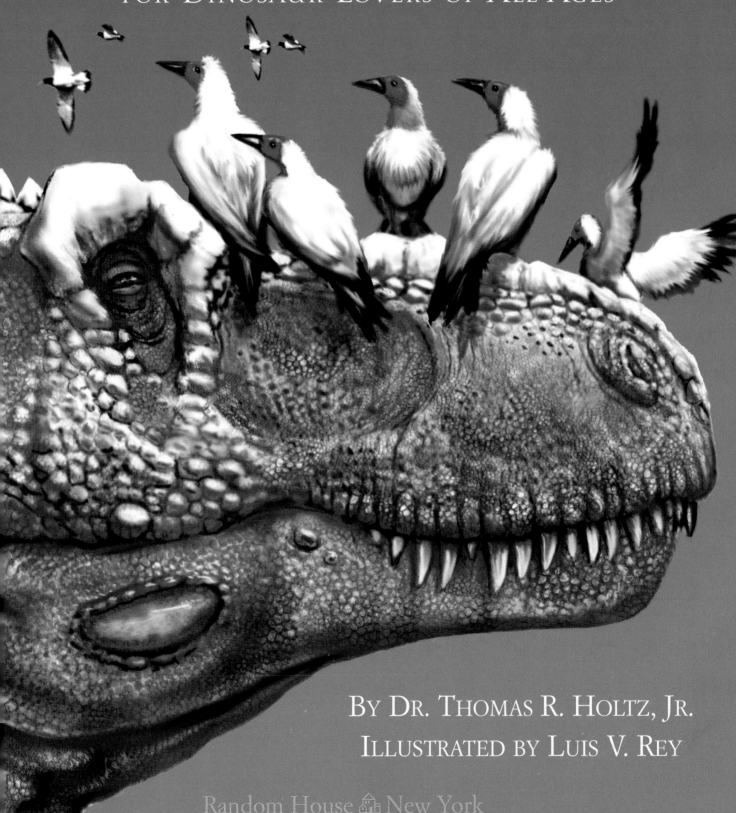

BY DR. THOMAS R. HOLTZ, JR.
ILLUSTRATED BY LUIS V. REY

Random House 🏠 New York

To the late Alan Charig, Ned Colbert, and John Ostrom, and to Bob Bakker,
Phil Currie, Jack Horner, Dave Norman, and Dave Weishampel,
and to all other fellow paleontologists who recognize the importance of reaching young minds.
To all who love dinosaurs (extinct and extant).
To all teachers of Science.
To Alice, for putting up with the fact that paleontologists sometimes
operate on a geologic time scale.
To Mom and Dad, for all your care and support.
And most of all, to Sue, with all my heart.
—T.R.H.

To my nieces and nephews all over the world (and in particular the ones in Metepec, Edo. de México)
and to the memory of Celsus and Charles Darwin.
—L.V.R.

Luis Rey would like to thank Leon Baird, Robert Bakker, L. V. Beethoven,
Eric Buffettaut, Sandra Chapman, Per Christiansen, Scott Hartman, Tom Holtz,
Alice Jonaitis and the rest of the Random House team, Mary Kirkaldy, Charlie and Flo Magovern,
David Martill, Darren Naish, Carmen Naranjo, James P. Page,
Marco Signore, Janet Smith, and Raoul Vaneigem
for invaluable help and general inspiration.

The editor would like to thank Artie Bennett, Godwin Chu, Shane Eichacker,
Melissa Fariello, Jan Gerardi, and Jenny Golub for their unstinting assistance with this book.
Many thanks also to Thom Holmes for editing and organizing the contributors' sidebars.

Text copyright © 2007 by Thomas R. Holtz, Jr.

Illustrations copyright © 2007 by Luis V. Rey.

Sidebars copyright © 2007 by their credited authors.

All rights reserved. Published in the United States by Random House Children's Books, a division of Random House, Inc., New York.

Photo credits can be found on page 427.

A portion of the publisher's profits from the sale of this book will go to the Society of Vertebrate Paleontology to support the publication of articles relating to dinosaur science in the *Journal of Vertebrate Paleontology*. Founded in 1940, the Society is the premier professional organization of scientists interested in dinosaurs and other extinct vertebrates (backboned animals). Its objective is to advance the science of vertebrate paleontology and to serve the common interests of all persons concerned with the history, evolution, comparative anatomy, and taxonomy of backboned animals, as well as the field occurrence, collection, and study of fossil vertebrates. The Society is also concerned with the conservation and preservation of fossil sites. For more information, please contact:

The Society of Vertebrate Paleontology
60 Revere Drive, Suite 500
Northbrook, IL 60062
USA

www.vertpaleo.org

www.randomhouse.com/kids

Library of Congress Cataloging-in-Publication Data
Holtz, Thomas R.
Dinosaurs : the most complete, up-to-date encyclopedia for dinosaur lovers of all ages / by Dr. Thomas R. Holtz, Jr. ;
illustrated by Luis V. Rey. — 1st ed.
p. cm.
Includes index.
ISBN: 978-0-375-82419-7 (trade) — ISBN: 978-0-375-92419-4 (lib. bdg.)
1. Dinosaurs—Juvenile literature. I. Rey, Luis V., ill. II. Title.
QE861.5.H645 2007 567.9—dc22 2006102491

Printed in the United States of America 10 9 8 7   First Edition

RANDOM HOUSE and colophon are registered trademarks of Random House, Inc.

CONTENTS

Introduction   **The World of Dinosaurs** 2

Chapter 1   **History of Dinosaur Discoveries** 6
    Frontiers of Dinosaur Science by Dr. Matthew C. Lamanna 12

Chapter 2   **Rocks and Environment** 13

Chapter 3   **Fossils and Fossilization** 18
    Getting the Drop on Dinosaur Dung by Dr. Karen Chin with Thom Holmes . 22

Chapter 4   **Geologic Time: How Old Is That Dinosaur, and How Do We Know?** 23
    How Old Is Old? The Evolution of Life on Earth by Dr. Raymond R. Rogers . 28

Chapter 5   **From the Field to the Museum: Finding Fossils** 29
    Putting Dinosaurs Together by Jason "Chewie" Poole 33

Chapter 6   **Bringing Dinosaurs to Life: The Science of Dinosaur Art** 34

Chapter 7   **Taxonomy: Why Do Dinosaurs Have Such Strange Names?** 41
    Digging Through Dinosaur Names by Ben Creisler 45

Chapter 8   **Evolution: Descent with Modification** 46

Chapter 9   **Cladistics: Figuring Out the Dinosaur Family Tree** 51

Chapter 10   **Evolution of the Vertebrates** 56

Chapter 11   **The Origin of Dinosaurs** 60

Chapter 12   **Saurischians (Lizard-Hipped Dinosaurs)** 68

Chapter 13   **Coelophysoids and Ceratosaurs (Primitive Meat-Eating Dinosaurs)** 76
    Small Theropods, Big Ideas by Dr. Ron Tykoski 86
    Diversity of Ceratosaurians by Dr. Fernando E. Novas 87

Chapter 14   **Spinosauroids (Megalosaurs and the Fin-Backed Fish-Eating Dinosaurs)** 88
    Fish-Eating Giants—the Spinosaurs by Dr. Angela C. Milner 97

Chapter 15   **Carnosaurs (Giant Meat-Eating Dinosaurs)** 98
    Giant Pack-Hunting Dinosaurs by Dr. Philip J. Currie 106
    Allosaurus Eating Habits by Dr. Emily Rayfield 107

Chapter 16   **Primitive Coelurosaurs (The First Fluffy Dinosaurs)** 108

Chapter 17   **Tyrannosauroids (Tyrant Dinosaurs)** 116
    Tyrannosaurus Tantrums—Growing Up with the Tyrant Lizard
        by Dr. Thomas D. Carr 128
    Bad to the Bone—*Tyrannosaurus rex* Bites Again
        by Dr. Gregory M. Erickson 129

Chapter 18   **Ornithomimosaurs and Alvarezsaurs (Ostrich and Thumb-Clawed Dinosaurs)** . 130
    Big Bird Imitators: Ornithomimosaurs by Dr. Yoshitsugu Kobayashi 139

Chapter 19   **Oviraptorosaurs and Therizinosauroids (Egg-Thief and Sloth Dinosaurs)** . . . 140

Chapter 20   **Deinonychosaurs (Raptor Dinosaurs)** 150

Chapter 21   **Avialians (Birds)** 162
    The Earliest Birds by Dr. Luis Chiappe 172
    The Origin of Flight in Birds by Dr. Kevin Padian 173

Chapter 22   **Prosauropods (Primitive Long-Necked Plant-Eating Dinosaurs)** 174

Chapter 23   **Primitive Sauropods (Early Giant Long-Necked Dinosaurs)** 182
    Survival of the Biggest: Adaptations of the Sauropods by Dr. Paul Upchurch . 189

Chapter 24   **Diplodocoids (Whip-Tailed Giant Long-Necked Dinosaurs)** 190
    Sauropod Evolution by Dr. Jeffrey A. Wilson 201

Chapter 25   **Macronarians (Big-Nosed Giant Long-Necked Dinosaurs)** 202

Chapter 26   **Ornithischians (Bird-Hipped Dinosaurs)** 212

Chapter 27   **Primitive Thyreophorans (Early Armored Dinosaurs)** 220

Chapter 28   **Stegosaurs (Plated Dinosaurs)** 226

Chapter 29   **Ankylosaurs (Tank Dinosaurs)** 234

Chapter 30   **Primitive Ornithopods (Primitive Beaked Dinosaurs)** 242

         Tough Little Dinosaurs by Dr. Patricia Vickers-Rich and Dr. Thomas H. Rich . . 249

Chapter 31   **Iguanodontians (Advanced Beaked Dinosaurs)** 250

Chapter 32   **Hadrosauroids (Duckbilled Dinosaurs)** 258

         Hadrosaurs by Dr. Michael K. Brett-Surman 267

Chapter 33   **Pachycephalosaurs (Domeheaded Dinosaurs)** 268

         Bone-Headed Dinosaurs—the Pachycephalosaurs
            by Dr. Ralph E. Chapman 275

Chapter 34   **Primitive Ceratopsians (Parrot and Frilled Dinosaurs)** 276

         Caught in the Act: The Fighting Dinosaurs of Mongolia by Dr. Mark A. Norell . . 283

Chapter 35   **Ceratopsids (Horned Dinosaurs)** 284

         Male and Female Dinosaurs—Can We Tell the Difference?
            by Dr. Scott D. Sampson 291

Chapter 36   **Dinosaur Eggs and Babies** 292

         How Fast Did Dinosaurs Grow? by Dr. John R. "Jack" Horner 300

         Dinosaur Growth: The Case of *Apatosaurus* by Dr. Kristina Curry Rogers . . . 301

Chapter 37   **Dinosaur Behavior: How Did Dinosaurs Act, and How Do We Know?** 302

         Walking and Running Dinosaurs by Dr. Matthew T. Carrano 308

         Keeping Up with *Tyrannosaurus rex*: How Fast Could It Run?
            by Dr. John R. Hutchinson 309

Chapter 38   **Dinosaur Biology: Living, Breathing Dinosaurs** 310

         Dinosaurs from the Inside Out: What the Bones Can Tell Us
            by Dr. Anusuya Chinsamy-Turan 321

         Hot- and Cold-Running Dinosaurs by Dr. Peter Dodson 322

         Dinosaur Paleopathology by Dr. Elizabeth Rega 323

Chapter 39   **Life in the Triassic Period** 324

Chapter 40   **Life in the Jurassic Period** 334

         Jurassic Detective by Dr. Robert T. Bakker 343

Chapter 41   **Life in the Cretaceous Period** 344

         South American Dinosaurs by Dr. Rodolfo Coria 354

         Dinosaurs of Europe by Dr. Darren Naish 355

Chapter 42   **Extinctions: The World of the Dinosaurs Ends** 356

         Will *Jurassic Park* Ever Happen? by Dr. Mary Higby Schweitzer 365

        Dinosaur Genus List 366

        Glossary 415

        Index 421

Welcome to the world! A baby *Triceratops* hatches.

Introduction

THE WORLD OF DINOSAURS

The world of dinosaurs is changing.

How so? you ask. After all, the world of dinosaurs ended 65.5 million years ago! How could something that ended so long ago be changing? What's done is done, right?

Not necessarily.

In truth, the world of dinosaurs itself isn't changing, but our understanding of it is. Facts and discoveries about dinosaurs and their world that we now take for granted would have *astonished* people at the beginning of the twentieth century! In fact, some of these facts were astonishing people just ten or fifteen years ago! For example, we now know that some dinosaurs (including the infamous *Velociraptor*) had long feathers on their arms, legs, and tail. We now know that it took giant dinosaurs like *Apatosaurus* only ten to twenty years to reach their immense adult size. Whole new groups of dinosaurs, like the little alvarezsaurids (who really *do* have hands that are almost "all thumbs") and big rebbachisaurids (long-necked plant-eaters with wide, flat mouths—like living lawn mowers), have

been discovered.

Every year new species of dinosaurs are found. And with each new discovery we ask more questions. How did the dinosaur live? What did it eat? Did anything eat *it*? We also ask questions about dinosaurs we've known for a long time. Was *Tyrannosaurus* a hunter or a scavenger? How big was the biggest dinosaur? Where did dinosaurs come from and what happened to them?

The way we answer these questions is through dinosaur science. Dinosaur science is part of the bigger science of paleontology—the study of extinct animals, plants, and other organisms. Paleontologists work with fossils—the remains of living things or traces of their behavior preserved in rocks. These fossils might be leaves, pollen, or wood from plants, shells from shellfish, or bones, teeth, footprints, or eggs from dinosaurs and other backboned animals.

Fossils are the raw material for paleontology, but they are just the beginning. A fossil sitting in a rock out in the wild or up on display in a museum exhibit isn't Science. It's just a fossil. In order for dinosaur science to begin, someone has to make observations about that fossil. We might study the shape of a fossil bone, comparing it to that of other fossil bones. We might measure the lengths of the bones or parts of the bones. We might look at the fossils with X-rays or CAT scans or slice them up with a saw to see the features inside. We might look at the rocks that the fossils were found in for clues about the environment in which the dinosaur lived and died.

But just making observations isn't doing science. Science is about asking and, hopefully, answering questions. We ask questions about patterns we see in nature. The possible answers based on those observations are called *hypotheses.* For example, we might hypothesize that a particular dinosaur species was a meat-eater. We test that hypothesis by checking it against what we can see. Do the teeth of the dinosaur have sharp edges or are they dull? Do its teeth match those of living animals that eat meat or living animals that eat plants? Are there any remains in the belly of the dinosaur fossil? And if so, are they bits of bone or are they chopped-up plants or are they something else? Do we have dinosaur dung from this species? And if so, is it full of bone chips or plant parts? Even if we don't have enough of a skeleton to answer these questions directly, we can compare the parts we *do* have to the parts of dinosaurs previously discovered.

Dinosaur science is about testing such hypotheses. By making more and more observations of fossils, we can build up a more complete picture of dinosaurs and the world they lived in. We can figure out which dinosaurs lived together and how they interacted. We can trace when new groups of dinosaurs appeared and when old ones died out. We can even figure out how the common ancestor of *all* dinosaurs gave rise—over 235 million years ago—to creatures as different from each other as lump-nosed *Pachyrhinosaurus,* spiky *Tuojiangosaurus,* immense *Argentinosaurus,* slender *Struthiomimus,* and feathered *Archaeopteryx.* We can examine how the world of dinosaurs ended 65.5 million years ago. And we can see that some dinosaurs survived that great disaster because they

are still with us today (although many people don't even know it)! Finding fossils, making observations, and testing hypotheses are all part of what we call research. And it's research that Science is all about.

There are times when scientists can make a reasonably good guess at an answer even when they can't directly make observations. This is called inferring the answer, and the best way to do it is to use reason. For example, we don't find the eyeballs inside dinosaur skulls (because eyeballs decay), but we can infer that dinosaurs had eyeballs because of different types of other evidence. For example, the skulls have an eye socket and other bones that surround the eye in living animals, and they have the holes in the skull that hold the nerves connecting eyeballs to the brain. Also, all the living relatives of dinosaurs have eyeballs, too. Here's another example: most dinosaur skeletons are incomplete. They often are missing a limb or a tail or a skull. We can reasonably infer that all dinosaur species had four limbs and tails because all their relatives also have those features. In fact, were we to claim otherwise, we'd better find some good evidence to support that idea.

There's something else to think about, too. Science can answer many questions, but it can't answer all of them. Sometimes the observations *do* point to just one answer, but sometimes the observations might lead to two or more *different* answers. In those cases, we have to admit that we don't know what the answer really is. We might be able to narrow it down to a couple of possibilities, but not down to one that's definitely true. That's okay. In Science, "I don't know" is sometimes the best answer available.

And sometimes we like to think about things to which there is no definite answer. We know that dinosaur skins were *some* color (they weren't transparent, after all!), but we can't tell from fossils what specific color any particular dinosaur was, and we will almost certainly *never* know. We can only guess what a *Triceratops* smelled like or what the sound of a baby *Massospondylus* was. In these cases, it's fine to *speculate,* as long as we are fair and recognize it is just speculation. It may be

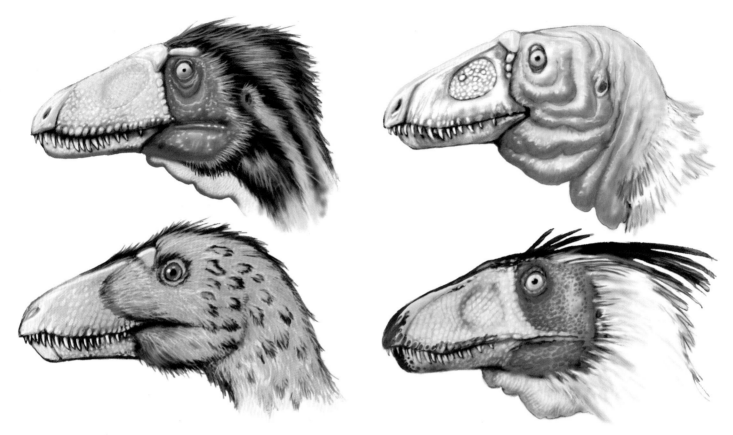

We can use Science to infer that the raptor *Deinonychus* had feathers, but because we don't know their color or pattern, it is up to artists to speculate on what these feathers looked like.

that future discoveries will show that our speculations were wrong. In that case, we have to return to the observations and perhaps give up some of our speculative ideas, no matter how much we like them.

Most people think of Science as just a bunch of facts. It's true that a lot of science books and science classes just present a bunch of facts to memorize. But I want to do more in this book. I want to help you understand how it is that dinosaur scientists—paleontologists—ask and answer questions about dinosaurs and their world.

I am a dinosaur paleontologist. Something that you might want to know is that a lot of dinosaur books aren't written by dinosaur paleontologists but by writers who talk to scientists. My favorite dinosaurs—the ones I've liked since I was a kid and the ones I do most of my research on—are the carnivorous dinosaurs, especially *Tyrannosaurus rex* and its closest relatives. (Actually, the first *T. rex* I ever saw was a plastic toy like the one on the top of page 2.) But even though I like the car-

nivores most of all, I'm interested in all kinds of dinosaurs—and almost anything having to do with the history of life. I'll try my best to explain what we understand about dinosaurs as directly and straightforwardly as I can.

But I don't have all the answers. In fact, nobody does: that's why we keep doing research! If I'm going to give you a good look at dinosaurs

Author Tom Holtz, age nine and already dino-obsessed.

the way scientists understand them, I need help doing that. So I've asked a number of other dinosaur scientists to provide short writings about the research they do. You'll find these writings through-

out the book. Not all paleontologists agree on the answers. After all, there is a lot of information missing when all we have to work with is fossilized

4

bones, teeth, footprints, and other remains. Sometimes the other dinosaur paleontologists and I agree on the answers; sometimes we disagree. In the end, it will be new discoveries and observations that will give us the answers.

Dinosaur bones, teeth, footprints, and other fossils are wonderful things to look at (at least *I* think so), but a lot of us want to see what dinosaurs looked like in the flesh. Dinosaur artist Luis V. Rey, one of the best dinosaur illustrators around, has helped bring them to life in this book. In a later chapter, we'll see how we go from fossils in the ground to paintings of dinosaurs in the flesh.

A final note of introduction: I've tried to make this book as up-to-date as I can while I've been writing it. But new dinosaur discoveries are being

Illustrator Luis Rey, age ten—and *Stegosaurus*—at the 1965 World's Fair in New York.

made all the time. Some of these will just add a species or two to the list of known dinosaurs, but some may be as amazing as finding the first dinosaur fossil with feathers, or the first dinosaur nest, or the first-ever fossilized dinosaur bone! As I said before, the world of dinosaurs is changing all the time.

Maybe, in the future, some of those discoveries will be made by *you*.

Compare the clunky 1960s image of dinosaurs on page 2 with our view of dinosaurs today.

HISTORY OF DINOSAUR DISCOVERIES

There once was a time when people didn't know anything about dinosaurs. In fact, there wasn't even the word "dinosaur" until 1842. But dinosaur fossils were found by people throughout history. In fact, dinosaur fossils were lying around on the surface of the Earth for millions of years before humans evolved. So why did it take until the 1800s for people to recognize dinosaur fossils as something special? And how have our ideas about dinosaurs changed since then?

DRAGON BONES OR FUNNY CRYSTALS?

Before anyone could discover dinosaurs for what they were, people had to realize that fossils—such as bones and footprints—really *were* bones and footprints. Which seems pretty obvious.

But the only reason we realize this is because we understand how rocks form. Before scientists figured it out, no one knew how rocks came to *be* rocks! People thought that rocks had always existed in the same shape and size as when they saw them. They didn't realize that rocks are actually produced by volcanoes or sediment.

So imagine that you are someone who doesn't know how rocks are made and you find something that looks like a bone sticking out of one. How could it have gotten there?

You might think that it was the bone of a creature that lived in the rock. Or that it was a fake bone placed into the rock by an evil spirit. Or maybe that it wasn't a bone at all but just a funny crystal. At one point or another in history, all of

Top: Hunting for dinosaurs in the American West in the nineteenth century.

these ideas were really suggested.

By the 1600s, however, enough scientific evidence had been gathered to convince people that rocks *were* once in a different form than they then appeared. The science of geology had finally been developed,

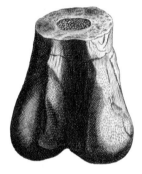

The lower end of a dinosaur thighbone found in England, once thought to be from a giant person.

and people were almost ready to discover dinosaurs for what they were.

MYSTERIOUS CREATURES AND VANISHED WORLDS

But first, two major discoveries had to be made: (1) people had to realize that fossils were the remains of creatures different from those around them, and (2) people had to realize that the reason the fossil specimens were different from modern-day creatures was that they came from animals that were extinct.

In the 1600s and 1700s, seagoing expeditions

from Europe brought back new types of animals and plants from all over the world. Scientists began to study the anatomy of these animals and to compare them to creatures with which they were already familiar. After enough different varieties of living things were studied, these scientists (called comparative anatomists) began to get a better idea of the diversity of creatures in the world.

Comparative anatomists could then look at the fossils already collected. Some were very similar to modern animals, but most were far different. These were truly mysterious animals. But why should they be found inside rocks and not out and about in the wild? Surely if these creatures were still around, someone would have seen them!

In the late 1700s and early 1800s, Baron Georges Cuvier—France's leading comparative anatomist—came up with the answer: extinction. The reason people didn't see these animals was that the animals were no longer alive. It was around this time that geologists realized the ancient age of Earth. Our planet was not just thousands of years old, like most people had thought, but millions (or even billions) of years old! Cuvier theorized that the mysterious creatures had lived on the Earth once but died out long ago. The only surviving remains were their fossils.

With this realization, Cuvier showed the world something important. Rocks and fossils proved that the ancient Earth was different from the modern Earth. There were different animals and plants than there are today, and different ones evolved and became extinct during different parts of Earth's history.

"FEARFULLY GREAT LIZARDS"
The first real dinosaur discoveries were made in the early 1800s in England. The Reverend William Buckland found the bones of a big reptile, which he named *Megalosaurus* (big lizard), in 1824. Buckland made some mistakes about what bones went where, but there were enough for him to tell that this creature was different from any reptile then known. It had sharp teeth like those of a monitor lizard, so it must have eaten meat. Unlike a lizard, however, its thighbone was shaped so that its hind legs were directly underneath its body, like a modern mammal or bird. *Megalosaurus* was the first fossil to be found of a giant land-living reptile of the ancient past.

At around the time Buckland was studying *Megalosaurus,* Dr. Gideon Mantell and his wife, Mary Ann, were making their own discoveries. Workmen had brought various fossil bones and teeth to the attention of the Mantells. Although the fossils were only a small part of the whole animal, they were clearly from an enormous reptile. Like *Megalosaurus,* this animal had hind legs that were directly underneath its body. Unlike *Megalosaurus,* however, its teeth were not sharp at all. In fact, they looked something like those of the plant-eating iguana. Mantell named the fossil reptile *Iguanodon* (iguana tooth) in 1825 and imagined it to look like a giant iguana.

In 1833, Gideon Mantell found the bones of a new fossil reptile, which he named *Hylaeosaurus* (woodland lizard), after the heavily wooded Weald region of England, where it was found. This partial skeleton showed that *Hylaeosaurus* had big spikes sticking out of its body. It was the first armored dinosaur discovered.

Iguanodon versus *Megalosaurus*, as pictured in the mid-nineteenth century.

Finally, in 1842, the word "dinosaur" was coined. The man who gave dinosaurs their name was Sir Richard Owen, the leading paleontologist in Great Britain. Owen had studied *Megalosaurus, Iguanodon,* and *Hylaeosaurus* and noticed several similarities. These three creatures had all lived on land. They had legs directly underneath their bodies and extra bones in the hip. And they were bigger than any living reptile.

A New Year's Eve party held *inside* Benjamin Waterhouse Hawkins's *Iguanodon* sculpture.

Owen decided that this was evidence that *Megalosaurus, Iguanodon,* and *Hylaeosaurus* together formed their own special group of reptiles. He named this group Dinosauria, from the ancient Greek word *deinos* (which means "fearfully great" or "terrible") and *sauros* (which means "lizard" or "reptile").

In hindsight, it turns out that "fearfully great lizards" isn't that good a description. Strictly speaking, dinosaurs aren't lizards, and for the rest of this book I'll generally translate *sauros* as "reptile." Also, as we now know, not all dinosaurs were big. Still, "dinosaur" is a good word.

THE FIRST "JURASSIC PARK"

Owen believed it was important to get the public interested in science, and in the 1850s he found a way to get people interested in dinosaurs. There was going to be a huge world's fair—known as the Great Exposition—in London. It would be a perfect way to show off the newest fossil discoveries.

Instead of putting the fossil bones on display, Owen wanted to bring the dinosaurs to life. So he teamed up with scientific artist Benjamin Waterhouse Hawkins to turn the fossil finds into sculptures of living animals. These sculptures were made life-size and were grouped together on a series of islands according to the time the dinosaurs lived in. In a sense, this was an attempt to create the first "Jurassic Park."

Before one of the two model *Iguanodon* specimens was put on display, Owen and Hawkins held a dinner party for twenty people inside its body! Even though *Iguanodon* was big in real life, the Hawkins model was bigger. (It would be hard to have more than two or three people eat dinner inside a truly life-size *Iguanodon*.) The size error wasn't the only problem with these statues. By today's standards, their anatomy is very inaccurate. But it's not fair to blame Owen and Hawkins. Surely some things we think about dinosaurs today will seem strange and inaccurate to future paleontologists.

Owen's plan was very successful. Millions of people saw the Hawkins statues. The word "dinosaur" became familiar to many people.

* * *

DINOSAURS STAND UP!

While the Great Exposition was going on, new discoveries were being made in America that would change the way people understood dinosaurs. Footprints of two-legged, three-toed creatures had been found in Triassic and Jurassic rocks from New England. When Professor Edward Hitchcock described these in detail in 1836, no one had considered that they might be from dinosaurs. After all, the descriptions of *Megalosaurus, Iguanodon,* and *Hylaeosaurus* showed that these were all heavily built, quadrupedal (four-legged) animals. So Hitchcock assumed that the tracks were those of birds, even if some of them were so big that the birds would have been over fifteen feet tall!

A discovery that helped link the dinosaur bones of England with the New England trackways was made in New Jersey in 1858. In that year, Dr. Joseph Leidy described a new dinosaur, which he named *Hadrosaurus* (heavy reptile). Many of the *Hadrosaurus* bones were very similar to those of *Iguanodon,* including the teeth. And even though it was not complete, this partial skeleton was *more* complete than the *Iguanodon* fossils. It showed that the forelimbs of *Hadrosaurus* were a lot more slender than the hind limbs, so *Hadrosaurus* probably spent a lot of time walking on just two legs. The concept of bipedal (two-legged) dinosaurs had been arrived at. Leidy predicted that when more-complete fossils of *Iguanodon* were found, they would have arms more slender than legs. In the 1870s, this prediction came true with the discovery of complete *Iguanodon* fossils in Belgium.

In 1866, Professor Edward Drinker Cope, a friend and student of Leidy, made a similar discovery. He found a fossilized carnivorous dinosaur, which he named *Laelaps* (after a mythical hunting dog) but which was later renamed *Dryptosaurus* (tearing reptile). *Dryptosaurus* had teeth and jaws that looked a lot like those of *Megalosaurus,* but its arms were so short compared to its slender legs that there was no way it could walk on all fours. So at least some of the meat-eating dinosaurs were bipedal, too.

THE *WILD* WILD WEST

The next big phase in dinosaur discoveries was made in America's Wild West. These days—the 1860s through the 1890s—saw battles between Native Americans and frontier settlers, the spread of the railroad, the growth of new towns and cities,

Edward Drinker Cope.

and the near extinction of the American bison. One of the strangest fights in the Wild West was between two East Coast paleontologists. One was Edward Drinker Cope and the other was Othniel Charles Marsh of Yale University. These two rivals sent teams out west to collect as many dinosaur fossils as they could find and ship them back east to their museums. They thought of this as a kind of race to see who could describe the greatest number of new species.

In a sense, Cope and Marsh were rather silly. They would often describe fossil species before they had extracted the fossils from the rocks. They acted dishonestly, including sending spies into each other's camps to learn what discoveries had

Othniel Charles Marsh and Chief Red Cloud.

been made. They even got various Native American tribes to harass the other's field teams to slow down their digs!

But one good thing about this rivalry was that many spectacular discoveries were made. The first really complete dinosaur fossils (*Allosaurus, Stegosaurus,* and *Triceratops,* to name just a few) were discovered by these teams. Dinosaurs were far more wonderful than people had even imagined! No one would seriously dismiss them as "big lizards" ever again.

These skeletons allowed scientists to better

understand the anatomy and diversity of dinosaurs. They could begin to make more serious speculations about how dinosaurs ate and how they moved. And they could use the newly discovered concept of evolution by natural selection to figure out how different dinosaurs were related.

And around the turn of the century, just after Cope and Marsh had passed away, another big discovery was made. Scientists found out that if you put dinosaur skeletons in a museum and positioned the bones the way they fit together in real life, people would pay to see them. Now there was a reason other than just science to collect dinosaur bones: dinosaur skeletons made great exhibits!

A WORLD OF DINOSAURS

While Marsh and Cope fought over the dinosaurs of the Wild West, discoveries continued to be made in Europe. The first fossil of a Jurassic bird (*Archaeopteryx*) and the first complete small dinosaur skeleton (*Compsognathus*) were found in Germany, and the first complete *Iguanodon* skeletons were unearthed in Belgium.

In fact, after 1900, museums began to send expeditions all over the globe to find dinosaur skeletons for display. Probably the most famous of these expeditions were the Central Asiatic Expeditions of the American Museum of Natural History in New York City. The museum's team went into parts of China and Mongolia for year after year in the 1920s and brought back many important finds.

Roy Chapman Andrews.

These include the first complete dinosaur nests and the first specimen of *Velociraptor*. This expedition faced powerful sandstorms and desert bandits, and its leader (zoologist Roy Chapman Andrews) carried a whip and a revolver like the fictional hero Indiana Jones.

THE DINOSAUR RENAISSANCE

But the Great Depression—and World War II afterward—slowed down dinosaur research. By the middle of the 1900s, there were actually very few dinosaur scientists around the world. Many scientists thought that dinosaurs were just "kid stuff," unworthy of real research. At best, they were useful for getting people into museums to see more "important" things.

Thankfully not everyone felt that way. One who didn't was John Ostrom of Yale University. In the 1960s, he was part of a team that went to Montana and Wyoming to explore rocks that had yielded a few dinosaur bones before. The most important discovery made by that team

John Ostrom.

was the dinosaur Ostrom named *Deinonychus* (terrible claws). This was the first nearly complete dromaeosaurid—aka "raptor"—skeleton ever found. It showed the famous sickle-shaped claw on the foot of *Deinonychus*. Ostrom reasoned that if *Deinonychus* had used this to hunt, it must have been very agile and active—more like a bird or a cat than an alligator. He had previously examined the jaws of duckbilled and horned dinosaurs and had shown that these dinosaurs were able to chew their food very finely, so that they could digest faster. And he had shown that dinosaurs were found in parts of the world that were cold even during the Mesozoic Era.

All this suggested to Ostrom that dinosaurs were not cold-blooded animals. Instead, he reasoned that they were more active, perhaps warm-blooded, animals, like modern mammals and birds.

In fact, Sir Richard Owen had thought the same thing and said as much in his 1842 paper, when he had coined the name Dinosauria. Marsh and Cope and their contemporaries had likewise agreed with this. It was the new generations of paleontologists from the early and middle 1900s—many of whom didn't think dinosaurs were that interesting—who regarded them as slow-moving, cold-blooded animals!

Ostrom compared the skeleton of *Deinonychus* to that of the early bird *Archaeopteryx*. He found that the raptor *Deinonychus* and *Archaeopteryx* had anatomies that were more similar to each other than either *Deinonychus* was to other carnivorous dinosaurs or *Archaeopteryx* was to modern birds. This led him to revive the idea that dinosaurs were the ancestors of birds.

In a sense, dinosaurs became "interesting" again, and a lot of new research got under way. This revival of interest led Ostrom's student Robert Bakker to call the new era the "Dinosaur Renaissance." Most of the information in this book comes from work taking place during this Dinosaur Renaissance.

The last couple of decades have seen a return of large expeditions going to far-off countries. But now, instead of bringing specimens back for display in Europe and America, these expeditions are helping to build up collections and exhibits in the countries where the fossils are discovered. Dinosaurs have now been found on every continent, including Antarctica. But even places that have been explored for over a century (like England and Montana) still yield new species.

DINOSAURS GO DIGITAL

The field of dinosaur science wasn't just limited to finding new species, though. New areas of dinosaur research, or new approaches to old topics, began to be developed. Jack Horner of Montana State University and his students made important advances in the study of dinosaur nesting behavior and the growth of dinosaurs, from hatching to adulthood. Research on the great extinction at the end of the Mesozoic Era increased with the discovery of a giant asteroid

A combination of lasers, CAT scans, and computer graphics allows scientists to peer inside the skulls of dinosaurs, such as this *Majungasaurus*.

impact site from that same time. The new field of cladistics allowed paleontologists to make better estimations of the evolutionary relationships among the different groups of dinosaurs. Scientists began to explore different ways of using math and engineering rules and observations of modern animal species to test ideas about the behavior of dinosaurs. (I happen to be interested in all of this myself! Most of my work has been on figuring out the family tree of tyrant and other carnivorous dinosaurs and how they ran, fed, and interacted with other dinosaurs.)

One major new approach to dinosaur science is the use of computers and related technology. Today some researchers enter measurements of the shapes and sizes of the bones of an individual dinosaur and predict how it might have moved. Others use CAT (computerized axial tomography) scans to peer inside dinosaur skulls to see the shape of the brain cavity or inner ear without harming any of the bones. Some have even used computers and sensors to find fossils while they are still buried.

Scientists will continue to make new dinosaur finds. But in order to understand them, they'll have to start at the beginning. How did the fossils get in the rocks, and what do those rocks tell us about the environment the dinosaurs lived in? That is the first thing we'll have to look at in order to understand dinosaur science.

Frontiers of Dinosaur Science

Dr. Matthew C. Lamanna
Carnegie Museum of Natural History

Photo by Ken Lacovara

Where are the frontiers of dinosaur science? What will the future hold? Like so many questions in paleontology, nobody knows for sure. But recent milestones give us some great clues about what to expect.

There are thousands of new dinosaur fossils to be found. Many will be unearthed in the deserts and badlands of faraway places, while others will be discovered right under our noses. Countries that have already been the home of many spectacular dinosaur finds—including the United States, China, Argentina, Canada, and Mongolia—will host countless more. Furthermore, paleontologists will uncover dinosaurs in dozens of other exotic lands: northern Africa, the Middle East, Siberia, India, and Madagascar, to name a few. I personally would like to take a closer look at Antarctica!

The way we look for fossils may change dramatically. New technology, such as ground-penetrating radar, may one day allow us to precisely locate dinosaur skeletons underground. A couple of years ago, radioactivity was used to find the missing skull of an Allosaurus buried under rock and sand.

Future fossil discoveries will bring us new and amazing kinds of dinosaurs. Some will be expected. Mark my words: someday someone will find another skeleton of a nonflying dinosaur preserved with feathers, but this time from the Jurassic Period! That would make it the earliest known feathered dinosaur by many millions of years and fill in another gap in the evolution of birds.

In addition to uncovering new types of dinosaurs, paleontologists will find better fossils of dinosaurs that we are already aware of. The gigantic Deinocheirus is currently known only from its 8-foot arm and shoulder bones. Who can say what

the rest of this amazing creature looked like? What other kinds of dinosaurs was it related to? We won't know for sure until someone finds a more complete Deinocheirus skeleton.

Discoveries of strange new dinosaurs will capture our imaginations, but there will be much more to the exciting future of dinosaur science. More than ever, innovative scientists will ask questions about what dinosaurs were like as living animals. What did the skin and organs of dinosaurs look like? How fast did dinosaurs grow? Were they warm-blooded? Did dinosaurs live in groups or by themselves? Did they care for their young? How did dinosaurs interact with their environment and with other living things? There is much to be learned about the biology and behavior of dinosaurs.

Many of these questions will be answered by fossil discoveries yet to come. For example, thanks to the discovery of a gigantic nesting ground in Argentina, we are beginning to learn how the huge long-necked dinosaurs laid their eggs and raised their babies. Startling new technology and fresh ways of studying fossils will provide other clues. Sophisticated X-ray machines called CAT scanners now let us peer inside dinosaur skulls without damaging them, allowing us to study what their brains were like. Comparisons with today's animals, especially birds and crocodiles, will offer other ideas about the daily life of dinosaurs.

Partnerships among paleontologists and other scientists will open a wide window onto the world of dinosaurs. Geologists and chemists are now working with us to figure out the environments that dinosaurs inhabited, while fellow paleontologists investigate the many animals and plants that lived with the dinosaurs.

Last but not least, a few pioneering scientists have begun the search for biological molecules, like DNA, preserved in dinosaur remains. Who knows, maybe someday we will be able to use techniques like cloning to bring dinosaurs back to life. It doesn't seem likely now, but you just never know.

What will the future of dinosaur science bring? Lots and lots of amazing discoveries. Discoveries we can't even imagine yet.

2
ROCKS AND ENVIRONMENT

No human ever saw a living *Stegosaurus* or *Argentinosaurus* or *Spinosaurus*, so how do we know they existed? We know this from fossils—the remains of ancient living things preserved in rock. In order to understand how fossils are made, we first need to know how rocks are made.

When we pick up a pebble, we don't normally think too much about where it came from. But if you understand how a pebble is formed, you can understand the history of the world.

A pebble or stone wasn't always a rounded thing. It is just a piece of a bigger rock that was broken off and rolled around in the water until its edges wore smooth. If we trace a pebble back to the rock from which it broke off, we might find a cliff or hill or mountain. But even these places can't be called the "birthplace" of the pebble because cliffs and hills and mountains are formed by previously existing rocks being pushed up and eroded away.

To geologists (scientists who study the structure and function of the Earth) "rocks" aren't just stones or mountains or cliffs. When geologists talk about rock, they mean the solid upper portion of the Earth. This solid layer, or crust, is tens of miles deep—from a thickness of a few miles under the ocean floor to over 62 miles (100 kilometers) under mountain ranges. That sounds like a lot, but it is really just a fraction of the almost 4,000 miles (6,380 kilometers) to the center of the Earth!

Top: Every pebble is a record of the Earth's history.

HOW TO MAKE A ROCK

Rock is made in three ways. Because of this, we say that there are three different classes of rock.

Some rocks start off as hot liquid deep below the surface of the Earth. This liquid, or molten rock, is called magma if it is below the Earth's surface or lava if it erupts onto land or into water (forming a volcano). Rocks that are formed when molten material cools down are called igneous rocks. In a sense, igneous rocks are like ice: they start as a liquid, but when they get cooler, they turn into a solid. There are many different types of igneous rocks, depending on the chemistry of the original molten material and whether it cooled under or above the ground.

Fossils aren't found in igneous rocks. Any part of a living thing that fell into hot molten material would burn up, so there wouldn't be anything left to make into a fossil. Nevertheless, igneous rocks are really important to scientists because they help us determine when ancient events took place. And, once in a while, the ash from a volcanic eruption will even preserve a fossil.

Another kind of rock is made when previously existing rocks are transformed by incredibly high temperature and pressure. When a rock is baked

Igneous rocks can form either on the surface of the Earth or deep underground. Black basalt, shown on the left, is formed when the hot, glowing lava from a volcanic eruption cools down. The pink granite on the right was formed when magma deep beneath the surface of the Earth cooled down. We see the granite now because it was pushed up and the weaker rock around it eroded away.

hot enough, buried deep enough, or squished hard enough by colliding landmasses, the atoms inside the rock can recombine in new ways. We call rocks changed by heat or pressure metamorphic rocks. Metamorphic rocks often contain crystals that can form only under high heat and pressure.

As you might imagine, heat and pressure intense enough to rearrange the atoms of a rock would obliterate any fossils that existed in it. So you won't find any fossils in metamorphic rocks—even if they were originally *in* the rock that metamorphosed.

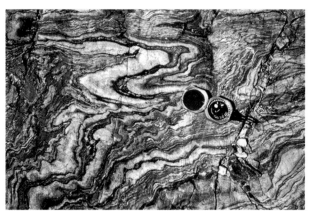

Metamorphic rocks—like this gneiss—are folded, crumpled, and otherwise highly transformed from their original state.

Thankfully, though (or I'd be out of work), there *is* a type of rock that contains fossils. These are rocks that are formed on the Earth's surface, in the same conditions and places where animals and plants live. These rocks are made when bits of previously existing rock, or the hard parts of living things (like skeletons or shells), accumulate in lay-

ers and become fused together. These bits of previously existing rocks and living things are called sediment, so we call these rocks sedimentary rocks.

MAKING A SEDIMENTARY ROCK

Sedimentary rocks can be produced in several different ways. In the oceans, there are many living things that make skeletons or shells out of the mineral calcium carbonate. When these creatures die, their skeletons fall apart, and some even dissolve into the seawater. These broken skeletons and dissolved minerals build up on the seafloor and form a layer of ooze. When this ooze is buried for a long time, the weight squeezes the ooze together to form the rock limestone. Fossils of seashells and other kinds of marine creatures are very common in limestone. In general, though, limestone is not a good kind of rock in which to find dinosaur or other land animal fossils. (Those that *are* found are from bodies that were washed out to sea.)

The most common way that sedimentary rocks are formed on land is when bits of old rock are moved from one location and deposited elsewhere. These locations might be the sides of cliffs, mountains, hills, and the like, which are pushed up and out of the ground by the same heat and pressure that produce magma and metamorphic rocks. The rocks at these locations are eroded by wind and rain, and parts of them fall off. These broken-off parts, or sediment, are then transported by water or wind or ice. Depending on the minerals

Sedimentary rocks are formed when bits of previously existing rocks settle into layers called strata.

in the original rock, and how far they travel, the sediment might include big cobbles and pebbles, smaller sand, even smaller silt, or very small bits of clay and mud. Eventually the sediment is deposited: the wind dies down and sand is dropped in the desert, or the river overflows its banks and deposits mud across the surrounding land. These layers of deposited sediment are called strata. Since floods and windstorms tend to happen over and over again, additional sediment is often deposited on top of older strata, forming layers.

If the sediment is just mud, then it can turn to rock simply by being buried and squished (like limestone). This kind of rock is called (not too creatively) mudstone, or shale if it has nice thin layers. Silt, sand, and pebbles, however, won't just stick together by themselves. They need some kind of glue, which nature provides. In most places in the world, water moves through sediment that contains various dissolved minerals. As this water flows between grains of silt or sand, some of the dissolved materials stick to the edges of these grains, holding them together. This is called cementation, and it changes loose sediment into sedimentary rock. Sedimentary rock that is made mostly of sand is called sandstone. Sedimentary rock that is made mostly of silt is called (surprise!)

siltstone. Sedimentary rocks made up of pebbles and cobbles are called conglomerate if the pebbles and cobbles are rounded, or breccia if they have sharper edges.

Now think about what you need to form sedimentary rock. You need original rocks that have been lifted up, eroded, and turned into sediment; you need wind, water, or ice to transport the sediment; and you need a place to deposit this sediment. Not every spot in the world has all these conditions at any given time. Some places are flat, so there is no source of sediment. Other places may not have enough wind, water, or ice to transport sediment. In other places the wind, water, or ice may be moving too fast for the sediment to be deposited. Because of this, only certain spots in the world will form sedimentary rocks at any given time. This is one reason why scientists know less about the ancient world than we would like. After all, if there are no sedimentary rocks forming in an area at a given time, then we won't get any fossils forming there, either. That means there are parts

The Sedimentary Rock Cycle

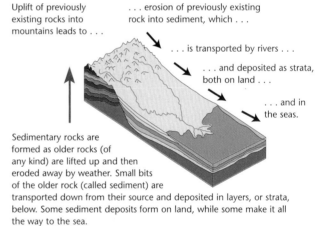

Uplift of previously existing rocks into mountains leads to . . .

. . . erosion of previously existing rock into sediment, which . . .

. . . is transported by rivers . . .

. . . and deposited as strata, both on land . . .

. . . and in the seas.

Sedimentary rocks are formed as older rocks (of any kind) are lifted up and then eroded away by weather. Small bits of the older rock (called sediment) are transported down from their source and deposited in layers, or strata, below. Some sediment deposits form on land, while some make it all the way to the sea.

of the history of regions in which there are blank spaces, or gaps, in the record. We simply don't know what happened there.

Note that there *are* a couple more ways sedimentary rocks can be formed. If a body of salt water—like a salt lake or lagoon—dries up, it can leave a layer of rock salt, a kind of sedimentary rock. Also, if lots of vegetation is buried faster than bacteria can decay it, the vegetation becomes compressed and can form the sedimentary rock coal. All these types of sedimentary rocks *could* contain fossils. However, because dinosaurs were land-living animals, it is most common to find their remains in rocks formed on land: mudstone, siltstone, sandstone, conglomerate, and breccia.

SEDIMENTARY STRUCTURES AND PALEOENVIRONMENTS

When sedimentary rocks are deposited, they are changed by the environment around them. The movement of waves or the drying effects of the sun change the surface of the layers and produce what are called sedimentary structures. We can use these sedimentary structures to reconstruct the paleoenvironment, or the way the environment was when the rocks were formed.

The most common sedimentary structures of all are layers, or strata. The thickness of the layers can reveal something about the amount of sediment being moved around in the environment, which in turn may give clues about how fast the water, wind, or ice was moving. Very thin layers mean a quiet environment, with no currents to disturb the sediment or worms to burrow through the layers. Thicker layers often mean more powerful flows that can transport a lot of sediment at once.

Ripple marks are a common form of sedimentary structure. These are made by flowing water or blowing air. We can tell from the shape of the ripple marks if water was flowing in one direction (like in a stream) or back and forth (like along a shore). We can tell if the marks were made by the small ripples of a stream or the giant sand dunes of a desert or beach.

Another kind of sedimentary structure is mud

Raindrop marks on a billion-year-old mudstone.

cracks. When mud gets dry, it shrinks and breaks along the edges. If another layer of mud covers these cracks, they can be preserved, so you can find the mud-cracked rock ages later. Similar to these are raindrop marks, where you can actually find the preserved impressions of raindrops from millions of years ago! When you find mud cracks and raindrop marks on rocks, you can tell that the paleoenvironment was wet enough to have mud but was not entirely underwater (or else the mud wouldn't dry and the rain wouldn't hit the mud).

These sedimentary structures—layers, ripples, mud cracks, and raindrop marks—are clues that geologists use to figure out what the paleoenvironment was like. They compare the ancient rocks with places in the present-day world where the same sets of sedimentary structures can be found. For example, if they find that a section of rock has thin layers in the middle, back-and-forth ripples around that, and mud cracks and raindrop marks on the edges, then this was probably a lake paleoenvironment.

Geologists find that the environment at any spot today can be very different from the paleoenvironment of the past. Also, by looking at the sequence of rocks from the bottom to the top, you can see that paleoenvironments can change a lot through time in any given place. For example, if you go to the Grand Canyon in Arizona, you can find rocks there that show the same spot was once shallow warm ocean, sandy desert, tropical swamp, and other paleoenvironments.

Ripple marks show that this sandstone was originally deposited under flowing water.

PLATE TECTONICS AND THE ROCK CYCLE

By looking at changing rock types and paleo-environments, as well as the shape and position of mountain ranges, the presence of volcanoes and earthquakes, and many other lines of evidence, geologists have pieced together the reasons and ways that the Earth is always changing.

Geologists have discovered that the upper portion of the Earth (the rocky crust and a less-solid layer underneath) is made up of dozens of enormous sections called plates. These plates float like gigantic sheets of ice over slowly moving material below. As the plates move, they brush, smash, and crash into each other. Sometimes plates spread apart from each other, and new crust (in the form of igneous rock) appears along great rifts on the surface. The geologic term for these motions is plate tectonics.

As plates move, they cause great disturbances on the Earth's surface. Some of these disturbances, like earthquakes or volcanic eruptions, happen quickly. Others, like the uplift of mountain ranges or the spreading of the ocean floor, happen slowly. Over millions of years, these disturbances have changed the entire surface of the planet.

For example, a map of the present-day world is very different from one of the Triassic Period, when dinosaurs first appeared. Today there are six major continents—North America, South America, Eurasia, Africa, Australia, and Antarctica—and a number of smaller landmasses. In the Triassic Period, there was only a single continent called Pangaea, or "all lands." During the end of the Triassic Period, Pangaea began to break apart, and the new Atlantic Ocean formed between the sections (see chapter 39). Over the many millions of years of the Mesozoic Era and through the Cenozoic Era, the plates continued to move, sometimes breaking apart and sometimes colliding.

In fact, these plates are still moving today! Using GPS (Global Positioning System) devices and satellites in orbit, geologists have shown that the Atlantic Ocean gets wider at about the same rate that your fingernails grow!

The changes caused by plate tectonics are what make rocks form. Magma underground or lava from volcanoes on the surface cools into igneous rocks. The great pressures created from the crumbling and crunching plates change old rocks into new metamorphic ones. Where mountains have formed, wind and water erode them into sediment, forming sedimentary rocks.

And it doesn't stop there. Old igneous and metamorphic and sedimentary rocks are melted to form new igneous rock; old igneous and metamorphic and sedimentary rocks are squished and baked to form new metamorphic rock; and old igneous and metamorphic and sedimentary rocks are broken down and fused together to make new sedimentary rock. This continual formation and re-formation of rocks is called the rock cycle.

So the next time you pick up a pebble or stone, think about this: before you found it, that piece of rock had been through the rock cycle at least once, and possibly many hundreds of times! Every stone in the world is ultimately made by the reshaping of the surface of the Earth.

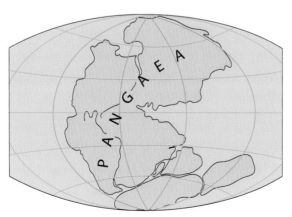

Earth in the Triassic.

Earth today.

3
FOSSILS AND FOSSILIZATION

Fossils are remains of living things or traces of their activities recorded in sedimentary rock. As we saw in the last chapter, sedimentary rock is formed in places where there is water or wind—the same kind of places that sustain animal and plant life. We've seen how sedimentary rock is formed. Let's now look at how animals and plants end up *inside* sedimentary rock.

INTO THE ROCKS

Paleontologists divide fossils into two major categories. Body fossils are actually parts of living things, like bones, teeth, shells, claws, leaves, and twigs. Trace fossils, on the other hand, are traces of the activities of living things, like footprints,

needed is a body—usually a dead one (shed teeth from living animals and leaves from live plants being two notable exceptions). Like animals today, dinosaurs died from all kinds of causes. Some were killed by other animals. Others were killed by disease or accident. And a few lucky dinosaurs

A *Stegosaurus*, wounded in a fight with a *Ceratosaurus*, sickens and dies . . .

burrows, and droppings. As you might imagine, body fossils and trace fossils are created and preserved in different ways.

In order to make a body fossil, the first thing

Top: A fossil, like this *Stegosaurus* skeleton, was once a living animal.

probably died of old age. But just because a dinosaur died doesn't mean that its body became a fossil.

The second thing needed to make a fossil is that the dead animal, tooth, plant, or whatever has to get buried, the sooner the better! The longer a dead thing is exposed to the elements, the greater the chance that scavengers will rip it apart, bacteria will cause it to decay, and weather will break it down.

So how does a dinosaur get buried? By the same things that bury animals today: flooding rivers, sandstorms, and any other situation where a lot of sediment is moving at once. A small dinosaur could be buried any number of ways. But big dinosaurs were usually buried in one of two ways. The first was by flood, like when a major river overflowed its banks or when a hurricane hit shore. The other way was by dropping dead at a dried-up watering hole. In the Mesozoic Era (as today), animals gathered at shrinking watering holes during the dry season. At the end of a particularly bad season, the bodies of many different animals who had died of dehydration could be found in the cracked mud of the dried-up hole, ready to be covered when the rainy season arrived.

The third thing that needs to happen in order to make a fossil? The sediment the body is buried in has to turn to rock. Soft parts of the body like flesh and skin decay quickly, often before a body is buried. But bones normally last a lot longer than flesh and skin. As water moves through the sediment, cementing the grains of dirt, sand, and min-

other fossils, there is so much of the sediment mixture inside the bone that it is stained black and breaks like a rock when dropped.

This same process preserves some types of trace fossils. If a nest of dinosaur eggs was buried in a flood or sandstorm, the eggs (and the bones of the embryo dinosaurs inside them) could become fossilized. Likewise, dinosaur droppings, or feces, could be buried and fossilized. Fossil feces are called coprolites, and they tell us a lot about what dinosaurs ate and how they ate it.

BITS AND PIECES

When you go to a museum or look at a dinosaur book like this one, you often see complete skeletons of dinosaurs. In the field, however, complete skeletons are almost impossible to find!

Think about the steps it takes to make a fossil. If a dinosaur died from the bite of another animal, then the bitten-off part would be missing from the fossil. If the body wasn't immediately buried, then some parts of it would probably be scavenged or weathered away. If the body was washed around for a while in water before burial, almost certainly even *more* parts would be missing. And finally, if the fossil is later exposed to the elements because of erosion (and most of the time, that's how fossils

. . . and is scavenged by meat-eating dinosaurs and pterosaurs . . .

erals together, it also flows through the pores inside the bones, leaving little bits of the mixture inside. This process is called fossilization. In some fossils, there is so little sediment added to the bone that it stays white and looks like it could have been buried seven (instead of 70 million) years ago! In

are found), the parts that stick out would be broken and further weathered by wind and rain.

Because of all of this, the vast majority of fossils are single teeth or broken bits of bone. Complete bones are rare. A couple of bones stuck together are even rarer. And rarer still are nearly complete skeletons: these had to have been covered very quickly after the dinosaur died but discovered very soon after the first bits of it were re-exposed on the surface of the Earth.

BEAKS, HORNS, SCALES, FEATHERS, AND MUSCLES AS HARD AS ROCK

In some really rare instances, other types of body tissue—like beaks and claws and feathers—are preserved. The surface of the beaks and horns of dinosaurs, like the surface of bird and turtle beaks or antelope horns, is made up of a substance called keratin—the same stuff that fingernails are made of. While keratin isn't as hard as bone or teeth, it is a lot tougher than skin, muscle, and other tissue. Once in a very rare while, the keratin of a dinosaur is preserved. In these cases, we can get a hint of the shape of the beak, the horns, or the claws of a dinosaur.

Normally, the skin of a dinosaur isn't preserved. But once in a while, a dinosaur body came to rest on some soft mud, and when the mud hardened, it took an impression of the animal. This is how we know that many types of dinosaurs were covered by little round scales. In fact, we know that dinosaur scales were not like lizard or snake

Skin impressions have also been found that show some dinosaurs were not covered in typical scales. For example, the tail of a few sauropods and the back of most duckbills had a series of boneless spines on them that are only known from impressions. The tail of the primitive little dinosaur *Psittacosaurus* sprouted a row of long quills. If it weren't for a recently discovered fossil, we would not have known that.

In the advanced meat-eating dinosaurs (the coelurosaurs), yet another kind of body covering is found—feathers! In the primitive coelurosaurs these were simple tufts, but in the more advanced groups these were true feathers. In some fossils the feathers are preserved as impressions; in others some of the original feather material remains as a film of carbon on the rock! The conditions needed to preserve these layers of carbon are extraordinarily rare. Since the early twentieth century, paleontologists (or at least a few of them) have speculated that coelurosaurs had feathers, but it was not until the discovery of *Sinosauropteryx* in 1996 (and other feathered dinosaurs since then) that this was confirmed.

Perhaps the rarest fossils of all are what paleontologists call mineralized soft tissues. This is when parts of the body that normally decay

. . . and the carcass is buried when nearby rivers rise during a flood . . .

scales (which overlap each other) but were instead more like the scales of turtles, crocodilians, or bird legs (which lie next to each other). In general, though, it is just the impression of the skin that is found and not the skin itself—because of this, we have no real idea of the color of dinosaur scales.

quickly, like muscles or tendons, are changed into rock with the help of certain bacteria. This can happen only in certain types of tropical lagoons or inside carnivore droppings. These fossils tell us something about the insides of dinosaurs.

* * *

WALKING WITH DINOSAURS

Body fossils (except for shed teeth) are made after a dinosaur dies; trace fossils, on the other hand, were made by dinosaurs while they were still alive. We've already seen some types of trace fossils: eggs and coprolites. These are preserved the same way that body fossils are preserved.

The most common type of dinosaur trace fossil is footprints. These were made when a dinosaur walked on mud that was wet enough to take an impression but not so wet that it immediately washed away. You find conditions like this on the shores of lakes and seas and along muddy riverbanks. Dinosaur footprints are a kind of sedimentary structure (like mud cracks or raindrop marks). Like other sedimentary structures, they have to be covered over in order to be preserved.

Dinosaur tracks can tell you a lot. First, they show what the bottom of dinosaur feet looked like—sometimes they even have scale impressions. Dinosaur trackways (series of dinosaur footprints) confirm that dinosaur legs were held directly underneath the body, not sprawling off to the side. Trackways also show that dinosaurs did *not* drag their tails as depicted in some old-fashioned illustrations. If they did drag their tails, where are the drag marks? Even an iguana (which is a heck of a

A fossil footprint is a record of tracks made by a dinosaur.

fast it was going when it made those tracks. As you might expect, most dinosaur trackways show them walking (after all, how often do *you* choose to run in mud?). But a few show dinosaurs moving pretty quickly. Some trackways in Texas of man-size theropods show they were moving at speeds up to 24 miles (38.6 kilometers) per hour. That's faster than the fastest Olympic runner!

Another set of trackways in Texas shows us something else about dinosaur behavior—hunting! These tracks show a giant predator (probably the carnosaur *Acrocanthosaurus*) chasing an even larger plant-eater (a sauropod, possibly *Sauroposeidon*). Where the two trackways come together, the predator tracks do a strange thing: instead of stepping left-right-left-right-left, the predator stepped left-right-right-left-right. Unless the three-ton meat-eater was playing hopscotch, the simplest explanation for the missing left footprint was that the *Acrocanthosaurus* grabbed on to the plant-eater with its powerful claws and was dragged a step before it was shaken loose. Did the plant-eater escape? We'll never know. The rest of the tracks were eroded away before we reached the end of the trail.

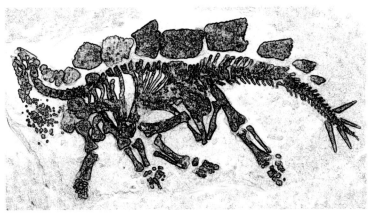

. . . and the skeleton becomes fossilized.

lot smaller than most dinosaurs!) leaves a tail drag mark, but dinosaurs do not.

More importantly, trackways can tell you how fast a dinosaur was moving. If you know how tall the dinosaur making the footprint was, then you can use a mathematical equation to figure out how

Body fossils and trace fossils are our only direct clues to extinct dinosaurs. And no fossil is a complete record of an animal: there is always something missing. Still, by putting together these bits and pieces, paleontologists can reconstruct how the dinosaurs looked, how they lived, and how they evolved.

Getting the Drop on Dinosaur Dung

Dr. Karen Chin
with Thom Holmes,
University of Colorado

Karen Chin is a dinosaur scientist with an unusual specialty. She studies what dinosaurs left behind—and I don't mean their bones. Karen is an expert on the fossilized feces, or droppings, of dinosaurs.

Everything in science has a fancy name, and dinosaur droppings are no different. They are called coprolites (KOP-ruh-lites). Coprolites are the fossilized feces of prehistoric animals. What can we learn from fossilized feces? Plenty. As Karen says, coprolites "teach us about the diet of ancient animals and about how those animals interacted with each other."

One way Karen studies coprolites is to observe them with her trusty microscope. "It is usually very difficult—if not impossible—to determine which type of animal produced a coprolite, but we can distinguish between meat-eaters and plant-eaters by studying the contents of the dung. Other clues such as age and geographical location may help point to the most likely producers of a coprolite. One speci-men from Saskatchewan, Canada, contained bone fragments and was probably left by a Tyrannosaurus. Other specimens from Montana contain tough plant tissues that were eaten by plant-eating dinosaurs—probably duckbilled dinosaurs."

Coprolites can also reveal evidence of relationships between dinosaurs and their environment. Karen has found burrows produced by dung beetles in some Late Cretaceous coprolites. "Now we know," she explains, "that dung beetles evolved with the dinosaurs and helped recycle the large quantities of dung that the dinosaurs surely produced." The biggest of all land creatures made it possible for some of the smallest creatures to survive.

Dinosaur coprolites are rather rare. Fossilization of the soft fecal matter only occurred when the droppings were buried under just the right conditions. "We usually don't have a good idea of the original size or shape of dinosaur droppings because feces from large animals are easily broken or deformed by rain erosion, trampling, or burial." The largest coprolites Karen has found are around seven quarts in volume.

Do coprolites smell when they are broken open? No. Karen explains that coprolites left behind by dinosaurs are just too old. They are rocks. "But dried dung from Pleistocene animals, from about 2 million years ago, still contains a lot of organic material and may smell when wet."

Giant dinosaurs made giant droppings: the 2-liter coprolite (fossilized dung) of *Tyrannosaurus rex*.

4

GEOLOGIC TIME: How Old Is That Dinosaur, and How Do We Know?

Two of the most amazing geological discoveries involve the vast age of the Earth and how long ago dinosaurs lived. We have found out that the Earth is *billions* of years old and that dinosaurs first appeared *millions* of years ago. These are stupendously large numbers. We refer to this long span of the history of the Earth as geologic time. But how did scientists figure out these numbers?

NUMERICAL TIME AND RELATIVE TIME

There are two main ways we measure time. One is in numerical time, or time expressed as numbers. These can be hours and minutes (4:50 PM) or dates (AD September 2, 2004). We use numbers to talk about the duration of events, whether it is setting a microwave oven for 3 minutes and 30 seconds to pop popcorn or to say that it takes 4.3 years for light to travel from Alpha Centauri to Earth. When we talk about dinosaurs, we talk about numerical time in terms of dates (*Tyrannosaurus rex* died out 65.5 million years ago) or durations (the Cretaceous Period lasted from 145.5 to 65.5 million years ago, for a total of 80 million years).

But we can also measure relative time, or time expressed as a sequence of events. We can say that we ate breakfast this morning before going to school or that the American Revolution happened before *Apollo 11* landed on the moon. These statements aren't any less true than measurements of numerical time. In fact, sometimes you can be more certain of relative time than you can about

numerical time. When I see a tree in the forest, I can be totally certain that it was an acorn before it became a fully grown tree (a sequence of relative time), even if I can't tell by looking at it when the acorn fell to the ground and sprouted into a tree.

In the 1600s, scientists began to realize that they could look at the Earth in the same way. They could try to figure out the sequence of events (that is, Earth history in terms of relative time). And they could try to figure out the dates when events took place (that is, Earth history in terms of numerical time). It turned out that the first was a lot easier to do than the second!

LAYERS OF TIME

The first key to figuring out how to read Earth's history in relative time was to understand how rocks form—in particular, to know how sedimentary rocks form in layers, or strata. These strata are just piles of sediment spread one on top of another as material is transported from a source rock to a region of deposition.

You can understand how to tell time by looking at layers of rocks by thinking about another region of deposition: the bedroom of someone

Top: The rocks of the Grand Canyon reveal millions upon millions of years of geologic time.

who leaves dirty clothes on the floor (hopefully not yours!). The clothes at the bottom of the pile are the ones that were dropped there first. On top of that will be the next layer of clothes in the pile. This pattern (with the oldest on the bottom) continues all the way to the top of the pile, where the most recently deposited clothes are found.

We can look at the pile and figure out the sequence in time. We might not know for certain *when* each particular piece of clothing was dropped, but we can tell the order in which they were thrown there.

That's the same principle we see in sedimentary rocks. The first, and oldest, layer of rocks deposited in an area is at the bottom; the layer above is younger than the layer below it, and so on, until the youngest is on the top.

As we learned in chapter 2, sedimentary rocks are the only ones that contain fossils. And a fossil found in a particular layer of rock is from a living thing that died while that layer was forming. So if we find a fossil in one layer and a second fossil in a layer that is higher up, we know that the second fossil is younger (closer to our time) than the first one. We might not know *how* much closer in time, but we do know the order.

When we look at layers of rock, we sometimes find that they have been folded or twisted and no longer lie flat. This can make it difficult to tell for certain which layer was on the bottom (and therefore the oldest) when they formed. However, if sedimentary structures like mud cracks, ripple marks, and footprints are present, they will tell you what the original "up direction" was. That's because these features only form on the top side of sediment layers. So if you find sedimentary structures, you can determine which strata are the youngest, as well as the ages of the strata relative to each other.

Folds and twists in the strata also tell us something else about relative time. They tell us that the rocks had to already have existed before they could get folded and twisted. So those changes had to occur even more recently than the rocks themselves!

We can use this last bit of information on more than just sedimentary rocks. For example, sometimes magma melts through other rocks and then chills to form sheets of igneous rock. Those sheets of igneous rock have to be younger (closer to us in time) than the rocks around them. Also, any time that a previously existing rock was eroded away and additional layers of new rock were deposited on it, we know that the eroded rock had to be older than the new rock.

FOSSILS AS PAGE NUMBERS

These observations about the positions of rocks are useful for figuring out the relative sequence of events at a given spot on the Earth (like at the Grand Canyon, for instance). But they don't help you relate events happening in one part of the world with those happening in another part. To do that, scientists need something else: something that is found in the rocks at both locations and lasted for only a limited period of time. In other words, it needed to have appeared, lasted for a certain amount of time, and then disappeared, never to be seen again.

In the early 1800s, a man named William "Strata" Smith (yes, his nickname was "Strata"!) realized there was, in fact, something in the rocks just like this—*fossils*! A particular fossil species appears in the strata for a certain amount of time, then goes extinct. We don't find those types of fossils in any other layer of rock below or above. So any rock that contains that particular fossil species had to have formed between the first appearance of that species and its extinction. In this way, a fossil can be used as a sort of "page number" in the Earth's history. These page-number fossils came to be called index fossils.

"Strata" Smith didn't actually know why fossils appeared in the particular order they did (the modern understanding of evolution wouldn't be proposed until 1859), but his work was very important.

In order to be a useful index fossil, a fossil has to be very common. You should be able to find it in its strata at many different locations. And that species should only have lasted for a relatively short amount of time.

This last part is very important. Remember that any rock containing the index fossil formed between the first and last appearance of that species. The shorter the amount of time the species existed, the more precise we can be about how close in time two distinct strata from different parts of the world are. So if a fossil species lasted from 500 million years ago to 250 million years ago, two discrete strata containing that species could be separated by as much as 250 million years. That's a lot of time! But if that species lived only from 251 to 250 million years ago, we'd know that the two rocks were separated by, at most, only a million years (still a long time from the point of view of a human being, but a lot better than a 250-million-year spread!).

NAMES FOR GEOLOGIC TIME

By using fossils, geologists of the nineteenth and early twentieth centuries went about creating names for parts of geologic time. The boundaries between these chunks of time were based on major changes in the index fossils. As it turned out, these changes often reflected the mass extinction of many species.

Geologists gave names to each of the different pieces of geologic time. They organized them so that each big unit of time contained a series of smaller units. This arrangement (with big units containing various smaller and smaller units) is called the geologic time scale.

The largest units of the geologic time scale are eons. We, and dinosaurs, and almost all living things that you can see without a microscope live in the Phanerozoic Eon (the most recent of the four eons). Phanerozoic means "visible life."

Eons are divided into eras. The Phanerozoic Eon is divided into the Paleozoic (ancient life) Era, the Mesozoic (middle life) Era, and the Cenozoic (recent life) Era. We are currently in the Cenozoic Era, but the Age of Dinosaurs was in the Mesozoic Era. The boundary between the Paleozoic and

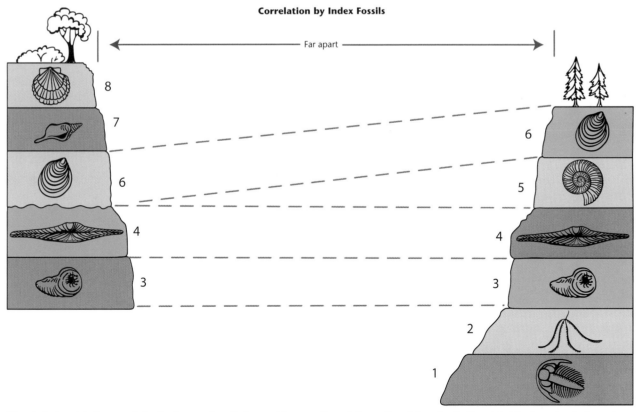

Correlation by Index Fossils

Far apart

All rocks that contain the same index fossils were deposited around the same time—between the origin and extinction of that fossil species. So the rocks that contain fossil 3 are about the same age, the rocks that contain fossil 4 are about the same age, and so on. Note, however, that no place in the world contains a complete history of time. For example, the section of rocks on the left includes younger strata (with fossils 7 and 8) than the one on the right, and the one on the right contains older strata (with fossils 1 and 2). Also, rocks of the age of fossil 5 are not found in the left section: either no rocks of that age were deposited there or they were eroded away before rocks of the age of fossil 6 were laid down.

Mesozoic eras represents the greatest mass extinction we know about in paleontology, when perhaps 95 percent of all animal species died out. The extinction that marks the Mesozoic and Cenozoic boundary wasn't as bad, but it ended the reign of the dinosaurs (but not—as we will see—the dinosaurs themselves!).

Eras are divided into periods. The Mesozoic Era contains the Triassic (three-part) Period, the Jurassic (after the Jura Mountains) Period, and the Cretaceous (chalk) Period.

Periods are divided into smaller chunks of time called epochs. There is an Early, Middle, and Late Triassic Epoch, and an Early, Middle, and Late Jurassic Epoch. Unfortunately, when the nineteenth-century geologists got to the Cretaceous Period, they only divided it into an Early and a Late Cretaceous Epoch. And because of the rules governing geological names, today we are stuck with only those two divisions of time in the Cretaceous.

Now here's something to think about: at no time above did I mention numerical time in terms of these eons, eras, periods, and epochs. That's because numerical time wasn't used to figure out the geologic time scale. It wasn't until the twentieth century began that geologists determined how to measure geologic time in numbers of years. That's because it wasn't until then that radioactivity was discovered.

RADIOACTIVE DATES

When we think about radioactivity, we often think about human-made objects like medical scanners, nuclear power plants, or atomic bombs. But many substances in nature are naturally radioactive. In other words, they break down from one type of element to another over time. Radioactivity is all around us.

About a hundred years ago, it was discovered that all radioactive atoms break down, or decay, in the same manner. After a certain period of time, half of the radioactive atoms in an object would decay into another type of atom called the daughter product. Then in another period of the same duration, half of the remaining radioactive atoms

would break down into the daughter product, leaving one-quarter radioactive atoms and three-quarters daughter product. And in another period of the same duration, half of the remaining radioactive atoms would break down, and so on. Scientists named this period of time the half-life of the radioactive element. After careful study, they found out that each radioactive element has its own unique, unchanging half-life.

Geologists realized that by measuring how much radioactive element and daughter product was found in a particular rock, they could tell how many half-lives ago it formed. By multiplying this number with the known half-life of the radioactive element, they could calculate the age of the rocks, or their radioactive date. And they could do this with each distinct radioactive element (each with its own unique half-life) for the same rock.

This realization got geologists very excited. The technique produced extremely consistent radioactive dates for rocks, even when elements with very different half-lives were used. Using different elements is important because you can then compare their dates against each other. When the elements match—even though their half-lives are very different—you can be certain that the date you calculate is correct. But for paleontologists, there was a problem. You can't get a radioactive date for a sedimentary rock! If you tried, you would be dating the age of the *source rock* that the sediment came from, not the sedimentary rock *itself*.

But paleontologists remembered how *sometimes* an igneous rock cuts through older sedimentary rocks and how *other times* sedimentary rock gets deposited over older igneous rock. In these cases, they could figure out a radioactive date for the igneous rock and know that the sedimentary rock—and thus any index fossils it contained—had to be older or younger than that igneous rock. That way they could use *relative* time and *numerical* time together.

A COMPLETE GEOLOGIC TIME SCALE

By using this procedure again and again in different parts of the world, geologists began to put numerical values onto the geologic time scale. Numerical time measurements, like most measurements in science, are always subject to change as new types of experiments are done. That is why some books say that the Cretaceous Period ended 65.5 million years ago, and some say 64 million, and some say 66 million.

Below is a chart of the geologic time scale showing when major events happened in the history of the Earth and evolution of life. Because this book is about dinosaurs, it shows the Mesozoic Era in the most detail. But paleontologists and geologists study other chunks of geologic time, too.

Using numerical time calculations, we see that the Age of Dinosaurs (the time between the earliest dinosaurs around 235 million years ago and the great extinction 65.5 million years ago) was about 170 million years long. We can see that *Tyran-*

nosaurus rex, which lived at the very end of the Age of Dinosaurs (65.5 million years ago), actually existed closer in time to us than it did to *Stegosaurus* (at 150 million years ago)! And the time between *T. rex* and *Stegosaurus* was just half of the Age of Dinosaurs.

So how old is a particular dinosaur? And how do we tell? There are a lot of different ways to approach that question. We can use the relative time scale to figure out that one particular dinosaur found on the side of a cliff was younger than another individual we found lower in the strata. We can use index fossils in the rock to figure out when in the geologic time scale those rocks formed. And we can use radioactive dates (either at the site where we found the fossil or from other places that have the same index fossil) to get a good idea of how old that dinosaur is in numerical time.

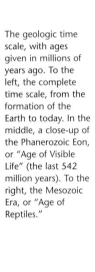

The geologic time scale, with ages given in millions of years ago. To the left, the complete time scale, from the formation of the Earth to today. In the middle, a close-up of the Phanerozoic Eon, or "Age of Visible Life" (the last 542 million years). To the right, the Mesozoic Era, or "Age of Reptiles."

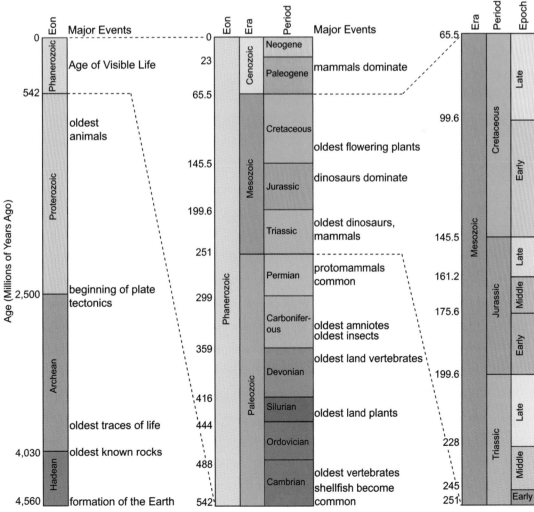

How Old Is Old? The Evolution of Life on Earth

Dr. Raymond R. Rogers
Macalester College,
St. Paul, Minnesota

Photo courtesy of Raymond R. Rogers

So how old are you, anyway? Clearly old enough to read, but still much younger than your parents or grandparents because they are really old. But the Earth—well, that is another category of OLD altogether. Geologists currently consider the age of the Earth to be approximately 4.6 billion years. It was way back then that our Earth and the other planets in our solar system first formed and began to orbit around the sun. The early Earth was undeniably a rather tough place to live, with seas of molten lava and a harsh pinkish yellow sky that lacked the oxygen that we need to survive. Fortunately for us, the Earth cooled over time, and as it cooled, lava turned to rock and water condensed from vapor, setting the stage for life.

Life on Earth started out small and simple. Single-celled organisms similar to today's bacteria were first on the scene. The fossil record indicates the presence of single-celled life dating back approximately 3.5 billion years. From these very modest beginnings along the shores of ancient oceans, life flourished and diversified. Soon (a few billion years later), at least in the opinion of a time-tolerant geologist, life evolved to include creatures more familiar to you and me, such as jellyfish and sponges.

Then, about 500 million years ago, fish were swimming among the sponges and, not too long thereafter, testing their jaws on the jellyfish. One type of fish was so bold that it ventured from its watery home to see how its sturdy lobed fins worked on land. This 375-million-year-old adventure by an ancient relative of today's lungfish paved the way for the evolution of amphibians and an assortment of land-dwelling animals, such as turtles, mammals, and yes, of course, the wonderful dinosaurs.

Now, as far as the dinosaurs are concerned, we have a very good handle on how old they are and how long they were around. Their fossil bones and teeth first show up in rocks approximately 235 million years old, and they disappear from rocks younger than 65.5 million years old. Simple math shows that they spent approximately 170 million years roaming the Earth in fantastic fashion.

Here are two important things to keep in mind as you explore the ancient world of dinosaurs. First, though amazing through and through, dinosaurs are only one part of life's long evolutionary history. This history continues to this day. The 170-million-year Age of Dinosaurs is only one exciting chapter in life's 3.5-billion-year story. And second, humans and our closest ancestors first walked this Earth only a few million years ago, and a few million years are little more than drops in the deep bucket of time.

5

FROM THE FIELD TO THE MUSEUM: *Finding Fossils*

We know *how* animals and plants become fossils. But how do we know *where* to find fossils? And when we do find them, how do we know *what to do* with them?

WHERE TO DIG?

When people hear about the discovery of a new species of dinosaur, a lot of them want to run out and dig one up. Problem is, dinosaur fossils are *very* hard to find and almost as difficult to remove from rock.

Dinosaur fossils only turn up in rocks that were formed when dinosaurs were alive. So it is no use looking for them in rocks from the Paleozoic Era or any part of the Precambrian Era because that is *long* before dinosaurs first appeared. The only dinosaur fossils you can find in Cenozoic Era rocks are of birds (which are actually a type of dinosaur) or ones that got eroded out of older rocks and then got redeposited into younger ones.

To find dinosaur fossils, you've got to first find rocks formed in the Mesozoic Era. These rocks can be found in many places, but not all of them will contain fossils. For example, neither igneous rocks nor metamorphic rocks contain fossils. And rocks that were formed in the ocean will only rarely have dinosaur fossils—and never dinosaur footprints or coprolites.

You need Mesozoic Era rocks *that were formed on land* in order to find dinosaur fossils. Thankfully, there are many places on the Earth where these kinds of rocks are exposed on the surface.

Top: Dinosaur-fossil-bearing sedimentary rocks near Shell, Wyoming.

That exposure is very important. If the rocks are entirely underground, there's no way to tell if there are fossils in them. It's only when fossils are close to the surface, or partially exposed, that people can actually find them. Once in a while, fossils become exposed accidentally—like when a new highway or building is constructed—but the best

The author, over a decade ago and in a more gracile morph (that is, a lot skinnier), helps to uncover Late Jurassic dinosaur bones near Shell, Wyoming.

Protecting fossils after they are excavated requires time and patience—*and* plaster and toilet paper.

SCRAPING AWAY

When dinosaur bones *are* found, you can't just dig them up with a shovel or backhoe. Dinosaur fossils are *very* fragile and will shatter if you don't treat them carefully. In fact, if you are lucky enough to find what you think are fossil bones, you should leave them in the ground and ask a professional scientist to come look at them. Many good fossils have been destroyed by people who impatiently tried to dig them up themselves!

way to find fossils is to let Mother Nature do the digging. That is, look for rocks that have been weathered by wind and rain. Over time, fossils in these rocks can become partially exposed. Working this way, you might find anything from the tip of a tooth to a field of dinosaur tracks!

On TV and in movies, we often see pictures of big expeditions of paleontologists looking for dinosaur fossils. While these expeditions *do* occur, most dinosaur fossils aren't found by people who are actually looking for them. They are found by accident! Sometimes they are found by someone who is digging up the ground for some other reason. For example, the first skeleton of *Hadrosaurus* was unearthed by people digging the foundation for a house to be built in New Jersey. Other times fossils have been found by people simply taking a walk! A famous *Tyrannosaurus* skeleton was found by a rancher in Montana who happened to be lucky enough to look at the ground at just the right moment. Still others are found by geologists or other scientists who are exploring the rocks for their own research and accidentally come across the bones or eggs or footprints. Only once in a while are dinosaur fossils actually found by dinosaur paleontologists who are exploring a region for the purpose of digging up their favorite creatures.

There is also more to consider about a fossil site than the fossils themselves. The position of the bones in the rocks can tell us something about what happened to the animal. Was it killed by a flooding river? Was the body pulled apart by scavengers or dried up in the sun? Also, there may be traces of skin impressions or other small details in the rocks around the fossils that can easily be destroyed.

That's why dinosaur digs should really be called "dinosaur scrapes." When the time comes to actually get the dinosaur fossils out of the rocks, professionals use dental picks and trowels and other delicate tools. Shovels and backhoes and jackhammers are only used to remove the tons of rock that might cover part of where you are digging, *never* rock that is close to the fossils themselves!

Starting with the bones that nature has exposed, a team of paleontologists and their helpers will move outward to see if there are other fossils nearby. Sometimes there might be just the one bone, but sometimes that bone will be connected to a whole skeleton. And once in a long while, that skeleton will be part of a whole group of skeletons! If you are lucky enough to find that, then you've got a dinosaur dig that will take years to work and that will probably have a lot of new information stored in it.

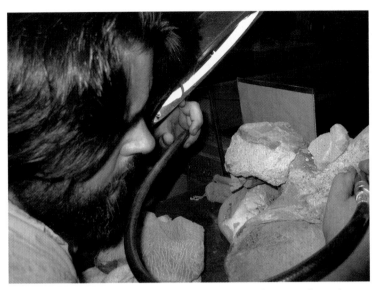

Back at the lab, the bones are revealed by carefully removing the surrounding rock.

It is also never a good idea to dig out fossil bones completely in the field. They are so fragile that they will probably fall apart when you try to move them. So instead, paleontologists jacket the fossils they find. That means they leave some of the sedimentary rock around the fossil and put layers of plaster or foam and burlap around the fossil and the rock for protection. They have to put something between the protective material and the bone to keep the material from sticking to the fossil: this is called a separator. In the "olden days," people used rice paper as a separator. Today it is a lot more common to use toilet paper, which works just as well—and serves another useful purpose, too!

BACK TO THE MUSEUM, INTO THE COLLECTIONS

Once information has been collected on the position of a fossil and the whole thing has been jacketed up, it's time to ship the specimen to a museum laboratory. There the fossil can be studied in greater detail.

The job of opening up fossil jackets and repairing any damage to the fossils belongs to a special group of paleontologists called preparators. Preparators don't necessarily do their own scientific research (although some do), but without them the rest of us wouldn't be able to do ours! Preparation requires a lot of skill and time. Because of that, many museums have jacketed fos-

sils from digs long ago that haven't been prepared yet. (There are some museums where jackets from over a hundred years ago are still sitting around!) But it is better to leave a jacketed fossil unprepared and safe than to have it destroyed because someone untrained or in a rush messed up when they were working on it.

As the fossil is being prepared, research paleontologists will come by to check on it and make notes about the details of its shape and other features. If there seems to be something special about the fossil—perhaps it's a new species or part of a skeleton that wasn't known before—the research paleontologist might start taking notes right away. If it turns out that the fossil *is* special, then the paleontologist will want to write up (and publish) a description of it to announce the discovery to other scientists.

Not all fossils teach us something new. But regardless of whether a fossil is a new discovery or just another hadrosaur rib, it has to be accessioned. That means that the specimen is given a unique number and put into the collections of the museum where it's being studied. As much information about that fossil as possible (what species it belongs to, what bone it is, when and where it was found, in which rock formation it was found, who collected it, who identified it, and more) is entered into a database so that researchers can go back and take a look at it in the future.

A museum may have many thousands of accessioned fossils in its collections, and there's no way it can display all of them. So behind the exhibit halls of the world's museums are warehouses packed to the ceiling with fossils. These warehouses might be boring to some people, but to researchers they are very important. The fossils housed in them might be useful in identifying a fossil fragment found elsewhere. They might also be needed to compare new discoveries to. Sometimes specimens that were once thought unimportant contain useful information, like signs of a predator's bite or of a disease. In fact, a lot of new dinosaur species are named when paleontologists are looking at specimens that were accessioned decades previously but were not understood to be new at the time.

THE FEW, THE PROUD, THE MOUNTED SKELETONS

Why shouldn't all of a museum's fossils be on display? Well, to start with, it would be pretty boring. After all, there are only so many ribs or toe bones people want to see. Also, there is a question of space: you can safely store a lot of specimens in the same amount of space that it takes to display a single skull.

So what does it take for a fossil to make it into an exhibit hall? Normally a fossil has to have something special about it—such as its size—that makes it important and worth being seen by a lot of people. And the more complete a dinosaur fossil is, the more likely it will be displayed. After all, most of us would rather see a complete skeleton than a single bone.

But putting together a complete skeleton for display isn't easy. Without muscles, tendons, and skin to hold the bones together, preparators have to build a structure to keep them in position. And since complete fossils are very rare, preparators usually have to fill in a bunch of missing parts. In the early days, preparators often did this by using whatever bones they had handy. This resulted in some weird, Frankenstein-like mounts, such as *Triceratops* skeletons with duckbill feet and *Stegosaurus* skeletons cobbled together from different-size specimens!

Today preparators create duplicate bones using plastic. In fact, with the help of computers and laser scanners, they can take a left upper-arm bone of a specimen and make a mirror-image copy to replace a missing right upper-arm bone.

Dinosaur skeletons mounted for display are also very costly to put together. So, unfortunately, they don't often get changed, even when new discoveries show that our old ideas about the way a dinosaur stood or held its arms were wrong. Because of this, most museums have some out-of-date dinosaur mounts. These might not be totally accurate, but they are still great to look at.

So the next time you go to a museum, take a little time out from admiring the exhibits to think about all the hard work and thought that went into setting them up. Preparators do pretty amazing work, but you almost never read about their efforts in dinosaur books or see them on TV.

Putting bones together to make skeletons for display is a *big* project!

Putting Dinosaurs Together

Jason "Chewie" Poole
Academy of Natural Sciences,
Philadelphia

When was the last time you looked at a dinosaur skeleton in a museum? Did you ever wonder who put the bones together?

Fossil preparators are people who work with the fossils of prehistoric animals and plants. Their job is to carefully remove or uncover fossils from the rock in which they are found.

Fossils of dinosaurs are often found in hard rock. It may take weeks or years to dig a fossil skeleton out of the ground. Bone diggers remove a few bones at a time. To protect the fossils, they are wrapped in a "field jacket" made of burlap bandages and soupy plaster, like a cast that a doctor puts on a broken arm or leg. Some rock is usually left around the bone to support it while it is shipped to the lab, where the preparators work.

Once the fossils arrive at the lab, preparators can begin the job of cleaning and making a fossil less breakable.

Putting a dinosaur together from all of these fossil pieces is like putting a jigsaw puzzle together without the picture on top of the box. To help the preparators in this task, the people who dug up the dinosaur fossil provide several kinds of information. They may have maps and photos of the dig site before and during the removal of the bones. They may also have sketches and notes explaining how the bones were found. All of these facts help the preparators put the bones back together in the correct way.

When the field jackets are first opened, the bones inside are still partially covered by rock, dirt, and mineral deposits. This material is carefully cleaned off the fossil with tools such as small chisels, awls, and picks like the ones a dentist uses to clean teeth. The rock and other residue must be removed without damaging the fossil.

Fossils are dry and delicate, and often crack. Cracks and breaks can be fixed using special glues and fasteners. A good fossil preparator learns many tricks for fixing damaged fossils without damaging them further. This work can take weeks or even months to complete.

The work of fossil preparators may seem exasperatingly slow. But the rewards are great. Imagine what it is like to be the first person to see a fossil after it has been put back together. Preparing fossils can be as exciting as finding them in the first place.

Once a dinosaur fossil has been cleaned and prepared for viewing, it is studied by a paleontologist. The paleontologist will decide what kind of dinosaur it is. Sometimes the fossils provide a surprise. They may show bite marks, signs of disease, or breaks in the bones. Each discovery provides one more piece to complete the puzzle of dinosaurs.

Some dinosaur skeletons will be put on display in a museum for people to see. Other specimens may go into a laboratory so that other scientists can examine them. A fossil collection is like a library of fossils for scientists to learn from.

When reassembling dinosaur skeletons, you sometimes have to use casts (plastic duplicates of the original bones).

6

BRINGING DINOSAURS TO LIFE: *The Science of Dinosaur Art*

I think it is safe to assume that if you're reading this book, you like looking at dinosaurs. And if you like looking at dinosaurs, chances are you have wondered why some pictures of dinosaurs look so much different from other pictures of the same dinosaurs.

Dinosaur restorations (at least the ones you see in museums and in this book)—the drawings, paintings, sculptures, and computer models of what dinosaurs looked like as living animals—are works of art done by people called paleoartists. But in order to create a *good* dinosaur restoration, paleoartists have to study dinosaur science.

START WITH THE SKELETON

Just as paleontologists have to start with dinosaur fossils in order to do their science, paleoartists have to start with fossils in order to do their restorations. The more fossil information we have about a particular species, the better our under-

standing of it will be, both artistically and scientifically. That's why pictures of dinosaurs created in the nineteenth century look wrong to us: scientists and artists had very incomplete material to work with and had to guess at what things looked like. So old restorations show *Megalosaurus* on four

Top: Luis Rey combines science and art to bring this *Styracosaurus* to life.

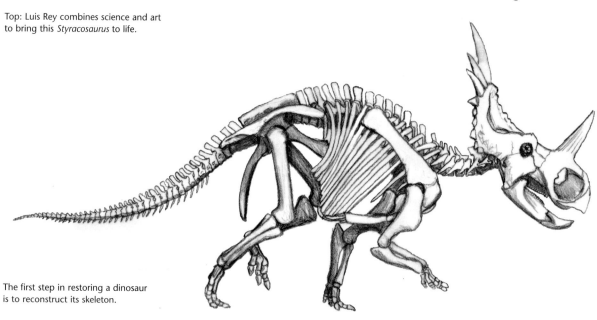

The first step in restoring a dinosaur is to reconstruct its skeleton.

legs instead of two and *Tyrannosaurus* with its tail dragging on the ground.

Ideally, it would be best to start a restoration with a complete skeleton. Problem is, not all dinosaurs are known from complete skeletons. In fact, very few of them are! And even when a complete skeleton *is* known, it has often fallen apart and only shows what the dinosaur looked like when it was dead. To know what the dinosaur looked like in real life, you need to create a dinosaur reconstruction first—that is, you need to put the skeleton back together (at least on paper) and fill in the missing bones to figure out what the complete skeleton looked like.

You might think that it is easy to create a good reconstruction when you have an entire skeleton to work with—that you simply fit each bone into the appropriate joint in the bone next to it—but there still can be some confusion. For example, shoulder blades don't actually attach to other bones at a joint but are held on by cartilage, which doesn't fossilize. So there is always some guesswork about getting the shoulder blades, and therefore the arms, into the right position.

Another cause for confusion: when a bone gets buried and preserved in sedimentary rock, it is often deformed and bent out of shape. Sometimes it's obvious that there was deformation, but other times it isn't. To do a good reconstruction, you need to be able to tell the difference.

If there are bones missing from a fossil, the best way to replace them in your reconstruction is to use information from other bones. For example, if the fossil you're reconstructing is missing a right leg, you can use the left leg to create a "mirror image" to complete the skeleton. Or if you need to fill in a missing back bone, you can use the bones in front of it and behind it to guess at the shape.

Often you have to use information from another skeleton of the same species or a closely related species to figure out the missing part. But you have to be very careful! After all, not all individuals of the same species are the same size, so their bones are going to be different sizes, too. Imagine if you were making a skeleton reconstruction of a human being and you used the top half of a six-foot weight lifter and the bottom half of a four-foot gymnast! It would look pretty goofy! (And some old dinosaur reconstructions *are* just this goofy!)

And then there are the times when you can't figure out what to do with the bones you *do* find. A famous case of this involved the spike thumb of *Iguanodon*. Its discoverers found an odd cone-shaped bone along with the *Iguanodon* remains, but they didn't know where it went. They thought it might have been a nose horn, so for many years artists drew this dinosaur with a horn. Only when more-complete fossils were found did they discover it was, in fact, a thumb.

Sometimes a paleoartist will leave blank spots or dashed lines on a fossil reconstruction to show

After reconstructing the skeleton, the artist adds in muscles and tendons.

the parts that are missing. That can be useful if you are doing just a reconstruction of a skeleton, but it won't do for a complete restoration.

MUSCLES AND GUTS

A skeleton creates the framework for a restoration, but it is only the beginning. A paleoartist then must work from the inside out and add the soft tissue of the animal: the muscles and tendons and various internal organs. (It is the muscles that are really important here. Knowing the position of the intestines and stomach and so forth will help fill out the belly region, but muscles define the shape of an animal.)

In order to place the muscles and guts, a paleoartist needs to know about the internal anatomy of modern animals. Because modern birds are a surviving part of the dinosaur family tree, they can give some information. But because birds have adapted to a very different set of environmental conditions, their shapes are very different from other dinosaurs. So you can't just use birds. Paleoartists also have to study the insides of modern reptiles, such as crocodilians and lizards.

Because all these animals—modern birds, dinosaurs, crocodilians, and lizards—share a common ancestor, they are all built along the same basic body plan. That means that they tend to have muscles in the same positions, even if the actual size of a particular muscle might be bigger or smaller in one group than in another. So a paleo-

artist can use that information to put the muscles in the right spot on a dinosaur skeleton. It helps that many muscles attach to bones at particular surfaces, bulges, bumps, or crests. If you correctly identify these muscle attachment points, you'll know where a particular muscle goes.

ADDING THE OUTSIDES

Once you've got muscles draped over the bones, it's time to tackle the outside of the dinosaur. This can be pretty tricky. Our understanding of what was on the outside of dinosaur skin has changed a lot in the past ten years.

Dinosaur skin itself, like the skin of all living animals, covers the muscles and guts. But different groups of animals have different kinds of integument, or coverings on the skin. Mammals tend to have fur; lizards and snakes have scales; turtles and crocodilians have scales and armor plates; birds have scales and feathers; and amphibians have "naked" skin (although sometimes it's pretty bumpy, like on a toad). Because dinosaurs are a type of reptile, scientists have long known that dinosaurs had scales. In fact, dinosaur skin impressions have been known for over a century, so we know that dinosaur scales were like those on the legs of crocodilians and turtles—that is, a series of bumps of various sizes. They didn't have scales like a lizard or snake, where one scale overlaps the next scale.

But it might be that there was more to the

The artist wraps the muscles in skin.

36

An impression of a dinosaur's skin shows us the size and shape of its scales, but not its color.

Some dinosaurs, like this *Microraptor*, had feathers as well as scales.

body covering of dinosaurs than scales. Over the past several decades, paleontologists discovered that modern birds are the living part of the dinosaur family tree. So paleontologists have speculated for decades about how many dinosaurs might have had that same special covering found on birds: feathers. Some thought that feathers didn't evolve until the very earliest bird, so none of the *other* dinosaurs in the Mesozoic had feathers. Others speculated that feathers might have been on many groups of dinosaurs, even some of the earliest and most primitive sorts.

Starting in the mid-1990s, a series of fossils—mostly from northeastern China—have helped solve this problem. These fossils were found in ancient lake deposits that had very fine-grained mud that preserved the remains of the outsides of the animals and plants that sank into it. So far, every single fossil of a carnivorous dinosaur found

in those particular lake deposits has revealed something other than just scales. In many species, there is a sort of fuzzy body covering. Scientists call this fuzz protofeathers because it represents the type of integument from which true feathers evolved. A variety of carnivorous dinosaurs with protofeathers have been found in these rocks, including the compsognathid *Sinosauropteryx* and the primitive tyrant dinosaur *Dilong*.

There are other dinosaurs, however, that show *true* feathers. These include birds and the dinosaurs most closely related to them: oviraptorosaurs like *Caudipteryx* and *Protarchaeopteryx* and deinonychosaurs (raptors) such as *Microraptor* and *Sinornithosaurus*. Birds, oviraptorosaurs, and deinonychosaurs are all part of the group of carnivorous dinosaurs called Maniraptora, and so far, every time people have found the body covering of any maniraptoran, it has had broad feathers on its

Texture is added to the skin based on scale patterns found on fossils, like the one above.

arms and tail (and sometimes legs), with smaller feathers over the rest of the body. So paleontologists and paleoartists can predict that all maniraptorans had this kind of body covering.

So far, no dinosaurs more distantly related to birds than *Sinosauropteryx* and *Dilong* have protofeathers. Where known, other groups of carnivorous dinosaurs show typical dinosaurian scales. But modern birds give us a warning: if all birds were extinct and we found impressions only of the legs of chickens or ostriches, we might think that birds only had scales and not feathers. In fact, all living birds have both scales *and* feathers. In order to show that a carnivorous dinosaur totally lacked feathers, we need to find a complete skin impression. And since even partial skin impressions are very rare, we can't, at present, say how many carnivorous dinosaurs had protofeathers and exactly where on their bodies the protofeathers were found. So we have to be cautious about our interpretation of the body covering of primitive carnivorous dinosaurs. Some may have had protofeathers, others only scales. At present, we don't know, so each restoration is a guess—a (hopefully) well-informed guess.

We can think of a piece of paleoart as a type of scientific hypothesis. As with other hypotheses, we use the best evidence available. So right now, nobody has found the integument of *Velociraptor,* but because all the closest relatives of *Velociraptor* currently known have broad feathers on the arms and tail and small feathers elsewhere, we can predict that *Velociraptor* did as well. In order to demonstrate that this is incorrect, we'll need to find an impression of the skin of this dinosaur that shows that such feathers were *not* there. Therefore, weird as it may seem to some, paleontologists accept that raptors were feathered, and the best paleoartists recognize this and paint them that way.

New discoveries have shown that some plant-eating dinosaurs had odd body coverings of their own. The little plant-eating ceratopsian dinosaur *Psittacosaurus* has been found in the same Chinese lake deposits as *Sinosauropteryx.* Skin impressions from over most of its body show typical dinosaur scales, but impressions of its tail are very *untypical!* They show a row of tall, slender, bendable shafts running along the top edge. These aren't scales, or feathers, or even protofeathers. They *might* be evolutionarily related to feathers, but they might also have evolved separately from protofeathers and true feathers. Who knows what other weird integument might have been present on other dinosaurs! Many of the more unusual features of modern animals—like the wattles of turkeys, the combs of roosters, or the manes of lions—cannot be seen on the skeletons of these animals. If we didn't see them alive today, we wouldn't know these things existed.

Before we get to coloring the dinosaurs, we have to consider the final details of the outsides of the dinosaurs. These are things like nostrils and cheeks. In current paleontology, there has been some debate about exactly where the fleshy parts of the nostrils of dinosaurs were, and whether or not some dinosaurs had cheeks. Dinosaur skeletons tend to have big nostril openings, and so many artists used to draw dinosaurs with great big fleshy nostrils. But the nostril opening in the skull is often filled with all sorts of living tissue—it isn't just a hole to the outside world. Larry Witmer of Ohio University and his colleagues looked at the skulls and soft tissues of living animals and found particular pits for the blood vessels and nerves that are associated with the fleshy nostril. When they looked at the skulls of dinosaurs, they found the same pits at the front of the snouts of dinosaurs, even those with their nostril openings on the tops of their skulls. So paleontologists and paleoartists now think that all dinosaurs had fleshy nostrils toward the end of their snouts.

And what about cheeks? Check out chapter 26 for the rest of that story!

THE QUESTION OF COLOR

Finally, what colors were dinosaurs? After all, the colors or color patterns on living animals are very distinctive. Think about the black-and-white feathers of a male ostrich, the brilliant colors of a

Opposite: A full-color restoration of *Sinornithosaurus* and a dead *Confuciusornis.*

Left and below: Because color doesn't normally preserve in fossils, an artist has to use his or her judgment, knowledge of modern animals, and imagination when finishing up a painting.

parrot, the stripes of a zebra, and the spots of a cheetah. Unfortunately, none of these colors and patterns are more than "skin deep," so there is no way to discern them from bones or integument impressions.

The same is true for the fossils of dinosaurs. There really is no way to tell what colors any of the dinosaurs of the Mesozoic were. Almost certainly some had showy patterns and others were plain, but we don't know which were which. We can make some reasonable guesses, though. Dinosaurs with big showy surfaces, like the plates of stegosaurs or the frills of ceratopsians, likely used these to display to other dinosaurs. So it is not unreasonable to think that at least some of the time these structures had bright colors to them.

Because all the closest living descendants and relatives of the dinosaurs of the Mesozoic (that is, birds and other reptiles) have good color vision,

we can infer that extinct dinosaurs did as well. Animals with good color vision often have brilliant colors, at least during times of the year when they want to attract members of the opposite sex.

On the other hand, it might have been problematic for a predatory dinosaur to be *too* showy when stalking other dinosaurs, or for a herbivore to be *too* brilliantly colored if predators were about. So we expect that a lot of dinosaurs had colors that helped them blend into the environment, too.

If you want to be a paleoartist, dinosaur color is one part of the restoration process where it is hard to be proven incorrect (at least without a time machine!). So use your imagination when you color them. But remember that what you are restoring was once a living, breathing animal—please try to make it realistic. Dinosaur art should always be based on dinosaur science.

7

TAXONOMY: Why Do Dinosaurs Have Such Strange Names?

One thing about dinosaurs that many young people find fascinating, and many older people find difficult, is their names. Whether they are short names (like *Mei*) or long ones (like *Micropachycephalosaurus*), dinosaur names are a lot different from modern animal names like "cat," "crocodile," and "horse." Why is that?

A SCIENTIFIC SYSTEM OF NAMES

The names "cat," "crocodile," and "horse" are examples of common names for animals. People have known about these critters for thousands of years, and they came up with these names a long time ago. Every culture comes up with common names for the living things that it encounters. After all, saying "cat" is a lot easier than saying "one of those triangular-eared, long-whiskered, furry creatures with sharp retractable claws."

The problem, however, is that *every* culture has its own common names for the living things that it encounters. So the animal called "cat" in English is *gato* in Spanish, *chat* in French, *Katze* in German, *neko* in Japanese, *mao* in Chinese, *paka* in Swahili, *felis* and *catus* in ancient Latin, *ailouros* in ancient Greek, and so forth.

Scientists and linguistic scholars in the 1600s and 1700s found all these common names problematic. What they wanted was a single name that people all over the world could use for the same animal or plant, regardless of what that animal or plant was commonly called in different places—that is, they wanted a taxonomy: a set of rules for giving scientific names to living things.

The main naturalist to develop the beginnings

Top: Carolus Linnaeus, who developed the Linnaean system of taxonomy. Above: Every language (such as those of ancient Egypt, nineteenth-century America, and twentieth-century France) has a different word for *cat*. But scientists around the world use the same name for this species: *Felis catus*.

of our modern system of naming was Carl von Linné of Sweden, who lived in the 1700s. Like many scholars of that time, he wrote his books in Latin, which most educated people in the world could read. So in his writings he isn't called Carl von Linné but rather by the Latin form of his name: Carolus Linnaeus. And the system for making scientific names that he came up with is called the Linnaean system of taxonomy.

Considering Linné gave himself a Latin pen name, it isn't too surprising that he used Latin to name animals and plants. (He actually gave Latin names to rocks and minerals, too, but geologists never really went for Linnaean taxonomy and instead developed their own system.)

Linnaeus's system had several different rules. One is that all the names would be in Latin or Greek, or at least in a Latin- or Greek-like form. Another is that all living things were grouped into small categories, called species, as well as larger categories, called genera. (Linnaeus grouped them into other larger categories, as well, but we'll deal with that in the next chapter.) We'll start by looking at genera.

The English words "generic" and "general" come from the Latin word *genera,* and they all mean the same basic thing: some broad category of things. Each genus (the singular form of "genera") contains at least one species, and many genera contain lots of different species. For example, when we say "crocodile" in English, we're actually talking about a genus called *Crocodylus* in the Linnaean system. *Crocodylus* contains twelve different species in the modern world and a bunch of ones known only from fossils. Each genus has a unique, one-word name. It should be capitalized and written in *italics.*

Species are literally more specific categories than genera. In fact, that is where the word "specific" comes from! In the Linnaean system, every genus has one or more species. And every species belongs to one genus. Species names are two-word names. The first part of a species name is the genus that it belongs to; the second part is an extra word that forms a unique combination with the genus name. So within *Crocodylus* there is *Crocodylus*

niloticus (whose common name is the Nile crocodile), *Crocodylus porosus* (the saltwater crocodile), *Crocodylus acutus* (the American crocodile), and so on. (If we want to write this in an abbreviated form, we can also say *C. niloticus, C. porosus,* and *C. acutus.*)

When fossil organisms were first discovered, scientists wanted to give them Linnaean names, too. And they did. But because no culture had seen these animals alive, they had no common names for scientists to translate into Latin. So instead, scientists came up with new names. These names might describe how the animal looked (*Triceratops horridus,* "rough three-horned face") or how it is thought to have acted (*Tyrannosaurus rex,* "tyrant reptile king"). Other names might honor the person who found the fossil or another scientist or someone else who helped the namer (*Lambeosaurus lambei,* after Lawrence Lambe). Other names may be based on a mythological character or a place: *Jobaria tiguidensis* refers to the Jobar, a mythical beast from North Africa, and the Tiguidi cliff, a place near where the first *Jobaria* skeleton was found.

Most of the time, we only refer to dinosaurs by their genus name. *Tyrannosaurus rex* is just about the only dinosaur that *everyone* knows by its species name. In fact, when we talk about a dinosaur genus, it might be that only one species is known, but it might also be that many species are known. For example, many paleontologists think that there are three different species of *Apatosaurus: A. ajax, A. excelsus,* and *A. louisae.* If these really are three different species, then they might have been as different from each other as lions, tigers, and leopards.

LUMPING AND SPLITTING

But why should only "many paleontologists" and not *all* paleontologists think that there are three different species? After all, we can easily tell lions apart from tigers, right?

Well, you might be able to tell lions from tigers from their outsides, but their insides (and, specifically, their skeletons) are pretty much identical. And with dinosaur fossils, bones are pretty much

Lions and tigers are easy to tell apart in the flesh and fur, but their skeletons are almost identical.

all we have (and in most cases, not even a complete skeleton!). So, if you have two fossils that are slightly different from each other, you are stuck with a couple of hypotheses about those differences. Maybe they are two entirely different genera? Maybe they are two different species in the same genus? Or maybe they are both members of the same species, but one was fully grown and one was younger, or one was male and the other female? And, let's face it, no two members of the same species are 100 percent identical anyway.

It would be great if I could whip out my Species Detector or Generometer and use it to tell if two different fossils belong to the same species or genus. But I can't, because there isn't such a thing. In fact, the problem of telling if two different individuals are from the same species isn't limited to paleontologists: even biologists who work on modern animals have this problem. (We just have it worse because we *never* get to see the whole animal!)

Since Species Detectors and Generometers aren't real, we have to use something else. One thing we can do is start by looking at how modern animals within a species differ from each other. We measure the differences, or variation, within populations of living animals that most biologists agree belong to the same species. Then we look at the fossils. If the differences between them are about the same as the range of variation in modern species, then we would agree that these two fossils belong to the same species. If the differences between them seem greater than what we see in typical modern species—but within the range we

see in modern genera—then we would say that the fossils are probably different species in the same genus. If the differences measured are even more than that, then we'd say that they are from different genera.

As you might guess, not all scientists agree on how much variation is species level and how much is genus level. It isn't that some scientists are definitely wrong and others are definitely right, but rather that we all have honest differences of opinion. Scientists who think that there is a lot of variation in any species or genus are called lumpers, because they "lump" lots of specimens into the same species or genus. Scientists who think that there is little variation in a given species or genus are called splitters, because they "split" those specimens into many different groups.

TYPES AND PRIORITY

Okay, so what do lumping and splitting mean for dinosaur names? Well, Linnaeus and the other early taxonomists knew that these sorts of disagreements might happen, so they set up rules to govern which names would be used.

The first rule is that each species has its own type specimen. This is a particular individual that the name goes with. Scientists can then compare other specimens to the type specimen when they are comparing amounts of variation. So, if a new fossil is found that has a lot of differences from the type specimen of a species, it's very likely it belongs to a different species. In fact, if the new fossil is very different from *all* the type specimens of already-named species, then it probably belongs to a whole new species and can become a whole new type specimen.

The second rule is the principle of priority, which in its simplest form means that the oldest name given is the one that must be used. So, if today we scientists decide to lump two different species or genera together, the oldest species or genus name has priority. In a famous case, *Brontosaurus excelsus* (which was named in 1879) was considered to belong to the same genus as *Apatosaurus ajax* (which was named in 1877). Even though *Brontosaurus* (thunder reptile) was a much more widely known—and, I happen to think, cooler—name than *Apatosaurus* (deceptive reptile), the latter (older) name has priority, and today we call the first dinosaur *Apatosaurus excelsus.*

Even with these rules, though, there is still disagreement between paleontologists about the exact classification of particular fossils. Because of this disagreement, some of the dinosaurs in this book may be called by different names in other books. In the table in the back of the book, I've tried to note where these disagreements have occurred.

* * *

BEYOND THE GENUS

Linnaeus and the other taxonomists didn't stop at the genus level. Linnaeus recognized something very interesting about the natural world. He noticed that each species fits into one—*just one*—genus. He also noticed that it was pretty easy to group genera together into larger groups, and those larger groups into even larger groups. In Linnaean taxonomy, each larger group could get its own name. These larger groups all had single-word Latin-style names, which were capitalized but (unlike genera) were not italicized. So the species *Tyrannosaurus rex* belongs in the genus *Tyrannosaurus,* which was part of the even larger groups Tyrannosauridae, Tyrannosauroidea, Coelurosauria, Theropoda, and Dinosauria.

But why do living things fit into these larger groups? Linnaeus never figured this out, but a century after him, a scientist named Charles Darwin did. And a century after Darwin, another scientist, Willi Hennig, figured out a way to combine Darwin's discoveries with a scientific method of grouping animals into larger and larger groups. In the next chapter, we'll see what Darwin discovered, and how Hennig's system changed the way we figure out who is most closely related to whom.

For many years, paleontologists regarded *"Brontosaurus"* as its own distinct genus, but now it is generally considered a type of *Apatosaurus.* Our knowledge of this dinosaur has changed, so pictures of it have gone from showing the blunt-faced, tail-dragging form (left) to depicting the more elegant animal below.

Digging Through Dinosaur Names

Ben Creisler
www.dinosauria.com

Photo courtesy of Ben Creisler

Why do dinosaurs have such long, complicated names?

I asked that question for the first time in kindergarten after the teacher showed pictures of creatures "as big as a house" that lived long ago. Dinosaurs made my imagination go, "Wow!" and I had fun learning their strange scientific names.

Those Greek and Latin names helped spark my interest in all kinds of languages. I studied about languages at different universities and later wrote articles about dinosaur names that had been misunderstood. After more work, I put lists of names of dinosaurs with their meanings and pronunciations on the World Wide Web and even helped paleontologists come up with scientific names for new dinosaurs.

Pronouncing such complicated Greek or Latin names is not easy. Different people may pronounce dinosaur names in different ways. For example, Deinonychus *is sometimes pronounced as die-NON-ick-us or die-no-NIE-kuss. Either way is correct, and they both mean "terrible claw." Some ways are better than others—even though people don't pronounce the p next to the t in* pterodactyl *(tair-uh-DAK-til), they should pronounce it in* Caudipteryx *(kaw-DIP-tuh-riks) (meaning "tail feather"), the same as they do in* helicopter.

Maybe the hardest names to pronounce contain words from Chinese. A few tips help: x sounds like "sh," q like "ch," and zh like "j," so: Xiaosaurus *(she-ow-SAW-rus) (meaning "dawn lizard"),* Qinlingosaurus *(CHIN-ling-uh-SAW-rus) (meaning "lizard from Qinling"), and* Zizhongosaurus *(dzuh-JOONG-uh-SAW-rus) (meaning "lizard from Zizhong").*

How do paleontologists choose the names for dinosaurs?

Names can describe how a dinosaur looked, such as Triceratops *(try-SEHR-uh-tops), which means "three-horned face." A name may describe how it behaved:* Maiasaura *(MY-uh-SAW-ruh) means "good mother lizard." Others may tell where a dinosaur was found, such as* Albertosaurus *(al-BERT-uh-SAW-rus), for "Alberta (Canada) lizard." Or a dinosaur name may honor a person, as in* Marshosaurus, *for "O. C. Marsh's lizard." A few are even jokes.* Gasosaurus *("gas lizard") was named for a gas-drilling company that found dinosaur bones in southern China, but the Chinese word for "gas" also means to "make trouble"—fitting for a meat-eating dinosaur!*

There are now (in 2007) over 800 names for dinosaurs. The longest is Micropachycephalosaurus *(MY-krow-PAK-ee-SEF-uh-low-SAW-rus), which means "little thickheaded lizard." There are two names consisting of only five letters each:* Khaan *(KAHN), a Mongolian word meaning "ruler," and* Minmi *(MIN-mee), for a place in Australia. One of the oddest names may be* Hudiesaurus *(HOO-dee-eh-SAW-rus), or "butterfly lizard," for a giant plant-eater from China! Parts of its backbone looked a bit like butterfly wings, so a Chinese scientist used the Chinese word* hudie, *meaning "butterfly."*

Sometimes you don't have to be a grown-up scientist to name a dinosaur. Fourteen-year-old Wes Linster found the skeleton of a little meat-eating dinosaur in Montana. He nicknamed it "Bambiraptor" ("baby robber") after the baby deer in a Disney movie—and paleontologists made Bambiraptor *(BAM-bee-RAP-tor) its official name!*

You can also have a dinosaur named for you. Byronosaurus *(BYE-ron-uh-SAW-rus) was named for Byron Jaffe, the son of a family who paid for dinosaur expeditions to Mongolia, and* Leaellynasaura *(lay-ELL-in-uh-SAW-ruh) was named for Leaellyn Rich, the young daughter of two paleontologists.*

The names for dinosaurs can be almost as surprising—and fun—as dinosaurs themselves!

8
EVOLUTION:
Descent with Modification

By around 1800, when scientists really began to understand fossils, they saw that the animals and plants whose remains were preserved in the rocks were different from the living animals and plants around them. Some were very similar and some were very different, but almost none were identical. So scientists proposed the idea of evolution: the theory that living things change over long periods of time. One of the best ways to describe evolution is "descent with modification" (a phrase used by Darwin himself). And the first step in understanding evolution comes from looking at the anatomy of different animals.

BARNYARD COMPARATIVE ANATOMY

Think about this before you read the next paragraph: Which farm animals have knees that point backward?

Did you guess horses, cows, sheep, and other four-legged mammals? Or did you guess chickens, ducks, geese, and other barnyard birds? Either way, you would be completely wrong! (Don't worry, though: almost everyone makes the same mistake!)

None of these animals—or *any* animal—has a knee that points backward. Some of them *seem* to have backward-pointing knees, but the part that's pointing backward isn't a knee at all. It's a backward-pointing ankle! Most people are mistaken about which parts of these animals correspond to which parts of our (human animal) bodies. To properly identify the body parts, you need

to understand the basics of comparative anatomy: the study of the common anatomical "blueprint" shared by closely related living things.

Comparative anatomists like Baron Georges Cuvier noticed over 200 years ago that barnyard animals and other vertebrates have the same basic body plan. For instance, they all have a single upper-leg bone that connects to the hip on the top and to the knee on the bottom; a pair of bones between the knee and the ankle; some small ankle-bones; long, slender bones between the ankle and the toes; and the various individual toe bones. Look at your own leg. It follows that same pattern.

Now if you were to look at the skeleton of a cow, dog, or chicken, you would find that same basic pattern. But you would find that the thigh is fairly short, so the knee is closer to the hip in these animals than it is in a human. What most people mistakenly think is a cow (or dog or chicken) knee is really its ankle, which points backward, just like our ankles do. In fact, cows, dogs, and chickens

Top: Charles Darwin, co-discoverer of evolution by natural selection.

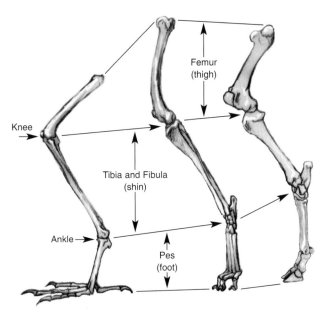

The legs of a chicken, cat, and cow are made of the same bones.

(and all other barnyard animals) actually stand on their toes and not the "soles" of their feet.

In comparative anatomy, we give the same name to the same bone in all different animals. So the thighbone is called the femur, the two bones in the shin are the tibia and fibula, and so on.

The reason that related animals have the same bones and other structures is that they had an ancestor who had that overall body plan. When we look at ancient mammal fossils or ancient bird fossils, we find the same bones as in living mammals and birds, respectively, but the exact shape and proportion of these bones are different. And some of these ancient animals had features that today are found in totally distinct groups. For example, *Archaeopteryx* had feathers like a bird but a long, bony tail, clawed fingers, and teeth like a typical reptile.

Why are there these anatomical differences between various related animals? What purpose do they serve? And what caused the changes?

ADAPTATIONS

Let's look at the forelimb (front leg or arm) of some dinosaurs. The forelimb of dinosaurs—and all other vertebrates—has a very similar pattern to the hind limb: there is a single upper-arm bone, a pair of forearm bones, a bunch of little wristbones, long bones of the palm of the hand, and individual

bones down each finger. However, the forelimbs of each animal are shaped differently for specific functions: that is, they are adapted to different ways of life. So we say that the differences in shape are adaptations. We also call these differences specializations because they help living things move or act in a particular way. For example, the long fingers and sharp claws of *Deinonychus* were specializations that allowed that carnivorous dinosaur to quickly grab prey. The heavy limb bones and broad front feet of *Stegosaurus* were specializations useful for supporting its heavy weight. The long, slender hand of *Anatotitan* could support some of its weight, but its opposable pinkie was a specialization that let it grab food as well. And compared to all of these, the hand of *Plateosaurus* was rather generic: it could grab a bit and support some weight, but it didn't show much in the way of specialization.

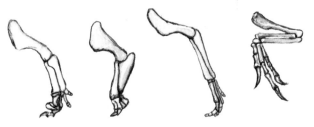

The forelimbs of *Plateosaurus*, *Stegosaurus*, *Anatotitan*, and *Deinonychus* contain the same bones but in different proportions based on the way they were used.

NATURAL SELECTION

The discovery of the process that explains how these adaptations occur was made independently by two British scientists named Charles Darwin and Alfred Russel Wallace in the mid-nineteenth century. Darwin and Wallace called the process they discovered natural selection. It works like this: every living thing (including members of the same species) is slightly different from every other living thing. Now some of those slight differences (called variations) might help an individual survive better in the wild. They might make it a little faster, or smarter, or smaller, or whatever. In the wild, far more individuals are born than can possibly survive, so any advantage an individual has gives it a slightly better chance of staying alive. Those individuals with a variation that helps them

to survive have a better chance of growing up to have kids of their own. And if that variation is genetic (that is, passed on by DNA), then at least some of an individual's offspring will also have that difference—they'll be faster, or smarter, or smaller, or whatever.

With enough time, these changes add up. Each generation varies slightly from the one before, until eventually descendants might not look or act any-

Some traits—like the frill of *Triceratops* and the plates of *Stegosaurus*—may have evolved to make dinosaurs more attractive to members of their own species.

thing like their ancestors. They will have different shapes and behaviors, and the features that were once just slight variations will become whole new specializations. In other words, the descendants will become a brand-new kind of living thing: they will have evolved into a new species.

You can see why natural selection couldn't have been discovered until *after* scientists figured out that the Earth was millions upon millions of years old. If the Earth were only a few thousand years old, there simply wouldn't be enough time for the vast number of generations needed to turn subtle variations into complex specializations.

Some people in Darwin's time, and even today, get confused about evolution. They think that it means that creatures are getting more "perfect" over time. Sometimes there *are* signs of major improvements from ancestors to descendants. For example, early feathered dinosaurs like *Microraptor* and *Archaeopteryx* were probably lousy fliers, if they could actually fly at all. But their feathered arms did help them to run up the sides of trees (as you'll see in chapter 19)! Later dinosaurs inherited these feathered flapping arms. Some continued to use them in the same fashion, but others (perhaps ones with slightly broader feathers) were able to use them for more: perhaps swooping down from trees or gliding from branch

Opposite: Jurassic *Archaeopteryx* had both the advanced feature of feathers and the primitive traits of toothed jaws and long, bony tails. As later birds evolved, they lost teeth within their beaks, and the tail became more specialized.

to branch. Over time, descendants of some of the ones with the bigger wings evolved other new traits, like bigger chest muscles so they could propel themselves better from tree to tree. In other words, they became true fliers.

But other times a descendant isn't really any more "perfect" at doing something than its ancestor was. Think about how natural selection works: those variations that do better in a particular environment are the ones that are the most likely to get passed on. But we know from geology that environments are changing all the time! So a variation that worked for your ancestors might not work best for you. And since the other living things in your environment are evolving, too, variations that were once not particularly helpful may suddenly be beneficial.

So the phrase "survival of the fittest" (a term that was used by people who studied business and was eventually applied to evolution) isn't really the best description of evolution. It's better to just use "descent with modification."

Darwin noticed something else: specializations were not limited to traits like speed or brains that helped an individual survive better in the wild. They could also be traits that made the individual more attractive! If an animal had some feature that the opposite sex happened to fancy (prettier feathers, bigger horns, or whatever), then that animal would be more likely to have children than other members of its population. Darwin named this sexual selection, and it explains many of the more bizarre (to our eyes) features in living things today, like the tails of peacocks. Sexual selection might help to explain things like the frills and horns of ceratopsid dinosaurs or the plates of *Stegosaurus*.

THE TREE OF LIFE

Many people—from before Darwin's time and up to the present day—think that evolution is one species evolving into just one more species, like a ladder or chain of species through time. But Darwin and company saw that it was more complex than that. One species could give rise to *just one* descendant species. Or it could go entirely extinct. Or it could give rise to *more than one* descendant species. It all depended on how many sets of variations were favored by natural selection.

Imagine if a species of plant-eater had some descendants that were smaller and better able to hide and others that were larger and better able to fight off predators. Over time, you would most likely get two descendant species, one smaller than the ancestor and one larger. So the pattern of evolution isn't like a ladder or chain but more like a tree. On the Tree of Life, time is represented by height. At the base of the tree's trunk is the common ancestor species. The ancestor survives for a while (that is, the trunk grows upward), but, eventually, the ancestral line splits into two or more branches. Each of these branches is now a whole new species. These species might continue to evolve and grow and give rise to new species themselves. Or they might become extinct. Over time, what was once a single trunk has given rise to many different branches and twigs.

The leaves at the tips of the smallest twigs are the living species of the modern world. If all we knew were the living species of the modern world, we'd just see a lot of leaves. We might notice that some of the leaves are close to each other (in other words, that some animals resemble each other), but we wouldn't see the connections between them. The woody part of the tree—the trunk and branches and twigs—is the past history of the modern species. We only see the woody part of the tree when we look at fossils. Some are ancestors of modern forms and lie directly on the branches that

lead to modern species. But others are side branches and twigs that had split off from the ancestors of modern creatures only to become extinct.

Darwin, Wallace, and their contemporaries tried to draw family trees—which they called phylogenies—of different groups of animals and plants. But in those days, it was mostly guesswork. They didn't have a scientific way (that is, testing hypotheses based on observations) of figuring out which branches connected with which other branches. A good method to figure that out would not be discovered until the middle of the twentieth century, just about a hundred years after Darwin and Wallace first put forth the idea of natural selection.

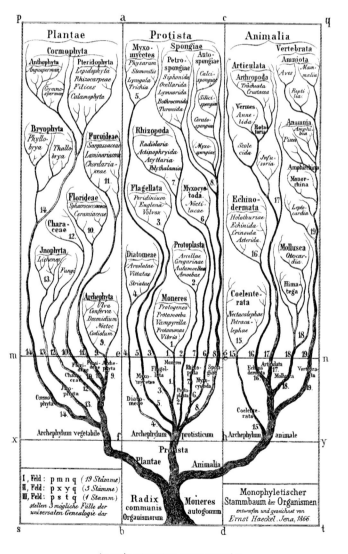

An early attempt to reconstruct the Tree of Life by German scientist Ernst Haeckel.

50

9
CLADISTICS: Figuring Out the Dinosaur Family Tree

In the 1700s, Carolus Linnaeus developed a way to organize living things into small groups, then into larger and larger ones. For example, lions, tigers, and house cats are all part of the group Felidae (the cat family). Felidae, Ursidae (the bear family), Canidae (the dog family), and others are grouped together in the larger group Carnivora (the meat-eating mammals). Carnivora, Rodentia (the rodents), Chiroptera (the bats), and others are grouped into the even bigger category Mammalia (the mammals). But Linnaeus didn't know *why* it was possible to do that. A hundred years later, Charles Darwin and Alfred Russel Wallace came up with a theory. The reason? Living things evolve through time, and Linnaeus's groups represent the descendants of common ancestors. The smaller Linnaean groups represent descendants of recent common ancestors, while the larger groups had ancestors further back in time.

Pretty simple. But how do we figure out which groups shared the most recent common ancestor? Darwin and Wallace suspected that specializations shared between related groups would be the main clue to understanding this. But neither of them developed a way to use specializations to determine relationships. That would not happen for about a hundred years, until German scientist Willi Hennig (who studied flies) created a way to use observations about an animal's physical features and other traits to determine the most likely relationships between it and animals in other groups. By using Hennig's technique—called cladistics—we can figure out the phylogeny, or family tree, for any group of living things: fungi, shrimp, cats, and, of course, dinosaurs.

Top: The features of dinosaurs are converted into computer codes to run a cladistic analysis.

TRACING THE SHAPE OF THE TREE OF LIFE

In 1859, Darwin observed that Linnaean taxonomy could be represented as an evolutionary Tree of Life. For example, smaller groupings, like species within a genus (such as *Panthera leo* and *Panthera tigris* within *Panthera*), represent animals or plants that had a recently shared common ancestor, but more distantly related categories, like genera within a family (such as *Panthera* and *Felis* in Felidae) or families within an order (such as Felidae and Ursidae in Carnivora), represent much older divergences. Or, to use Darwin's Tree of Life comparison, closely related species are leaves connected by twigs. And more distantly related groups are twigs connected by longer branches. And eventually, *all* living things are connected to each other at the base of the tree! So even leaves on opposite sides of the tree are connected to some degree.

As living things evolved—or as the Tree of Life grew—new specializations appeared in each branch and were passed on. This was about as far as Darwin got—he recognized that there would be a pattern of specialization, but he never really figured out how to *use* that pattern.

Building on Darwin's observations, in the 1950s and 1960s Hennig recognized that you can work backward down the Tree of Life (that is, starting at the leaves, working down through the twigs and branches to the trunk) by looking at shared specializations. These shared specializations are like markers left by evolutionary history. Hennig showed that we can look at which species have which markers and figure out their evolutionary relationships.

For instance, bears, zebras, duckbilled platypi, and lizards do not have retractable claws, but lions and tigers do. So lions and tigers share a common ancestor distinct from the others. Lions and tigers evolved retractable claws from an ancestor with nonretractable claws. This specialization evolved *after* the common ancestor of lions and tigers had split from the ancestors of all these other animals, but before that common ancestor had split into lions and tigers.

Zebras, platypi, and lizards do not have molar teeth with a specialized shearing shape that helps them to eat meat, but lions, tigers, and bears do. So there was an ancestor of lions, tigers, and bears that evolved this specialization after it had split off from the ancestors of the other creatures. Lions, tigers, and bears are descendants of that modified ancestor.

Going further down the Tree of Life, lions, tigers, bears, and zebras have live births. Platypi and lizards lay eggs. So the specialization of live birth shows that lions, tigers, bears, and zebras had a common ancestor. Furthermore, lions, tigers, bears, zebras, and platypi have fur and give milk. Lizards do not.

By making these kinds of observations of how animals share some features but not others, we can make a hypothesis of the shape of the family tree.

Here it goes: the common ancestor of lions, tigers, bears, zebras, and platypi was an animal that evolved fur and milk. That ancestor had at least two descendant branches—one eventually leading to platypi and one to the rest. That second descendant evolved live birth and had one descendant line that eventually led to zebras and another that led to the ancestor of lions, tigers, and bears. Again, that latter ancestor eventually split into two different lines, one leading to bears and one to cats. And that latter ancestral line includes the ancestors of tigers and lions.

We can show this hypothesis of relationship in a couple of different ways. We can show it by putting the different animals that share particular features in the same bubbles, like this:

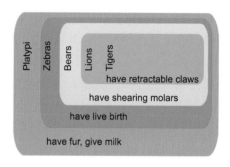

But another way is to draw a sketch of the branching pattern. This sketch is called a *cladogram* (from *klados*, Greek for "branch") and represents a hypothesis of the shape of the Tree of Life. Here's the cladogram for the animals we have been discussing:

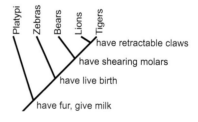

(Note: this isn't the complete Tree of Life *by any means*! It is just a subset of the complete tree. It doesn't include all the other cats, or dogs, or raccoons and other bear relatives, or all the other types of mammals. It doesn't show any of the extinct mammals, either. Its purpose here is to trace the shape of the branches joining the individual leaves—that is, species—we are looking at.)

Cladistics, which is basically the process of making and studying cladograms, is now the main method used by biologists (including dinosaur paleontologists) for figuring out which creatures are most closely related to which other creatures. Some people find cladistics a bit complicated, and it is true that it takes a lot of work to fully understand it. But when we look at its basic principles, cladistics is straightforward.

Hennig recognized that not all features of living things were useful in figuring out which are most closely related. Using the example from before, we might notice that lizards, platypi, bears, tigers, and lions all have five fingers on each hand, but zebras have only one. So we might think that all five-fingered animals are more closely related to each other than they are to zebras. But when we look at additional animals (like turtles and crocodilians and opossums and others), we see that five-fingered hands are common to most: they represent the *ancestral,* or *primitive,* condition. That means that this is the condition that was found in the common ancestor of all the animals we're looking at, both the five-fingered ones and the one-fingered zebra. The reason that bears and lizards both have five fingers isn't that they share a five-fingered ancestor that zebras don't. They simply never evolved a different condition than their ancestors. So ancestral conditions don't let us figure out who is most closely related to whom.

Also, the single-toed foot is just a *unique* specialization on the line to the zebra not found in the other animals. It doesn't show us if zebras are closer to tigers or to lizards. So unique specializations don't help us determine the shape of a cladogram, either. Only those specializations that are shared by some, but not all, of the animals are useful.

Both tigers and zebras have stripes, so we might think that they are more closely related to each other than to the other animals (through one that evolved stripes). But when we look at more features (like retractable claws and shearing teeth), we see that tigers are closer to lions and bears than to zebras. The stripes of tigers and zebras must

have evolved *independently,* or *convergently.* Therefore, because convergently evolved features might mislead us, biologists look at many different features in the animals concerned. If we just looked at one, we might get a false impression about the evolutionary relationships of those animals.

The best way to reconstruct the shape of the Tree of Life is to look at as many different specializations as possible. The example I've given here might seem complex, but it is *a lot* simpler than what a biologist would really do to figure out the relationships between lions, tigers, bears, zebras, platypi, and lizards. In a real *cladistic analysis,* there might be dozens of species, and dozens or hundreds of specializations, to be examined.

Because this is a time-consuming task, scientists use computers to do their cladistic analyses. They enter their observations of animals and their specializations into software programs, and the programs evaluate different possible cladograms for those animals. The software programs calculate how many changes from the primitive condition to the specialized one are needed on each branch of a cladogram to match what we observe in nature. Scientists follow the rule called Occam's razor: when given the choice, always pick the simpler explanation over the more complex ones. For this reason, the cladogram or cladograms that require the fewest number of changes are preferred. They might not be correct, but they are the "best guess" we can make with the data currently available. And by adding in new information (new specializations, observations, and species), we can check our previous results and hopefully improve the accuracy of our answers.

ADVANTAGES OF CLADISTICS

Before Hennig, most people who tried to draw family trees of living things were concerned when they couldn't find the direct ancestors of each species in the fossil record. What Hennig showed is that you can reconstruct the shape of the Tree of Life even when you don't include all the ancestors and descendants.

Because you can make a cladogram by

examining the specializations found in a limited number of species rather than finding every last ancestor and descendant, cladistics is very useful for paleontologists. After all, only a tiny fraction of the creatures that ever existed have become fossils and been discovered! So even if we don't find every ancestor and descendant in the fossil record, we can still get an *approximation* of the shape of that part of the Tree of Life.

Making a cladogram is also more scientific than the old way of drawing phylogenies. Remember that to be scientific, a hypothesis has to be something that can be tested. When scientists perform a cladistic analysis, they have to state what observations of specializations they made on each particular species. Then they use a computer to find the one cladogram (or sometimes a bunch of cladograms) that most simply explains the observations they made. Another scientist should be able to take the same data and find the same answer.

Cladistics also lets a paleontologist "fill in the gaps" of missing information in some cases. Below is the cladogram for the Tyrannosauroidea, or tyrant dinosaurs:

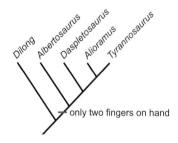

We see that the common ancestor of *Albertosaurus, Daspletosaurus,* and *Tyrannosaurus* had the specialization of a two-fingered hand, so their common ancestor evolved from a three-fingered hand (like *Dilong*) to a two-fingered one. (Most carnivorous dinosaurs related to the tyrant dinosaurs, such as dromaeosaurid raptors, ornithomimosaurs, and allosaurs, have three-fingered hands, so the three-fingered hand is the ancestral condition.) *Alioramus* is only known from a partial skull and some foot bones, so we don't have its hand skeleton. However, from the cladogram we see that it is also a descendant of the

two-fingered ancestor, so it almost certainly had only two fingers per hand. In fact, to argue that it had a three- (or four- or five-) fingered hand is to argue for an evolutionary change for which we don't have evidence. In science, we should never argue for things for which we don't have evidence (either directly or inferred from other information).

DIFFERENCES BETWEEN LINNAEAN AND CLADISTIC TAXONOMY

When Linnaeus set up his system of taxonomy, he used overall similarity as the basic principle for joining groups together. Cladistic taxonomy, following the ideas of Darwin and Hennig, looks to create groups that are based on *common ancestry*.

Sometimes the Linnaean system actually matches an analysis based on common ancestry. Relabeling the first cladogram in the chapter, we find that it matches the traditional classification of mammals:

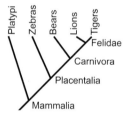

But sometimes Linnaeus and his followers were misled. They grouped creatures together based on primitive features rather than on common ancestry as revealed by specializations. Look at the cladogram below:

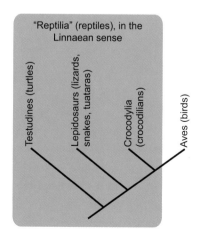

In Linnaean taxonomy, birds have their own group, Aves, because they are so different from other creatures. For example, birds are warm-blooded and have feathers, and most of them can fly. Turtles, lizards, and crocodilians were grouped together as Reptilia because they were scaly, cold-blooded, and laid eggs on land rather than in the water. But being scaly and cold-blooded and laying eggs on land are all primitive features, not specializations. There are no unique specializations shared by turtles, lizards, and crocodilians that aren't also shared by birds. But to most people, crocodilians look more similar overall to lizards than they do to birds.

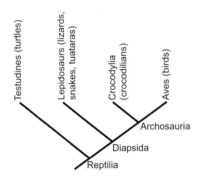

But when we use the evolutionary relationships revealed by specializations, we get a different set of groupings. We see that birds are *part* of Reptilia, which isn't defined by primitive features but by specializations that are also found in birds.

So even though they don't look very similar, crocodilians are more closely related to birds than either are to lizards.

This doesn't mean that birds are any less "birdy" than they were before people started using cladistics. They are still their own special group. But now we can tell that birds aren't something totally different from reptiles: they are a really specialized group *of* reptiles.

A cladogram can be a very useful tool for understanding the relationships between different

animals. It can also be used to figure out which creatures had which specializations. Below is a cladogram of Ceratopsia (the frilled, horned dinosaurs) labeled so that you can understand how to read this information:

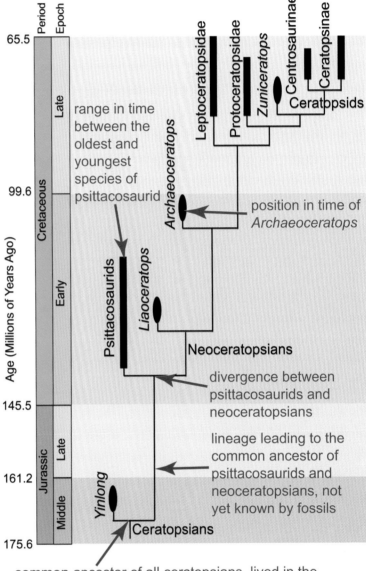

common ancestor of all ceratopsians, lived in the Middle Jurassic (at the latest), not yet known by fossils

This is a *really* brief look at cladistics. There is a lot more you can learn about it and from it. But this is enough to get you started. In the next chapter, I'll show how we use cladistics to see where dinosaurs fit in the family tree of the vertebrates. And in the Saurischia and Ornithischia chapters, I'll show the cladograms of these groups of dinosaurs as they are currently understood.

10
EVOLUTION OF THE VERTEBRATES

Dinosaurs are just one of many branches on the family tree of vertebrates—animals with an internal skeleton. Their skeletons—and ours—show the traces of our shared evolutionary history. Surprisingly, that history begins underwater.

All life, including all vertebrates, first evolved in the sea and got oxygen from the water. Today we have a name for vertebrates that get their oxygen from the water: we call them fish. But they don't represent a single, discrete branch of the Tree of Life. Instead, there are many different branches of "fish," some of which are more closely related to you and dinosaurs than they are to other fish.

The history of the vertebrates is a *huge* topic—we would need many, *many* more volumes the size of this one to do the story justice. So I'm afraid

Above: One of the many aquatic stegocephalians, *Crassigyrinus*, chases a lungfish in a Carboniferous lake.

Top: Like all vertebrates, this snake's skeleton is made up of many different individual bones.

you'll have to settle for this very brief review:

The first vertebrates appeared in the Cambrian Period, more than 500 million years ago. They had a head and a tail, but no bones or fins or jaws. Over the course of the next 100 million years, each of these traits evolved and was passed on to their various descendants. In one lineage, simple lungs evolved. The lungs helped these fish to gulp air if they couldn't get enough oxygen from the water. (If you have pet goldfish, you might see them doing this from time to time.)

One of these groups of fish with bones, jaws, and lungs evolved specialized fins with wrists and ankles. These are called the stegocephalians and they first appeared in the Devonian Period. Their wrists and ankles could help them to push through the dense vegetation in swampy waters and also to push along the land if they needed to get to a different pond or stream. (Today there are fish such as the mudskipper and snakehead that do this with just fins. With wrists and ankles, the stegocephalians were able to move much more easily.)

To the right, you can see a cladogram showing the evolution of the stegocephalians. As you can see, this group includes amphibians, synapsids (our own group!), and many different types of reptiles. And one of these types of reptiles was the dinosaurs.

Evolution of the Stegocephalians

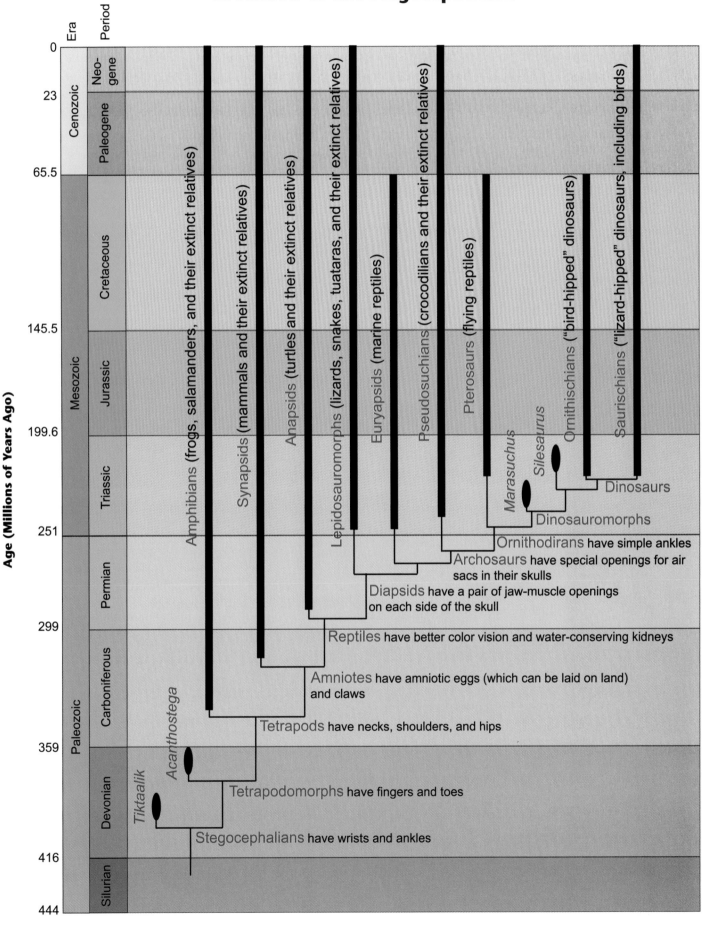

SKULL ANATOMY

On the previous pages, you saw the cladogram of the vertebrates. And you saw how new anatomical features—including different parts of the skeleton—were added on by evolution. In order to understand more about dinosaurs, their evolutionary relationships, and their biology, we need to know the details of their anatomy.

Most amniotes have a similar basic skeletal structure. The skeleton is divided up into the *skull* and everything else (the *postcranial* skeleton). The skull houses the brain and many sense organs (nose, eyes, tongue, and ears). Skulls are made up of many different bones, with openings for the sense organs and other soft-tissue structures.

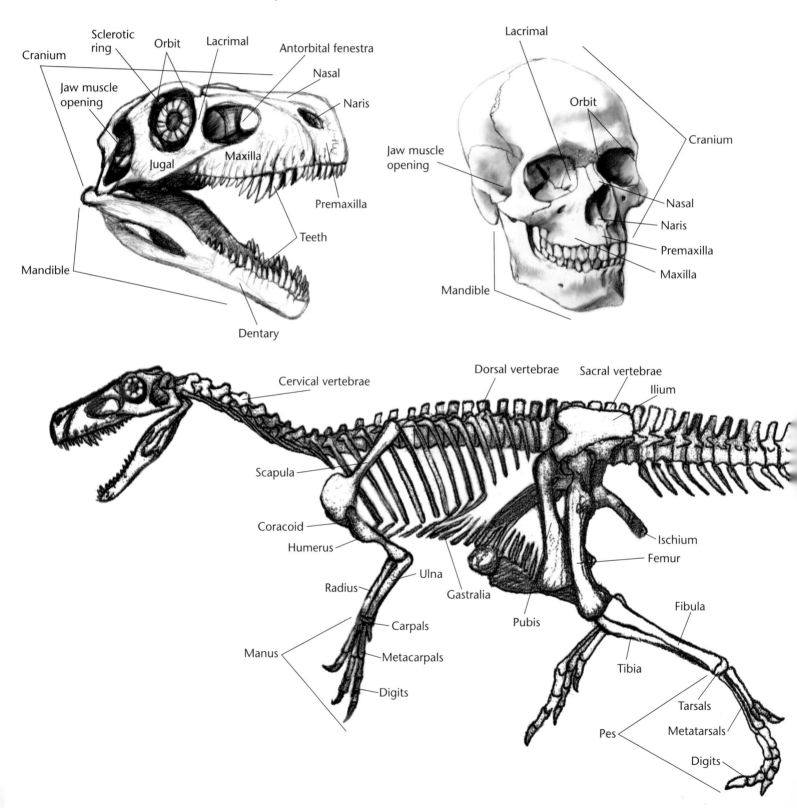

POSTCRANIAL SKELETAL ANATOMY

The postcranial skeleton—everything behind the skull—of a dinosaur or other vertebrate is composed of two basic parts. The *axial skeleton* is made up of the backbone and other bones along the trunk of the body. The *appendicular skeleton* is made up of the limbs and the bones that attach the limbs to the axial skeleton.

Understanding the differences in the size and shape of the various bones in the skeleton allows a paleontologist to make hypotheses about how different dinosaurs lived, moved, and acted.

Nearly all the bones and structures found in the dinosaur skeleton are found in the human skeleton.

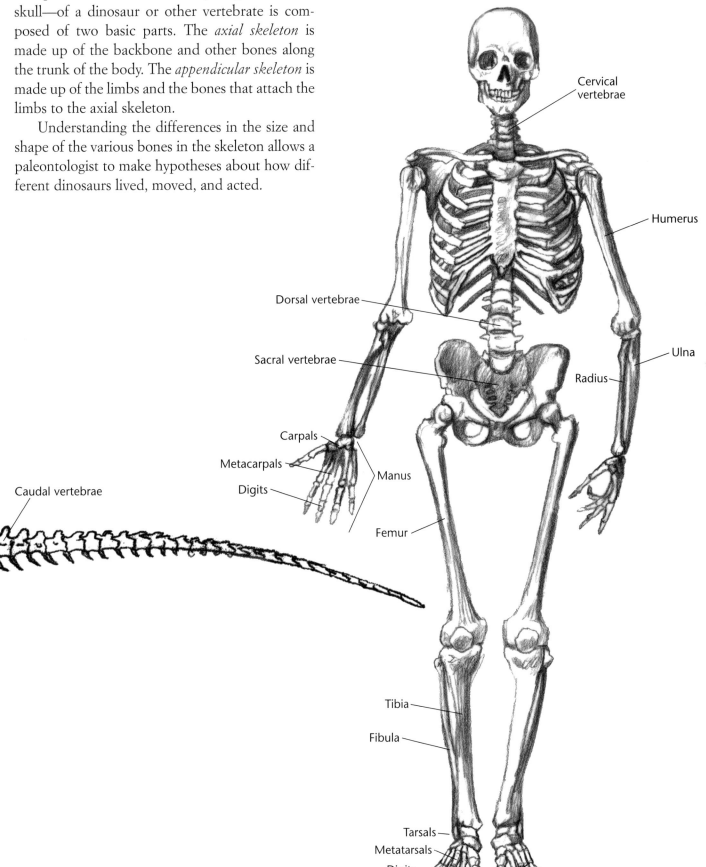

Lagerpeton

Silesaurus

Marasuchus

11

THE ORIGIN OF DINOSAURS

Before we look at the various types of dinosaurs, let's look at where dinosaurs came from. It will help you understand what makes a dinosaur a dinosaur.

DO DINOSAURS EXIST?

To scientists today, a biological group is said to "exist" or to be a "natural" group if all its members are the descendants of a creature that is also a member of that group. For example, whales and dolphins and porpoises are all descendants of a common ancestor, and so they form a natural group named Cetacea. So for a group of animals called dinosaurs, or Dinosauria, to exist, the common ancestor of all dinosaurs would have to be a dinosaur.

When someone groups together a bunch of animals whose common ancestor would *not* belong to that group, scientists consider this an "unnatural" group: one that doesn't exist in nature. For example, people once classified elephants, rhinos, and hippos together in a group they called Pachydermata (thick-skinned ones). But later discoveries showed that elephants were more closely related to sea cows, rhinos to horses, and hippos to pigs, so that the common ancestor of the pachyderms wouldn't have been a pachyderm at all! Therefore, Pachydermata is considered an unnatural grouping of animals.

From the late 1800s through the 1970s, most paleontologists thought that dinosaurs were like pachyderms: an unnatural group. They thought that different reptiles gave rise to the different groups (such as ornithischians, sauropods, and theropods) that we now call dinosaurs. These paleontologists thought that dinosaurs were not a natural group and that Dinosauria didn't exist. In their minds, *Triceratops, Tyrannosaurus,* and *Saltasaurus* were no more closely related to each

Pachydermata is an unnatural grouping of giant mammals. Hippos, rhinos, and elephants each separately evolved giant body size from entirely different small mammals, none of which would be considered pachyderms.

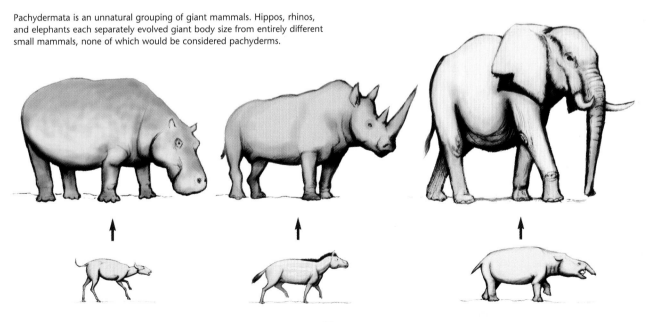

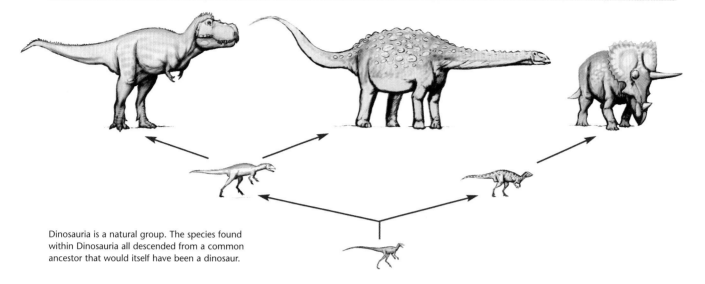

Dinosauria is a natural group. The species found within Dinosauria all descended from a common ancestor that would itself have been a dinosaur.

other than *Triceratops* was to an alligator.

So if dinosaurs were not a natural group, how did paleontologists explain features like an upright stance and extra hip bones that dinosaurs had in common? Well, before the 1970s, most paleontologists thought that these features evolved separately in different groups of reptiles because of similar lifestyles. This pattern is called *convergent evolution,* that is, when two or more groups that look different in the beginning evolve into similar forms. Scientists know many cases of it.

Convergent evolution happens when features that help one animal do better in a particular lifestyle independently evolve in another animal group with the same lifestyle. For example, dolphins and sharks have similar body shapes, back fins, and flippers, even though the dolphin is a descendant of four-legged, land-dwelling mammals and the shark is a descendant of bottom-dwelling cartilaginous fish. These two different groups independently evolved a similar body shape because that shape helped them move faster through the water.

Paleontologists made a prediction based on this idea of convergence. If each group of dinosaurs evolved these features separately from different non-dinosaur groups, we would expect the oldest of each of the dinosaur groups to look very different from each other—and to look more like those other, non-dinosaurian reptiles.

In the 1970s, however, the convergent evolution idea of dinosaur origins ran into trouble.

Paleontologists like Robert Bakker and Peter Galton in America and José Bonaparte in Argentina found evidence that the common ancestor of all dinosaurs was itself a dinosaur: a creature that had many of the same features found in other dinosaurs.

Part of this discovery came from their observation that the earlier you go in dinosaur history, the more similar the different types of dinosaurs become. During the Late Triassic, the earliest and most primitive members of each of the major groups were about 4 to 6 feet (1.2 to 1.8 meters) long, while later dinosaurs were as big or bigger than elephants. The earliest dinosaurs walked on two legs, while many of the later dinosaurs (like *Stegosaurus, Triceratops,* and *Apatosaurus*) walked on all fours. And even though the hands of later dinosaurs could be as different as the two-fingered claws of *Tyrannosaurus* and the broad foot of *Ankylosaurus,* the hands of the earliest dinosaurs were all five-fingered and built for grasping.

Bakker, Galton, and Bonaparte saw that the exact opposite of convergent evolution was taking place: that the earliest dinosaurs in each group were more similar to each other, and that they became more different from each other as time went by.

But these similarities were only part of the answer. Bakker, Galton, and Bonaparte also found evidence for the common ancestry of dinosaurs in newly discovered fossils from the Middle Triassic.

* * *

THE MIDDLE TRIASSIC ZOO

Think about the types of animals you see today at a typical zoo. Most of them are mammals: furry animals that give milk. You probably see a lot of birds, too. If you go into the reptile house, you will see the main types of living reptiles: turtles, lizards and snakes, and crocodilians. There might be the modern types of amphibians—frogs, toads, and salamanders—in the reptile house, too.

Now if you could go to a zoo during the Age of Dinosaurs (from the end of the Cretaceous through the Late Triassic), you'd see some different animals. Instead of elephants and tigers and other big mammals, you'd see a lot of big dinosaurs. The few mammals you'd see would be no bigger than a badger. These little mammals would be different from any modern mammal, but they would still be furry and give milk. You would also see some of the same groups of reptiles and amphibians that are in the modern world. They would be different species of reptiles or amphibians than you'd see today, but they would still be turtles or lizards or frogs.

But what if you went even further back in time to the origin of the dinosaurs? In a zoo from the Middle Triassic, the animals would be *very* different. None of the creatures in a modern zoo would have been around: no mammals, no birds, no turtles, no lizards and snakes, no crocodilians, no frogs, no toads, no salamanders. There would be reptiles and amphibians, but none of these would belong to any modern group. And there would be animals that were neither reptiles nor amphibians but something else entirely.

Not all the strange creatures of the Triassic were dinosaurs. On the left is a dicynodont protomammal, in the background is a plant-eating armored aetosaur, with its head at the top is a giant meat-eating rauisuchian, and at the bottom right is a crocodile-like parasuchian.

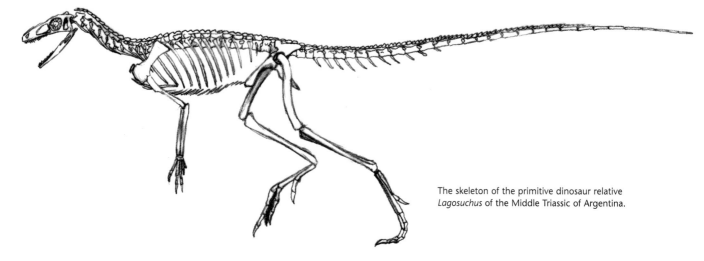

The skeleton of the primitive dinosaur relative
Lagosuchus of the Middle Triassic of Argentina.

One of the strangest groups of these animals in the Middle Triassic zoo would be plant-eating dicynodonts. These were very weird creatures, ranging from cat- to ox-size and looking like a cross between a turtle, a walrus, and a bulldog. Dicynodonts were related to the ancestors of mammals, the cynodonts. Cynodonts would also be common in the Middle Triassic zoo. These were cat- to wolf-size meat-eaters and omnivores with doglike snouts and sprawling legs. They may have been furry. These dicynodonts and cynodonts were the last surviving groups of the many types of protomammals that once ruled the Earth.

There would also be many different types of archosaurs, or "ruling reptiles," in the Middle Triassic zoo. Modern archosaurs include crocodilians and birds, but in the Triassic there were many other kinds. Lurking in lakes and rivers were parasuchians, long-snouted fish-eaters that looked (and probably acted) like crocodiles. On land were aetosaurs, plant-eating, armored archosaurs with spikes jutting out of their sides. And the top dogs (or, rather, "top crocs") were the giant meat-eating rauisuchians. All these creatures ran around on all fours and had legs that stuck out of the sides of the body, like they do in modern lizards and crocodiles.

But none of these big archosaurs were the ancestors of dinosaurs. In order to have seen them, you would have had to look down at your feet. We might think of dinosaurs as giants, but they came from animals that could have been beaten up by a house cat!

ANCESTORS OF THE DINOSAURS

The archosaur ancestors of dinosaurs were small animals with long hind legs directly underneath their bodies. This meant that they could run quickly and for a long time (a useful trait when you lived in a world full of big, hungry rauisuchians and cynodonts and lumbering herds of aetosaurs).

These little, long-legged archosaurs are the primitive ornithodirans (bird necks). Later ornithodirans include dinosaurs and (possibly) the flying pterosaurs. Like these later creatures, early ornithodirans had legs directly beneath the body and ankles that were like simple hinges.

As chance would have it, almost all we know about the early ornithodirans comes from fossils found in South America. There is no known complete ornithodiran skeleton because, for some reason, the hips and legs stay pretty well preserved, but not the rest of the body. The best fossils we have show that they had very short arms and may have been bipedal. Most of them had short, triangular heads with small, pointed teeth suited for eating insects.

In the 1970s, paleontologist Alfred Sherwood Romer discovered and named several different early ornithodirans. The most famous of these are *Lagosuchus,* the closely related *Marasuchus,* and the somewhat larger *Lagerpeton.* The first two of these were quite small, running bipedal animals that probably ate insects. *Lagerpeton* was larger but unfortunately is only known from its hips, legs, feet, and part of the backbone. Based on the shape

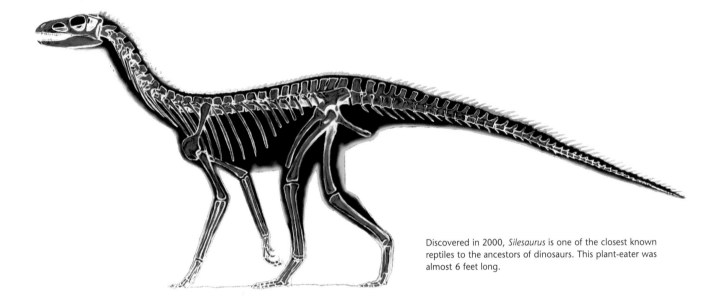

Discovered in 2000, *Silesaurus* is one of the closest known reptiles to the ancestors of dinosaurs. This plant-eater was almost 6 feet long.

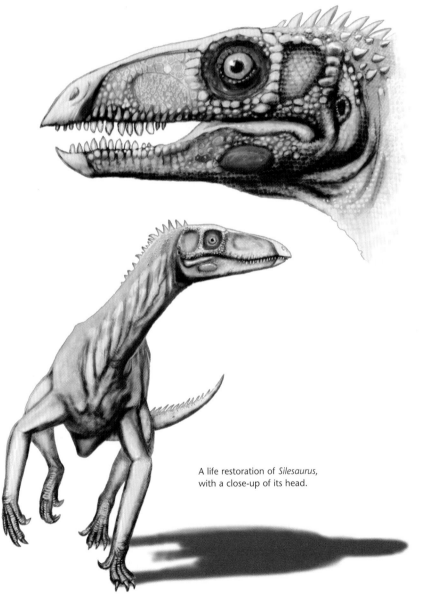

A life restoration of *Silesaurus*, with a close-up of its head.

of the feet and backbone, some paleontologists think that it may have hopped like a rabbit!

Larger still were *Lewisuchus* and *Pseudolagosuchus*. *Lewisuchus* had a bigger head compared to its body than the others. It looks like it probably hunted animals bigger than insects: in fact, it might have killed and eaten *Lagosuchus, Marasuchus,* and *Lagerpeton*! Based on certain features of the legs, some paleontologists think that it is the same species as *Pseudolagosuchus;* others, however, think that it isn't even an ornithodiran and is instead a relative of the ancestors of crocodiles.

The newest discovery of a dinosaur relative is also probably the closest creature so far to an actual dinosaur ancestor. This is the 5.6-foot (1.7-meter) *Silesaurus* of Poland. It was discovered in 2000 and named in 2003. Unlike most close dinosaur relatives, this one is known from most of the skeleton, and in fact at least four individuals of *Silesaurus* were found in the same spot. Unlike the other close dinosaur relatives, it has leaf-shaped

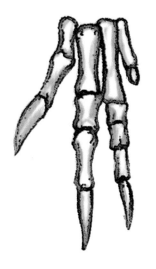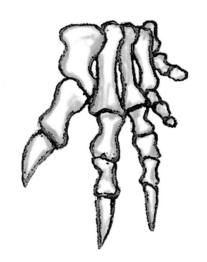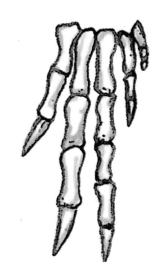

Dinosaur hands, like these left hands of *Megapnosaurus* (left), *Plateosaurus* (middle), and *Heterodontosaurus* (right), are different from those of other reptiles. The thumb was opposable, and the fourth and fifth fingers (the ring finger and pinkie) were much smaller than the others.

teeth like those of herbivorous lizards and herbivorous dinosaurs, so paleontologists suspect it was a plant-eater, too. Like dinosaurs, but unlike *Lagosuchus, Marasuchus,* or *Lagerpeton,* it has hips with long, slender pubis and ischium bones; this suggests that it was more closely related to dinosaurs than those Argentine reptiles. Its long, slender arms suggest that it could walk on all fours some of the time, but on just the hind legs when it wanted to go fast. Because it comes from the Late Triassic Epoch, though, *Silesaurus* is too late in time to be an actual ancestor of Dinosauria.

These creatures were closely related to dinosaurs, but they still hadn't evolved features that are found in all true members of Dinosauria. Together with true dinosaurs, these Triassic reptiles form the group Dinosauromorpha. The oldest true dinosaurs first appeared around 230 million years ago, toward the beginning of the Late Triassic. These early dinosaurs were not much different from their closest ornithodiran relatives. They were all less than 6 feet (1.8 meters) long and stood on their hind legs (particularly when they wanted to run). The primitive ornithodirans couldn't last long in the same world as their more advanced relatives: the dinosaurs had new adaptations that would make them better able to run, get food, and so forth. By the end of the Triassic Period, the primitive ornithodirans had all died out. The world was left to the true dinosaurs.

WHAT MAKES A DINOSAUR A DINOSAUR?

Many people (*including* some scientists!) are confused about what is or isn't a "dinosaur." They think that flying pterodactyls or fin-backed *Dimetrodon* or seagoing plesiosaurs or woolly mammoths are dinosaurs. THEY ARE WRONG! To a paleontologist, the word "dinosaur" is used *only* to describe an animal that is the most recent common ancestor of plant-eating *Iguanodon* and meat-eating *Megalosaurus* (two of the first Mesozoic dinosaurs known to science) or any of that ancestor's descendants.

That said, how do you recognize a dinosaur? Dinosaurs have a few features that make them special. The first is their hands. Look at the palm of your hand and touch the tips of any of your fingers to your thumb. See how the tip of your thumb can meet your other fingers? You can do this because you have an opposable thumb. Dinosaurs had a kind of opposable thumb, too. But dinosaur hands weren't like your hands. Look at the palm of your hand again and touch your thumb to any of your other fingers. You see how the thumb moves all the way down to the wrist? In dinosaur hands, the bones of the palm all stayed in place. Dinosaurs were able to grasp with their hands because the thumb was set at a different angle than other fingers. When dinosaurs closed their hands, their thumb and fingers would meet.

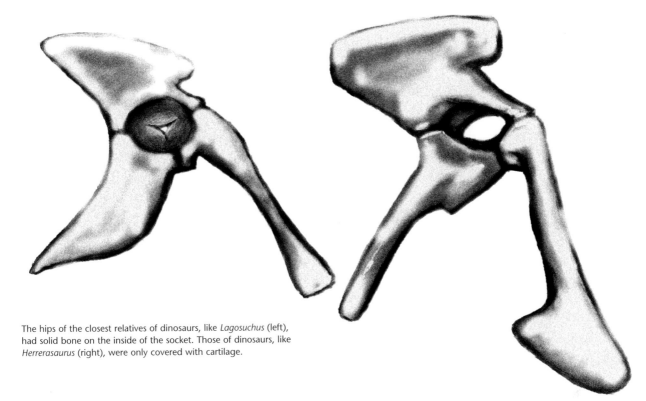

The hips of the closest relatives of dinosaurs, like *Lagosuchus* (left), had solid bone on the inside of the socket. Those of dinosaurs, like *Herrerasaurus* (right), were only covered with cartilage.

Why did dinosaurs evolve grasping hands? It may have helped them climb. It mostly would have helped them catch prey or gather plants. Dinosaurs could evolve such good grasping hands because they had ancestors who were already two-legged. Since these ancestors were able to move around without using their front paws, the paws were free to do something else.

The other big difference between dinosaurs and their ancestors is their hips. If you look at the hips of most living animals, the place where the thighbone fits into the hip socket has a solid wall of bone on the inside. Dinosaurs are different. Their hip sockets didn't have a wall of bone but only soft tissue called cartilage. Since cartilage rarely fossilizes, dinosaur hip fossils don't have anything inside the sockets, so paleontologists call them "open."

Why did dinosaurs have open hip sockets? No one has yet figured out a good answer. It probably wasn't to save weight, because the first dinosaurs to have this feature were still small. One likely reason is that having only cartilage on the inside of the hip socket made the leg move more smoothly.

Although dinosaurs began as small animals, they later became much larger. With their ances-tors' legs already underneath their bodies, dinosaurs were, literally, in a good position to become larger! See, if you have sprawling legs like a crocodile and you get really big, it becomes hard to move around on land because your legs have to hold up your weight at an angle. But if your legs are underneath you, they can support a lot more weight. Because of this, almost every group of dinosaurs had descendants that grew to giant size.

Paleontologists recognize two major branches of the dinosaur family tree, both of which evolved from a common ancestor, and both of which were present in the Late Triassic. The first of these are the saurischians, or "lizard-hipped" dinosaurs. Saurischians include the giant, long-necked sauropods and their smaller ancestors, and also the great number and variety of carnivorous theropods. Ornithischians, or "bird-hipped" dinosaurs, were all plant-eaters, as far as we know. The armored dinosaurs, the duckbills and their relatives, the domeheaded pachycephalosaurs, and the horned ceratopsians are all types of ornithischians. But we should keep in mind that all these different kinds of dinosaurs evolved from small running creatures you could hold in your hands.

Herrerasaurus

Eoraptor

12

SAURISCHIANS
(Lizard-Hipped Dinosaurs)

The saurischians make up one of the two main branches of the dinosaur family tree. Included among them are both the largest and the smallest dinosaurs known to science. Saurischia contains two diverse groups—the long-necked plant-eating sauropodomorphs and the blade-toothed meat-eating theropods. It also includes some Triassic species whose exact evolutionary position is far from certain. Most amazing of all, saurischian dinosaurs are not extinct! Today's living dinosaurs—birds—are a type of saurischian.

LIZARD HIPS AND HOLLOW BONES

Throughout the nineteenth century, paleontologists discovered various dinosaur fossils. Although the first skeletons found were very incomplete, nearly complete ones were found from the 1860s onward. With these new discoveries, paleontologists felt confident that they could begin to recognize groups within the dinosaurs: that is, to figure out which dinosaurs were most closely related.

Since that time, scientists have proposed many different ways of grouping, or classifying,

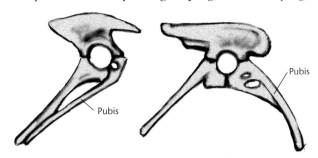

The pubis of ornithischians—like *Lesothosaurus* on the left—points toward the tail, while that of most saurischians—like *Megapnosaurus* on the right—points toward the head.

dinosaurs. The most famous of these (and the one still in use today) was that of Harry G. Seeley of England. In 1887, Seeley wrote a short paper (only seven pages) that is still one of the most influential treatises in dinosaur science.

Why was this little article so influential? Prior to 1887, paleontologists recognized some general groups of dinosaurs. In particular, American paleontologist O. C. Marsh of Yale University had named four groups of dinosaurs that we still use today. These were Stegosauria (for the armored dinosaurs like *Stegosaurus* and *Polacanthus*— today we call this whole group Thyreophora), Ornithopoda (for beaked plant-eaters like *Hypsilophodon, Iguanodon,* and the duckbills), Sauropoda (for giant, long-necked plant-eaters like *Camarasaurus* and *Diplodocus*), and Theropoda (for two-legged meat-eaters like *Allosaurus* and *Compsognathus*). Marsh, however, did not suggest how these four different groups were related.

But Seeley did. He recognized that Stegosauria and Ornithopoda had many features in

Most saurischians had hollow chambers in their vertebrae, as in this sauropod.

common, especially a backward-pointing pubis bone in the hip. Because birds also have a backward-pointing pubis bone in the hip, Seeley gave the name Ornithischia (bird hips) to the scientific order containing the groups Stegosauria and Ornithopoda.

In contrast, the pubis bone of sauropods and theropods (or at least all the ones Seeley knew about) points forward. This is what the pubis bone does in lizards, so he named this order Saurischia (lizard hips), and it contains the groups Sauropoda and Theropoda. Of course, the pubis bone also points forward in crocodiles, turtles, *and* mammals, so he could have named these the croc-hipped dinosaurs, turtle-hipped dinosaurs, or mammal-hipped dinosaurs. But the name Saurischia was the one he chose, so we use it.

Seeley also recognized other features of sauropods and theropods that made the group more similar to each other than either was to ornithischian dinosaurs. In particular, the vertebrae of sauropods and theropods had a lot of hollow chambers in them. Ornithischian vertebrae, in contrast, are solid. Seeley compared the hollow vertebrae of saurischians to those of birds and thought that (like those of living birds) these hollow dinosaur back bones would have been filled with air. Discoveries in the last few years have shown that Seeley was right. In fact, what Seeley had recognized was the first stages in the evolution of modern birds' special air-sac system.

Seeley argued that the differences between ornithischian and saurischian dinosaurs were too great for them to be closely related. He proposed that they were separate branches of the reptile family tree that had been mistakenly put together as the single group Dinosauria.

For almost a century, most paleontologists agreed with Seeley. However, discoveries in the 1970s showed that Dinosauria was a "real" group—that is, that all dinosaurs came from a common ancestor that was itself a dinosaur. Even so, Seeley's two major groups are still recognized as the main branches of the dinosaur family tree.

LONG NECKS AND POINTER FINGERS

Following publication of Seeley's paper, many more types of dinosaurs were found, both ornithischians and saurischians. Among the saurischians, discoveries showed that some Triassic long-necked dinosaurs previously thought to be theropods (in particular, *Plateosaurus* and *Anchisaurus*) were really close relatives of the Sauropoda, so a new group was recognized: Sauropodomorpha (sauropod forms). Now scientists recognized the two main groups in Saurischia as Theropoda and Sauropodomorpha.

As more skeletons of each group were discovered, paleontologists could begin to better trace the evolutionary history of the saurischians. This became much easier as more Triassic theropods and sauropodomorphs were found. These early forms had less time to evolve from the original common ancestor of all saurischians, so they still retained a lot of primitive (ancestral) features.

One feature that Triassic theropods (like *Coelophysis* and *Procompsognathus*) and Triassic sauropodomorphs (like *Plateosaurus* and *Riojasaurus*) had in common was long necks. If you compare the necks of these dinosaurs to those of primitive ornithischians (like *Lesothosaurus*), you can see that the saurischians had really stretched-out necks. In particular, the longest neck bones of the early saurischians were those located near the shoulders. That is different from most of their relatives, whose middle bones of the neck are the longest.

For the early sauropodomorphs, a long neck meant that they could reach higher than any other plant-eater of their time. For the early theropods, a long neck meant they could snap quickly at small

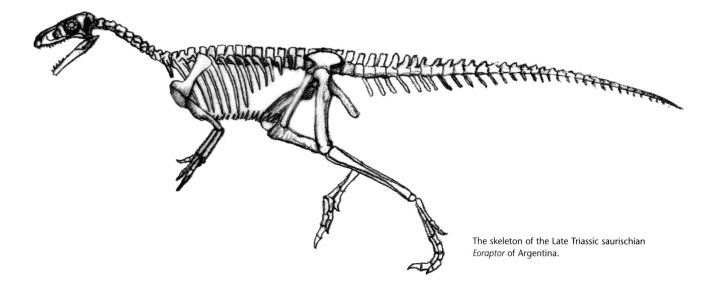

The skeleton of the Late Triassic saurischian *Eoraptor* of Argentina.

prey on the ground but also hold their heads up high to look out for larger, meaner meat-eaters.

Another way that early saurischians were different from their relatives was the shape of their hands. In all early dinosaurs, the hand was built for grasping, with long fingers and a thumb built to clutch. Ornithischians keep the ancestral feature of having the middle finger be the longest.

Saurischian hands were different. If you look at the hands of most lizard-hipped dinosaurs, you'll see that the second finger, or index finger, is the longest in the hand. Also, the thumb claw of most early types of saurischians is very big. Primitive sauropodomorphs, and most theropods, kept this special saurischian hand. In sauropods, though, the hand was used only to walk on, so it looked more like a pillar.

EORAPTOR AND THE HERRERASAURIDS

Most saurischians are clearly either theropods or sauropodomorphs. Since both of these groups were already around at the beginning of the Late Triassic Epoch, the common ancestor of Theropoda and Sauropodomorpha must have lived earlier (in the Middle Triassic).

However, there *are* some Late Triassic saurischians that are harder to place on the family tree. The best known of these "problem saurischians" are little *Eoraptor* and larger *Herrerasaurus* from Argentina. Enough fossils of these two have been found that we know what almost every bone in their bodies looked like. There are bits and pieces known of a few other dinosaurs (*Staurikosaurus, Chindesaurus,* and *Caseosaurus*) that closely

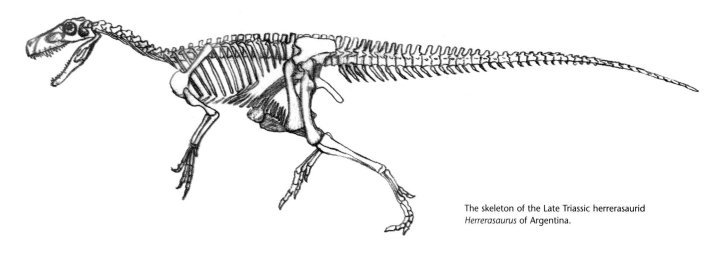

The skeleton of the Late Triassic herrerasaurid *Herrerasaurus* of Argentina.

resemble *Herrerasaurus,* and all of these are put into the group Herrerasauridae.

Eoraptor and *Herrerasaurus*—and a few other dinosaurs like them—had the bladelike serrated teeth of carnivores, so they are often considered early types of theropods. But many of the close relatives of dinosaurs (such as rauisuchians and other primitive crocodile relatives) *also* had bladelike serrated teeth, so we expect that the earliest dinosaurs had them, too. The leaf-shaped teeth of ornithischians and sauropodomorphs are believed to be specialized features that evolved separately in the two groups to help them eat plants. So bladelike teeth don't make a dinosaur a theropod. They just make it a meat-eater.

These problem saurischians also lack some of the features found in definite theropods. For example, the first toe (aka the big toe of a human being) in a theropod is shortened so that it doesn't normally touch the ground when an animal walks. And the metatarsal—the long bone of the foot—doesn't extend to the ankle. *Eoraptor* and the herrerasaurids are like non-theropods, with a first toe that is low on the foot and a metatarsal that extends to the ankle.

Also *Eoraptor* and the herrerasaurids lack the long necks (with long vertebrae near the shoulders), big thumbs, and long pointer fingers of sauropodomorphs and theropods. But they do have hollow vertebrae! This leads some paleontologists to think that these dinosaurs branched off from the saurischian family tree earlier than the split between sauropodomorphs and theropods.

On the other hand, the claws and some of the finger bones of herrerasaurids and *Eoraptor* are more similar in shape to those of true theropods than are those of sauropodomorphs. And the shape of the chambers inside the vertebrae of these dinosaurs reminds paleontologists of those inside true theropod vertebrae. So some paleontologists think that *Eoraptor* and the herrerasaurids were very primitive early theropods. Personally, I think the jury is still out, but new specimens will help to resolve this question, one way or the other.

Regardless of whether they were theropods or just primitive saurischians, neither *Eoraptor* nor the herrerasaurids nor any of the other non-sauropodomorph, non-theropod saurischians survived into the Jurassic. However, as you'll read about in the next thirteen chapters, the sauropodomorphs and theropods continued to flourish in the Jurassic and Cretaceous.

The Late Triassic predatory saurischian
Herrerasaurus of Argentina.

The saurischian *Eoraptor* examines an early mammal in Late Triassic Argentina.

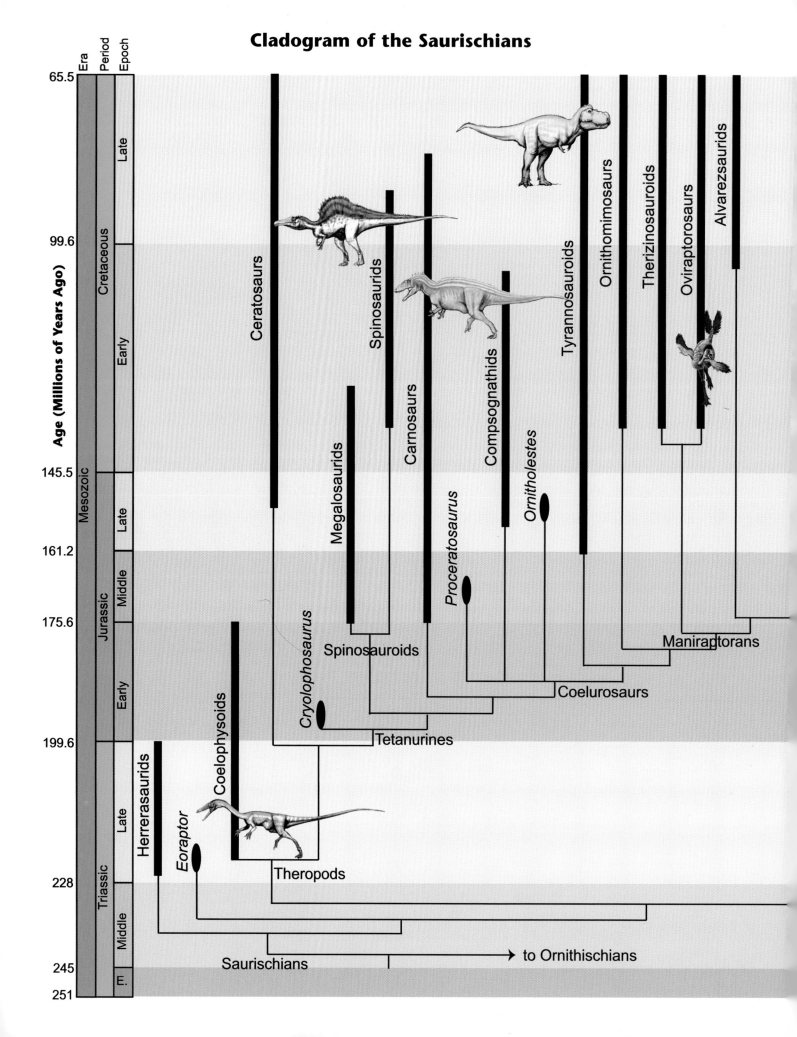

Cladogram of the Saurischians

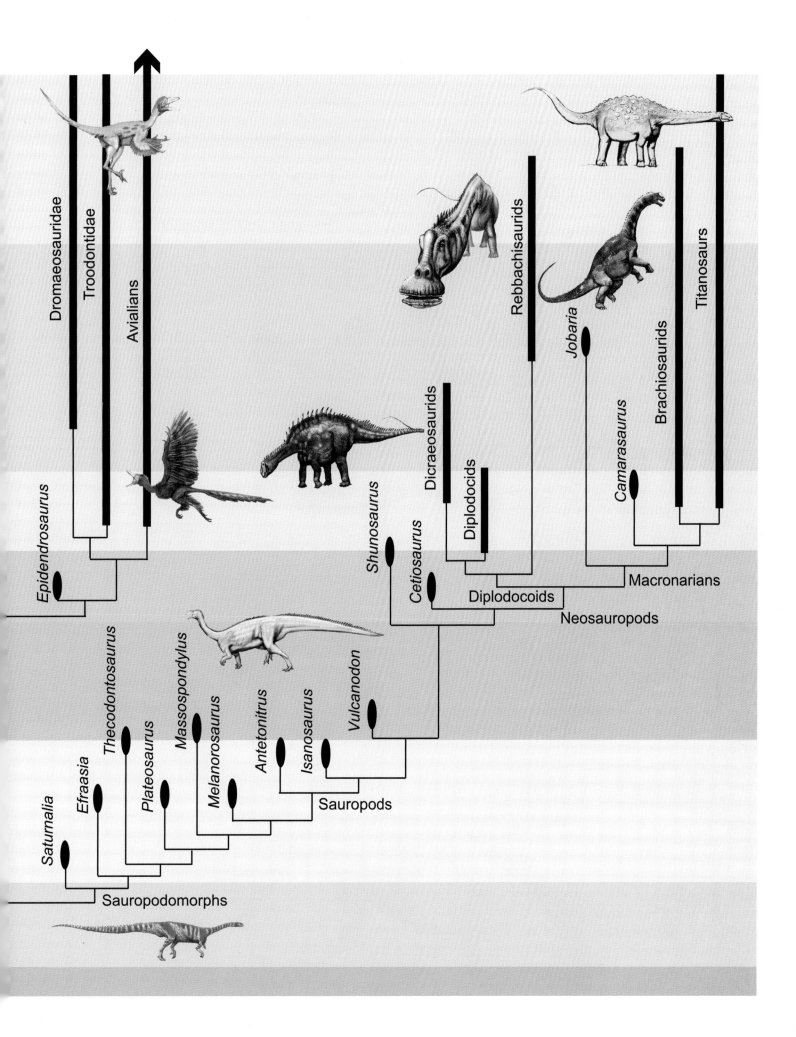

Rugops

Ceratosaurus

Masiakasaurus

Coelophysis

13

COELOPHYSOIDS AND CERATOSAURS
(Primitive Meat-Eating Dinosaurs)

Carnivorous, or meat-eating, dinosaurs belong to a group called Theropoda (beast feet). They are in one of the two main branches of Saurischia (the other being the long-necked plant-eating Sauropodomorpha). Theropods came in many shapes and sizes, from toothy giants like *Tyrannosaurus* and *Spinosaurus* to tiny stalkers like *Sinosauropteryx* and *Mei*. From the beginning of the Jurassic Period until the end of the Cretaceous Period, they were the top predators on land. Theropoda also includes all the feathered animals in the history of the Earth, from *Caudipteryx* through *Velociraptor* to modern birds. So theropods are still with us today.

This chapter reviews the basics of theropod anatomy and behavior, and looks at two of the first groups of theropods to branch off the family tree. These are the slender Coelophysoidea—the first major group of theropods to appear—and the more diverse and long-lasting Ceratosauria.

BIG BRAINS AND FAST FEET

As you might imagine, a carnivorous animal needs to be well armed to hunt, kill, and eat another animal. All you need to do is look at a shark, tiger, or wolf to see that it's true. It was the same with the species of Theropoda. This group of dinosaurs shares a number of traits that helped them find, catch, and kill their food.

First, theropods had big brains, or at least big brains for dinosaurs. When compared to other dinosaurs of the same weight, theropods had larger brains than those of plant-eating sauropodomorphs or ornithischians. This is because being able to track, hunt, and kill another animal takes more skill than finding and eating a plant, and so requires a bigger "computer," or brain, to process information. Throughout the family tree—in roughly the same order as the chapters in this book—theropod brains evolved to become larger and more sophisticated. That's not to say that any Mesozoic theropod was as brainy as a modern mammal or bird. Even the brainiest of theropods during the Mesozoic Era were probably only as smart as some of the dumbest modern mammals and birds, like opossums and emus. I know that this isn't particularly flattering, and as a dinosaur fan myself, I wish that weren't the case.

The Early Jurassic coelophysoid *Dilophosaurus* of western North America.

But that seems to be what the evidence comparing brain to body size shows. Still, their brainpower was greater than that of their contemporaries, including Mesozoic mammals.

Theropods needed to *catch* prey, too, and not just *think* about it! In general, meat-eating dinosaurs were faster than plant-eaters. Their legs were typically slender and long, giving them big strides. Their feet were narrow, like the feet of most fast-running animals today. In fact, in order to keep their feet narrow, their first toe—the equivalent of our big toe—was reduced in size until it was basically useless, at least for running. (It may have helped them grasp food.) Theropods were effectively three-toed, with a little first toe on the side.

Theropods weren't just swift; they were also agile. The rear half of the tails of primitive theropods was stiffened by prongs of bone that helped them balance when making quick turns. In later groups of theropods (especially the dromaeosaurid raptors), this adaptation was taken to an extreme. Carnivorous dinosaurs were able to run down plant-eaters and to turn quickly after them as they tried to get away.

THE JAWS THAT BITE, THE CLAWS THAT CATCH

But brains and speed do not a predator make. Theropods needed to actually *kill* their victims before eating them!

Ever since the discovery of *Megalosaurus* (the first Mesozoic theropod found), paleontologists have known that the carnivorous dinosaurs had bladelike serrated teeth. It was these teeth that indicated these dinosaurs *were* carnivores, since similar teeth are found in the jaws of modern flesh-eating lizards. A bladelike serrated tooth cuts through meat like a steak knife.

One problem with a steak-knife-shaped tooth is that it can be easily broken when twisted. But losing a tooth wasn't as big a problem for a dinosaur as it is for a mammal because dinosaurs grew new teeth throughout their lives. Even so, it would be useful to have an adaptation to help keep the teeth from getting too damaged by struggling prey. Theropods evolved such an adaptation in the form of the intramandibular joint. This long name simply means that their lower jaw (or mandible) had a joint in it. That joint—between the toothy part of the jaw and the bones that connected the lower jaw to the upper jaw—acted as a kind of shock absorber. If the animal a theropod was biting started to struggle, the intramandibular joint would flex to keep the teeth from becoming too stressed.

Carnivorous dinosaurs didn't just use their jaws to catch prey, however. Most of them could also use their hands. In fact, theropods are the one group of dinosaurs that were all strictly bipedal. So far as is currently known, no theropod evolved into a quadruped, the way that sauropodomorphs and ornithischians did.

The common ancestor of all dinosaurs had a grasping hand, and in the theropods these hands became specialized for killing. Theropod claws were curved like the talons of birds of prey. Theropods could use their claws to hook into the meat of their victims, and perhaps to slash the sides of the prey in order to wound them. Big cats today use their sharp claws in both these ways.

The hands of theropods are specialized in another way. They have fewer fingers than most dinosaurs, which have five. In primitive theropods, like coelophysoids and ceratosaurs, the pinkie has been lost, and the fourth finger—equivalent to our ring finger—is generally reduced. This gave primitive theropods a four-fingered hand. In more advanced theropods, other fingers were sometimes lost as well, so you can find three fingers on *Allosaurus* and *Velociraptor* (for example) and only two on *Tyrannosaurus.*

Like biting into a victim, grabbing hold of one can be pretty tough on a predator. Theropods evolved a way of dealing with this. Their collarbones—which in most animals, including ourselves, are two separate bones—fused together into a single unit. This single bone is technically called a furcula, but most of us know it as a wishbone. In birds, the wishbone is used as a spring so the flapping wings use less energy while flying. In the ancient theropods, the wishbone seems to have also served as a spring, but in this case as a shock absorber and brace. It would allow the carnivorous dinosaur to hold on to an animal it was trying to kill without hurting its arms as much.

HOLLOW BONES AND AIR SACS

Like their plant-eating relatives the sauropodomorphs, theropods had hollow vertebrae. In fact, theropods had lots of hollow bones. The long bones of the arms and legs of carnivorous dinosaurs had hollow spaces, and there are various holes and chambers in their face and braincase bones. These openings were spaces for air sacs.

In today's living theropods—birds—air sacs make the animal very light, so many people mistakenly think that these structures must have

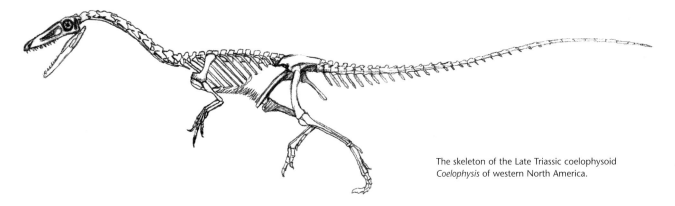

The skeleton of the Late Triassic coelophysoid
Coelophysis of western North America.

79

evolved to help birds fly. But birds simply inherited their air sacs from larger, nonflying, ground-dwelling ancestors. What purpose would the air sacs serve in these animals?

Birds use their air sacs for a lot more than staying lightweight. The air sacs are used to help rid their bodies of excess heat. And some air sacs are used to pump extra oxygen into the lungs. It appears that both the heat-dumping and oxygen-pumping features of birds were present even in the earliest theropods.

FIRST OF THE FEARSOME: COELOPHYSOIDS

What *were* the earliest theropods? That is a matter of some debate. Some paleontologists regard *Eoraptor* and the members of Herrerasauridae—discussed in the previous chapter—as the oldest and most primitive theropods. They certainly are "carnivorous dinosaurs," as they were carnivores and they were dinosaurs. But were they really part of the theropod family tree? Some traits that *Eoraptor,* herrerasaurids, and theropods share—such as hollow bones—are also found in other saurischian dinosaurs. And herrerasaurids have an intramandibular joint similar (although not identical) to that of theropods. But as mentioned in chapter 12, sauropodomorphs and theropods share some traits that *Eoraptor* and herrerasaurids lack. That suggests that sauropodomorphs are closer relatives to theropods than *Eoraptor* and herrerasaurids are. If eventually a furcula (rather than individual collarbones) is found in these Late Triassic carnivores, that will clinch it and show that they were theropods. But for now, the issue is unsettled.

The oldest and most primitive group of theropods that everyone *agrees* is theropod is called Coelophysoidea, after the best-known genus, *Coelophysis* (hollow form). Coelophysoids show up in the Late Triassic a little after *Eoraptor* and the members of Herrerasauridae, and thus are some of the oldest dinosaurs known. The last coelophysoids disappeared at the end of the Early Jurassic Epoch, after which their more advanced relatives replaced them.

The Late Triassic coelophysoid *Zupaysaurus* of Argentina.

When coelophysoids first evolved, they were not the top predators in their ecosystem. Indeed, no dinosaur was. For most of the Late Triassic, other groups, especially giant land-dwelling relatives of crocodilians, were the largest and most powerful meat-eaters. Coelophysoids were just one among many groups of small- and medium-size hunters. But at the end of the Late Triassic there was a mass extinction, and the dinosaurs' competition died out. Starting in the Early Jurassic, dinosaurs became the major group of large land animals, and coelophysoids were the top carnivores.

Coelophysoids, in general, were rather slender, with long necks and tails. Their skulls were long and narrow and filled with bladelike teeth. A particular feature shared by coelophysoids was a kink

A young *Ceratosaurus*.

in the front of the upper jaw and a corresponding swelling in the lower jaw. Larger-than-normal teeth in the lower jaw would come out of the swelling and fit inside the upper-jaw kink. This arrangement is seen in some modern crocodilians, which use this spot in their snouts to hold on to struggling victims. Coelophysoids probably used their jaw kinks in the same way.

Another unusual feature of the skulls of at least some coelophysoids was their crests. In many coelophysoid species, there was a pair of thin bony semicircular crests along the snout. These crests were very frail and probably used only for show.

The smallest coelophysoids—dinosaurs like *Segisaurus* and *Procompsognathus*—were only 3.5 to 5 feet (1.1 to 1.5 meters) long, and about half of that was tail. That's about the size of a wild turkey! Larger coelophysoids were 10-to-13-foot (3-to-4-meter) *Coelophysis* and *Megapnosaurus,* and 20-foot (6.1-meter) *Zupaysaurus* and *Liliensternus.* The biggest known coelophysoids were *Gojirasaurus* and *Dilophosaurus,* which grew to perhaps 23 feet (7 meters) long. These were the first

big dinosaur predators, although they were small compared to some of the later theropods.

INTRODUCING THE CERATOSAURS

During the 1980s and 1990s, the coelophysoids were considered one branch of a larger group of theropods called Ceratosauria, after *Ceratosaurus* (horned reptile). However, most recent cladistic studies show that coelophysoids were actually an earlier branch, and that the features that were shared between coelophysoids and true ceratosaurs were common to the ancestor of all theropods.

Ceratosaurs first appear in the fossil record in the Late Jurassic and last until the end of the Late Cretaceous. Ceratosaurs share a number of features, such as extra hip vertebrae, a specialized socket between some of the hip bones, and rather short fingers. Most ceratosaurs, such as the abelisaurids and *Ceratosaurus,* had short, deep skulls, not long, shallow ones like coelophysoids.

But beyond these features, most ceratosaurs were fairly different from each other. *Ceratosaurus* is one of the oldest known ceratosaurs (and, incidentally, one of the first discovered). It was up to 23 feet (7 meters) long, from the Late Jurassic Morrison Formation of the American West, and possibly from the same-age Tendaguru Formation of Tanzania. Although not as big as some of its more advanced theropod neighbors—*Allosaurus* and *Torvosaurus*—*Ceratosaurus* was still a predator to be reckoned with. Its teeth were quite large for its size, and it had a short but powerful neck. Its name comes from the narrow crest down the

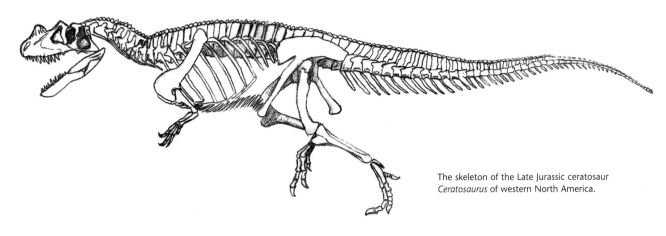

The skeleton of the Late Jurassic ceratosaur *Ceratosaurus* of western North America.

81

middle of its snout and a pair of smaller crests in front of each eye.

In contrast, 20-foot (6.1-meter) *Elaphrosaurus* (also from the Morrison and Tendaguru formations) was built more like a coelophysoid. It had a long neck, slender tail, and very long, slender legs. Based on its limb proportions, it was probably the fastest dinosaur of the Jurassic Period. Unfortunately, no one has found the skull of *Elaphrosaurus,* so we don't know the shape or proportions of its jaws and teeth.

Some Cretaceous ceratosaurs seem to resemble *Ceratosaurus* or *Elaphrosaurus.* For example, Early Cretaceous *Genyodectes* of Argentina is known only from a partial snout, but what has been discovered suggests that it was very similar to *Ceratosaurus.* And the recently named *Spinostropheus* of the Early Cretaceous of Niger is another long, slender—and, sadly, skull-less!—ceratosaur. But there were other groups of ceratosaurs that were different from these forms. And for at least some of these, we *do* have skulls! These were dinosaurs of Noasauridae and Abelisauridae.

MYSTERIOUS NOASAURIDS

Although some of the individual species of noasaurids have been known for decades, no one thought to bring them together into a single group until very recently. That is because before the discovery of *Masiakasaurus* of the Late Cretaceous of Madagascar, no one had found a noasaurid skeleton that linked all the bits and pieces together.

Previously, each of the noasaurid species was known only from very incomplete skeletons, and some were thought to be entirely different sorts of theropods. For example, *Deltadromeus,* by far the biggest of all, was thought to be a long-legged coelurosaur (an advanced birdlike theropod dinosaur). But with *Masiakasaurus*'s skeleton as a guide, we now have a much better idea of the anatomy of these dinosaurs.

Noasaurids range from 7-foot (2.1-meter) *Noasaurus* to 26.5-foot (8.1-meter) *Deltadromeus.* They are known only from the Cretaceous Period of South America, Africa, India, and Madagascar. All these lands were connected together as a supercontinent called Gondwana during that time. Noasaurids appear to have been very fast runners. Their feet were long, with the side metatarsals (the long bones of the feet) especially slender. It was once thought that noasaurids had a sickle-shaped claw on one toe (as did the dromaeosaurid raptors), but it turns out to have actually been a hand claw.

The most unusual thing about noasaurids, however, is their face. So far *Masiakasaurus* is the only one for which most of the skull is known, and it is a very weird skull! The back half isn't that unusual for a theropod, but the front half *is.* The lower jaw droops downward, and the teeth there point forward. These teeth are also peculiar for a theropod. They are conical, with a bit of a curve at the end. (Those in the rear of the jaws are typical bladelike theropod teeth.) How *Masiakasaurus* used these strange teeth isn't certain. Some paleontologists suggest that it may have stabbed fish with them. Others suggest that they were used to catch insects.

The Late Cretaceous noasaurid *Masiakasaurus* of Madagascar.

LORDS OF THE SOUTHERN WORLD: ABELISAURIDS

Noasauridae included the most important smaller theropods in Gondwana during the last epoch of the Age of Dinosaurs. But the top predators of the southern continents at that time were their relatives in Abelisauridae.

Like the noasaurids, individual abelisaurid species had been known since the beginning of the twentieth century, but it wasn't until *Abelisaurus* and *Carnotaurus* were discovered and described in 1980 that paleontologists were able to link the Late Cretaceous southern giants. Abelisaurids share a number of odd traits. The bones of their faces have a wrinkled texture: whether this means that they had wrinkled skin or keratin (the material in fingernails and horns) covering most of their heads is not known at present. Also, compared to those of other theropods, their teeth were rather small. In at least some abelisaurids, there were a pair of stout hornlike projections coming out of the top of their heads. And they had short but powerfully built necks.

Abelisaurid arms are ridiculously short. Neither hand could touch the other. They had four fingers, like other ceratosaurs and coelophysoids, but these fingers were extremely stubby. And their forearm bones were so reduced they were practically just wrist bones. Their distant cousins, the tyrannosaurid coelurosaurs, are infamous for their tiny arms. But compared to the stumpy forelimbs of abelisaurids, those of tyrannosaurids look powerful! It is likely that abelisaurid arms were essentially useless. It's interesting to speculate that if

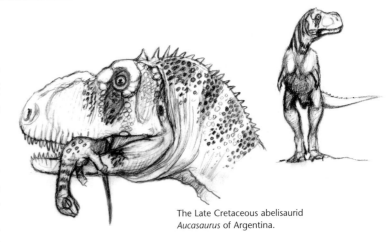

The Late Cretaceous abelisaurid *Aucasaurus* of Argentina.

they hadn't become extinct, perhaps abelisaurids would have lost their arms entirely after a few more tens of millions of years.

Abelisaurid legs were thicker and somewhat shorter than those of other theropods, and so they probably weren't very fast. But abelisaurids may not have needed much speed. Unlike their distant tyrannosaurid cousins—which had to chase relatively swift prey like horned ceratopsids and duck-billed hadrosaurs—abelisaurids lived in environments where saltasaurids and titanosaurs were the main herbivores. Although saltasaurids may have been somewhat faster than the other giant long-necked sauropods, they still weren't as fast as horned and duckbilled dinosaurs. So abelisaurids had to be strong, but not particularly fast.

Like their smaller noasaurid neighbors, abelisaurids survived until the very end of the Age of Dinosaurs, long after most other large southern theropods (like carcharodontosaurids and spinosaurids) had gone extinct. In their time, they were the rulers of the southern world. But their reign,

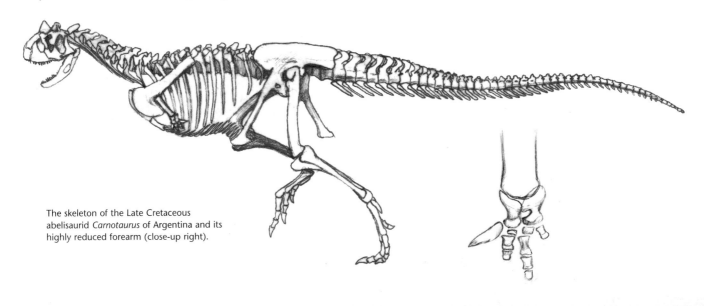

The skeleton of the Late Cretaceous abelisaurid *Carnotaurus* of Argentina and its highly reduced forearm (close-up right).

like that of the tyrannosaurids in the north, came to an end 65.5 million years ago, with the great extinction at the end of the Cretaceous.

COELOPHYSOID AND CERATOSAUR TRACE FOSSILS

The footprints of coelophysoid dinosaurs are one of the most common fossils in rocks from the Late Triassic and Early Jurassic epochs. One such type of track, given the technical name *Eubrontes,* is even the official state fossil of Connecticut! Paleontologists have studied these tracks since the 1800s, when American scientist Edward Hitchcock first described them in detail. Recent studies by Paul Olsen of Columbia University and his colleagues have used these tracks to show the rise of theropods to their status as top predators on land. They have shown that coelophysoid tracks in the Connecticut River Valley of New England are rel-

atively small until the end of the Triassic Period. At that time there is a major extinction, and most of the competitors of the dinosaurs are wiped out. From that point onward, the tracks of the theropod dinosaurs become much larger.

Skin impressions are known from the Argentine abelisaurid *Carnotaurus.* They show that its body was covered by round scales of various sizes, as are the bodies of herbivorous dinosaurs.

One interesting set of trace fossils is associated with the abelisaurid *Majungasaurus* from Madagascar. On some *Majungasaurus* bones, there are bite marks that definitely come from other *Majungasaurus.* This is the first definite evidence of cannibalism in dinosaurs. (There are fossils of the coelophysoid *Coelophysis* that were thought to show it had eaten babies of its own species. New

Abelisaurids like *Carnotaurus* may have used their thickened skulls in tests of strength, as do many animals today.

evidence shows that some of these fossils were bones of non-dinosaur reptiles it had eaten. In other cases, the babies weren't actually inside the bellies of the adults; the bones were simply mixed together after both were dead.) It wouldn't be a surprise if *all* carnivorous dinosaurs were cannibals, at least occasionally. Most living meat-eaters—including lions and wolves—will eat other members of their own species if they are hungry enough. That is part of the way of being a predator.

The abelisaurid *Majungasaurus* attacks the titanosaur *Rapetosaurus* in Late Cretaceous Madagascar.

Small Theropods, Big Ideas

Dr. Ron Tykoski
University of Texas at Austin

Giant carnivorous theropods hold a special place of awe and terror in our imagination. However, small theropods are of even greater interest to some dinosaur paleontologists than the menacing multi-ton tyrannosaurs and allosaurs that grip the public's fascination.

How big is a "small" theropod? "Small" is a deceptive term when speaking of dinosaurs. Theropods less than about 10 feet (3 meters) and weighing under 220 pounds (100 kilograms) in mass are generally considered "small."

Much of our knowledge about dinosaur relationships, anatomy, and lifestyles has come from the discovery and study of small theropods. The first nearly complete theropod skeleton ever found was that of the chicken-size Compsognathus, *described in 1861.* Compsognathus *showed scientists that not all dinosaurs were large. Details of its skeleton provided some of the first clues that extinct dinosaurs and living birds were closely related.*

Most of the earliest theropods were not large. Coelophysis *was a lightly built, 10-foot (3-meter) predator that lived during the Late Triassic Epoch (about 220 million years ago) in North America. Remarkably, the remains from many dozens of skeletons were collected from a single quarry in northern New Mexico.* Coelophysis *is known from more fossils than any other extinct theropod. The study of* Coelophysis *and its closest kin provides important details about the early evolution of theropods and their spread across the Earth.*

The description of Deinonychus in 1969 inspired a resurgence in dinosaur science and the popularity of dinosaurs with the public. At 10 feet (3 meters) from nose to tip of tail, Deinonychus weighed about as much as a large wolf. This killer possessed many birdlike features in its skeleton, sparking a new debate about whether birds had evolved from dinosaurs. Evidence supporting this relationship continues to build with more fossil finds. Among the most spectacular are specimens from China with traces of feathers around the skeletons of several different small theropods.

If history provides a guide for predicting the future of dinosaur paleontology, it is likely that many of our biggest finds will continue to come from some of the smallest predatory dinosaurs.

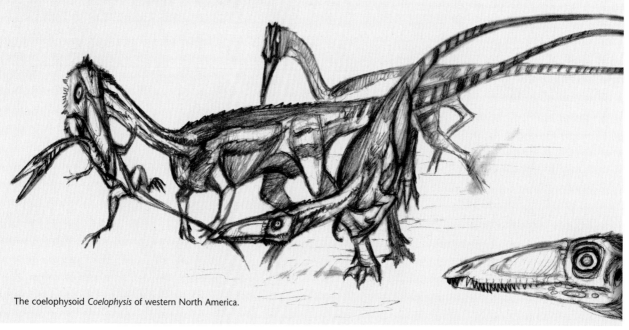

The coelophysoid *Coelophysis* of western North America.

Diversity of Ceratosaurians

Dr. Fernando E. Novas
Museo Argentino de Ciencias
Naturales, Buenos Aires, Argentina

Photo by Hernán Canuti

Ceratosauria is the name for a group of predatory dinosaurs that inhabited the Earth during the Jurassic and Cretaceous periods. All ceratosaurians had some kind of horn on their heads. The best examples of horned meat-eating dinosaurs are Ceratosaurus *from the western United States and* Carnotaurus *from southern Argentina.*

Paleontologists once thought that some early predatory dinosaurs from the Late Triassic and Early Jurassic epochs were ceratosaurs. These included Coelophysis *and its kin* Syntarsus, Halticosaurus, *and* Dilophosaurus. *Closer examination of these fossils showed that they retained a more primitive pelvic structure and hind limbs than* Ceratosaurus *and* Carnotaurus. *Because of this, these earlier meat-eaters are now thought by many paleontologists to represent their own branch of theropod evolution, which is not closely related with the evolution of true ceratosaurians.*

Ceratosaurs originated during the Jurassic Period, but only a few of these early examples are known. They include Ceratosaurus *as well as the slender and bizarre* Elaphrosaurus *from central Africa.*

Ceratosaurs evolved into many forms in the Cretaceous Period. They were most successful and populous on the supercontinent of Gondwana. This giant landmass was the cradle of abelisaurs, a group of ceratosaurs that roamed South America, Africa, Madagascar, and India. It was during the Cretaceous Period that the landmasses of Laurasia in the Northern Hemisphere and Gondwana in the Southern Hemisphere became disconnected. Because most dinosaurs could no longer migrate between the Northern and Southern hemispheres, different forms of meat-eaters dominated each half of the world. While tyrannosaurs and velociraptorids dominated the northern continents, abelisaurs were the most common predators in the southern continents.

Abelisaurs vary widely in size and shape. Ligabueino, *discovered near the Andes Mountains in Argentina, was no bigger than a chicken.* Masiakasaurus, *from the island of Madagascar near Africa, was a little longer at about 7 feet (2.1 meters). Another small abelisaur from Argentina was* Noasaurus, *which was remarkable for its dangerous sickle claw on the second toe of its foot, a characteristic that evolved separately from the sharper toe claw of the velociraptorids. It was about 8 feet (2.4 meters) long.*

The best known and most spectacular abelisaur is Carnotaurus, *the villain in the Disney movie* Dinosaur. Carnotaurus *inhabited Patagonia around 70 million years ago. It combined the horns of a bull above a very stubby face, with forelimbs that were even shorter than those of* Tyrannosaurus. Carnotaurus *had a stout, muscled neck and could swing its head with great power and fury. It probably used its head and horns to butt other meat-eaters away when they gathered around a carcass. One can also picture* Carnotaurus *engaged in combat with members of its own species, using its horns to fight for mates and food and to defend its turf. There is an important clue in the backbone that supports this interpretation of* Carnotaurus *behavior. The sturdy spine is constructed to limit side-to-side movement, presumably to counter the violent shocks made when the dinosaur rammed its horny head into a rival.*

Carnotaurus *belongs to a group of monstrous abelisaurs that also included* Majungasaurus *from* Madagascar, Indosuchus *from India, and* Aucasaurus *from Patagonia.*

Suchomimus

Spinosaurus

Megalosaurus

14

SPINOSAUROIDS
(Megalosaurs and the Fin-Backed Fish-Eating Dinosaurs)

Theropoda (two-legged meat-eating dinosaurs) contains many different groups. Two of the first to branch off of the family tree—coelophysoids and ceratosaurs—were discussed in chapter 13. All the remaining theropod types belong to a large group called Tetanurae. Tetanurines (sometimes spelled "tetanurans") include a wide variety of species, among them the famous theropods *Allosaurus, Velociraptor,* and *Tyrannosaurus.* Tetanurines also include all species of birds, living and extinct.

Among the major branches of tetanurines is Spinosauroidea, named after its most famous member, *Spinosaurus*—one of the most spectacular of all meat-eating dinosaurs, and quite possibly the largest. Spinosauroids also include *Megalosaurus,* the first Mesozoic dinosaur known to science.

STIFF TAILS
The name Tetanurae—"stiff tails"—comes from one of the main adaptations found in this group. Almost all theropods have little projections of bone in the vertebrae of the tail that help keep it stiff. In coelophysoids and ceratosaurs, these projections are fairly small and are only found in a few tail bones. In tetanurines, they are larger and are found in half or more of the tail bones. These stiff tails evolved to be used as balancing tools, allowing the tetanurines to turn more easily while chasing prey.

Another feature found in tetanurines is big hands. Compared to their more primitive relatives, the tetanurines had longer hands with stronger fingers, typically ending in larger claws. They probably used them to clutch on to prey. In coelophysoids and ceratosaurs, there are four fingers on each hand. In tetanurines, these hands did not have a fourth finger. So far, all known hands for this group have three or fewer fingers.

So how do spinosauroids differ from other tetanurines? First of all, spinosauroids have longer snouts. In fact, they are longer than those of almost all other theropods. And the places on their arms for muscles to attach are exceptionally large, so they probably had very strong forelimbs.

So spinosauroids are a subset of the tetanurines, and tetanurines are a subdivision of the theropods. What types of spinosauroids are there? Spinosauroidea contains a group of advanced species called Spinosauridae and a number of more primitive species. Some paleontologists

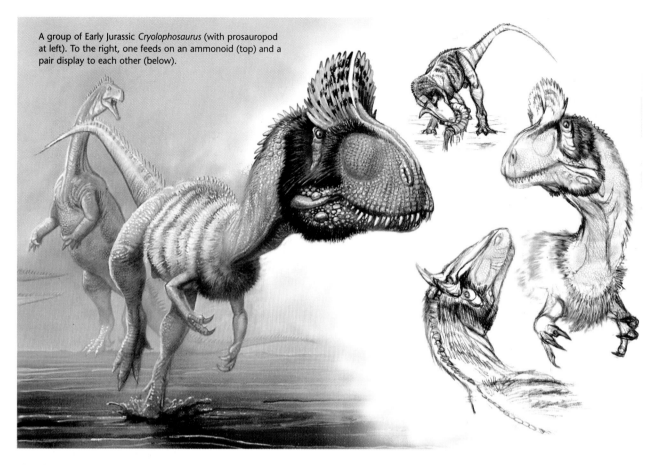

A group of Early Jurassic *Cryolophosaurus* (with prosauropod at left). To the right, one feeds on an ammonoid (top) and a pair display to each other (below).

think that these primitive species belong to a single evolutionary branch, for which the proper name would be Megalosauridae because it would include *Megalosaurus.* But other paleontologists think that some of these "megalosaurids" are closer to spinosaurids, that some—the true members of Megalosauridae—are closer to *Megalosaurus,* and that still others are more primitive than either spinosaurids or true megalosaurids.

A FROZEN DINOSAUR?

The oldest and most primitive known tetanurine is *Cryolophosaurus.* It comes from the Early Jurassic of Antarctica.

Antarctica today is arguably the toughest place in the world for any animal to live. Nearly all of the continent is under miles of ice. The only vertebrates living there are seals, penguins, flying seabirds, and human explorers and scientists. Two of these scientists are William Hammer and William Hickerson. In 1991, they were looking for fossils in some of the few rocks that poke through the ice when they found a series of dinosaur and other bones from the Early Jurassic Epoch. Among those bones were parts of a plant-eating prosauropod and a bizarre theropod.

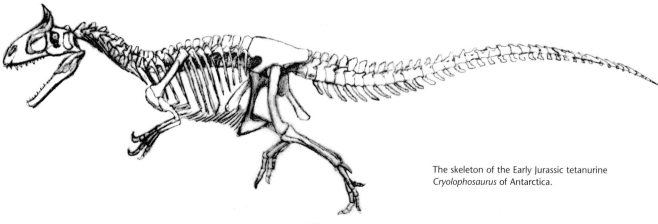

The skeleton of the Early Jurassic tetanurine *Cryolophosaurus* of Antarctica.

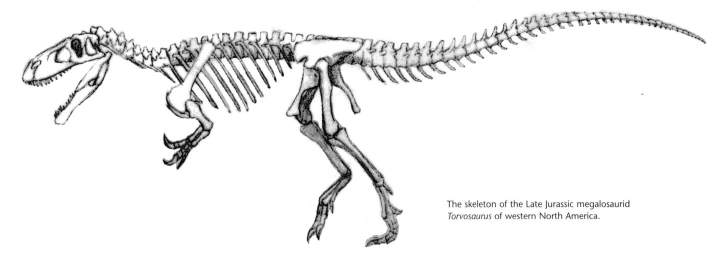

The skeleton of the Late Jurassic megalosaurid *Torvosaurus* of western North America.

Although only parts of the theropod's skull and skeleton were found, that was enough to show that this was an entirely new species. The most unusual thing about this dinosaur is its crest. While many theropods have crests, these projections normally are parallel to the skull. But in this new dinosaur, which they named *Cryolophosaurus* (frozen crested reptile), the crest curls forward. It looks a little like the pompadour of the famous singer Elvis Presley, leading some paleontologists to nickname the dinosaur "Elvisaurus."

At present, a comprehensive study of *Cryolophosaurus* has not been completed. Some paleontologists have thought it was a primitive member of Carnosauria (the subject of the next chapter). Others thought it was a ceratosaur. But most recent evidence suggests it is a primitive tetanurine, and possibly even a megalosaur. Only future analyses will show which of these is most likely accurate.

What would a medium-size meat-eater be doing in such a frozen wasteland? Well, when this dinosaur was alive, the Antarctic wasn't frozen! During the Jurassic Period, and indeed well past the end of the Mesozoic Era, Antarctica was farther north than it is today. The continent wasn't covered with ice, but instead had forests and hills and streams and all the other kinds of landforms we see in the rest of the world. It was only

much later that the continent drifted to the South Pole, and even later that the climate changed and the landmass got covered in ice. Who knows what other strange dinosaur fossils might still be there, hidden under the glaciers?

Another early tetanurine, and possibly early megalosaur, doesn't even have a proper name yet! *"Dilophosaurus" sinensis* of China was first thought to be a new species of the coelophysoid *Dilophosaurus*. Like the true *Dilophosaurus*, it lived in the Early Jurassic Epoch, and like the true *Dilophosaurus*, it had a pair of crests on its head. But unlike the features of the true *Dilophosaurus*, the structure of the face, vertebrae, and limbs of the Chinese species are not like those of coelophysoids. Instead, they are more like those of megalosaurids. This is another

The Late Jurassic megalosaurid *Torvosaurus*.

dinosaur currently under study. Hopefully, paleontologists will determine what sort of theropod it is and give it a proper name.

BUCKLAND'S BIG LIZARD

The oldest definite spinosauroids known are from the Middle Jurassic Epoch. One of these is also the first dinosaur known from fossils. *Megalosaurus* was discovered by the Reverend William Buckland in England in the early 1800s. Only a few bones were discovered at that time, but they were enough to show that this was an animal different from anything else known before. Its teeth were like those of today's meat-eating monitor lizards, and Buckland (not very creatively) named it "big reptile," or *Megalosaurus*. He pictured it looking something like a giant monitor lizard, but with the legs held directly under the body rather than sprawling out to the sides.

To date, no one has found a complete skeleton of *Megalosaurus*. This has caused some problems. Many paleontologists have thought they found a new species of *Megalosaurus* when in fact they found an entirely different sort of theropod. For example, the coelophysoid *Dilophosaurus,* the ceratosaur *Majungasaurus,* and the carnosaur *Carcharodontosaurus* were all once thought to be new species of *Megalosaurus* until additional comparisons showed that they were from other groups.

It's also possible that some of the bones that Buckland found in the Middle Jurassic rocks of England, or the ones that others have found there since, may belong to more than one kind of theropod! A recent examination by paleontologists Julia Day and Paul Barrett show that there are probably at least two different species represented in Buckland's specimens. One, a heavily built primitive tetanurine, would be a true *Megalosaurus.* The other might be a ceratosaur, but it is not at all certain.

Thankfully, there is more to Megalosauridae than *Megalosaurus*! Many other megalosaurids are known from the Middle Jurassic through the Early Cretaceous from around the world. Some seem to be very similar to Buckland's big reptile. These include *Poekilopleuron* from the Middle Jurassic of France and *Edmarka* and *Torvosaurus* from the Late Jurassic of the western United States. Two new species in this group, not yet named, have been found in the Middle Jurassic rocks of Italy and Germany. The second of these is probably the largest theropod currently known from Europe. These are all heavy dinosaurs with large, well-muscled arms. They probably went after slower prey like stegosaurs and sauropods rather than faster-moving ornithopods.

Other megalosaurids were more lightly built. These include *Piatnitzkysaurus* of the Middle Jurassic of Argentina, *Dubreuillosaurus* from the Middle Jurassic of France, *Eustreptospondylus* of the Middle Jurassic of England, and *Afrovenator* of the Early Cretaceous of Niger. The skulls of *Calvadosaurus* and *Eustreptospondylus* are the most complete of any megalosaurid. They are long and not terribly deep. It seems likely that their bite was not as strong as ceratosaurs' or carnosaurs' (and it was definitely weaker than tyrannosaurs'). They may have relied more on their stout but well-muscled arms to catch and kill prey.

* * *

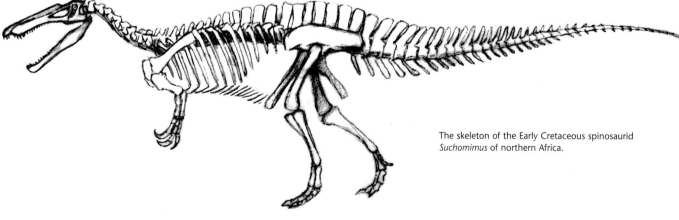

The skeleton of the Early Cretaceous spinosaurid *Suchomimus* of northern Africa.

The Early Cretaceous spinosaurid *Baryonyx* of Europe.

A MYSTERY OUT OF EGYPT

We often associate Egypt with ancient and mysterious things: hieroglyphic writings, mummies, and pyramids, for example. But the sands (or, in this case, the sandstones) of Egypt contain a secret thousands of times older than the oldest pharaoh. And like the hieroglyphs, which were once unreadable to modern people until a key was found to translate them, this even more ancient mystery didn't make much sense until other "keys" were found.

The mystery was the dinosaur *Spinosaurus.* It was discovered in 1912 by a team led by German paleontologist Ernst Freiherr Stromer von Reichenbach and his field assistant, Richard Markgraf. In 1915, Stromer published his description of this strange new dinosaur from the beginning of the Late Cretaceous Epoch of Egypt. Although less than 10 percent of the animal had been found, there were many features on it that showed it was very unusual. First was its size. Where bones could

be compared between it and *Tyrannosaurus* (at the time the biggest known theropod), *Spinosaurus*'s were as big if not bigger than the tyrant dinosaur's. And unlike the teeth of most theropods, *Spinosaurus*'s were cone-shaped and not like steak knives. In fact, they looked like giant crocodile teeth.

But strangest of all was its back bones. The neural spines—projections that come out of the top of the vertebrae—were tall. Really, *really* tall! The tallest were nearly 6 feet (1.8 meters) long. They were arranged to form a sail along the back of the dinosaur. Some later dinosaur discoveries—such as the diplodocoid sauropods *Rebbachisaurus* and *Amargasaurus* and the iguanodontian ornithopod *Ouranosaurus*—also had tall sails, as did the protomammal *Dimetrodon*. But *Spinosaurus*'s sail dwarfed the others.

Unfortunately, there was little else discovered

of this dinosaur. Only one drawing of the bones in position was made, and since there were so many missing bones, Stromer used *Allosaurus* and *Tyrannosaurus* as models for the missing parts. That's why most older drawings and models of *Spinosaurus* made it look like a *Tyrannosaurus* with a sail.

What was also unfortunate was the fate of this specimen, at the time the only one of a spinosaurid known. The skeleton of *Spinosaurus* was destroyed when the museum it was in was bombed during World War II. For many years, all paleontologists had to go on in order to understand these dinosaurs were drawings of their bones that had been published in technical articles. It would not be until the 1980s that new, much more complete spinosaurid fossils were discovered.

WHY THE LONG FACE? FISH-EATING DINOSAURS!

The new discovery was made in England, and it began as a mystery, too. In 1983, amateur fossil hunter William Walker found an enormous claw in a clay pit. A team from London's Natural History Museum went to look for the rest of the skeleton. What they uncovered was a new Early Cretaceous dinosaur species, which they named *Baryonyx walkeri* (Walker's heavy claw). While they were studying this fossil, it became apparent that this was a smaller, slightly older relative of mysterious *Spinosaurus.* And it began to fill the gaps in our knowledge of spinosaurid anatomy. Soon other specimens were found, including new fragmentary fossils of *Baryonyx* and *Spinosaurus,* as well as Early Cretaceous *Irritator* of Brazil and *Suchomimus* of Niger. (Because *Suchomimus* is so similar to *Baryonyx,* some paleontologists think that they may even be the same dinosaur.)

No other spinosaurid has a sail quite like that of *Spinosaurus,* but they all have taller neural spines than nearly every other type of theropod dinosaur. These sails might have been used to make them look bigger and fiercer. They might also have been used to tell related species apart. Or, since many of these dinosaurs lived in regions that were hot, even by the standards of the Meso-zoic Era, the sails might have helped them get rid of excess body heat.

Spinosaurid snouts are probably their second-most distinctive feature. They don't look like the snouts of other theropods. What they look like is crocodile snouts! That is where *Suchomimus*—which means "crocodile mimic"—got its name. Their snouts are long and relatively tubular and full of big, conical teeth. These teeth have very deep roots. This is not a good tooth pattern for slicing through meat, but an excellent one for holding on to struggling prey and tearing it apart. That is the way modern crocodilians feed, too: they don't slice through meat like a monitor lizard; they grab on to it, hold tight, and twist. And like crocodilians—and coelophysoids, too—spinosaurids have a curve in the upper jaw matched by big teeth in the lower jaw to serve as a point to get a good grip on their food.

What sort of food would a 50-foot (15.2-meter), 8-ton *Spinosaurus* eat? Anything it wanted. And that's no joke! While we don't have direct fossils from inside the belly of *Spinosaurus,* we *do* have such remains from *Baryonyx.* Inside its belly were the partially digested bones of a young *Iguanodon.* But also inside were the partially digested scales of large fish. It seems that spinosaurids had a diet similar to that of big modern crocodilians. Just as today's Nile crocodile and American alligator eat a mixture of land mammals, birds, turtles, and *a lot* of fish, so, too, the spinosaurids could eat both land vertebrates (like dinosaurs) and aquatic vertebrates (like turtles and fish).

Spinosaurids were well adapted for catching fish. Because they were big dinosaurs, they could wade into the water like giant herons or grizzly bears. They had fairly long necks, making it easy for them to dip their snouts into the water. In all spinosaurids, but especially in *Spinosaurus* and *Irritator,* the nostrils seem to have been placed far back on the snout, so they could keep the front of their noses underwater while still breathing. Like the teeth of some crocodilians, but unlike those of nearly all other theropods, the teeth at the front of the snout were much larger than those behind, the better to snag a big fish.

And there were some pretty big fish in those waters. The same rocks that contain the bones of *Spinosaurus* and *Irritator* also have fossils of 10-foot (3-meter) fish! If their jaws alone weren't enough to capture these monsters, the spinosaurids could use their giant hooklike claws and massively muscled arms to pull the fish out of the water.

But we know that *Baryonyx* ate *Iguanodon,* too. And teeth and snouts that are good for grabbing on to big fish are also good for grabbing the legs and necks of other dinosaurs. Spinosaurids had the best of both worlds. They could get food from the water *and* from the land. The more "normal" theropods would have a problem getting

fish, and the giant crocodilians of their time couldn't easily catch dinosaurs up on land.

MEGARAPTOR: LAST OF THE SPINOSAUROIDS?

Nevertheless, the spinosaurids' world came to an end about 95 million years ago. Spinosaurids lived in shallow swampy areas in the equatorial regions. From about 110 million to 95 million years ago, the world was *very* hot, and the sea levels were very high, so the spinosaurids had a lot of habitat. But after 95 million years ago, the world began to change. The climate became cooler (although still hot by modern standards) and the sea levels dropped. These changes drained off the swamps.

The Late Cretaceous theropod *Megaraptor*—a possible spinosaurid relative—attacks the titanosaur *Saltasaurus.*

Although the spinosaurids were well adapted for their own environment, it seems they were not able to compete with other large theropods in drier times. *Spinosaurus* wasn't merely the largest of the spinosaurids; it was the last of all species in Spinosauridae.

But discoveries made since 2003 suggest that close relatives of the spinosaurids and megalosaurids may have survived a little later, until 90 million years ago. These discoveries were fossils of a dinosaur called *Megaraptor,* found in 90-million-year-old rocks from Argentina. Only a few bones of *Megaraptor* were found at first, including an enormous claw. Many paleontologists thought that it may have been similar to the dromaeosaurid raptors, and in fact nearly every illustration ever drawn of this theropod shows it like that. But more recently found specimens show us a different picture. That talon didn't come from the foot but was instead from the hand! Also, other bones show that *Megaraptor* isn't a dromaeosaurid after all.

Some features of *Megaraptor* are similar to those of the carcharodontosaurid carnosaurs. But others are like those of both megalosaurids and spinosaurids. So it might be that the forests of Argentina, rather than the swamps of Egypt, were the last place spinosauroids stalked.

The Late Cretaceous spinosaurid *Spinosaurus* swallows a 6-foot (1.8-meter) *Mawsonia* fish.

Fish-Eating Giants— the Spinosaurs

Dr. Angela C. Milner
Natural History Museum,
London, England

We are all familiar with meat-eating dinosaurs—but the idea of fish-eating dinosaurs might sound strange. One group of very large dinosaurs, the spinosaurs, specialized in eating fish.

I was lucky enough to be involved in the study of the most complete spinosaur discovery to date, that of Baryonyx walkeri. It was found only 30 miles from London, England, in rocks dating from the Early Cretaceous Epoch, from about 120 million years ago. When we were uncovering the jawbones in the lab at the Natural History Museum, several paleontologists looked at them and said, "Those are the jaws of a crocodile." But I suspected that they were something different. They turned out to be part of the first discovery of the skull of a fish-eating dinosaur.

Spinosaur skulls were shaped like those of fish-eating crocodiles. They had very long, low skulls up to about 3 feet (0.9 meters) long. At least half of that length was made up of the slender jaws, which had a large number of teeth and a spoon-shaped end to help keep a grip on slippery fish. Spinosaurs also had very powerful forelimbs and huge, hooked claws. I suggested that the claws on their hands might have been used to help catch fish—just like the claws of grizzly bears that fish for salmon.

Even more evidence for a fishy diet was found with Baryonyx. We discovered partly digested scales and teeth of a large fish inside the dinosaur's rib cage—the remains of its last meal.

Spinosaurs were very large animals. Our Baryonyx specimen was about 33 feet (10 meters) long, and it wasn't fully grown. Spinosaurus was much bigger. There is no complete skeleton, but it must have been at least as big as Tyrannosaurus. Could such large animals live only on a diet of fish? I have no doubt about that. The fossil remains of spinosaurs, which lived in Europe, Africa, and South America, have only been found close to seacoasts or where there were lakes, rivers, and swamps. Their remains are always found near abundant fish fossils, including giant 20-foot coelacanths and lungfish. Spinosaurs would have a plentiful food source and, as there were no other fish-eating dinosaurs, they had it all to themselves.

The Late Cretaceous spinosaurid *Spinosaurus*.

Giganotosaurus

Allosaurus

Monolophosaurus

15

CARNOSAURS
(Giant Meat-Eating Dinosaurs)

Carnosauria (meat-[eating] reptiles) was one of the longest-lasting groups of big carnivorous dinosaurs. From their first appearance in the Middle Jurassic until the beginning of the Late Cretaceous, carnosaurs were the top predators in most parts of the world. Some of them—like *Giganotosaurus*—grew even bigger than *Tyrannosaurus* and may have rivaled *Spinosaurus* as the largest meat-eating dinosaur of all time.

Carnosaurs represent a group of theropods—the two-legged meat-eating dinosaurs. Specifically, they are part of Tetanurae. Tetanurines (sometimes spelled "tetanurans") have three-fingered hands and stiff tails. The other groups of tetanurines are the primitive long-snouted spinosauroids and the advanced, diverse coelurosaurs.

MORE THAN JUST BIG THEROPODS

In most dinosaur books of the twentieth century, the word "carnosaur" is used to describe all types of large-bodied theropods. According to this usage, *Dilophosaurus, Ceratosaurus,* the abelisaurids, the megalosaurids, the spinosaurids, and the tyrannosaurids are all considered types of carnosaurs. But since the mid-1990s, paleontologists have agreed that this isn't the proper use of the name. Modern scientists only use a technical name in classification if that name describes a "natural" group, or clade—a complete branch of the Tree of Life. The old-fashioned Carnosauria wasn't a complete branch. The group that modern paleontologists call Carnosauria, however, *is* a natural group.

Specifically, it is the clade comprised of *Allosaurus* and its closest relatives—that is, species that are more closely related to *Allosaurus* than they are to modern birds. Ever since German paleontologist Friedrich von Huene named Carnosauria in 1920, *Allosaurus* has been considered a carnosaur.

The closest relatives to the dinosaurs of Carnosauria are found in the group Coelurosauria (which makes up the next several chapters). Carnosaurs and coelurosaurs are more similar to each other in some ways than either are to spinosauroids, ceratosaurs, or coelophysoids. Carnosaurs and coelurosaurs have extremely hollow vertebrae with very complex chambers. These are just like the complex chambers found in bird vertebrae (in fact, birds *are* a type of coelurosaur!), and show that carnosaurs and coelurosaurs both had complex air sacs. Modern birds use air sacs to help them breathe fast, to cool their bodies, and to keep their lungs from getting too dry. Carnosaurs probably did the same. (Other primitive theropods and sauropodomorphs also had chambers in their vertebrae, but they weren't the complex ones that carnosaurs and coelurosaurs had.)

Carnosaurs, and their cousins the coelurosaurs, were more advanced in their skulls than other theropods, too. Both carnosaurs and coelurosaurs had more complex air sacs in their heads than did more primitive theropods, which probably also helped to cool their bodies (especially their heads) and keep their lungs moist. We can recognize the greater complexity of these air sacs because there are extra holes in the facial bones of advanced theropods that aren't found in other dinosaurs.

DIVERSITY OF THE CARNOSAURS

In fact, carnosaur facial bones have *a lot* of extra holes in them. Some are as small as a dime. Others are as big as a pizza. These holes are one of the features that help us recognize whether a theropod is a true carnosaur. Additionally, the nares—the openings in the skull for the nasal passages—are bigger in carnosaurs than in other theropods.

Many members of Carnosauria have a crest or ridge on their faces. In the case of *Monolophosaurus,* a hollow crest of bone runs down the center of the top of the head. The advanced group of carnosaurs, called *Allosauroidea,* is characterized by a pair of ridges, one on each side of the face. Additionally, in *Allosaurus* itself there are little triangular hornlets that flare up in front of the eyes. In all these cases, the crests were probably for show. That is, they helped the dinosaurs recognize other members of their own species.

The carnosaurs first appeared in the Middle Jurassic Epoch. Chinese *Monolophosaurus* and *Gasosaurus* are two of the oldest forms. They

The Late Jurassic sinraptorid *Yangchuanosaurus* of China.

probably do not belong to the advanced group Allosauroidea. Similar non-allosauroid carnosaurs include the Late Jurassic *Lourinhanosaurus* from Portugal (which may actually be a megalosaurid), Early Cretaceous *Fukuiraptor* from Japan, and Early Cretaceous *Siamotyrannus* from Thailand. None of these are particularly giant animals. They range from 15 to 20 feet (4.6 to 6.1 meters) long.

The remaining carnosaurs—the allosauroids— are typically bigger. Allosauroids have three main branches. Sinraptoridae is best known from the Late Jurassic of China. *Yangchuanosaurus,* the biggest sinraptorid, grew over 35 feet (10.7 meters) long and weighed nearly 3.5 tons. Allosauridae is a group that ranged from the Late Jurassic into the Early Cretaceous. Its largest member is *Saurophaganax* from Oklahoma, reach-

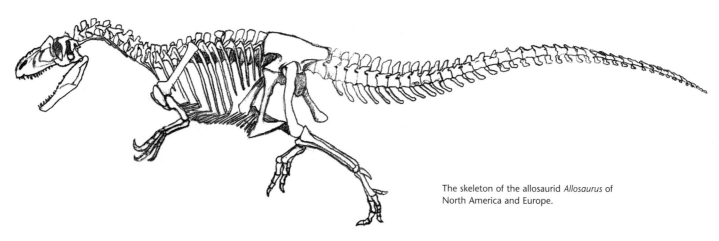

The skeleton of the allosaurid *Allosaurus* of North America and Europe.

Allosaurus is the best-studied carnosaur.

ing almost 40 feet (12.2 meters) long; its most famous, and best-studied, member is *Allosaurus*. Carcharodontosauridae is a group known only from the Cretaceous. Carcharodontosaurids range from 26-foot (8-meter) *Neovenator* to gigantic 46-foot (14-meter) or longer *Giganotosaurus*. The latter weighed about 8 tons, making it longer and heavier than *Tyrannosaurus*.

Nevertheless, the anatomy of all carnosaurs was basically the same. They might have different crests, slightly differently shaped skulls, or smaller or larger forelimbs, but otherwise carnosaurs tended to look the same. Because carnosaurs changed very little over 100 million years (other than in size), they must have been very good at what they did. And what they did was hunt, kill, and eat sauropods.

* * *

WEAPONS OF THE GIANT SLAYERS

Wherever carnosaurs are known, sauropods are also found. There are sometimes other types of plant-eaters present—stegosaurs, ornithopods, or ankylosaurs—but always sauropods. This suggests that carnosaurs had a taste for the giant long-necked plant-eaters.

There are some trace fossils that document carnosaurs ate sauropods. For example, carnosaur tooth marks have been found on sauropod bones. But these bite marks could also have been made if the carnosaurs were scavenging an already-dead giant herbivore. What we need to show that carnosaurs actually *attacked* sauropods are trace fossils made while both animals were alive—in other words, footprints. And it turns out that just such trace fossils exist.

There is a famous trackway from Paluxy, Texas, that shows the footprints of the 40.2-foot (12.2-meter) carcharodontosaurid *Acrocanthosaurus* chasing the brachiosaurid sauropod *Sauroposeidon.* The trackway shows that the carnivore struck at the plant-eater, was carried for a step before it was shaken off, and then continued the pursuit.

This isn't to say that carnosaurs didn't eat other plant-eaters, too. There is a fossil of *Allosaurus,* for instance, that shows the meat-eater was clobbered by the thagomizer tail spikes of *Stegosaurus.* Since a *Stegosaurus* would have little reason to pick on a giant meat-eater, it is likely that the plated plant-eater was defending itself from attack.

How would a carnosaur attack a herbivorous dinosaur? With steak-knife teeth and eagle-like talons. Carnosaur teeth are like those of megalosaurids, ceratosaurs, and other primitive theropods. They were flat on the sides, with a cutting row of serrations up the front and down the back. This kind of shape was good for slicing through meat.

Carnosaur skulls were deep and narrow, and some paleontologists have compared their shape to meat cleavers or hatchets. In fact, computer studies by Emily Rayfield of the University of Cambridge in England and her colleagues show that a hatchet isn't a bad analogy. Because of the openings on the sides of the skull and the lack of a hard palate (roof of the mouth), carnosaur heads weren't especially strong. That is, they were weak if the carnosaurs tried to hold on to struggling prey with just their jaws. But the computer studies show that striking like a hatchet, a carnosaur skull was pretty strong. *Allosaurus* and its kin probably snapped at their victims, slicing off big ribbons of meat and causing massive blood loss. This blood loss would make the animal weaker and easier to kill.

Could a carnosaur control its strike? Against smaller animals, like young sauropods, ornithopods, and stegosaurs, it wouldn't be too hard. Carnosaurs were typically taller than these animals. But against adult sauropods, it was probably harder to get in a good bite. Here's where the carnosaur arms would help out. Although not very long, carnosaur forelimbs were strong and ended with claws like eagle talons. These claws were literally meat hooks: carnosaurs could use them to pierce the flesh of their victims and hold on tight. While holding on, they could better aim their strikes against the flanks of a sauropod. (In fact, the *Acrocanthosaurus-Sauroposeidon* tracks might actually record such an attempted bite!)

* * *

The skeleton of the enormous Late Cretaceous carcharodontosaurid *Giganotosaurus* of Argentina.

KING OF THE JURASSIC

The best known and best understood of all carnosaurs is *Allosaurus*. We have more skeletons of this dinosaur than of any other large theropod, including *Tyrannosaurus*. Definite specimens of *Allosaurus* are known from the Late Jurassic Morrison Formation of western North America and from rocks of the same age in Portugal. Presumably, it lived in every place in between as well.

Allosaurus fossils outnumber other theropod fossils in the Morrison Formation two to one. And there are at least eleven other theropod species in the Morrison! Most of these *Allosaurus* fossils are of an individual skeleton or of partial skeletons. But at a site called the Cleveland-Lloyd Quarry, in Utah, more than forty different *Allosaurus* individuals were found together. The rocks from this site were not deposited in a flood or storm, so this probably doesn't represent a pack that died at the

The Late Cretaceous carcharodontosaurid *Carcharodontosaurus* of northern Africa attacks a herd of sauropods.

same time. Instead, the place may have been a predator trap. Predator traps work like this: you need some "bait" and something for the predator to get stuck in. The shale at the Cleveland-Lloyd Quarry was once sticky mud, and fossilized with the many *Allosaurus* (and a few other theropod) skeletons are a few skeletons of plant-eaters. These herbivores must have wandered into the mud and gotten stuck. The cries of the trapped plant-eaters, or the rotting smell after they died, would attract *Allosaurus* and other predators. One by one, the meat-eaters wandered in to get what they thought was an easy meal, only to get stuck themselves and to become "bait" for even more predators! (Similar conditions happened in the much younger La Brea Tar Pits of Los Angeles, California. As with the Cleveland-Lloyd Quarry, most of the La Brea

Early Cretaceous *Acrocanthosaurus* feed on the carcass of a brachiosaurid while much smaller deinonychosaurs get ready to steal some scraps.

fossils are of predators and just a few are of the plant-eater "bait.")

Allosaurus was a good-size predator, averaging about 30 feet (9.1 meters) in length and weighing up to 1.7 tons. A second Morrison allosaurid—*Saurophaganax*—grew even larger, but it is known from only a single site. In fact, some paleontologists regard it as only a giant species of *Allosaurus.*

SHARK DINOSAURS

The largest of the carnosaurs were the members of Carcharodontosauridae. *Carcharodon* is the scientific name of the modern great white shark, and *Carcharodontosaurus*—the Late Cretaceous northern African carnosaur—got its name because its teeth resemble shark teeth, only bigger. And just as the great white preys on animals that vary in size, from small fish to big whales, *Carcharodontosaurus* probably fed on dinosaurs from little ceratosaurs to giant titanosaurs.

There were several other carcharodontosaurs living around the world during the Cretaceous. The most completely known one is *Acrocanthosaurus* of North America, although some paleontologists consider it to be the last allosaurid rather than a true carcharodontosaurid. Regardless of its exact position on the family tree, this big carnosaur had powerful hooklike claws and a long skull. Its most famous features, though, are the tall

spines on its back. These tall spines formed a crest or ridge from the back of the head to the end of the tail.

More carcharodontosaurids are known from South America than from any other part of the world. *Tyrannotitan* was bigger than *Acrocanthosaurus* and more heavily built. Larger and more famous is *Giganotosaurus.* This aptly named "giant southern reptile" is currently the biggest meat-eating dinosaur known, although parts of a *Spinosaurus* skeleton hint that the Egyptian dinosaur may have been even larger.

Another Argentine carcharodontosaurid—*Mapusaurus*—is from a little later than *Giganotosaurus.* It seems to have been about the same size as its earlier cousin, only with a shorter and stockier skull. What is most impressive about it, however, is the possibility that it was a pack hunter. Its discoverers, Rodolfo Coria and Philip Currie, found several individuals of this new species fossilized together. From the sedimentary structures in the rock, it appears that they were buried at the same time, suggesting that they lived (or at least died) as a group. What could such giant 8-ton monsters eat? Not coincidentally, perhaps, these rocks also contain the fossils of *Argentinosaurus,* a herbivore and the largest of all known dinosaurs.

In fact, the other big carcharodontosaurids are *also* typically found with some of the biggest of all sauropods: *Acrocanthosaurus* with the brachiosaurid *Sauroposeidon; Carcharodontosaurus* with the titanosaur *Paralititan; Giganotosaurus* with the rebbachisaurid *Limaysaurus* and the titanosaur *Andesaurus; Mapusaurus* with the titanosaur *Argentinosaurus* and an unnamed rebbachisaurid; and an unnamed Argentine carcharodontosaurid with the saltasaurids *Antarctosaurus, Neuquensaurus,* and *Saltasaurus.* It seems likely that these giant carnosaurs were specialists in eating the largest of all herbivores.

THE LAST CARNOSAURS

This taste for big titanosaurs may have been the carnosaurs' downfall. The last carnosaur disappeared around 85 million years ago. It was around this same time that the last of the super-giant titanosaurs died out as well. Only smaller (although still big) saltasaurids were left among the sauropods.

It may be that the disappearances were linked. Something killed off the super-giant sauropods—perhaps a climate change—and the carnosaurs were left without their main food supply. It's true that there were still plenty of smaller herbivores around, but it is also true that more newly evolved groups of theropods had appeared. These newer groups were the abelisaurids in the Southern Hemisphere and the tyrannosaurids in the Northern Hemisphere. Perhaps the big, bulky carnosaurs could not compete with these newfangled predators when hunting for the remaining types of prey. During the last 20 million years of the Cretaceous, it was these other theropods that ruled the Earth. The long reign of Carnosauria was at an end.

Giants hunting giants: the enormous Late Cretaceous carcharodontosaurid *Mapusaurus* of Argentina hunts a juvenile *Argentinosaurus* while a herd of adult *Argentinosaurus* looms in the distance.

Giant Pack-Hunting Dinosaurs

Dr. Philip J. Currie
Royal Tyrrell Museum,
Alberta, Canada

Some of the most terrifying scenes in any dinosaur movie, including Jurassic Park, are those of a gigantic, flesh-eating dinosaur bearing down on its supper. But just imagine how much more horrifying those scenes would be if the lone hunter were replaced by a pack of these ferocious beasts! One can picture the drama as the unfortunate prey tried to evade its pursuers. Even if it were able to escape the jaws of the largest of the predators, smaller, more agile, and faster members of the pack would dash in to cut off any retreat.

Although such scenes remain speculative, considerable evidence has been collected by paleontologists to suggest that many species of large meat-eating dinosaurs may have been pack hunters. Perhaps they did this all the time. Or perhaps the carnivores only gathered together twice a year, when enormous herds of plant-eating dinosaurs migrated through their territories.

Some of the earliest evidence for pack hunting in dinosaurs came from footprint sites. Trackways sometimes indicate that several large carnivores were moving in the same direction at the same time. Once, while cleaning off a huge slab of footprint-covered rock, I realized that I was witnessing evidence of a dramatic pursuit many millions of years ago. Three large carnivores had been walking together, crisscrossing each other's path in an apparent hunting strategy.

In 1910, Barnum Brown of the American Museum of Natural History in New York led an expedition to the Red Deer River of Alberta, Canada. There he found a bed of fossil bones that was dominated by the remains of Albertosaurus. This predator is a close relative of Tyrannosaurus, only slightly smaller. Brown collected partial skeletons of nine animals, but never completed his research. After we rediscovered the locality, we gathered more evidence to show that the tyrannosaurs had died together at the same time. At the time of death, they were almost certainly traveling together as a pack. The youngest individuals were less than half grown, and were as lightly built as ostriches. They must have been extremely fast and aggressive! Although tyrannosaurs are relatively rare as fossils, we now have sites in Canada, Mongolia, and the United States that suggest other tyrannosaur species (including Tyrannosaurus) were also pack hunters.

There are fossils of flesh-eating dinosaurs that were as large or larger than Tyrannosaurus. Two of these animals, Carcharodontosaurus and Giganotosaurus, probably hunted long-necked sauropods. It is not surprising that they were so large, considering they were hunting the largest animals that have ever walked on Earth! Even so, we were extremely surprised to discover the remains of a pack composed of seven of these horrific hunters in the wilds of Patagonia, Argentina, in 1997. It probably took more than one of these huge meat-eaters to bring down an animal as large as Argentinosaurus, a sauropod that may have weighed a hundred tons.

A trio of *Giganotosaurus.*

Allosaurus Eating Habits

Dr. Emily Rayfield
University of Cambridge

Photo courtesy of Emily Rayfield

Allosaurus was a meat-eater, and a particularly messy one at that. Around 150 million years ago, this dinosaur could be found roaming the floodplains, rivers, and lakes of North America and Europe in search of a bite to eat.

We cannot be absolutely sure about what *Allosaurus* ate. A partial Apatosaurus backbone, apparently scraped by *Allosaurus* teeth, is about all the evidence we have. Perhaps *Allosaurus* hunted in packs to capture large sauropods such as Diplodocus and Camarasaurus. Or maybe it stalked smaller prey such as Stegosaurus and Camptosaurus. We do not know for sure. But *Allosaurus* certainly had a rough-and-tumble lifestyle because some skeletons contain many broken and rehealed bones.

The skull of *Allosaurus* provides many clues to how this animal may have captured and fed on its prey. Its jaw muscles were attached to the lower jaw near the jaw joint. This means that the skull was specialized for rapid chopping rather than forceful biting. The bite of *Allosaurus* was maybe three to four times weaker than the estimated bites of Tyrannosaurus and alligators, and similar in strength to the bites of modern-day big cats such as lions and leopards. *Allosaurus* teeth were strong and blade-like, with serrations along the front and back edges to grip and rip through flesh. To create maximum carnage while biting, the serrated edges were twisted along the tooth to churn through flesh with every bite. A weaker bite force and narrower teeth made it unlikely, however, that *Allosaurus* could splinter bone in the same way as Tyrannosaurus. *Allosaurus* was a snapper, not a bone crusher.

Although the normal *Allosaurus* bite was quite weak for an animal of its size, the skull was exceedingly strong. Like the pillars of an arch, struts of bone helped contain stress generated during biting. Other thickened regions of bone and flexible joints helped further reduce physical stress caused by biting, so that the *Allosaurus* skull could have withstood up to 6 tons in weight before fracturing! *Allosaurus* also had a very powerful S-shaped neck. It seems that it used its strong neck muscles to thrust the head and drive the teeth of the upper jaw down into the hide of its unlucky prey. The strong skull helped it withstand the jarring impact. Once hooked into the prey, the jaws could be clamped together. Then *Allosaurus* tugged its ripping teeth through the flesh to tear away a bite to eat. The prey would rapidly grow weak because of shock and blood loss, making it only a matter of time before *Allosaurus* could dine at leisure on its helpless victim.

The deadly teeth and claws (close-up lower right) of *Allosaurus*.

Ornitholestes

Sinosauropteryx

Scipionyx

16

PRIMITIVE COELUROSAURS
(The First Fluffy Dinosaurs)

Not all dinosaurs were giants. Many of them were smaller than a human being. This is true of many plant-eating dinosaurs as well as meat-eaters. Early *Eoraptor* was only about 3 feet (0.9 meters) long, as were the coelophysoids *Procompsognathus* and *Segisaurus* and the ceratosaurs *Noasaurus* and *Velocisaurus*. The most famous small-bodied dinosaurs of all, though, are the coelurosaurs.

These advanced theropods began as chicken-to-turkey-size predators. From them—the dinosaurs in this chapter—evolved a whole host of advanced species. Some became ferocious hunters, from smaller dromaeosaurid raptors to enormous tyrannosaurids. Others evolved into plant-eaters, like the ornithomimosaurs and therizinosaurs. And some evolved into birds. One of the most remarkable discoveries in modern science is that coelurosaurs, even the most primitive ones, were actually fluffy rather than scaly!

Coelurosaurs are part of the group of theropods called Tetanurae. Tetanurines (sometimes spelled "tetanurans") have three-fingered hands (not four-fingered like coelophysoids and ceratosaurs, or five-fingered like most other dinosaurs) and stiff tails. The other groups of tetanurines are the primitive, long-snouted spinosauroids and the large, big-skulled carnosaurs.

JURASSIC JACKALS, CRETACEOUS COYOTES

People once used the name "coelurosaur" to describe all the small-bodied theropods. But this wasn't a natural grouping. After all, little *Procompsognathus* and medium-size *Coelophysis* are evolutionarily more closely related to large *Dilophosaurus* than they are to little coelurosaur *Compsognathus* or medium-size coelurosaur *Ornitholestes*. And Friedrich von Huene, the paleontologist who created the name Coelurosauria in 1914, recognized that the gigantic tyrant theropods—Tyrannosauridae—were actually coelurosaurs. There is more to being a coelurosaur than size.

In addition to certain detailed features of the skull, some traits shared by all coelurosaurs include a narrow (rather than broad) hand and a slender rear portion of the tail. Most (but not all) coelurosaurs also have long arms compared to other theropods. And coelurosaur brains tend to be two or more times bigger than those of other theropods with the same size body.

The name Coelurosauria comes from *Coelurus* (hollow tail), one of the oldest and first-discovered coelurosaurs. This 6.5-foot (2-meter) dinosaur is typical of many early members of this group. It had a fairly long neck; a very long tail; and long, slender arms and legs. It was much smaller than most of the other predators in its community, the Late Jurassic Morrison Formation of the American

The Late Jurassic coelurosaur *Ornitholestes* of western North America.

West. If we were to compare that ecosystem to today's Serengeti Plain of Africa, then *Allosaurus* and *Torvosaurus* would be like the mighty lions, *Ceratosaurus* would be a smaller predator like a leopard, and little *Coelurus* would be like a jackal or fox. In fact, there were other "Jurassic jackals" in this environment: 6-foot (1.8-meter) *Ornitholestes* and 11.5-foot (3.5-meter) *Tanycolagreus*.

Today's jackals hunt little things like mice, rabbits, and snakes, not big things like antelope, rhinos, or elephants. So, too, the little coelurosaurs would not have gone after big prey like *Camptosaurus* and *Stegosaurus* and would have avoided giants like *Brachiosaurus* or *Apatosaurus*—who could easily step on and crush them! Instead, coelurosaurs would have hunted for frogs, mammals, lizards, and the occasional baby dinosaur. While a coelurosaur didn't risk being smashed, spiked, or flattened by such prey, catching little animals poses a different set of problems. Little animals might not have a lot of stamina, but they are often agile. They can turn quickly and dash into the ferns or between rocks or into ponds. How could the little coelurosaurs get their prey?

Think about modern animals that hunt such prey—jackals and coyotes, raccoons and cats, hawks and snakes. Although they are all very different, they share some traits in common. They are all pretty clever, at least when it comes to food. They are all agile. And they all strike very fast.

Primitive coelurosaurs were the same way. They captured their prey with quick wits, fast hands, and swift legs. Their big eyes and big brains meant they could find and track a running lizard or scampering mammal. Their long, nimble arms could strike quickly and reach between rocks or branches. And their slender legs and tails meant they could run fast and turn suddenly while chasing prey. (This also helped the coelurosaurs from becoming the prey of bigger theropods!)

COMPY, KIRKY, AND SKIPPY: THE PRIMITIVE COELUROSAURS

The oldest-named coelurosaur is *Proceratosaurus* from the Middle Jurassic of England, although there are many fragments and bits of coelurosaur bone from that epoch from many parts of the

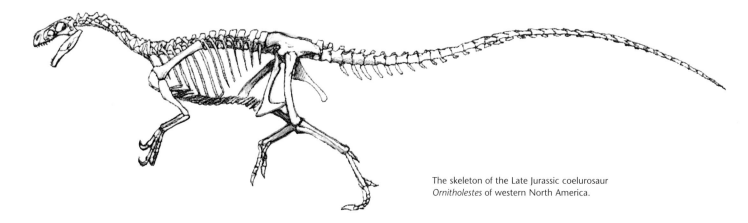

The skeleton of the Late Jurassic coelurosaur *Ornitholestes* of western North America.

world. This dinosaur, known only from a skull, seems to be quite similar to the younger North American *Ornitholestes.*

There were more coelurosaurs around by the Late Jurassic. You've already been introduced to *Coelurus, Ornitholestes,* and *Tanycolagreus* of North America. One of the most famous of the primitive coelurosaurs lived at nearly the same time in Europe. This is *Compsognathus.* It grew up to 3.6 feet (1.1 meters) long, but more than half of that was tail. In fact, this dinosaur was only the size of a barnyard chicken! For many years—before the discovery of tiny Chinese forms and before paleontologists realized that birds were a type of dinosaur—"Compy" was the smallest known dinosaur species.

Compsognathus is one of a group of early coelurosaurs called Compsognathidae. "Compy" itself was the first dinosaur known from a nearly complete skeleton, found in 1861. Compsognathids lived during the middle part of the Age of Dinosaurs, with *Compsognathus* in the Late Jurassic and its relatives—English *Aristosuchus,* Brazilian *Mirischia,* and Chinese *Sinosauropteryx* and *Huaxiagnathus*—in the Early Cretaceous. Unlike most other types of coelurosaurs, compsognathids had short arms. Additionally, the hands of the more advanced compsognathids (such as

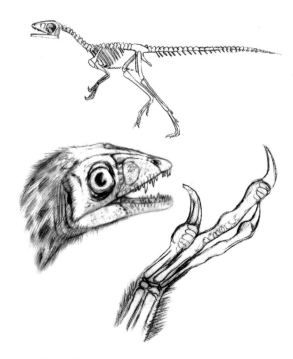

A dead *Scipionyx* (left) from the Early Cretaceous of Italy, its skeleton (top right), its head (middle right), and a close-up of its slender, three-fingered hand (bottom right).

"Skippy" and family: the Early Cretaceous coelurosaur *Scipionyx* of Italy.

Compsognathus and *Sinosauropteryx*) had an enormous, thick thumb.

This latter trait was also found in South African *Nqwebasaurus,* which some paleontologists consider a compsognathid. The scientists who discovered *Nqwebasaurus* gave it the nickname "Kirky" because it was found in the Kirkwood Formation from the early part of the Early Cretaceous. The tiny dinosaur that was found was less than a meter long, but the development of its back bones suggests that it may not have been an adult when it died. And since only one skeleton of *Nqwebasaurus* is known, we have no idea yet how big it would have been when it was fully grown.

The same situation exists for another primitive coelurosaur. *Scipionyx* is a cute little dinosaur from the Early Cretaceous of Italy. It had a big head with great big eyes. It was probably less than a foot (0.3 meters) long when it died. However, its bone texture and teeth suggest that it was just a hatchling. Again, we really don't know how big *Scipionyx* would have been when it was fully grown.

Scipionyx (Scipio's claw) gets its name from two different people: the ancient Roman soldier Scipio Africanus, who defended the Italians from Hannibal's Carthaginians; and Scipione Breislak, a naturalist who in 1798 first described fossils from the same rocks that *Scipionyx* would be found in nearly 200 years later. When I first read about this dinosaur and its name, I nicknamed it "Skippy," because it's a cute name for a tiny dinosaur, and because in ancient Latin the name Scipio is pronounced "SKEE-pee-oh." However, Cristiano Dal Sasso and Marco Signore—the Italian scientists who discovered it—point out that this name is pronounced "SHIH-pee-oh" in modern Italian, and they use the nickname "Ciro" for the tiny dinosaur. Even so, I still think of the little guy as "Skippy."

But by any name, *Scipionyx* is an interesting little fossil. Some of its body tissues were petrified, or turned into stone, soon after death. There are bits of muscle and other tissue that are now rock. One of the most outstanding features of the spec-

Multiple views of the Early Cretaceous compsognathid *Sinosauropteryx* of China.

imen is the fact that you can see its intestines! (Everyone knew that dinosaurs had intestines, but they aren't something that normally gets preserved.) However, it might not actually be the intestine tissue itself that was petrified. Instead, it may be that limy mud entered the guts after death and created an internal mold of the intestines. Only further research will show for sure.

THE MANY VARIETIES OF ADVANCED COELUROSAURS

From primitive coelurosaurs evolved many wondrous forms—the dinosaurs that make up the next five chapters. Each of these later groups represents a type of advanced coelurosaur—that is, they are still part of Coelurosauria. The first to branch off was Tyrannosauroidea. Early tyrannosauroids, like *Dilong* of China, aren't much different from compsognathids or *Ornitholestes,* except that their skulls were stronger and they had front teeth shaped like scrapers. But the small tyrannosauroids eventually evolved into the enormous tyrannosaurids, giant two-fingered hunters that were the top predators of North America and Asia during the last 20 million years of the Cretaceous.

Another branch of the coelurosaur family tree is the ostrich-like Ornithomimosauria. These small-headed fast-running theropods were one of the first to evolve away from eating meat.

Most of the advanced coelurosaur groups, however, belong to a large clade called Maniraptora. This name means "hand grabbers," and refers to one of these dinosaurs' main adaptations. In the maniraptorans, the arms became especially long—sometimes nearly as long as the legs. Long arms can be useful when catching food, but they are a drag when running (literally!). So in maniraptorans, the semilunate carpal (a special wrist bone found in tetanurines) became quite large, allowing the hand to fold up tightly. And the shoulder joint was oriented more out to the side than backward (like in most theropods). When a maniraptoran folded its arms and hands up, they would tuck closely to the body. This would keep those long forelimbs out of the way and let the dinosaurs run faster.

We'll explore the maniraptorans in greater detail in chapters 19 to 21. The best-studied maniraptorans are ones that for a long time people didn't even realize were dinosaurs. These are the *Avialae,* or birds and their ancestors. Over the past 130 years, paleontologists have amassed a lot of evidence showing that birds evolved from coelurosaurian dinosaurs. But for a long time, people thought that there was one very important difference between birds and their coelurosaur ancestors. Birds, after all, have feathers. And no other type of dinosaur had feathers, right?

ENTER THE CHINESE DRAGONS

Actually, some paleontologists—such as Robert Bakker and Greg Paul—*did* think that coelurosaurs other than birds might have had feathers.

But there was no proof until the 1990s, when a series of important discoveries was made in rocks from the Early Cretaceous of northeastern China. In Liaoning Province, the extremely fine-grained sedimentary rocks of the Yixian Formation (and some other similar places) were once mud in ancient lakebeds. When animals and plants died and settled onto the lake floor, they were covered by this fine-grained mud. Because of the particular nature of the lake bottom and the sediments, many details normally lost in fossilization were preserved as a thin black layer of carbon. Flowers, leaves, insects, hair, and scales can all be clearly seen.

In 1996, Chinese paleontologists Ji Qiang and Ji Shuan described little *Sinosauropteryx* from the Yixian Formation in a Chinese scientific journal. Unfortunately, very few scientists outside of China knew of this paper. Ji and Ji considered this creature to be a bird rather than a compsognathid, however, because of what they saw in the fossil.

A dead Early Cretaceous compsognathid *Sinosauropteryx* of China.

Around the skeleton of this little dinosaur were a bunch of hollow fibers. When looked at under a microscope, they seemed to be very primitive versions of feathers! And since Ji and Ji reasoned that only birds had feathers, *Sinosauropteryx,* they concluded, *must* have been a bird.

Later that year, Canadian paleontologist Philip Currie was visiting China and was shown this specimen. He became very excited because he realized that despite the fuzz around it, this was the skeleton of a compsognathid. It was the long-predicted feathered dinosaur! I remember when I saw Currie after he got back from China. At the annual meeting of the Society of Vertebrate Paleontology that year, he showed me and others the photographs of this fossil. We were all very excited, just like he was.

The reason for the excitement: this showed that feathers—or *something* from which modern bird feathers evolved—were present in primitive coelurosaurs. Since the 1980s, skeletal evidence had convinced most dinosaur paleontologists that birds were an advanced kind of maniraptoran coelurosaurian dinosaur. But we still didn't know where on the dinosaur family tree feathers evolved. Maybe all the nonbird coelurosaurs were scaly, and feathers didn't appear until the very first birds? Many scientists and paleoartists thought that it was best to take this cautious approach, and this is why almost all older coelurosaur pictures show them with just scaly skin. But maybe deinonychosaurs (birds' closest relatives among the coelurosaurs) had feathers as well? Or maybe all coelurosaurs had them (like Bakker and Paul had suggested)? Without body impressions, no one could say for certain. And until the discovery of the Yixian Formation specimens, no one had such fossils.

Since 1996, many coelurosaurs have been found from the lake deposits of Yixian and similar formations in China. And every time a body impression is found, it has some sort of feather. The primitive coelurosaurs—compsognathids like *Sinosauropteryx* and tyrannosauroids like *Dilong*— only have simple fluffy structures. Since these structures are more primitive than any type of feather found on modern birds—even the down on baby chicks—the fluff seems to represent an intermediate stage between true reptile scales and modern bird feathers. While some have called these structures "dinofuzz," a more professional-sounding term is "protofeathers."

Perhaps more surprising than the protofeathers of primitive coelurosaurs is what is found on the bodies of the maniraptorans from the Yixian Formation. The avialians (early birds) have true feathers, which was no surprise. But oviraptorosaurs (such as *Caudipteryx*) and deinonychosaurs (such as *Microraptor* and *Sinornithosaurus*) *also* have honest-to-goodness true feathers! The feathers on their arms and tails (and on the legs of the deinonychosaurs) look just like the wing and tail feathers of modern birds, even at the microscopic level.

Given this evidence, paleontologists now predict that the common ancestor of all coelurosaurs had protofeathers over at least part of its body. In primitive coelurosaur groups, that is the only type of fuzzy covering the dinosaurs had. But in maniraptorans, the protofeathers evolved into true feathers, at least on the arms, legs, and tail.

I should add here that we don't know if more-primitive theropods—carnosaurs or spinosauroids or ceratosaurs or coelophysoids—also had protofeathers. Skin impressions of these dinosaurs are very rare, and so far we haven't found any from lake deposits that would preserve feathers. There are a few patches of scaly skin known from the carnosaur *Allosaurus,* and a lot of scaly skin is reported to have been found with the skeleton of the ceratosaur *Carnotaurus.* Some paleontologists have said that since there were scales on these dinosaurs, they must have evolved from nonfeathered ancestors, and that protofeathers would have been found only in coelurosaurs. That may not be the case, though. We know that big tyrannosaurids had patches of scaly skin, but we also know that these big tyrant dinosaurs evolved from earlier fuzzy coelurosaurs like *Dilong.* So it *is* quite possible that *all* theropods had fuzzy ancestors, from the coelophysoids on up. In fact, it may be that baby *Allosaurus* and *Carnotaurus* were fuzzy, but

lost their fuzz as they grew up. Without more fossils, we won't know for certain.

WHAT GOOD ARE PROTOFEATHERS?

We know that true feathers are good for flying. (We'll see in chapter 19 that they are also good for another form of locomotion.) But what good are the fuzzy protofeathers of *Sinosauropteryx* and other primitive coelurosaurs?

One likely answer is insulation. A little animal loses heat a lot faster than a big animal. So if you were a little animal that needed to keep warm, it would help if you had a body covering that trapped heat inside the body. Modern birds use feathers, modern mammals use fur, and modern bees use fuzz for just this reason. So it may be that little dinosaurs with an active lifestyle, like fast-running coelurosaurs, evolved protofeathers so that they could keep from losing too much heat.

A fuzzy coating is also useful for showing off. If you look at the fur of mammals and the feathers of birds, you'll see that many of them have special patterns and colors. Sometimes these patterns are used to attract members of the opposite sex. Sometimes they are used to ward off attackers. Other times they might help camouflage an animal. A dinosaur might use colored and patterned protofeathers to do any or all of these things.

Also, primitive coelurosaurs may have incubated their eggs by lying directly on top of them. This habit, called brooding, is known to have been present in maniraptoran coelurosaurs and may have been present in primitive coelurosaurs, too. Protofeathers would help keep the eggs warm, and also would cushion the eggs when the parent dinosaur sat on them. But until we find a brooding primitive coelurosaur, we won't be certain that this is the way they nested.

Regardless of how they nested, these primitive coelurosaurs were amazing little creatures. They may not have been very impressive by themselves, but from these dinosaurs evolved some of the most wonderful of all creatures: *Tyrannosaurus, Velociraptor,* the chicken, and the hummingbird.

Gorgosaurus

Dilong

Eotyrannus

17

TYRANNOSAUROIDS
(Tyrant Dinosaurs)

Unquestionably the coolest, most spectacular of all dinosaurs—indeed, of all living things in the history of the Earth—is *Tyrannosaurus rex.* (Okay, I'm biased. *T. rex* and its closest kin are my professional specialty, and it's been my favorite dinosaur since I was a kid.) But really—it even has the best name, which translates as "king of the tyrant lizards"! *Tyrannosaurus* was the last of a very successful branch of the theropod family tree known as Tyrannosauroidea, or tyrant dinosaurs. When they first appeared, tyrannosauroids were small, fast-running meat-eaters. But during the last 20 million years of the Cretaceous Period, one group of tyrannosauroids—the giant, two-fingered Tyrannosauridae—evolved into the top predators of Asia and North America.

There is more to the tyrant dinosaurs than their great size, giant teeth, and inherent coolness, however. They are in many ways the most specialized of the big carnivorous dinosaurs. That is to say, of all the big predators, they evolved the most new traits from the ancestral condition of all theropods. This combination of size and specialization makes the tyrant dinosaurs very interesting to paleontologists, especially me! Many types of scientific analyses—from computer models to microscopic studies to biochemical tests—have been done on tyrannosaurid fossils.

Additionally, due to the work of many paleontologists and others collecting fossils in the United States, Canada, Mongolia, and China, there are now more skeletons of dinosaurs from Tyrannosauridae in museums than almost any other group of theropod. Because of this, we know more about tyrants than we do about ceratosaurs or spinosauroids or most carnosaurs (with the exception of *Allosaurus*).

ORIGINS OF THE TYRANTS

Fossils of giant tyrant dinosaurs from western North America have been known since the 1850s, and relatively complete skeletons have been known since the 1910s. But for most of that time, paleontologists didn't have a clear picture where the species of Tyrannosauridae fit in the evolutionary family tree of carnivorous dinosaurs. Some scientists—like Henry Fairfield Osborn of the American Museum of Natural History, who named *Tyrannosaurus rex* in 1905—thought that tyrannosaurids were the last surviving members of Carnosauria. That is, they thought tyrannosaurids were descendants of *Allosaurus* or a close relative that grew larger and larger while its arms grew smaller and smaller.

The Late Jurassic tyrannosauroid *Guanlong* of China.

But other scientists—including German paleontologist Friedrich von Huene and the American Museum of Natural History's Barnum Brown (who discovered the specimens from Wyoming and Montana that Osborn described)—recognized that tyrannosaurids were not "super carnosaurs." Certain details of the skulls, hips, hind limbs, and so forth showed that they were instead members of Coelurosauria. Most types of coelurosaurs—like compsognathids, ornithomimosaurs, and deinonychosaurs—were small. In fact, many were smaller than human beings. But von Huene, Brown, and their colleagues saw that tyrannosaurids were coelurosaurs grown to gigantic size.

For most of the twentieth century, paleontologists thought that Osborn was correct, and a lot of dinosaur books show *T. rex* and its kin as the last of the carnosaurs. But starting in the late 1980s, several paleontologists—such as Argentine Fernando Novas, Canadian Philip Currie, and me—

The Early Cretaceous tyrannosauroid *Dilong* of China.

showed that it was von Huene and Brown who were correct. When we looked at the details of the anatomy of theropod dinosaurs and used the method of cladistics to reconstruct their family tree, the giant tyrannosaurids turned out to be members of Coelurosauria.

Our understanding of tyrannosaurids changed yet again in 1996 with the discovery of the primitive coelurosaur *Sinosauropteryx*. This little Chinese compsognathid dinosaur was covered with primitive fuzzy structures called protofeathers. These bits of fluff are the earliest stage in the evo-

lution of the true feathers that are found in the more advanced maniraptoran coelurosaurs, including the living group of maniraptorans called birds. Because both compsognathids (like *Sinosauropteryx*) and maniraptorans (like *Microraptor* and birds) have some sort of feather structure, scientists recognized that their common ancestor would have had protofeathers, too.

Previous cladistic studies had shown that tyrannosaurids were more closely related to birds than were compsognathids like *Sinosauropteryx*.

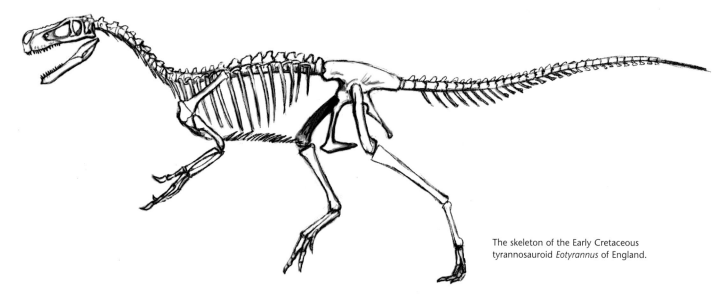

The skeleton of the Early Cretaceous tyrannosauroid *Eotyrannus* of England.

So if the common ancestor of birds and compsognathids had protofeathers, then the tyrant dinosaurs were descendants of that same fuzzy common ancestor! In the mid-1990s, I and my colleagues made a prediction. When someone eventually discovered an early member of the branch of the family tree that led to Tyrannosauridae, it would be—like all primitive coelurosaurs—a small dinosaur with long arms and slender, three-fingered hands. And like all other primitive coelurosaurs, it would be covered with protofeathers. If only someone could find such a dinosaur.

FLUFFY TYRANTS: PREDICTED FIRST, DISCOVERED LATER

And as it turned out, someone *did* find such a dinosaur! Our prediction turned out to be true when *Dilong* was discovered and described in 2004. *Dilong* was indeed a little dinosaur, about 5 feet (1.5 meters) long. It is from the Early Cretaceous Yixian Formation of China, the famous formation that often preserves the impressions of feathers, hair, scales, or other soft structures of the fossils that are found in it. And *Dilong*'s fossils showed protofeathers.

But was *Dilong* really on the line leading to Tyrannosauridae? That is, was it a member of Tyrannosauroidea? In general, *Dilong* looked like many other primitive coelurosaurs. Its arms were fairly long, and it had three-fingered hands. It had a thin tail. It did not have the specialized feet or the bone-crunching teeth that characterize tyrannosaurids. But it *did* have several features found in those giant predators that aren't seen in other coelurosaurs.

For example, the bones along the top of its

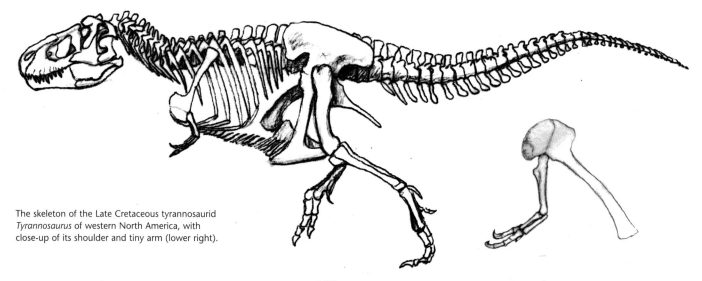

The skeleton of the Late Cretaceous tyrannosaurid *Tyrannosaurus* of western North America, with close-up of its shoulder and tiny arm (lower right).

snout were fused together, as with the dinosaurs in Tyrannosauridae. Also, the teeth in the premaxillae—the pair of bones at the front of the lower jaw—were not shaped as they are in most theropods. Instead, they were shaped like little scrapers. These teeth would have been useful for nipping and scraping meat off bones. Also, the head of *Dilong* was pretty big for the size of the dinosaur, which is characteristic of the species in Tyrannosauridae as well. These features led paleontologists to conclude that *Dilong* is indeed an early, primitive member of the line leading to Tyrannosauridae. In other words, it is an early tyrannosauroid.

By studying the skeleton of *Dilong,* we can tell something about the behavior of primitive tyrannosauroids. *Dilong* was a small hunter that could both grab prey with its hands and snatch it up with its jaws. Its prey would have included the many lizards, mammals, and other small vertebrates that lived in northeastern China at that time. It may even have eaten other little coelurosaurs. Most of all, however, *Dilong* probably hunted *Psittacosaurus,* an early ceratopsian dinosaur that was one of the most common animals in Early Cretaceous Asia. It is interesting to note that this predator-prey relationship continued throughout the next 65.5 million years of tyrannosauroid history, culminating with the giant relatives of these two dinosaurs—*Tyrannosaurus* and *Triceratops,* respectively.

Dilong was one of the first early tyrannosauroids known from a nearly complete skeleton. But it isn't the only early tyrant dinosaur known. It isn't even the oldest. There are a few bones of Late Jurassic tyrannosauroids known. These include *Stokesosaurus* of western North America and *Aviatyrannis* of Portugal. But no one has yet found a complete skeleton of either of these.

Today's special: fresh *Anatotitan*! A mother *Tyrannosaurus* feeds her young some tasty duckbill while other adults round up one more.

But in 2006, the nearly complete skeleton of a Jurassic tyrannosauroid was finally described. *Guanlong* from western China is known from two very good fossils from the beginning of the Late Jurassic. It showed some traits that were expected in early tyrannosaurids—for example, scraping front teeth, fused nasals, and long arms ending in three-fingered hands. But unexpectedly, its skull was crowned by a tall crest. This crest is very thin, and presumably was simply for show.

Tyrant dinosaurs have been hunting horned dinosaurs from their beginnings: *Guanlong* prepares to attack *Yinlong* in Jurassic China.

The next stage in tyrant dinosaur evolution is represented by *Eotyrannus*. This more advanced tyrannosauroid stalked the forests of Europe at about the same time *Dilong* lived in Asia. The only *Eotyrannus* specimen known so far is 15 feet (4.6 meters) long. And that specimen may not have been fully grown. This dinosaur is from the Isle of Wight, off the southern coast of England. Like *Dilong,* but unlike the later tyrannosauroids, *Eotyrannus* had long arms and hands. More like the members of Tyrannosauridae than *Dilong,* it had legs and feet that were fairly long for its body size. Clearly, it could catch smaller dinosaurs with them. It had the fused nasal bones and scraper front teeth found in all tyrannosauroids. Like the members of Tyrannosauridae, but unlike *Dilong,* it had legs and feet that were exceptionally long for its body size. It was probably a fast runner, perhaps the fastest meat-eater in its environment. This would have been useful for going after fast-running prey, like the small ornithopod *Hypsilophodon.* It also would have been useful to keep *Eotyrannus* from *becoming* the prey of much larger hunters, namely the spinosaurid *Baryonyx* and the carnosaur *Neovenator.* Because at this time, tyrannosauroids were still only minor predators.

* * *

THE TRUE TYRANT KINGS

In the Late Cretaceous, the tyrant dinosaurs grew larger still. *Dryptosaurus* was a primitive tyrannosauroid from the Late Cretaceous of New Jersey. Although known from only a few bones, it was clearly bigger than the Early Cretaceous tyrants. It was probably 20 feet (6.1 meters) long or more. And unlike the earlier tyrannosauroids, it had very short arms. In fact, its complete arm and hand may have been shorter than its thighbone. That is very different from typical coelurosaurs—including the primitive tyrannosauroids—but it *is* similar to its closest relatives, the most advanced of the tyrants, the true species of Tyrannosauridae. Like its more specialized cousins, *Dryptosaurus* seems to have been the largest hunter in its environment.

We know a lot more about the true members of Tyrannosauridae than about the other tyrant dinosaurs. Most of the tyrannosaurids are known from multiple specimens, including juveniles and adults. In terms of their overall anatomy, tyrannosaurids are all similar to each other. They have very large skulls for their body size. Tyrant dinosaurs also have very blunt snouts. The eyes of most tyrannosaurids (especially *Tyrannosaurus*) were aimed more forward than were the eyes of typical theropods. This meant that tyrant dinosaurs had better overlapping vision and could focus better on things in front of them (a very useful trait for a hunter). The back of the skull of the most advanced tyrannosaurids was very wide, giving tyrants extremely large and powerful neck muscles. Tyrannosaurids were also the only big theropods that had a solid roof to their mouths. This strengthened the tyrannosaurids' jaws against the forces of twisting and turning while they were feeding. Many tyrannosaurids had small projections on the bones above the eye socket, and some had bumps or little horns on their noses. Each particular species seems to have had head bumps of a different shape and size.

Like all tyrannosauroids, the advanced tyrant dinosaurs had scraper teeth in the front of their upper jaws. But the other teeth—those in the sides of the jaws—were unique. They were not the blade-shaped teeth found in most other theropods. The advanced tyrannosaurids had teeth that were thick side to side. In large individuals, they could be thicker side to side than front to back in cross section. These thick teeth had very deep roots: two-thirds of the tooth was root, rather than one-half as in most meat-eaters. Tyrannosaurid teeth were also long—some reaching the size of a big banana! The size and shape of tyrannosaurid teeth made them very strong. They could pierce strong hides, crush bones, and (importantly for dinosaurs with tiny little arms) hold on to struggling prey.

Tyrannosaurids are famous for their arms. They were almost ridiculously small. These arms were so short that the hands barely reached past the chest muscles, and they couldn't touch each other. A tyrannosaur couldn't even use its arms and claws to pick its own teeth. The hands couldn't reach the mouth! And they had only two fingers per hand.

In contrast to their dinky arms, tyrannosaurids' legs—especially the shinbones and long bones of the feet—were longer than those of other giant theropods. This suggests that they were fast movers. In fact, the proportions of the legs of small tyrant dinosaurs are the same as those of fast-running ornithomimosaurs, or ostrich dinosaurs, of the same size. And as with ostrich dinosaurs, the long foot bones of tyrannosaurs were locked together so that they could better absorb the twists and turns of running fast. Overall, the shape of the legs of tyrant dinosaurs suggests they were *very* good runners, particularly at the smaller size. Recent computer studies suggest that the largest tyrannosaurs (like an adult *Tyrannosaurus*) would have been unable to run very fast, but the same studies show that smaller tyrannosaurs (including a young *Tyrannosaurus*) would have been among the fastest theropods. But even a full-grown *Tyrannosaurus* was better built for running than the duckbilled hadrosaurs, horned ceratopsids, and enormous titanosaurs that were their likely food.

Because they had protofeathered ancestors, tyrannosaurids may have had protofeathers themselves. Some paleontologists (such as me) have suggested that baby tyrants may have been covered in fuzz like earlier coelurosaurs. However, we know from patches of fossilized skin impressions that at least some of an adult tyrannosaurid's body was covered with small, round scales. Would it make sense for an animal to grow from fuzzy to scaly? This type of change makes sense if protofeathers evolved for insulation. A small animal needs more insulation to keep it warm than a

Tyrannosaurids are characterized by extremely short, two-fingered arms.

big animal. (For instance, compare the giant and relatively hairless rhinos and elephants of Africa to smaller and furrier antelope.) And note also that baby elephants are more hairy than their parents.

There are two primitive tyrannosaurids (in fact, some paleontologists would say they aren't quite true members of Tyrannosauridae) named *Alectrosaurus* and *Appalachiosaurus*. The former is from Mongolia and China, and the latter is from Alabama. They are small for tyrannosaurids. *Alectrosaurus* was 16.5 feet (5 meters) long, and *Appalachiosaurus* 21 feet (6.4 meters) long. But they seem to have all those traits mentioned above, so I'll consider them tyrannosaurids for now.

Later, more advanced tyrannosaurids got much larger. They split into two main branches. The dinosaurs of Albertosaurinae—such as *Albertosaurus* and *Gorgosaurus*—were somewhat more slender and had longer necks. These grew to about 28 feet (8.5 meters) long. The big bruisers of the tyrants belong in Tyrannosaurinae. These dinosaurs had shorter necks and wider, stronger skulls. *Daspletosaurus* was a little longer than the albertosaurines, at 30 feet (9.1 meters). Larger still was Asian *Tarbosaurus*, at over 33 feet (10.1 meters). Dwarfing all of these was the last and most advanced, *Tyrannosaurus*. The biggest specimen of this dinosaur found so far was 41 feet (12.5 meters) long and probably weighed about 6 tons.

HADROSAUR HUNTERS AND CERATOPSIAN SLAYERS (AND CARRION CRUNCHERS, TOO)

It's clear that tyrant dinosaurs—like most theropods—were meat-eaters. Nearly all scientists agree that they were predators, capable of killing other dinosaurs for food. However, a few paleontologists have suggested that tyrannosaurids, or *Tyrannosaurus* in particular, would have been incapable of killing their own food. They think that *T. rex* was strictly a scavenger. There is little direct evidence to support this notion, however, and considerable evidence to demonstrate that tyrant dinosaurs could (at least on occasion) hunt and kill other animals. For example, a duckbilled *Edmontosaurus* skeleton from Montana bears a wound at

the base of its tail that matches the shape of the mouth of an adult *Tyrannosaurus*. What is interesting is that this wound had healed over, indicating that the hadrosaur was alive during and after the time the tyrant dinosaur bit into it! It was lucky for the *Edmontosaurus* that the *Tyrannosaurus* didn't get a better bite. And lucky for paleontologists to have discovered this fossil to find out about how that *Tyrannosaurus*, and probably other tyrants, hunted living animals, at least some of the time.

A recently discovered specimen of the horned dinosaur *Triceratops* similarly shows that it was bitten by a *Tyrannosaurus* and lived. But this particular horned dinosaur actually lost part of its horn in the process. This shows a major difference between tyrannosaurids and other giant meat-eating dinosaurs—the tyrants were bone crunchers! This is almost certainly the reason that the tyrannosaurids evolved their thicker, more deeply rooted teeth. The fused nasal bones would have also helped keep the skull strong. Mechanical studies and studies of bite marks on bones of hadrosaurids, ceratopsids, and even armored ankylosaur skulls show that tyrannosaurids had extremely powerful bites. In fact, a coprolite (fossilized feces) from the latest Cretaceous of Saskatchewan, Canada—almost certainly produced by *Tyrannosaurus*—is made up mostly of the partially digested bones of a young cow-size ornithischian dinosaur. The shape of the broken bones shows that the tyrannosaur smashed the prey into a pulp before swallowing it.

With their long legs and strong jaws, tyrannosaurids would have been able to run down and kill any other dinosaur in their environment. However, like modern carnivorous animals, tyrannosaurids would have eaten carrion as well as hunted. There aren't many animals who will pass up a free meal! In the places where the tyrannosaurids lived, they were the largest carnivorous dinosaurs by far, so they could easily chase away any other meat-eater from their kills. (Sometimes—if you're a wild animal—it pays to be a bully.)

While early tyrannosauroids probably caught prey with their arms, the dinky forelimbs of tyrannosaurids would have been useless in hunting. It would have been far easier for them to use their mighty jaws and massive teeth to capture and kill prey. Denver paleontologist Ken Carpenter, however, has shown that the small arms may have been strong enough to hold on to the sides of a struggling animal while the tyrannosaurid's jaws ripped it apart.

HABITS OF THE TYRANT KINGS

The arms may have had another function, though. In modern flightless birds, the wings are still useful in signaling to other members of the species. It might be that tyrannosaurids also used these little arms to signal. (In fact, I wonder if even the largest tyrannosaurids may have retained some protofeathers on their arms to make them more "showy.")

How social were tyrant dinosaurs? Did they hunt alone or in packs? Fossil discoveries show that groups of different individuals of various ages (little young ones, half-grown "teenagers," and full-grown adults) of *Albertosaurus* and of *Tyrannosaurus* at least sometimes lived together, because they were buried together. It may be that these tyrant dinosaurs, and maybe some of their relatives, hunted in family packs like modern wolves and lions. Some scientists suggest that the faster young tyrants could chase their prey toward the waiting jaws of their powerful parents, but without a time machine such ideas are just speculation.

Even if they did live together, it's clear that tyrannosaurids didn't always get along. Many skulls show bite marks on their snouts where one tyrant snapped at another. These bites weren't fatal, but they were deep enough to scar the bone. In fact, some of these bites got infected. We can't tell for sure what provoked those attacks, but it's easy to imagine a couple of tyrants squabbling over a fresh kill until one drives the other away with a well-placed snap. (Such fights and wounds are found in many modern carnivores, from lions to vultures to Komodo dragons.)

Like all dinosaurs, tyrant dinosaurs probably guarded their eggs and watched over their

The Late Cretaceous tyrannosaurid *Gorgosaurus* of western North America.

125

offspring. Tyrannosauroids were obviously too big to brood, or sit on, their eggs, but they might have used rotting plants to protect the eggs and keep them warm, as do modern alligators and some birds.

Although no one has yet found a hatchling tyrannosaurid, there are small individuals known. In fact, some paleontologists have considered (and still consider) these small individuals to be adults of their own small species. Others think that these are just the partially grown young of larger species. Personally, I think that the weight of the evidence shows that the dinosaurs once called *"Nanotyrannus,"* for instance, are really just *T. rex* kids. A new series of studies by several different teams of paleontologists has shown us how long it took for a tyrannosaurid to grow up and how they changed as they got older. As with all dinosaurs, their babies would have been very small. And like most animals, they hit an age when they started growing really fast and their bodies began to change shape. In most dinosaurs, this period of rapid growth began before the dinosaurs were ten years old (sometimes much sooner). In tyrannosaurids, like in human beings, this rapid growth didn't start until they were about twelve years old and finished when they were eighteen or nineteen. During that time, the tyrannosaurid's skull would get deeper and more powerful, its teeth would grow proportionately longer, and the various head bumps would show up.

Why did tyrannosaurids have a longer childhood than most other dinosaurs? I propose this has to do with a strange aspect of the environments in which the tyrannosaurids lived. In earlier times (the Late Triassic through the Early Cretaceous), it was normal for several different types of large theropods—even of the same body size—to live in the same region at the same time. And there were lots of intermediate-size carnivores. For example, in the Late Jurassic of western North America, giant *Allosaurus, Saurophaganax, Torvosaurus,* and *Edmarka* made up the top of the food chain, followed by medium-size *Ceratosaurus,* slender *Elaphrosaurus,* and a whole host of smaller species. In the Late Cretaceous of western

North America and eastern Asia, however, tyrant dinosaurs are the only large-bodied meat-eating theropods known. The next largest theropods (therizinosauroids, ornithomimosaurs, and oviraptorosaurs) were all omnivores or herbivores. In fact, wherever the true tyrannosaurids are found, the next largest carnivorous dinosaurs are dromaeosaurid raptors or troodontids, and these were only one-fiftieth the size of the tyrants at most.

Where were the middle-size predators? My studies suggest that young tyrant dinosaurs, at less than a half ton, filled in this ecological gap. Based on their extremely long leg proportions, young tyrant dinosaurs would have been among the fastest dinosaurs of all the Mesozoic. They could probably catch and kill even the ornithomimosaurs and troodontids—two other fast-legged theropods from their environment. While most dinosaurs seem to have had a very short childhood, tyrannosaurids benefited from spending many years as medium-size predators. But eventually they got older and grew up, becoming the top predators of their world. As full-grown adults, tyrannosaurids were capable of killing duckbills, horned dinosaurs, ankylosaurids, and saltasaurid sauropods.

But there was one danger that even *Tyrannosaurus rex* couldn't defeat. The last individuals of that species were present at the very end of the Cretaceous Period. We know that *T. rex* lived in the southern parts of western North America. So it is possible that some individuals of this species may have even been looking south one day 65.5 million years ago and seen the flash of the impact of an asteroid crashing into the sea, bringing the reign of the tyrant kings to an end. And while it is probably a good thing that the tyrannosaurids were long dead before the first humans appeared, I still feel sad that I'll never get to see a living *Tyrannosaurus rex.*

Opposite: Even though they were fearsome predators, young *Tyrannosaurus* were themselves threatened by other carnivores such as giant crocodilians. Hungry pterosaurs look on hopefully.

Tyrannosaurus Tantrums— Growing Up with the Tyrant Lizard

Dr. Thomas D. Carr
University of Toronto

Photo by Dino Pulerà

Tyrannosaurus rex first enchanted me when I was two years old. Learning about this mysterious dinosaur is now at the heart of my work as a dinosaur scientist.

I have been studying changes in the skulls of tyrannosaurs as they grew up. At one point, my work took me to the Cleveland Museum of Natural History to examine a spectacular skull of a small tyrannosaur specimen. Measuring only about 23 inches (58 centimeters) long, this skull was thought to be from a pygmy dinosaur—an adult that stopped growing at a small size.

The Cleveland skull was so different from that of an adult tyrannosaur that scientists had assumed it might have been from a unique kind of tyrannosaur. It was small, delicate, and sleek, whereas big adult tyrannosaurs looked a bit like warthogs—they had a knobby skull and a gaping mouth with protruding teeth. I discovered that the skull was similar in many ways to that of a juvenile Albertosaurus, a tyrannosaur from Canada. It also resembled the skull of an adult T. rex in many ways. Putting these observations together, I concluded that the Cleveland skull was probably that of a juvenile T. rex.

The Cleveland skull reveals that T. rex went through enormous changes as it grew up. It lost several teeth, its jaws deepened, its teeth became long and wide, and the bones of its face became puffed up by air sacs inside the snout. Also, T. rex became adorned with age by growing a horn above and behind its eyes. The Cleveland skull, while not being from a new kind of tyrannosaur, has proven to be invaluable by showing us an important stage in the growth of the world's most famous dinosaur.

I am now working on a study of the evolution of T. rex and its relatives. Along the way, I've had the thrill of naming new species of North American tyrannosaurs and pachycephalosaurs (domeheaded dinosaurs). Discovering new dinosaurs is exciting, but it is not the end goal for a paleontologist. If you want to be a paleontologist one day, you should be open to new paths of discovery. Ask yourself, What are the big unanswered questions about dinosaurs that I want to figure out? Most important of all, if science is your dream, you must stay in school and learn, learn, learn.

A young *Tyrannosaurus*.

Bad to the Bone—
Tyrannosaurus rex
Bites Again

Dr. Gregory M. Erickson
Florida State University

Photo by Ken Womble

Tyrannosaurus rex *sported the most lethal dentition of any dinosaur. These animals had sixty serrated daggers in their mouths. The longest of these teeth were exposed a full six inches. Every pale-ontologist agrees that these teeth show that the king of tyrants fed upon other dinosaurs. Nevertheless, just how the teeth were used has been a matter of debate. Could tyran-nosaur teeth endure the enormous force required to plunge them through bone, or were they solely suited for stripping flesh?*

One way to answer this question is to examine possible victims of T. rex. *Bones recently found in Montana suggest that* T. rex *may have left its mark on two plant-eating dinosaurs, the giant three-horned dinosaur* Triceratops *and the duckbilled dinosaur* Edmontosaurus. *The telltale signs of* T. rex *feeding include large bone punctures several inches in depth and long bone scrapes. One of the dinosaurs had been bitten nearly eighty times. We compared several aspects of these bite marks to the size and spacing of* T. rex *teeth. The size of the bites, the spacing of the serration marks made as the teeth grazed bones, and a dental putty casting (from the same material your dentist uses to cast your teeth) of the puncture marks all perfectly matched* T. rex *teeth. Based on this evidence, my colleagues and I were able to conclude that* T. rex *was responsible for the bite marks. This also told us that* T. rex *fed on horned dinosaurs and hadrosaurs—two of the most common herbivorous dinosaurs of the time. We could also see that the bite of* T. rex *was powerful enough to bite through bone, and that* T. rex *had the capacity to attack prey with great force. It certainly didn't worry about hurting its teeth!*

What was the actual bite force of Tyran-nosaurus rex? How strong were the teeth? To answer these questions, we needed more than just the bones of animals that T. rex *ate. I teamed up with a group of engineers from Stanford University's biomechanical engineering department to deter-mine the bite force of* T. rex *during feeding.*

By examining the microstructure of the bitten bones and comparing them to bones of living ani-mals, we determined that pelvic bones of cows were a perfect match for Triceratops *bones. We then molded and cast exact-scale copies of adult* T. rex *teeth using a combination of the metals bronze and aluminum. Using a mechanical testing frame (a machine that can accurately measure how much force is required to penetrate an object) we then drove the metal teeth into fresh cow bones whose dimensions were similar to those of the bitten* Tricer-atops *bones. We stopped each test at the exact depth of the deepest bite mark we were trying to simulate.*

To our amazement, the bite marks produced by the experiment were exactly like the bite marks in the dinosaur bones. T. rex *was "feeding" again for the first time in 64 million years! From our exper-iments, we determined that the minimum bite force generated by* T. rex *was on the order of 3,300 pounds. This is equivalent to the weight of a small pickup truck pressing down on each tooth. For com-parison, this is about three times greater than the biting forces of large carnivores today, like the king of the beasts, the lion, and the bone-crushing cham-pion, the spotted hyena. Clearly* T. rex *teeth were not weak in comparison to those of today's animals and were more than capable of doing considerable damage to any creature in the tyrant's realm.*

Deinocheirus

Gallimimus

Shuvuuia

18

ORNITHOMIMOSAURS AND ALVAREZSAURS
(Ostrich and Thumb-Clawed Dinosaurs)

Paleontologists sometimes compare dinosaurs to modern animals to give people a sense of what a dinosaur's behavior and anatomy were like. So I might compare spinosaurids to crocodiles or deinonychosaurs to cats. If I were to compare the species of Ornithomimosauria and Alvarezsauridae to modern animals, the best comparison would be to ostriches and chickens, respectively.

Most people don't find the dinosaurs in this chapter very impressive. When I talk to kids and ask them what their favorite dinosaur is, I never get *Pelecanimimus* or *Struthiomimus* or *Shuvuuia* as an answer. But just because a dinosaur isn't as spectacular as *Tyrannosaurus, Velociraptor,* or *Triceratops* doesn't mean it isn't interesting. There are a lot of very weird features in the anatomy of ornithomimosaurs and alvarezsaurids. And understanding them gives us a more complete picture of the Mesozoic world.

Both ornithomimosaurs and alvarezsaurids are part of Theropoda—the group of bipedal, mostly meat-eating dinosaurs. More specifically, they are members of Coelurosauria—the advanced group of theropods containing birds and their kin. Other coelurosaurs include the tiny compsognathids, the giant tyrannosaurids, the catlike deinonychosaurs, the slothlike therizinosauroids, and the just plain weird oviraptorosaurs. Those last three groups—along with birds—form a larger category called Maniraptora, the "hand grabbers." Most maniraptorans had very long arms that could fold up close to the body and long feathers on their arms and tails. Alvarezsauridae *might* be a group within Maniraptora. It might also be closer to Ornithomimosauria.

Whatever the case may be, alvarezsaurids and ornithomimosaurs are very different from most other theropods. When we talk about theropods, most people imagine either gigantic killers like *Tyrannosaurus* and *Allosaurus* or swift little hunters like *Velociraptor* and *Deinonychus*—in other words, dinosaurs with big skulls, sharp teeth, and slashing claws. But while alvarezsaurids and some ornithomimosaurs did have teeth, those teeth were very tiny. Their skulls were small and beaky. And although their hands ended in claws, they definitely weren't used for slashing. Like the oviraptorosaurs and therizinosauroids (which we'll meet in chapter 19), ornithomimosaurs and alvarezsaurids were definitely not hunters. They probably didn't even eat meat!

BIRD MIMICS
The first fossils of Ornithomimosauria were

The Late Cretaceous ornithomimid *Gallimimus* of Mongolia.

recognized in 1890. O. C. Marsh, a paleontologist from Yale University, described some hand and foot bones of a Late Cretaceous dinosaur that had been discovered in Colorado. Marsh noted the way the long bones of the foot—the metatarsals—were bundled tightly together. These reminded him of the way that the metatarsals of modern birds were fused together. Because the dinosaur feet were similar to, but not exactly the same as, bird feet, he named this new discovery *Ornithomimus velox,* the "swift bird mimic."

Although other paleontologists found bits and pieces of *Ornithomimus* bones—and those of related dinosaurs—over the next few years, a complete skeleton was not found during Marsh's lifetime. This caused a lot of confusion when Marsh described some other incomplete coelurosaur fos-

sils. For example, in 1892 he thought the hip and leg bones of *Tyrannosaurus* were from a giant new species of *Ornithomimus*! (That isn't as crazy as it sounds. Except for their difference in size, the hind limbs of *Ornithomimus* and *Tyrannosaurus* are extremely similar. As we'll see in a bit, this has some important implications about how these two groups of dinosaurs lived.) So he never knew how right he was when he called *Ornithomimus* a "bird mimic."

Discoveries made between 1900 and 1916 showed that *Ornithomimus* had a body shape *a lot* like a modern bird, specifically the modern ostrich! The most complete of these fossils was a skeleton of a slightly older Canadian relative of *Ornithomimus* that was given the name *Struthiomimus,* or "ostrich mimic." That's an even more accurate name than "bird mimic," because ornithomimosaurs may not have looked much like a robin or blue jay or hummingbird, but they *were* built like an ostrich! In fact, many paleontologists (including me) use the nickname "ostrich dinosaurs" for this group.

Ornithomimosaurs were like ostriches in many ways. Most species were actually about the same size as an ostrich. They had small heads with slender snouts at the end of long necks. Their eyes were quite large. Their bodies were short, and their legs were extremely long. And the advanced ornithomimosaurs were toothless.

Ostrich dinosaurs differed from true ostriches in other ways, however. Primitive ornithomimosaurs had small teeth in their beaks. And instead of wings, all ornithomimosaurs had long arms ending in three-fingered hands. They also had long, slender bony tails.

In older dinosaur books, the author would now explain that another difference between ostrich dinosaurs and ostriches was that one had scales, while the other (the birds, of course) had feathers. But we can't say that anymore. This is because feathers have been found in maniraptoran dinosaur fossils, and protofeathers have been found in more primitive coelurosaur fossils (like compsognathids and tyrannosauroids). Cladistic studies show that the common ancestor of all coelurosaurs, including the ancestor of ornitho-

mimosaurs, would have had a covering of simple protofeathers. Therefore, ostrich dinosaurs were the descendants of fuzzy dinosaurs, and were probably fuzzy themselves.

Unfortunately, we can't be certain if ornithomimosaurs had any true feathers or just protofeathers. As of 2007, no one has found a good impression of an ornithomimosaur's body covering. We *do* have an impression of the throat pouch of an early ostrich dinosaur called *Pelecanimimus,* and it has neither scales nor protofeathers *nor* feathers. But that doesn't tell us what the rest of its body was covered with. After all, the throat pouch of modern pelicans, for instance, doesn't have feathers or scales on it, even though the rest of a pelican's body has one or the other.

MOSTLY HARMLESS

Ornithomimosaurs had long and fairly weak jaws. The jaws of primitive ornithomimosaurs such as *Pelecanimimus* and *Shenzhousaurus* had peglike teeth. Indeed, *Pelecanimimus* had the most teeth (220) of any known theropod. But these teeth were incredibly small. In more advanced ornithomimosaurs, such as *Garudimimus* and the highly specialized members of Ornithomimidae like *Ornithomimus* and *Struthiomimus,* there were no teeth at all. Instead, their beaks were covered by keratin (the same material that covers the beaks of modern birds and turtles).

The skeleton of the Late Cretaceous ornithomimid *Gallimimus* of Mongolia, with close-ups of its characteristic hand with three long palm bones (left) and foot with arctometatarsus (right).

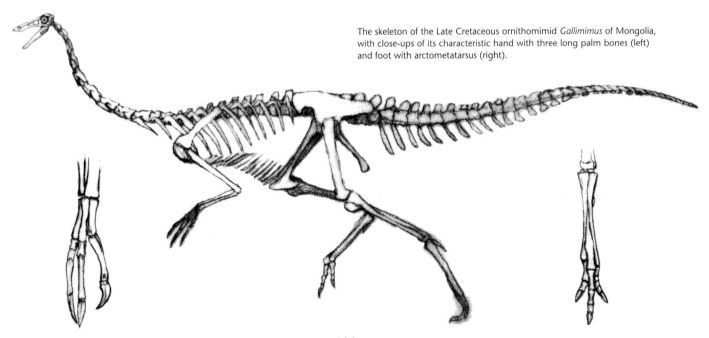

The long, slender legs of ornithomimids helped them flee from meat-eaters like tyrannosaurids.

What did ornithomimosaurs eat? Tiny peg teeth and flat, toothless beaks would have been pretty useless for ripping apart a meaty carcass or slashing open a living dinosaur. But they were probably good enough to bite plants and snatch up small animals like lizards, frogs, and mammals.

Ornithomimosaur hands also differed from those of classic predatory dinosaurs. Instead of the grasping hands and slashing claws of most theropods, the hands of ornithomimosaurs formed a hook, or clamp, and their claws were rather straight. The closest modern comparison would be the hands and claws of South American tree sloths. But unlike tree sloths, ornithomimosaurs were too big to hang from the trees. They must have used their clamping hands to grab and pull down branches to get at tasty leaves and fruit.

Paleontologists look at the beaks and hands of ornithomimosaurs to try to figure out what they ate. Some suggest that ostrich dinosaurs dabbled like ducks for small aquatic invertebrates. Others propose that they were strict herbivores. *Pelecanimimus* is thought by some to have gulped up small fish and swallowed them whole. Ostriches (and their modern relatives, like rheas and emus) are probably our best models for understanding the diet of ornithomimosaurs. Those big, flightless modern birds are omnivores. They eat fruit, seeds, insects, small vertebrates (like lizards and frogs), eggs, and plants—which make up the vast majority of their diet. The same seems to have been true for ostrich dinosaurs.

Ornithomimosaurs—and, in particular, mem-bers of the advanced group Ornithomimidae—had long legs. The ornithomimids especially had longer metatarsals than any of their same-size contemporaries, with one major exception—young tyrannosaurids. Indeed (as was sometimes confusing to Marsh back in the 1890s), the legs of advanced ostrich dinosaurs and tyrannosaurids are nearly identical in detail. In Ornithomimidae and Tyrannosauridae, the metatarsals are very long, and the middle metatarsal has a special shock-absorbing shape. As research by myself and others—notably Eric Snively at the University of Calgary—has shown, this adaptation allowed ornithomimids and tyrannosaurids to run swiftly

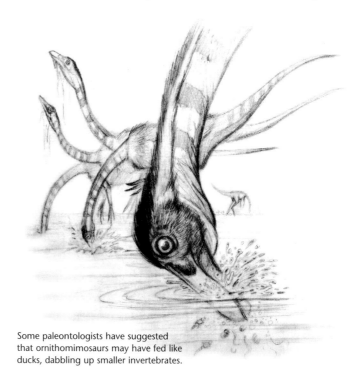

Some paleontologists have suggested that ornithomimosaurs may have fed like ducks, dabbling up smaller invertebrates.

on very slender feet. I researched this particular adaptation for my doctoral dissertation, and in 1992 I formally named this shock-absorbing structure the arctometatarsus (meaning "pinched long bones of the foot").

This adaptation of the foot evolved independently in advanced ostrich dinosaurs and advanced tyrant dinosaurs, because both the primitive ornithomimosaurs and the primitive tyrant dinosaurs do not have an arctometatarsus. In both groups, the arctometatarsus evolved at about the same time (around 80 to 85 million years ago) in the same region (Asia). This suggests these adaptations (the long legs and the arctometatarsus) are related. It may indicate an evolutionary arms—or, rather, foot—race! That is, the specialized running feet of the mostly harmless ornithomimids may have evolved so that they could run away from the tyrannosaurids, and the specialized running feet of the definitely harmful tyrant dinosaurs evolved so that they could catch ostrich dinosaurs.

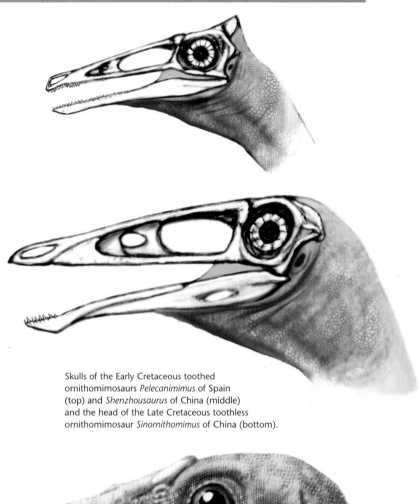

Skulls of the Early Cretaceous toothed ornithomimosaurs *Pelecanimimus* of Spain (top) and *Shenzhousaurus* of China (middle) and the head of the Late Cretaceous toothless ornithomimosaur *Sinornithomimus* of China (bottom).

DIVERSITY OF ORNITHOMIMOSAURIA

At present, ornithomimosaurs are known only from the Cretaceous Period. Paleontologists once thought that the leggy *Elaphrosaurus* of the Late Jurassic of eastern Africa was a primitive ornithomimosaur, but detailed study of its skeleton shows that it is instead a ceratosaur. Primitive ornithomimosaurs are definitely known from Europe (*Pelecanimimus*) and Asia (*Shenzhousaurus* and *Harpymimus*) in the Early Cretaceous. Less certain are fragmentary fossils of medium-size theropods from North America and Australia that some paleontologists think may be Early Cretaceous ostrich dinosaurs. The only known Late Cretaceous ostrich dinosaurs are from Asia and North America. These later ornithomimosaurs are toothless.

Pelecanimimus and *Shenzhousaurus* are fairly small dinosaurs, 6 to 8 feet (1.8 to 2.4 meters) long. Later ornithomimosaurs were larger, typically more than 13 feet (4 meters) long. At 20 feet (6.1 meters), *Gallimimus* of the Late Cretaceous of Mongolia was the largest member of Ornithomimidae, but a primitive ornithomimosaur in its environment dwarfed it. Known only from its enormous 8-foot (2.4-meter) arms and a few other bones, *Deinocheirus* was a giant. Its claws were blunt at the end, however, and couldn't do much damage. Like other ornithomimosaurs, it probably

Alvarezsaurids like *Shuvuuia* may have eaten ants and termites.

ate mostly plants. Hopefully someday someone will find the rest of *Deinocheirus* so we can see what an ostrich dinosaur as big as (or bigger than?) *Tyrannosaurus* looked like!

THE MYSTERIOUS ONE-CLAWED DINOSAUR: IS IT A BIRD?

Deinocheirus had the longest arms of any theropod; *Mononykus* had the shortest. Like *Deinocheirus*, *Mononykus* was also from the Late Cretaceous of Mongolia. Partial skeletons of this and closely related dinosaurs had been collected in the Djadokhta Formation since the 1920s and filed away in museums in New York and Ulaanbaatar. There they lay, labeled "birdlike dinosaur" or "coelurosaur," for decades. Perhaps because they were small—about the size of a big chicken or a small turkey—they didn't interest the paleontologists who had found them.

But in 1992, a new specimen of *Mononykus* was discovered by Malcolm McKenna of the American Museum of Natural History; it was

described and named in 1993 by a team led by Mongolian paleontologist Altangerel Perle and Mark Norell of the AMNH. These scientists were interested in the origins of birds and knew that fossils of coelurosaurs—the category of dinosaur that birds belong to—could contain important information for figuring out those details.

In some ways, this little dinosaur was extremely birdlike. It had a pubis (hip bone) that pointed backward, as in birds. The shape of the vertebrae in the neck, back, and hip was like that of birds, as were some of the leg bones. The braincase had a lot of features like those of modern birds, and the breastbone had a big birdlike ridge down the middle. (Next time you're eating a chicken or turkey, you can find this ridge. It's what the white meat is connected to.) But there were also some important differences. The tail was long and bony. The middle metatarsal bone was even more specialized than in tyrannosaurids and ornithomimids. Its arms were very short but strong. And weirdest of all, its hands seemed to have only one single finger: a thumb.

Perle, Norell, and colleagues initially named this dinosaur *Mononychus,* or "one claw." They had to change the spelling of the name to *Mononykus,* however, because there was already an insect named *Mononychus.* Soon after the spelling change, more skeletons of this dinosaur were found—some out in the field and some sitting in storage in the collections of museums. Additionally, new species of related dinosaurs were found, including *Parvicursor* and *Shuvuuia.* With the discovery of a nearly complete *Shuvuuia,* it was noted that these dinosaurs actually *did* have three fingers rather than just one. But the other two fingers were extremely small, making their hands just about the strangest body part of any dinosaur.

At first, paleontologists thought that *Mononykus, Shuvuuia,* and *Parvicursor* were totally unlike all previously found dinosaurs. But people began to look at previously discovered dinosaur specimens and realized that other members of this group had already been found and named. For example, in 1994, I noted that O. C. Marsh had found the foot of a North American *Mononykus*-like dinosaur in the 1890s and had named it *Ornithomimus minutus.* More importantly, a coelurosaur from Argentina, which paleontologist José Bonaparte had named *Alvarezsaurus* back in 1991, was recognized as a primitive relation to these strange dinosaurs. Since Bonaparte had already coined the word Alvarezsauridae, that name is now used for this unusual group. Additionally, Argentine paleontologist Fernando Novas named *Patagonykus,* a dinosaur intermediate in form between *Alvarezsaurus* and the advanced group Mononykinae (the North American and Asian weirdies).

What kind of dinosaur were the alvarezsaurids? They were definitely some kind of coelurosaur. But they had a strange combination of features that make them difficult to place. When Perle and colleagues first described *Mononykus* and *Shuvuuia,* for instance, they thought that the two were some new type of Cretaceous bird. It is true that mononykine alvarezsaurids have a lot of features more like those of modern birds than like those of most dinosaurs. But more primitive alvarezsaurids (like *Patagonykus* and *Alvarezsaurus*) do not have all these birdlike features. So the similar traits found in both Mononykinae and birds appear to have evolved independently.

Most recent studies show that alvarezsaurids are not actually a type of early bird, but in fact are a different type of maniraptoran. (To be fair, a few studies do indicate that they were actually closer

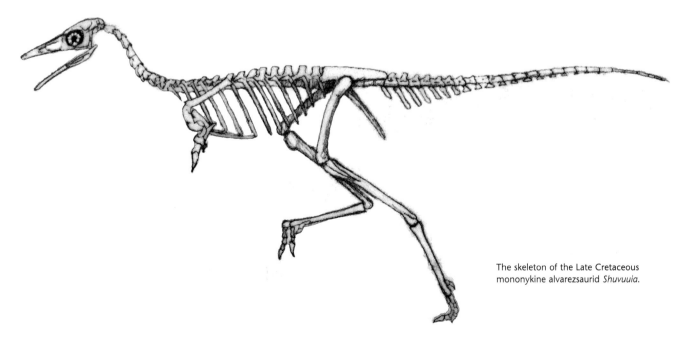

The skeleton of the Late Cretaceous mononykine alvarezsaurid *Shuvuuia.*

relatives of the species in Ornithomimosauria.) My own analyses place this group in Maniraptora, but I admit that their beaky skulls and peglike teeth are similar to those of ostrich dinosaurs.

ANTEATER DINOSAURS?

The evolutionary position of the big-thumbed dinosaurs isn't the only confusing thing about Alvarezsauridae. Another is figuring out how they lived and fed.

Some things are fairly clear. They had long legs—especially mononykines—and were almost surely very fast. In particular, the members of Mononykinae had a metatarsus similar to that of ornithomimids and tyrannosaurids, but even more specialized. Also, their small, beaky faces and tiny teeth strongly suggest that these weren't predators. Instead, they may have eaten plants or perhaps insects.

The arms and bizarre hands of the species in Alvarezsauridae are hard to figure out. If you just looked at the shape of the arms, and not their tiny size, you'd think they'd be great for digging. The arms were very powerfully built and had huge muscle attachments (for their size). So they could make strong repeated blows against something. And their stout thumb with its strong claw might be useful for cracking into termite nests.

But the arms are *so* tiny! The dinosaurs would have to press their chests up against a termite nest in order to smash into it! At present, that seems to be the best model of how they lived. They would break holes through the hard mud of a termite mound or an anthill and snatch up the insects with their jaws as they came rushing out. Still, I wonder if there might be something else to their feeding that we haven't yet figured out.

Alvarezsaurids are among the last group of theropods to have appeared during the Cretaceous Period. So far, they have been found in North America, Asia, and South America and possibly in Australia and Europe. Because they are already in all these regions, I wouldn't be surprised if alvarezsaurids were eventually found on all the continents.

The ostrich dinosaurs and alvarezsaurids may not be the show-stopping wonders of the dinosaur world. In museums, people might pass by their skeletons quickly on the way to see the sexier *Apatosaurus* and *Tyrannosaurus.* But they do show us what strange and wonderful and downright puzzling dinosaur fossils are *still* being discovered. Who knows what future paleontologists might find?

Alvarezsaurids are among the stranger dinosaurs discovered in recent years.

Big Bird Imitators: Ornithomimosaurs

Dr. Yoshitsugu Kobayashi
Fukui Prefectural Dinosaur Museum, Japan

In 1890, the paleontologist Othniel C. Marsh described the first ornithomimosaur dinosaur ever discovered. All he had to work with was parts of the foot and hand. Even so, he noted how similar they were to bird bones and named them Ornithomimus, *which means "bird mimic." When more-complete skeletons of ornithomimosaurs were eventually discovered, their similarity to birds became even more surprising. These dinosaurs closely resembled large flightless birds such as the ostrich. They had a small head, a long neck, and long hind limbs.*

*During the Late Cretaceous Epoch, ornithomimosaurs flourished in North America (*Ornithomimus, Struthiomimus, *and* Dromiceiomimus*) and Asia (*Garudimimus, Archaeornithomimus, Sinornithomimus, Anserimimus, *and* Gallimimus*), and they went extinct with the rest of the dinosaurs before 65.5 million years ago. The earliest ornithomimosaurs lived in Spain (*Pelecanimimus*) and Mongolia (*Harpymimus*) during the Early Cretaceous Epoch, about 130 million years ago. Unlike their descendants, these early ornithomimosaurs had teeth.*

The behavior of ornithomimosaurs is a hot topic of debate among dinosaur scientists. Because of their long, nimble legs, ornithomimosaurs were probably the fastest-running dinosaurs. Why did they need to run so fast? Were they running to catch prey or trying to escape a predator?

*Even though ornithomimosaurs are classified as theropods, they did not have dagger-shaped teeth like other known meat-eaters. Instead, ornithomimosaurs had either small, stubby teeth or a hard beak with no teeth at all. Evidence from the fos-*silized stomach contents of Sinornithomimus *even suggests that it was a plant-eater.* Gallimimus *preserves a comblike structure in the beak that was probably used to filter out food from rivers and lakes like a fishing net. These clues about eating habits don't suggest a ferocious meat-eater in search of prey. They ran probably to escape from predators.*

Another clue that ornithomimosaurs may have had a peaceful lifestyle is that some of their fossils have been found in bone beds consisting of many individuals. These bone beds contained both adults and juveniles. This suggests that ornithomimosaurs may have lived in herds, a social structure that would be useful for protecting individuals from predators. In this way, these quirky theropods were more like plant-eating dinosaurs than hunters.

The feeding behaviors of ornithomimosaurs are still poorly understood.

139

Therizinosaurus

Citipati

Caudipteryx

19

OVIRAPTOROSAURS AND THERIZINOSAUROIDS
(Egg-Thief and Sloth Dinosaurs)

The species in the groups Oviraptorosauria and Therizinosauroidea are among the weirdest of all dinosaurs. They are plant-eating meat-eating dinosaurs. That may sound like a contradiction, but it really isn't. Paleontologists often use the phrase "meat-eating dinosaur" to refer to the dinosaurs in Theropoda. And it's true that many types of theropods were meat-eaters. But we classify groups of animals based on their evolutionary position, not on their diet. The two groups in this chapter seem to have been primarily herbivores, so that makes them plant-eating members of Theropoda, the so-called meat-eating dinosaurs.

Yes, I know that the idea sounds peculiar. But the same situation exists today. The group of mammals that contains cats, hyenas, dogs, bears, seals, and their kin is called Carnivora—the carnivores. But pandas (a type of bear) eat only bamboo and so are "herbivorous carnivores," or plant-eating meat-eaters!

In addition to their strange dietary habits, oviraptorosaurs and therizinosauroids are just plain strange-looking. Oviraptorosaurs typically had short skulls, and many of them had no teeth (although they had a pair of projections coming out of the roof of the mouth). Some had tall crests on their heads. Some had very long arms, while others had very short ones. They ranged from the size of a chicken to bigger than an ostrich. Therizinosauroids, on the other hand, had pointed skulls, long necks, and heavy bodies, and all had big arms. They ranged from the size of an ostrich to as big as *T. rex*! But strangest of all is the fact that they all had honest-to-goodness feathers!

Like compsognathids, tyrannosauroids, and ornithomimosaurs, the dinosaurs in this chapter belong to Coelurosauria (the fuzzy theropods). Specifically, they are part of a group of coelurosaurs called Maniraptora, or "hand grabbers." (The other main groups are deinonychosaurs and birds.) Maniraptorans typically had very long arms. They had a special half-moon-shaped wrist bone that allowed them to fold their arms and hold them close to the body. This kept them from getting tangled in the underbrush while running. As we'll see, however, there are other things they could do with their long, folding arms. One was to brood their eggs. The other was to get up into trees in a very surprising way.

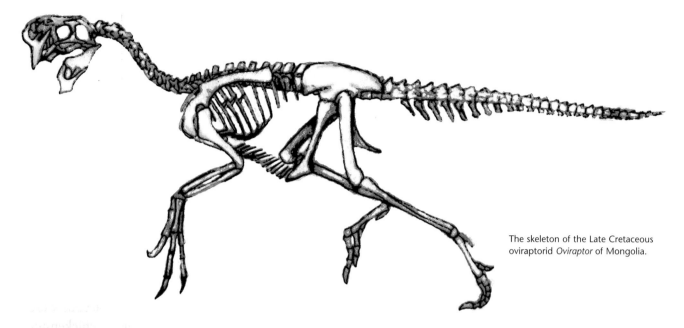

The skeleton of the Late Cretaceous oviraptorid *Oviraptor* of Mongolia.

EGG THIEVES?

The first fossil of *Oviraptor*—the oviraptorosaur after which the group is named—was found in Mongolia in the 1920s. When Roy Chapman Andrews and others from the American Museum of Natural History first saw its skull, they noticed it was very different from most theropod skulls. It was short, deep, and full of big openings. And it

Incisivosaurus of the Early Cretaceous of China is among the oldest and most primitive oviraptorosaurs. Its skull (close-up top) has strong incisor-like teeth in front and small leaf-shaped teeth (good for eating plants) behind.

didn't have any teeth. In fact, they weren't really sure which end was front and which was back!

More significantly, though, they noticed that there were eggs buried with the toothless theropod. Andrews and his team had previously found many of these eggs and assumed that they came from *Protoceratops,* a small ceratopsian (horned dinosaur) that was the most common species from that formation. They figured that the toothless theropod was an egg-eater that had stolen the eggs from a *Protoceratops,* and so they named this new species *Oviraptor philoceratops*—"egg thief that loves ceratopsians."

As it turned out, Andrews and his colleagues had made a mistake. Various expeditions to Mongolia and China in the 1990s uncovered additional *Oviraptor* specimens (and related species) nesting on the very same type of egg. And eventually, one of these eggs was found with a fossilized *Oviraptor* embryo inside. *Oviraptor* wasn't an egg thief but an egg protector! But just because *Oviraptor* didn't eat its own eggs doesn't mean it never ate *any* eggs. Its skull was well built to snatch and crack open dinosaur eggs.

OVIRAPTOROSAURS AROUND THE WORLD

Species of oviraptorosaur are known from many parts of the world. Fossils of this group have been

The Early Cretaceous *Caudipteryx* of China was one of the first oviraptorosaurs found with feathers preserved.

found in Asia, North America, and Europe, and possible oviraptorosaurs are known from Australia and South America. So far, all the definite oviraptorosaur specimens are from the Cretaceous Period, although there is a fossil from the Late Jurassic of North America that *might* be from this group. (However, it looks like this unnamed specimen may be an ancestor of both Oviraptorosauria and Therizinosauroidea.)

The most primitive known oviraptorosaurs are *Protarchaeopteryx* and *Incisivosaurus,* both from the Early Cretaceous of China. *Protarchaeopteryx* is known from a skeleton with a very damaged skull, and *Incisivosaurus* from a complete skull without a skeleton. (Some scientists think that these are actually the same species, which wouldn't surprise me at all.) The body of *Protarchaeopteryx* is like those of most oviraptorosaurs. It had a moderately long neck; long arms with

large, three-fingered hands; moderately long legs; and a short tail. The skull of *Incisivosaurus* was boxy and had long, incisor-like teeth in front and leaf-shaped teeth behind. The big gnawing teeth in front make it look something like a rabbit or a rodent. Regardless of its appearance, these are not the teeth of a flesh-eater. Instead, it probably ate mostly—or maybe *only*—plants.

A more advanced oviraptorosaur lived alongside these two (or one?). *Caudipteryx* differs from *Protarchaeopteryx* by having short arms and long legs, and from *Incisivosaurus* by having short teeth in front and no teeth behind. Similar species, such as *Microvenator* of western North America and *Thecocoelurus* of Europe, lived a little later in time.

Oviraptorosaurs of the Late Cretaceous were especially diverse. *Avimimus* was a chicken-to-turkey-size dinosaur with small teeth in the front of its jaw; big eyes; a long neck; a fat, round body; a short tail; and short arms with small, stubby fingers. Its legs were very long. Like the advanced alvarezsaurids, ornithomimids, tyrannosaurids, and other fast-running theropods, it had a specialized middle metatarsal (long bone of the foot) that served as a shock absorber. This same metatarsal adaptation was also present in Caenagnathidae, a group of Late Cretaceous oviraptorosaurs from Asia and North America. Ranging from chicken-size *Elmisaurus* to an ostrich-size (and presently unnamed) species from western North America, caenagnathids differ from *Avimimus* by having skulls with crests and toothless jaws, and by having very long arms with large, powerful hands. Similar skulls and forelimbs were found in Oviraptoridae—the Asian subgroup of oviraptorosaurs to which *Oviraptor* itself belonged.

There are a lot of similarities between true birds and oviraptorosaurs. For example, the tail of the oviraptorid *Nomingia* ends with several bones fused together. This feature, called a pygostyle, is also found in some therizinosauroids and in most species of birds. In fact, several oviraptorosaur species were originally thought to be primitive birds when they were first discovered. A few paleontologists even consider Oviraptorosauria to be a group of primitive flightless birds. While I agree

Oviraptorosaur heads came in a variety of shapes. Top row (left to right): A currently unnamed caenagnathid from western North America, *Rinchenia,* and another as-yet-unnamed oviraptorosaur from western North America. Bottom row: *Khaan,* an as-yet-unnamed form from Mongolia, and *Conchoraptor.*

that there are a lot of similarities between advanced oviraptorosaurs and advanced birds, my research (and that of many other paleontologists) shows that the closest relatives of birds are the deinonychosaurs (whom we will meet in the next chapter), and that the closest relatives of the oviraptorosaurs are the mysterious therizinosauroids.

SLOTH DINOSAURS

Paleontologist Michael Brett-Surman of the Smithsonian Institution has called the therizinosauroids "dinosaurs designed by committee."

In other words, they seem like they were put together by a bunch of people with very different ideas of what a dinosaur should be and, as a result, look like a hodgepodge of various groups. Since their discovery, therizinosauroids have been considered theropods, sauropodomorphs, and ornithischians (a neat trick!). But there is now enough known about these dinosaurs for us to be sure that their parts really *do* go together, and that they are a type of maniraptoran coelurosaurian theropod.

Falcarius from the Early Cretaceous of Utah is

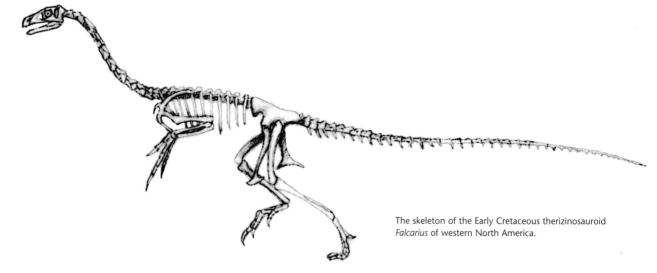

The skeleton of the Early Cretaceous therizinosauroid *Falcarius* of western North America.

144

Even more oviraptorosaur heads. Top row (left to right): *Citipati* and two as-yet-unnamed forms from Mongolia.
Bottom row: *Nemegtomaia, Heyuannia,* and *Oviraptor.*

the most primitive therizinosauroid known. In fact, the remains of dozens of *Falcarius* are known. It had a long skull with small, leaf-shaped teeth similar to those of *Incisivosaurus.* It had a very long neck, typical long maniraptoran arms, coelurosaurian legs, and a long, slender tail. It was about the size of an ostrich when fully grown. As with most theropods, its pubis (one of the pelvic bones) pointed forward.

Like *Falcarius,* the more advanced therizinosauroids had a toothless beak in the front of their jaws and leaf-shaped teeth behind. Their arms and hands were proportionately even larger, and the hands broader. Their claws were very large, and in the case of the gigantic *Therizinosaurus,* they were the same size and shape as the blades of an old-fashioned farmer's sickle. (This is where *Therizinosaurus*—the "scythe reptile"—got its name.) The tails of most therizinosauroids were very short, and at least one ended in a pygostyle.

The later therizinosauroids were typically as long or longer than *Falcarius,* and were much more

The Early Cretaceous therizinosauroid *Falcarius* of western North America.

145

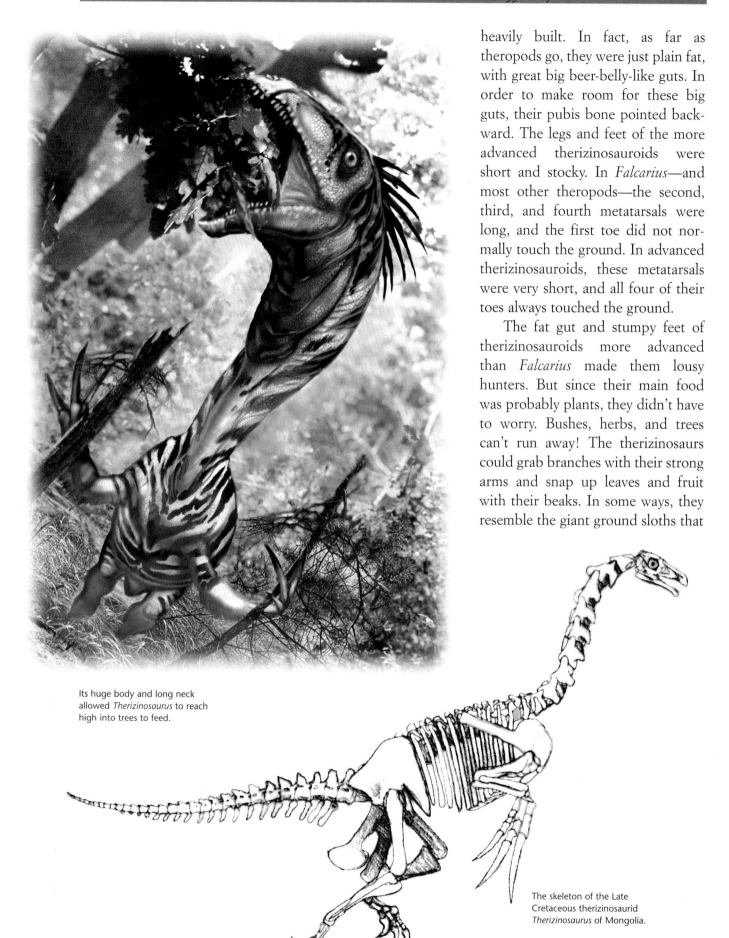

heavily built. In fact, as far as theropods go, they were just plain fat, with great big beer-belly-like guts. In order to make room for these big guts, their pubis bone pointed backward. The legs and feet of the more advanced therizinosauroids were short and stocky. In *Falcarius*—and most other theropods—the second, third, and fourth metatarsals were long, and the first toe did not normally touch the ground. In advanced therizinosauroids, these metatarsals were very short, and all four of their toes always touched the ground.

The fat gut and stumpy feet of therizinosauroids more advanced than *Falcarius* made them lousy hunters. But since their main food was probably plants, they didn't have to worry. Bushes, herbs, and trees can't run away! The therizinosaurs could grab branches with their strong arms and snap up leaves and fruit with their beaks. In some ways, they resemble the giant ground sloths that

Its huge body and long neck allowed *Therizinosaurus* to reach high into trees to feed.

The skeleton of the Late Cretaceous therizinosaurid *Therizinosaurus* of Mongolia.

lived in the Americas until 4,000 years ago or so. So I, and some other paleontologists, call them "sloth dinosaurs."

Both giant ground sloths and therizinosauroids were big, heavy, slow-moving plant-eaters with powerful forelimbs ending in long claws. Those claws were probably used to grab branches. But they no doubt served another function, too—defense. Because they were slow, ground sloths and therizinosaurs couldn't run away from predators. Instead, they both probably stood their ground and used their strong clawed hands to guard themselves. This might explain the nearly 3-foot (0.9-meter) claws of *Therizinosaurus.* They seem way too big for getting plants but just right for keeping tyrannosaurids at bay.

At present, therizinosauroids are known only from the Cretaceous Period of Asia and North America. However, I wouldn't be surprised if they turned up in European rocks from the Early Cretaceous, like their close relatives the oviraptorosaurs and more distantly related cousins like ornithomimosaurs and tyrannosauroids. There is a possible therizinosauroid from the Early Jurassic of China. This dinosaur, called *Eshanosaurus,* is known only from a lower jaw. Since prosauropods are very common in the Early Jurassic of China, and since they have lower jaws that are very similar to those of therizinosauroids, I expect that we will eventually find out that *Eshanosaurus* is a member of Prosauropoda. (If it *does* turn out to be a therizinosauroid, then this group has a history millions of years longer than we currently know.)

MORE THAN JUST PLANT-MUNCHERS

Therizinosauroids (sometimes called segnosaurs) were first thought to be fish-eaters, but not because of any direct evidence. It was simply because their discoverers assumed they must have been carnivores (they're theropods, right?) and because they were clearly too slow to catch animals on land. But their teeth show that the sloth dinosaurs were indeed primarily, if not exclusively, herbivorous. *Falcarius* might be an exception, because its long legs and tail suggest that it was a

fast runner. So this early sloth dinosaur may have chased and eaten small animals as well. (Of course, being a fast runner is a good defense, too.)

Most oviraptorosaurs were probably plant-eaters, too. That definitely seems to be the case with *Protarchaeopteryx, Incisivosaurus, Caudipteryx,* and *Avimimus,* because the teeth of these species were not shaped right to eat meat. There is, however, evidence that at least some of the toothless oviraptorosaurs ate meat. A lizard was found in the belly of the original *Oviraptor* skeleton, for instance. Also, paleontologists discovered the remains of two baby troodontid deinonychosaurs in a nest of the oviraptorid *Citipati.* Maybe the baby troodontids were brought to the nest as food for the about-to-hatch babies? A few paleontologists have suggested that oviraptorosaurs were shellfish-eaters, but their jaws seem too weak to have cracked open shells. Most oviraptorosaurs

The giant therizinosaurid *Therizinosaurus* defends itself against the tyrannosaurid *Tarbosaurus* in Late Cretaceous Mongolia.

have a pair of projections coming out of the roof of their mouths, and while these were too weak to smash a clam, they might have worked to crack open eggs. It may be that they were egg thieves after all!

Falcarius and *Avimimus* both lived in large groups. Skeletons of the therizinosauroid *Falcarius* and footprints of the oviraptorosaur *Avimimus* indicate that they lived in herds of dozens of individuals. It is uncertain if any of their relatives gathered in such large numbers.

Therizinosauroids are known only from regions that had a lot of water, like lakeshores and forests. Oviraptorosaurs are found in these environments, too, but also in sandy deserts. Those sandy desert deposits are important for understanding oviraptorosaur behavior, because it is in those sandstones that the nests of these dinosaurs were discovered.

BROODING DINOSAURS

Oviraptorosaurs, even ones like *Citipati* that were nearly as big as adult humans, brooded their nests. We have enough specimens of these dinosaurs

Oviraptor broods its nest and defends its eggs from the lizard *Estesia*.

found in position on top of their eggs to know something about this behavior. They laid their eggs in a ring in the desert sands, partially buried. Then the parent (we don't know if it was the mother, the father, or both) would sit in between the eggs, covering them with its sides, tail, and arms. The arms were well adapted for this, because, as with most maniraptorans, they stuck out to the side rather than facing backward, as in other theropods. Even more importantly, the long arm feathers would cover the tops of the eggs. The soft body feathers would also keep them warm and protected.

We know that oviraptorosaurs had long arm and tail feathers because they are preserved in *Protarchaeopteryx* and *Caudipteryx.* The rest of the body was apparently covered in smaller feathers. Whether these smaller feathers were simple protofeather fuzz (as in compsognathids and tyrannosauroids) or more complex body feathers (such as on modern bird bodies) isn't currently known. The long, fuzzy protofeathers are found in the early therizinosauroid *Beipiaosaurus,* but some of what seems to be protofeathers may actually be imperfectly preserved true feathers.

What do I mean by "true feathers"? Almost all the feathers of modern birds, and especially those of the wings, the tail, and most of the body, have the same basic structure. There is a hollow shaft attaching the feather to the skin. Off this shaft come smaller branches. If you look at them under the microscope, you'll see that those smaller branches have even smaller branches, with hooks coming off those. These hooks help hold the shape of the feather. The best-preserved arm and tail feathers of oviraptorosaurs show exactly this structure.

Why would such elaborate traits as true feathers evolve from protofeathers? One possibility is that they were for show. The tail and arm feathers of oviraptorosaurs, and probably therizinosauroids, would make good displays. These could be used for defense or to attract mates. Also, larger true feathers would help in brooding eggs. The longer and broader the arm and tail feathers, the more eggs they cover.

INTO THE TREES WITH WAIR

By flapping their feathered arms, early maniraptorans ran up trees to escape predators.

Another possible use for the evolution of true feathers is suggested by a recent discovery about modern birds. You might think that we know all there is to know about living animals, but zoologists are constantly discovering surprising facts about even familiar creatures. The discovery in question here was made by zoologist Ken Dial of the University of Montana. He has found that birds use their wings in a surprising fashion. We all know about flying birds. But it turns out that birds also use their wings for a different form of locomotion. And this form of locomotion may have been useful for baby oviraptorosaurs and therizinosauroids, too.

Many species of bird—such as peacocks, turkeys, and tinamous—live mainly on the ground but nest in trees or on rocks to keep safe from predators. It had always been assumed that birds simply flew up into the branches to get there. But Ken Dial discovered that there is another way for birds to get up into trees, even baby birds that haven't learned to fly. They run up the sides of trees! But they wouldn't be able to do this using just their feet, because they would fall down. What Dial discovered is that their wings help them run up the trunks, but in a very unexpected way. They don't use their wings to cling to the tree or anything like that. Instead, they flap their wings back and forth (rather than up and down, as when flying) to generate traction to keep themselves from falling off. As long as they flap their wings back and forth, the force they make presses their feet against the tree. This means they can literally *run* up the tree trunk!

Dial calls this behavior "wing-assisted incline running" (or WAIR), and he experimented to see how it actually worked. He found that without flapping, birds could only run up 45-degree-angle surfaces. Anything steeper and the birds fell off. But when they were flapping, the birds could run up steeper angles. He also found that the bigger the size of the wing feather, the steeper the angle the birds could run up. When they were flapping full-size wing feathers, the birds could run straight up a vertical tree trunk!

When Dial first presented this work at the Society of Vertebrate Paleontology in 2001, I and a lot of other paleontologists were very impressed. He had found a behavior that was probably not just limited to birds. It turns out that every single trait needed to do WAIR was also present in oviraptorosaurs and (probably) in therizinosauroids. They had arms that stuck out to the side, and they could make the same forward-and-backward flap as WAIRing birds. They had big feathers on the arms to help generate traction. And they even had large breastbones to support the strong chest muscles needed for this action.

An adult oviraptorosaur or therizinosaur would be too big to run up a tree like this. (If a *T. rex*–size *Therizinosaurus* tried it, the tree would probably collapse.) But baby dinosaurs were very small, and they were on the menu of predators. So early maniraptorans, including the ancestors of oviraptorosaurs and therizinosauroids, may have evolved their long, folding arms, big breastbones, and true feathers so that they could escape into the trees as babies.

Just because they could escape using WAIR doesn't mean that these dinosaurs could fly. Other branches of the maniraptoran family tree did evolve true flight, however. We know that birds did. And a recent surprise is that the closest relatives of birds, the deinonychosaurs, may also have had some flight ability. But even in nonflying maniraptorans, having WAIR as a method of defense would have helped these groups survive. And both oviraptorosaurs and therizinosauroids survived until the very end of the Cretaceous Period.

Microraptor

Deinonychus

Troodon

DEINONYCHOSAURS
(Raptor Dinosaurs)

Probably the most popular carnivorous dinosaur after *Tyrannosaurus* is *Velociraptor.* Made famous by the *Jurassic Park* series of books and movies, this little dinosaur (actually a lot smaller than shown in the movies!) was a swift, smart, and agile hunter. The public found *Velociraptor* so exciting that they began to use the name "raptor"—which means "thief," "grabber," or "plunderer"—to describe *all* the species in Deinonychosauria. Not all scientists were happy with this new nickname, but I think it is fine.

Incidentally, the name "raptor" is *also* used to describe modern birds of prey like hawks, eagles, and falcons. In both modern raptor birds and extinct raptor dinosaurs, the foot serves as a deadly weapon: clutching talons in the modern birds, and a slashing sickle-shaped claw in the extinct dinosaurs.

Deinonychosauria is broken down into two main branches: Dromaeosauridae and Troodontidae. Both groups began as crow-size fast-moving hunters with grasping hands and a distinctive foot. This foot had a second toe (equivalent to the one known as "the little piggy that stayed home" in humans) that could be raised up from the ground. In other words, it was retractable, like the toes of modern cats. And like the toes of modern cats, the second toe of deinonychosaurs ended with a sharp, curved claw.

SOME VERY IMPORTANT DINOSAURS

One of the most important discoveries in dinosaur paleontology was when John Ostrom of Yale University found *Deinonychus* in 1964. This dinosaur—whose name means "terrible claws"—was the first raptor dinosaur known from a relatively complete skeleton. Indeed, it is the one after which the whole group Deinonychosauria is named.

The discovery of *Deinonychus* led Ostrom to propose several significant ideas about dinosaur biology. At the time, many paleontologists regarded dinosaurs as being slow and sluggish. Carnivorous dinosaurs were pictured as clumsy and stupid, at best able to take a few good bites and/or swipes at their equally clumsy and stupid prey. But Ostrom argued that in order to use its toe claw as a deadly weapon, *Deinonychus* had to be swift and agile. If it was slow and stupid, the claw would be good for little more than scratching the ankles of other dinosaurs. But if *Deinonychus* was fast and active, the claw would be good for tearing and ripping, again and again. And active combat like that isn't typical of cold-blooded predators. It is, however, similar to the attacks of warm-blooded hunters, like modern predatory

Some small maniraptorans, like *Epidendrosaurus* (left) and the dromaeosaurid *Microraptor* (behind and right), may have lived in the trees.

birds and mammals. Ostrom also noticed that the anatomy of this raptor was very similar to that of the primitive Jurassic bird *Archaeopteryx.* For example, the forelimbs were practically identical in every detail but size. And as in birds, the pubis bone in the hip of this dromaeosaurid pointed backward. So Ostrom brought back an idea first proposed in the 1870s: that dinosaurs were the ancestors of birds. Specifically, he hypothesized that deinonychosaurs were the closest relatives to birds among the various groups of dinosaurs.

It is worth pointing out here that Ostrom did not argue that *Deinonychus*—or any deinonychosaur—was the *ancestor* of birds. He recognized that deinonychosaurs have too many of their own specializations—like the retractable sickle claw, for instance—that are not found in early birds. And he knew that all the deinonychosaur fossils available at that time were younger than

Archaeopteryx, the oldest known bird. What Ostrom proposed, and additional data has since demonstrated, is that deinonychosaurs and birds both came from a common ancestor that wasn't also shared with oviraptorosaurs, therizinosauroids, and earlier branches of the theropod dinosaur family tree. So deinonychosaurs weren't the ancestors of birds, nor birds the ancestors of deinonychosaurs. Instead, birds and deinonychosaurs were each other's closest relatives.

During the past ten years, newly discovered dromaeosaurid and troodontid species have shown that the earliest deinonychosaurs were even more similar to *Archaeopteryx* than was wolf-size *Deinonychus.* Since 2001, we have known that

152

deinonychosaurs had true bird-style feathers on their arms, legs, and tail. And recent discoveries indicate that at least some small raptors may have been capable of limited flight!

DINOSAURS IN THE TREES

Deinonychosauria is a group within the larger category of dinosaurs called Maniraptora. Other maniraptorans include avialians (birds), oviraptorosaurs, therizinosauroids, and probably alvarezsaurids. Maniraptora means "hand grabbers" or "hand snatchers," and maniraptorans do share a number of specializations of their forelimbs. Their arms are longer than those of other coelurosaurs (the group of dinosaurs including maniraptorans, ornithomimosaurs, tyrannosauroids, and related species). Their shoulder joints face sideways, like in birds or humans, rather than backward, like in cats or most dinosaurs. Special half-moon-shaped bones in their wrists allowed their long, slender hands to tuck in close against the body when folded up. And their breastbones were very large, helping to support strong chest muscles.

Maniraptorans also share the trait of true feathers. While their more primitive relatives among the coelurosaurian theropods had simple protofeather fuzz, maniraptorans had feathers with a shaft down the middle, branches coming off of the shaft, and smaller structures coming off the branches to hold the feathers' shape. Deinonychosaurs had long feathers on their arms, at the end of their tail, and on their legs. The rest of the body was covered either with protofeathers or with small body feathers (like those found on modern birds).

As discussed in chapter 19, this combination of specialized arms and feathers was useful for brooding on nests of eggs. It also enabled a special type of locomotion called wing-assisted incline running, or WAIR. Discovered by Montanan zoologist Ken Dial, WAIR is a behavior used by modern birds that combines flapping the wings back and forth while running up the sides of trees. This flapping motion pushes the feet of the bird against the surface of the tree, allowing it to run vertically up the trunk. Most maniraptorans had all the anatomical features needed to do WAIR, and it is very probable that they did so when they were small.

The ability to run up a tree is a great advantage. It helps you get away from predators. In fact, this is one of the reasons modern birds that live and feed mostly on the ground use WAIR. Their ancient cousins would have faced the same problem. Although these dinosaur species—like modern chickens, partridges, and peacocks—were too big to actually dwell in the trees, they may have used WAIR to get up into the branches to save themselves. (Also, the branches make a safe place to rest for the night.)

The ability to get up into the trees would protect small maniraptorans from their larger carnivorous kin.

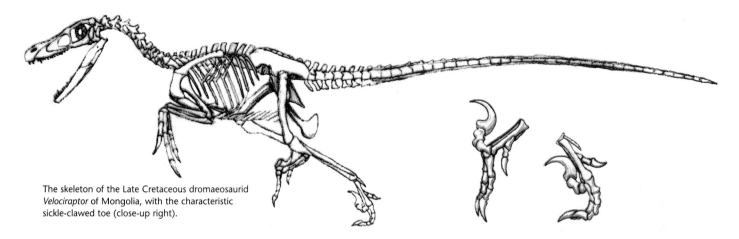

The skeleton of the Late Cretaceous dromaeosaurid *Velociraptor* of Mongolia, with the characteristic sickle-clawed toe (close-up right).

In the past, few paleontologists thought that there were Mesozoic dinosaurs that spent most of their lives in the trees. Today there are many birds that live that way. Nearly all of these species, however, are quite small, and most of them are smaller than the ground-dwelling birds. (Some highly specialized birds like parrots and woodpeckers are exceptions.) Since even small Mesozoic maniraptorans like *Caudipteryx* were bigger than most tree-dwelling birds, it was thought that they all had to be ground dwellers (even if they might escape into the trees using WAIR). But in the early 2000s, new evidence of small tree-dwelling dinosaurs was discovered. Like many of the other famous feathered dinosaur specimens, these new discoveries are small species from China. But the lake mudstones that these small maniraptorans were found in may be a lot older than the ones in which *Microraptor* and *Sinornithosaurus* were found. A recent analysis shows that they may be from either the Late Jurassic or the very beginning of the Early Cretaceous epochs.

Regardless of their exact age, the little maniraptoran dinosaurs *Pedopenna* and *Epidendrosaurus* are neither deinonychosaurs nor birds, but they may be close relatives of the common ancestor of both groups. *Pedopenna* is known only from a leg and part of an arm, but both of these have long feathers on them (as do deinonychosaurs and early birds). *Epidendrosaurus* is currently known from two tiny skeletons about 4.5 inches (11.4 centimeters) long, which may be only hatchlings. The most interesting feature of this dinosaur is its hand. Unlike most other theropods (in which the second finger is the longest), it has an extra-long third finger. Some paleontologists have advanced the idea that this finger was used to pick insects out of tree bark, like the similarly weird finger of the aye-aye (a primate from Madagascar).

In any case, *Pedopenna*, *Epidendrosaurus*, primitive dromaeosaurids, and birds all have a first toe placed very low on the foot. Such a toe enables grasping on to branches to perch. Other theropods do not have this arrangement, so it seems likely that the common ancestor of this combined group of advanced maniraptorans spent much of its time in trees.

In addition to the Chinese forms, there are some isolated bones and teeth from North America and Europe that suggest that deinonychosaurs may have already evolved by the Late Jurassic, maybe even by the Middle Jurassic. But the oldest definite deinonychosaurs are from the Early Cretaceous.

FLYING RAPTORS?

Dromaeosauridae—the group in Deinonychosauria to which both *Velociraptor* and *Deinonychus* belong—is very diverse. It includes jackal-to-grizzly-bear-size predators. In recent years, though, many primitive species of dromaeosaurids have been discovered, and these have given us a better idea of what the early members of this group looked like. Dromaeosaurids started off as crow-size dinosaurs, with arms almost as long as their legs. Their skulls were not particularly strong, but they were full of small, sharp teeth. The chevron bones along the base of their tails fit

The Late Cretaceous unenlagiine dromaeosaurid *Buitreraptor* of Argentina.

together more tightly than did those of other theropods. And the feathers on the arms and legs of primitive dromaeosaurids were very long.

A recent analysis by paleontologist Peter Makovicky of the Field Museum in Chicago and his colleagues shows that there were four main branches of the dromaeosaurid family. These are the long-snouted creatures of Unenlagiinae, the tiny members of Microraptorinae, the svelte species of Velociraptorinae, and the stout dinosaurs of Dromaeosaurinae.

Unenlagiines were the first to branch off from the others. They are so far only known from South America, Africa, and Madagascar. All these land-masses were once joined together as part of a single supercontinent called Gondwana. Unenlagiines, unlike other deinonychosaurs, had very long snouts with many small teeth. This suggests that they hunted animals a lot smaller than themselves. Crow-size *Rahonavis* of Madagascar and turkey-size *Buitreraptor* of Argentina represent the smaller unenlagiines. Larger are South American *Unenlagia, Neuquenraptor* (which might simply represent a different growth stage of *Unenlagia*), and *Unquillosaurus,* at about 8 feet (2.4 meters) long. A giant unenlagiine has been discovered by

Some small deinonychosaurs—like the Late Cretaceous unenlagiine *Rahonavis*—may have had limited flying or gliding ability. (Riding on a swimming *Rapetosaurus* is pure speculation, however!)

A pack of the Early Cretaceous velociraptorine dromaeosaurid *Deinonychus* attacks the iguanodontian *Tenontosaurus*.

Argentine paleontologist Fernando Novas. He has not yet named or fully described this dinosaur, but it is about 20 feet (6.1 meters) long, making it one of the largest raptors.

Rahonavis was originally described as a primitive bird. Although its skeleton was incomplete, it was apparent that its arms were very long compared to its body size. Along the ulna (the lower bone in the forearm) were bumps that indicated the attachment of big feathers. This little dinosaur clearly used its arms for flapping. In fact, it appears to have been at least as good a flier as the primitive bird *Archaeopteryx*. (Which isn't saying too much, since *Archaeopteryx* was probably a lousy flier compared to modern birds!)

The other unenlagiines were probably too big to fly, at least when fully grown. But it might be that their offspring could glide or flap from tree to tree, or from the trees down to the ground.

The Microraptorinae were another group of raptors that probably could fly. As the name implies, the known microraptorines were small. They share with their larger cousins, velociraptorines and dromaeosaurines, extra-long projec-

tions of bone from the tops of their tail vertebrae and along their chevrons. This means that their tails were very stiff, except for right at the base. Also, like the larger dromaeosaurids, microraptorines had shorter snouts and larger teeth than unenlagiines.

All definite microraptorines discovered so far are from the Early Cretaceous of China. They include *Sinornithosaurus* and *Microraptor* itself. (Little *Bambiraptor* of the Late Cretaceous of North America might be a late-surviving microraptorine or a small velociraptorine.) The fossils show that the arm and leg feathers of the species in Microraptorinae were particularly long. In fact, some people call these the "four-winged dinosaurs." At first some paleontologists imagined these little raptors sticking their legs out to the side like their arms, but that can't work. In order to do that, they would have had to pop their thighbones out of their hip sockets!

(You can test this at home using a roast chicken or turkey. The arrangement of the thigh-

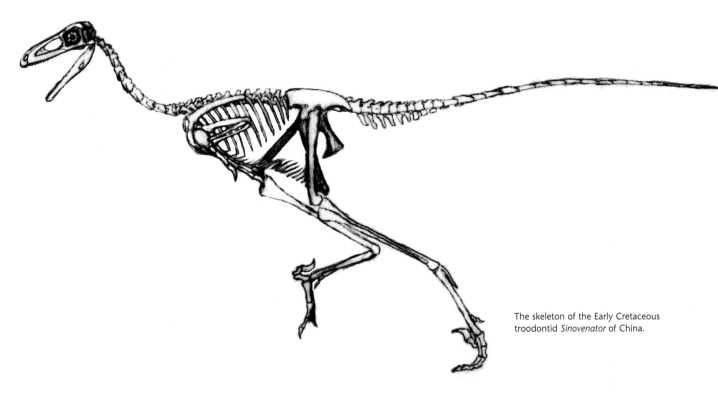

The skeleton of the Early Cretaceous troodontid *Sinovenator* of China.

bone and the hip socket is very similar in birds and microraptorines. If you lift the thigh off to the side to make it horizontal, the leg will come right off!)

Since the legs couldn't stick out to the side without dislocating their bones, they must have been held in some other position while gliding. Perhaps they were tucked close to the body? But then the leg feathers wouldn't have to be so big. Maybe they let their legs hang down while flying to give them better control (like the vertical tail fin of an airplane)? Maybe they stretched their legs

The Late Cretaceous troodontid *Troodon* of western North America, with close-ups of foot (left) and teeth (right).

backward so that the feathers lined up along the tail to form a "tail fin"? Paleontologists are still trying to figure this out.

There are some modern birds with very big leg feathers, too. Some hawks and eagles (today's "raptors"!) have them. They may be only for show, or they may help these birds control their movements as they swoop down out of the sky to catch their prey. Perhaps primitive dromaeosaurids did the same?

CRETACEOUS CATS

More familiar to paleontologists and the public are the larger dromaeosaurids, the velociraptorines and dromaeosaurines. Velociraptorines tended to have more lightly built skulls and limbs, while dromaeosaurines were more solidly built and bulkier. Both groups are known only from North America and Asia, but probably lived in Europe as well.

Deinonychus is an 11.5-foot (3.5-meter) velociraptorine from the Early Cretaceous of North America. *Velociraptor* is a later, smaller relative, only 7 feet (2.1 meters) long or less, from the Late Cretaceous of Mongolia. Other velociraptorines were the even smaller Late Cretaceous North American species *Saurornitholestes* and possibly

Three individuals of the troodontid *Sinovenator* chase *Psittacosaurus* in the Early Cretaceous of China.

Bambiraptor (which may instead be the last of the microraptorines). Dromaeosaurines include the largest and most heavily built deinonychosaurs: 23-foot (7-meter) *Utahraptor* of the Early Cretaceous of North America and 17-foot (5.2-meter) *Achillobator.* Other dromaeosaurines were shorter, such as Late Cretaceous *Atrociraptor* and *Dromaeosaurus* of Canada and *Adasaurus* of Mongolia, which were all comparable in size to *Velociraptor.*

While baby dromaeosaurines and velociraptorines may have been able to glide or fly out of trees, adults were too big to do this. But the adaptations that served their ancestors (and babies?) for traveling through the air helped them hunt on the ground. For example, their long, stiff tail also served as a counterbalance while running. By flipping it one way or another, they could turn very quickly when chasing prey. Their long arms (end-

ing with sharp claws) could unfold and snap forward, grabbing a victim. Adult dromaeosaurids could leap onto the backs or sides of their prey. Grasping the animal, they would use their big sickle claw to slash open its throat or rip into its guts. Dromaeosaurids would have been very effective hunters.

If that scenario of attack sounds familiar, then you probably know something about big cats. Modern lions, tigers, leopards, cheetahs, and their relatives hunt in a similar fashion. In fact, I think that if the nickname "raptor" hadn't been given to this group, "panther dinosaurs" would have been a pretty good name.

How do we know about these hunting scenarios? Partly from the features of anatomy—the long, unfolding arms; stiff tail; huge, retractable sickle claws; and so on. But also because of the spectacular "Fighting Dinosaurs" fossil from Mongolia. This was a fossil of a *Velociraptor* preserved in the midst of using its sickle claw to rip into the throat of the small ceratopsian (horned dinosaur) *Protoceratops.*

RAPTOR PACK

Did dromaeosaurids hunt in packs? That seems to have been the case with *Deinonychus* at least. There are several examples of fossil quarries where many individuals of this species were found buried with a single skeleton of the large iguanodontian herbivore *Tenontosaurus*. While this could be because the dromaeosaurids were scavenging in a group when they got buried, some evidence suggests that that is not the case. Specifically, no one has found a similar grouping of many *Deinonychus* together with a single skeleton of *Sauropelta,* the ankylosaur that also lived in the same environment. It seems that packs of *Deinonychus* would attack the larger, but mostly defenseless, *Tenontosaurus* rather than the heavily armored *Sauropelta.*

If a pack of wolves or a pride of lions loses a couple of members during an attack, the group may become too weak to hunt effectively. But dinosaurs were not mammals. Because each adult female could lay a dozen or more eggs every year, they could replenish their numbers more easily than mammals. So a raptor pack could lose more hunters every year than a lion pride and still be successful.

But just because *Deinonychus* lived in a pack doesn't mean that *all* dromaeosaurids did! After all, lions live in prides, but the very closely related leopards and tigers are mostly solitary animals. So some dromaeosaurids may have been solitary, with others hunting in pairs and others in packs. It makes sense that *Deinonychus,* which lived in an environment with lots of plants—and thus lots of big herbivores to eat—could afford to live in packs.

Desert-dwelling *Velociraptor* would probably starve if there were too many mouths to feed, so it was more likely a solitary animal. We know that once in a while *Velociraptors* did get together, but not always to cooperate. There is a *Velociraptor* skull with evidence of a fatal bite that did damage to its brain, and the tooth mark appears to be that of another *Velociraptor.*

CONFUSING TROODONTIDS

Not as famous as the dromaeosaurids, the troodontids were actually the first group of deinonychosaurs discovered. When *Troodon* was named in 1856, only its teeth were known. In fact, it was at first thought to be a lizard and not a dinosaur at all. Later on, similarities between the teeth of *Troodon* and pachycephalosaurs led to confusion, and the name Troodontidae

The Early Cretaceous troodontid *Sinusonasus* of China.

159

was used for the domeheaded, head-banging plant-eaters! Eventually more-complete skeletons of true troodontids were discovered, and it was recognized that they were coelurosaurian theropods.

The confusion didn't end there, however. For a long time, the only troodontids known were advanced Late Cretaceous species like North American *Troodon* and Mongolian *Saurornithoides*. These seemed to show a mix of traits seen in totally different groups of theropods. In some ways, the braincase was like that of birds, for example, and in other ways it was like that of ornithomimosaurs. Troodontid feet had retractable sickle claws, like dromaeosaurid feet, but also had a pinched middle metatarsal bone, like ornithomimid and tyrannosaurid feet. Unlike dromaeosaurids and birds but like primitive theropods, they had a forward-pointing pubis. Like most other maniraptorans, they had a big half-moon-shaped wrist bone; unlike most maniraptorans, they had fairly short arms. So up until recently, troodontids were the "problem children" of cladistic analyses. Some studies showed them as the closest relatives to birds. Others placed them closest to ornithomimosaurs (as mine used to). Still others placed them as the cousins of dromaeosaurids.

Part of the problem was that before the mid-1990s all we had to study was the most specialized troodontids from the very end of the Late Cretaceous. What was needed was early, primitive troodontid fossils that would show which traits were present in the ancestor of all Troodontidae and which evolved later in troodontid history. Happily, in the 1990s and 2000s, just such fossils were found in Early Cretaceous rocks from Asia: *Sinornithoides, Sinovenator, Mei,* and *Jinfengopteryx.* We now know that primitive troodontids had a backward-pointing pubis, as in dromaeosaurids and birds. The similarities in their skulls to those of ornithomimosaurs occurred only in the later forms, so those similarities are examples of independent evolution. Most of the current information shows that troodontids are closely related to dromaeosaurids. In other words,

Deinonychosauria is a complete branch of the Tree of Life. The discovery of these primitive troodontids helped us understand where they fit in the family tree (and relieved a lot of us who had been confused before!).

Caution should be observed, however. Some troodontids, such as *Mei,* have particularly bird-like features in the skull, so new discoveries could show that troodontids were actually closer to birds than they were to dromaeosaurids. Future analyses and discoveries will hopefully help to resolve these problems.

There is also much confusion over what troodontids ate. Their arms are typically small compared to those of maniraptorans and wouldn't have been very good for snatching prey. Only a few have teeth that are bladelike and good for eating meat. Various troodontid species have no serrations on their teeth at all. Serrationless teeth are also known in some insect-eating lizards as well as ornithomimosaur and alvarezsaurid dinosaurs. *Troodon* itself—and a few of its closest kin—has teeth with big bumps rather than small serrations. These bump-ridged teeth are similar to the teeth of plant-eating reptiles like iguana lizards and ornithischian and sauropodomorph dinosaurs. All this suggests a varied diet for the troodontids: small vertebrates, insects, eggs, and maybe even plants. In any case, it is unlikely they hunted animals their own size or larger, the way their velociraptorine and dromaeosaurine relatives did.

Most troodontids had very long legs. As with ornithomimids, tyrannosaurids, the oviraptorosaur *Avimimus,* and other fast-running theropods, the middle metatarsal bone in the foot of troodontids had a special adaptation to absorb shock. Some unenlagiine and microraptorine dromaeosaurs had similar feet, and so were also fast runners. These long legs and shock-absorbing feet may have helped troodontids catch small animals, but those features would also have helped them run away from dromaeosaurids and young tyrannosaurids! (Despite having a name that means "fast thief" and being portrayed in movies running as fast as cheetahs, *Velociraptor* lacked either especially long legs or shock-absorber feet and were almost certainly slower than troodontids.)

Troodontids were generally small dinosaurs. None known are as heavy as an adult man. The largest is *Troodon* itself, 10 feet (3 meters) long but weighing only 110 pounds (50 kilograms) or so. Tiny *Mei* is only 21 inches (53 centimeters) long, about the same size as *Rahonavis,* one of the species of *Microraptor,* and the early bird *Archaeopteryx.* The others ranged in between.

RAPTOR BEHAVIOR

Deinonychosaurs of both groups are known from wet *and* dry environments, including deserts. Nests and eggs of both groups are also known. Like oviraptorosaurs and birds, deinonychosaurs brooded their eggs. Also like birds, deinonychosaurs slept with their heads tucked underneath their feathered arms. We know this because two troodontid skeletons (one of *Sinornithoides,* the other of *Mei*) have been found in this position, with the tail wrapped around the body.

In the 1970s, the relative brain size of *Troodon* (then called *Stenonychosaurus*) was found to be the largest of all dinosaurs other than birds. This gave troodontids the reputation of being the smartest dinosaurs of the Mesozoic. To be fair, none of the other groups of maniraptorans were examined in that study, and it is likely that oviraptorosaurs and dromaeosaurids would have been found to be similarly brainy. Those big brains would have been useful in coordinating the complex motions of chasing after prey. They would also have helped tree-dwelling deinonychosaurs navigate among the branches while gliding down from trees. But as brainy as they were, deinony-

chosaurs did not have a big brain by the standards of modern mammals and birds. Despite what some science fiction movies might say, they were not smarter than dolphins or primates!

Neither dromaeosaurids nor troodontids were ever the top predators in their environment. In some cases, they were the smallest dinosaurs in their world. These highly specialized theropods lived for most of the Cretaceous, and bones and teeth of both groups make it all the way up until 65.5 million years ago. At that point they died out. Their closest relatives, however, survived and lived to become the most successful of all groups of dinosaurs. We call them "birds."

We do not know what soft tissues may have adorned the heads of dinosaurs. While the turkey-like face of this *Deinonychus* is purely speculative, the real dinosaur may have been equally strange-looking.

161

Longipteryx

Confuciusornis

Archaeopteryx

21

AVIALIANS
(Birds)

I f you have been reading this book from the beginning, you are well aware by now that birds are dinosaurs. If not, you may be thinking, Why is there a chapter on birds in a book about dinosaurs? Well, remember what a dinosaur is. It isn't just a "prehistoric animal." It isn't a "scaly creature from the Mesozoic Era." It isn't even a "reptile from the Mesozoic Era that lived on land and had legs directly underneath its body."

To modern scientists, an animal is a dinosaur if it is a descendant of the most recent common ancestor of *Iguanodon* and *Megalosaurus*. The size or era or shape of the animal doesn't matter. All that matters is ancestry. And one of the most important discoveries in paleontology of the past forty years is that birds are descendants of the most recent common ancestor of *Iguanodon* and *Megalosaurus*. In other words, birds *are* dinosaurs!

Some people think that paleontologists say "birds are dinosaurs" because it is fun to talk about watching dinosaurs in the backyard or to say that dinosaurs taste like chicken. Let me tell you now, saying "birds are dinosaurs" is *not* fun! It causes all sorts of headaches! For example, how am I to answer the following questions: What is the smallest dinosaur? What is the fastest dinosaur? What is the smartest dinosaur? Why did dinosaurs become extinct?

If I am true to my scientific principles, then I have to answer these questions as follows: the smallest dinosaur is the Cuban bee hummingbird (*Mellisuga helenae*) at 0.07 ounces (2 grams). The fastest-flying dinosaur is the peregrine falcon (*Falco peregrinus*), which can reach 200 miles (322

kilometers) per hour in a dive. And the fastest-running dinosaur is the ostrich (*Struthio camelus*), at more than 40 miles (64 kilometers) per hour. The smartest dinosaurs are various species of parrots and crows. And because birds live today, dinosaurs never did become extinct.

These may not be the kind of answers you want to find in a dinosaur book, but they *are* the best answers if we recognize that being a dinosaur—like being a mammal or being a vertebrate—is based on who your ancestors are. And all the evidence today points to birds being a type of dinosaur.

Modern birds belong to a group called Aves, which is Latin for "birds." The various extinct species of birds throughout the Cenozoic Era, and even some from the end of the Cretaceous Period of the Mesozoic Era, are also avians (that is, members of Aves). But there are many species of extinct birds from the Cretaceous Period, and one or two known from the Jurassic Period, that are more primitive than Aves. In 1986, paleontologist Jacques Gauthier coined the name Avialae—"bird wings"—for the group that contains both Aves proper (modern birds) and these older primitive

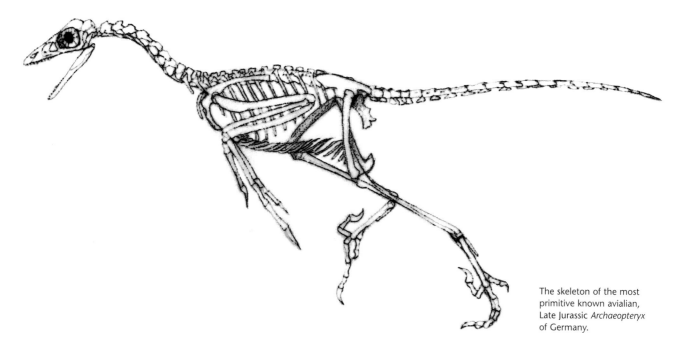

The skeleton of the most primitive known avialian, Late Jurassic *Archaeopteryx* of Germany.

birds. Avialae includes not only Aves but also the famous Late Jurassic *Archaeopteryx,* the toothless Early Cretaceous *Confuciusornis,* the diverse species in Enantiornithes, and some odd seabirds of the Cretaceous Period.

WHEN IS A BIRD A BIRD?

So what makes birds so special? How do you recognize when an animal is a bird? You might be tempted to say "birds fly," but hopefully you remember that bats and insects fly, as did the

We know from the latest studies that *Archaeopteryx* had long feathers on its legs as well as on its wings and tail.

Birds like *Confuciusornis* (top left and right) were not the only feathered dinosaurs in the Early Cretaceous of China. The primitive ceratopsian *Psittacosaurus* (center and left) had long, feather-like quills on their tail; the compsognathid *Sinosauropteryx* (bottom right) was covered in protofeather fuzz; and the dromaeosaurid *Microraptor* (fighting pair, middle right) and therizinosauroid *Beipiaosaurus* (background) had honest-to-goodness feathers.

extinct pterosaurs and possibly even some deinonychosaurian dinosaurs. And perfectly good birds, like ostriches and penguins, are totally incapable of flight.

If there were no fossil record—if dinosaurs had never been discovered—birds would be very easy to distinguish from other living things. That's the way it was, in fact, before there was a science of paleontology. Birds have always been one of the most recognizable groups of modern animals, because they are *so* different from every other animal alive. Birds have feathers, of course. And in the modern world, *only* birds have feathers, and *every* bird species has them. But there are other specialized traits in their anatomy.

Let me list some of the important ones for you here. Birds have a complex system of air sacs that helps them breathe more efficiently and control their body temperature and moisture loss. These air sacs form lots of complex hollow spaces in bird skulls, vertebrae, and limb bones. Birds have huge brains and toothless beaks. Birds have a wishbone, or furcula. The large breastbone of most birds has a great big ridge, or keel, down the middle—this is what the white meat of chicken and turkey attaches to. The forelimbs of birds—their wings— are normally very long. The half-moon-shaped wrist bone and the bones of the palm of the hand of birds are all fused together. Birds have only three fingers in their hands, the middle of which is the longest, and none of those fingers have claws (except in babies of a type of South American bird called a hoatzin). The hip bones of the birds are fused together. The pubis bone of the hip points

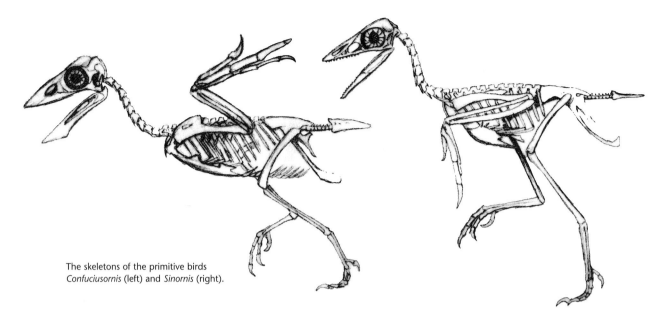

The skeletons of the primitive birds
Confuciusornis (left) and *Sinornis* (right).

backward, and the tips do not touch. All birds stand only on their hind legs, which are held directly underneath the body. The long bones of the foot—the metatarsals—are all fused together. Birds have only four toes, the first of which faces backward and the other three of which face forward (although this pattern is modified in certain climbing and paddling birds). The tail vertebrae of birds are very short and are mobile right near the hips, but fuse together into a single structure called a pygostyle at the end.

That sure sounds like a lot of distinctive features! And it would be a lot, *if* all we knew about was the anatomy of modern animals. But that isn't the case, of course. We have more than just the anatomy of modern animals to take into account. We also have all the different extinct species to consider. And it turns out that recognizing what is a bird and what isn't a bird becomes *a lot* more complicated when you add the creatures preserved in the fossil record! Many of them are far more birdlike than crocodilians, which are evolutionarily the closest living relatives of birds. The most important of all these birdlike fossil forms, of course, are the different species of dinosaurs. As you can see in this book, many traits that are only found in birds today are found in various types of dinosaurs as well. In fact, these traits help us determine the place of birds in the dinosaur family tree.

As with all dinosaurs, the legs of birds are held directly underneath the body. Birds are saurischian dinosaurs, and like other saurischians, they have hollow vertebrae containing air sacs and have the middle (second) finger as the longest. Birds are theropod saurischian dinosaurs, as seen by their wishbones, air sacs in their skulls, and feet with three main toes and a smaller first toe. Birds are tetanurine theropod saurischian dinosaurs, in that they have only three fingers, their tails are stiff, and the chambers in their vertebrae are very complex. Birds are coelurosaurian tetanurine theropod saurischian dinosaurs, which you can see because they have feathers as well as scales, and because their hand is long and narrow. Birds are maniraptoran coelurosaurian tetanurine theropod saurischian dinosaurs, as revealed by their true branching feathers, their long forelimbs with half-moon-shaped wrist bones, their big breastbones, and their big brains. Among the maniraptorans, the closest relatives to birds are the deinonychosaurs, or raptors. Both groups share a backward-pointing pubis bone, tail vertebrae that are mobile right next to the hips, and a first toe placed at the bottom of the foot.

So where does that leave us? There are still a lot of features to distinguish Aves from Deinonychosauria. Avians—modern birds—have toothless beaks, enormous brains, keeled breastbones, fused wrist and palm bones, no claws on their fingers, fused hip bones, pubis bones that don't meet in the middle, fused metatarsals, a first toe that points backward, and very short tails ending in a pygostyle.

If all those features appeared together at one point in the evolution of birds, it would be easy to say what is and what isn't a bird. But nature doesn't work like that. Different traits evolve at different points in the history of a lineage. This is true for the features listed above. Some are found in various avialians—modern and Mesozoic birds— but none are found in *all* the avialian groups other than Aves itself. In other words, birds started off very similar to their closest cousins, but gradually evolved new and distinctive features throughout the rest of the Mesozoic Era. This chapter deals with those Mesozoic birds and their evolution.

ARCHAEOPTERYX AND OTHER HANDY BIRDS

For a long time, the study of Mesozoic birds centered on *Archaeopteryx,* the oldest known member of Avialae. There is a good reason for this. Scientists have known about it since the 1860s. It was the first fossil discovered that showed the impressions of feathers. And there are several good skeletons of it that have been found (although some people think a few of these skeletons represent different species).

But *Archaeopteryx* is just one—okay, some people say as many as three, but I think probably one—species. Today we know of a lot more Mesozoic birds than just *Archaeopteryx.* Still, it is an important species, so we should take a closer look at it.

All *Archaeopteryx* fossils found so far are from southern Germany. They are from Late Jurassic rocks called the Solnhofen Formation. These rocks are made of limestone that settled in the warm, shallow seas and lagoons that covered much of Late Jurassic Europe. There was no oxygen at the bottom of these seas and lagoons, so worms and other creatures that could disturb the bodies of dead animals settled there couldn't survive. Because of this, impressions of soft tissues, like the wing skin of pterosaurs and the feathers of *Archaeopteryx,* are often preserved.

Archaeopteryx was a crow-size dinosaur, about 23.6 inches (60 centimeters) from the tip of its toothy snout to the end of its bony tail. Its jaws had small, pointy teeth at the front rather than a beak. Its brain was about the same size as that of deinonychosaurs and oviraptorosaurs. Its wrist and palm bones were unfused, and its fingers were long and ended in very sharp claws. The hip bones of *Archaeopteryx* were unfused, and the pubis bones met together at the tip. Its metatarsals were unfused, and it isn't entirely certain if the first toe pointed backward. Its tail had fewer bones than in most deinonychosaurs, but it did not have a pygostyle.

How can we tell that *Archaeopteryx* was really a bird? Honestly, at present it is difficult to know for certain that it *was* a bird! With the discovery of primitive deinonychosaurs like *Rahonavis* and *Microraptor,* we know that many features that were once only known in *Archaeopteryx* and other avialians were found in raptors, too. For example,

The Early Cretaceous Chinese bird *Confuciusornis.*

Archaeopteryx has long feathers on its arms and legs, but so do raptors. Raptors also have a first toe at the bottom of their feet. Many paleontologists agree that *Archaeopteryx* could fly—although nowhere near as well as modern birds—but small primitive raptors seem to have had just as many adaptations to flight as this avialian.

Right now, there are only a couple of details of the braincase, a small number of teeth at the front of the jaw, a small number of tail vertebrae, and a possibly backward-pointing first toe that show that *Archaeopteryx* is more closely related to modern birds than are primitive raptor dinosaurs. I wouldn't be surprised if future discoveries showed that the species in Deinonychosauria are really more closely related to Aves than is *Archaeopteryx*.

Archaeopteryx had a poorly developed breastbone and arms that weren't particularly well adapted to flight, so it was at best a lousy flier. Like other maniraptorans, it likely used its feathered arms for wing-assisted incline running. In terms of its skeleton, it is very similar to other small coelurosaurs (such as *Microraptor* or *Mei*), and like them, it may have hunted mostly on the ground. The diet of *Archaeopteryx* is uncertain, but the sharp teeth suggest that it might have eaten fish, small land vertebrates, and maybe insects. Since pterosaurs are very common in the same rocks as *Archaeopteryx*, I suspect that this little dinosaur may have hunted small flying reptiles when they landed.

The next branch on the family tree of early birds is the little dinosaur *Jeholornis* (and the closely related—if not identical—*Shenzhouraptor* and *Jixiangornis*). *Jeholornis* is also the oldest and most primitive bird known to have been a plant-eater. *Jeholornis* is a turkey-size long-tailed bird from the Early Cretaceous of China. The belly of one specimen contains fifty or so small seeds, so it ate plants at least some of the time. In many ways, it was similar to *Archaeopteryx*. Its fingers still had claws, and its tail had individual bones instead of a pygostyle. But *Jeholornis*'s breastbone was well developed, as were its shoulder bones. So it may not have been as good a flier as modern birds, but it was probably better than its Jurassic relative.

Many species of birds are known from the Early Cretaceous of China. The most numerous is *Confuciusornis,* of which thousands of skeletons have been discovered. This bird had a toothless beak, and may have been a seed-eater or a fruit-eater. It, like all later birds, had a true pygostyle. But the breastbone of *Confuciusornis* had only a very small keel, and its hand bones and metatarsals were still unfused. In fact, its big, three-fingered hands still look a lot like the hands of deinonychosaurs or oviraptorosaurs, and it could probably use them to hold on to branches or food.

One interesting feature about *Confuciusornis* is that some of the adults have a pair of long tail feathers. Many adults, however, did not. This might mean that the long tail feathers were only found in males, and that they used them to show off to potential mates, like peacocks do today.

ENANTIORNITHES AND PATAGOPTERYX

Most of the Early Cretaceous birds belong to a more advanced group of birds called Enantiornithes, or "opposite birds." Indeed, enantiornithines are the most common group of Cretaceous birds in the world. There are dozens of species already known, and even more are currently being described by paleontologists. Enantiornithines first appeared near the beginning of the Cretaceous and lived until the very end of that period. They have been found on every continent.

Enantiornithines resemble avians in having partially fused hand bones, partially fused metatarsals, a keeled breastbone, and extra hip vertebrae. A few enantiornithines still have a claw on one or two fingers. All enantiornithines share particular details of shoulder, palm, and shinbone shape.

Enantiornithines include many different-size species with many different habits and habitats. The smallest were the size of sparrows, but the largest had wingspans of about 40 inches (102 centimeters). There were short-snouted forms that may have eaten bugs or plants, long-snouted ones that probed for water invertebrates, other long-snouted ones that caught fish, and even possibly flesh-eating species. Most members of Enantior-

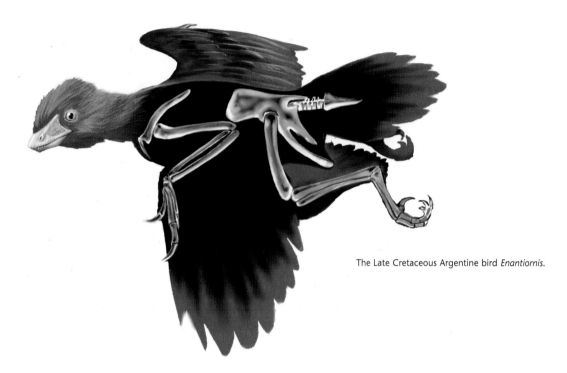

The Late Cretaceous Argentine bird *Enantiornis*.

nithes had teeth, but a few had toothless beaks. Some lived in lakes, some in forests, and some have been found in ancient deserts. These birds were probably very good fliers compared to more primitive species.

But just as there are today many species of flightless birds, there were also Cretaceous birds that lost the ability to fly. One is *Patagopteryx.* This species is from the Late Cretaceous of Argentina and stood about 20 inches (50 centimeters) high. Like modern ostriches and kiwis, it had ancestors that could fly. But *Patagopteryx*'s wings were far too small, so it could only run. It is more similar to Aves than were enantiornithines, in that its palm bones, metatarsals, and hip bones are completely fused (although not all together!), and its pubis bones do not meet in the middle.

SEABIRDS OF THE CRETACEOUS

There are a great many species of birds today that live near and feed in the sea. There are gulls that catch fish near the surface and scavenge on the shores, pelicans that use their enormous pouches to capture fish, albatrosses and frigate birds that fly way out over the oceans looking for food, boobies and gannets that dive deep into the water to

catch their prey, and many others. Some seabirds, like penguins, have even lost their ability to fly and have evolved into fast-swimming predators.

The Cretaceous oceans were also full of tasty food for birds that could catch it, and there were a couple of groups of seabirds that evolved at this time. Unlike today's seabirds, the Cretaceous ones were not members of Aves proper. Still, they were more closely related to the species in Aves than all the Mesozoic birds we've seen so far. For example,

The Late Cretaceous flightless Argentine bird *Patagopteryx*.

169

they have fewer vertebrae in the back, and more vertebrae in the hips, than other avialians.

These Mesozoic marine avialians still had teeth to capture fish and squid. Some—such as *Ichthyornis* and *Iaceornis*—were good fliers. They probably swooped over the water and grabbed small fish to eat. These birds were the size of modern terns, about 10 inches (25.4 centimeters) or so long.

Bigger, and more unusual, were the members of Hesperornithes, or "western birds." These were birds that swam after fish and squid, using their feet to propel themselves through the water like modern loons, grebes, and flightless cormorants. In fact, at least some hesperornithines had extremely reduced wings. In *Hesperornis* and *Baptornis,* the hand and forearm parts of the wing had been entirely lost. Hesperornithines ranged in size from that of a duck to nearly 6 feet (1.8 meters) long. They have been found in Europe, Asia, and North America, and possible hesperornithines are known from Antarctica and South America. Most lived in the seas, but some species lived in lakes and streams. Like all birds, they would have had to lay their eggs on land, but they could probably only waddle around at best. They would have spent most of their time in the water, like many of today's species of penguins.

Incidentally, some people mistakenly think that marine reptiles like plesiosaurs and ichthyosaurs were "seagoing dinosaurs." Others say that there were no marine dinosaurs. Both groups of people are wrong! It is true that plesiosaurs and ichthyosaurs were not types of dinosaurs—that is, they weren't descendants of the most recent common ancestor of *Iguanodon* and *Megalosaurus.* But hesperornithines *were* descendants of that ancestor. So they really were a type of seagoing dinosaur. In fact, they are the only Mesozoic dinosaurs we know of that were adapted to life in the water.

MODERN BIRDS IN THE MESOZOIC

The species in Aves proper have toothless beaks, and many of their skull bones are fused together. They have the most complex air-sac chambers in their skulls, vertebrae, and limb bones of all

dinosaurs. There are also features of vertebrae and limb bones that allow us to distinguish a member of Aves from other avialians.

Although I use the nickname "modern birds" for Aves, I don't want to confuse you. Perhaps "modern-style birds" is better, because members of this group actually go all the way back into the Mesozoic Era. The oldest definite modern-style birds are from the beginning of the Late Cretaceous Epoch, although there are some Early Cretaceous Chinese forms that might be close relatives or even direct ancestors of Aves. Very few of the early modern bird species are known from more than a few bones, so it is difficult to say what their habits were like. They are found in many environments: at sea, in deserts, in lakes, in forests, and in between.

Some of these species might be early representatives of present-day groups. For example, there are paleontologists who argue that there are bones of Cretaceous albatrosses, petrels, loons, parrots, flamingos, ducks, and pheasants. But not all paleontologists agree, and it is likely that many of these fossils belong to now-extinct species of Aves. Even so, these fragmentary remains show that there was a fairly high diversity of modern-style birds around by the end of the Age of Dinosaurs.

And finally, I should offer an apology: if this book were a *really* thorough review of the diversity of dinosaurs, it should include a lot of details about modern birds. However, there are over 9,000 living bird species. If I gave each modern bird group the amount of space I give to the fossil dinosaur groups, this book would be about ten times as thick as it is now! Since you probably are reading this book because you are interested in Mesozoic dinosaurs (and I'm writing it for the same reason), I won't go into all those details. But when you get a chance, check out books about living birds. They are really interesting creatures! And remember, they are just as much dinosaurs as are *Triceratops, Saltasaurus,* and *Tyrannosaurus*!

Opposite: *Hesperornis*, a flightless diving bird of the Late Cretaceous seas of Kansas, was one of the few marine dinosaurs of the Mesozoic.

The Earliest Birds

Dr. Luis Chiappe
Natural History Museum of
Los Angeles County

The Mesozoic Era—the time of the dinosaurs—witnessed the first half of the evolutionary history of birds. The earliest bird was the 150-million-year-old Archaeopteryx, found in Germany. It was about the size of a seagull and had sharp teeth, wings with claws, and a long, bony tail. Although Archaeopteryx is the only known bird from the Jurassic Period, many other primitive birds have been discovered in slightly younger rocks.

Birds blossomed in many different shapes and sizes during the Early Cretaceous Epoch. Among the most primitive birds is the Chinese seed-eater Jeholornis. This 125-million-year-old bird still had a long, bony tail, but its wings looked more like those of modern birds.

Long-tailed birds were common during most of the Mesozoic Era, but the typical stumped tail of modern birds also evolved very early in their history. Another Chinese fossil bird, Sapeornis, lived at the same time as Jeholornis. This large, toothed bird had a stump at the end of its short tail. Its wings were proportionally much longer than those of Archaeopteryx and Jeholornis, which tells us that it was a good flier.

As the evolution of birds advanced, some forms no longer had the teeth found in their dinosaurian ancestors. The earliest toothless bird was Confuciusornis, found in rocks of the Early Cretaceous Epoch of China. The crow-size Confuciusornis is known from thousands of fossils. It probably used its beak to crush seeds.

Even more advanced than Confuciusornis are the Enantiornithes, a branch of birds that flew as gracefully as today's birds. The Enantiornithes also had many different eating habits. This we know from their variety of skulls and beaks, as well as from fossilized gut contents found in some fossils. The different kinds of Enantiornithes ate such things as seeds, insects, tree sap, and crustaceans. We also know that the earliest Enantiornithes were small—only about the size of a common songbird. Later Enantiornithes were much larger. By the end of the Mesozoic Era, some of these birds had reached the size of a turkey vulture.

By the end of the Age of Dinosaurs, birds existed in many forms and had many different lifestyles. A form of large, flightless bird, best represented by Hesperornis, first appeared around 100 million years ago. They were excellent divers and used their long toothed jaws to snatch fish underwater. They shared the shorelines with Ichthyornis, a much smaller flying bird that also fed on fish.

By the end of the Mesozoic Era, the diversity of birds had grown dramatically. About the time of the demise of the last dinosaurs, evidence begins to appear of a new group of birds, one that in due course led to the colorful varieties that fly all around us today.

Another view of the Late Cretaceous Argentine bird *Enantiornis*.

The Origin of Flight in Birds

Dr. Kevin Padian
University of California, Berkeley

What makes a bird able to fly? The simple answer is a pair of feathered wings that can be flapped. But wings would be of no use if a bird didn't also have a smart brain and physical endurance to keep it aloft.

Birds make flying look easy, but how did this ability originate?

Feathers first evolved in dinosaurs that were the ancestors of the first birds. Some kinds of small carnivorous dinosaurs had a hairlike covering all over their bodies. Other kinds had real feathers on their hands and along their tails. These feathers were very much like those of today's birds. Some were probably colored with a banded pattern. Maybe these colors helped them recognize others of their species, attract mates, or even camouflage themselves from predators. Feathers may have also helped a parent dinosaur provide cover for its nest of eggs.

The small dinosaurs most closely related to birds had feathers on their arms. Over millions of years, these feather-covered arms evolved into wings.

Why did feathers help form wings when they were already doing other things? Feathers probably helped bird ancestors move better. If these animals lived in trees, feathers might have slowed a fall or jump. If these bird ancestors lived on the ground, the feathers might have given them a little lift as they ran and jumped over objects.

Landing softly from a tree or jumping over obstacles on the ground is not the same as flying. For flight, a bird uses a motion of the wing called the flight stroke. The flight stroke begins with a down-and-forward motion of the wings followed by an up-and-backward motion that brings the wing back for the next stroke. As the wing cuts through the air, it creates a wake of air that propels the bird forward.

Flapping the wings requires a large amount of energy. Most of this energy comes from the action of the bird's wrist. The wrist joint is round, and it swings the hand in a half circle. You can see the wrist joint at the base of the pointy end of a chicken wing (the hand bones). It's the joint to which the flight feathers attach.

Other than birds, the only animals that have ever had this rounded wrist joint were the small carnivorous dinosaurs most closely related to birds.

What were these dinosaurs doing with this joint if they didn't fly? It seems that they were able to whip the hands forward as they chased down and grabbed prey. If they made such motions in the air while running after prey—or away from predators—there could well have been an aerodynamic advantage that lifted them in the air or moved them faster along the ground.

There is much more to learn about the origin of flight in birds, but we have a lot of the pieces of the puzzle in the skeletons of the small dinosaurs most closely related to them.

The Late Cretaceous American seabird Ichthyornis.

Riojasaurus

Plateosaurus

Massospondylus

22

PROSAUROPODS
(Primitive Long-Necked Plant-Eating Dinosaurs)

Some of the oldest dinosaurs, and among the first to be discovered, are the primitive prosauropods. These were long-necked plant-eaters from the Late Triassic and Early Jurassic epochs. At the beginning of the Age of Dinosaurs, the prosauropods were the most common big plant-eaters. In fact, they were the first dinosaur group to become major players in their ecological community. While the first theropods (meat-eaters) were tiny compared to other Late Triassic predators, and ornithischians (bird-hipped dinosaurs) were rare, the prosauropods were the largest and most common herbivores in their habitats.

All long-necked plant-eating saurischian dinosaurs are grouped together in Sauropodomorpha (sauropod forms). The most famous sauropodomorphs are the enormous species found in Sauropoda (lizard feet), the largest dinosaurs of all time and the largest animals ever to live on land. But there are other sauropodomorphs that are more primitive than the sauropods. The exact relationships among these early primitive sauropodomorphs are uncertain. For simplicity's sake, I'm calling *all* these early forms "prosauropods": it's easier than saying the more accurate "primitive sauropodomorphs." But understand that the cladogram shown on pages 74–75 is only one possible arrangement for these dinosaurs. In some cladistic analyses, they are all clustered into a single clade called Prosauropoda (before the sauropods). But other analyses show that some primitive sauropodomorphs are closer to Sauropoda. And still other studies show that many are each other's closest relatives (Prosauropoda

proper), but that some—such as *Saturnalia, Efraasia,* and *Thecodontosaurus*—branched off the family tree prior to the Prosauropoda-Sauropoda split. Yes, this is all confusing, even to paleontologists! More work definitely needs to be done on prosauropod history.

FIRST DISCOVERIES OF EARLY DINOSAURS

In 1836, medical doctor Henry Riley and geologist Samuel Stutchbury discovered various fossilized reptile bones and teeth in Bristol, England. They thought they had found a new species of extinct lizard. Because its teeth were set in sockets (like the teeth of mammals or crocodiles) and not just attached to the top or insides of the jaws (as with most lizards), they named it *Thecodontosaurus* (socket-toothed reptile). Later discoveries showed that all dinosaur teeth were set in sockets, so this name isn't particularly descriptive. And, in fact, the animal they discovered didn't *look* like a lizard

The Late Triassic prosauropod *Plateosaurus* of Europe, with a close-up of its hand (right).

MIXED-UP MONSTERS

Additional specimens of *Plateosaurus* and other prosauropods were later found in Germany. These included much more of the skeleton than the fossils studied by von Meyer. In fact, paleontologists eventually discovered many complete *Plateosaurus* skeletons, so now it is one of the few dinosaurs of which we know every bone in the body. It is because of these *Plateosaurus* skeletons that we know *a lot* about the anatomy of prosauropods as a group.

But between von Meyer's first specimen and the discovery of a complete *Plateosaurus* specimen, a paleontological mix-up happened. Some *Plateosaurus* bones were found along with skull bones and teeth from meat-eating reptiles, and a few paleontologists thought that these were the skull bones and teeth of the prosauropods. A picture began to emerge in the late nineteenth and early twentieth centuries of a weird-looking creature with a long neck, a heavy body, big clawed hands and feet, and a head full of sharp teeth. This creature was given the name *Teratosaurus* (monster reptile) and was thought by some to be the link between carnivorous dinosaurs and sauropodomorphs.

In reality, this was just a badly mixed-up monster! In the 1980s, paleontologists José Bonaparte, Michael J. Benton, and Peter M. Galton recognized that *Teratosaurus*'s skull and teeth belonged to a giant predatory relative of the crocodiles. That animal, which kept the name *Teratosaurus,* was fairly short-necked. It was an interesting animal and the top predator of its time, but it *wasn't* a dinosaur. The rest of the skeleton of *"Teratosaurus"* was from real prosauropods. The paleontologists had mixed up the predator and its prey!

Thankfully, later discoveries of more-complete fossils allowed paleontologists to figure out what an actual prosauropod looked like. And once the scientists understood that, they could begin to determine how prosauropods lived, what they ate, and what happened to them.

at all! Later fossils would show that *Thecodontosaurus* was an 8-foot (2.4-meter) bipedal dinosaur with a small head, a long neck, grasping hands at the end of long arms, and a long tail. It was a small, primitive prosauropod.

The next prosauropod discovery occurred a year later, in Nuremberg, Germany. A medical doctor named Johann Friedrich Engelhardt found some large fossil bones, and he brought them to paleontologist Christian Erich Hermann von Meyer. Von Meyer recognized that these were unlike the bones of any reptile, living or extinct, known to science. Although only a few parts of the body were known (some skull bones, leg bones, back bones, and others), he was able to tell from the shape of the thighbone that this animal's legs were held directly underneath the body, like those of *Megalosaurus* and *Iguanodon* (both of which had been discovered). But the shape of this thighbone was different from either *Megalosaurus*'s or *Iguanodon*'s. Because this new animal seemed to be bigger than an ox, and maybe as big as a hippo or rhino, von Meyer named it *Plateosaurus,* "broad reptile."

* * *

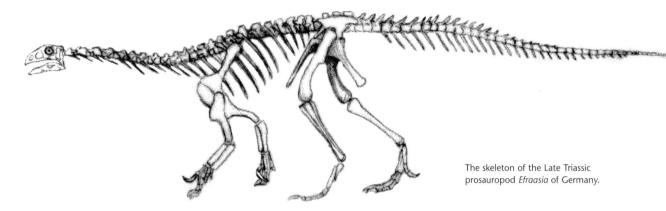

The skeleton of the Late Triassic prosauropod *Efraasia* of Germany.

PROSAUROPODS— THE *REAL* PICTURE

Prosauropods ranged in size from about 6 feet (1.8 meters) up to 33 feet (10.1 meters). They were the first group of dinosaurs to really become big. In fact, the biggest ones may have been the first land animals on Earth to weigh more than one to two tons.

Compared to the heads of most dinosaurs (except for the sauropods), prosauropod heads seemed small in relation to their body size. Their skulls had leaf-shaped teeth with big bumps (denticles) along the sides. This sort of tooth is found in most plant-eating reptiles, and it shows us that these dinosaurs ate mostly plants. The row of teeth in the lower jaw fit entirely within the row of teeth in the upper jaw, giving them what I call the "wraparound overbite." Many types of dinosaurs had this sort of arrangement. When the prosauropod closed its jaws, the teeth would act something like scissors, slicing up the plants it was biting. Compared to the skulls of sauropods, those of prosauropods look fairly long. In fact, they look a

lot like the skulls of primitive saurischians like *Eoraptor*. That isn't too surprising because prosauropods hadn't evolved much since the days of the first primitive saurischians.

Prosauropods tended to have long, flexible necks, and their bodies were fairly heavy. They were not built for speed. The proportions of their front and hind limbs fell somewhere between those of dinosaurs that were strictly bipedal (like theropods and primitive ornithopods) and those that were strictly quadrupedal (like sauropods). This suggests that prosauropods could walk on four legs when they were moving slowly and on two when they wanted to run. Counterbalancing their heavy front end was a long tail.

One important thing about the hands of prosauropods is their thumb. Like primitive theropods, prosauropods had a great big thumb claw. They probably didn't use it to tear into meat (unless some were omnivores rather than strict herbivores). And they couldn't use it to rip into fruit because prosauropods died out long before the first fruit had evolved. Perhaps they used it to

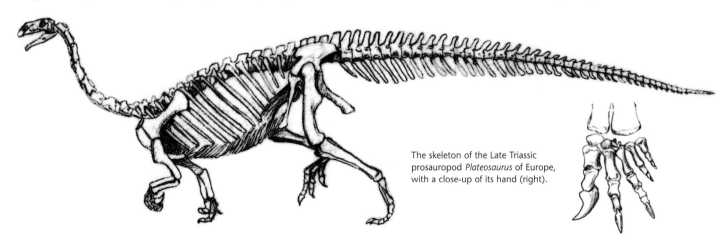

The skeleton of the Late Triassic prosauropod *Plateosaurus* of Europe, with a close-up of its hand (right).

177

Prosauropod heads: Late Triassic *Plateosaurus* (top) and Early Jurassic *Massospondylus* (bottom).

break open other kinds of plants or to defend themselves from attackers. Whatever the case, it probably served one or more important functions because all known prosauropod species had a big thumb claw.

In addition to whatever it was they were doing with their thumbs, prosauropods retained the grasping function that we see in the hands of most primitive dinosaurs. But their hands were also pretty broad, and they could stretch their fingers out in such a way that they could walk on their palms. There are good prosauropod fossil trackways that show that they did walk like this, at least occasionally.

Prosauropods were "all-purpose" dinosaurs. They could walk on just two legs or all four. They could feed near the ground or up high. And some paleontologists have suggested that they may have even eaten some meat, although there is no strong evidence for this at present. There is one thing that definitely sets prosauropods apart from their contemporaries, though: they got tall!

THE BENEFITS OF BEING TALL

If you look at the other creatures in the world of the Late Triassic, you'll notice that most of them are built low to the ground. Some were big four-legged animals, including predators like *Teratosaurus* or herbivores like the armored croc relatives called aetosaurs or the two-tusked dicyn-

odonts. Others were two-legged but pretty small, like early ornithischians and theropods. Prosauropods, on the other hand, had very long necks. And they could stand on their hind legs to reach even higher.

What advantages are there to being tall? The first one is food. A tall animal can reach food that short ones can't, like leaves on trees. Aetosaurs and dicynodonts—the main potential rivals of the prosauropods—were low-built, heavy plant-eaters. They could eat shrubs, bushes, and ferns, but they couldn't get to the leaves of trees unless the tree fell over. Prosauropods could stick their necks up to munch on those leaves. And their only competition for that would be tiny herbivores such as early mammals, which could climb, and (most importantly) other prosauropods.

Another advantage to having a long neck is being able to see farther. There is a reason that lookouts always go to the top of boats, castles, and lighthouses. The higher up you are, the fewer things will block your view and the longer distance you can see. A prosauropod with its neck up could spot a tasty plant—or an approaching predator—far before a smaller rival could.

Over time, several species of the prosauropod family became taller and taller, and it would have become harder for them to walk on just their hind

Prosauropods may have used their large thumb claws in combat against each other, like modern roosters do with their spurs.

A debate remains as to whether some prosauropods were strictly bipedal or walked both on all fours and on two legs as conditions required.

legs. The very largest prosauropods probably walked on four legs and reared up just to feed. Their descendants, the Sauropoda, were permanent quadrupeds. I'll discuss those giant dinosaurs over the next few chapters.

EARLY LONG-NECKS AROUND THE WORLD

When the prosauropods were alive, the world was basically one place. All the continents had come together to form the supercontinent Pangaea. So it

The Late Triassic prosauropod *Saturnalia* of Brazil is among the most primitive sauropodomorphs known.

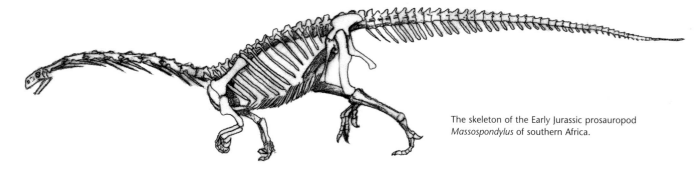

The skeleton of the Early Jurassic prosauropod *Massospondylus* of southern Africa.

shouldn't be too surprising that prosauropods are found all over the world, and that similar species are often found in places that today are very far apart.

Many excellent prosauropod skeletons have been found in South America. The small (6-foot [1.8-meter]), very primitive form *Saturnalia* and the later and larger *Unaysaurus* are known from Brazil. From Argentina come medium-size *Coloradisaurus,* the giants *Lessemsaurus* and *Riojasaurus,* and small *Mussaurus.* The last one, whose name means "mouse reptile," was first known from the skeleton of a little baby dinosaur. *Mussaurus* babies (and other baby prosauropods) had short faces with big eyes, while the adults had longer snouts.

North America, on the other hand, has not yielded many prosauropod fossil finds. The best are two small forms from New England: *Ammosaurus* and *Anchisaurus.*

European prosauropods include some of the most famous, especially *Thecodontosaurus, Plateosaurus,* and *Sellosaurus.* These three are among the best studied of the entire group because many skeletons are now known of each type.

The countries of southern Africa are some of the best spots in the world to find terrestrial rocks dating from the Late Triassic and Early Jurassic. It is no surprise that we have a lot of good prosauropod fossils from there. These include *Massospondylus* (known from at least eighty individuals) and the giants *Melanorosaurus* and *Euskelosaurus.*

Probably the best place in the world to find prosauropods, however, is in China. At present, there are at least five different species of these dinosaurs known from good skeletons in China. Incomplete specimens might yield a few more.

These range from little 7.5-foot (2.3-meter) *Gyposaurus* to nearly 30-foot (9.1-meter) *Yimenosaurus.*

END OF THE ALL-PURPOSE DINOSAURS

If prosauropods were so successful, why are they only found at the beginning of dinosaur history? It seems likely that their success was in fact their downfall.

Prosauropods could do lots of things moderately well. They were able to grow fairly big; they could stand tall or feed low; they could be bipeds or quadrupeds; and they might even have been able to eat meat. But unlike other groups of dinosaurs, they didn't do any one of these things *really* well.

During the Late Triassic, the prosauropods didn't have any serious competition, except for other prosauropods. But by the very end of the Late Triassic, that competition had produced a new sort of sauropodomorph. One branch of the "prosauropods" had evolved into the true Sauropoda. These more advanced forms could reach higher and bite better and were safer from predators because of their gigantic size.

In the Early Jurassic, the ornithischians were also becoming more advanced. The ornithopods evolved more complex jaws than the prosauropods. The thyreophorans evolved body armor that made them better protected from attack than their long-necked distant cousins.

So the prosauropods had gone from being the most advanced herbivores for most of the Late Triassic to one of the most primitive to survive into the Early Jurassic. To make matters worse, the new Jurassic meat-eating dinosaurs were more advanced predators than the croc relatives and the small theropods of the Triassic. By the time the Middle Jurassic arrived, the prosauropods had died out.

The prosauropods left an important legacy, though. Of course they left many bones and foot-prints and even some eggs as fossils. But they also left behind their descendants—the sauropods. And those descendants evolved into some of the most awesome creatures ever to exist in the history of the Earth.

Plateosaurus defends itself from attacking coelophysoids.

Omeisaurus

Isanosaurus

Shunosaurus

23

PRIMITIVE SAUROPODS
(Early Giant Long-Necked Dinosaurs)

The largest dinosaurs belong to a group called Sauropoda. These were immense long-necked, four-legged plant-eaters. All sauropods were big as adults. (The smallest adults were bigger than elephants, which are the largest animals on land today.) Some grew up to 115 feet (35 meters) long, longer than the longest whales. The heaviest weighed 100 tons, as much as a *herd* of elephants! Sauropods dwarfed the other land animals that lived before and after them. They even dwarfed their contemporaries, the other dinosaurs! Only the very largest ornithischians (bird-hipped plant-eaters) and theropods (meat-eaters) were as big as the smallest sauropod.

Not only were sauropods giants, they also survived for a long time. The first sauropods appeared right before the end of the Triassic Period, about 205 million years ago. And the last sauropods died out at the great extinction 65.5 million years ago. That means sauropods roamed the Earth for around 140 million years. In comparison, ceratopsids (the true horned dinosaurs) were around for about 20 million years, only one-seventh as long. Sauropod fossils have been found on all continents except Antarctica (and they were almost certainly there, too).

Sauropoda is a group within the larger category of herbivorous saurischian dinosaurs called Sauropodomorpha. You read about the earlier sauropodomorphs—the prosauropods—in the previous chapter. The true sauropods inherited from their prosauropod ancestors a small head, a long neck, and a heavy body with a big gut for digesting plants. But unlike most prosauropods, the sauropods couldn't walk on just their hind legs. They weighed too much and had to walk on all fours. They were quadrupeds.

The name Sauropoda is unfortunate. It means "lizard feet," but the only thing sauropod feet have in common with lizard feet is they both have five toes. That is one more toe than on most dinosaur feet (which normally have only four), and it *is* the same as on lizard feet. But it is also the same as on crocodile feet, or opossum feet, or human feet! Other names have been proposed for this group (such as Cetiosauria and Opisthocoelia), but they never really caught on. So we call them "sauropods" and ignore the fact that their feet are no more like lizard feet than are yours and mine.

Sauropods are very distinctive, and they don't look like anything alive today. They all had a small head, a long neck, a huge body on four legs, and a long tail. The basic shape always stayed the same.

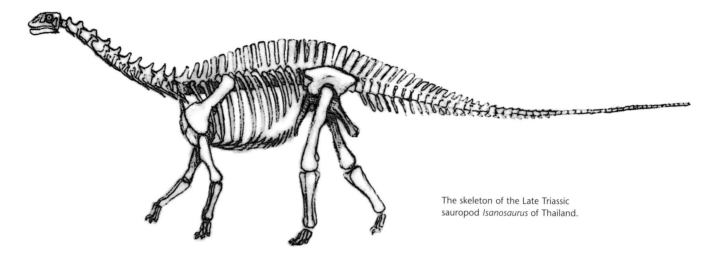

The skeleton of the Late Triassic sauropod *Isanosaurus* of Thailand.

Nevertheless, there were a lot of differences among the various sauropods—enough to justify devoting three chapters of this book to them!

This chapter covers the origin of the sauropods and the early members of the group. The bigger and more famous advanced sauropods—the whip-tailed diplodocoids and big-nosed macronarians—are covered in the next two chapters.

WHALE CROCS? FLIGHTLESS PTERODACTYLS? NO, GIANT DINOSAURS!

For the past hundred years or so, sauropods have been one of the most familiar of all types of dinosaurs. In fact, if you ask people to draw a dinosaur, half of them will probably draw a sauropod.

That wasn't always the case. When Sir Richard Owen named Dinosauria in 1842, neither he nor anyone else had a clue that sauropods existed. But it wasn't because nobody had found sauropod fossils. Plenty of them had been discovered. In fact, Owen had already discovered and described some of them himself. But he didn't know what kind of animal the fossils were from.

The sauropod fossils that Owen had found in England included leg bones and vertebrae. The vertebrae in particular reminded him of crocodilians. But these bones were immense—far larger than any modern crocodilian. They were the size of whale vertebrae. So Owen proposed that they were the bones of a giant seagoing crocodile that

he named *Cetiosaurus* (whale reptile) in 1841. The idea of a giant "whale croc" isn't as crazy as it sounds. Jurassic fossils of much smaller sea-living crocodilians were known since the 1810s. Some had even been found in the same rocks as the *Cetiosaurus* fossils.

Paleontologist Harry G. Seeley unknowingly described other English sauropod vertebrae in 1870. Because they were full of hollow chambers, like the vertebrae of birds and pterosaurs (flying reptiles), he named them *Ornithopsis* (bird-looking). Seeley suggested that these were the vertebrae of pterodactyls (a type of pterosaur). Because these back bones were far, far larger than those of any known pterodactyl, he hypothesized that they must have been from a giant pterosaur that had lost the ability to fly. Again, this isn't a terribly bad idea. There are many types of large birds—like today's ostriches and emus, and the recently extinct moas and elephant birds—that lost the ability to fly. But no one has ever found the remains of a flightless pterodactyl, especially not one bigger than an elephant!

At the same time Seeley was describing *Ornithopsis,* other paleontologists were beginning to suggest that *Cetiosaurus* and similar remains were actually from some giant dinosaur—one "even bigger than *Iguanodon* and *Megalosaurus!*" (From today's point of view, that almost sounds silly. Nobody considers *Iguanodon* or *Megalosaurus* to be big dinosaurs anymore.) And yet still no one had a good idea of what these animals looked like.

It took discoveries in the United States to figure this out. Fossils found in the 1870s, like *Camarasaurus,* described by Edward Drinker Cope, and *Diplodocus* and *Apatosaurus,* named by Othniel Charles Marsh, showed the world what complete skeletons of these dinosaurs were like.

BABY FACES WITH THE RIGHT BITE

Sauropods look something like giant prosauropods, which in a sense is what they were. The smallest sauropods were about the same size as the biggest prosauropods, 26 to 33 feet (8 to 10.1 meters) long. And like the biggest prosauropods, even the smallest sauropods were stuck walking on all fours.

If you examined their faces, though, you would begin to see some differences. Sauropod faces don't look a lot like prosauropod faces. Or rather, they aren't that much like *adult* prosauropod faces. They *do* resemble those of baby prosauropods, though.

In baby prosauropod skulls, the snout is very short, especially compared to an adult prosauropod. And from above, the shape of the baby's snout is more round than pointed. Also, the jaw joint doesn't extend as far back in a baby prosauropod skull as in an adult's. Sauropods (both babies and adults) have skulls that are a lot more like newly hatched prosauropods than grown-up ones. So in a sense, sauropods are baby-faced.

But sauropods have some advanced skull features, too. In more primitive dinosaurs, including prosauropods, there is a "wraparound overbite." The prosauropod lower jaw fits entirely within the tooth row of the upper jaw. When a prosauropod closed its jaws, the teeth from the upper jaw would shear past those of the lower jaw, giving them a scissor-like action.

In sauropods, there was no overbite. Instead, when a sauropod closed its mouth, the tips of the upper teeth met the tips of the lower teeth, like the bite of a mammal. This gave them a more advanced, precise bite, and they could be choosier about what they ate.

Sauropod teeth were different, too. Instead of

Isanosaurus feeding.

the broad leaf-shaped teeth of prosauropods and most ornithischians, the teeth of primitive sauropods were spoon-shaped. These big, fat spoon-shaped teeth were useful for chomping through twigs and branches, so the sauropods could bite off the best bits (the leaves, for instance).

BEING BIG

The prosauropods had an advantage over other plant-eaters in their world. They could feed higher than everyone else. Sauropods took that advantage to an extreme. By the Middle Jurassic, there were already some sauropods—like *Omeisaurus*—that could munch on leaves 33 feet (10.1 meters) above the forest floor just by reaching their necks up. That's about as high as a three-story building!

185

The sauropods' giant size also gave them extra protection against predators. So as the primitive predators of the Late Triassic and Early Jurassic (including coelophysoids like *Coelophysis* and *Dilophosaurus*) gave way to the advanced predators of the Middle Jurassic (like *Monolophosaurus* and *Megalosaurus*) the giant sauropods survived where the prosauropods did not.

Sauropod necks were long. Unlike giraffes, which have the same number of neck bones as other mammals, sauropods had many extra neck vertebrae. Typical dinosaurs had nine or ten neck bones, but sauropods had twelve to seventeen. These necks were not as heavy as they might appear, however. Sauropod vertebrae—especially in the neck area—had lots of hollow chambers. Based on comparisons with living birds and with fossils of theropod dinosaurs, we can predict that these spaces were filled with the complex air sacs that modern birds have. Living birds use their air sacs for several different things. The sacs help them pump air through the lungs. They help birds keep their body temperatures down while exerting themselves. And they make the birds lighter than they otherwise would be. Sauropods probably used their air sacs for all these purposes.

The limb bones of sauropods are heavy but relatively slender. They don't have big, complex muscle attachments, like the limb bones of some big mammals, like rhinos, or of big theropods. Most sauropods had long forelimbs and even longer hind limbs. Sauropod feet were short and squat, with a very large claw on the first toe. Sauropod hand skeletons looked like their foot skeletons, but when the flesh was on them, the hands did *not* look like their feet! We know this from trackways. The feet of sauropods had a big oval pad of fat underneath them, making them something like elephant feet. Their footprints are shaped like an oval. But trackways of their hand-

The Late Triassic sauropod *Antetonitrus* of South Africa.

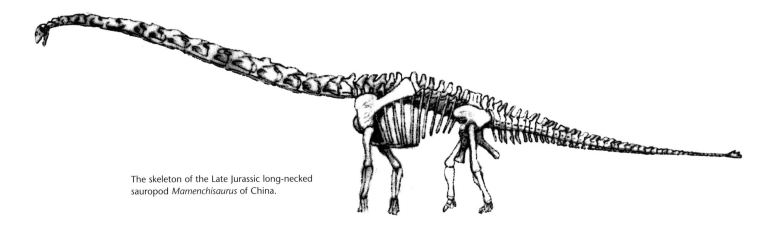

The skeleton of the Late Jurassic long-necked sauropod *Mamenchisaurus* of China.

prints show no fat pad underneath. Sauropod handprints are shaped like a horseshoe.

THE FIRST GIANTS

For a long time, there were no definite sauropods known from the Triassic. There was a dinosaur called *Blikanasaurus* from the Late Triassic of South Africa, but paleontologists are uncertain if it was a giant advanced prosauropod or a primitive sauropod. Discoveries from the 1990s and 2000s—in particular, *Isanosaurus* of Thailand and *Antetonitrus* of South Africa—prove that there were sauropods in the latest part of the Triassic Period, and now most paleontologists agree that *Blikanasaurus* is one of these. A word of caution, however: no good skulls are known for any of these Triassic sauropods. Therefore, it might be the case that the baby face and special bite appeared sometime after the sauropods evolved from the prosauropods.

Additional primitive sauropods are known from the Early Jurassic—*Vulcanodon* of Zimbabwe, *Gongxianosaurus* of China, *Kotasaurus* and *Barapasaurus* of India, and *Ohmdenosaurus* of Germany. These fossils show that sauropods were already living in many parts of the world, but at this time they were still outnumbered by their smaller primitive kin, the prosauropods.

That changed in the Middle Jurassic, however. The prosauropods had died out, probably outcompeted by more advanced dinosaurs, and sauropods became one of the two most common dinosaurs in their world. (Stegosaurs were the other most common type.) It was during this time

that *Cetiosaurus* of England lived, as well as *Patagosaurus* of Argentina. But most of the best fossils of Middle Jurassic sauropods come from China.

CHINESE LONG-NECKS

If you went back in time 165 million years ago to China, you would find two very different kinds of sauropods living side by side. Both of these are known from many good fossil skeletons, so we know a lot about them.

The smaller of the two was *Shunosaurus*. It was only about 40 feet (12.2 meters) long with a relatively short (for a sauropod) neck. It was a pretty typical early sauropod, but it had a club at the end of its tail, something like those of ankylosaurids. And like those tank dinosaurs, *Shunosaurus* probably used its club to bash at predators.

The larger, and more impressive, of the Middle Jurassic Chinese sauropods was *Omeisaurus*. It was around 56 feet (17.1 meters) long and had an enormously long (even for a sauropod) neck. It would have been able to feed much higher in the trees than *Shunosaurus*. In fact, these two relatives probably evolved so that they didn't eat each other's food, but instead specialized in feeding at their own level. We see the same sort of thing happening with modern related plant-eaters, where some feed on low-growing plants and others on higher-growing ones.

Omeisaurus wasn't the only superlong neck in China. In the Late Jurassic, there were two dinosaurs with even longer necks: *Euhelopus* and *Mamenchisaurus*. The latter dinosaur was very large. It grew to over 82 feet (25 meters) long, and its neck made up half that length. In fact, this is the longest neck of any animal (dinosaur or otherwise) known to science!

Why were the necks of Chinese dinosaurs so long? There isn't any evidence that the trees of Jurassic China were that much taller than in the rest of the world. Most likely, it was just the solution they evolved to the problem faced by all the big sauropods: how to reach even higher up into the trees. When there were lots of sauropods present, the largest species in each region tended to develop newer ways to get to leaves the "little" giants couldn't. Their necks were relatively light and easy to lift up high, and their heavy, round bodies kept them from toppling over. In the next two chapters, we'll see how other groups of sauropods evolved different solutions to reach especially high in the trees.

THE NEW SAUROPODS

The new sauropods, or Neosauropoda, eventually replaced the primitive sauropods. Neosauropods were different from their ancestors in that their hands were shaped like a column rather than being short and squat. Their teeth were all positioned at the front of the snout. And the bony openings for their nostrils were placed farther back on the face, toward the top of the head.

Neosauropods first appear in the Middle Jurassic, but they don't become common until the Late Jurassic. It is among these dinosaurs, which include the whip-tailed diplodocoids and the big-nosed macronarians, that we find the greatest diversity, the biggest sizes, and the most specializations. We'll see more about these neosauropods in the next two chapters.

Mamenchisaurus had one of the longest necks of any animal in the history of the Earth!

Survival of the Biggest: Adaptations of the Sauropods

Dr. Paul Upchurch
University of Cambridge

Sauropods were big—in fact, they are the largest known land animals. I'm nearly six feet tall, but when I stand next to the skeleton of Brachiosaurus, my head barely reaches its elbow! Sauropods ranged from 20 feet (6.1 meters) in length and weighing a couple of tons (such as Vulcanodon) to the gigantic Sauroposeidon and Argentinosaurus, which reached about 131 feet (40 meters) long and weighed 40 to 50 tons. In the Jurassic Period, when sauropods passed through your neighborhood, they would be very hard to miss!

But why were sauropods so large? And why did their size vary? One explanation concerns defense. There were some very big predators, such as Tyrannosaurus, in the times of the sauropods. Some sauropods were protected by having body armor, spikes, tails with clubs, or long whiplike tails that could be snapped at a hungry predator. But most sauropods did not have such protection. They relied on their large size to keep them safe. But there is a problem with this explanation for the large size of the sauropods—they had evolved into gigantic animals before there were many big predators around.

Another idea for explaining the size of the sauropods is that their large mass allowed them to maintain a warm body—and keep functioning—even through the night. Imagine a pebble and a boulder on a beach. The sun heats the pebble much faster than the boulder. After sunset, however, the boulder takes much longer to cool down than the pebble. The same effect is seen in animals. Provided the animal can keep its body at the preferred tem-

perature, all of its systems will work in the most efficient way. But if being large is so great, why haven't all animals become as big as sauropods? There may be another way to explain the gigantic size of the sauropods.

My favorite explanation for giant sauropods concerns food. First, most sauropods needed a long neck, a large body, and strong legs so that they could feed on leaves from the tops of trees. Second, the plants available to sauropods were rather tough and difficult to digest. Sauropods had to grind up the leaves in a special extra stomach (the gizzard) packed with stones. Then the food passed to the main stomach, where it stayed several days while it was slowly broken down. Small animals need energy very quickly, whereas larger ones can afford to digest over a longer period of time. If you want to eat tough leaves, you need to be big. This idea also explains why some of the last sauropods had evolved to a smaller size. Smaller sauropods may have given up eating treetop leaves, instead specializing on more nutritious plants close to the ground.

Sauropods may have become giants because it helped them feed on tough leaves from the tops of trees—something that most other dinosaurs could not do. Protection from predators and a constant body temperature were also important, but these were bonuses that came with their large size. Plants and climates have changed considerably since the Cretaceous Period—sadly, it is unlikely that anything quite like a sauropod will ever appear again.

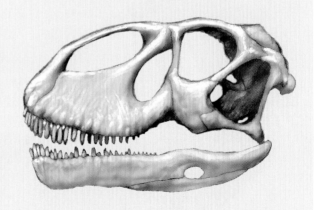

The skull of the Middle Jurassic Chinese sauropod Shunosaurus.

Apatosaurus

Amargasaurus

24

DIPLODOCOIDS (Whip-Tailed Giant Long-Necked Dinosaurs)

The largest dinosaurs, and the largest land animals of all time, are found in Sauropoda. These were enormous long-necked saurischian dinosaurs that walked on four legs. All sauropods were plant-eaters. The sauropod family tree contains various primitive species as well as two advanced groups: the whip-tailed Diplodocoidea and the big-nosed Macronaria. Macronaria is discussed in the next chapter. In this chapter, we'll look at Diplodocoidea, which includes the longest animals that have ever lived on land.

Diplodocoids first appeared in the Middle Jurassic Epoch and died out around the beginning of the Late Cretaceous Epoch. Their name comes from the genus *Diplodocus,* which means "double beam." It refers to the weird shape of the chevron bones (small bones that attach underneath the vertebrae of the tail). Unlike most dinosaur chevrons, these bones are split down the middle, so they have two shafts, or "beams."

PENCIL-SHAPED TEETH BUT NO SNORKELS

Double-beamed chevron bones can also be found in some other sauropods, but diplodocoids have many more specialized features that help us recognize them.

One specialization is their teeth. Primitive sauropods and most macronarian sauropods have spoon-shaped teeth. Diplodocoids, on the other hand (in the other mouth?), have pencil-shaped teeth. Actually, "crayon-shaped" might describe them better. Particularly if you imagine a crayon that has been used a lot so that the end is

blunt. Several paleontologists—especially Paul Upchurch and Paul Barrett from Great Britain, Jorge Calvo from Argentina, and Anthony Fiorillo from the United States—have studied how diplodocoids used their odd dentition. Based on microscopic scratches on the teeth, as well as the shape of diplodocoid skulls, these scientists have concluded that diplodocoids didn't bite leaves off branches. Instead, they raked their teeth along the branches and *pulled* off the leaves and needles.

Diplodocoid skulls are long, with a squared-off muzzle. They only had teeth at the very front of their snouts. Strangely, the openings in the skull for the nasal passages, or nares, are located at the top of the head, above the eyes. In most vertebrates—including humans—these openings are at the front of the skull, close to the fleshy nostril. But don't assume diplodocoids had fleshy nostrils on top of their heads. Recent work by paleontologist Larry Witmer shows that the nostrils in diplodocoids were *not* near the nares. Instead, as in most living animals, the fleshy nostrils would have been in the front of the snout, which makes

Whiplash! The long, slender tail of diplodocoids may have been a useful defense against attackers.

sense because that way they could sniff what they were eating! The air would flow into the nostril at the front of the snout, up through a tube of soft tissue on the face, then down the nares at the top of the head and into the windpipe.

For a long time, however, paleontologists thought that the diplodocoids' fleshy nostrils were on the very tops of their heads, and that they might have been used as snorkels. Why would a land animal need a snorkel? Many paleontologists between the mid-1800s and the 1970s thought that diplodocoids and other sauropods lived in the water. It was assumed that these dinosaurs were too big and heavy for their legs to support them on land, and that instead they were strictly aquatic! In the 1960s, Robert Bakker (then a student at Yale University) presented evidence showing that sauropods were actually far better adapted to life

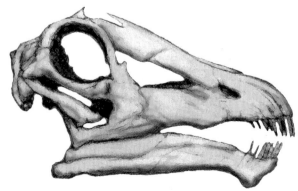

The long skull of *Diplodocus*.

on land. Their feet were compact and narrow compared to their body size, and not splayed out and wide like the feet of aquatic animals. Their rib cages were narrow, rather than round, and their legs were generally quite long. In fact, Bakker showed that sauropods were built more like giant land animals such as elephants and giraffes than like big aquatic animals such as crocodilians and hippos.

Back to those "snorkels." The idea was that most of the sauropod would be underwater with just the top of the head—where the nostrils were *thought* to be located—sticking out for it to breathe. In 1951, British paleontologist K. A. Kermack proved that the snorkeling hypothesis wouldn't work. The dinosaur's lungs would have been so deep in the water that not even its powerful muscles and bones could push hard enough for the animal to draw a breath. The water pressure would have simply killed it. These days, no one takes the idea of snorkeling sauropods seriously.

Diplodocoids differ from other sauropods in terms of their legs, too. Their front legs are much shorter than their hind legs, to a greater degree than in any of their relatives. Some paleontologists have suggested that this made them better at rearing up on their hind limbs. Because their front legs were shorter, their center of mass (or point of balance) would be just around the hips, and they could more easily rock back onto just their back legs. While they almost certainly were incapable of *walking* on two legs, they may have *stood* on two legs to feed higher in trees. Some paleontologists have suggested that they may have even taken a "tripod" pose, using their tails as a sort of third leg to support them. While this is difficult to test directly, there are some diplodocoid specimens with fused vertebrae at the spot where they might have used the tail as the third base of the tripod. Perhaps these bones fused because they had to support the massive weight of the dinosaurs?

WHIP TAILS

Diplodocoids are also characterized by long, whiplike tails. While the part of the tail near the hips of these dinosaurs was thick and deep like

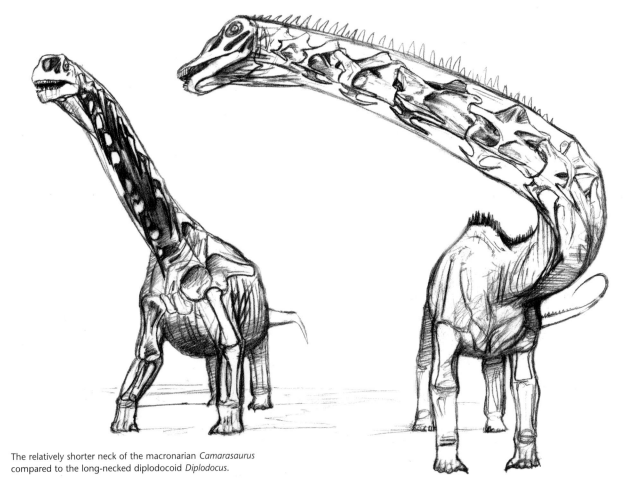

The relatively shorter neck of the macronarian *Camarasaurus* compared to the long-necked diplodocoid *Diplodocus*.

most sauropod tails, the rest of it was very narrow. And very, very long! In fact, these are the longest tails known to science. A very big diplodocoid such as a 115-foot (35-meter) *Diplodocus* would have had a 69-foot (21-meter) tail!

What were these tail whips used for? Well, an obvious idea is that they were actually used *as* whips. That is, diplodocoids may have used them to smack attacking theropods the way the (admittedly *much* smaller) monitor lizards of today use their tails to whack attackers. The blow from such a gigantic sauropod tail would likely have crushed bone and muscle. Indeed, a specimen of the predator *Allosaurus* on display at the Smithsonian Institution's National Museum of Natural History shows damage along its left jaw, left shoulder blade, and left ribs that might be from a *Diplodocus* tail smack.

However, computer specialist Nathan Myhrvold and paleontologist Phil Currie have suggested an alternative. They calculate that the tip of a diplodocoid tail, like the tip of a bullwhip, would have broken the sound barrier and made a very *loud* crack. They suggest that this might have been a way of signaling among diplodocoids, or a warning to would-be attackers. But paleontologist Ken Carpenter points out that bullwhips tend to get frayed at the ends. He thinks that a diplodocoid with a supersonic "whip" would wind up destroying the end of its own tail!

FLEXIBLE NECKS (MAYBE NOT?)

How flexible were sauropod necks? Could they all be held up high? Some paleontologists and paleoartists have illustrated sauropods with swanlike necks held erect, while others have shown them with necks straight out.

There are skeletons of sauropods that show that, at least in death, the neck could be held up high. However, this position might be due to the drying of ligaments rather than the way the necks

Diplodocus was one of the most common dinosaurs in the Late Jurassic of western North America.

were held in life.

Paleontologists Kent Stevens and Michael Parrish have tried to test the range of motion in sauropod necks using computers. They have taken measurements of the shapes of sauropod vertebrae and made computer models of the necks. They then determined the limits of motion between each pair of vertebrae. *Their* models show that sauropod necks could not take a swanlike posture but that most of them had a relatively horizontal position. (Not all paleontologists agree with this, and some still consider a swanlike neck reasonable.)

In any case, Stevens and Parrish discovered something unusual in the flexibility of diplodocoid necks. They found that the necks were pretty flexible downward. It is unlikely that diplodocoids were adapted for looking at their own bellies, so what might account for the pliancy of their necks? If they were just looking at the ground, one would expect the flexibility to stop around the point required for them to look down. But diplodocoids could flex their necks beyond that point. Downward neck flexibility makes sense if diplodocoids did rear up on their hind legs. They could then stand stationary in front of a tree and move their

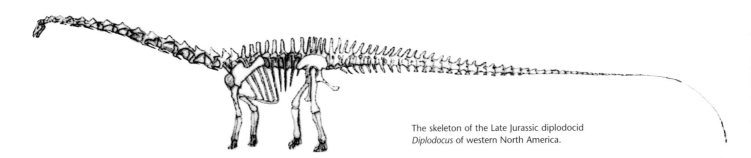

The skeleton of the Late Jurassic diplodocid *Diplodocus* of western North America.

necks up and down to find the best and tastiest branches to strip.

DIPLODOCOID DIVERSITY

There are three main types of diplodocoids: the very long-necked Diplodocidae, the sail-backed, short-necked Dicraeosauridae, and the highly specialized but poorly known Rebbachisauridae.

Additionally, there are a few diplodocoid species that do not seem to fall into any of these categories. These include the earliest diplodocoids, such as Middle Jurassic *Cetiosauriscus* of England. But some later diplodocoid forms are also of uncertain evolutionary position, including Late Jurassic *Suuwassea* and *Amphicoelias* of the western United States, Late Jurassic *Dinheirosaurus* of Portugal, Early Cretaceous *Losillasaurus* of Spain (although this might actually be a relative of the Chinese dinosaur *Mamenchisaurus*), and Early Cretaceous *Amazonsaurus* of Brazil (which might be a rebbachisaurid).

At present, these primitive diplodocoids are only known from incomplete specimens. One famous fossil of this sort was so incomplete it apparently fell apart before it could get from the field to the museum! This was a gigantic specimen of *Amphicoelias* that Edward Drinker Cope named *Amphicoelias fragillimus*. If his measurements are correct, this single partial vertebra was from a dinosaur that dwarfed even *Diplodocus, Sauroposeidon,* and *Argentinosaurus.* This would have been a dinosaur perhaps 140 feet (42.7 meters) long and weighing 150 tons (assuming it had the same proportions as smaller diplodocoids). That's as heavy as the largest individuals of the biggest animal known—the modern blue whale! Sadly, this bone can no longer be located,

so no one can confirm that it was really as enormous as Cope said. It hints at the possibility of truly tremendous diplodocoids, in any case.

JURASSIC GIANTS: THE DIPLODOCIDS

Most diplodocoid species are known from just one or two incomplete skeletons. However, the members of Diplodocidae (the "family" of *Diplodocus*) are known from many very good skeletons. If you've gone to a museum with dinosaur fossils, you've probably seen one of these. Paleontologists have even found the skeletons of baby diplodocids, which have not been found for other diplodocoid groups. Almost all good skeletons of this group are from the Morrison Formation, a Late Jurassic rock unit from the western United States.

Diplodocidae includes the familiar *Diplodocus* and *Apatosaurus.* In the past, some very big individuals of *Diplodocus* were mistakenly identified as new species—such as *"Supersaurus"* and *"Seismosaurus."* (In fact, there are paleontologists who still regard these as unique types rather than as *Diplodocus.*) The same thing happened with *Apatosaurus,* named by O. C. Marsh in 1877. When Marsh found a new and even more complete *Apatosaurus* specimen in 1879, he named it *Brontosaurus.* Up until the 1970s, many paleontologists still regarded this as a valid name. Today most paleontologists consider the various species of *"Brontosaurus"* to belong to *Apatosaurus,* and because the latter name was the first one used, we have retired the *much* cooler name *Brontosaurus.* (A few paleontologists, however, still regard *Brontosaurus* as a distinct form.)

Diplodocus is the basic model for the

The long neck spines of *Amargasaurus* may have been for display.

diplodocids. It is a slender but big dinosaur, with the largest individuals growing up to 115 feet (35 meters) long and weighing about 50 tons. More typical specimens are smaller, at 72 to 80 feet (22 to 24.4 meters) long and weighing a mere 20 tons.

Apatosaurus was more of a bruiser than *Diplodocus,* with a heavier neck and thicker limbs. A 72-foot (22-meter) *Apatosaurus* is estimated to have weighed about 30 tons, and there are individual bones suggesting that *Apatosaurus* may have grown much larger! Some paleontologists have suggested that instead of just rearing up to feed in trees, *Apatosaurus* may have used its strong limbs and impressive weight to knock trees down! This

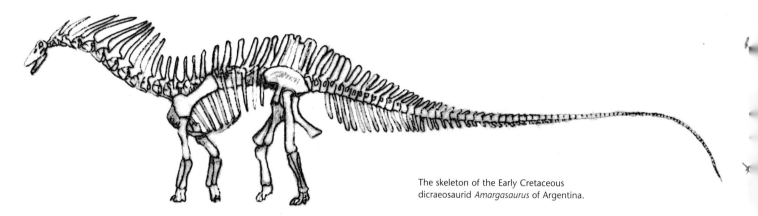

The skeleton of the Early Cretaceous dicraeosaurid *Amargasaurus* of Argentina.

is an interesting speculation, but it would be very difficult to test from the fossil record.

The third Morrison diplodocid, *Barosaurus,* is smaller than the other two but has a proportionately longer neck. Diplodocid necks and tails are longer than the necks and tails of other diplodocoids. While most diplodocids had necks that were about two-thirds the length of their tails, *Barosaurus*'s neck and tail were almost equal in length.

America in the Late Jurassic would have been an astonishing place. Not only were there at least three diplodocids and two primitive diplodocoid species present, there were also three species of macronarians (*Haplocanthosaurus, Camarasaurus,* and *Brachiosaurus*). That's the most sauropods in one place at one time that we know of. Imagine eight different types of animals, all of them bigger than elephants, wandering around in the same region!

The diplodocids may have been diverse in the United States, but they are poorly known elsewhere. An East African close relative of *Barosaurus* called *Tornieria* has been found in rocks dating from the Late Jurassic. And there are a few isolated bits and pieces from the Late Jurassic of other lands that might be diplodocids. Spectacular as they were, it seems that members of Diplodocidae had a short duration compared to other whip-tailed sauropods.

DOUBLE-SAILED DINOSAURS

In Diplodocidae, the neural spines—the ones that stick up from the tops of the vertebrae—are split down the middle. It is likely that a series of ligaments ran down the split from the hips to the back of the neck. These ligaments held the neck in a horizontal position without the dinosaur having to use its muscles. Similar split neural spines are found in a few other sauropods and are taken to extremes in Dicraeosauridae.

Only three types of dicraeosaurids are known. These are *Dicraeosaurus* of the Late Jurassic of eastern Africa, *Brachytrachelopan* of the Late Jurassic of Argentina, and *Amargasaurus* of the Early Cretaceous of Argentina. These were smaller than the diplodocoids, between about 20 and 33 feet (6.1 to 10.1 meters) and have shorter necks than most sauropods.

What makes the dicraeosaurids stand out is

The dicraeosaurid *Brachytrachelopan* of the Late Jurassic of Argentina had the shortest neck known in any sauropod.

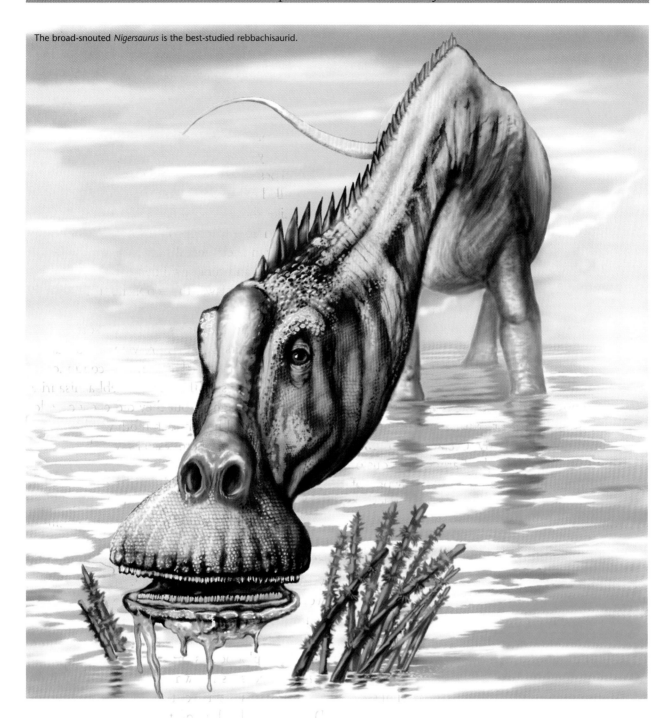

The broad-snouted *Nigersaurus* is the best-studied rebbachisaurid.

their unusual neural spines. Not only are these spines split, they are also tall. In *Dicraeosaurus,* they were about 2 feet (0.6 meters) tall, and in *Amargasaurus* they were 4 feet (1.2 meters) tall. They would have formed a "sail" along the necks and backs of these dinosaurs. There is some question as to whether a web of skin stretched between the longest neural spines in *Amargasaurus* or if (as shown on page 196) the individual spines formed big points sticking out of the sail. Until we have a

skin impression of an *Amargasaurus* neck, we won't know for certain.

Other dinosaurs—such as the iguanodontian *Ouranosaurus* and the theropod *Spinosaurus*—had sails. But those dinosaurs had unsplit neural spines, so they only had a single sail. The dicraeosaurids had split neural spines, so they had a double sail! As with all the sailed dinosaurs, we don't know exactly what the sails were used for. They could have been useful in gaining heat from the sun or losing it to the wind and so helping the dinosaurs maintain their body temperature. They would also make them appear bigger, perhaps scaring off potential attackers. They may have been used to attract mates. Or it could be some combination of all of these.

WHAT DO YOU GET WHEN YOU CROSS A SAUROPOD AND A RODENT?

The answer is a rebbachisaurid. Rebbachisauridae contains a very weird group of Cretaceous diplodocoids from Africa and South America. At the time of this writing, no one has put together a complete rebbachisaurid skull or skeleton, so we aren't sure what they looked like. But enough is known from different body parts to begin to understand them.

There are at least four types of rebbachisaurid dinosaurs known. These are *Nigersaurus* from the Early Cretaceous of northern Africa, *Rebbachisaurus* from the Early Cretaceous of Morocco, *Rayososaurus* from the Early Cretaceous of Argentina, and *Limaysaurus* from the early part of the Late Cretaceous of Argentina. The newly discovered *Amazonsaurus* from Brazil might be one of these dinosaurs as well, as might the fragmentary *Histriasaurus* from the Early Cretaceous of Croatia and some newly discovered but unnamed sauropods from Spain.

These are medium-size sauropods, around 50 feet (15.2 meters) long. They have fairly tall neural spines (particularly so in *Rebbachisaurus*), which are not split as in diplodocids and dicraeosaurids. They seem to have relatively short necks, similar to those of dicraeosaurids.

What makes rebbachisaurids unusual is their mouths. The other diplodocoids have squared-off snouts, but in rebbachisaurids, the snout is *really* straight, with pencil-like teeth in a straight row right at the front of the snout. In other diplodocoids, there are eighteen to thirty-two teeth in the lower jaw; in rebbachisaurids, there are sixty-eight! And those are just the teeth you can see! In the jaw behind each tooth are seven more ready to be used, one after another. A *Niger-*

saurus would have had 600 teeth in its mouth at one time!

This peculiar arrangement is an example of a dental battery. Dental batteries are specialized sets of teeth where each individual tooth acts as part of a single major unit, and as soon as one tooth is worn away, another is there to replace it. Two other types of dinosaurs have dental batteries: the duckbilled hadrosaurids and the horned ceratopsids. Like those dinosaurs, rebbachisaurids must have been able to chop up a lot of plants pretty quickly with their dental batteries. But while the hadrosaurid and ceratopsid dental batteries are on the sides of the jaws, the rebbachisaurids' are in the front.

That's why rebbachisaurids are sort of like rodents. Rodents have ever-growing incisors at the front of their jaws so that they can continuously gnaw without losing their teeth. Rebbachisaurids probably didn't gnaw, but they did chew on a lot of plants. And although each tooth would eventually be worn away, there was always a brand-new one ready to replace it.

Why did they need such specialized teeth? We really don't know. If they lived today, we might guess that they were grazers, because big animals that eat lots of tough grass (like horses and rhinos) often have a wide set of teeth up front that can withstand a lot of wear and tear. Rebbachisaurids would be perfectly reasonable grass-eating sauropods. The problem is, grass hadn't yet evolved by the Early Cretaceous!

The diplodocoids include some of the most bizarre dinosaurs known, but as far as we know now, none made it to the end of the Age of Dinosaurs. The last of the diplodocoids (*Rebbachisaurus* and *Limaysaurus*) lived around 95 million years ago, at the very beginning of the Late Cretaceous. But even after this group died, other sauropods lived on for another 30 million years. These others were all members of Macronaria, the big-nosed sauropods.

The gigantic diplodocid *Supersaurus* rears up at the threatening megalosaurid *Torvosaurus* in Late Jurassic Colorado.

Sauropod Evolution

Dr. Jeffrey A. Wilson
University of Michigan

The first sauropod was discovered more than 160 years ago in Oxford, England. It was a humble collection of a few large tail bones that were so large they were thought to belong to an ocean-dwelling animal like today's whales. For that reason, the first sauropod was called Cetiosaurus, or the "whale lizard." More and better sauropod skeletons were soon discovered in western North America and eastern Africa, and it was soon realized that sauropods were not whale-like at all. By the end of the 1800s, paleontologists had a detailed picture of the sauropod skeleton.

Sauropods have a deep, barrel-shaped chest supported by four column-like legs. An extraordinary neck that held up a small skull was balanced by an equally long tail that became quite narrow toward its end. This basic body plan, or evolutionary "blueprint," is shared by all sauropods, but no two sauropods look exactly alike. Both small and large differences in all parts of the skeleton allow us to recognize about seventy different sauropods that lived all over the world during most of the dinosaur era.

Compared to the skulls of other dinosaurs, those of sauropods are a bit plain: they have no horns, no crests, no beaks—a no-frills design! Sauropod skulls were well equipped for eating plants, and lots of them. Most sauropods had fewer than 100 large, strong teeth, but some sauropods packed more than 600 narrow teeth into their jaws. In sauropods, the top and bottom rows of teeth ended at the same place at the back of the jaws, allowing each top tooth to match a bottom tooth. This formed a continuous surface to cut plant matter before it was swallowed. Sauropods probably did not chew their food very well—like today's plant-eaters, they probably had long guts and housed microorganisms that helped them break down their food.

The sauropod neck is truly extraordinary, both in its length and in the shape of the neck bones that support it. All sauropods had long necks, but large and small differences in neck length may have allowed different sauropods to feed in different places—high in the trees, low to the ground, or somewhere in between. Perhaps part of the secret to sauropod necks is that every neck bone was partly air-filled, or pneumatized. As in birds today, tiny extensions from the lungs fit like balloons into hollows in the sauropod neck bones. Air-filled neck bones may have reduced the weight of the bone without sacrificing its strength.

Sauropod bodies were heavy and supported by thick legs that were held upright, like tree trunks or the columns in front of a building. Because of their extreme weight, we think that sauropods were not agile and could not run, much like elephants today. But although they could not run, we know that they were good walkers because we find their footprints all over the world. We can easily recognize sauropod footprints because they walked on four legs and had five fingers and five toes. Fossilized trackways from Colorado tell us that sauropods sometimes traveled in herds.

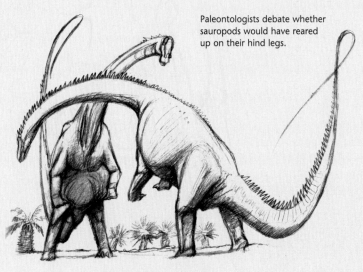

Paleontologists debate whether sauropods would have reared up on their hind legs.

Brachiosaurus

Jobaria

Saltasaurus

25

MACRONARIANS
(Big-Nosed Giant Long-Necked Dinosaurs)

The group of giant long-necked plant-eating saurischian dinosaurs is Sauropoda. It contains many different types. There were extremely long-necked primitive forms, like *Omeisaurus;* the enormous whip-tailed diplodocids; the spine-backed species in Dicraeosauridae; and the lawn-mower-mouthed members of Rebbachisauridae. But the most diverse of all sauropod dinosaur groups is Macronaria.

Species in Macronaria range from basic blunt-nosed types like *Camarasaurus* and *Jobaria* to the long-armed species in Brachiosauridae and the many different types in Titanosauria. Titanosauria was the most successful of all sauropod groups, running in time from the Middle Jurassic to the very end of the Late Cretaceous, and in size from the "dwarf sauropod" *Magyarosaurus* (only 18 feet [5.5 meters] long) to 100-foot (30.5-meter), 100-ton giants like *Argentinosaurus* and *Antarctosaurus.* There were even spoon-billed titanosaurs and armored titanosaurs.

WHERE THE NOSE GOES

Macronaria means "big noses," and the species in this group get this name because the opening in their skull for the nose is *huge,* often much bigger than the eye socket. And while even primitive sauropods had nose openings farther back from the front of the snout than typical dinosaurs, it was *way* far up in macronarians. Basically, they had great big nose openings in their foreheads!

But that doesn't mean that their nostrils were *on* their foreheads. This was a reasonable assumption in the past, however, and almost any illustration of a macronarian from the nineteenth or twentieth century shows just that. For instance, there is a memorable scene in the movie *Jurassic Park* when a *Brachiosaurus*—one of the most famous macronarians—sneezes on a little girl who is hiding up in the trees. The snot flies out of its forehead.

But newer studies, led by Ohio University paleontologist Larry Witmer, have shown that the actual fleshy openings for the nasal passages were almost certainly at the end of the snout, just as they are in most living animals. He observed that the little openings in the skull for the nerves and blood vessels associated with nostril muscles are located down at the front of the snout and not up near the macronarian's big nose opening on its forehead. This led Witmer to conclude that the big nose opening of macronarians was filled with a fleshy nasal chamber, and that the actual nostril was located farther down the face, near the end of the snout.

Why did they have such big nasal chambers? We don't know for certain, but many types of

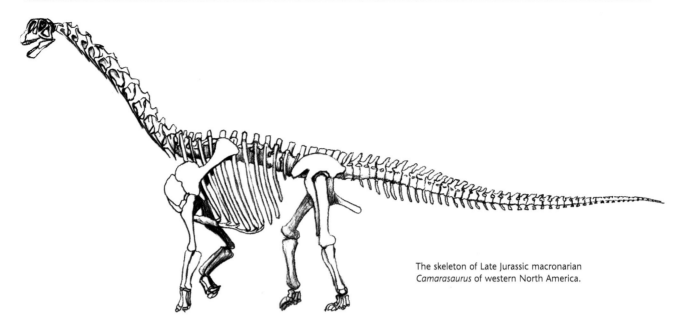

The skeleton of Late Jurassic macronarian *Camarasaurus* of western North America.

dinosaurs did—dinosaurs such as the horned ceratopsids and the beaked iguanodontians. One possibility is that this space contained a fleshy chamber or sac that might have been inflated to make loud sounds. Another is that tissue in the nose—living tissue, not paper!—may have helped rid the body of excess heat or trap moisture to keep the lungs and throat from drying out. I suspect it was a combination of some, or all, of these reasons.

BASIC BIG-NOSES

Besides their giant noses, the most primitive macronarians are not much different from early sauropods of other groups. In fact, not all paleontologists agree on which sauropods are primitive macronarians and which ones are distantly related types of sauropod that happen to have big noses. In general, though, the primitive macronarians have blunt snouts and big, strong, spoon-shaped teeth.

Most of the oldest macronarians (from the Middle Jurassic Epoch) belong to this "basic big-nose" type. These include *Abrosaurus* and *Bellusaurus* of China and *Atlasaurus* of Morocco. Very similar to these dinosaurs is *Jobaria* from Niger, but it is from much later (the Early Cretaceous). In between these dinosaurs in time is *Haplocanthosaurus* of the Late Jurassic of western North America, which some phylogenetic studies suggest is a macronarian, too.

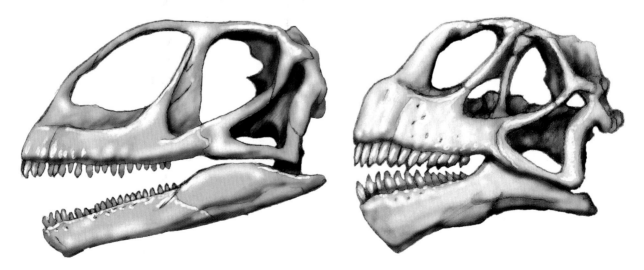

Skulls of the primitive macronarians *Jobaria* of Early Cretaceous northern Africa (left) and *Camarasaurus* of Late Jurassic western North America.

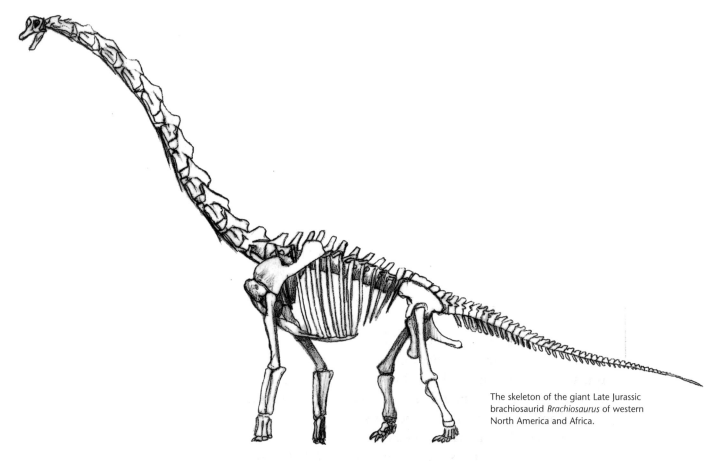

The skeleton of the giant Late Jurassic brachiosaurid *Brachiosaurus* of western North America and Africa.

But by far the best-known and best-studied primitive macronarian is *Camarasaurus* of the Late Jurassic. This sauropod is known from dozens of almost-complete skeletons and many hundreds (or possibly even thousands) of isolated bones. In fact, in the Morrison Formation of the American West—the rocks that contain more Jurassic dinosaurs than any others in the world—this is the most common dinosaur of all. Many museums around the world have mounted skeletons of this famous sauropod. At 60 feet (18.3 meters) long and up to 25 tons, it was smaller than many of its contemporary relatives, such as *Brachiosaurus, Diplodocus,* and *Apatosaurus.* Nevertheless, it was still much larger than any of the carnivorous dinosaurs.

These basic big-noses don't show much in the way of specializations, other than the features commonly found in all macronarians. In fact, they seem to have evolved themselves out of existence, because they were eventually replaced by their more advanced relatives: the tall brachiosaurids and the diverse titanosaurs.

BRACHIOSAURIDS: TALLEST OF THEM ALL

One of the most distinctive dinosaurs of all is *Brachiosaurus.* Although no one complete skeleton has ever been found, good partial material from the American West and from Tanzania, in eastern Africa, gives us a good idea of what it looked like.

First of all, it was big. For many decades it was thought to be the biggest of all sauropods, with a weight of up to 50 tons and a length of perhaps 86 feet (26.2 meters). More spectacularly, it was tall! The biggest *Brachiosaurus* could probably hold its head up 60 feet (18.3 meters) high at the tallest, although it would have more typically held it at a "mere" 30 to 33 feet (9.1 to 10.1 meters)!

How did *Brachiosaurus* reach such great heights? In part because it had a pretty long neck, even by sauropod standards. About half the length of this dinosaur was neck. But mostly *Brachiosaurus* was tall because it was built uphill! In general, dinosaurs had shorter forelimbs than hind limbs, so their shoulders were lower than their hips. But that wasn't the case with *Brachiosaurus.*

Brachiosaurus was built uphill, allowing it to feed higher than most other dinosaurs.

Its forelimbs were longer than its hind limbs, making its shoulders much higher than its hips. Even if *Brachiosaurus* held its neck out straight, its head would be 20 feet (6.1 meters) above the ground, enabling it to look onto the roof of a two-story building. Probably a more natural posture would have been to hold its neck at a 45-degree angle. Craning its neck up all the way, it could peer into a fourth- or maybe even fifth-floor window. (If you want to see the world like a *Brachiosaurus,* look out a fourth-story window and imagine your feet are on the ground!)

That's as high as *Brachiosaurus* could reach, though. Unlike the diplodocoids, and possibly the titanosaurs, *Brachiosaurus* and its closest relatives probably couldn't rear up and stand on their hind legs. Too much of their weight was in front of their hips, and their arms were too slender to take the impact when they came back down. So despite what you see in the movies, *Brachiosaurus* most likely kept to all fours, even when feeding.

Brachiosaurus's skull is a bit odd, even by sauropod standards. It looks puny from four stories away, but in fact it is pretty big. The head of *Brachiosaurus* was 5 feet (1.5 meters) long. It had big, spoon-shaped teeth, as did the more primitive macronarians. The nose openings formed a bulge, or dome, on the top. At *Brachiosaurus*'s other end, it had a short (by sauropod standards) tail. Its arms were long and relatively thin, and its hand formed a tall pillar.

Some paleontologists consider the extremely large bones of *Brachiosaurus* to belong to a dinosaur named *"Ultrasauros."* Others say that the African species should be given the name *Giraffatitan.* Most paleontologists, however, don't see

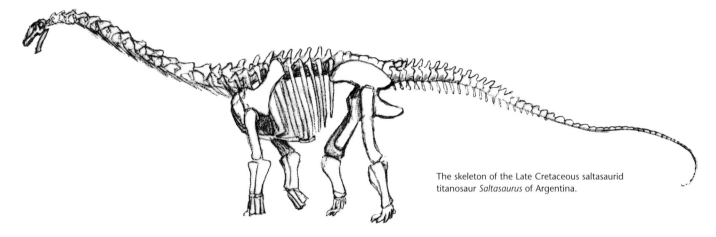

The skeleton of the Late Cretaceous saltasaurid titanosaur *Saltasaurus* of Argentina.

these new names as justified, so I'll stick to calling all of them *Brachiosaurus* for now!

Brachiosaurus is the best known of the brachiosaurids. Few of the others are known from even half a skeleton, so we don't know how many of the features of *Brachiosaurus* are found in all of them. The other brachiosaurids seem to all have shoulders higher than their hips. And most of them are pretty big dinosaurs.

Brachiosaurid skeletons have been found from many parts of the world, and all are from the Middle Jurassic through the Early Cretaceous. The most recent, and mightiest, of all brachiosaurids is *Sauroposeidon* from the Early Cretaceous of the American West. Named after the Greek god of earthquakes (Poseidon's "side job"; he's more famous as god of the seas), *Sauroposeidon* was one of the largest of all dinosaurs. At perhaps 98 to 107 feet (30 to 32.5 meters) long and weighing 70 to 80 tons, it was shorter than the giant *Diplodocus* and lighter than *Argentinosaurus,* but not by much. And because it seems to have been built along a

The head of the Late Cretaceous saltasaurid *Bonitasaura* of Argentina.

similar pattern as *Brachiosaurus, Sauroposeidon* would have been the tallest of all dinosaurs. That makes it the tallest animal known. If it could crane its neck up, it might have been able to hold its head 66 to 69 feet (20 to 21 meters) high or more. That's the height of three and a half of the tallest giraffes stacked one on top of the other.

But hard as it is to believe, *Sauroposeidon* wasn't immune from attack! There is a wonderful fossil trackway in Paluxy, Texas, that shows a brachiosaurid (probably *Sauroposeidon,* but possibly a close relative) being chased by the giant meateater *Acrocanthosaurus.* At one point the trackways converge, and the predator seems to have grabbed on to the side of the herbivore. It then apparently lost its grip and continued to chase it. Sadly, the trackway ends before we can see if the sauropod got away.

THE TITANS: BIGGEST OF THE BIG

The longest-lasting of all the macronarian groups is Titanosauria, and the oldest known titanosaur is *Janenschia* from the Late Jurassic of Tanzania. Some titanosaurs, such as the American *Alamosaurus,* the Romanian *Magyarosaurus,* and the Indian *Isisaurus,* were alive at the time of the great extinction 85 million years later. That means that *Alamosaurus* lived closer in time to you and me than it did to *Janenschia.* Titanosaurs have been found on every continent except Antarctica (and paleontologists predict it is only a matter of time before they are found there).

As you'll see, there is a lot of variety to the

The Late Cretaceous saltasaurid *Rapetosaurus* of Madagascar.

titanosaurs. But there *are* a few common features. Their chests are pretty broad, not narrow as in the brachiosaurids. Also different from the brachiosaurids, the bones of their forearms—between the elbow and the wrist—are particularly thick

Rapetosaurus faces danger at the watering hole in the form of the crocodilian *Mahajangasuchus*.

and heavy. The ilium (upper hip bone) of titanosaurs flares out sideways, and the ischium (rear lower hip bone) is shorter than the pubis. (In other sauropods, the ilium doesn't flare out, and the ischium is as long as or longer than the pubis.)

And the hind limbs of titanosaurs are farther apart than the hind limbs of most sauropods. Paleontologists Jeff Wilson and Matt Carrano have speculated that these hip and leg changes would have allowed titanosaurs to sit back and stand more easily on their hind legs.

Another feature found in at least some titanosaurs is body armor. Since the late 1800s, paleontologists have found armor plates unlike those of thyreophorans (armored ornithischian dinosaurs) that were too big to be from anything but dinosaurs. Who grew this

The spiny-armored Early Cretaceous titanosaur *Agustinia* of Argentina.

armor? The mystery was solved in 1980 with the discovery and description of *Saltasaurus,* a titanosaur sauropod. It turned out that the armor plates came from its back. Since then armor has been found in many other titanosaurs. At present, we don't know if all titanosaurs, or only certain species, had it. In most titanosaurs, the armor consisted of round disks with rough edges, ranging from the size of a cookie to the size of a personal pizza. But in at least one species, the armor was more than round disks. The Early Cretaceous *Agustinia* from Argentina had many different types of spikes, plates, and projections. In fact, it seems to have been as impressively armored as a stegosaur!

As sauropods go, some titanosaurs were quite small. The most notable of these is "little" *Magyarosaurus,* which was only about as big as a rhino.

It may have been small because it was stuck living on an island in what is now Transylvania, Romania. When members of a large animal species are trapped on an island, there often isn't enough food for the largest individuals to survive. Evolution selects for smaller and smaller animals, until you get dwarf descendants from a giant ancestor. Paleontologists have records of this happening many times among fossil elephants and their relatives (mammoths and mastodons), and *Magyarosaurus* appears to be a dinosaurian case.

But some titanosaurs were quite large. In fact, the largest known dinosaurs are members of Titanosauria. Based on fossils currently described, the biggest of all was *Argentinosaurus* from the earliest part of the Late Cretaceous of Argentina. Comparing the parts known from this dinosaur with those of smaller, but more complete, titanosaur skeletons, paleontologists estimate *Argentinosaurus* weighed between 80 and 100 tons. It was perhaps 100 to 110 feet (30.5 to 33.5 meters) long. Not much smaller than *Argentinosaurus* was the Egyptian *Paralititan* from the same age and the much younger *Antarctosaurus* (which, despite its name, is from Argentina). These dinosaurs were ten times the size of the largest carnivorous dinosaurs. The present-day blue whale is the only animal known that grows larger than this.

SALTASAURIDS: LAST OF THE LONG-NECKS

At present, there is a lot of confusion over the evolutionary relationships among the titanosaurs. Very few of them are known from relatively complete material, making it hard to compare the different species. In fact, only *Rapetosaurus* from the Late Cretaceous of Madagascar is known from both good skull and good body material.

Most studies agree, however, that there is a group of very advanced titanosaurs. This is Saltasauridae. Saltasaurids have some odd features. For example, they don't have any fingers. Instead, their pillar-shaped hands end in a stump. Also, they have pencil-shaped teeth. This caused a lot of confusion in the past, because diplodocoids *also* have pencil-shaped teeth. For a long time, paleontologists thought that diplodocoids and titanosaurs must have been close relatives, but now better fossils show that titanosaurs were much more closely related to brachiosaurids. The pencil-shaped teeth just evolved independently in the two lineages.

Saltasaurids have heads shaped a little like those of ducks or duckbilled dinosaurs. They are round at the front of the snout, pinched in the middle, and then wider again in back. They have a lot of teeth concentrated at the front of the jaws, although not as many as in rebbachisaurid diplodocoids.

Saltasaurids were the last group of sauropods to evolve. All the titanosaurs that are definitely saltasaurids are from the last 20 million years or so of the Cretaceous, after all of the non-titanosaur sauropods had died out. Although smaller than their more primitive titanosaur relatives, at least some saltasaurids—like *Alamosaurus*—reached 30 tons.

Older dinosaur books say that sauropods were rare at the end of the Age of Dinosaurs. In fact, they were only rare in North America and in Asia. Everywhere else that dinosaurs are known—Europe, India (then its own island continent), Madagascar, and most especially South America—titanosaurs, and especially saltasaurids, are the most common type of dinosaur found. Even when the end came, this group of long-necks was still going strong.

MACRONARIAN TRACE FOSSILS

Not all sauropod fossils are bones and teeth. Remains of their behavior, called trace fossils, are also known. Earlier I mentioned the famous Paluxy trackway. Sauropod tracks of all sorts are known from around the world. It is often hard to tell which sauropod types made which trackways. However, those of titanosaurs are very distinctive, with their footprints farther apart than those of normal sauropods because their bodies were proportionately wider.

Some of the best macronarian trace fossils are nests. The eggs and nests of titanosaurs have been found in Europe, South America, and Asia. The best-known nest site is Auca Mahuevo from Patagonia, Argentina. Literally *thousands* of dinosaur eggs are known from this location, and some of these contain the fossils of unhatched baby saltasaurids. Even though the babies inside these would grow up to be perhaps 30 tons, the eggs were only 6 inches (15.2 centimeters) in diameter.

Another, somewhat less appealing, trace fossil of a titanosaur was described in 2005. This is a coprolite, or piece of fossilized feces, from the end of the Late Cretaceous Epoch of India. It contains the remains of a seed: one of the last meals of one of the last of the largest animals ever to walk the Earth.

Opposite: *Astrodon* defends itself against a pack of the dromaeosaurid *Utahraptor*.

Lesothosaurus

Pisanosaurus

26

ORNITHISCHIANS
(Bird-Hipped Dinosaurs)

One of the two major branches of the dinosaur family tree, ornithischians, or bird-hipped dinosaurs, were all primarily plant-eaters. Some of the most spectacular dinosaurs ever—plate-backed stegosaurs, armored ankylosaurs, horned ceratopsians, domeheaded pachycephalosaurs, and hollow-crested duckbills—were ornithischians. What might surprise you, though, is that although birds are dinosaurs, they are *not* bird-hipped dinosaurs!

BIRD HIPS AND LOWER BEAKS

When paleontologists first discovered dinosaur fossils, their most important job was to describe them and give them names. After all, they needed to know what bones they were looking at, and what to call these strange, ancient creatures. Over time, however, as more and more dinosaur fossils were found, scientists started thinking about how the dinosaurs were related to each other.

By the 1880s, enough dinosaur skeletons had been found to recognize that there were several major body types. There were four-legged long-necked plant-eaters, two-legged carnivores, four-legged shorter-necked plant-eaters (often with armored bodies), and two-legged plant-eaters. Yale University paleontologist O. C. Marsh named these four types Sauropoda (lizard feet), Theropoda (beast feet), Stegosauria (roofed reptiles), and Ornithopoda (bird feet).

In 1885, British paleontologist Harry G. Seeley noticed that Marsh's Stegosauria (which included dinosaurs we now include in Ankylosauria) and Ornithopoda had a number of features in common, and that Sauropoda and Theropoda, in turn, also had a number of features in common. For example, the dinosaurs in Sauropoda and Theropoda each had a pubis bone that pointed forward and had hollow-chambered vertebrae.

In contrast, the vertebrae of the dinosaurs in Ornithopoda and Stegosauria were solid. And their hips were very strange. All dinosaurs and other vertebrates with legs have hips made from three main bones. The ilium is on top, and it attaches the hip to the vertebrae. The other two bones attach on the bottom of the ilium. The ischium is the bone that attaches farther back on the bottom of the ilium and points toward the tail end of the animal. The pubis is the bone that attaches on the front part of the bottom of the ilium. In almost all these animals, the pubis points forward or down. Because the hips of the dinosaurs in Sauropoda and Theropoda reminded Seeley of the hips of lizards, he named the group Saurischia (lizard hips).

In contrast, the pubis of stegosaurs and ornithopods was unusual. Instead of pointing forward or down, it pointed backward like the

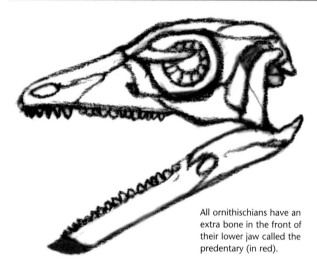

All ornithischians have an extra bone in the front of their lower jaw called the predentary (in red).

ischium. This was like the pubis in the hips of modern birds, so Seeley called this group of dinosaurs Ornithischia, or "bird-hipped." However, the hips of "bird-hipped" dinosaurs weren't exactly like those of birds. Some ornithischians (duckbills and horned dinosaurs, for instance) had a projection coming out of the front of the pubis. No bird has a hip like that.

A later discovery showed another similarity between ornithopods and stegosaurs. This was the predentary bone: an extra bone connecting the front ends of the two sides of the lower jaw. The predentary bone is found only in ornithischian dinosaurs. In fact, O. C. Marsh suggested that the ornithischians be renamed Predentata (the predentary dinosaurs), but this idea was never really accepted. The predentary bone was covered with a horny beak.

In the late 1880s and onward, new types of ornithischians were discovered. Ceratopsians (horned and frilled dinosaurs) and pachy-cephalosaurs (domeheaded dinosaurs) were particularly weird new groups. As better skeletons of ankylosaurs were found, paleontologists saw that they were different from stegosaurs, so they were moved out of Stegosauria and given a group (Ankylosauria) of their own.

Around this same time, paleontologists noted something else that most ornithischians had in common: leaf-shaped teeth. In the modern world, leaf-shaped teeth are found in reptiles that eat a lot of plants (like many species of iguana). This was one clue that ornithischians were plant-eaters. Another clue was their backward-pointing pubis bone. How's that? you might ask. The most likely answer is that they had a lot of guts. Literally.

Digesting plants is hard work. It takes the body more time to break down vegetable matter than it does to break down meat. And meat generally has a lot more nutrients per bite than plants. So plant-eating animals have to have longer and bigger intestines to make sure they get as much nutrition as possible out of the plants they eat.

Because of this, herbivores tend to be fat. If you look at a big plant-eater—like a cow or a horse—from the front, you'll see the belly sticking out to the sides. However, if you look at a big meat-eater—like a lion or a wolf—from the front, it will only have a big belly if it just fed; otherwise, the meat-eater will have a smaller belly. That's because carnivores have shorter intestines than herbivores.

Like cows and horses, plant-eating dinosaurs had to have big guts, too. However, the early plant-eaters were all bipedal (two-legged) animals,

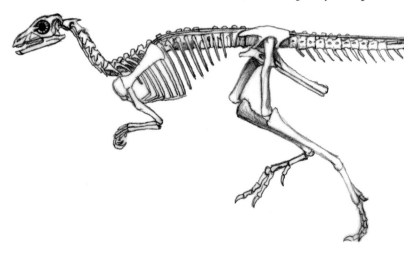

The skeleton of the Early Jurassic ornithischian *Lesothosaurus* of southern Africa.

The Middle Jurassic ornithischian *Agilisaurus* of China.

their armor that "pushed" them down on all fours. In the case of the horned dinosaurs, it was their huge, heavy heads.

EARLY ORNITHISCHIANS

The ancestors of all dinosaurs had a forward-pointing pubis. So, if ornithischians evolved from dinosaurs with a forward-pointing pubis, shouldn't we have found something like an ornithischian with such a bone? In fact, we have. And, not too surprisingly, it's the oldest and most primitive of all ornithischians.

Pisanosaurus of the Late Triassic Epoch of Argentina is the first ornithischian in the fossil record. (A few paleontologists suspect that the dinosaur relative *Silesaurus* might be an even more primitive one, but that doesn't seem to be the case based on what is currently known in 2007.) *Pisanosaurus* is only known from fragments, but those fragments show it is an ornithischian. Its hip is not complete, but what there is shows that its pubis pointed forward. (The paleontologist who described this dinosaur, José Bonaparte, actually thought the pelvis pointed backward. Later work showed that he was incorrect.)

There are a few other known fragments of Late Triassic ornithischians. Most of these are just teeth. So while we can figure out where early ornithischians lived, we can't say much about what they looked like.

When you look in slightly younger rocks, you get luckier. A number of ornithischians are known from good Early Jurassic specimens. While most belong to early members of the more advanced branches of the family tree of Ornithischia, a few are very primitive. The best known of these are *Fabrosaurus* and *Lesothosaurus*. (In fact, these might be the same dinosaur species.) While *Fabrosaurus* is known only from a jaw, much of the skeleton of *Lesothosaurus* is known. It shows that this was a little bipedal dinosaur that could run very fast. Its pubis points backward, so it is more closely related to the more advanced ornithischians than was *Pisanosaurus*. However, it lacks some of the special features of these more advanced forms.

so they couldn't get a big wide belly and still remain bipedal. The sauropodomorphs (long-necked plant-eating saurischians) eventually got a wide belly and became permanently four-legged animals. Early ornithischians evolved a different solution. They increased their gut size by having the pubis move backward. The farther back the pubis moved, the more space there was for intestines. Eventually, the pubis moved back as far as it could go—all the way back to the ischium.

By expanding their guts back rather than out to the side, ornithischians could keep the center of their mass close to their hips so they could still be two-legged walkers. In fact, the groups of ornithischians that became permanently four-legged animals didn't do so because of their big guts. In the case of the armored dinosaurs, it was the weight of

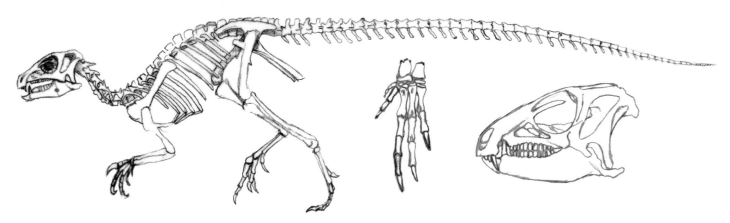

The skeleton of the Early Jurassic heterodontosaurid *Heterodontosaurus* of southern Africa, with close-ups of its grasping hand and powerful skull.

There are a few dinosaurs that are about as primitive as *Lesothosaurus* but lived later in time. These include the Chinese *Xiaosaurus* (from the Middle Jurassic), *Gongbusaurus* (from the Late Jurassic), and *Jeholosaurus* (from the Early Cretaceous). However, it may be that these dinosaurs were primitive members of the group Ornithopoda. New research is being done on these dinosaurs, so hopefully we will know more about these little plant-eaters soon.

HETERODONTOSAURS

One of the earliest important groups of ornithsichians is Heterodontosauridae. They are best known from *Heterodontosaurus* from the Early Jurassic Epoch of southern Africa, but fossils are known up to *Echinodon* of the Early Cretaceous Epoch of England.

Heterodontosaurs had hands with long grasping fingers and a semi-opposable thumb. Because saurischians have the same hand type, this seems to be the ancestral condition for dinosaurs. Later types of ornithischians evolved stubbier fingers, which were not as good for grasping. In fact, heterodontosaurs have some of the longest hands relative to their arm length of any ornithischian. Some paleontologists have suggested that they used their hands to dig for roots and tubers.

The heterodontosaurid skeleton is pretty similar to other early ornithischian skeletons. What makes heterodontosaurids different are features in their skulls, which are more strongly built than in most of their relatives. This suggests that they could eat pretty tough plants. Also, the teeth of the

heterodontosaurids are not the typical leaf-shaped teeth. Instead, their cheek teeth (the ones *not* at the front of the jaw) are shaped like little chisels— another clue that they fed on tough plants.

And at least some heterodontosaurids had fangs. This sounds pretty weird for a plant-eater, but there are some small deer and antelope today (which are about the same size as *Heterodontosaurus*) that have fangs. They don't use their fangs to hunt, but instead use them to show off to female deer and antelope and to intimidate other males. Did *Heterodontosaurus* do the same? We can't be sure, because we don't have enough skulls of this dinosaur to see if only some of them (presumably the males) had fangs.

CHEEKY DINOSAURS?

Pisanosaurus and *Lesothosaurus* represent the most primitive types of ornithischians. More advanced ones have a number of special features in their skeletons, especially in their mouths. The tooth row is inset: that is, the teeth are not exactly along the sides of the jaws but moved slightly in toward the tongue. Why might this be?

Paleontologist Peter Galton suggested an answer in 1972: cheeks! He hypothesized that the advanced ornithischians had cheeks along the sides of their jaws. Most reptiles are cheekless, so for a long time, paleontologists assumed that no dinosaur had cheeks. If you watch a plant-eating reptile without cheeks—like a turtle or an iguana—eat, you'll see that a lot of the food slops out of its mouth.

Galton suggested that ornithischians had

The fangs of *Heterodontosaurus* may have been used for display or defense.

cheeks that were attached along the outside of the face. He pointed out that if ornithischians had cheeks, they could swallow more of the food they were eating and so be more efficient eaters. This might explain why the cheeked ornithischian groups (thyreophorans, marginocephalians, and ornithopods) were so successful, while cheekless ones were rare.

While most paleontologists agree that ornithischians had cheeks, a few remain cautious. Larry Witmer of Ohio University and his team remind the rest of us that no one has actually shown that the bones of ornithischian jaws have attachment surfaces for cheeks. He cautions that the inset tooth row could have other explanations—for example, a longer beak extending far back in the jaws. His team is working to see if it can find clues

on the surface of these jawbones to demonstrate if either of these ideas is true.

(Personally, I suspect that Galton was correct, and Luis Rey has drawn most of the ornithischians in this book with cheeks. New data may eventually show that this is incorrect. That is part of the fun—and frustration—of doing dinosaur science. Sometimes new discoveries can radically change what you think of as "normal" for a dinosaur!)

Cheeks or no cheeks, ornithischians were a very diverse group of dinosaurs. While not the tallest or the fastest, they spanned a wide range of sizes and a wide variety of forms.

Cladogram of the Ornithischians

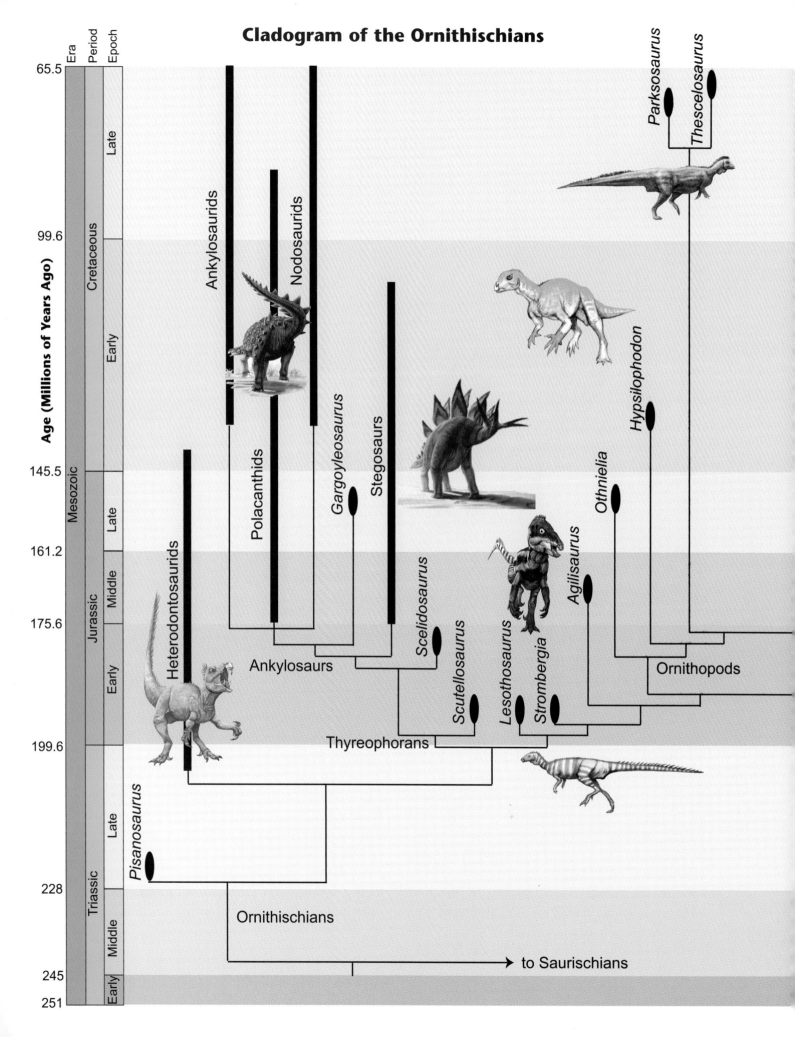

Age (Millions of Years Ago)

Era	Period	Epoch
		65.5
	Cretaceous	Late
		99.6
		Early
		145.5
Mesozoic		Late
		161.2
	Jurassic	Middle
		175.6
		Early
		199.6
	Triassic	Late
		228
		Middle
		245
		Early
		251

Parksosaurus
Thescelosaurus
Ankylosaurids
Nodosaurids
Polacanthids
Gargoyleosaurus
Stegosaurs
Hypsilophodon
Othnielia
Agilisaurus
Scelidosaurus
Scutellosaurus
Lesothosaurus
Strombergia
Heterodontosaurids
Ankylosaurs
Ornithopods
Thyreophorans
Pisanosaurus
Ornithischians
→ to Saurischians

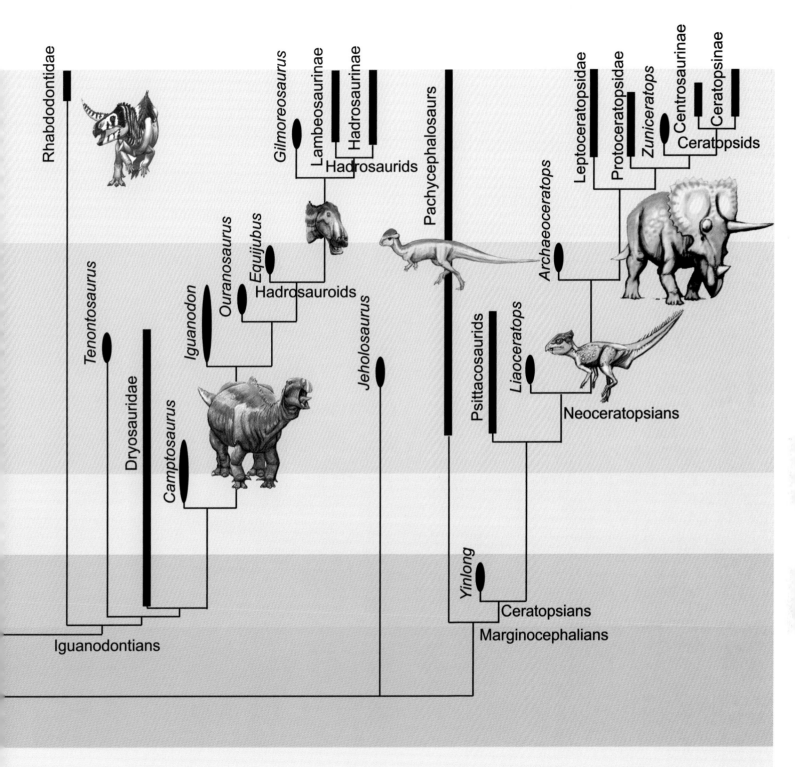

Rhabdodontidae

Tenontosaurus

Dryosauridae

Camptosaurus

Iguanodon

Ouranosaurus

Equijubus

Gilmoreosaurus

Lambeosaurinae

Hadrosaurinae

Hadrosaurids

Hadrosauroids

Jeholosaurus

Pachycephalosaurs

Psittacosaurids

Yinlong

Liaoceratops

Archaeoceratops

Leptoceratopsidae

Protoceratopsidae

Zuniceratops

Centrosaurinae

Ceratopsinae

Ceratopsids

Neoceratopsians

Ceratopsians

Marginocephalians

Iguanodontians

Emausaurus

Scelidosaurus

Scutellosaurus

27

PRIMITIVE THYREOPHORANS
(Early Armored Dinosaurs)

In a world populated by numerous types of dangerous carnivorous dinosaurs, there were several different ways for herbivores to survive. Some were relatively fast, so they could run away. Others were small enough to hide. Still others were giant-size and hard to kill. A few had horns to fight back. And then there were the ones that developed armor. The main group of armored dinosaurs is Thyreophora (shield bearers), named by Romanian paleontologist Ferenc Nopsca in 1915. Most thyreophorans belong to either the plated Stegosauria or the tanklike Ankylosauria. But the early armored dinosaurs were not members of either of these advanced groups.

SCUTELLOSAURUS: THE EARLIEST THYREOPHORAN

Thyreophorans are one of the major branches of the ornithischian family tree. The early armored dinosaurs are known from the Early Jurassic Epoch; all thyreophorans from the Middle Jurassic onward are either stegosaurs or ankylosaurs.

The most primitive of the early thyreophorans is *Scutellosaurus,* from the early part of the Early Jurassic of western North America. In general, *Scutellosaurus* resembles primitive ornithischians like *Lesothosaurus* or *Yandusaurus* in size and shape. It was about 5 feet (1.5 meters) long and walked mostly on just its hind legs. It had a rather long tail. What little is known of its skull shows that it was probably fairly short-snouted and had the typical leaf-shaped teeth of plant-eating dinosaurs. Its legs were somewhat shorter and stockier than *Lesothosaurus* and *Yandusaurus,* so it probably wasn't very fast.

What made *Scutellosaurus* different were the armor plates on its body. These armor plates are called scutes, or more technically osteoderms (skin bones). There were dozens of these scutes in the skin of *Scutellosaurus.* Some were flat, but others had a raised ridge, or keel, facing outward. They ranged in size from about a dime to a half-dollar. The scutes were not connected to each other or to the other bones in the skeleton. Instead, they would "float" in the skin of the dinosaur. This meant that the scutes could protect the body, but didn't make the skin so rigid that it couldn't bend.

Why would a dinosaur evolve armor? The answer: other dinosaurs! By the time the thyreophorans evolved, most non-dinosaurian predators on land had gone extinct, but there were still plenty of carnivorous dinosaurs around. In order to survive in such a world, the plant-eaters had to find some way to live and reproduce.

Theropods (carnivorous dinosaurs) were

Primitive armored *Scutellosaurus.*

pretty fast and agile. So the ancestors of the thyreophorans might have evolved to become faster still. However, there were already other plant-eaters that were faster (the early ornithopods). So thyreophorans probably wouldn't have been very successful if they tried to compete with the ornithopods.

Instead, the early thyreophorans evolved scutes. These were particularly helpful against smaller predators, especially the slender, agile coelophysoids that were the most common Early Jurassic theropods. If a small meat-eater tried to bite the surface of an early thyreophoran, it would have most likely broken its teeth. And because there had been a major extinction event between the Triassic Period and the Jurassic Period, most of the larger predators—such as the gigantic rauisuchians—had died out. So protection against smaller predators would have been useful indeed.

* * *

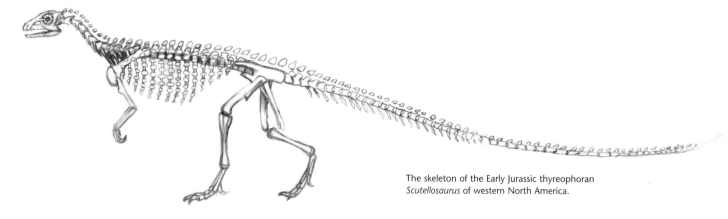

The skeleton of the Early Jurassic thyreophoran *Scutellosaurus* of western North America.

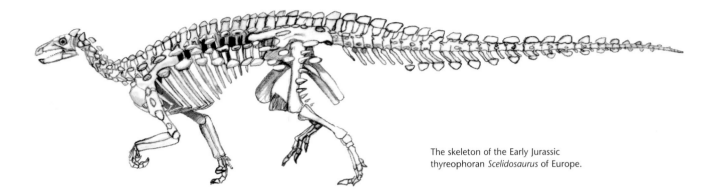

The skeleton of the Early Jurassic thyreophoran *Scelidosaurus* of Europe.

A CLOSER LOOK AT OSTEODERMS

Thyreophorans are not the only animals with osteoderms. Some titanosaur sauropods, for example, have osteoderms, as do some extinct non-dinosaurs, like plant-eating aetosaurs and crocodilian-like parasuchians. Many modern animals have osteoderms, too: armadillos and crocodilians, for instance. The most extreme form of osteoderms in living animals is found in turtles, where they interlock to form the shell.

If we look at an osteoderm close up, we see that most of it is made of bone. This is all we find in the skeletons of thyreophorans. But there is more to an osteoderm than bone. If you cut through the osteoderm of a modern armored animal, you see that the bone is covered with living tissue. And on the outside of that living tissue is keratin, the substance that makes up fingernails, hooves, and the surface of cow horns. Keratin is "dead" tissue. New keratin can be added from beneath, but the old keratin (the part that faces the outside world) doesn't have any nerves or blood vessels, and doesn't feel or heal.

This makes keratin pretty useful for protection. It can absorb the damage from an attacking animal's teeth and claws, keeping the armored animal from getting hurt. And as old keratin wears away, new keratin is created by the living tissue underneath.

We can also look at modern armored animals to see how they use their osteoderms. In most cases, they use them as simple defense. That is, if they are attacked, they hunker down and let the predator attack them. If their armor holds up, the would-be killer generally gets tired and goes away, leaving the armored animal alone. It was probably like that for the early thyreophorans, too. However, as we'll see in the next couple of chapters, some later thyreophorans did more than just sit around and take it!

THE PRICE OF DEFENSE

Although most predators in the early part of the Early Jurassic (when *Scutellosaurus* lived) were small, not all of them were. For example, rocks that contain the fossils of *Scutellosaurus* also contain the remains of long, slender *Syntarsus* (about 10 feet [3 meters] long), as well as its much larger and more powerful relative *Dilophosaurus* (20 feet [6.1 meters]) long. The armor of *Scutellosaurus* would probably hold up against an attack by *Syntarsus*, but a full-grown *Dilophosaurus* could probably rip a *Scutellosaurus* apart.

The same problem faced another early small thyreophoran, *Emausaurus*, from the later part of the Early Jurassic Epoch of Europe. Because *Emausaurus* was about twice as big as *Scutellosaurus*, it was a little better protected by size alone. More importantly, some of its scutes had bigger ridges. In fact, some were true spikes! This would make *Emausaurus* more "prickly" if a big theropod tried to bite it. But this thyreophoran was still fairly small, and a big determined predator might not be deterred even by these spikes.

The next stage in thyreophoran evolution can be found in *Scelidosaurus*. It was much bigger than either *Scutellosaurus* or *Emausaurus*—13 feet (4 meters) long. Some of the bones of its face were wrinkled, suggesting that it had some keratin

The heavy armor of *Scelidosaurus* forced it to walk on all fours . . .

osteoderms it wouldn't have to: it would simply let its plates do their work. And if an attacker wasn't deterred just by its armor, *Scelidosaurus* could swat at it with its armor-plated tail. *Scelidosaurus* represented the basic form from which all the later types of thyreophorans evolved: heavy, four-footed, relatively slow, but well armored.

Scelidosaurus had an interesting history in human times, too. It was one of the first dinosaurs known from a nearly complete skeleton, found in England in 1858 and studied by Sir Richard Owen (the man who named Dinosauria). But the original specimen of *Scelidosaurus* was found in very tough limestone that was hard for paleontologists in the nineteenth century to remove without destroying the skeleton. So for many decades the fossil of *Scelidosaurus* was mostly untouched.

In the middle of the twentieth century, British paleontologist Alan Charig began the process of preparing this specimen using new techniques, including utilizing weak acids that slowly dissolved the limestone without damaging the fossil itself. But this process takes a lot of time. In fact, the final complete description of this fossil hasn't even been published! Although Alan Charig has passed away, fellow British paleontologist Dave Norman is finishing up that report. So after a century and a half since its discovery, we'll finally know what most of this fossil looks like.

armor on its head. It had more scutes than these other dinosaurs, and the scutes were much bigger—some as big across as a playing card. But this armor came at a price. So many heavy plates over its body forced *Scelidosaurus* onto all fours. It couldn't walk on just two legs, or at least not for long, before the weight of all that armor would make it come back down on its front legs.

That armor would also have made it pretty slow. It wouldn't have been able to run fast to get away from an attacking theropod. But with its

LIFESTYLES OF THE EARLY AND ARMORED

Like other ornithischians, thyreophorans were herbivores. Because they were small (in the case of *Scutellosaurus* and *Emausaurus*) or stuck on all fours (like *Scelidosaurus*), they could only browse on plants low to the ground. Examinations of the wear on the teeth of *Scelidosaurus* show that it would grind its food differently than just mashing it together like a big lizard does, or more primitive ornithischians like *Lesothosaurus, Scutellosaurus,* and *Emausaurus* did.

No one has yet found nests of primitive thyreophorans, so we don't know much about their eggs or babies. Based on fossils of baby stegosaurs and ankylosaurs, we can predict that the scutes of baby primitive thyreophorans were much smaller and less developed than in adults.

Primitive thyreophorans lived in a variety of environments. *Scutellosaurus* fossils, for instance, were found in rocks that were formed in forests near deserts, so it may be that some *Scutellosaurus* or its relatives occasionally wandered into the desert. *Scelidosaurus* fossils have been found in limestones formed in the sea. Paleontologists don't think that *Scelidosaurus* was aquatic but that it lived along the shore. The fossils are just the remains of dead dinosaurs that washed out into the sea. (In fact, one partial *Scelidosaurus* skeleton was found inside the guts of a marine reptile that made a meal of the chewy carcass!)

. . . but was useful protection against attacking theropods.

Stegosaurus

Huayangosaurus

28

STEGOSAURS
(Plated Dinosaurs)

Easily one of the most recognizable and popular dinosaurs is *Stegosaurus*. It is definitely the best known of the Thyreophora (the armored dinosaurs, which also include the tanklike ankylosaurs and primitive armored forms like *Scelidosaurus* and *Scutellosaurus*). Its distinct plate-backed, spike-tailed image graces countless cartoons, movies, TV shows, postage stamps, toys, and models. But what do scientists really know about this famous plant-eater? And just how "distinct" was it, really?

A ROOFED REPTILE?
THE SHINGLE-SAURS

While *Stegosaurus* is familiar to us today, that wasn't always the case. In fact, when O. C. Marsh and his team first found fossils of this animal in the American West, they weren't even sure it was a dinosaur! Marsh thought that they were possibly the bones of a giant turtle!

Part of Marsh's confusion was a misunderstanding about the animal's most distinctive feature: its huge bony plates. Without other clues to guide him, Marsh didn't know how these plates fit onto the body. His initial guess—which he wrote about when he first described *Stegosaurus* in 1877—was that the plates lay flat on the animal's back. Marsh pictured these plates like the shingles on a roof, and in fact that is why he named the creature *Stegosaurus,* or "covered reptile."

Soon afterward, though, Marsh's team collected more-complete specimens of this reptile, and he recognized that it was a dinosaur and not a turtle. With more specimens, he also recognized that the plates pointed upward.

It is easy to understand why Marsh was confused about the plates of *Stegosaurus*. These osteoderms (pieces of bony armor) were not connected to the skeleton, but were instead held in the skin by cartilage. So when a stegosaur died and its body decayed, the plates would fall away and could be easily moved. In fact, Marsh only figured out the position of the plates after finding a specimen that had died in a dried-up watering hole that was then covered by mud, holding the bones in place.

STEGO-MYTHS

Stegosaurus may be popular, but it has been the subject of more than its share of misunderstandings.

For instance, since the late 1800s, some books (and nowadays some Web sites) have asserted that *Stegosaurus* had two brains. This is just plain nonsense! No serious paleontologist ever thought that this was true, and yet many books and Web sites about dinosaurs (which, in general, are not written

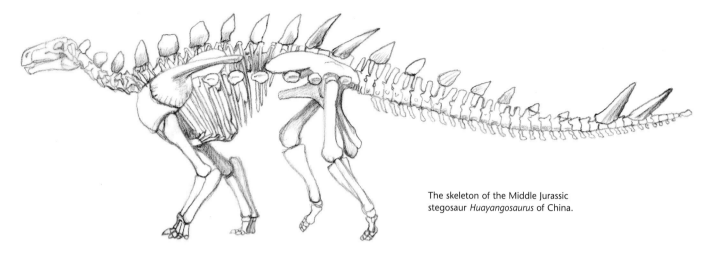

The skeleton of the Middle Jurassic stegosaur *Huayangosaurus* of China.

or created by paleontologists) keep perpetuating this tired tale.

The myth began because of two misunderstandings. The first started with the discovery in the late nineteenth century that the space inside the hip vertebrae of *Stegosaurus* (and some other dinosaurs) where the spinal cord was contained was very big. Some paleontologists—including Marsh—suggested that this enlarged space held an extra-large bundle of nerves. All vertebrates—including us—have these bundles, called ganglia, which help control the reflexes of the limbs and workings of the organs. Marsh and other paleontologists suggested that a single, exceptionally large ganglion located in the hip would help *Stegosaurus* reflexively swat attacking predators with its spiked tail.

It turns out that Marsh and the other nineteenth-century paleontologists were probably incorrect. In the 1990s, American paleontologist Emily Buchholtz examined the hips of living relatives of *Stegosaurus* (birds and crocodilians) and found that they also have an enlarged space in their hip vertebrae. But these animals don't have an extra-large ganglion there. Instead, that space is filled with fatty tissue. Although biologists aren't certain about the function of this tissue, it probably isn't for reflexes!

The second misunderstanding happened when people writing about dinosaurs misconstrued what a ganglion is. Marsh and other scientists described the ganglion as "a big nerve cluster." Now, the brain is basically a big cluster of nerves, so some

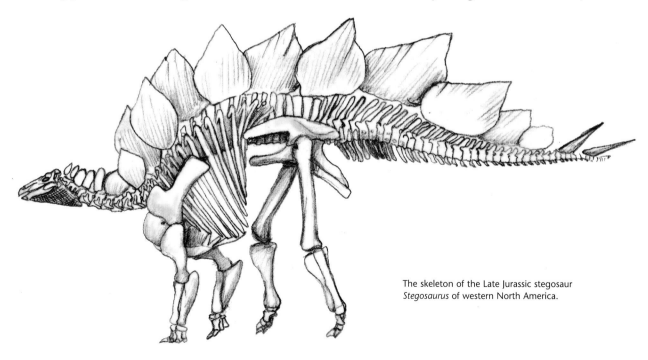

The skeleton of the Late Jurassic stegosaur *Stegosaurus* of western North America.

228

people read about the "big nerve cluster" in the hips and thought Marsh and company *actually meant* there was an honest-to-goodness brain located there! In fact, they thought it was amusing that this "brain" was bigger than the one in the stegosaur's head, so they said *Stegosaurus* had a "butt-brain"! And so the myth of the two-brained *Stegosaurus* was spread. But please don't *you* spread it! We know that *Stegosaurus*—and all other dinosaurs—had only one brain.

Another *Stegosaurus* myth is that it lived at the end of the Age of Dinosaurs, in the Late Cretaceous. The source of this myth is more subtle than words. Often it is spread in illustrations or in movies (like the classic Disney film *Fantasia*) that show *Stegosaurus* fighting *Tyrannosaurus. This never happened! Stegosaurus* lived about 150 million years ago, in the Late Jurassic, while *Tyrannosaurus* lived only 65.5 million years ago, at the end of the Late Cretaceous. In fact, if you do the math, you see that *Tyrannosaurus* lived closer in time to us humans than it did to *Stegosaurus*. So in terms of geologic time, a picture showing *Tyrannosaurus* running down the street where you live is actually more realistic than one showing *Tyrannosaurus* fighting *Stegosaurus*!

For the same reason, any picture that shows *Stegosaurus* watching the great asteroid impact at the end of the Age of Dinosaurs is also wrong. *Stegosaurus* itself had been extinct for over 80 million years when the asteroid hit!

Yet another *Stegosaurus* myth is that it's a "one of a kind" dinosaur. While it certainly had a few features that were unique to it, *Stegosaurus* is just one out of many different types of plated dinosaurs who make up Stegosauria.

INTRODUCING STEGOSAURIA

Stegosauria is one of two major branches of Thyreophora (the other being Ankylosauria). All stegosaurs have the same basic shape. Stegosaurs were four-legged dinosaurs, with hands that had evolved into broad feet with blunt hooves instead of claws. Their skulls were rather long and pointy, although primitive stegosaurs (like *Huayangosaurus* and *Hesperosaurus*) had shorter and

Stegosaurus armor included plates, the spiked thagomizer (close-up left), and small armored knobs under the neck (close-up right).

broader skulls than the advanced ones (like *Tuojiangosaurus* and *Stegosaurus*). The teeth of stegosaurs were leaf-shaped and showed that they ate plants. In *Huayangosaurus* (the most primitive known stegosaur), the teeth go all the way to the front of the upper jaw, but in all others, the front of the snout (the premaxilla bone) was covered with a toothless beak.

With the exception of *Huayangosaurus,* all stegosaurs had front limbs that were much shorter than the hind limbs. This gave their bodies a tall, arched shape from the neck to the hip. The vertebrae of the back (between the shoulders and the hips) in stegosaurs are very unusual. They are stretched upward, making the dinosaurs even taller. Stegosaur tails are fairly deep from top to bottom and narrow from side to side.

Based on the relative length of their front legs to their back legs, and from their feet to their shins to their thighs, it's unlikely that stegosaurs were fast runners. They could, however, probably move side to side fairly well. This would have helped them use their most famous feature: their armor.

STEGOSAUR ARMOR

Stegosaurs evolved from a dinosaur similar to *Scelidosaurus,* with big osteoderms, or scutes, that lay flat in the skin over much of its body. Some of these scutes in *Scelidosaurus* were flat-topped; others were topped with a low ridge. Stegosaurs had some scutes of both sorts. For example, the most

Heads of the stegosaurs *Hesperosaurus* (top), *Huayangosaurus* (middle), and *Tuojiangosaurus* (bottom).

complete skeleton of *Stegosaurus* shows flat and ridged scutes covering its thighs.

Stegosaurs (or at least some of them) also had a sort of neck armor. This consisted of many very small scutes embedded in the skin of the neck. This arrangement kept the neck flexible but protected (should a theropod try to rip the stegosaur's throat out). This combination of flexibility and protection worked like the chain mail of a medieval soldier.

But the armor that makes stegosaurs most spectacular is their plates and spikes. Each type of stegosaur had a different number, shape, size, and pattern of plates and spikes on its body. This makes each type of stegosaur very distinctive. A plate is an osteoderm that is tall and flat, like a bony pancake sticking out of the dinosaur's back. Stegosaurs had plates running down their backs. In more primitive stegosaurs, these plates were paired and not terribly big. In more advanced stegosaurs, these plates were tall, and in *Stegosaurus* (at least) they weren't paired but alternated right and left. Stegosaur plates came in a

variety of shapes: oval, triangular, and some that looked like a French symbol called a fleur-de-lis.

Unlike plates, spikes were always pointed. Some stegosaurs (although apparently not *Stegosaurus*) had spikes sticking out of their shoulders. In some, the spikes followed the plates in pairs down the back. But most significantly, all stegosaurs had at least a pair of spikes facing sideways at the end of the tail. When swung back and forth, these spikes made an impressive weapon that could pierce the flesh of an attacking theropod.

Cartoonist Gary Larson once drew a *Far Side* cartoon showing a bunch of cavemen being warned about the danger of stegosaurs, and he called their tail weapon a "thagomizer." Denver paleontologist Ken Carpenter thought that "thagomizer" was a good name, so he used it in his 1993 scientific presentation of the most complete *Stegosaurus* ever found. That name stuck, and now it is accepted scientific nomenclature to say that stegosaurs are characterized by having a thagomizer.

And here are another couple of stego-myths to dispel. Marsh drew a famous picture of *Stegosaurus* with its thagomizer spikes facing upward, and for over 120 years everybody assumed that this was their correct position. If you have a *Stegosaurus* toy, it probably shows thagomizer spikes like that. But in 1993, Ken Carpenter pointed out that the bones of his newly discovered complete *Stegosaurus*—as well as some that had been known even to Marsh—showed that the spikes faced sideways and backward. This solved a bit of a mystery, since stegosaur tails were not particularly flexible enough to strike like a scorpion (as implied by Marsh's upward-facing spikes). However, a side-to-side swat would have been easy for a stegosaur to do. The other thagomizer myth has to do with the number of tail spikes. Because he didn't have complete skeletons to work with, Marsh thought that at least some species of *Stegosaurus* had four pairs of thagomizer spikes. Carpenter has gone back to examine the evidence and shown that there is no sign that any *Stegosaurus* species had more than two pairs of

Spiky *Tuojiangosaurus* of the Late Jurassic of China.

active defense than their relatives. They had spikes and thagomizers facing backward, so if they were attacked, they would have tried to keep their prickly tail end facing their attacker. The stegosaur could then try to get away and if chased take a swipe at its pursuer. There is direct evidence that stegosaurs used their thagomizers to defend. In a recent study, it was shown that about one out of every ten thagomizers collected shows signs of damage, probably from striking the bone of an attacker. This would have been painful to both the meat-eater and the stegosaur. Even more impressive is the new discovery of an *Allosaurus* tail bone showing that it had been pierced by a *Stegosaurus* thagomizer spike. (The *Allosaurus* must have lived after it had been hit, because the bones had rehealed. We don't know, however, if the *Stegosaurus* survived the attack.)

STEGOSAURS AROUND THE WORLD

The oldest traces of stegosaurs are some fossil footprints from the Early Jurassic Epoch of France and Australia. The oldest known stegosaur *bones* are those of *Huayangosaurus* from the Middle Jurassic Epoch of China. It is one of the smallest stegosaurs, at 15 feet (4.6 meters) long. Slightly younger and larger, at 20 feet (6.1 meters) long, was *Lexovisaurus* of Europe.

spikes on its thagomizer.

And how was the armor used? In other four-legged armored dinosaurs, like *Scelidosaurus* and typical ankylosaurs, the armor was strictly passive. If attacked, those dinosaurs would hunker down and let the attacker waste energy (and maybe break some teeth) trying to bite through their scutes. Stegosaurs seemed to have done things differently. They evolved lighter and more specialized plates and spikes than their heavily armored ancestors (which probably closely resembled *Scelidosaurus*), allowing them to be more maneuverable. This leads us to believe that they used a more

The Late Jurassic saw a great flourishing of stegosaurs around the world. In Europe, there was *Dacentrurus;* in North America, there was smaller *Hesperosaurus,* and *Stegosaurus* itself, the largest of the stegosaurs at 30 feet (9.1 meters) long (and *possibly Hypsirophus,* if it really is a different dinosaur than *Stegosaurus*); in Africa, there was spiky *Kentrosaurus;* and in Asia, there was *Chialingosaurus, Chungkingosaurus,* and *Tuojiangosaurus.* In fact, stegosaurs are among the most common dinosaurs found at Late

The spikes and thagomizer of *Tuojiangosaurus* are used as a defense against marauding *Yangchuanosaurus.*

Jurassic Epoch dinosaur sites—only sauropods are more common.

Stegosaurs continued to survive in the Early Cretaceous, but they were less common. *Wuerhosaurus* of Asia, *Paranthodon* of Africa, and *Craterosaurus* and *Regnosaurus* of Europe are all Early Cretaceous stegosaurs. But unlike in the Jurassic, stegosaurs weren't the most common armored dinosaurs in the Cretaceous. Their ankylosaur relatives were becoming more numerous.

This brings me to yet another stego-myth: the supposed "lost world of stegosaurs" in Madagascar and India. There are some teeth, pieces of armor, and bones from Madagascar and India that until the 1990s were thought by some to come from stegosaurs. These were far younger than any other stegosaur fossil found in other parts of the world. Because Madagascar and India were isolated from all other lands (although originally connected to each other) during the Late Cretaceous, some paleontologists speculated that these were "lost worlds" where stegosaurs survived after going extinct everywhere else.

Sadly, we now know that this probably never happened. Closer examination of the Indian fossils in the 1990s showed that some were from the armor of titanosaur sauropods, and the others were mistakenly identified bones of marine reptiles (plesiosaurs). And at the same time, it was found that the Madagascan teeth came from the weird herbivorous crocodilian relatives of the Cretaceous (such as *Simosuchus*). So the "lost world of the stegosaurs" idea, while reasonable and exciting, isn't based on any physical evidence.

LIFE HABITS OF PLATED DINOSAURS

Although no one has yet found and described a stegosaur nest, there are known baby stegosaurs. These look a lot like their parents, but their armor is much smaller in proportion to their body size.

Because their forelimbs were generally much shorter than their hind limbs, stegosaurs had heads that were fairly low to the ground. This meant they mostly would have eaten smaller shrubs and other small plants rather than trees.

Some paleontologists have speculated that stegosaurs might have reared up on their hind legs to feed higher in the trees, but while this might have been possible, most of their anatomy suggests that they fed low to the ground. (And besides, there were plenty of iguanodontians and sauropods feeding higher than the stegosaurs, so it would make sense that instead of competing with these other dinosaurs, the stegosaurs were low-feeding specialists.) Because their snouts were narrow rather than broad, they were probably picky about which plants they fed on (rather than munching on different plants at once, as ankylosaurs probably did).

And what about those famous plates down the stegosaurs' backs? What purpose did they serve? If they were for defense, why evolve from spikes (which seem to be the original shape of the big osteoderms) to plates? Spikes, after all, could cause serious injury if a theropod ran into them, while plates would have not hurt the attackers at all.

A number of ideas have been suggested for the change from pointed spikes to flat plates. Some paleontologists think that the spikes became broader so that the stegosaurs could catch and

The thagomizer of *Stegosaurus* provided a powerful defense . . .

. . . but against many attackers even that might not be enough.

release more heat. A stegosaur could face its plates into the sun to warm itself when it was cold. And it could face them into the wind to lose heat if the animal was hot. An alternate hypothesis is that stegosaurs could change the color of their plates, perhaps as a warning sign. According to this idea, the stegosaur would flush blood into skin covering the plates and quickly change their color.

The problem with these two hypotheses is that the plates, like spikes and all thyreophoran osteoderms, would not have been covered with skin. Instead, there would have been a layer of living tissue and then a layer of horny keratin covering them. And keratin, as dead tissue, would not be full of blood vessels. So a stegosaur plate couldn't gain heat, lose heat, or change color quickly.

Probably the most important characteristic of a stegosaur plate is that it is broad, like a roadside billboard. And like a billboard, it might have been

used as a sign. Perhaps stegosaur plates were a sign that said, "Stay away!" to theropods, because they made the stegosaur look bigger from the side than it really was. Or maybe the sign said, "Hey, I'm a *Stegosaurus stenops* and not a *Stegosaurus ungulatus*." In other words, because each species of stegosaur had a different number, pattern, and size of plates and spikes, any stegosaur could tell at a glance if another stegosaur was one of its own species or not. We may never be able to exactly read the signs of a stegosaur plate, but it seems most likely that these distinctive dinosaurs evolved their big plates precisely *to be* distinctive. And even millions of years later, we can still recognize the different species from their plates.

Sauropelta

Euoplocephalus

29

ANKYLOSAURS
(Tank Dinosaurs)

One of the most successful of all the ornithischian groups is Ankylosauria, the tank dinosaurs. They are known from every continent except Africa, and lived from the Middle Jurassic Epoch until the very end of the Cretaceous Period. While some ankylosaurs were only 10 to 13 feet (3 to 4 meters) long, others were the largest of all the Thyreophora (the armored dinosaurs). The biggest ankylosaurs were even bigger than the biggest stegosaurs—their closest relatives among thyreophorans. The key to the group's success was probably its extreme armor. No other dinosaur group was so well protected.

DEFENSE, DEFENSE, DEFENSE

The first known fossil of an ankylosaur was *Hylaeosaurus,* described by Gideon Mantell in 1833. It was one of the original three members of Sir Richard Owen's Dinosauria. But *Hylaeosaurus* was known only from the back of the skull to the middle of the torso, so paleontologists didn't have a good idea of what it looked like. In fact, we still don't know what the complete skull or hind end of *Hylaeosaurus* looked like.

Over the decades, though, more-complete tank dinosaur fossils were found. Among them was *Ankylosaurus* (fused reptile) of the very end of the Cretaceous Period. *Ankylosaurus* was one of the largest of the ankylosaurs, at 30 feet (9.1 meters) long, and the one that gave the group its name. They were called fused reptiles because they had what seemed to be scutes fused onto their skull bones. New studies suggest that most of this head armor, though, was really produced by growth outward from the skull bones themselves

rather than being armor from the skin that grew down into the skull.

The bodies of ankylosaurs were covered with osteoderms (bony armor in the skin). Some of these, like the ones on the neck, were joined together in big rings. Others, like those over the hips of some ankylosaurs, fused together to form big shields. Many ankylosaur osteoderms were like those of *Scelidosaurus,* embedded in the skin. But ankylosaurs had far more osteoderms than did *Scelidosaurus.* Some even had armored eyelids!

FUEL FOR A TANK

There is more to tank dinosaurs than their armor, however. They had other features that made them special among the dinosaurs. Their legs tended to be short, thick, and stocky, and their hands and feet were broad. They probably were not very good runners. No one has ever suggested (as some have about stegosaurs) that ankylosaurs could rear up on their hind legs to feed higher in the trees.

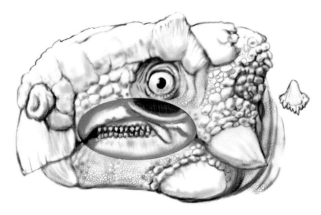

The skull of the ankylosaurid *Pinacosaurus,* with a close-up of its tiny teeth.

It's agreed they must have fed low to the ground.

But what did they feed on? In the mid-twentieth century, a few paleontologists suggested that ankylosaurs were ant-eaters. (Perhaps they were reminded of armadillos or armored lizards that eat ants.) But most paleontologists—then and now—agree that tank dinosaurs were plant-eaters. In fact, the fossil of the small Australian ankylosaur *Minmi* contains the remains of its last meal: various types of plants.

Ankylosaur teeth look like those of herbivorous lizards. In fact, some of the first ankylosaur teeth found were thought to come from a big extinct herbivorous lizard. Except for the more primitive forms, ankylosaurs had broad snouts, suggesting that they weren't picky about what they ate and munched on whatever low-lying plants they could find. Their hips were particularly wide and broad, and they had very wide bellies. This would have helped them digest all the different leaves they found.

For a long time, it was thought that ankylosaurs just mashed up their food like modern plant-eating lizards rather than chewing or grinding it up like a mammal or a hadrosauroid. But recent studies by Paul Barrett, Natalia Rybczynski, and Matthew Vickaryous have shown that not to be the case. By studying the wear on ankylosaur teeth, as well as the shape of the joints in the lower jaw, these paleontologists have shown that there was some motion forward and backward, and side to side, when an ankylosaur fed.

The discovery of the moving joints in the ankylosaur lower jaw surprised many paleontologists but also helped explain something. Ankylosaurs have very small teeth compared to their body size, and paleontologists had wondered how they got enough food to survive. (This is one reason why it was thought that they might have been insect-eaters, because insects provide more energy per biteful than plants.) Now we know that ankylosaurs did more chewing than previously thought, which would have helped them digest faster, so they could get enough energy from plants alone.

TYPES OF TANKS

Figuring out the evolutionary relationships between the different ankylosaur groups has been very difficult. This is, in part, because we know a lot about some of the ankylosaur groups from the end of the Late Cretaceous of North America and Asia, a fair amount about those from the Early Cretaceous of North America, and much less about those from the Jurassic of North America or those of any age from other parts of the world. (Thankfully, that is beginning to change.)

Paleontologists have long recognized two major groups of tank dinosaurs. One, called

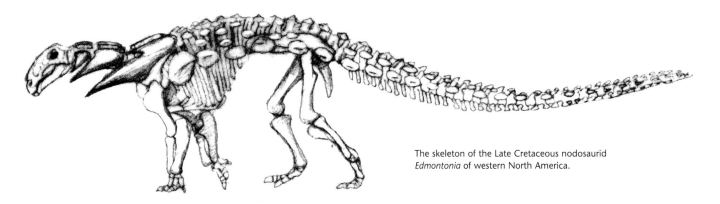

The skeleton of the Late Cretaceous nodosaurid *Edmontonia* of western North America.

236

The skeleton of the Late Cretaceous ankylosaurid *Euoplocephalus* of western North America.

Nodosauridae, is best known from the Late Cretaceous North American dinosaurs *Nodosaurus, Panoplosaurus, Silvisaurus,* and *Edmontonia,* and the Early Cretaceous North American *Sauropelta.* This group probably contains the Late Cretaceous European *Struthiosaurus* and the recently discovered forms from Utah, Early to Late Cretaceous *Animantarx* and gigantic *Cedarpelta,* which was 33 feet (10.1 meters) long (making it the biggest thyreophoran), plus a few others. Nodosaurids were notable for having very large shoulder spines and lots of other spines as well. Nodosaurid heads were smoother over the top and back than those of other ankylosaurs, lacking the little horns that are found in the others.

Traditionally, all other tank dinosaurs are placed in the group Ankylosauridae. Ankylosaurids include many well-known genera of Late Cretaceous dinosaurs, such as the North American forms *Ankylosaurus, Euoplocephalus,* and *Nodocephalosaurus* and the Asian dinosaurs *Pina-*

cosaurus, Talarurus, Tarchia, Saichania, and *Tsagantegia.* Early representatives of this group are the Early Cretaceous Asian *Shamosaurus* and *Gobisaurus.* Ankylosaurids are the so-called club-tailed ankylosaurs because they have a bunch of osteoderms fused together at the end of the tail, forming a massive, powerful club. This club was supported by strongly interlocking tail vertebrae and (unlike most pictures in books or movies!) was not very flexible. All of the flexibility was at the base of the tail, right behind the hips. So the ankylosaurid tail club would swing stiffly from side to side. This would have been an effective active defense, similar to the thagomizer of stegosaurs. In a big ankylosaurid (like *Ankylosaurus*), the blow from the tail club would be devastating: it could crush a dromaeosaurid raptor's body and break the leg or snout of an attacking *Tyrannosaurus.*

Ankylosaurids were more than just their tail clubs, though. They also had shorter, deeper snouts than nodosaurids and small horns on the

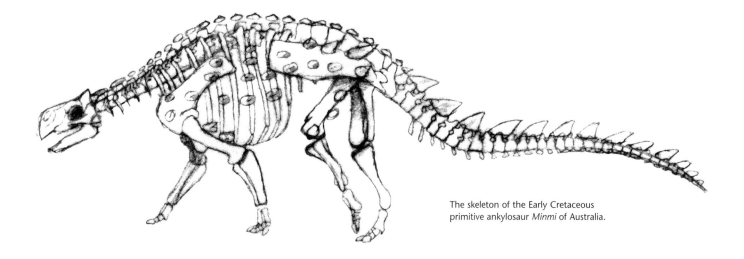

The skeleton of the Early Cretaceous primitive ankylosaur *Minmi* of Australia.

back of their skulls. And here is where some confusion comes in. Some Late Jurassic forms (like *Gargoyleosaurus* from Wyoming) and Early Cretaceous ankylosaurs (like *Minmi*) have these same little horns but otherwise have narrower skulls and no tail clubs. Recent cladistic studies by Matthew Vickaryous, Teresa Maryaska, and Dave Weishampel suggest these smaller, earlier ankylosaurs were more closely related to *Ankylosaurus* than to *Nodosaurus:* in other words, they were early *clubless* ankylosaurids. Although this is a very reasonable hypothesis, other studies come up with an equally reasonable idea: that the two groups Nodosauridae and Ankylosauridae were more closely related to each other than either was to *Minmi* or *Gargoyleosaurus.* This is also a reasonable hypothesis. In fact, the recently discovered Chinese tank dinosaur *Liaoningosaurus* very likely branched off from other ankylosaurs before the ankylosaurid-nodosaurid split.

Minmi of Australia.

Gastonia, a polacanthid, is menaced by *Utahraptor* (the largest known dromaeosaurid).

Other confusing tank dinosaurs are the so-called polacanthids. These include Late Jurassic and Early Cretaceous ankylosaurs, including *Polacanthus, Dracopelta,* and *Hylaeosaurus* of Europe, and *Gastonia* and *Mymoorapelta* of North America. Some analyses place some of these genera closer to definite nodosaurids and others closer to definite ankylosaurids, in which case these don't form their own group. But other studies show them as each other's closest relatives—a group called Polacanthidae, which itself might be closer to Ankylosauridae or to Nodosauridae. This situation is currently unresolved and represents an important field of dinosaur research.

And just to mess things up further, a few paleontologists have suggested that *Scelidosaurus* was actually a very primitive ankylosaur!

So take the above as both a message and a warning. The message: there was a lot of diversity among the tank dinosaurs, which were an important group. The warning: the ankylosaur cladograms shown in this book are a hypothesis based on a particular set of analyses, and new information may instead support a different cladogram in the future.

MYSTERY NOSES

There is another, rather surprising, field of interest in tank dinosaur studies: figuring out what they did with their noses. Paleontologists have spent a lot of time peering into the nostril regions of ankylosaurs, which are more complicated than the simple holes in the skulls of most other dinosaurs.

Nodosaurids, ankylosaurids, and other ankylosaurs have complex chambers in their nasal passages. The purposes of these chambers are uncertain, as their structure differs in different types of tank dinosaurs. Perhaps they increased the surface area for the sense of smell? Or supported tissue that would help keep the lungs moist? Maybe they helped generate particular sounds? At present we do not know.

One new set of discoveries is particular to certain members of Ankylosauridae. Paleontologists—including Larry Witmer—have been examining the nostril region of the desert ankylosaurid *Pinacosaurus.* For many years, it has seemed that *Pinacosaurus* (strangely) had more than one nostril opening on each side of the face. But in 2003, Larry Witmer used a CAT scan of a *Pinacosaurus* skull to show that only one opening per side was really a nostril. The others housed some sort of tissue. But what? Work is still going on in this project, but the initial results suggest that there was some sort of inflatable structure associated with these openings. Did *Pinacosaurus* have an inflatable trunk like an elephant seal? Or something even weirder, unlike any living animal? Work continues on this mysterious nose.

Edmontonia of the forests of the Late Cretaceous of western North America.

The Late Cretaceous ankylosaurid *Tarchia* of Mongolia.

TANK DINOSAURS AT HOME

Fossils of ankylosaurs of all age groups, from little babies to full-grown adults, are known. The armor of baby ankylosaurs was much less well developed than it was in young ones, and that of young ones was less well developed than that of adults. In fact, the babies and juveniles didn't have any head armor at all.

We do know that at least some baby tank dinosaurs lived with each other. In one famous fossil find, several baby *Pinacosaurus* were found to have been buried together in a sandstorm. No adult skeletons were found nearby, so we don't know if the babies lived together on their own as a group, or if one or both parents were separated from them during the sandstorm.

Ankylosaurs lived in a variety of environments. Some were at home in deserts, while others came from forested regions with rivers and lakes. Sev-

eral species seem to have lived near the seashores, and in fact several nodosaurid species are only known from skeletons that floated out to sea and were buried in marine mud. But these dinosaurs were not sea creatures by any means! It is just that the armor of a dead tank dinosaur would help preserve its body and keep it floating in the sea longer than an unarmored dead dinosaur.

Armor (and the occasional tail club) was the ankylosaurs' only defense against theropods. But because ankylosaur history is so long, different tank dinosaur genera had to stand up to different meat-eating attackers. Sometimes these predators would have been much larger than they were, as in the case of little *Gargoyleosaurus*: only 10 feet (3 meters) long in a world patrolled by giants like *Allosaurus* and *Torvosaurus.* In other cases, the

Ankylosaurus defends itself against *Tyrannosaurus.*

ankylosaur was bigger than its most common predator. *Sauropelta* was much larger than the dromaeosaurid *Deinonychus,* for instance, and seems to have been pretty well protected from that pack-hunting raptor. Finding evidence of *Deinonychus* feeding on *Sauropelta* is very rare, but it is common to find evidence of *Deinonychus* feeding on the nonarmored ornithopod *Tenontosaurus.*

The later ankylosaurids had a particularly fearsome set of foes in the form of the tyrannosaurids. In fact, it may be that the big tail club of the later ankylosaurids evolved especially to defend against the slender legs of the tyrant dinosaurs. However, the tyrannosaurids managed to get to the head of the armored dinosaurs in at least some cases. In fact, there is a skull of the giant ankylosaurid *Tarchia* with a wound that was almost certainly produced by the bite of the even larger tyrannosaurid *Tarbosaurus.*

Ankylosaurs were still present on many continents all the way up to the end of the Mesozoic Era. Then, 65.5 million years ago, they faced a threat from which even their armor couldn't save them.

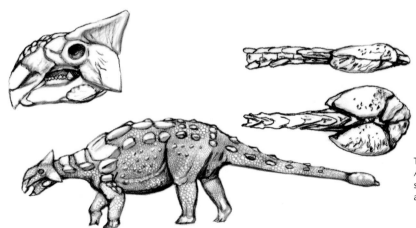

The Late Cretaceous ankylosaurid *Ankylosaurus,* with close-ups of its skull (top left) and tail club (side and bottom view right).

Drinker

Hypsilophodon

30

PRIMITIVE ORNITHOPODS
(Primitive Beaked Dinosaurs)

When someone says "dinosaur," we usually think of the really impressive ones like the giant sauropods, or the meat-eaters *Tyrannosaurus* and *Spinosaurus,* or those with weird features like *Stegosaurus* with its plates and spikes. But not all dinosaurs were that impressive. Among the ones that don't look very interesting—but that are very important nevertheless—are the primitive members of the group Ornithopoda, the beaked dinosaurs.

A POOR CHOICE OF NAMES

Ornithopoda isn't a very good name. It means "bird feet," but the feet of ornithopods are not particularly birdlike. Advanced ornithopods (the iguanodontians, including the duckbilled hadrosauroids) *do* have three main toes (as do birds), but lack a reduced first toe like the one that faces backward in most birds. And primitive ornithopods—like the ones in this chapter—walked on four forward-facing toes. Nevertheless, we are stuck with the name that O. C. Marsh gave them in 1881.

What makes an ornithopod an ornithopod isn't its feet, however, but its mouth. Like most ornithischians, all ornithopods had a beak in the front of their jaws. But ornithopods differ from other ornithischians by having a premaxilla bone (the front bone of the upper jaw) that reaches farther down than the maxilla bone (the second bone in the upper jaw). And the jaw joint of ornithopods is placed farther down than in other dinosaurs. This combination of features means that ornithopods had a very powerful bite. So "beaked dinosaurs" would have been a better name than "bird feet."

Regardless of their name, the primitive ornithopods (those *not* part of the advanced group Iguanodontia, covered in the next two chapters) mostly had simple leaf-shaped teeth, like those in other primitive ornithischians (*Lesothosaurus,* thyreophorans, and pachycephalosaurs). So, like other ornithischians, these dinosaurs were plant-eaters. Primitive ornithopods were all fairly small: most were just about 3 feet (0.9 meters) long—smaller than a human kid—while a few got up to 8 feet (2.4 meters) long.

These dinosaurs kept the primitive dinosaur habit of walking on their hind legs. In fact, given that most of these dinosaurs had fairly long legs, they were probably swift runners. This was most likely one of their defenses. Another defense may have been that they simply bred rapidly. If there are many individuals of a species around, some probably *won't* get eaten by predators. So chances are pretty good that the species will survive. In fact, their defense might have been a combination of the two—modern rabbits, for example, are fast runners and can also increase their population in a hurry.

The Early Cretaceous ornithopod *Hypsilophodon* of Europe and North America.

Whatever their defenses, primitive ornithopods were a very successful kind of dinosaur. They first appear in the Early Jurassic and persist all the way until the end of the Cretaceous. In fact, there are some Middle Jurassic primitive ornithopods that are nearly identical to the latest Cretaceous primitive ornithopods—a span of roughly 115 million years!

The dinosaurs in this chapter do not represent a single complete group. Instead, these are all the different kinds of ornithopods, except for the bigger, more advanced Iguanodontia. In the older Linnaean system, the dinosaurs in this chapter were grouped together into "Hypsilophodontia." But some "hypsilophodonts" were actually more closely related to iguanodonts than they were to other "hypsilophodonts." And, in fact, some recent studies suggest that other dinosaurs (in particular, the pachycephalosaurs and ceratopsians) might also be descendants of some "hypsilophodonts."

A TREE-DWELLING DINOSAUR? (PROBABLY NOT)

The "hypsilophodonts" are named after *Hypsilophodon* from the Early Cretaceous of Europe and North America. These dinosaurs don't have any particular specializations in common that aren't also found in Iguanodontia. Some of the features that the two share are stubby fingers and long, bony tendons in the hips and tail. Primitive beaked dinosaurs had fairly light skulls, and so they probably ate relatively soft vegetation.

The skulls of *Hypsilophodon* and its relatives were lightly built with good reason. Like their descendants (the iguanodontians), these primitive ornithopods had upper jawbones that would move slightly outward when the lower jaw came up. This

The toothy beak of *Hypsilophodon* allowed it to chop up plants.

trees. These tree-dwelling marsupials might have inspired early paleontologists to think that *Hypsilophodon* was a tree ornithopod.

However, when later paleontologists examined the feet of *Hypsilophodon,* they didn't have the traits of a tree climber. Climbing animals normally have longer toe bones toward the tips of their toes. But *Hypsilophodon* had the feet of a ground dweller, with shorter toe bones toward the tips. (It's hard to say why earlier paleontologists didn't notice this.)

There is other evidence that *Hypsilophodon* and its close relatives were runners. Most of the bones in their tails (particularly the parts toward the end) were bound together by tendons that had turned to bone. This means that their tails were very stiff. Stiff tails are used by various animals (such as some modern lizards, and dinosaurs such as dromaeosaurid raptors) as a counterbalance to turn quickly while running. Having a good counterbalance meant that a primitive ornithopod would be fairly agile, a helpful trait when being chased by a predator!

FATHOMING FOSSILS

We know from many skeletons that baby *Hypsilophodon* and other baby ornithopods are like smaller versions of the grown-ups, with bigger eyes and smaller snouts. You may have seen pictures, movies, or TV shows depicting these big-eyed babies living in nests. In fact, in some well-known TV documentaries you may have seen many nests of primitive ornithopods arranged in a colony and the parents living in a complex social structure. That is certainly possible, but at present there is no evidence to support it. As of now, we don't actually know what primitive ornithopod nests are like. Paleontologists once *thought* they had found the nests of the ornithopod *Orodromeus,* but these turned out to be from the theropod *Troodon.*

Another possibly mistaken ornithopod fossil is the "heart" of one of the last of the primitive ornithopods, *Thescelosaurus.* The most complete fossil of this dinosaur, found in 1993 and nicknamed "Willo," had a lump found in its chest area.

meant that their teeth would slide past each other, helping them to chew their food. This sort of skull joint was only slightly developed in the primitive ornithopods, but it would have helped them chew their food and digest it faster.

Hypsilophodon was one of the first small dinosaurs recognized by science, and it has long intrigued paleontologists. How did it live? One idea proposed early on was that it might have been a tree dweller. Today there are tree kangaroos in Australia and nearby islands that are about the same size and shape as *Hypsilophodon* (approximately 5 feet [1.5 meters] long) and that climb in

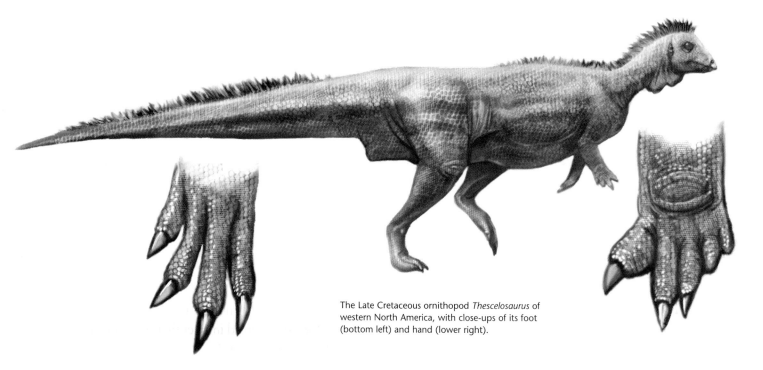

The Late Cretaceous ornithopod *Thescelosaurus* of western North America, with close-ups of its foot (bottom left) and hand (lower right).

Some paleontologists suggest that this is a petrified heart. Other paleontologists suggest it is just a lump of stone. (No one doubts that *Thescelosaurus had* a heart, only that this lump was the fossilized remains of it.) In any case, "Willo" is a very special fossil in that it shows skin impressions of a primitive ornithopod. Like other ornithischians, it had round scales of various sizes all over the body.

LOTS OF LITTLE DINOSAURS

Hypsilophodon is the most famous of this general type of dinosaur with good reason. This genus is known from many fossils, from babies to adults. It has also been known for a long time. But it is far from the only one of this type. In fact, there are lots of these little dinosaurs. Dinosaurs of this sort have been found on every continent.

There are several small ornithischians known from China that might be primitive ornithopods. However, they might instead be even more primitive branches of the ornithischian family tree. These include *Agilisaurus, Hexinlusaurus,* and *Xiaosaurus* from the Middle Jurassic; *Yandusaurus* from the Late Jurassic; and *Jeholosaurus* from the Early Cretaceous. Late Jurassic American *Othnielia* and *Drinker* were tiny little ornithopods that lived in the shadow of larger and more famous

dinosaurs, such as *Brachiosaurus, Stegosaurus,* and *Allosaurus. Zephyrosaurus*—named after the swift Greek god of the west wind—hopefully lived up to its name when being chased by the raptor *Deinonychus* in Early Cretaceous North America.

In the Early Cretaceous, Australia seems to have been crawling with little ornithopods: *Atlascopcosaurus, Fulgurotherium, Leaellynasaura,* and *Qantassaurus.* Interestingly, because the continents have been moving, these dinosaurs actually lived south of the Antarctic Circle and so would have gone for months without light. But they would have been rewarded during the summer, when the sun would shine twenty-four hours a day for months, and the plants they ate would flourish. (That doesn't happen today because the Antarctic has become too cold for plants to grow at all.)

There are few ornithischians known from the Late Cretaceous of South America, but the primitive ornithopods were definitely there. *Anabisetia, Gasparinisaura,* and *Notohypsilophodon* are known from that time and place.

Even at the end of the Age of Dinosaurs, primitive ornithopods were still present. In western North America, some genera—like *Orodromeus*—were very similar to Jurassic and Early Cretaceous primitive ornithopods in size and shape. But

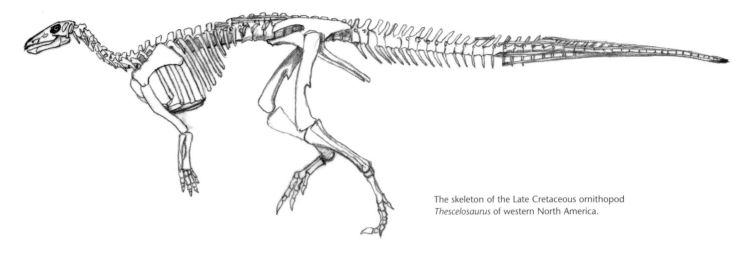

The skeleton of the Late Cretaceous ornithopod *Thescelosaurus* of western North America.

others, like *Parksosaurus, Bugenasaura,* and *Thescelosaurus,* were larger (up to 8 feet [2.4 meters] long) and had longer snouts. These last dinosaurs would have been food for young tyrannosaurs or full-grown raptors. *Bugenasaura* and *Thescelosaurus* were among the last ornithischians to live, and it is possible that some individuals of these genera actually witnessed the terrible hours and days after the asteroid impact that brought the Age of Dinosaurs to its end.

A group of *Hypsilophodon* is attacked by the tyrannosauroid *Eotyrannus* in Early Cretaceous Europe.

Tough Little Dinosaurs

Dr. Patricia Vickers-Rich
Monash University,
Melbourne, Australia
and Dr. Thomas H. Rich
Museum of Victoria,
Melbourne, Australia

Photo courtesy of Thomas H. Rich

Some dinosaurs had it tough. When most people think of dinosaurs, they think of them in steaming swamps or arid uplands. They usually think of them as big—like Tyrannosaurus rex. But some of the toughest dinosaurs were little, and they lived in places that had winter snow and ice and darkness for three months of the year.

One group of little dinosaurs, the hypsilophodontids, thrived and diversified in one of the most difficult places on Earth—near the South Pole of the time, at what is now about 38 degrees south, not far from the Australian city of Melbourne. Today this place has a temperate climate. It is mild with no winter snow or ice. But during the Early Cretaceous Epoch, from about 120 to 105 million years ago, this region lay at about 75 degrees south. Structures in the rocks tell that at times the ground was permanently frozen—it had permafrost. Great rivers snaked across a vast floodplain that separated the south coast of Australia from Antarctica to the south. Isotopic studies of these waters today tell scientists that these streams were once cold.

In this cold place, the sun did not shine for three months during the winter because of the high latitude. The hypsilophodontids (meaning "high-crowned tooth") thrived in this region. Most hypsilophodontids were about the size of a chicken, although a few kinds reached the size of an emu. These little dinosaurs probably did not hibernate—bone studies show that they continued to grow all year long. They had huge eyes, and the optic lobes—the parts of the brain that helped them see—were immense. Paleontologists have suggested that these little dinosaurs were probably warm-blooded and could see in the dark. One of these dinosaurs, Leaellynasaura amicagraphica, is named after our daughter, Leaellyn Rich, who has found a number of new dinosaur sites in Australia and Patagonia.

The hypsilophodontids were tough—but so were the people who discovered them and dug them up. One site in Australia named Dinosaur Cove has yielded many different kinds of dinosaurs from these frozen wastes. The bones were found underground, and we had to work the site like a mine. Our digging crew used explosives, rock drills, and heavy mining equipment to dig many meters underground, following an old stream channel that contained concentrated bones. These fossiliferous rocks lay at sea level along a rugged coastline, so work could only progress when the tide was out and had to stop before the high tide, when the tunnels were underwater.

These tough little dinosaurs were not the easiest to find and dig up, but they give us some ideas about the kinds of severe climatic conditions dinosaurs could endure. They suggest that whatever happened at the end of the Cretaceous, which led to the extinction of so many dinosaur groups, must have happened over a longer period than a year or so—because dinosaurs like these that lived in polar regions could have dealt with a shorter-lived catastrophe.

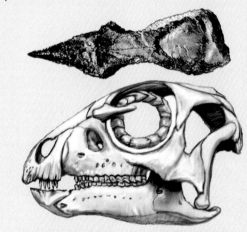

The original specimen of *Leaellynasaura* (top) was the upper part of its skull. The fossil showed that it resembled *Hypsilophodon* but had enormous eyes (reconstructed skull below).

Iguanodon

Ouranosaurus

Camptosaurus

31

IGUANODONTIANS
(Advanced Beaked Dinosaurs)

In the previous chapter, we looked at primitive ornithopods. These dinosaurs were mostly small, and included among them are both the earliest and some of the latest beaked dinosaurs. You may have come away from that chapter thinking that primitive ornithopods were boring. I confess, I sometimes think that myself. But while it's true some of them were pretty much unchanged from the Middle Jurassic until the end of the Late Cretaceous, the primitive ornithopods actually *did* do something rather exciting. They evolved into the advanced ornithopods, or Iguanodontia!

The iguanodonts are named after *Iguanodon,* one of the first dinosaurs discovered. In fact, *Iguanodon* is one of the best understood of *all* dinosaurs because many complete *Iguanodon* skeletons have been discovered. But there are many other iguanodonts beyond *Iguanodon* itself. Some were small plant-eaters barely distinguishable from more primitive types of beaked dinosaurs. Others were giants with strange fins, stumpy legs, or tall noses. A fair number had very peculiar—but useful—hands. And iguanodonts belonging to Hadrosauroidea, or duckbill dinosaurs, were *so* specialized and so diverse that they rate an entire chapter to themselves! In this chapter, we'll look at the beaked dinosaurs that fit on the family tree between primitive forms (like *Orodromeus, Hypsilophodon,* and *Thescelosaurus*) on one side and the duckbills on the other.

HUMBLE ORIGINS, GREAT SUCCESSES

The oldest iguanodont—*Callovosaurus* of the Middle Jurassic Epoch of England—is known only from a thighbone, so we can't say much about it. But other primitive (and more complete) iguanodont specimens from later in time give us an idea of what *Callovosaurus* probably looked like. *Dryosaurus, Valdosaurus,* and *Talenkauen* are all good examples of the least specialized sorts of iguanodonts.

At first glance, these dinosaurs seem to be hard to differentiate from *Hypsilophodon,* a typical primitive beaked ornithopod. And, in fact, when they were discovered, they *were* considered hypsilophodonts. But if you look in their mouths, you'll see why they are not. Their premaxilla (the front bone of the upper jaw) has no teeth: it is just a toothless beak. This is different from more primitive ornithopods (and from most other dinosaurs and, for that matter, from you and me), who have teeth in the premaxilla. The lower jaws of the iguanodonts are also deeper and heavier than in their primitive cousins.

So the iguanodonts were clearly chopping up their food differently than their kin. But exactly *how* differently is unclear. Perhaps they fed on

Part of this success was due to the iguanodontians evolving into many different body types. One of the earliest types to split off from the others was *Tenontosaurus*. In some ways, *Tenontosaurus* looks like a great big *Hypsilophodon* or *Dryosaurus* with a really long tail. On average, it was almost 15 feet (4.6 meters) long, considerably bigger than its 8-foot (2.4-meter) relatives. But there were other differences than size. *Tenontosaurus* seems to have spent most of its time on all fours. Its front limbs are proportionately thicker than those of *Dryosaurus* because they had to absorb some of the dinosaur's weight. *Tenontosaurus* remains are often found with the teeth of the dromaeosaurid raptor *Deinonychus,* which seemed to have fed regularly on the iguanodontian. But the raptors didn't always survive the attack. Paleontologists have identified some sites where *Deinonychus* were preserved alongside *Tenontosaurus.*

Another primitive iguanodontian is *Muttaburrasaurus.* It had an arched nose, much like the advanced iguanodontian *Altirhinus* and some of the hadrosauroids. As in those dinosaurs, the arch may have helped support a nose sac that generated sound or controlled the temperature and humidity of the air *Muttaburrasaurus* breathed.

The Late Cretaceous rhabdodontid *Zalmoxes* of Europe.

different plants or could break down and digest their food more efficiently? Whatever the difference was, it allowed these dinosaurs to become very successful. In fact, when you consider that duckbills are just *one* branch of the iguanodontian family tree, they were the most successful and diverse group of ornithischian dinosaurs.

One of the most recently recognized branches of Iguanodontia is Rhabdodontidae. As iguanodonts go, rhabdodontids were small (only 10 feet [3 meters] long), and they were strictly bipedal. They had massively built skulls and teeth better built for shearing (like those of the horned

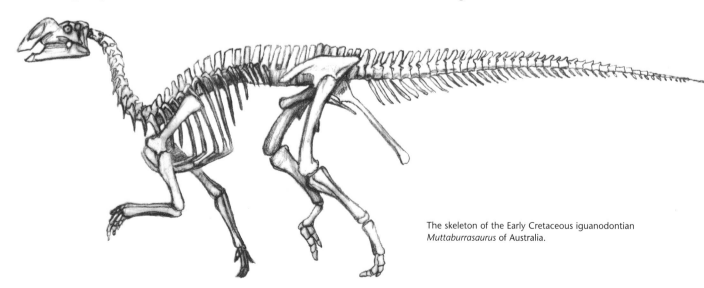

The skeleton of the Early Cretaceous iguanodontian *Muttaburrasaurus* of Australia.

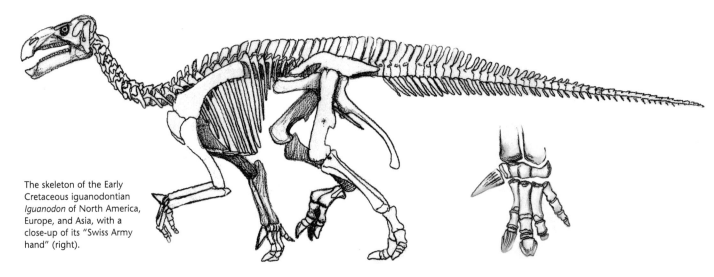

The skeleton of the Early Cretaceous iguanodontian *Iguanodon* of North America, Europe, and Asia, with a close-up of its "Swiss Army hand" (right).

dinosaurs or of *Muttaburrasaurus*) than for grinding (like those of most other iguanodonts). In fact, when parts of the skull of *Zalmoxes* (the most completely known rhabdodontid) were discovered in Transylvania in the 1980s and 1990s, rumor spread through the paleontological community that the first European horned dinosaur had been found! But *Zalmoxes* is a true iguanodontian, not a ceratopsian (horned dinosaur). Its solid skull and shearing bite are simply examples of convergence, the evolution of the same features in distantly related groups with the same ecological habits.

(Incidentally, other than the hadrosauroids and Argentina's *Talenkauen,* rhabdodontids are the only group of iguanodontians to make it all the way to the very end of the Cretaceous Period.)

SLIDING JAWS AND SWISS ARMY HANDS

The remaining iguanodontians have a number of important specializations. For one thing, they are the dinosaurs that could chew the best! When biologists say "chew," they mean something very specific—to grind the teeth past one another to break the food apart. Many ornithischians might have been able to chew a bit by slightly rotating the sides of the lower jaw, using the predentary bone at the tip as a pivot. And some—like armored ankylosaurs and ceratopsians—show specializations of the teeth for some type of advanced feeding. But only the more advanced beaked dinosaurs show a true chewing motion.

The grinding jaws of iguanodontians are different from our grinding jaws and those of other mammals. When we chew, our upper jaw stays in place while the lower jaw moves back and forth and side to side. In the iguanodontians, the lower jaw moved pretty much straight up and down while the upper jaw slid sideways at the same time. This way the teeth in the upper jaw would grind against those in the lower jaw, breaking the food in between into little bits. And food that is broken into little bits can be digested faster, so the iguanodont got more energy and could be more active.

But how was the upper jaw able to slide back and forth? In the 1980s, paleontologists Dave Norman (working on *Iguanodon*) and Dave

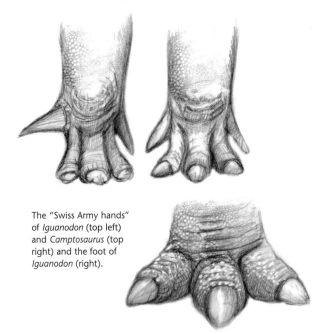

The "Swiss Army hands" of *Iguanodon* (top left) and *Camptosaurus* (top right) and the foot of *Iguanodon* (right).

253

The heavily built Early Cretaceous iguanodontian *Lurdusaurus* of northern Africa.

Weishampel (working on hadrosauroids) both recognized special joints between the upper jaw and the other skull bones in their respective dinosaurs. Using cladistics, they were able to track this feature to a very primitive stage in *Hypsilophodon* and other ornithopods that branched off the family tree very early. While a simple version was present in primitive ornithopods, the joint became well developed in the Late Jurassic and Early Cretaceous iguanodontian *Camptosaurus*.

Camptosaurus was one of the most common dinosaurs in North America and England during the Late Jurassic and earliest Cretaceous. Typical *Camptosaurus* skeletons are about 13 feet (4 meters) long, but some individuals are almost double that size. Compared to more primitive ornithopods, *Camptosaurus* had a longer, somewhat horselike face. In fact, this trait was found in the later iguanodontians, which all typically had long snouts.

The hand of *Camptosaurus* was interesting, too. It is the first example of what I call the "Swiss Army hand." A Swiss Army knife is a tool that has many separate parts with very different functions: blades, corkscrews, files, and more. The hands of *Camptosaurus* and more advanced beaked dinosaurs also had separate parts with totally different functions. The middle three fingers are hooflike, and the metacarpals (the bones in the palm of the hand) are built to help support weight. So we know that *Camptosaurus* and other advanced iguanodontians spent a lot of time walking on all fours, even though they were probably able to run on their hind legs alone. The pinkie of the Swiss Army hand was long and opposable. It could bend to touch the palm of the hand, so the iguanodontian could pick up things (probably plants). And the thumb had evolved into a cone-shaped spike. It is unclear how the spike was used, however. It may have been used to defend against

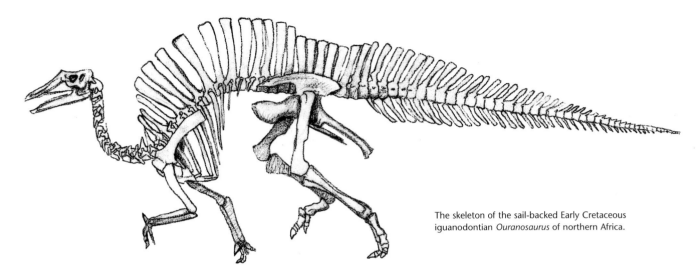

The skeleton of the sail-backed Early Cretaceous iguanodontian *Ouranosaurus* of northern Africa.

attackers, but if a predator was close enough to get stabbed by the thumb, it would probably be close enough to bite the ornithopod! Maybe it was used in combat with others of the same species, like roosters use their spurs on other roosters? Or maybe it was used to pry open seeds or plants to get at something tasty inside.

Iguanodon looked very much like a big *Camptosaurus*. It lived later, in the Early Cretaceous, and is also known from both Europe and North America. The largest specimens are 33 feet (10.1 meters) or more long—making it the biggest known ornithopod other than hadrosauroids. *Iguanodon* and other advanced iguanodontians typically had longer and wider beaks and longer metacarpals than *Camptosaurus*. Their middle three fingers are even more hooflike. *Iguanodon* is by far the most common dinosaur from Europe in the Early

Ouranosaurus in the flesh.

255

Iguanodon is the best studied of all iguanodontians.

Cretaceous Epoch. In fact, one quarry in Belgium yielded at least thirty-eight individuals! Yet despite what many other books say, the evidence shows that this *wasn't* a single herd that died all at once. Dave Norman's study of the position of these skeletons, and the fact that different layers of sediment separated them, shows that there were at least three different episodes of burial at the quarry. But these cases—as well as other sites in Germany and many trackways—show that *Iguanodon* probably *was* a herd animal.

If they lived in herds, young *Iguanodon* probably had to run to keep up with their parents. And they probably did so on their hind legs. Study of the proportions of the front limbs to the back limbs shows that young *Iguanodon* individuals were built more like typical bipedal animals, while adults were more likely quadrupeds most of the time. (If you think about it, this is the opposite of humans. We're quadrupeds as babies and only walk on two legs when we're older.)

Part of the success of *Iguanodon, Camptosaurus,* and their relatives is that they were (kind of) two plant-eaters in one. When they walked on all fours, they could forage for herbs, ferns, and other low-lying plants. (If grass had existed in the Mesozoic, they would have been good grazers. Unfortunately for the iguanodontians, grass didn't evolve until well after the last ornithopod died out.) But when they walked on their hind legs, they could reach fairly high into the trees. So they could compete with herb-munching stegosaurs, ankylosaurs, and ceratopsians and tree-browsing sauropods at the same time, all because of their highly specialized chewing jaws.

TALL NOSES AND SAIL BACKS

Although *Iguanodon* is the best known and most thoroughly studied of the advanced iguanodonts, there are many others known. In Asia in the Early Cretaceous lived *Altirhinus.* Its name means "high nose," and a glance at the skull shows how it got that name. That tall snout would have supported a large fleshy nose. Otherwise, *Altirhinus* is very similar to its European and North American cousin, *Iguanodon.*

In Africa during the Early Cretaceous lived some of the most spectacular iguanodontians. *Ouranosaurus* was one of the most lightly built of the group. It had a long, narrow skull and slender arms and legs. Most amazing, though, was its sail. The neural spines—the part of the vertebrae that stick up from the back—grew to 3 feet (0.9 meters) tall. In some species of *Iguanodon,* the neural spines are also tall, but never anything like this! In fact, one of the few dinosaurs that had an even bigger sail—the theropod *Spinosaurus*—also lived in northern Africa a few million years later. Some paleontologists speculate that the environment of the tropical regions during the end of the Early Cretaceous and the beginning of the Late Cretaceous was so hot that big dinosaurs like *Ouranosaurus* and *Spinosaurus* needed some extra way to dump body heat. A sail would have been very useful for this purpose because it could be turned into the wind to let the heat blow away.

However, other giant dinosaurs from the same regions did not need such great big sails. So perhaps some other function was more important. For example, the sail of *Ouranosaurus* could have made each individual distinctive, so members of the same species could have instantly recognized each other.

Living in the same environment as slender *Ouranosaurus* was another advanced iguanodontian, *Lurdusaurus.* But where *Ouranosaurus* was graceful, *Lurdusaurus* was massive and stocky. It was the widest, shortest-limbed iguanodontian

known. It was presumably fairly ponderous, but that doesn't mean it was necessarily super slow. After all, a hippopotamus is ponderous, too, but hippos can move very fast when they need to, on land or in the water. In fact, *Lurdusaurus* may have been a dinosaur equivalent to a hippo. Unlike the hands of other advanced iguanodontians, its hand was short, broad, and splayed outward, like a hippo's foot. (Of course, *Lurdusaurus* might have evolved this splayed hand simply to support the dinosaur's massive weight.)

FATHERS (AND MOTHERS) OF THE DUCKBILLS

The remaining iguanodontians in this chapter represent the transition toward the true duckbills, but, in fact, it's hard to figure out where iguanodontians end and Hadrosauroidea begins. Some paleontologists think *Equijubus* and *Probactrosaurus,* for instance, are not hadrosauroids and should technically be discussed as primitive iguanodontians. I consider them to be probably primitive duckbills, so I've put them in the next chapter.

Something that non-hadrosauroids generally don't have but hadrosauroids do is narrow, diamond-shaped teeth. The teeth of *Iguanodon* are fairly broad and have big bumps called denticles on the side. They look something like the teeth of the modern lizards belonging to the genus *Iguana* (hence the name *Iguanodon,* meaning "iguana tooth"). Hadrosauroid teeth have smaller denticles, or none, and the teeth are narrower, with a diamond shape on the side. This lets them be packed together very closely.

Two Chinese dinosaurs—*Jinzhousaurus* and *Shuangmiaosaurus*—seem to represent the closest relatives of the hadrosauroids. In fact, *Jinzhousaurus* is early enough that it could be the ancestor of the duckbills. Both these dinosaurs have very broad snouts—the feature that gave duckbills their nickname—but their teeth are still fairly wide. So (provisionally) I'm keeping them in this section. However, these two hint at what was to come: a great explosion of specialized, sophisticated (and to tyrannosaurs—*tasty!*) iguanodontians called Hadrosauroidea.

Shantungosaurus

Parasaurolophus

Corythosaurus

32

HADROSAUROIDS
(Duckbilled Dinosaurs)

Duckbills—or Hadrosauroidea, as the group is scientifically called—were the last, and most advanced, type of ornithopod (two-legged, beaked, plant-eating dinosaur) to evolve. Paleontologists know more about the lives and anatomy of these creatures than about any other group of extinct dinosaur. Besides being the most common dinosaurs of Late Cretaceous North America, hadrosauroids have been found in Asia, Europe, South America, and Antarctica. Duckbill skeletons of all ages are known—from embryos inside eggs to old adults. In fact, whole *herds* of duckbill skeletons (literally *hundreds* of them!) have been found in great piles called bone beds. Even duckbill skeletons surrounded by impressions of their skin—so-called dinosaur mummies—have been discovered!

Hadrosauroids were part of a larger group of ornithopods called Iguanodontia. Like other iguanodontians, hadrosauroids spent most of their time walking on all fours, but they could also walk on just their hind legs. While some duckbill species (particularly the earliest and most primitive) weren't much bigger than a horse, most ranged in size from that of a rhino to that of an African elephant. A few were even bigger than that. In fact, the biggest duckbills were probably among the largest animals ever to walk on land. The only bigger land animals were their distant cousins, the sauropod dinosaurs.

Duckbills get their nickname—no surprise here—from the shape of their snouts. Many iguanodontians had long faces, and the hadrosauroids were no exception. In the duckbills, however, the end of the snout got broader and was more rounded. In some cases, it actually *did* look something like a duck's bill.

ORIGIN OF THE DUCKBILLS

The ornithopods included a number of different types of plant-eating dinosaurs. Primitive ornithopods (discussed in chapter 30) were mostly small animals that ran around only on their hind legs. The species in Iguanodontia (discussed in chapter 31) were larger, and many of them spent at least some time walking on all fours. The more specialized types of iguanodontians evolved a structure I like to call the "Swiss Army hand." Like today's Swiss Army knives, the hands of these iguanodontians had many different functions. The thumb was a spike, which may have been used to defend the dinosaur or to pry apart plants it wanted to eat. The pinkie was opposable to the

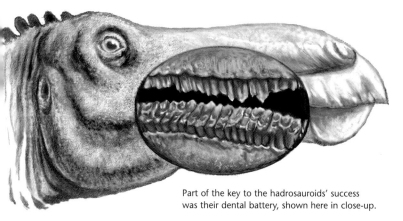

Part of the key to the hadrosauroids' success was their dental battery, shown here in close-up.

palm of the hand, so the dinosaur could grab on to branches or other bits of food. The three middle fingers functioned as hooflike toes, making it easier to walk on them. In fact, it seems that the middle toes of at least some iguanodontians (including the hadrosauroids) were entirely covered over with skin, making the dinosaurs look like they were wearing mittens, only backward!

These iguanodontians also evolved specialized grinding jaws. Unlike most reptiles, whose jaws simply mash up and down on food, iguanodontians were able to chew their food because of a joint in the facial bones. When the mouth closed, the upper jaw would swing outward, scraping the teeth of the upper jaw against those in the lower jaw. This is different from the way that we, and other mammals, chew our food. In our case, our upper jaw stays in place, and our lower jaw moves up and down, front to back, and side to side. Because hadrosauroids and other iguanodontians ground their food (plants of various types) into a mush, they could digest their food more quickly than other plant-eating dinosaurs.

The ancestors of hadrosauroids were iguanodontians closely related to *Jinzhousaurus*—if not that species itself. The species in Hadrosauroidea include a number of primitive dinosaurs as well as the advanced group Hadrosauridae. The hadrosaurids, which include most of the known species of duckbills, are divided into two major branches: the broad-snouted, large-nosed Hadrosaurinae and the smaller-snouted, hollow-crested Lambeosaurinae. (As you can see, a lot of these names are similar but with slightly different endings. This is because they were coined back in the nineteenth and twentieth centuries, when there was a set of rules for different "ranks," or levels of taxonomy. Superfamilies typically ended in "-oidea," families in "-idae," and subfamilies in "-inae." Although most scientists don't use ranks anymore, we still use the names themselves.)

The earliest and most primitive duckbills lived near the end of the Early Cretaceous Epoch and the beginning of the Late Cretaceous Epoch. Many different species of these primitive hadrosauroids are known, such as *Nanyangosaurus, Equijubus, Probactrosaurus, Bactrosaurus, Eolambia,* and *Protohadros.* Most of these were medium-size dinosaurs, 10 to 20 feet (3 to 6.1 meters) long. *Eolambia* grew to be as long as 30 feet (9.1 meters). Like their primitive iguanodontian ancestors, these hadrosauroids had multifunction "Swiss Army hands": spike thumb, opposable pinkie, and hooflike middle fingers. The primitive duckbills also had the deep beaks of their iguanodontian ancestors. In other words, they looked, in general, like typical iguanodontians. (In fact, some paleontologists don't consider all of them to really *be* hadrosauroids!) These primitive duckbills had evolved the traits that make the group Hadrosauroidea distinct from other types of iguanodontians. The ends of the snouts of these first hadrosauroids were wider and more rounded than in typical iguanodontians so they could crop up more vegetation. In other words, they had evolved the duckbill.

TOOTH GRINDERS

The next important feature in hadrosauroid history, and one that made them distinct from the other types of advanced iguanodontians, was the dental battery. This was an adaptation that helped them chew their food even better and finer than did their ancestors. One change from the ancestral state was that advanced duckbills had more teeth in their jaws. Grinding quickly wears teeth down, so hadrosauroids needed extra teeth. Use your tongue and feel around the inside of your own mouth. You probably have twenty-eight teeth in your mouth: fourteen on top and fourteen on the bottom. Adults who have never had their wisdom

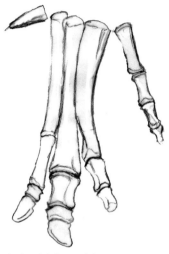

The hand skeleton of the Early Cretaceous hadrosauroid *Probactrosaurus*.

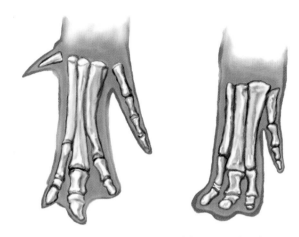

The "Swiss Army hand" of *Probactrosaurus* (left) compared to the thumbless hand of a true hadrosaurid (right).

teeth removed have thirty-two. Early hadrosauroids had 80, and true hadrosaurids had 120 or more. Underneath each of those teeth, six or more replacement teeth were formed and ready for use as soon as the topmost tooth wore away. As duckbills evolved, the many individual teeth in each side of the jaw got compressed together until they formed a true dental battery, which worked like two giant rasps grinding against each other on each side. Duckbills could grind down leaves, twigs, fruit, and stems into a pulp and digest it quickly.

Despite all those teeth along the sides, the front end of a hadrosauroid's jaw was toothless. Instead, both the upper jaw and lower jaw were covered with a horny beak at the front. Traces of this horny material have been found with the fossils of some specimens.

Hadrosauroids like *Claosaurus, Telmatosaurus, Secernosaurus,* and *Gilmoreosaurus* were the first ones to evolve a true dental battery. They are more specialized than *Equijubus, Bactrosaurus,* and the like, but they are still not members of the even more advanced Hadrosauridae. Many paleontologists include a dinosaur in Hadrosauridae only if it belongs to the subgroups Hadrosaurinae or Lambeosaurinae, and these four don't seem to belong to either one. The first three of these hadrosauroids were only about 10 to 13 feet (3 to 4 meters) long, but *Gilmoreosaurus* was over 26 feet (8 meters) long and may have weighed up to 2 tons.

Another difference between these hadrosauroids and the more primitive sort like *Equijubus, Probactrosaurus,* and *Bactrosaurus* is in their hands. These dinosaurs (and the later true hadrosaurids) were thumbless. The thumb spike found in primitive hadrosauroids and in older iguanodontians had disappeared. Whatever that spike was for, the hadrosaurids apparently didn't need it!

The most famous *and* common types of duckbills were the hadrosaurids. Hadrosaurid dental batteries had even more teeth than those of their ancestors: 120 or more single teeth grinding together at once. Directly underneath were rows and rows of new teeth. When a tooth on top was worn away or broken, a new tooth would take its place from below. This meant that hadrosaurids had *hundreds* of teeth in their jaws at all times! It is also one reason why hadrosaurid teeth are such common fossils. These stupendous grinding jaws allowed hadrosaurids to get more energy out of food faster and may be the reason why the hadrosaurids became so successful. (Note: that's what happens when you thoroughly chew your food!)

There are two main divisions of Hadrosauridae. The first of these, Hadrosaurinae, includes *Hadrosaurus* itself (making *Hadrosaurus* a hadrosaurine hadrosaurid hadrosauroid!). Hadrosaurines had the broadest snouts among the hadrosauroids; in other words, they were the "duckbilliest" duckbills. Hadrosaurines were a very diverse group. Some had shorter, deeper snouts, like *Brachylophosaurus* and *Kritosaurus*. Others, like *Prosaurolophus* and *Maiasaura,* had bigger, broader bills. The longest and broadest snouts are found in *Anatotitan, Edmontosaurus,* and

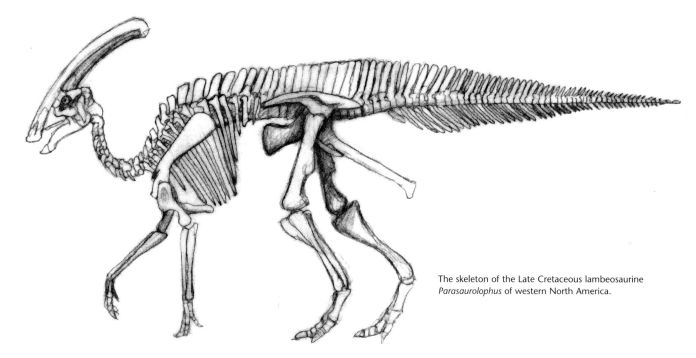

The skeleton of the Late Cretaceous lambeosaurine *Parasaurolophus* of western North America.

Shantungosaurus. Most hadrosaurines were big, typically 30 feet (9.1 meters) long or more when fully grown. In fact, *Shantungosaurus* may have reached 50 feet (15.2 meters) and weighed 13 tons, making it the biggest bipedal animal known to science! (In comparison, the largest bipedal predatory dinosaurs weighed probably only about 8 tons.) Hadrosaurines are known mostly from North America, but some Asian and Argentine hadrosaurines have also been discovered.

Lambeosaurines have shorter, narrower snouts than hadrosaurines, as well as differences in some other bones. The most famous and distinctive fea-

ture of the lambeosaurines is their hollow crest. (This feature actually hadn't appeared in the oldest and most primitive lambeosaurine—the Asian *Aralosaurus*—but it is in all the later forms.) While the hadrosaurine *Saurolophus* had a spikelike crest sticking out the back of its skull, only the lambeosaurines had hollow crests. These structures were actually the bones surrounding the nasal passages (the paths that connect the nostrils to the windpipe). The crests came in a variety of shapes and sizes. In some, like *Parasaurolophus* and *Tsintaosaurus,* the crest looked like a tube. In others, like *Lambeosaurus, Corythosaurus,* and *Hypacro-*

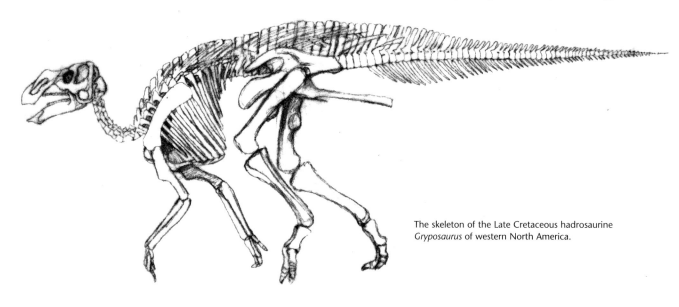

The skeleton of the Late Cretaceous hadrosaurine *Gryposaurus* of western North America.

262

saurus, the crest looked like a helmet. *Olorotitan* had a crest that looked like a tubular helmet! Lambeosaurines were common in both Asia and North America, but some fossils are also found in Europe.

BIG HONKING NOSES

Like other iguanodontians, hadrosauroids had big noses. They were especially prominent in the hadrosaurines. But these big noses didn't come with giant nostrils. In fact, most of the inner nose space would have been filled with fleshy tissue to help keep the dinosaurs' lungs moist. (In lambeosaurines, most of this tissue would have been inside the hollow crest.)

The fleshy tissue may have served another function, though. Like the inflatable throat sacs of frogs or the snouts of male elephant seals, the big noses of duckbills might have been used to make loud sounds.

The calls of the hadrosauroids would be useful in attracting mates, but they probably served other purposes as well. Parents could call to their babies, and one member of the herd could call to the others if it saw trouble. And there was plenty of trouble in the world of the hadrosauroids! Baby duckbills would be prey for many types of meat-eaters, and the adults could be killed by tyrannosauroids (in Asia and North America) and abelisauroids (in Europe and the southern continents). In fact, there are duckbill fossils with tyrannosauroid bite marks on them. An individual adult duckbill had no real defense other than its size, although in some cases, that might have been enough. Their legs weren't built for running, and they didn't have horns or armor or sharp claws. What duckbills *did* have, however, was strength in numbers. In a herd, each individual could keep a lookout for big meat-eaters and alert the others if it saw one coming.

Lambeosaurines were probably the most specialized sound-makers of all the hadrosauroids— or, indeed, perhaps of all the dinosaurs except for songbirds! Each species of lambeosaurine had a unique crest shape. Just as wind instruments of different sizes and shapes make different sounds, it seems that each species of lambeosaurine had its own unique sound.

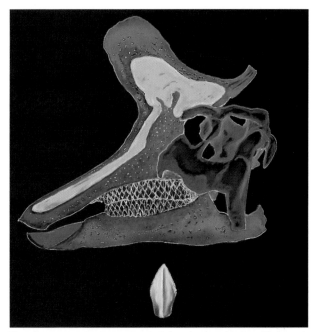

There is more to a lambeosaurine skull than the dental battery. Their crests are actually filled by hollow nasal passages, which may have been used to generate sounds or to moisten their lungs.

Baby lambeosaurines did not have a crest. As a young lambeosaurine got older, the crest started out as a bump on the front of the face and became bigger and more pronounced as the dinosaur grew up. Adult male lambeosaurines seem to have had bigger and more fancy crests than adult females. In fact, in the early twentieth century, paleontologists thought that because male adult lambeosaurines, female adult lambeosaurines, "teenage" lambeosaurines, and juvenile lambeosaurines had such different crests, they all must be different species! Later studies showed that these changes in shape and size were due to the differences between males and females and between animals of different ages. The variation in crest shape between males and females provides some clues to lambeosaurine behavior. Because the crests of males were bigger, males probably used them to show off to the females. The male with the fanciest crest probably got the girls.

Lambeosaurine crests weren't just for show, however. Remember how duckbill crests could generate different sounds? This means that even within a single species, males and females had different songs, or calls.

* * *

DUCKBILL NESTS

Paleontologists have discovered fossils of hadrosauroids from eggs to full-grown adults. Hadrosauroid eggs were smaller than soccer balls, which is pretty small for such big animals. Females laid a dozen or so eggs per nest, and they didn't lay them alone! Discoveries in North America and Europe show that hadrosauroids nested in colonies, where dozens (or hundreds, or maybe even thousands!) of nests were built in the same area. Duckbill mothers built their nests with their hands or feet, making shallow pits in the mud. Since a mother hadrosauroid weighed tons, it couldn't incubate the eggs by sitting on them. Most paleontologists believe that hadrosauroids—like modern crocodilians and some birds—covered their nests with vegetation to keep them warm.

The bone joints of newly hatched duckbills were not fully formed. This means that the babies were nest-bound. They couldn't walk around on their own. Because of this, their parents must have brought them food. Sometimes you see paintings of mother duckbills carrying mouthfuls of plants to their babies to eat, but truth be told, this probably didn't happen. When modern birds (the closest living relatives of duckbills and other extinct dinosaurs) bring their babies food, they mostly swallow it first and regurgitate it for the babies to eat. This may not be *your* favorite way to eat dinner, but the baby duckbills probably liked it!

Like many animals, duckbill youngsters looked different from their parents. Size was one difference, but a big one: they grew from babies that could fit in a soccer-ball-size egg to grown-ups that weighed several tons. But hadrosauroids went through other changes, too. All baby duckbills—primitive ones, hadrosaurines, *and*

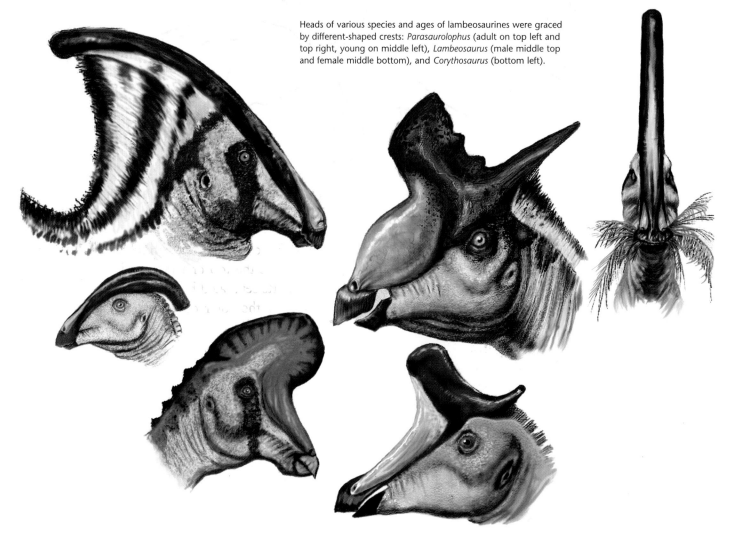

Heads of various species and ages of lambeosaurines were graced by different-shaped crests: *Parasaurolophus* (adult on top left and top right, young on middle left), *Lambeosaurus* (male middle top and female middle bottom), and *Corythosaurus* (bottom left).

Eggs (close-up bottom left), babies, and nests of the Late Cretaceous lambeosaurine *Olorotitan* are protected by the adults.

lambeosaurines—had short, narrow bills. It was only as they got bigger that their bills took on their adult shape.

HABITS AND HABITATS OF HADROSAUROIDS

Some hadrosauroids have even been preserved as "mummies." These aren't mummies like in Egyptian tombs, in which the flesh is actually present but dried. Dinosaur mummies don't have the flesh preserved; only the impression of the skin around the skeleton remains. Hadrosauroids had pebbly scales all over their bodies. And some—maybe all—had a crest or ridge of bigger scales down

their backs. In some of the duckbills, this back ridge looked like the top of a castle, with raised rectangular parts separated by short open spaces. We don't know the color of the scales of these ridges or crests. However, it seems reasonable to speculate that if the ridges and crests were a type of display to get the attention of other hadrosauroids, then they would have been brightly colored.

In the early days of dinosaur studies, paleontologists got a little carried away with the similarities between duckbills and ducks. Some thought that hadrosauroids spent most of their time paddling around in the water rather than walking on land. Some even thought that they could only feed on soft swamp plants. (You have to wonder if they ever even *looked* at a dental battery!) In the 1960s, Yale University paleontologist John Ostrom re-examined the fossil evidence and demonstrated that duckbills *really* weren't very ducklike and that they could eat tough plants. Their feet weren't built well for paddling (they had short, stubby toes, not long, broad ones) but were perfectly good for walking on land.

We know what duckbills ate because we have found their skeletons and mummies with fossilized plants where the dinosaurs' stomachs would be. We've also found their fossilized feces. Hadrosauroids were definitely plant-eaters. They ate the needles and branches of pine trees, the leaves of broad-leafed trees, and all sorts of seeds and fruit. Their dental batteries could break down even tough plants so that they could digest them easier. Even so, adult hadrosauroids were big animals and needed a lot of food. The life of a duck-bill was mostly spent walking around and chewing.

Hadrosauroids lived in a wide variety of environments. Some, in fact, *did* live in swamps (like people once thought), but probably behaved a lot more like a moose than a duck. Others lived in forests, and still others in hills and in highlands. It's unlikely that duckbills would live in the desert (since there wouldn't be enough food for them), but they seemed to thrive in most other places. Duckbills were the most successful group of big dinosaurs in the Late Cretaceous Epoch.

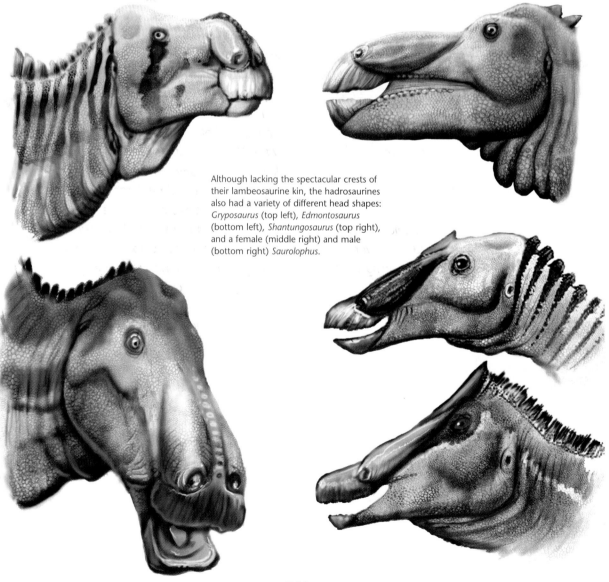

Although lacking the spectacular crests of their lambeosaurine kin, the hadrosaurines also had a variety of different head shapes: *Gryposaurus* (top left), *Edmontosaurus* (bottom left), *Shantungosaurus* (top right), and a female (middle right) and male (bottom right) *Saurolophus*.

Hadrosaurs

Dr. Michael K. Brett-Surman
National Museum of Natural History,
Washington, D.C.

Photo by Kimberly Moeller

The hadrosaurian (duck-billed) dinosaurs represent the pinnacle—and end-point—of ornithopod evolution. They first appeared in the Early Cretaceous Epoch and became extinct at the end of the Late Cretaceous Epoch. Their origins appear to be in Asia, and by the end of the Cretaceous Period, they were on every continent, including Antarctica. A few reached the size of smaller sauropod dinosaurs. In some ways, they were better designed than humans.

The ancestors of the hadrosaurs were the iguanodonts. Like iguanodonts, hadrosaurs were plant-eaters. One key difference between the hadrosaurs and their ancestors was the way they processed plant food before swallowing. They had become highly efficient plant-eating machines.

Hadrosaurs had three rows of teeth in use at one time, perfectly interlocked into a dental battery. The whole assemblage of teeth slowly emerged from the jaws as the upper part of the teeth wore away. You might picture this like an escalator moving in slow motion. As one set of teeth was worn away, another moved into position. The chewing surface of the upper and lower teeth was angled down and out to increase the surface area for grinding. This made the hadrosaurs the only group of herbivorous dinosaurs to "chew" food in the true sense. (Ceratopsians "chopped" plants, but did not chew them.)

Another feature unique to hadrosaurs was the hinge in their upper jaws. Every time they chewed plants, the upper jaw swung outward, as if on a hinge. This allowed the jaws to simultaneously chew food in two directions at once—up and out.

Hadrosaurs were the largest of all the ornithopods. They continued several evolutionary trends first seen in their ancestors, the iguanodonts. Because of their large size and weight, they had extra vertebrae to reinforce the lower back. The back end of the ilium (upper hip bone) was longer for the attachment of the large muscles that powered the legs. Both the pubic and ischial bones were relatively larger to support the muscles of the belly and tail. The tail also had two sets of ossified tendons that overlapped each other. The tendons made the tail stiff, and also added strength to the spine from the middle of the back to the first third of the tail. This improved the animal's balance and mobility while walking or running. Although hadrosaurs could not outrun any theropods of a similar size, they could outmaneuver them because of their wider stance and smaller turning radius.

Paleontologists recognize three main groups of hadrosaurs. The first was a transitional group that evolved from the family Iguanodontidae. These early hadrosaurs had some, but not all, of the features that later define the family.

The most well-known group is made up of the lambeosaurs. They are easily recognized by their different forms of hollow head crests. The crest itself was an extension of the nose, consisting of premaxillary and nasal bones. The crests served many functions. Being a greatly enlarged nose, head crests increased a lambeosaur's sense of smell. A lambeosaur could make sounds by blowing air through its crest, allowing it to communicate with others of its kind. The distinctive crests also made the lambeosaurs easily recognizable to others.

The last group to appear were the hadrosaurines. They had no hollow crests but did have the largest number of teeth—up to 720 functioning at any one time—and the longest muzzles.

Ecologically, hadrosaurs were the equivalent of a giant horse or moose. Before their extinction, they shared their world with ceratopsians and tyrannosaurs. It was not until 15 million years after the demise of the dinosaurs that their ecological role would be filled again.

Pachycephalosaurus

Stygimoloch

Homalocephale

33

PACHYCEPHALOSAURS
(Domeheaded Dinosaurs)

In a weird way, members of Pachycephalosauria (thickheaded reptiles) look somewhat human. Most species are smaller than an adult person, and they all walked on their hind limbs. Their heads are placed fairly upright on their necks, and most of them have a tall, domed head. They are a little like scaly, bald-headed senior citizens, albeit ones with pointy faces and tails!

But there is one very important difference. Our tall, domed human skulls are filled with an enormous brain, covered by a thin layer of bone. Pachycephalosaurs' tall, domed skulls held a very modest brain, covered by a thick layer of bone. You might think that some people are "boneheads," but these dinosaurs were the real thing!

BONEHEADS

Pachycephalosaurs are ornithischian (or bird-hipped) dinosaurs. Their most characteristic feature is their thickened skulls. In primitive forms, like *Wannanosaurus* and *Homalocephale,* the skull is just about twice as thick as what you would expect in a normal ornithischian. But in most pachycephalosaurs—including *Stygimoloch, Prenocephale, Sphaerotholus, Stegoceras,* and *Pachycephalosaurus*—the skull is at least twenty times thicker than the skull of a comparable-size normal ornithischian!

In fact, these bone domes are so hard and durable, they are often the only part of a pachycephalosaur to have fossilized. Indeed, when the first specimen of *Stegoceras* was discovered, only the dome was found. No one had a clue what the rest of that dinosaur looked like for nearly a quarter century! (Incidentally, in case you are confused by the name, *Stegoceras* is a typical pachycephalosaur and is *not* the same thing as its famous distant relative with a similar-sounding name, *Stegosaurus.*)

Pachycephalosaurs have a lot of nicknames. "Boneheads" is a good one, since all of them have these thickened skull roofs. "Domeheads" works for most, except the primitive flat-skulled forms. But my favorite name for them is "buttheads," not just because it sounds rude but because it describes what at least some paleontologists think they did with their weird heads.

HEAD-BANGERS?

When paleontologists find a strange feature in a fossil, they speculate about how that feature was used. This is definitely the case with the thickened skulls of the domeheaded dinosaurs.

One suggestion, first proposed by science fiction writer L. Sprague de Camp in the 1950s, was that pachycephalosaurs used them the way bighorn sheep use their horns: for bashing together! Rams run at each other and slam their

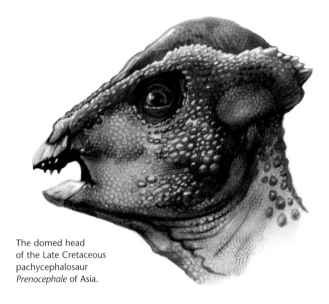

The domed head of the Late Cretaceous pachycephalosaur *Prenocephale* of Asia.

heads together as a test of strength. The one that emerges the strongest at the end of the fight is the winner. He gets the female sheep and the territory. The loser is forced to try his strength, luck, and skill elsewhere, if he isn't too injured.

Certainly having a thick skull roof is useful for protecting the brain from an impact with another pachycephalosaur skull. But is there any other evidence that these dinosaurs butted heads? There do seem to be some supporting features. A mathematical study of the skulls of pachycephalosaurs showed that in any population there was one set with tall domes and another with lower domes. This suggests a difference between male and female pachycephalosaurs, which might be expected if the dino-rams spent time and energy fighting over the dino-ewes. Of course, differences between the sexes could also exist if the males were just showing off rather than actually fighting. After all, male peacocks have big showy tails that females lack, but they don't use their tails to smack each other!

There is other evidence supporting the butthead hypothesis. The joint that attaches the skull to the body is oriented differently in pachycephalosaurs than in most other ornithischians. It is more vertical in pachycephalosaurs. That means when they straightened their necks out, the dome of the pachycephalosaur pointed forward, as would be necessary if one were going to ram another dinosaur. At present, however, we don't know much about pachycephalosaur necks. But the vertebrae of their backs are built solidly enough to absorb impacts, with well-developed grooves and ridges to hold the bones in place. And, as is found in primitive ornithopods and dromaeosaurid theropods, the tails were very stiff toward the end. This would act as a counterbalance while running and turning.

Still, not all paleontologists agree that pachycephalosaurs butted heads. Some have suggested that because of the rounded shape of the domeheads, they might have tried to smack each other on the sides instead. But computer models by paleontologist Ralph Chapman show that even tall, domed pachycephalosaurs could probably bang heads straight on without rolling off wildly to the left or the right. Also, there is no reason to think that all, or even any, pachycephalosaurs actually charged at each other before hitting heads. Many species of lizards, deer, antelope, and even

Two *Stygimoloch* battle while an *Edmontonia* looks on.

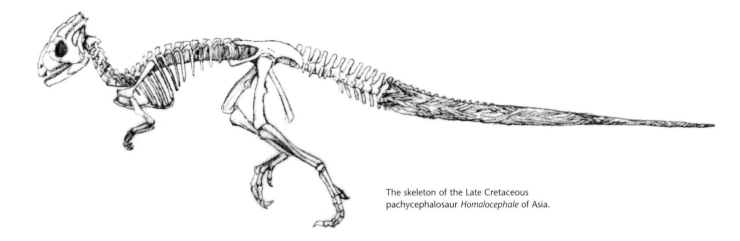

The skeleton of the Late Cretaceous pachycephalosaur *Homalocephale* of Asia.

fruit flies push heads against one another in fights between males without running into each other. They simply face off, place their heads together, and start pushing.

Perhaps pachycephalosaurs didn't use their domes against other pachycephalosaurs, but how about against predators? Rams today certainly use their horns against attackers. These domes might have been useful against small predators like dromaeosaurid raptors, but against a tyrannosaur (the top predator in the world of the domeheads) they wouldn't have been very effective. In fact, ramming into a tyrannosaur would be like *asking* it to eat you!

There are also a few paleontologists who doubt that pachycephalosaurs used their domes to bang into anything. They suggest that there is nothing about the bone (beyond its being thick) to make it good for absorbing impacts. Instead, they suggest that these domes were mostly just visual signals to help different species identify each other. Indeed, different species of pachycephalosaurs have differently shaped domes. And many of them have small bumps, or even horns, around the edges of the skull, making the shapes even more distinctive.

While there almost certainly *was* a visual-signal aspect to these domes, the evidence is pretty strong that at least some head-banging was going on. But there is no reason to have to choose one hypothesis over the other here, since many animals have features with multiple functions. In fact, some of the best visual signals in modern animals

are the distinctive horns of each antelope species. But these horns are also used for fighting each other, and for warding off predators, too.

DIVERSE TEETH AND AFTERBURNER GUTS

There is more to Pachycephalosauria than domed heads, though. These dinosaurs have the narrow snouts of choosy eaters. They have some of the most diverse teeth within the ornithischians. Their teeth are nowhere near as complex as the dental batteries of hadrosauroids or ceratopsids, but every pachycephalosaur had several different tooth types in its jaw. That's different from most dinosaurs, which typically only have a single type of tooth.

For example, the teeth in the front of the upper jaw are cone-shaped. They were probably useful for nipping. The teeth in the sides of the upper and lower jaws are more like those of typical ornithischians—leaf-shaped with bumps called denticles on the edges. These side teeth also resemble those of the troodontid theropods. In fact, during the early twentieth century, there was some confusion about what sort of dinosaur *Troodon* was, so older books will call the domeheaded dinosaurs "Troodontidae"! We now know that troodontids are close relatives of the dromaeosaurids and birds and not very much like the domeheaded plant-eaters. In a few pachycephalosaurs—like *Wannanosaurus* and *Goyocephale*—there are also tall, cone-shaped teeth in the lower jaw. There is a gap in the upper

The business end of *Pachycephalosaurus*.

jaw of those domeheads for the lower cone-shaped teeth to fit. All this together suggests that pachycephalosaurs were doing some very specialized feeding, but exactly *what* was special about it has not been fully figured out.

Because they were generally small, pachycephalosaurs had to eat low-lying plants. But their different tooth forms might have helped them eat a wide variety of plants and maybe other food like small animals or eggs.

The bodies of pachycephalosaurs generally look like those of primitive ornithopods like *Hypsilophodon*. They were all bipedal. But there is something peculiar about their hips. Instead of

getting narrow past the legs, the hip bones actually widen outward. In fact, this region at the base of the tail is expanded at the sides. This evolution probably happened to make space for extra guts. Some paleontologists have referred to this as their "afterburners."

THE RIDGE HEADS

Pachycephalosaurs have a rather restricted range in time and space. One probable pachycephalosaur (based on the shape of its hips; its skull is unfortunately not known) is *Stenopelix* of the Early Cretaceous of Germany. All other pachycephalosaurs are known only from the last 20 mil-

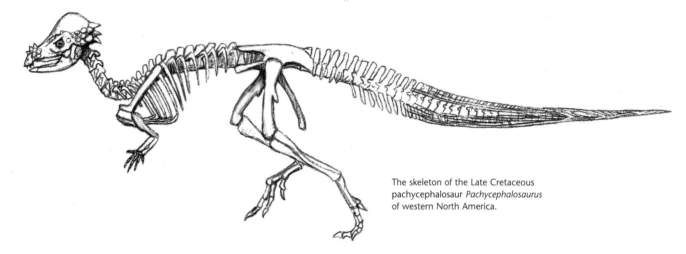

The skeleton of the Late Cretaceous pachycephalosaur *Pachycephalosaurus* of western North America.

lion years of the Cretaceous, from Asia and western North America.

Where did the pachycephalosaurs come from? And what are their closest relatives?

Because their body is generally shaped like a fat *Hypsilophodon,* paleontologists used to consider them a type of ornithopod. Others compared their thick skulls to the armored skulls of ankylosaurs, and so considered them a type of thyreophoran (armored dinosaur).

In the early 1980s, however, paleontologist Paul Sereno did one of the first cladistic analyses of Ornithischia. He observed many features shared between pachycephalosaurs and the species in Ceratopsia, the group containing the parrot-beaked, frilled, and horned dinosaurs. In particular, both these groups (Pachycephalosauria and Ceratopsia) share a shelf of bone extending off the back of the skull. So Sereno named this larger group Marginocephalia, or "ridge-headed ones."

It seems, then, that the ceratopsians were the closest relatives of the pachycephalosaurs. (Not all paleontologists agree with this, but no one has yet shown an alternative arrangement by means of a cladistic analysis.) If this idea is correct, then there is a little mystery to solve. Ceratopsians are now known from the Middle Jurassic, in the form of *Yinlong.* But the earliest pachycephalosaurs are known only from 25 million years or more later. The immediate ancestors of the pachycephalosaurs must have lived at some point during those 25 million years, but no one has found them yet.

There are a couple of possibilities. Maybe some of the primitive ornithischians of the Jurassic Period, such as *Xiaosaurus* or *Hexinlusaurus* or *Yandusaurus,* will turn out to be protopachycephalosaurs. In that case, then in a sense the old model was correct: the ancestors of Pachycephalosauria might indeed have been dinosaurs that we would have once called "hypsilophodonts."

But it may be instead that the ancestors of the pachycephalosaurs lived in an environment where fossils did not easily form. For example, many types of animals live in the mountains today and presumably did so back in the Jurassic Period, too. But mountains are lousy places to form fossils. Fast-moving mountain streams would tend to destroy the bodies of animals that fell into them by dashing them against rocks, rather than covering them with sand and mud.

Or it may be that they lived in some region of the world for which we haven't found good fossils from the Jurassic Period. For example, we don't yet have good Jurassic dinosaur fossils from Siberia or Mongolia. If the protopachycephalosaurs lived only in these regions, we wouldn't know unless someone found rocks of that period from northern Asia.

Hopefully, someday a cladistic analysis or a new fossil discovery will reveal the origins of Pachycephalosauria. But regardless of where they came from, pachycephalosaurs represent an interesting, if weird, bunch of dinosaurs. Not bad for a bunch of "boneheads"!

273

A rogues' gallery of head-bangers: female *Pachycephalosaurus* (top left and bottom left), *Stegoceras* (middle left), male *Pachycephalosaurus* (top right), and *Dracorex* (bottom right), which might prove to be a juvenile *Pachycephalosaurus*.

Bone-Headed Dinosaurs— the Pachycephalosaurs

Dr. Ralph E. Chapman
Idaho State University

Photo courtesy of Ralph E. Chapman

One of the things that make dinosaurs so interesting is that so many of them exhibit such extremes in the way they look. Some are simply incredibly large, as seen in the immense sauropods. Some have dramatic shapes and defensive adornments to them, such as the huge neck frill and horns of Triceratops. Even within this context, pachycephalosaur skulls stand out as extremely odd.

The pachycephalosaur dome is an expansion of the back of the top of the skull. It can be more than six inches thick! The odd shelf of bumps and spikes that rings the back and sides of the skull completes the bizarre look. One species of pachycephalosaur looked so sinister that paleontologists Peter Galton and Hans Sues named the animal Stygimoloch, which means "demon from the River Styx" (in the Greek mythological underworld).

The thick skull dome gives the impression that pachycephalosaurs had large brains, but the dome is solid bone and their brains were actually rather small. If the dome wasn't to house a large brain, what was its purpose?

Paleontologists have puzzled for well over half a century about the function of the dome. Early suggestions ranged from a pathological (that is, disease) condition to Edwin Colbert's idea that it was used as a battering ram. Current thinking is that males used the dome during contests for mates. There are two schools of thought in this regard. One group of scientists suggests the dome was used like the horns of mountain sheep and that pachycephalosaurs banged their heads together in combat to win mates. The other group suggests that the domes were too steep and fragile to allow this combat to take place without damaging both rivals. Instead, they suggest that the dome was for display. In this way it would serve the same purpose as frills, horns, and inflatable pouches seen in some living species of mammals, reptiles, and birds. In this theory, the look of the dome was most important; the meanest-looking animal won.

The great variety of dome shapes seen in different pachycephalosaurs suggests that the answer combines a little bit of both of these ideas. The more ornate and inflated domes probably were only used for display, while the more rounded domes could have been used in combat. The very flat domes seen in more primitive pachycephalosaurs may have even been used for attacking the sides of an opponent rather than for head-to-head butting. Testing these ideas is difficult because we cannot observe pachycephalosaur behavior directly; after all, they are all dead. Nor do we have many skeletons of these creatures to examine. However, as more pachycephalosaur skeletons are discovered, we may find the evidence we need to fully understand the function of their domes.

Fighting *Pachycephalosaurus*!

Zuniceratops

Psittacosaurus

Protoceratops

34

PRIMITIVE CERATOPSIANS
(Parrot and Frilled Dinosaurs)

Nearly everyone in the world is familiar with *Triceratops,* and a lot of people have seen spike-frilled *Styracosaurus* in cartoons, even if they don't know its scientific name. Where did these strange four-legged dinosaurs with horned faces, big beaks, and bony frills come from? That is the subject of this chapter—the origin of Ceratopsia, or horn-faced reptiles.

Ceratopsians are one of the two main types of Marginocephalia, or ridge-headed dinosaurs. The other main type is Pachycephalosauria, the dome-headed dinosaurs. (Marginocephalia itself is a subgroup of Ornithischia, the plant-eating bird-hipped dinosaurs.) Ceratopsians are only known from the Cretaceous of Asia and western North America, although some questionable ceratopsian fragments are found in Australia and eastern North America. They are one of the last major groups of dinosaurs to have appeared in history and were very successful in their time.

PUT YOUR BEST BEAK FORWARD

Ceratopsians are often called the horned dinosaurs, but not all ceratopsians had horns. In fact, only Zuniceratops and members of the advanced group Ceratopsidae had them! More primitive ceratopsians *did* have a frill of bone sticking out of the back of their heads. But the most primitive known ceratopsians lack even that. So how do we know that any of them are ceratopsians at all? Because of a special bone in the snout.

All ceratopsians—and *only* ceratopsians among *all* vertebrates—have an extra bone at the end of the upper jaw. This extra bone is in front of the premaxillae, which are normally the bones at the very front of the upper jaw of all vertebrates. (The premaxillae hold the incisors. The maxillae hold the canines and are the next bones in the upper jaw.) In you and me, or cats or dogs, or *anything* but a ceratopsian, the right and left premaxilla meet each other in the middle. In ceratopsians, though, the right and left premaxilla connect to a single triangular bone in the jaw. Because the name "pre-premaxilla" sounded silly, paleontologist O. C. Marsh (who first recognized this feature) named this triangular bone the rostral, or beak, bone. If a skull has no rostral bone, it isn't from a ceratopsian.

If you remember, all ornithischian dinosaurs have a similar bone (called the predentary) at the front end of the *lower* jaw. The predentary was covered by a horny beak. Well, the rostral bone is sort of a mirror image of the predentary bone, only on the upper jaw, and it was also covered by a horny beak. Ceratopsian snouts all had a toothless, beaky front end, which let them snap off plants to eat and snap at predators who tried to eat *them.*

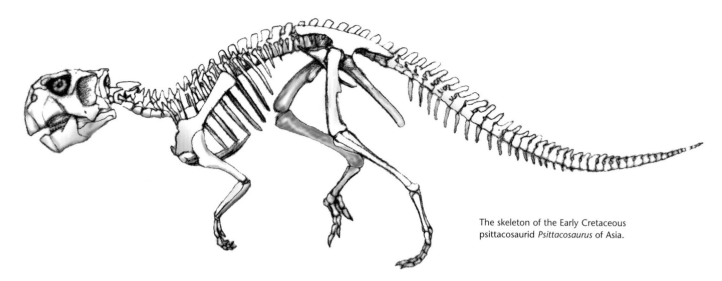

The skeleton of the Early Cretaceous psittacosaurid *Psittacosaurus* of Asia.

(Some ceratopsians *do* have teeth in the premaxilla, and all have teeth in the lower jaw's dentary bone. But the rostral and predentary bones were always toothless.)

BRUSH-TAILED, PARROT-BEAKED DINOSAURS

The most primitive known ceratopsians are the psittacosaurids, or parrot dinosaurs. These are some of the most common small dinosaurs of the Early Cretaceous of Asia. At present, only two types have been named: the rare *Hongshanosaurus* and the very common *Psittacosaurus.*

Most species of *Psittacosaurus* were 5 feet (1.5 meters) long or less, but a few grew up to 6.5 feet (2 meters). Their hind legs could support all of their weight, but their arms were also pretty strong. *Psittacosaurus* may have been a facultative biped—an animal that can choose to walk either bipedally or quadrupedally. Its body was chunky compared to those of relatives like pachycephalosaurs and primitive ornithopods, and it probably wasn't a fast runner.

Psittacosaurus had a deep skull with stout jaws. It probably had a very strong bite, and may have preferred tough plants to softer ones. We know that it didn't just rely on its beak and teeth to break up its food because *Psittacosaurus* skeletons are often found with gastroliths (stomach stones) inside their bodies. Gastroliths are stones that animals swallow to help break down food. They are kept in special parts of the digestive system called the crop and the gizzard.

Many baby *Psittacosaurus* skeletons are known. They are tiny—only about 6 inches (15.2 centimeters) long. In one case from China, an adult *Psittacosaurus* was found buried with thirty-two babies. This may have been a parent with its offspring that were covered over by volcanic ash or mud.

Another famous Chinese *Psittacosaurus* find shows us what the *outside* of this dinosaur looked like. This specimen, from the Early Cretaceous Yixian Formation, is from rocks that have also preserved feather impressions from birds and other carnivorous dinosaurs, the hair of mammals, and the scales of lizards. In this case, the impressions show that most of the body was covered by different-size round scales. These scales were con-

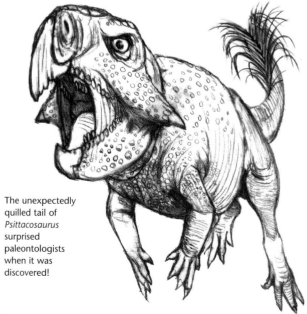

The unexpectedly quilled tail of *Psittacosaurus* surprised paleontologists when it was discovered!

278

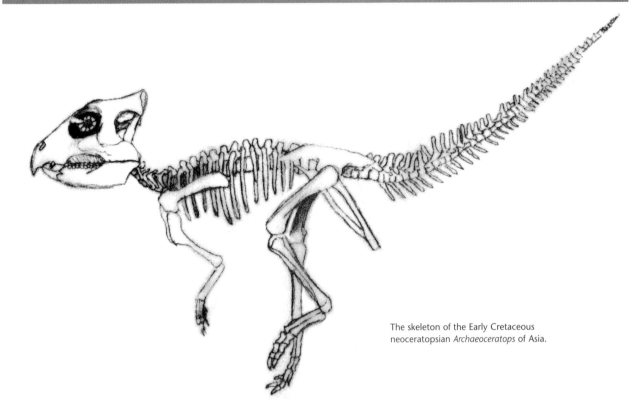

The skeleton of the Early Cretaceous neoceratopsian *Archaeoceratops* of Asia.

sistent with scales found in previously discovered ceratopsian skin impressions. But this specimen showed something else. Sticking out of the top of the tail were many long plumes, or quills. These were hollow, flexible rods, like the shafts of the wing feathers of a bird, minus the soft fringing parts.

Were these structures related evolutionarily to the feathers of birds and various carnivorous dinosaurs? Possibly, but they might also have convergently evolved. What function did this brush of quills serve? Were they for display? Defense? Did only adults have them? Males *and* females? Were they present all year round? Were they limited to *Psittacosaurus,* or might other ceratopsians (even giant *Triceratops*!) have had a brush tail?

At present, we can't answer *any* of these questions because all we have is a single fossil to go on. This goes to show that even dinosaurs as familiar to scientists as *Psittacosaurus*—known from complete skeletons since the 1920s—still hold a lot of surprises!

DINOSAURS WITH ALL THE FRILLS

The remaining ceratopsians, including all the ceratopsians of the Late Cretaceous, belong to a group called Neoceratopsia (new horned faces). Neoceratopsians include the giant species of Ceratopsidae—the true horned dinosaurs—discussed in the next chapter. But there were many genera of neoceratopsians that weren't ceratopsids. In older books, those ceratopsians in between Psittacosauridae and Ceratopsidae on the cladogram were called "Protoceratopsia." But these dinosaurs didn't really have any specialization in common with each other that they didn't also share with the dinosaurs of Ceratopsidae. Indeed,

Eggs, babies, young and full-grown male, and young and full-grown female *Protoceratops* (in order from left to right) have all been discovered in Late Cretaceous rocks of Asia.

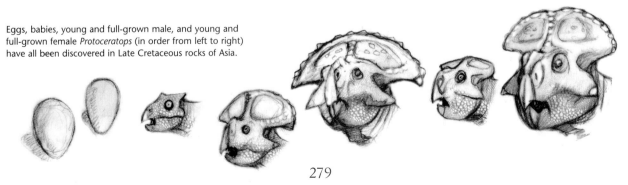

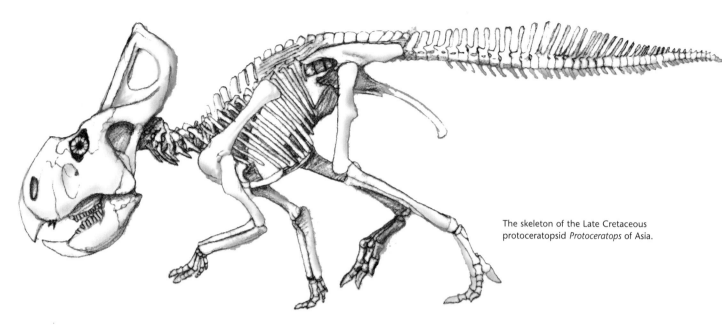

The skeleton of the Late Cretaceous protoceratopsid *Protoceratops* of Asia.

some "protoceratopsians" are more closely related to Ceratopsidae than they are to other "protoceratopsians"!

All the dinosaurs of Neoceratopsia share one major trait. Instead of a little shelf of bone on the back of the head—as in *Psittacosaurus* and the species in Pachycephalosauria—they have an actual *frill* made of skull bones.

What was the frill for? In the early neoceratopsians (like *Chaoyangsaurus, Archaeoceratops,* and *Liaoceratops*), it was probably there to increase the size of the jaw muscles. In all dinosaurs and their relatives, there is a set of jaw muscles that pass inside the skull and attach to an opening on the top of the head. By increasing the area of this opening, as well as providing for a bigger area to attach the muscles, the early neoceratopsians would have had bigger, stronger jaws and a better bite. In fact, many neoceratopsians had teeth that were not leaf-shaped (like typical ornithischians) but had more of a shearing surface at the top. This meant that these dinosaurs had a very strong, sharp bite. While a couple of modern paleontologists have suggested that these dinosaurs might have eaten some meat, most researchers think this shearing bite was for slicing up tough plants.

Primitive neoceratopsians had relatively small heads and slender arms, and so probably spent at least some time walking on just their back legs. But later neoceratopsians, like *Zuniceratops* and the

dinosaurs of Leptoceratopsidae, Protoceratopsidae, and Ceratopsidae, all had heads that were one-fifth to one-fourth the size of their whole body. This weight forced them down onto all fours. To support their massive skulls, the advanced neoceratopsians had specialized neck bones that were fused together for added strength.

Most species in Leptoceratopsidae, like *Montanoceratops* and *Leptoceratops* of North America, had frills just a little bigger than those of the earlier neoceratopsians. But *Zuniceratops* and the dinosaurs of Protoceratopsidae and Ceratopsidae all had very big frills. (As you might have noticed by now, almost all types of ceratopsians have "ceratops" somewhere in their names!) Sometimes these frills had big holes in them that would have been covered with skin. These very big frills were too big (and the surface texture wasn't right) for muscle attachments. So what else might they have been used for?

In the early days of dinosaur paleontology, many paleontologists thought that these frills were used as shields to protect the neck. But frills with big holes in them would have been useless as shields: a predator could bite right through to the neck.

It is more likely that the frills of the advanced ceratopsians were used for display. Because they were big flat areas, they could work like dinosaurian billboards! Instead of advertisements for restaurants or movies, these billboards would say things like, "Hi, I'm a friendly *Bagaceratops!*"; "Stay away, I'm a mean *Zuniceratops!*"; or, "Check me out, ladies, I'm a good-looking male *Protoceratops!*" These sorts of displays—for identifying species, warning off attackers, or attracting mates—are common in all sorts of animals. A large flat area would make a good place for a large display pattern. Sadly, because we don't have skin impressions of their frills, nor *any* hint of the colors or color patterns from any dinosaur fossils, we won't ever know exactly what these patterns (if there *were* patterns) were like.

DUEL IN THE DUNES

Primitive ceratopsians have been found in rocks from a variety of different environments. Some lived on lakeshores, others in forests. Many (particularly in what is now Mongolia and China) lived in deserts. In fact, perhaps the most famous primitive ceratopsian fossils of all came from a desert deposit.

In 1971, a team of paleontologists from Poland and Mongolia were exploring the Gobi Desert. The rocks they were searching in had long been known to contain many dinosaur species. These rocks, called the Djadokhta Formation, formed when Mongolia was also a desert back in the Late Cretaceous Epoch. (By the way, in between then and now, Mongolia became wetter. In fact, younger dinosaur fossils found there were from a forested environment.)

The fossil find in question contained two dinosaurs locked together. One was a specimen of *Protoceratops,* the best-known primitive neoceratopsian; the other was the dromaeosaurid *Velociraptor.* The *Velociraptor* was preserved with its right arm trapped in the jaws of the plant-eater and its left hand holding on to the plant-eater's frill. The right leg of the predator was pinned to the ground, but the left leg was pointed at the neck of the herbivore. From the position of the meat-eater's foot, we can see that its infamous sickle claw was actually well within the flesh of the neck of the frilled dinosaur. In other words, it was about to rip out the plant-eater's throat!

If the claw of the *Velociraptor* had torn through the neck of the *Protoceratops,* the plant-eater would have quickly died. But its last act would have been to snap its sharp jaws and cut off the *Velociraptor*'s arm. Because the nearest veterinarian was 80 million years away, the raptor would have almost certainly died from that wound.

But perhaps mercifully, the sand dune on which the dinosaurs were fighting collapsed. It covered both of them in the moment of their final battle. This duel in the dunes is one of the most amazing discoveries in dinosaur paleontology, and it shows us something about the behavior of both the predator and the plant-eater. We can only hope that there are other equally spectacular fossils waiting to be found!

THE OLDEST HORNED CERATOPSIAN

Most primitive neoceratopsians were fairly small, only 2 to 6 feet (0.6 to 1.8 meters) long. Some of these forms—like *Leptoceratops*—survived all the

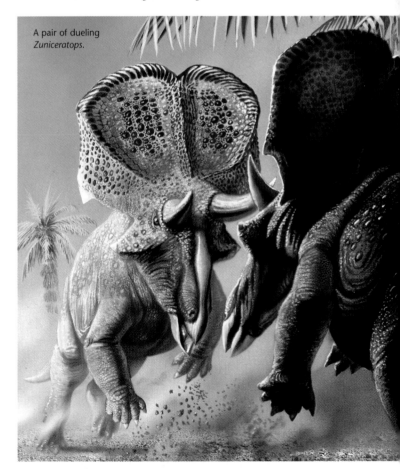

A pair of dueling *Zuniceratops.*

Duel in the desert! *Velociraptor* might have a nasty reputation, but *Protoceratops's* bigger body and powerful beak make it dangerous prey.

way to the end of the Cretaceous Period. But about 90 million years ago, one branch of the neoceratopsian family tree started evolving to a bigger size. This was a strictly American branch. The oldest hint of this is *Zuniceratops,* a 10-foot (3-meter) form. Like the leptoceratopsids and protoceratopsids, it walked on all fours. Like the protoceratopsids, it had a big frill. But unlike them, it had a horn over each eye. These horns had a core of bone, and in life they would have been covered with keratin (the substance in our fingernails and what covers the horns of antelope).

Zuniceratops wasn't quite a true member of Ceratopsidae. It hadn't yet evolved all the features that the later, larger group had. But it was on the path of evolution to the last great success story in the history of the ornithischian dinosaurs. For that story, the life and times of the true horned dinosaurs, you'll have to read the next chapter.

Caught in the Act: The Fighting Dinosaurs of Mongolia

Dr. Mark A. Norell
American Museum of Natural History, New York

Photo by Mick Ellison/AMNH

One of the most perplexing and spectacular dinosaur fossils ever collected was discovered in 1971 by a Polish-Mongolian expedition to south-central Mongolia. At first, the excavators thought they had only found a well-preserved skeleton of Velociraptor. *After more digging, they found a second skeleton, a herbivorous* Protoceratops. *Finding two specimens next to one another is not that unusual, but these were not just two skeletons that had washed together. Their pose suggested that they had died in a death struggle, and they immediately became known as the Fighting Dinosaurs.*

Many paleontologists have tried to explain why the Fighting Dinosaurs came to be preserved in this way. Some thought it was merely by chance. Others thought that the predatory Velociraptor *was eating a dead* Protoceratops. *Still other explanations have included death caused by a quick burial by a sandstorm, simultaneous drowning, and even that the* Protoceratops *was eating the* Velociraptor!

Adding to the challenge of deciphering this specimen is the fact that it rarely travels out of Mongolia—where it is an object of national pride—and has not been closely studied by many scientists. The geology of the region where it was found is not well understood, either. This makes it difficult for paleontologists to understand what may have happened to these two creatures about 80 million years ago.

One can understand the Fighting Dinosaurs better by first taking a close look at the specimen. The first—and most remarkable—thing is that the two dinosaurs were not just found together, they were touching one another. The Protoceratops *was in a crouched position and the* Velociraptor *was lying on its right side. The left arm of the* Velociraptor *was gripping the neck frill of the* Protoceratops. *Also, the* Velociraptor's *right forearm ran through the mouth of the* Protoceratops, *and its right hand raked across the left side of the* Protoceratops's *face. Finally, the* Velociraptor *had embedded its deadly foot claw into the neck of the crouching* Protoceratops, *near where the blood supply would flow to and from the head.*

Evidence from other localities in this part of Mongolia suggests that animals were sometimes buried alive by the sudden collapse of sand dunes. This would occur when the towering dunes became waterlogged and too heavy to remain standing. They would then collapse, the wet sand instantaneously burying whatever was beneath in a mixture like concrete. This was much like what happens to sand castles at the beach. Animals that were killed so suddenly in this way were often preserved in remarkable detail. In addition to the Fighting Dinosaurs, fossils have been found of oviraptorid dinosaurs brooding on nests of eggs, lizards curled in spirals (a common defense posture among some lizards today), and groups of juvenile Pinacosaurus *all pointing in the same direction. These uncommon finds are not just fossils but observable snapshots of behaviors of Late Cretaceous animals. The Fighting Dinosaurs find is one of these, a behavioral artifact of a very violent encounter between two dinosaurs and the sand dune that buried them both.*

Triceratops

Einiosaurus

Torosaurus

35

CERATOPSIDS
(Horned Dinosaurs)

In the previous chapter, we looked at the primitive members of the Ceratopsia group, which includes the psittacosaurids and the neoceratopsians. The diagnostic feature of ceratopsians (the trait that they all have) is a rostral bone at the front of the upper jaw, which formed part of a toothless beak. One diagnostic feature of the neoceratopsians—members of Neoceratopsia, a subset of Ceratopsia—is a frill of bone sticking out of the back of the skull. Another diagnostic feature of neoceratopsians is that—compared to the bipedal psittacosaurids—their heads are very large. So large that most of them could walk only on all fours. And finally, in the most advanced of the primitive neoceratopsians, *Zuniceratops,* there is the diagnostic feature of a horn over each eye.

In this chapter, we will look at the advanced ceratopsians, or Ceratopsidae—the *true* horned dinosaurs. They had all the diagnostic features mentioned above, plus a few of their own. Compared to their primitive relatives, ceratopsids were all big. The smallest of them was the size of a modern rhino, over 13 feet (4 meters) long. The biggest—*Pentaceratops, Torosaurus,* and *Triceratops*—grew to be as big as the biggest bull African elephants, over 26 feet (8 meters) long and weighing 11 tons!

Ceratopsids were one of the last groups of ornithischian dinosaurs to evolve. The oldest is from only about 80 million years ago, so they lasted only 14.5 million years before the great extinction 65.5 million years ago. And as they have only been found in rocks from western North America (Canada, the United States, and Mexico), they had one of the most restricted geographic ranges of any dinosaur group. But even with this limited range in time and space, ceratopsids were very successful, and we know a lot more about this group than about many other types of dinosaurs.

HORNED FACES
The first thing you notice in a ceratopsid is its horns. All ceratopsids have two brow horns and a single nose horn. Now, many of you may know that the name of the most famous ceratopsid, *Triceratops,* means "three-horned face." This was the first ceratopsid whose skull was discovered, so a three-horned face looked pretty distinctive. But now we know that *all* ceratopsids had three-horned faces, at least as kids! As we'll see later on, some of them had their horns shrink and vanish when they grew up, but all ceratopsids were three-horned early in life.

Ceratopsid horns varied in size from small

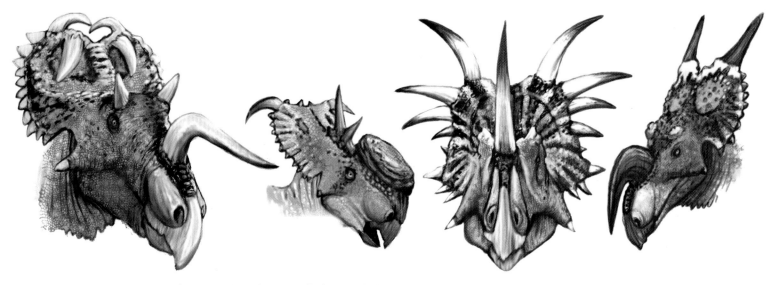

Meet the centrosaurines: *Centrosaurus brinkmani*, *Pachyrhinosaurus*, *Styracosaurus*, and *Einiosaurus* (from left to right).

lumps just a few inches tall to 5 feet (1.5 meters) long or more, depending on the species. In life, the horns would have been covered by a layer of keratin (the material that your fingernails and the surface of cow and antelope horns are made of). These horns served several purposes, depending on the size and shape of the horns in a specific species. The horns could be used as visual signals for ceratopsids to identify each other. They could also be used to frighten off potential predators. And if that didn't work, they could be used to defend against attacking predators.

Of course, a ceratopsid could also use its horns against another member of its own species—for example, in fights over mates or territory. In fact, there is direct evidence supporting this hypothesis. Some ceratopsid skulls have been found with puncture marks on the face or frill. These wounds match the size and shape of another ceratopsid's brow horns.

These might seem like *a lot* of different functions, but that's perfectly normal. After all, today's horned and antlered mammals—like antelope and deer—use their horns for the same sets of behaviors.

SHEARING BITE

The horns might be the first thing you notice in a ceratopsid, but the frills would be a close second. As in other neoceratopsians, the frills were proba-bly for show. Many of them—like those of *Chasmosaurus* or *Centrosaurus*—were thin and had big openings in the bone. Those openings were covered with skin in life, and the frills would have been too weak to stop the bite of a tyrannosaur or the blow from another ceratopsid's horns. But some of the frills were solid—like those of *Triceratops*—and may have actually served as shields for the neck.

Another important specialization of the ceratopsids was in the jaw. Like the primitive ceratopsians, they had a strong bite. Similarly, as with primitive neoceratopsians, their teeth were shaped to shear through food rather than to mash it to a pulp. But shearing tends to wear down teeth pretty quickly. So the ceratopsids evolved an advanced feature in their jaws. This specialization, called a dental battery, was an arrangement where all the teeth in each jaw were closely packed together. The tops of the teeth formed a single continuous surface, so when the horned dinosaur closed its jaws, its teeth acted like giant scissors. And underneath each tooth was another tooth already in position to take its place. (Hadrosaurids, or duck-bill dinosaurs, and rebbachisaurid sauropods also evolved dental batteries. But their dental batteries are each unique, and different from the shearing dental battery of ceratopsids.)

With these jaws, horned dinosaurs could slice their food into very small pieces. This would help

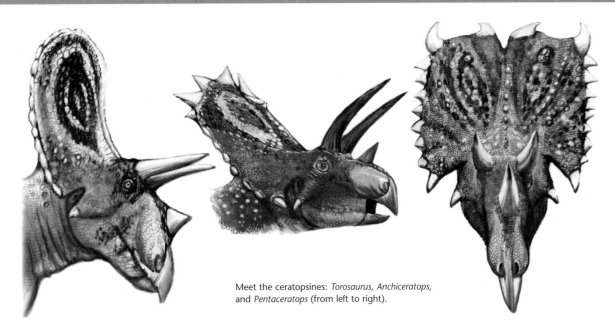

Meet the ceratopsines: *Torosaurus, Anchiceratops,* and *Pentaceratops* (from left to right).

animals with a big appetite because they could digest faster.

ALL-(NORTH)-AMERICAN DINOSAURS: THE DIVERSITY OF CERATOPSIDS

The horned dinosaurs are grouped into two major branches. The first is Centrosaurinae. The newly discovered centrosaurine *Albertaceratops* had long brow horns, which had already evolved in primitive relatives of the ceratopsids such as *Zuniceratops* (chapter 34). But in other centrosaurines, the brow horns were typically smaller than the nose horn. In fact, in some adult centrosaurines the brow horns are entirely gone. Their frills were normally shorter and often had large prongs sticking out of them. Their snouts were normally short and fairly deep.

Within this basic framework, there was a lot of diversity. *Centrosaurus* and *Styracosaurus* both had relatively slender nose horns, but you can easily tell them apart. *Centrosaurus* had a pair of frill prongs pointing downward, while *Styracosaurus* had three extremely long frill prongs pointing backward. The other centrosaurines had a pair of short frill prongs pointing backward. *Einiosaurus* had a thick nose horn that curved downward like a giant can opener. *Achelousaurus* and *Pachyrhinosaurus* didn't even have nose horns as adults. Instead, they had huge masses of knobby bones

covering their noses. In life, these massive wrinkled areas were probably covered with keratin, and may have been used to push each other back and forth. *Pachyrhinosaurus* was the last and largest of all the centrosaurines, but it wasn't as big as the largest of all ceratopsids (*Pentaceratops, Torosaurus,* and *Triceratops*).

The second branch of the ceratopsids is called Ceratopsinae, although some books call it Chasmosaurinae instead. Both names are used by paleontologists, but I prefer the first one. In ceratopsines, the brow horns are normally longer than the nose horn. The frill is typically very long and normally has great big open spaces in it. Ceratopsine snouts are normally longer and less deep top to bottom than those of centrosaurines. At first glance, most of the ceratopsines look pretty much the same, but there are differences in the size and shape of their horns and frills. Ceratopsines didn't have frill prongs, but instead had small triangular bones along the edge of the frill that gave each species a slightly different shape. Ceratopsines were typically larger than centrosaurines, and in fact the biggest ceratopsids were all ceratopsines. These dinosaurs were also the last of the horned dinosaurs to survive. *Pachyrhinosaurus* (last of the centrosaurines) died out about 68 million years ago, but *Triceratops* and *Torosaurus* (both ceratopsines) lived until the great extinction 65.5 million years ago.

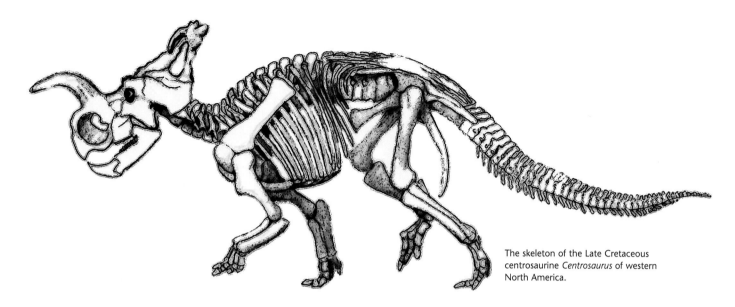

The skeleton of the Late Cretaceous centrosaurine *Centrosaurus* of western North America.

GROWING UP CERATOPSID

Baby ceratopsids of all species look pretty much alike. In fact, it's almost impossible to tell baby centrosaurines of one species apart from baby centrosaurines of another. They simply weren't born with their distinctive horns or frill ornaments. Even partially grown ceratopsids—dinosaur kids—didn't have all their adult features.

This has caused a number of problems. In the late nineteenth and early twentieth centuries, some paleontologists considered baby centrosaurines to be one species and partially grown ones to be another species. You can still go to some museums or look in books and see skeletons and pictures of *"Brachyceratops"* and *"Monoclonius."* But now we know that *all* centrosaurines looked like *"Brachyceratops"* as babies and *"Monoclonius"* as kids. Little *"Brachyceratops"* babies have small brow and nose horns; half-grown *"Monoclonius"* kids have small brow horns and a great big nose horn, but no special prongs or hooks coming out of the frill. Only when the youngsters were fully grown did the species-distinctive features of the horns and frill show up. Because of this, we now know that *"Brachyceratops"* and *"Monoclonius"* weren't distinct species of dinosaurs; they were just growth phases!

In fact, finding kid specimens of *Pachyrhinosaurus* helped solve a dinosaur question. For a long time, only a single skeleton—an adult—of

this knobby-nosed dinosaur was known. Some paleontologists thought that the wrinkled bone on the nose of this dinosaur wasn't the normal condition but was instead caused by an illness. That was difficult to test with only a single specimen. But in the 1980s, a whole herd of *Pachyrhinosaurus* skeletons was found in Alberta, Canada. This discovery was studied by Phil Currie and Darren Tanke of the Royal Tyrrell Museum and their colleagues. They showed that baby *Pachyrhinosaurus*es had the basic *"Brachyceratops"* form, with small nose and brow horns, and that kids had the *"Monoclonius"* form, with reduced brow horns but a good-size nose horn. Then, in the dinosaur equivalent of a teenage *Pachyrhinosaurus,* the nose horn changed into a knobby, wrinkled lump. This wasn't caused by a disease but was just a characteristic that developed at puberty.

Notice that it took finding a fossilized herd for paleontologists to solve this mystery. Herding seems to have been an important part of the behavior of at least *some* ceratopsid species. So far, paleontologists have found herds of *Centrosaurus, Styracosaurus, Einiosaurus, Pachyrhinosaurus,* and *Anchiceratops. Chasmosaurus, Triceratops,* and *Achelousaurus* have been found in small groups. It might be that other ceratopsids also lived in herds, but we haven't found those fossil sites yet. Alternatively, they may have been solitary. For comparison's sake, note that some modern deer species,

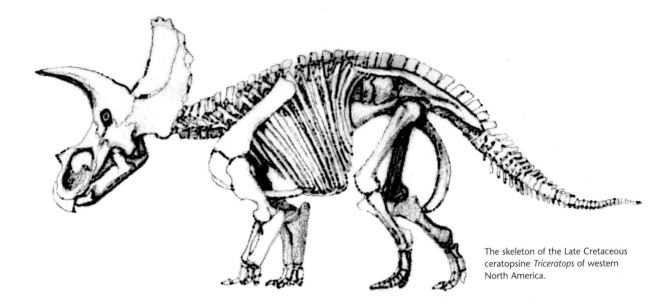

The skeleton of the Late Cretaceous ceratopsine *Triceratops* of western North America.

like caribou, live in vast herds; others, like white-tailed deer, live in small groups; and still others, like moose, live solitary lives.

How do paleontologists know when they find a herd? First, they have to recognize that they have discovered a bone bed. Bone beds are single layers of rocks with many skeletons in them, showing that many animals all died at the same time. Bone beds might be caused by a number of different events, but an important one is storms. Powerful storms like hurricanes can (and *do*) kill many creatures all at once.

Some bone beds contain the remains of multiple species, and these give us a clue to the diversity of animals living in an environment at a particular time. But some bone beds contain only a single species. And these bone beds typically have individuals of all ages: babies, kids, "teenagers," and grown-ups. Because they died together, they must have lived together at least part of the time. And because individuals of all different ages died together, it suggests that they normally lived in a group. They were herd animals.

Why live in a herd? There are advantages and disadvantages. Because all members of a herd eat the same stuff, they run the risk of starving if there isn't enough of that food around. But if there *is* a lot of food around, a herd can be good for protection. While you have your head down to eat, your brother or cousin might have his head up to look around. If he spots a predator (like a tyrannosaur) coming, he can alert the rest of the herd. And you can do the same if you have your head up at the right time. Also, the chances that an individual in a herd is going to be picked out by a predator for attack are pretty small. On your own, you are a much easier target.

So because at least some species of ceratopsids lived in herds, we know a couple of things about their lives. They must have had plenty of food, and there had to have been plenty of threatening predators around. There is only one group of large predatory dinosaurs that lived in the same time and place as the horned dinosaurs. Those were the giant tyrannosaurids, the most sophisticated and largest-brained of the big meat-eaters. So the world of the Late Cretaceous of western North America was probably a pretty exciting one, with herds of elephant-size herbivores with enormous horns on the lookout for elephant-size carnivores.

Now, it's true that a herd of ceratopsids probably didn't get attacked by a tyrannosaur every day. But it must have happened often enough for horned dinosaurs to evolve the behavior of grouping into herds.

One last thing to think about while picturing a herd of ceratopsids is their environment. When we think of the great herds of the modern world—the bison of North America or the zebras, elephants, and antelope of Africa—we think of creatures that live in grasslands. But there were no grasslands in the Cretaceous. In fact, there wasn't even any *grass*! Grasslands are a new environment that only appeared less than 10 million years ago, long after the last ceratopsid or tyrannosaurid. Instead, ceratopsids lived in woodlands separated by streams, rivers, and "prairies" of ferns and herbs.

Ceratopsids—along with their distant relatives, the hadrosaurids, or duckbilled dinosaurs— were the last great examples of ornithischian dinosaurs. Each group was the largest and most advanced of their lines (the marginocephalians and the ornithopods, respectively). When they died out, it was tens of millions of years before herd behavior and elephant-size plant-eaters evolved again. Perhaps had it not been for the great extinction, there would still be ceratopsids living in North America today.

Clash of the titans! *Tyrannosaurus* versus *Triceratops*.

Male and Female Dinosaurs— Can We Tell the Difference?

Dr. Scott D. Sampson
Utah Museum of Natural History

Photo by J. A. Borowczyk

There are many ways to tell the difference between the males and the females of living animals. Color is one. In birds, such as the mallard duck, the males are often more brightly colored than the females.

Size and adornment may also be clues to separate males from females. Among deer, for example, the males tend to be larger than females, and they have antlers, whereas the females do not.

Behavior may also be a clue. In many kinds of animals, including numerous species of birds and insects, the males have a distinct call or "song."

All of these characteristics—color, size, adornment, and behavior—are used by the animals themselves to distinguish between the sexes. They are also vital factors in the competition for mates.

Can these same rules apply to distinguishing male dinosaurs from female dinosaurs? This turns out to be a difficult challenge for several reasons. First, remember that, except for rare occurrences, the only kinds of tissues preserved from dinosaurs are the hard parts—bones and teeth. Even in the few instances where the fossils include impressions of skin or feathers, there is no direct evidence of color.

Size also proves to be an unreliable clue to the gender of a dinosaur. We cannot assume that males were always bigger than females. In some living animals, females can be bigger than males. Perhaps even more important, dinosaurs grew continually throughout their lives, so we find a great range of body sizes, from little juveniles to large adults. This means that greater size may simply indicate an older dinosaur of either gender.

Because female dinosaurs laid eggs, some paleontologists have tried to find bony characteristics that indicate egg laying. So far, this search has been unsuccessful.

As for the sounds that dinosaurs may have made, we certainly don't know if dinosaur males had different calls than females.

Where does this leave us in the quest to differentiate between male and female dinosaurs? The best clues may be found in dinosaur adornment. Fortunately, a few groups of dinosaurs preserve special bony features that probably differed between males and females. Horned dinosaurs (ceratopsians) such as Triceratops had horns over the nose and eyes and a large bony frill projecting from the rear of the skull. Similarly, duckbilled dinosaurs (hadrosaurs) had elaborate noses and bony crests on top of their heads. Domeheaded dinosaurs (pachycephalosaurs) possessed thickened bony caps on top of their heads. Within these dinosaur groups, each species had its own unique configuration of these bizarre features. It has been suggested that these skull adornments—like the longer antlers seen in male deer—were a way for the males to be distinguished from the females. Males may have had the more elaborate headgear in order to attract the attention of female mates, as well as to intimidate or even combat rival males.

Perhaps the biggest obstacle in telling males from females is sample size—that is, the number of specimens known for a particular dinosaur species. There are very few fossil specimens known for most kinds of dinosaurs. As a result, there is simply not enough information to suggest a clear pattern of differences between males and females. In a handful of cases, such as the Asian horned dinosaur Protoceratops, so many skulls and skeletons are known that two distinct types can be clearly seen. These probably represent males and females. But Protoceratops is the exception. Dinosaur paleontologists still have much work to do before they can confidently distinguish the boys from the girls. Maybe you can be the one to solve this paleo-puzzle!

36

DINOSAUR EGGS AND BABIES

Let's face it: baby animals are *cute*! Puppies, kittens, chicks, and hatchling turtles are all pretty darn appealing. So it should come as no surprise that a lot of people—including paleontologists—are very interested in baby dinosaurs.

But scientists are interested in dinosaur babies for reasons besides cuteness. You simply can't understand an animal's biology if you study only adult specimens. Every dinosaur—even the biggest sauropod—was once a tiny baby that had to grow, feed, and survive until it was full-size.

EGGS

The best place to start looking at dinosaur babies is the same place *they* started: inside eggs. Like most modern reptiles—including all living birds—dinosaurs were egg layers. Specifically, they laid shelled eggs on land, as do crocodilians, lizards, snakes, turtles, and egg-laying mammals, rather than laying eggs in the water, as do fish and amphibians. Some paleontologists once speculated that a few groups of dinosaurs—especially the gigantic sauropods—might have retained their eggs inside the body (like some modern snakes, for instance). However, fossilized eggs of every major group of dinosaurs have now been discovered, so scientists are pretty secure in our conclusion that all dinosaurs laid eggs.

The first dinosaur egg fossils were found in France in the 1800s, but were thought to be from giant seagoing crocodiles. In the 1920s, complete nests of dinosaurs were discovered in the Gobi Desert of Mongolia, and additional discoveries were made over the next several decades. Paleontologist Jack Horner's discovery of duckbill and raptor nests in Montana in the 1970s began an "egg rush," and now fossil eggs and nests have been found all over the world.

Dinosaur eggshells were crisp and brittle, like those of modern birds, and not leathery, like those of most turtles, lizards, snakes, or mammals. (Mammal eggs? Yes! *Most* species of mammals do not lay eggs, but the present-day duckbill platypus and the two different species of echidnas *do*. These weird creatures of Australia and New Guinea are the only surviving egg-laying mammals, although most kinds of mammals in the Mesozoic Era probably reproduced this way.) Like their modern representatives—birds—different species of Mesozoic dinosaurs laid different-shaped eggs. Some were spheres, some were symmetrical ovals, and some were pointed at one end and rounded at the other—what we call egg-shaped (by which we *really* mean chicken-egg-shaped). Modern bird eggs come in different colors, and some have different color patterns on them, too. The eggs of extinct dinosaurs probably

Opposite: A nesting site of the saltasaurid *Saltasaurus* in Late Cretaceous Argentina.

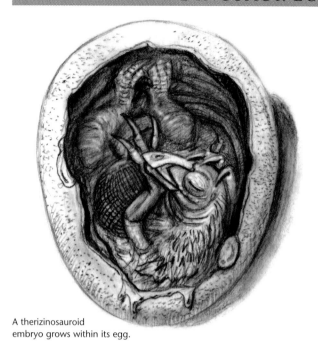

A therizinosauroid embryo grows within its egg.

really *Oviraptor* eggs.

You might think that dinosaur eggs were big. Moviemakers and cartoonists certainly do! (I've seen a lot of movies and cartoons in which dinosaur eggs are as big as people!) In fact, they tended to be pretty small. Little dinosaurs could obviously lay only little eggs, but even big dinosaurs laid fairly small eggs. Gigantic titanosaurs (which might grow to 100 tons) came from eggs only about 1 to 2 quarts (1 to 1.9 liters) in volume. The biggest eggs of any Mesozoic dinosaur known are the 1-gallon (3.8-liter) eggs of the lambeosaurine duckbill *Hypacrosaurus* and similar-size eggs from an Asian carnivorous dinosaur (possibly a tyrannosaurid, possibly a therizinosauroid—without the embryo we don't yet know!). While these are a heck of a lot bigger than chicken eggs to be sure, they are dwarfed by the eggs of the recently extinct *Aepyornis,* or elephant bird, of Madagascar, which laid 2.4-gallon (9.1-liter) eggs!

To put this into a more familiar perspective, most dinosaurs—even the very largest—came out of eggs the size of softballs to soccer balls. And since baby dinosaurs had to fit inside these eggs, this tells us something *very* important about dinosaurs: *all* dinosaurs were small, at least when they were born! This is different from big modern animals like hippos or rhinos or elephants. A newborn baby elephant is bigger than just about all other animals that live in Africa, but a baby *Argentinosaurus* or *Giganotosaurus* would have been a lot smaller than just about all the other dinosaurs that lived in its world.

NESTS: SUNNY-SIDE UP?

Dinosaurs didn't just lay their eggs randomly. Like present-day animals, they deposited them in nests. Modern egg-laying mammals, turtles, lizards, and snakes typically make nests by digging holes in sand and then burying their eggs. Dinosaurs (including birds) and their close relatives, the crocodilians, developed a different method. Although they may partially bury their eggs in sand, they often also use plants to construct nests. In crocodilians and some primitive birds, eggs are

also came in different colors and patterns, but those features don't get preserved in fossils. One thing that does get preserved, however, is the surface of the eggs. Some dinosaurs laid smooth-shelled eggs, but many laid ones with wrinkles, bumps, and other tiny structures. This makes each type of eggshell distinctive, so a single piece can help you recognize the egg type from which it came.

Unfortunately, although we know a lot about many different types of dinosaur eggs, it is more difficult to tell which dinosaur species laid which egg type. Once in a while it is very easy. For example, when you find the fossilized eggs inside the skeleton of the mother dinosaur, or when you find the skeleton of the embryo inside the egg, the connection is obvious. But these fossils are rare. Because of this, paleontologists give each egg type its own "species" name without knowing the actual dinosaur species it belongs to.

Paleontologists sometimes guess at which dinosaur species goes with which egg. They take into account which dinosaur species are known from that region and time, as well as the size of the egg in relation to the dinosaurs. But this can lead to big mistakes. Most famously, eggs thought to be from the small ceratopsian *Protoceratops* were found near the skeleton of the theropod *Oviraptor.* Later discoveries showed that those eggs were buried under big mounds of vegetation. As this vegetation decays, it keeps the eggs warm. Also, the big mound helps protect the eggs from predators.

Paleontologists suspect that most dinosaurs made this kind of nest. After all, if most dinosaurs tried to sit on their eggs to keep them warm, they would crush the eggs! However, although there are some hints of vegetation found with a few dinosaur nests, these hypothesized mounds are normally not preserved. In fact, it may be that many dinosaurs had nests that were partially exposed.

We know that some dinosaurs—all of them man-size or smaller—*did* sit directly on top of their eggs. Specimens of oviraptorosaurs and troodontids have been found on top of their own nests, with their arms outstretched to cover the eggs. This behavior is called brooding, and many modern bird species protect and warm their eggs this way. So far, all the brooding dinosaurs discovered have been from the group Maniraptora, the advanced group of theropods with true feathers and arms that would extend sideways. It might be that brooding didn't appear until the maniraptorans had evolved these traits (which would help them more fully cover their nests). But it could also be that more primitive small dinosaurs—including theropods like *Sinosauropteryx* and *Procompsognathus,* early sauropodomorphs like *Thecodontosaurus,* and small ornithischians like *Hypsilophodon* and *Psittacosaurus*—may have brooded as well. In fact, an adult specimen of the little ceratopsian *Psittacosaurus* was found with thirty-four babies underneath it, possibly trying to protect them (unsuccessfully) from volcanic ashfall. But these were babies, not eggs. Until we find an adult non-maniraptoran dinosaur directly over its own eggs, we can't be sure that any of these other small dinosaurs were brooders.

Where did Mesozoic dinosaurs lay their eggs? It is unlikely that *any* of them built nests in trees, not even the Mesozoic birds. Most of us think of birds' nests as something we find in trees, but in

Baby *Saltasaurus* hatching.

A mother *Citipati* feeds her chicks.

Like modern egg-laying mammals and reptiles (including birds), baby dinosaurs probably hatched from their eggs with the help of a caruncle, or egg tooth, a small projection from the end of the snout that babies use to cut and break their way out from the inside. The egg tooth falls off shortly afterward.

In modern animals, there are some types of babies that can run around within minutes of being born. Most ground-dwelling birds (such as chickens and ostriches), living reptiles other than birds, and mammals like elephants, horses, and antelope are all capable of walking around soon after hatching or birth. But there are also species—like most tree-dwelling birds, all egg-laying mammals and marsupials, and many other mammals (from mice to bears to humans)—that give birth to babies that are totally helpless. What was the case for dinosaur babies?

It depends on the species. Horner and various colleagues have studied different types of dinosaur embryos and hatchlings. In some maniraptorans, including *Troodon* and oviraptorosaurs, the joints on the limb bones were fully formed at the time they hatched. This probably means the babies could run around and start pestering their parents right away. In other species, such as the duckbill *Maiasaura,* the joints were not yet developed enough to support the babies' weight. They would be nest-bound, like newly hatched robins or newborn puppies. Like today's nest-bound babies, newly hatched *Maiasaura* would need their parents to feed them. In fact, this was some of the first evidence that dinosaurs had parental care.

But just because *Troodon* and *Oviraptor* could run around from birth doesn't mean they didn't have parental care. After all, chickens look after their chicks, and alligators look after their babies, even though the younglings can walk soon after they hatch. Like these modern relatives, dinosaur parents may have helped their young get food and shooed them toward safe hiding places when predators came by.

Movies, cartoons, and TV shows about dinosaur babies often show a mother, a father, and one or two babies together. We don't know

fact only the more advanced modern groups of birds are tree nesters. All the primitive groups of living birds—flightless groups like kiwis and ostriches, tinamous, chickens and other members of the pheasant group, and geese and other members of the duck group—make their nests at, or very close to, ground level. So *Confuciusornis, Archaeopteryx,* and bird-size dinosaurs like *Microraptor* and *Epidendrosaurus* were probably ground nesters, just like their enormous cousins. But dinosaurs nested on the ground in all kinds of environments. Dinosaur nests are known from deserts, forests, uplands, lakesides, seashores, and nearly every place in between.

STAY AT HOME OR RUN AROUND?

As discussed in the chapter on dinosaur behavior (chapter 37), we can infer that all kinds of dinosaurs stayed near their nests as the eggs were developing, and stayed with the babies shortly after they hatched.

whether both the mother and father or just the mother helped protect the young (both cases are known for birds and their relatives), but we *do* know that one or two babies is very unrealistic. Dinosaur nests had *a lot* more eggs than that. Unlike the nests of many modern songbirds—which typically have just four to six eggs at a time—most Mesozoic dinosaur nests held one or two *dozen* eggs together. (If the thirty-four babies found with the *Psittacosaurus* are from a single clutch, then that species had about three dozen—the size of a typical alligator litter.)

Even after hatching and leaving their nests, baby dinosaurs seem to have stuck together. There have been several cases where a dozen or more baby dinosaurs were found buried together. These were probably brothers and sisters who followed each other around. It might be that they were on their own, but it is also possible that one or both parents were with them but were too big to be

buried by the sandstorm or flood that entombed the little ones. The case of the *Psittacosaurus* and its young ones is at least one example of a parent buried with its babies. And there are discoveries of many other species, from herds of duckbills and ceratopsids to tyrannosaurid and carnosaur packs, where young, partially grown, and fully adult dinosaurs were buried together.

GROW FAST, DIE YOUNG

All dinosaurs were small when they were babies, but many were definitely *not* small when they grew up! How long did it take them to reach their gigantic size?

For many decades, scientists could speculate

A nursery in the Early Cretaceous of China. The ceratopsian *Psittacosaurus* (back left) and the oviraptorosaur *Caudipteryx* (front center) guard their nests, while the latter is harassed by a trio of *Jixiangornis*. A stealthy *Sinosauropteryx* hopes to steal a *Caudipteryx* egg. In the tree to the left is *Jeholornis*, and in the background a pack of *Microraptor* flutter down from the trees.

about this but lacked the information needed to figure it out. Some predicted that dinosaurs grew like modern cold-blooded animals such as turtles, snakes, and crocodiles. These animals have relatively slow rates of growth and keep on growing for almost all their lives.

But other paleontologists predicted that dinosaurs grew more like modern mammals or birds. These animals start growing while they are children, go through a stage of very rapid growth, and then stop growing (or at least slow it *way* down) when they reach adult size. In nearly all birds, this growth happens in just a few months. Small mammals have a similar pattern. In larger mammals, it might take a couple of years (in species like horses and cows) or a decade or more (in gorillas and elephants, for example). To take a very familiar example, humans have about ten to twelve years of childhood, six to eight years of adolescence, and then growth—at least vertically—ceases.

So what were dinosaur growth patterns like? Jack Horner, Florida State University paleontologist Greg Erickson, and other scientists have used the fact that dinosaurs had growth rings in their bones—as do many living animals—to answer that question. Similar to tree rings, one ring of bone developed per year while the dinosaurs were growing. These paleontologists discovered that dinosaurs grew with a mammal- or birdlike pattern, but with a difference. Typically they had a few years of childhood, then several years of rapid growth. Many little species were fully grown within two to three years. Duckbills like *Maiasaura* were adults by age seven. Even the gigantic *Apatosaurus* began its rapid growth phase at age five or so and was fully grown between ten to fifteen years old! So most species of dinosaurs did not get to enjoy long childhoods. In this way, dinosaurs were like most mammals and birds. But unlike those creatures, typical dinosaurs continued to grow a tiny bit every year of their lives, so the bones of adult dinosaurs have a bunch of narrow growth rings at the very edge.

(An exception is Tyrannosauridae, or tyrant dinosaurs. Erickson and his colleagues' studies showed that these species didn't start growing fast until age ten or twelve, similar to a human.)

It is pretty certain, though, that most dinosaur babies didn't make it to adulthood. Today in the wild, each parent of any species has on average only one offspring that survives long enough to have babies of his or her own. (If that weren't the case, the populations would get bigger and bigger until the animals ran out of food and space!) Since dinosaurs were born in clutches of a dozen or more, and a mother dinosaur might lay a clutch a year during her entire adulthood, most of the babies would die sometime before reaching their full size.

During that time, they not only had to reach adult size, but they also had to develop all their distinctive characteristics. Most baby dinosaurs of related species are very similar to each other. Only toward the end of their growth spurt do their specific features—horns, crests, and so on—fully develop. We see the same pattern in modern animals, too.

Once they were fully grown, how long did dinosaurs live? Again, until people started counting their growth rings, no one knew for certain. Nearly everyone suspected that dinosaurs were like big animals of today. These species tend to live a very long time, often many decades. This is true for many mammals—whales, elephants, rhinos, horses, and so on—as well as many large reptiles, from big birds like large parrots and albatrosses to crocodilians, lizards, snakes, and turtles. The champion is the Aldabra tortoise (*Geochelone gigantea*). One individual lived for over 150 years as a full-grown adult in captivity before it died from an accident, and another individual that records say was born in 1755 is still living in a zoo in India!

But to most paleontologists' surprise, it was found that dinosaurs typically died pretty young. The oldest known *Tyrannosaurus,* for instance, was less than twenty-nine years old. Most duckbills and ceratopsians were only a decade or so old when they died. Even big sauropods lived only to about age fifty, not to seventy or more like elephants.

So the life cycle of the dinosaurs was different

from that of either big modern reptiles or big modern mammals. Unlike modern reptiles, dinosaurs grew up fast. Unlike modern mammals, dinosaurs produced *a lot* of offspring. Unlike both, dinosaurs died relatively young.

There is still a lot to learn about dinosaur eggs, babies, and growth. What is the function of the little knobs and bumps on their eggshells? Did dinosaurs cover their nests with vegetation, and if so, which species? Did any dinosaurs other than maniraptorans brood their nests? Did both par-

ents or just one protect the young? How long did baby dinosaurs stay with their parents?

These questions would seem to be difficult to answer. But during the last decade or two, we've learned a lot more about dinosaur eggs and babies than I think many people would have predicted. Hopefully, even more techniques will be developed to help us understand what it was like to grow up a dinosaur.

A *Tyrannosaurus* brings lunch to her babies.

How Fast Did Dinosaurs Grow?

Dr. John R. "Jack" Horner
Museum of the Rockies

Photo by Celeste Horner

Dinosaurs grew like most warm-blooded animals today. Some small dinosaurs, like the primitive hypsilophodontids, grew slowest. Giant dinosaurs, like the tyrannosaurs and sauropods, grew the fastest.

Scientists learn how fast dinosaurs grew by studying the inside of their bones. We slice the fossil bone with diamond saws and then grind down the slices to make paper-thin samples. These slices can be put on microscope slides. We then view the transparent bone slices with a microscope to study the bony structures.

The inside of dinosaur bones looks identical to the inside of most bird bones, except that dinosaur bones sometimes have rings like trees. The bones of modern reptiles also have such rings. New layers of both tree rings and the rings in reptile bones are formed every year. To determine how old a tree or reptile is, one only has to count the rings.

Dinosaur bones have rings as well. We count the rings to see how old a particular dinosaur was when it died. Modern birds don't have rings because they are all fully grown in less than one year—too short a time for growth rings to form. Many extinct birds also have rings in their bones, so we know that they grew similarly to dinosaurs.

Counting the rings in dinosaur bones reveals that most groups of average-size dinosaurs, such as the duckbills, took seven or eight years to reach adulthood. Newly hatched duckbills were only 30 inches (0.8 meters) long. They grew to be 9 feet (2.7 meters) long after their first year and to be 25 feet (7.6 meters) by their seventh year. The long-necked sauropods hatched at small sizes and took between ten and twelve years to reach adulthood.

Tyrannosaurus rex *grew up in about eight years. Some of the primitive small dinosaurs, such as the hypsilophodontid* Orodromeus, *grew more slowly than larger dinosaurs. It took three years to grow to only about 3 feet (0.9 meters) in length.*

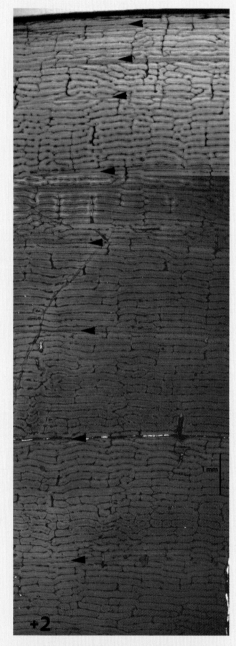

A microscopic view of the femur (thighbone) of *Tyrannosaurus*. The arrows show growth rings, one per year.

Dinosaur Growth: The Case of Apatosaurus

Dr. Kristina Curry Rogers
Science Museum of Minnesota

Photo courtesy of Kristina Curry Rogers

Sauropod dinosaurs were the biggest of the big, the most gigantic of all dinosaurs. But how fast did they grow? This question has fascinated dinosaur scientists ever since the first good skeletons of sauropods were unearthed over 120 years ago.

Many scientists first thought that sauropods grew at a slow rate like today's reptiles. If that were true, the largest animals ever to walk the planet would have reached their full size only after they'd had their hundredth birthday! There is evidence today to suggest that sauropods grew much faster than that.

In college, I worked hard to "clock" the childhood growth of dinosaurs, and my favorite dinosaur to study was the long-necked sauropod Apatosaurus. I wondered if Apatosaurus grew fast early in life, only slowing once it reached its adult size. That is the case with modern birds and mammals. Or was there some truth to the old idea that dinosaurs like Apatosaurus grew slowly for their entire lives, occasionally pausing, even when they were still "kid" dinosaurs? Since there aren't any Apatosauruses roaming around today that I could catch, weigh, and watch, I had to come up with a different way of measuring the speed of growth. I knew that the microscopic pattern of bones sometimes told the story of an animal's growth. After I took a close-up look at thin slices of Apatosaurus bones, the picture of Apatosaurus growth became clear.

What can bones tell us about growth? Bones in all backboned animals grow much like trees—out and up. As bones grow, proteins and minerals are laid down in patterns that show how fast the new bone is deposited. Blood vessels traveling around the outer margins of bones get trapped as new bone surrounds them. The patterns of bone minerals, proteins, and blood vessels provide an estimate of the speed of bone growth. Since we know how fast certain patterns are established in many modern animals, we can easily draw conclusions about similar patterns in Apatosaurus.

Under the microscope, Apatosaurus bones are disorganized, with many blood vessels going in all directions. This pattern is completely different from the patterns in living reptiles, but it is identical to the patterns we observe in mammals (including us!) and birds. Reptile bones under the microscope look much like trees when you cut them down. There are few blood vessels, and distinct rings indicating seasonal growth slowdown line the bones. In Apatosaurus, there weren't any rings. This meant that Apatosaurus grew quickly throughout the year and was not affected by seasonal changes. This also showed that Apatosaurus grew quickly until it reached adult size. These microscopic patterns allowed me to conclude that Apatosaurus wasn't just a scaled-up reptile—it grew just as fast as living mammals and birds. With a growth rate that speedy, Apatosaurus would have been half grown by the time it was five years old, and would have reached its full adult size—75 feet (22.9 meters) long from head to tail, and weighing 30 tons!—by the time it was only ten or twelve years old.

The Late Jurassic diplodocid *Apatosaurus*.

DINOSAUR BEHAVIOR:
How Did Dinosaurs Act, and How Do We Know?

I think most people understand how paleontologists figure out the size and shape of a given dinosaur by examining and measuring its fossilized bones, teeth, spikes, and so on. After all, these are the parts that are typically preserved as fossils, and they are the framework upon which the body of the dinosaur was built. So it isn't too difficult to understand that by measuring the length of the backbone, for instance, you get a good approximation of the length of the dinosaur in life. But there is *so* much more to an animal besides just its size and shape!

What people really want to know about is animal *behavior.* That's the reason why we go bird-watching, or watch television programs about wildlife, or go to zoos. Live animals are simply more interesting than dead ones. But how can paleontologists possibly figure out the behavior of dinosaurs?

It can be done, but it isn't as easy as measuring a dinosaur's length or figuring out its shape. After all, except for modern birds, dinosaurs are extinct. We can't go out with a pair of binoculars and wait for a pair of domeheaded male pachycephalosaurs to fight over breeding rights. We can't go on safari and watch herds of duckbills stalked by packs of tyrant dinosaurs.

So studying dinosaur behavior might seem hopeless. But it turns out there are several different approaches to figuring it out. Some of them are based on the physical evidence from body fossils (bones and teeth that were actually part of the dinosaur) and from trace fossils (footprints,

coprolites, nests, and other remains of the dinosaur's interaction with the world). Other approaches rely on comparisons made with modern animals, either ones with similar shapes or ones that are closely related to the extinct dinosaurs. We can also use models and mathematics to try to understand the way dinosaurs moved and how their bodies worked.

But first, we need to think about what we mean by "behavior." If a parent or teacher tells you to behave, they probably want you to stop doing something. In a sense, that's the exact *opposite* of the behavior that scientists are interested in. We want to know what dinosaurs *did* when they weren't standing around and doing nothing!

Opposite: The iguanodontian *Ouranosaurus* using its sailed back in display.

Footprints are fossilized imprints of tracks made by animals when they were alive.

Pentaceratops likely used their horns and frills to intimidate each other . . .

PHYSICAL EVIDENCE OF YOUR BEST BEHAVIOR

We can start with a relatively easy behavior: feeding. Probably the first question people ask about a dinosaur is whether it was a meat-eater or plant-eater. (A more savvy person might ask if it was an omnivore, too!) Feeding behavior was in fact one of the original aspects of dinosaur life that paleontologists addressed. When William Buckland deduced that *Megalosaurus* was a carnivore and Gideon Mantell reasoned that *Iguanodon* was a herbivore, they were *hypothesizing* about the feeding behavior of these first-discovered dinosaurs. They used comparisons with the teeth of modern reptiles—the bladelike, knife-edged teeth of monitor lizards and the leaf-shaped, bumpy-edged teeth of iguanas, respectively—to predict the feeding behaviors of their discover-

ies. More recently, paleontologists have observed the microscopic wear patterns on fossil teeth and compared them to the wear patterns on modern animals' teeth. Since feeding on flesh, on soft plants, and on hard plants all produce different sorts of wear, we can test our predictions based on the shape of the teeth against what we see in their microscopic wear patterns.

Coprolites, or fossilized dung, are also physical evidence of feeding. They tell us what an animal ate and how it was digested. Only a handful of coprolites can be traced to particular dinosaur species, unfortunately. That's because it would be very rare for a dinosaur to die at the very moment it was pooping—and be buried completely without the poop being disturbed.

Locomotion is another important aspect of dinosaur life. Was a dinosaur a biped, a quadruped, or a little of both (technically speaking, a facultative biped, like a bear)? Could it run, or just walk? Climb a tree? Fly? And if so, how fast? Paleontologists use various clues to figure out dinosaur locomotion: among them, the shape, size, and strength of various limb bones and the poten-

. . . while the troodontid *Sinusonasus* flapped its feathered arms and flashed its sickle claws.

tial size and shape of the muscles. Trace fossils, in the form of trackways, are one of the best types of evidence for locomotion. From a trackway, a scientist can calculate how fast a dinosaur was moving at the time it made those prints.

But a lot of the time when we ask about behavior, we mean, How did a dinosaur interact with other animals? Some of these interactions might have involved physical contact. For example, the horns of a male *Triceratops* might have been used to fight other male *Triceratops* in tests of strength to impress females. Or they might have been used to fend off attacks from *Tyrannosaurus*. We can try to test ideas like these by looking for physical evidence. And, in fact, we have evidence for both behaviors. There are puncture marks in the frills of some *Triceratops* that match the size and shape of the horns of *Triceratops*. And there are specimens of the horned dinosaur where the horns have been bitten off by a *Tyrannosaurus* and then rehealed.

Some behavior, though, doesn't involve direct contact. Probably the most important category of this is display. A display is a form of communication among animals. There are warning displays, like a cat puffing up and hissing, or a rattlesnake rattling. There are sexual displays, like a peacock showing off its tail feathers to a peahen, or male bullfrogs croaking to lady bullfrogs. There are species-identification displays, such as different-shaped horns on different species of African antelope, or a different song for each species of songbird. There are displays between parent and offspring, like the call of a sea lion pup or the scent of a baby rat.

Not all displays would be directly preservable in the fossil record. For example, many animals today use sound or smell to communicate, but neither sound waves nor scent molecules leave physical traces. Some visual displays, equivalent to the puffing up and hissing of a cat or the rattling of a rattlesnake, would also not be easily recorded. But sometimes visual displays use large structures made of bone, and these *are* preserved in the skeleton. In fact, many of the big, showy structures on dinosaur skeletons—horns, crests, frills, plates, and so forth—are interpreted as serving for com-

munication. In cases where there are differences in the shapes of these structures in closely related species, there almost certainly was a species-identification function. Where the crests or plates or other displays were small or absent on the babies but present on the adults, these features were probably for sexual display. This is doubly likely if the shapes are different on adult males and adult females. And many of these features may have served as warnings. It is important to remember, too, that most structures in modern animals help in multiple behaviors.

COMPARISONS WITH CURRENT CREATURES

As you can see, even when we use the direct physical evidence of fossils, we are almost always also comparing dinosaurs to modern animals. This is because studying modern animals is still the best way to figure out how living things actually work!

Sometimes these comparisons are pretty straightforward. Tooth form, for instance, is almost always associated with the type of food that an animal eats, so we use the shape of a fossil-species tooth to predict how and what it ate. We know which holes in the skull hold the eyeball, nasal passage, ear, jaw muscles, and so forth in living creatures, so we can use the size and shape of those holes in dinosaur skulls to estimate their features.

Other comparisons are somewhat more difficult. Large, showy structures, such as ceratopsian frills and stegosaur plates, are inferred to be used for display because that is the way that modern animals use them. But while teeth leave bite marks and horns leave puncture wounds, display structures don't leave "display traces." You can't look at physical evidence to demonstrate that a frill was *definitely* used for show. So in these cases, the concept that a frill or plate was *likely* to have been used as a display is less certain than the idea that a tooth was used to slice meat. And if we were to declare that a frill was used in a very specific type of display (like two shakes to the right, two to the left, one up and down, then repeat), we would be engaging in pure speculation. Sure, it *might* be

The lambeosaurine *Parasaurolophus* may have used its crest as a visual display and to make sounds. The large inflated sac shown on the male on the top middle is a speculation by the artist.

true, but we would have no way to test this. It can be fun to speculate, but it goes beyond what science can accurately, or even reasonably, predict.

Normally, we make comparisons between dinosaurs and modern animals because they might share similar body sizes or ecologies. For example, it is common to compare ceratopsids to modern horned herbivores like antelope and rhinos. This is not unreasonable, because of convergent evolution—distantly related groups evolving similar traits and behaviors because they have similar lifestyles. But we have to be cautious in doing this, because for all their similarities, horned dinosaurs are *not* horned mammals. For instance, unlike modern big-horned land animals, ceratopsids laid eggs, had proportionately smaller brains, and lived in a world without grass. These differences mean that we can't just think of *Triceratops* as a scaly rhinoceros. Dinosaurs were different animals in a different world.

We don't always have to compare dinosaurs with animals of similar sizes or shapes. We can also use related animals, even if they are radically different in size and shape. This is because behavior, like physical features, is a collection of traits passed on from ancestor to descendant. Today's birds are a type of dinosaur—specifically, avialian maniraptoran coelurosaurian theropods—and modern crocodilians are the closest non-avian living creatures to the Mesozoic dinosaurs. Lizards and snakes are next closest, followed by turtles, then mammals, then amphibians (see also chapter 10). Any trait—including a behavioral trait—that is found in both modern birds and crocodiles was almost certainly found in the common ancestor of both groups. And *that* ancestor was also the ancestor of all dinosaurs! So we can predict that all extinct species of dinosaurs had that trait, unless there is good physical evidence that suggests the species evolved away from that condition.

Here's a set of good examples. These are traits

that make crocodilians and birds, the two living members of the larger group Archosauria, different from most other vertebrates. Modern crocodilians and modern birds use complex vocal calls—songs—as well as different postures and poses when courting. They construct nests that are often made with vegetation rather than just holes in the sand. They hang around the nest as the eggs develop, protecting them from would-be thieves. When the embryos are about to hatch, they make peeping sounds to the parents, and the parents make sounds back to the embryos. After the eggs hatch, the parents (or sometimes just the mother) stay with the babies for at least a few weeks, watching over them until they are old enough to care for themselves. (Of course, in some bird species the babies and parents might stay together all their lives as part of a bigger flock.)

Because these behaviors are found in all the living archosaurs, the prediction is that fossil archosaurs such as extinct dinosaur species *also* had these traits. We don't know what exactly the courtship song of *Ankylosaurus* or the peeping call of a *Massospondylus* embryo sounded like, but we can infer that they did make sounds in these cases.

MODELS

Another way to approach questions about dinosaur behavior is to make models. These can be physical scale models, or computer graphics, or complex mathematical equations. Models are often most useful in trying to figure out the limits of dinosaur behavior.

Since dinosaurs lived in the physical world, just like all real things past, present, and future, they were subject to the laws of physics. Since we know from experiments how strong bone and muscle are, how blood gains and loses oxygen, what sounds are made in tubes of different sizes and shapes, and so on, we can use this information to help understand dinosaur behavior.

For example, paleontologist Dave Weishampel of Johns Hopkins University made a physical scale model of the internal tubes in the crest of the lambeosaurine duckbill *Parasaurolophus.* He did this to figure out what sounds that dinosaur would make when it blew air through the crest. Weishampel found a deep, bassoon-like sound. More recent computer models of *Parasaurolophus* crests, using scans of the actual internal structure of the fossil, have produced similar sounds.

Various paleontologists, such as John Hutchinson of the University of London and Donald Henderson of the University of Calgary, have used mathematical and computer models to predict the possible speed limits of different-size dinosaurs. Emily Rayfield of the University of Cambridge has used computers to test the possible bite strength of various carnivorous dinosaurs. These and similar experiments are very useful and help give us ideas about the possible range of dinosaur behaviors.

Like all computer programs, though, they are limited by the information the scientists can program into them. That is why one of the most important elements of dinosaur-behavior studies—even high-tech ones—is comparison with modern animals. A good computer, mechanical, or mathematical model of behavior should be able to calculate the real behaviors we see in modern animals before we should trust the values they predict for extinct dinosaurs. A lot of this sort of work is just getting started, so over the next few years, we should have a better idea of how accurate these methods are.

But even at their best, models, comparisons with living animals, and physical evidence will only give us a partial picture of dinosaur behavior. Much of the lives of dinosaurs will always be a mystery. Sometimes this makes me a little sad, because I would love to be able to understand *Tyrannosaurus, Triceratops,* and *Anatotitan* behaviors as well as a field ecologist can understand the behaviors of lions, rhinos, and elephants. But even though we will never have a totally complete understanding of how dinosaurs acted, we can still use the limited evidence we *do* have to make predictions. That is, after all, what science is all about.

Walking and Running Dinosaurs

Dr. Matthew T. Carrano
National Museum of Natural History,
Washington, D.C.

How did dinosaurs walk? How fast were they? Did they all move alike?

These are simple questions, but in many ways they are among the hardest for a paleontologist to answer. How can we learn about movement in dinosaurs? Walking and running are types of behavior, and behavior is difficult to decipher from fossils. It is a bit like trying to figure out a player's batting average just by looking at his photograph on a baseball card.

Aside from fossil skeletons, dinosaurs sometimes left other traces for us to find. Among the most common are footprints preserved in stone. With a trail of dinosaur footprints, we can sometimes figure out an animal's speed by measuring how far apart the tracks are. Dinosaurs stepped farther and farther apart the faster they ran. Other footprints show whole herds of dinosaurs walking together, and some actually show dinosaurs sitting down to rest.

We also have many dinosaur skeletons. The shapes of bones tell us many things about how they work in living animals. An animal that runs fast will have longer and thinner leg bones than a heavier, slower animal. The bones of digging animals also look different from those of climbing ones. By studying many kinds of living animals such as birds, reptiles, and mammals, we can find connections between how they move and the shapes of their bones. The patterns that we see can be used to "interpret" dinosaur bones.

How did dinosaurs walk? As it turns out, dinosaur legs are not so different from those of mammals and birds. They had the same bones and joints, and could move their legs back and forth about the same way. Dinosaurs stood straight on their legs, not crouched like reptiles. But dinosaurs differed from humans because they walked on their toes, with their heels off the ground. In this they were more like birds or horses.

How fast were dinosaurs? Big dinosaurs such as sauropods were probably not very fast, but they didn't really need to be; few predators could have hurt a fully grown sauropod. Most plant-eating dinosaurs were built like elephants and rhinos, but a few of the smaller ones may have been fast—perhaps they could run 15 to 20 miles per hour. A big meat-eater such as Tyrannosaurus was fast for its size, but it was probably too big to run very often or very quickly.

Did all dinosaurs move alike? Most dinosaurs were built in much the same way, so they probably walked similarly. They didn't live in the water and probably did not dig or climb; there were no dinosaur whales, no dinosaur moles, no dinosaur monkeys. Most of them walked or ran wherever they went, and like animals today, they probably walked more often than they ran. But even though many dinosaurs were basically similar, when alive they surely would have shown an impressive array of sizes, shapes, and speeds.

Could *Triceratops* run? Many artists like to draw them that way, but scientific studies are still ongoing to determine if they could.

Keeping Up with *Tyrannosaurus rex*: How Fast Could It Run?

Dr. John R. Hutchinson
University of London

Tyrannosaurus rex *was a huge dinosaur, but could it run fast? Henry Fairfield Osborn, the scientist who first described* T. rex, *was impressed by the long, slender legs of the king of the meat-eaters. He thought that it combined great "destructive power and speed." Some scientists who agree with Osborn think that* T. rex *could have run 25 miles per hour, as fast as a human Olympic sprinter, or even much faster than that. But not all paleontologists agree. They wonder whether the enormous size of* Tyrannosaurus *permitted great speed, or running at all.*

Some scientists who don't think that T. rex *could run quickly like to compare it to the modern-day elephant. Elephants can weigh about 13,000 pounds, a similar weight to that of an adult* Tyrannosaurus. *Based on what we know about the physical limits of elephants and other living animals, a creature weighing this much is simply too heavy to run very fast.*

Scientists who think that T. rex *could run fast point to its long legs as one of the features found in fast-running animals today. They argue that elephants are poor models for tyrannosaurs despite their similar weight because the two animals have very different kinds of legs. These scientists originally suggested that* Tyrannosaurus *running speeds may have been as high as 45 miles per hour (as fast as a racehorse), but more recently have put on the brakes at around 25 miles per hour.*

My research has tried to advance our understanding of this problem by using the methods of biomechanics: the physics of animal movement. My colleague Mariano Garcia and I have used simple computer models to estimate the forces involved in walking and running in a variety of animals. We know that for any animal to run, its leg muscles must be big enough to produce the force needed to support the body. We asked ourselves, If T. rex *could run fast, what size leg muscles would it have needed? Our computer model gave us a surprising and impossible answer. We found that a fast-running* T. rex *would have needed legs that made up as much as 86 percent of the animal's total body weight! Because this is not possible, we concluded that* T. rex *was probably a slower animal that could not run fast. Perhaps* T. rex *walked quickly or ran slowly with straighter legs than our model suggested, or perhaps science still doesn't understand tyrannosaurs enough. The investigation of running speed in dinosaurs will continue as we learn more about tyrannosaurs and about the biomechanics of all big animals.*

When Hutchinson and Garcia used computer models to figure out how fast *Tyrannosaurus* could move, they made comparisons with various modern animals (including a chicken!).

DINOSAUR BIOLOGY:
Living, Breathing Dinosaurs

Dinosaur skeletons are great! I *love* looking at them. I can gaze at them for hours upon hours in the field, in a lab, in collection cases, and on exhibit at museums. If I couldn't, I'd definitely be in the wrong job! But dinosaurs weren't just skeletons. They were living, breathing animals. Each dinosaur had skin, muscles, tendons, lungs, guts, a heart, veins, nerves, a brain—in short, all the gooey stuff packed around (and sometimes inside) the bones. And inside that gooey stuff is where the "living" took place.

There are *many* questions about dinosaur biology that paleontologists want to answer. For example: How did dinosaurs reproduce? How did they behave? How were the different species related? How did they move? How did they interact? What did they eat? Those topics are covered in other parts of this book.

I saved some general questions about dinosaur biology for here, however. These relate to that part of biological sciences called physiology—the functioning of living things and their various parts. This includes issues of metabolism (the digestion of nutrients and the removal of waste), breathing, circulation of blood, and growth of new tissue. All these functions are closely interrelated. And one of the most important questions concerning them is, How quickly did they occur?

HOT- OR COLD-RUNNING DINOSAURS?

Because one group of dinosaurs survives in the

form of birds, and more distant relatives of dinosaurs exist in the form of crocodilians and other reptiles, mammals, and so forth, we can often use these modern animals to explore our ideas about the physiology of dinosaurs. This helps us figure out, roughly, the size and shape of different organs in the dinosaurs' bodies. We know where the eyeball would go, for instance, based on the presence of the eye socket. And we can approximate how big the brains of dinosaurs were from the size of the braincase and space inside it.

One question about the physiology of dinosaurs that people have debated for a long time is whether dinosaurs were warm-blooded or cold-blooded. But before we *begin* to approach that question, we need to know what those phrases mean.

Despite what one might logically assume, being warm-blooded or cold-blooded has nothing to do with the temperature of an animal's blood. Instead, these two different types of physiology are about how an animal gets most of its energy. Modern warm-blooded animals include mammals

Opposite: Dinosaurs were not limited to tropical climates. Here an *Albertosaurus* pursues an *Edmontosaurus* in the snowy landscape of northern Alaska.

Cold-blooded animals (like frogs) use much less food than warm-blooded animals (like hamsters) of the same body size.

and birds, but also tuna and some other fish, as well as pythons while they are brooding eggs. Warm-blooded animals generate most of their energy internally—or, as scientists would say, they are endothermic. Because they produce their heat internally, warm-blooded animals tend to have a stable body temperature independent of the ups and downs of the outside environment—technically, they are homeothermic. But being endothermic and homeothermic comes at a cost. Warm-blooded animals need to eat *a lot* of food and to breathe very quickly in order to maintain that heat, so they have a fast metabolism—in other words, they are tachymetabolic.

Typical modern cold-blooded vertebrates include crocodilians, lizards, snakes, turtles, amphibians, and most fish. Although they get some heat from inside their bodies, cold-blooded animals normally rely on heating from the sun, warm rocks, or other outside sources—they are ectothermic. (This is why animals in the reptile house at a zoo usually just lie around under heat lamps.) Since cold-blooded animals rely on outside energy for heat, their body temperature fluctuates with their environment—they are poikilothermic. However, since cold-blooded animals do not need their insides to make most of their heat, they can survive on much less food and oxygen—what scientists call being bradymetabolic.

So what does it matter if a modern animal is warm-blooded (endothermic, homeothermic, and tachymetabolic) or cold-blooded (ectothermic, poikilothermic, and bradymetabolic)? Well, it makes a *big* difference in where the animal can live and how active it can be! Warm-blooded animals tend to be active for more of the day than cold-blooded ones. And they can survive in environments—such as high mountains and cold regions—that are too chilly for cold-blooded animals. But warm-blooded animals need a lot of food to survive. So a patch of ground—providing it is not in a chilly place—can support a lot more cold-blooded animals than it can warm-blooded ones.

Sir Richard Owen got people thinking about dinosaur physiology back in 1842, in the very same paper where he named Dinosauria. At the end of that article, he wondered whether dinosaurs—with their long, upright legs, more like those of modern birds and mammals than like those of sprawling lizards and crocodiles—might have been warm-blooded. This idea has been debated back and forth since then. We'll take a look at some of the evidence for and against warm-bloodedness, but first we need to know some basics about how physiology works.

THE ENGINES OF LIFE

When I said that warm-blooded animals (and to a much lesser extent, cold-blooded ones) generate heat inside their bodies, I didn't say *how*. Some of the heat comes from the action of the guts and muscles. But at the most basic level, animals generate internal heat from tiny structures found inside their cells. Those microscopic structures, called mitochondria, combine nutrients and oxy-

Animal Cell

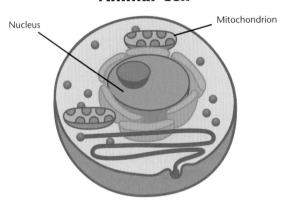

A simplified view of an animal cell. The nucleus contains the main DNA of the animal, while the mitochondria generate the power for the cells to do their work.

gen to release heat. In a very real sense, they are the "engines of life." Just like a car needs an engine to combine fuel (gasoline) and oxygen in order to move, animals need mitochondria to combine fuel (nutrients) and oxygen in order to live.

But mitochondria are very, very, *very* small, only 0.00008 to 0.0003 inches (0.002 to 0.008 millimeters) long. If you lined up a bunch of them end to end, you would need many thousands to make a line just one inch long. So you can't just shove a steak or potato into a mitochondrion for it to use as fuel! The purpose of the digestion process— biting a piece of food, breaking it apart with the teeth, gizzard (if you happen to have one), and stomach, dissolving it in digestive acids, and absorbing those dissolved bits through the intestinal walls and into the bloodstream—is simply to break down food into small enough pieces for the mitochondria to use as fuel. And the reason we breathe is to get oxygen absorbed into the bloodstream and transported to the mitochondria to burn that fuel.

All animals have mitochondria, not just warm-blooded ones. (Plants, fungi, and many types of single-celled animals have mitochondria, too.) However, warm-blooded animals have a lot more mitochondria in their cells than cold-blooded animals. It is these extra mitochondria that use food and oxygen to produce energy in mammals and birds.

At this point you might think, Wow, it should be easy to tell if dinosaurs were warm-blooded or not! All you have to do is count the mitochondria in their cells. Unfortunately, it is nearly impossible for individual cells to survive the fossilization process unchanged. The vast majority of dinosaur cells decayed millions of years ago. And the few little bits of preserved tissue that have been discovered also seem to have broken down. So we can't really be sure what the inside of those cells was originally like.

You might also think, But birds are a type of dinosaur. And if they're warm-blooded, shouldn't dinosaurs be warm-blooded? Well . . . while it is true that birds are living dinosaurs, they are also very specialized and advanced dinosaurs. There's a danger in using this argument. It's kind of like saying that birds fly, so therefore all dinosaurs—even *Stegosaurus* and *Brachiosaurus*—could fly! So we can't be certain if warm-bloodedness is something birds inherited from nonbird ancestors, or if they evolved it after the bird lineage had split off from other carnivorous dinosaurs.

What we need to do is see what clues we can find in the fossil record to help us answer the questions regarding dinosaur physiology.

WHAT'S FOR DINNER? AND HOW MUCH?

If a dinosaur were to be warm-blooded, it would have to have some means of getting more food over a given period of time than a cold-blooded animal of the same size. After all, those little mitochondrial engines had to be fueled. It turns out that there are various adaptations that suggest dinosaurs had such means.

Probably the first, and certainly the longest known, of these adaptations is the long vertical limbs of dinosaurs. Unlike modern crocodilians, lizards, turtles, and amphibians, and *like* modern mammals and birds, dinosaurs had limbs directly underneath their bodies. This means that they were all pretty good striders and could cover a lot of area. This adaptation was noticed by Owen back in 1842, and suggested to him that dinosaurs might have been more mammal-like than lizard-like in terms of their physiology.

Even the biggest sauropod and bulkiest

ankylosaur were still decent striders. And many dinosaurs—from little compsognathids to big duckbills—seem to have been able to move fairly quickly. So all dinosaurs, in general, would have been able to range over wide areas of land looking for food.

But more importantly, at least some types of dinosaurs had specialized feeding adaptations. The most spectacular of these are the dental batteries of hadrosaurid ornithopods, ceratopsid ceratopsians, and rebbachisaurid sauropods. These dinosaurs could grind, slice, or gnaw plants into extremely small bits very quickly, the better to digest faster.

In the late 1960s and early 1970s, paleontologist Robert T. Bakker examined another approach to the question of dinosaur—and specifically theropod—feeding. He observed that in the modern world, a given amount of food can support far more cold-blooded animals than it can warm-blooded ones. So if you compare the number of predators to the amount of food (meat) available in an ecosystem, you can get an idea of whether the predators were warm- or cold-blooded. The same amount of meat would support many more cold-blooded carnivores than warm-blooded ones.

Bakker looked at fossil populations of mammals from the Cenozoic, which everyone agrees

American paleontologist Robert T. Bakker.

were warm-blooded. He found that only a small amount—about 5 percent—of those populations were meat-eaters. Similarly, he looked at populations of land vertebrates from the Early Permian Epoch, when primitive sail-backed protomammals were the top predators. In these communities, between one-third to one-half of the population were carnivores. These had to have been cold-blooded, because at those numbers warm-blooded meat-eaters would quickly run out of food!

Bakker found that more advanced protomammals from the Late Permian Epoch and early crocodilian relatives from the Triassic Period had numbers in between these, suggesting that they were more warm-blooded than modern lizards and so forth, but less warm-blooded than mammals. His studies of dinosaur communities, however, found the same numbers as he found for mammals. In other words, they suggested that dinosaurs—or at least theropods—were fully warm-blooded.

Not everyone agrees with Bakker's analyses, though. Some say that it is too difficult to tell if the proportions in which the different fossil species are recovered accurately reflect what those proportions were in real life. However, it is intriguing that, based on the same technique as he used with dinosaurs, his fossil mammal communities had numbers that make sense for warm-blooded animals. If the technique works for fossil mammals, it might well work for dinosaurs, too.

Bakker's studies are useful for understanding the physiology of the meat-eaters, but they don't directly address the question of the plant-eaters. Some researchers think that there might have been too many tons of plant-eating dinosaurs in any one area for them to be truly warm-blooded. That is, the researchers think that based on how many nutrients are produced by plants over a given area and how many tons of warm-blooded plant-eaters those plants can support, there would have been too many warm-blooded herbivorous dinosaurs in a given place and time. Perhaps, they argue, plant-eating dinosaurs were only partially warm-blooded.

One recent study, though, has called one of the assumptions in those analyses into question. Based

The large nose sacs of *Muttaburrasaurus* may have helped to conserve moisture during breathing, as well as make a big honking sound!

on studies of fossil plankton and other evidence in the rock, it appears that the amount of oxygen and carbon dioxide in the atmosphere of the Mesozoic Era was different from today. North Carolina State University graduate student Sara Decherd and her colleagues wondered if the difference in atmospheric composition might mean that plants made different amounts of nutrients in a given period of time than they do today. They grew ginkgo trees—a type of plant that lived in the Mesozoic Era and is still alive today—in prehistoric-style atmospheres and found that the plants produced nutri-

ents two to three times as much as normal! So it may be that plants in the Age of Dinosaurs made enough food to support more tons of dinosaurs per acre than modern plants would be able to. This is really exciting research, and I and others are very interested in seeing further work of this sort!

TAKE A DEEP BREATH
Speaking of atmospheres, it is important not to forget that there is more to physiology than eating. The mitochondria need oxygen to combine with

Snort! Many larger dinosaurs, such as *Triceratops,* had big nasal chambers.

nutrients to produce energy, so extra nutrients by themselves can't give an animal a higher metabolic rate. Is there any evidence that dinosaurs might have been good breathers?

In fact, there is good evidence that dinosaurs—and some of their closest relatives—were able to get oxygen into their lungs and waste gases out of them very quickly. Biologists Colleen Farmer, Richard Carrier, and Elizabeth Brainerd and paleontologist Leon Claessens have been studying various aspects of breathing among modern and extinct vertebrates, including dinosaurs. One discovery they've made is that the common ancestor of archosaurs, the group including modern birds and crocodiles and their extinct relatives—including the various types of dinosaurs other than birds—had a special way of breathing. The gastralia, or belly ribs, of prehistoric archosaurs fit together so that when the muscles of the belly tightened, it caused the belly and chest to bellow outward. This caused the lungs to inflate faster, and with more air, than simply expanding the rib cage. Relaxing these muscles pushed the air out.

So the early archosaurs—which Bakker's evidence suggested had a slightly warm-blooded metabolism—had a special way of breathing faster. And dinosaurs were even more advanced in having extra-long pubis and ischium bones in the hips, which helped them move even more air through their lungs.

Additionally, early archosaurs seem to have a prototype of the special air-sac system that birds use to breathe more efficiently. This system is a series of sacs connected to the throat and lungs that help keep air flowing quickly. The sacs might also have been used to reduce water loss and to get rid of excess heat. In primitive archosaurs, these air sacs are found in the head and parts of the vertebrae, and this is what is also found in ornithischian dinosaurs. The system in saurischian dinosaurs is even more specialized, with parts of the sacs expanding to fill up more of the vertebrae. So dinosaurs seem to have been able to breathe a lot of air in and out very quickly.

Air sacs also probably played a role in trapping water that the dinosaurs exhaled. This would help keep the dinosaurs from drying out because of the fast breathing. In addition, many large dinosaurs of different groups—ornithischians, sauropodomorphs, and theropods—had another way to recycle moisture. They had extra-large nose regions. Some paleontologists have suggested that these big nose regions were filled with tissues that also helped trap moisture.

One question that is only beginning to be explored by scientists is what role the different levels of oxygen and carbon dioxide in the Mesozoic atmosphere might have had on dinosaur (and pterosaur) physiology. Higher oxygen levels may have allowed these reptiles to be even more active than they would have been if the atmosphere had been exactly the same as ours. While I'm writing this book, research is going on with modern archosaurs—birds and crocodilians—to see the effects of different atmospheres on their physiology.

THE PULSE OF THE DINOSAURS

Extra nutrients and oxygen can only fuel the mitochondria if they can get from the intestines and lungs, respectively, to all the cells of the body. That transport is the job of the circulatory system—the heart, arteries, and veins. Can we determine if the hearts of dinosaurs were up to the task?

Paleontologist John Ostrom once showed that dinosaurs had to have had efficient hearts, because they were so tall. In order to get the blood into the brains of dinosaurs, the heart had to pump against gravity. The brains of even relatively small dinosaurs like *Hypsilophodon* and *Velociraptor* were higher off the ground than those of modern crocodilians and turtles, so their hearts would have had to work harder to keep them from fainting all the time. And truly tall dinosaurs, especially the sauropods, would have needed very strong hearts.

In order to pump blood to these heights, dinosaurs had to have four-chambered hearts. Turtles, lizards, and snakes have hearts with only three chambers. The blood going into the lungs and the blood going to the rest of the body is not separated by any valve. If any of these three-chambered-heart animals grew too tall, their blood pressure would get too high and the creature would die. In contrast, animals with four-chambered hearts—mammals, crocodilians, and birds—have valves that separate the blood going to the lungs and the blood sent to the rest of the body. A four-chambered heart means that those animals could potentially grow much taller than three-chambered-heart animals.

Because both crocodilians and birds—today's living archosaurs—have four-chambered hearts, we can infer that extinct dinosaurs did, too. In fact, to say otherwise is to suggest an evolutionary change for which we don't have any evidence. The possible fossil of a four-chambered heart was found recently in a specimen of the ornithopod *Thescelosaurus.* However, many scientists think that this is not a fossilized heart but actually a lump of rock. Even so, paleontologists agree that dinosaur hearts were almost certainly four-chambered.

GROWING BONES

We often think of bones as simply scaffolding that holds the body together. In fact, bones themselves are living tissues. They change as an animal grows, and not just in size. There are changes in the microscopic details of bone, too. Some of these may reflect the physiology of the animal. Most importantly for paleontologists, these changes can be preserved in fossils.

Bones are where the body stores its minerals—particularly calcium and phosphorus. When the body needs these nutrients, it sends special cells to dissolve a little bit of bone into the bloodstream. Somewhat later, other cells move into the spaces and "plaster" new bone to fill the holes. If they didn't do this, the bones would become too brittle. This pattern of dissolving and patching bone is called reworking. In general, animals with lower metabolic rates—like most cold-blooded creatures—have only a little reworking in their bones. Those animals with higher metabolic rates—like warm-blooded creatures—have a lot more.

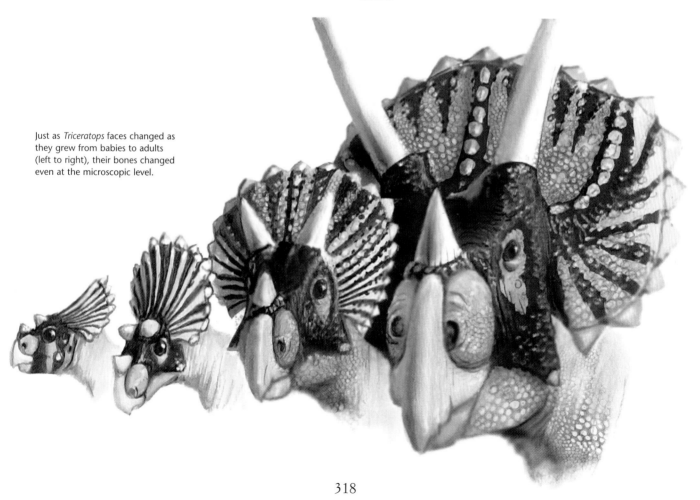

Just as *Triceratops* faces changed as they grew from babies to adults (left to right), their bones changed even at the microscopic level.

There is another difference inside the bones of low- and high-metabolism animals. Bone that is being grown very quickly—suggesting a high metabolic rate—looks different under the microscope than bone that is grown slowly. In other words, the *texture* of the bone is different depending on whether it was grown quickly or slowly. Typical modern warm-blooded animals have bone with a lot of reworking and with the fast-growing bone texture. Typical modern cold-blooded animals have only a little reworking and mostly the slow-growing bone texture.

Many paleontologists, especially Armand de Ricqlès, Kevin Padian, Jack Horner, Anusuya Chinsamy-Turan, Kristina Curry Rogers, and R.E.H. Reid, have studied the microscopic features of dinosaur bones to see what they could determine about dinosaur physiology. Since the early twentieth century, scientists have noticed that dinosaur bones show a lot of reworking. Also, it has been observed that dinosaur bones show almost only the fast-growing bone texture. So at least some paleontologists consider this to be evidence that dinosaurs were warm-blooded. Others disagree, however, and note that occasionally cold-blooded turtles and crocodilians show fast-growing types of bone, too. So the bone evidence is strong, but not certain.

Many dinosaur bones also show growth rings. These seem to have formed at the rate of one ring per year, like tree rings. Sometimes bone grew so fast that rings didn't form, and other times rings were formed but were then reworked as the bone was modified by later use. Growth rings typically only formed when the dinosaurs were growing.

Since we typically see these growth rings today in cold-blooded animals rather than warm-blooded ones, they were once thought to show that dinosaurs were cold-blooded. But now we know that such growth rings are also found in some definitely warm-blooded mammals and birds. We don't normally see them in birds because they are fully grown before they are a year old, but some giant birds of the Cenozoic Era show typical dinosaur-type rings.

* * *

The brains (blue) and spinal cords (green) of dinosaurs and their relatives: the avialian *Archaeopteryx* (top left), the deinonychosaur *Velociraptor* (middle left), the modern crocodilian *Crocodylus* (bottom left), the pterosaur *Pterodactylus* (top right), and the ceratopsid *Triceratops* (bottom right).

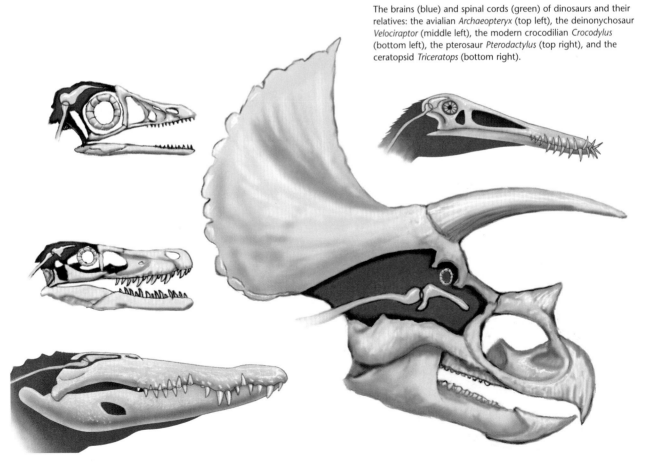

BRAINS

What do dinosaur brains tell us about their biology? Although the brains themselves are not preserved—they have long since decayed—the space inside the braincase shows us the size and shape of this organ.

Dinosaurs are famous for their tiny brains. It has often been pointed out that stegosaurs and sauropods had very tiny brains for the size of their bodies. That is certainly true. If you grew a crocodile to the size of *Stegosaurus* or *Apatosaurus,* it would probably have a brain twice as big as those of these dinosaurs.

But not all dinosaurs were small-brained. Ornithopods, and especially theropods, had larger brain sizes. Within the theropods, the fuzzy coelurosaurs had the biggest brains, and the maniraptoran coelurosaurs had bigger brains than non-maniraptoran coelurosaurs. One type of maniraptoran—the birds—has the biggest brains of all dinosaurs.

None of the Mesozoic dinosaurs had brains as big as modern birds and mammals. Although brain size and intelligence aren't exactly connected, the relative size of the brain is a good general indicator of how smart a creature is. So most dinosaurs were probably not as smart as modern mammals. They certainly weren't smarter than dolphins and primates, like some movies say! (This is particularly silly, as humans are a type of primate.) That isn't to say that they were stupid, though. Most dinosaurs seem to have had as much or more brainpower as the other land animals in the Mesozoic Era, and the maniraptorans were probably as brainy as any of the mammals of their time.

Fossil brain spaces tell us more than intelligence level, though. Different parts of the brain control different types of functions. So examining the spaces in the braincase helps paleontologists understand the senses of dinosaurs. For instance, the relative size of the smelling portion of the brain shows that *Tyrannosaurus* had a very good sense of smell, but *Troodon* did not. Small maniraptorans like *Archaeopteryx* had a very good sense of balance, which makes sense for a tree-climbing and flying animal. Bipedal dinosaurs still had fairly good balance, but quadrupedal ones had less specialized balance control (probably because they were already more stable).

The study of dinosaur brains is only now getting research attention. That is because the tools to study them have changed. In the past, you had to saw open a dinosaur skull to look at the features inside the braincase. And as you might imagine, not many museums would let scientists saw open rare dinosaur skulls like that! But now CAT scanners can probe the braincase without damaging the skull. It will be interesting to find out what new discoveries will be made looking inside the heads of old dinosaurs.

SO WHAT'S THE ANSWER?

Were dinosaurs warm-blooded or cold-blooded? That's a good question. It's also a question that hasn't been answered to everyone's satisfaction. Almost nobody today would say that dinosaurs were just like modern lizards or turtles in terms of their biology. There is just too much evidence that indicates otherwise, such as the features discussed in this chapter, as well as the observation that dinosaurs grew far faster than did big cold-blooded animals in their world (chapter 36).

Some paleontologists think that dinosaurs were fully warm-blooded, like modern mammals and birds. Others, however, wonder if they might not have been some sort of intermediate between crocodiles and birds in terms of their physiology.

I'll admit that I strongly favor the fully warm-blooded hypothesis, but I think there is still reason to be cautious. For instance, we are only beginning to appreciate the role that the changing atmosphere might have played in dinosaur biology. And there is still plenty of research to be done on the ancestors and other extinct relatives of the dinosaurs. But overall, I would say that the moving, feeding, breathing, circulating, and growing evidence shows that dinosaurs were much more like their modern representatives, the birds, than like their more distant crocodile and lizard relatives. This is still an unsettled, and therefore very exciting, field of dinosaur science.

Dinosaurs from the Inside Out: What the Bones Can Tell Us

Dr. Anusuya Chinsamy-Turan
University of Cape Town, South Africa

Dinosaurs are mostly known from the preserved hard parts of their skeletons, usually bones and teeth. By studying the anatomy and structure of such remains, paleontologists have gained a reasonable understanding of the diversity of dinosaur forms. The biology of dinosaurs is still much debated, and many lines of evidence have been proposed. Of these, it is well recognized that the microstructure (also known as histology) of preserved bones provides direct insight into how a dinosaur grew. Bones also offer clues about factors that affected the growth of a dinosaur.

Even though dinosaur bones have been subjected to the process of fossilization for millions of years, the bone microstructure is usually preserved intact. A paleontologist can examine a thin section of dinosaur bone under a microscope. Although organic matter is no longer present, important clues about dinosaur growth can still be found in the bones. This is because the inorganic mineral structure of a bone—made up of a calcium compound called hydroxyapatite—can still be preserved in a fossil. The direction of mineral bone crystals—or apatite—and the kinds of channels in the bone where blood once flowed both tell us something about dinosaur growth.

The organization of apatite tells us about the arrangement of the collagen fibers (which decomposed during fossilization) and the rate at which the bone formed. For example, if the bone texture consists of a woven pattern and the collagen fibers are haphazardly oriented, this suggests that the bone formed at a relatively fast rate. This contrasts with the pattern seen when bone forms more slowly. When growth is slow, the pattern of collagen fibers is more parallel.

The vascularization, or growth, of dinosaur bone can be deduced by studying the arrangement of the channels preserved in the fossilized bone that once contained blood vessels. When bone forms quickly, a woven texture results, and spaces are left around the blood vessels. Later, a distinctive ring of bone—called an osteon—forms around each blood vessel. This type of bone is called fibro-lamellar. When bones grow slowly, blood vessels are incorporated into the surrounding bone as it forms.

It is fascinating to note that dinosaur bone predominantly consists of fibro-lamellar bone, indicating fast growth. However, what is true for one kind of dinosaur may not be true for others. Although most dinosaurs have fibro-lamellar bone, many of them show periodic interruptions in their growth. Such interludes can be detected as lines of arrested growth and/or layers of lamellar bone tissue. These lines are often called growth rings. Seasonal or episodic growth like this is common among modern reptiles such as crocodiles, turtles, and lizards. In studies of different-size individuals of the same dinosaur species, the number of growth rings has been found to increase as the dinosaur gets older. By using a technique called skeletochronology, which involves counting the number of growth rings present in the bone, the age of the individual and its growth pattern can be determined.

Even though we will never be able to study a living dinosaur, studies of bone microstructure provide direct evidence of how dinosaurs grew.

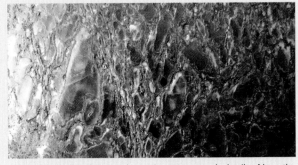

Looking at dinosaur bone under a microscope reveals details of how the animal grew.

Hot- and Cold-Running Dinosaurs

Dr. Peter Dodson
University of Pennsylvania

Our direct knowledge of dinosaurs comes from the bones they left behind, but we desperately want to understand these marvelous bygone creatures as living animals. This raises two separate but related questions that are the cause of much debate: Were dinosaurs warm-blooded or cold-blooded, and what difference does it make?

The short answer to the first question is that all dinosaurs had warm bodies. How do we know? Because all dinosaurs were at least as warm as the world they lived in, and the world of the Mesozoic Era was much warmer than the world we know today. There was no ice and snow during the time of the dinosaurs. But we would like to know more than that.

Did dinosaurs have rapid metabolic rates like warm-blooded birds and mammals today, or slow metabolic rates like cold-blooded reptiles today? One way that we have answered this question is to construct engineering models of dinosaurs using a computer. With the help of a computer, we have tested various metabolic rates on cyber-dinosaurs of different sizes. By changing virtual conditions such as blood flow patterns, wind speed, and sunlight strength in the computer, we can calculate body temperatures of dinosaurs and determine which metabolic rates place dinosaurs in temperature comfort zones, and which place them in temperature danger zones.

Our results show that body size is very important. For small dinosaurs like the 5.5-pound (2.5-kilogram) Compsognathus or 170-pound (77.1-kilogram) Deinonychus, body temperatures are affected little by whether the metabolic rate is slow or fast. But for very large dinosaurs, such as a 33-ton Apatosaurus, body temperature is extremely sensitive to metabolic rate.

High metabolic rates place the creature in grave danger of overheating. Without shade or water, a large sauropod dinosaur with a mammal-like metabolism could not get rid of body heat fast enough to avoid perishing. Even a 3-ton hadrosaur with a souped-up metabolism would need to be cautious about choosing its environment. Shade and water were always beneficial.

A dinosaur's rate of growth is an indicator of metabolic rate. Scientists study the microscopic patterns on the inside of bones to understand how fast dinosaurs grew. Studies of bone structure suggest that hadrosaurs and sauropods may have grown to adult size in only a few years, an amazing feat for such large animals. After they reached adult size, their rate of growth stabilized and they grew at a slower pace. Rapid growth may indicate high metabolic rates as the animals grew up, but slower metabolic rates for adults of large species.

Evidence for the migration of dinosaurs also suggests that they were active, warm-bodied creatures. Some familiar dinosaurs from Alberta and Montana (Edmontosaurus, Pachyrhinosaurus) have also been found in Alaska. This suggests that they migrated north in spring and migrated south again in the fall to avoid winter darkness and cold. Migratory ability turns out to be related to body size: larger animals can cover longer distances. Migration is costly in energy. Migration would have been easier for dinosaurs with a low metabolic rate because they could use existing fat stores for energy, stretching them over a long period of time. Dinosaurs with high metabolic rates would not have enough energy to go the distance.

We visualize our dinosaurs as warm-bodied, happy wanderers purring along with the engines of mini-compact cars, not gas-guzzling SUVs!

Reference

J. R. Spotila, M. P. O'Connor, P. Dodson, and F. V. Paladino. 1991. "Hot and Cold Running Dinosaurs: Body Size, Metabolism, and Migration." *Modern Geology* 16:203–27.

Dinosaur Paleopathology

Dr. Elizabeth Rega
College of Osteopathic Medicine
of the Pacific and College of
Veterinary Medicine,
Western University of Health Sciences,
Pomona, California

Photo by Jess Lopatynski

Can fossil bones show signs of dinosaur disease or injury? Yes, if you know what to look for.

Of the many dinosaur bones excavated by paleontologists, only a small number show abnormalities. A bone may be the wrong shape—its shaft may look "swollen" or eroded. Sometimes adjacent bones may be fused together. Extra bony bridges may be present, either between bones or at spots where muscles or ligaments were probably once attached. There may be holes that look like punctures, or even a false joint where no joint should have existed.

These are all evidence of disease or injury found in dinosaur fossils. The study of ancient disease is called paleopathology. There are many types of diseases and injuries that affected dinosaurs. Among them, broken bones and other traumatic injury are the most common. Infection of bones is also common, as well as ossification (transformation into bone) of soft tissues, such as ligaments and tendons, that once attached bones and muscles together. Cancer seems quite rare in dinosaurs. Strangely, wear and tear on joint surfaces (that which we call degenerative joint disease or osteoarthritis) seems to be completely absent. Arthritis is common in older humans and some animals, like dogs, but even older dinosaurs seem to show no evidence of this disease.

Studying dinosaur diseases is limited by what we have to work with in the fossil record. The only diseases we can see in dinosaurs are those that affected the bones. They could have had many other diseases that didn't affect the bones. We know from ourselves that most serious, life-threatening diseases don't affect the bones at all. They move too quickly for the bone to respond, or they only affect soft tissue, like guts or skin or the brain. Therefore, the vast majority of illnesses suffered by dinosaurs are probably invisible to us because their soft tissue was not preserved. For this reason, it is usually impossible to tell the cause of death.

Even though we can see signs of disease in dinosaur bones, we really don't know much about the health of a particular dinosaur. Bones are usually affected as a response to recovery from disease or injury. If a frail or weak dinosaur died quickly from an infection, its bones would look perfectly normal to us. It would not show that the dinosaur had been unhealthy. In contrast, a dinosaur with a strong immune system would have survived long enough to mount a response to the infection. Its fossils could show pathological changes on the bones. Therefore, even though this second specimen would look "diseased" to us, it could have been healthier than the dinosaur that died quickly.

Another challenge is identifying the kind of disease that infected a dinosaur. We assume that dinosaur bones responded to disease the same way as bones in modern animals, but we do not know if this is actually true. We also compare dinosaur diseases to diseases we know about in today's animals. But they may not actually be the same diseases because disease-causing organisms from the time of the dinosaurs may have evolved or become extinct. Dinosaur diseases may have changed over time in ways that we just can't see.

Even with our limited knowledge, diseases in dinosaurs are a fascinating source of speculation about ancient ways of living. One famous theropod dinosaur, the T. rex "Sue," suffered from many afflictions that show in its bones. It had an infected and healed lower leg bone (fibula), multiple broken ribs on both sides, injuries to an arm and shoulder blade, multiple fused parts of the backbone, and a number of holes at the back of both lower jaws. Scientists are still debating whether the latter are bite marks or the result of an infection.

39

LIFE IN THE TRIASSIC PERIOD

The Triassic Period (251–199.6 MYA) was the first part of the Mesozoic Era (251–65.5 MYA). It was then that dinosaurs first appeared. But much more happened during the Triassic than that. Many animal groups that we are familiar with today—frogs, mammals, turtles, crocodiles—first appeared in their earliest forms during this period. The Triassic also saw the origins of groups that were important in the Mesozoic but that have long since vanished—pterosaurs, marine reptiles, and so forth. And it was at the end of the Triassic that the Atlantic Ocean was born.

THE GREATEST EXTINCTION

The Triassic Period begins and ends with a mass extinction—the disappearance of many distantly related animal and plant species. In fact, extinctions are the basis for nearly all boundaries between the periods. But the one at the beginning of the Triassic, separating the Paleozoic Era (542–251 MYA) from the Mesozoic Era, was the largest mass extinction of all.

Most people know about the mass extinction at the end of the Cretaceous Period (145.5–65.5 MYA), which saw the end of the Age of Dinosaurs. In that event, perhaps 65 percent of all species died out. That was a very serious extinction, but it is still little compared to the one that separates the Permian Period (299–251 MYA) of the Paleozoic Era and the Triassic Period of the Mesozoic Era. During this *Permo-Triassic mass extinction,* about 90 to 95 percent of all species died out! And since

Opposite: The Late Triassic theropod *Coelophysis* eats a primitive mammal while trying to avoid being eaten by a parasuchian. Early pterosaurs fly overhead.

a species can survive so long as just a few of the millions of individuals survive, that means far more than 95 percent of the individual living things on the Earth died at that time. In fact, this may have been the closest life on Earth ever came to being totally destroyed!

What could cause this devastation? Right at this time, a gigantic series of volcanic eruptions occurred in what is now Siberia. These eruptions formed an immense field of lava known as the Siberian Traps. ("Traps" doesn't mean that things got trapped! It's a geological term for a particular type of preserved lava field, from a Dutch word meaning "steps.") The Siberian Traps are evidence of the largest volcanic eruptions in the history of life. Between 0.4 and 1 million cubic miles (1.6 to 4 million cubic kilometers) of lava flowed onto the surface of Siberia in a geologically short period of time. If you spread that much lava over modern North America, it would form a layer 243 to 614 feet (74 to 187 meters) deep!

But other than the poor animals and plants of

Permian Siberia, the lava didn't kill directly. Instead, gases that were expelled from the volcanoes along with the lava changed the atmosphere around the world. Because some of these gases acted like the glass in a greenhouse, heat from sunlight was trapped on the surface of the Earth rather than radiating out into space. Other gases released from the volcanoes and shaken up from the seafloor caused oxygen levels to crash both on land and in the sea. Many animals around the world asphyxiated. That is, they ran out of oxygen to breathe. (We sometimes forget that animals in the water need oxygen, too. But shellfish and fish and so forth do "breathe" oxygen, which is dissolved in the water. That's why a "bubbler," or some source of underwater oxygen, is so important for your aquarium: without it, the fish would die!) On top of this, ash and dust from the eruptions blanketed the world, cutting off the sunlight that plants and algae need to survive.

In this harsh environment, the only creatures that could survive were those that did not need much oxygen or those better able to extract the little oxygen that was there. In the water, many types of shellfish died out entirely, including the trilobites—relatives of modern crustaceans and arachnids that were among the most common animals in Paleozoic seas. On land all the species larger than a small dog seem to have perished. Most of the protomammals, which had been the most important Paleozoic land vertebrates, were wiped out. However, there were protomammals that *did* make it through. The ones that lived show adaptations indicating they could breathe faster and with bigger breaths than their relatives. Other survivors were amphibians and true reptiles.

RECOVERY OF THE REPTILES

Among the reptile groups to survive was a type that had just recently evolved. These were the archosaurs, the group that eventually evolved into crocodilians, pterosaurs, and dinosaurs (including birds). Archosaurs had adaptations such as specialized belly ribs and air sacs that allowed them to

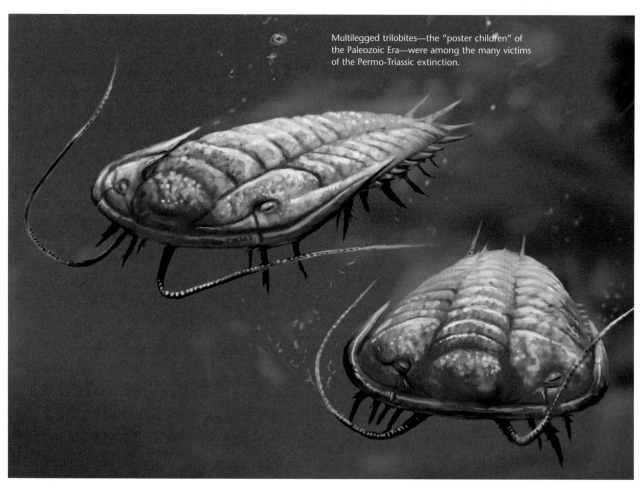

Multilegged trilobites—the "poster children" of the Paleozoic Era—were among the many victims of the Permo-Triassic extinction.

The Permo-Triassic mass extinction was the end of one world and the beginning of another.

get faster and bigger breaths than most land vertebrates. Although they were newcomers to the world, they became more common as the Triassic went on.

The world after the Permo-Triassic mass extinction took a while to recover. Sedimentary rocks record that much of the land surface was barren at that time, but eventually the surviving plants grew to cover the land again. These plants included many types of ferns and some woody plants like ginkgo trees, cycads, and conifers such as pines, cypresses, redwoods, and their relatives. But there was no grass, no flowers, and no fruit. These types of plants had not yet evolved.

Marine reptiles of the Late Triassic: shellfish-eating *Placodus* (bottom), long-necked *Tanystropheus* (middle), a pack of little *Keichousaurus* (top right), and a pair of ichthyosaurs (background).

The beginning of the Triassic was in some ways a good time for the survivors. Many different descendants of the same species might find a way of living with no competitors. So in a very short period of time, at least from a geological point of view, the surviving groups produced many diverse descendants—what scientists call an adaptive radiation. The amphibians, the protomammals, and the reptiles all had an adaptive radiation at this time. For example, during the Early Triassic Epoch, the first frogs appeared. But amphibians were limited because they had to go back to ponds to reproduce, so they never became the dominant group of land vertebrates. At first, the protomammals looked as if they might have the upper hand, just as they did in the Permian, but the reptiles eventually became more common and more diverse.

This may have been due to the general conditions of the world. During the Triassic, all the continents had combined together to form a single supercontinent called Pangaea (sometimes spelled Pangea). Much of Pangaea was hot, in part because of the greenhouse warming of the world. And the interior was very dry, because the interior of this landmass was so far from the sea. (In general, the farther away from the sea, the drier the land, because rain clouds don't easily reach it. Think about the American West or the Gobi Desert, for modern examples.)

Reptiles tend to do better in hot, dry environments than do mammals or amphibians, because reptile skins are less porous on the outside and because they have special water-conserving kidneys. Paleontologists infer that protomammals had skin and kidneys that resembled those of their surviving descendants, the mammals. So the reptiles did better in the hot Triassic than their neighbors.

* * *

DRAGONS OF THE SEA AND AIR

Many types of Triassic reptiles would have looked vaguely lizard-like, especially to people who don't know all the specializations that make lizards unique. In other words, many Triassic reptiles were quadrupeds with sprawling legs and long tails. But from such ancestors many different new forms appeared.

Some of these reptiles—most of them cousins of the archosaurs—began to colonize the seas. At first, they lived near the seashores, looking for fish to eat. Their descendants became better swimmers, just as the modern Galápagos marine iguana is a better swimmer than your typical lizard. These aquatic reptiles were something like modern otters, although probably a lot less fun. (Otters are just about the most playful living creatures I know of.) Some of these reptiles—such as *Tanystropheus* and *Dinocephalosaurus*—evolved extremely long necks and needle-like teeth, which they might have used to snatch fish. Others—like the pachypleurosaurs and the nothosaurs—developed stout conical teeth to catch bigger fish and fast squid. One type, called placodonts, evolved very strong grasping teeth in front and heavy crushing teeth behind. Placodonts were shellfish-eaters, pulling up mollusks from the seafloor and breaking the shells in their massive jaws to get at the tasty meat inside.

Even though they fed in the water, all these animals had to come up onto the surface in order to breathe. These first Triassic aquatic reptiles had arms and legs with fingers and toes (although they were probably *webbed* fingers and toes) so they could walk along the shores. For a long time, paleontologists assumed they crawled up onto beaches to lay their eggs. That might be true of the group in which *Tanystropheus* and *Dinocephalosaurus* belonged. But the others, which were among the first members of the marine reptile group called Euryapsida, had developed a new way of reproducing. Newly discovered pachypleurosaur fossils from China show the oldest evidence for this change, which has already been discovered in more advanced euryapsids. The change is this: instead of being laid on land, the eggs were retained and hatched inside the body of the mother. There they could develop until the young were old enough to swim and feed on their own. Only then would the young be born.

This adaptation allowed the euryapsids to become more seaworthy, since they wouldn't have to come up onto land. During the Middle Triassic Epoch, the most sea-adapted of all the marine reptiles had evolved. These were the ichthyosaurs. This group had long snouts with small, cone-

Late Triassic *Eudimorphodon*, one of the oldest known pterosaurs.

shaped teeth, and their gut contents show that they hunted fish and squid. Their eyes were enormous and well adapted to seeing even in the dark depths of the sea. Their hands and feet had evolved into flippers, useless on land but great help in swimming. Triassic ichthyosaurs ranged from just about 3 feet (0.9 meters) long to whoppers nearly 50 feet (15.2 meters) long. That's as big as a sperm whale! Most Triassic ichthyosaurs were long and sort of eel-shaped. They used their broad, flattened tail to propel them through the seas, and their flippers were mainly used for steering. The giant ichthyosaurs, in contrast, had extremely long flippers, which were probably used for swimming as well as steering. Toward the very end of the Triassic, new fast-swimming ichthyosaurs had evolved, but as this type had its heyday in the Jurassic Period, I'll talk more about them in chapter 40. Regardless of the type of ichthyosaur, they all retained their eggs inside their bodies until they were ready to hatch.

Another type of euryapsid that appeared at the very end of the Triassic was the plesiosaurs. These fully marine reptiles were more common in the Jurassic and Cretaceous, so you'll learn about them in those chapters.

Reptiles hadn't just colonized the Triassic seas, though. They also colonized the Triassic trees. There were several different types that had evolved into tree climbers. Some, like *Megalancosaurus* and *Drepanosaurus,* were probably just climbers looking for insects to eat. But some evolved the ability to glide down from the trees, just as today's *Draco* lizard does. Some of the Triassic gliders, such as *Longisquama* and the coelurosauravids, used long structures coming out from the side of the body as "wings." Others, like *Sharovipteryx,* had skin stretched between their legs for this purpose.

Most of the Triassic gliders were just that. They could glide from one tree to another, or from a trunk to the ground, but they couldn't get up above the forest. One type of Triassic reptile, though, did evolve true powered flight. These were the pterosaurs. Like *Sharovipteryx,* pterosaurs had skin stretched from limb to limb to form their wings. Their front legs were extremely long, and the fourth finger was *very* stretched out. In other words, their ring finger was their wing finger! Toward the ends of the wings, there were stiffening fibers inside the skin, so they weren't as loose as the wings of bats. Skin also stretched between the two hind legs, at least in early forms. But these were no mere gliders. Pterosaurs had very strong chest and arm muscles, so that they were powered fliers like modern bats and birds.

Pterosaurs were probably a type of archosaur (although a few researchers actually consider them closer to the weird long-necked Triassic swimmers like *Tanystropheus!*). They had hollow bones, and almost certainly had a complex air-sac system like birds. Their body was covered with fuzz, similar to the hair of mammals or the protofeathers of coelurosaurian dinosaurs. As in those other cases, the fuzz may have served to keep them warm. In fact, many paleontologists think that pterosaurs were probably warm-blooded, or at least more warm-blooded than modern crocodilians and lizards.

A recent discovery shows that pterosaurs laid their eggs in the sand. When their babies were born, they already had well-developed wings. So it seems that these flying reptiles could get into the air soon after hatching. Some paleontologists wonder if they even had parental care at all, and suggest instead that the mothers laid the eggs and left them. The babies would then hatch and fly away to live on their own.

Triassic pterosaurs were generally small, no bigger than a seagull. They had long tails and long snouts with pointed teeth for catching fish, insects, or other small prey. During the Jurassic and Cretaceous periods, the pterosaurs would get more diverse. During the Late Jurassic, the most famous sort of pterosaurs, the pterodactyls, evolved (see chapter 40).

WHEN DINOSAURS SHARED THE EARTH

The reptiles—and, in particular, the archosaurs—ruled the land during the Triassic, as well as the sea and the air. The protomammals were still present,

A Late Triassic scene in the American Southwest: a pair of the herrerasaurid *Chindesaurus* is threatened by the parasuchian *Smilosuchus* while rauisuchian *Poposaurus* looks on.

but overall it was the archosaurs that were the dominant group of land vertebrates. Many of these were types closely related to the ancestors of the crocodilians. One branch of the archosaurs that appeared during the end of the Middle Triassic, or perhaps the beginning of the Late Triassic, was Dinosauria.

The origin of the dinosaurs is discussed in chapter 11. By the Late Triassic, the ornithischians, sauropodomorphs, and theropods had all evolved. But even though the dinosaurs were pres-

ent, they were not yet masters of the land. During the Late Triassic, dinosaurs shared the Earth. While prosauropods were indeed the largest herbivores around—and in fact the largest land animals to have appeared up to that time—the early carnivorous dinosaurs like *Herrerasaurus* and the coelophysoids were not the top predators. Instead, they had to watch out for bigger carnivorous croc relatives. And the early ornithischians like *Pisanosaurus* had to compete with armored aetosaurs and various protomammals for plants.

There were new small animals present, too. The first turtles appeared during the Late Triassic. And so did the first mammals. These were rat-size or smaller creatures that would have looked something like modern shrews. But they were more primitive than any modern mammal. In fact, like the most primitive living mammals, the Triassic mammals would have been egg layers.

Although reptiles might have flourished because there were so many dry spots on the Earth, that is not to say that the whole Earth was a desert. Far from it! True, some of the best places to hunt for fossils of Late Triassic land vertebrates were once deserts. This includes the Ischigualasto Formation of Argentina, which produced *Eoraptor, Herrerasaurus,* and *Pisanosaurus,* and other younger Argentine deposits. It also includes the Chinle Formation of the American Southwest. Dinosaurs such as *Coelophysis* and a diverse community of reptiles, protomammals, and amphibians are known from the Chinle. But the most famous fossils from these rocks are the trees of the Petrified Forest. These huge trunks, once giant conifers, were preserved as the colorful mineral agate. You can still see their massive remains in Arizona, showing that what is now the dry Painted Desert was once a well-watered forested region.

BIRTH OF THE ATLANTIC

During the Triassic, things were pretty much the same everywhere. That is, animals and plants from one part of the world could also be found in all the other parts of the world. This is because the continents were still connected to each other. The world was just one big place. There were no seas to get in the way of animals moving from one region to another.

That isn't to say it was *exactly* the same everywhere. For example, the earliest sauropods (chapter 23) at the end of the Triassic are known mostly in southern Pangaea. Rocks of the same age in North America and Europe do not show signs of these giant dinosaurs (or at least they haven't been discovered). There would have been differences in rainfall, temperature, and seasons from place to place, and these would have meant that some species stayed in one region while others remained in another. But still, the Triassic world was much more similar from spot to spot than the modern—or even the Cretaceous—world.

At the very end of the Triassic, though, things began to change. A series of earthquakes and volcanic eruptions signaled the beginning of the breakup of Pangaea. Across the center of the supercontinent, a series of large cracks formed as the northern regions began to split from the southern ones. Plate tectonics, which had pushed Pangaea together in the Late Paleozoic, were now tearing it in half. New ocean crust began to form from the volcanic rifts across the middle. The seas came in to cover this crust. The Atlantic Ocean was born.

The split between the two parts of Pangaea produced two supercontinents. The northern part, which contained modern North America, Greenland, Europe, and most of Asia, has been called Laurasia. The southern landmass, containing South America, Africa, Madagascar, India, Antarctica, and Australia, is known as Gondwana. By the end of the Triassic, Laurasia and Gondwana were still very close. In fact, the Atlantic Ocean of 200 million years ago would have been not much wider than today's Red Sea. But throughout the rest of the Mesozoic Era, the Atlantic continued to widen, slowly but surely. It is still widening today, at about an inch (2.5 centimeters) or so a year.

A NEW EXTINCTION

As well as signaling the end of Pangaea, the volcanic activity that caused the birth of the Atlantic Ocean may have had a role in the end of the Triassic Period. There was a mass extinction between the Triassic and Jurassic periods. Although not as severe as the one at the end of the Cretaceous Period, and not even close to the one at the end of the Permian Period, it still saw the disappearance of many species.

Various types of sea creatures, including most marine reptiles except for ichthyosaurs and plesiosaurs, died out. On land, the protomammals vanished, leaving only mammals and their nearest relatives. Many groups of archosaurs died out, with crocodilians and their closest kin, pterosaurs, and dinosaurs as survivors. A host of other reptiles also vanished.

The cause of this extinction, and how quickly it occurred, is still a matter of scientific debate. Some think that it actually happened in a couple of stages, but others think that it happened all at once. Since there was a peak of volcanic activity right at the end of the Triassic, some paleontolo-gists suggest that a miniature version of the Permo-Triassic mass extinction took place. Others point to possible indications of an asteroid hitting the Earth at the time, which would make this a preview of the events 65.5 million years ago.

Regardless of the cause, or causes, the world was once again changed. And when the extinction was over, it would be the dinosaurs' turn to rule the Earth.

Make a wish! Two *Coelophysis* struggle over a tasty bit of reptile.

40

LIFE IN THE JURASSIC PERIOD

T he Jurassic Period (199.6–145.5 MYA) was the second part of the Mesozoic Era (251–65.5 MYA). It began with the mass extinction that ended the Triassic Period and allowed dinosaurs to become the rulers of the land. During this period, dinosaurs evolved into a wide variety of forms. Some became enormous giants, others armored tanks. Still more became powerful hunters. And one group of small dinosaurs took to the air.

Marine reptiles and pterosaurs also continued to flourish during the Jurassic. Mammals, too, diversified. In many ways, paleontologists regard the Jurassic as the golden age of the dinosaur world.

TRIUMPH OF THE DINOSAURS
Whatever caused the mass extinction at the end of the Triassic—a long, drawn-out event or a few *really bad* centuries; a volcanic eruption or an asteroid impact, or a combination of both—it resulted in a world where dinosaurs had few competitors. Protomammals were essentially wiped out. Only their smallest descendants—the early mammals and their kin—survived. Pterosaurs still ruled the skies, but they were relatively helpless on land. The various archosaurs that had once been the main hunters and competitors of the dinosaurs were gone, and only the crocodilians and their nearest relatives were present. And while turtles and lizards and frogs are interesting animals, they were not much competition for the Dinosauria.

So the earliest Jurassic dinosaurs found themselves in a world where they were on top. They were the swiftest predators and the largest herbivores. The reign of the dinosaurs had truly begun.

These earliest Jurassic dinosaurs would have been familiar to a visitor from the Late Triassic. The most common carnivorous dinosaurs were the coelophysoids, which had first appeared in the Triassic. They essentially remained unchanged, although some—like *Dilophosaurus*—had grown larger. The prosauropods and primitive sauropods, which had been the largest land animals of the Triassic, were still happily munching away on trees, although the sauropods, especially, continued to grow. Primitive ornithischians had not changed much, either. There were new groups of dinosaurs as the Early Jurassic continued, however. Among the predators, the first tetanurines appeared. And the Early Jurassic Epoch saw the first armored thyreophorans and beaked ornithopods evolve.

Just as in the Triassic Period, but unlike today, animals—including dinosaurs—were similar the world over. Nearly the same types of dinosaurs—coelophysoids, prosauropods, and primitive

Opposite: The Late Jurassic of the American West: a family of *Allosaurus* watches as a *Stegosaurus* and a herd of *Apatosaurus* go by.

Late Jurassic pterosaurs: primitive long-tailed *Rhamphorhynchus* (front left) and pterodactyloid *Pterodactylus* (front right).

ornithischians—are found in southern Africa, the American Southwest, China, and places in between. Even though the Atlantic Ocean had begun to form at the end of the Triassic, animals were able to move freely to all distant parts of the Earth. So, in many ways, if you saw the dinosaurs from one spot of the Earth in the Early Jurassic Epoch, you knew pretty much what all the others looked like elsewhere.

NEW BREEDS

As the Early Jurassic Epoch gave way to the Middle Jurassic Epoch, the world of the dinosaurs began to change. The coelophysoids seem to have died out, as did the prosauropods and the most primitive ornithischians. These groups were replaced by more specialized dinosaurs. For exam-

ple, the tetanurines—especially the spinosauroids and carnosaurs—became the top large predators, and the fuzzy coelurosaurs the top small forms. Various types of sauropods, including early diplodocoids and macronarians, replaced the older long-necked plant-eaters. In China, in particular, several super-long-necked sauropods appeared.

Among the ornithischians, the more primitive varieties were replaced by armored stegosaurs and ankylosaurs (which could better defend themselves) and by more advanced ornithopods (which were better at processing food).

During the Middle and Late Jurassic, the most abundant dinosaurs were carnosaurs, stegosaurs,

The Late Jurassic plesiosaur *Cryptoclidus*.

and sauropods. It is these groups that probably best characterize the golden age of dinosaurs.

PTERODACTYLS AND MARINE GIANTS

Over the heads of the dinosaurs flew the pterosaurs. Many of these Jurassic pterosaurs were, like their Triassic ancestors, long-tailed forms. They were typically small—the size of a mockingbird or gull—but a few grew to eagle size. However, during the Jurassic Period, the first pterodactyls evolved. Pterodactyls—technically called Pterodactyloidea—were the most advanced specialized types of pterosaurs. Pterodactyloids had shorter tails and longer necks than more primitive flying reptiles. Their brains were proportionately larger, and they might well have been more sophisticated fliers. Many had some sort of snout or head crest. These may have served as a sort of rudder but probably were also used for display.

Some pterodactyloids were small, but most Jurassic species were the size of modern eagles—in other words, most of them were as big as the largest of the long-tailed pterosaurs. During the Cretaceous, however, some would grow to gigantic size.

While a few Jurassic pterosaur species had teeth adapted to eating insects, many were fish-eaters. And they had plenty of fish to eat! The Jurassic oceans teemed with life. Squid and their relatives were very common, especially the armored ammonoids and the naked belemnoids. Ammonoid shells and belemnoid guards (solid structures from inside their bodies) are among the most abundant Jurassic marine fossils in the world.

Clams and oysters thrived on the Jurassic seafloor, and the first reefs of modern-type corals appeared. (There were corals in the Paleozoic Era, but they were only distantly related to modern corals. Those Paleozoic coral types died out at the Permo-Triassic extinction.) During this time, the earliest crabs and lobsters evolved.

Fish were also abundant in Jurassic oceans. Primitive sharks about 6 feet (1.8 meters) long swam the seas. Despite what a lot of books and TV shows say, modern sharks are *not* unchanged from before the Age of Dinosaurs! Sharks that would have resembled and acted like the big hunters of the modern oceans did not appear until the Cretaceous. One type of shark that is still present today and that first appeared in the Jurassic is the ray. (It turns out that rays—like today's stingrays and mantas—are actually a type of very flat shark!)

Far more impressive than any Jurassic shark, though harmless to anything but plankton, was *Leedsichthys*. This was a primitive ray-finned fish. The ray-finned group includes everything from mackerel and herring to tuna and sea horses and, well, pretty much any fish you can name that isn't a shark! *Leedsichthys* is the largest ray fin known. From its enormous gaping mouth to the tip of its half-moon-shaped tail, it was nearly 40 feet (12.2 meters) long. The tail alone was 16 feet (4.9 meters) from top to bottom! *Leedsichthys* swam through clouds of plankton, straining the tiny creatures from the water with specialized gills. Both the largest of all modern mammals and the largest of all sharks—the baleen whales and the whale sharks and basking sharks, respectively—are giant plankton-eaters in today's seas, so this way of life can support big marine animals.

Ichthyosaurs never came onto land and even gave birth in the water.

A family of *Ceratosaurus* scavenges the carcass of a *Camarasaurus*.

Swimming alongside peaceful *Leedsichthys* were marine reptiles of a decidedly less harmless disposition. As far as we know, no marine reptile evolved the plankton-gulping habit. Instead, they were hunters, chasing everything from small fish to the largest sea creatures, including each other! They were the kings of the Jurassic seas. In particular, the ichthyosaurs and plesiosaurs were the dominant groups. Both were types of fully marine euryapsids, aquatic cousins of the archosaurs that kept their young entirely inside the body of the mother until they could swim on their own. Because of this, the ichthyosaurs and plesiosaurs were able to remain in the water all the time.

Like their ancestors, Jurassic ichthyosaurs were fish- and squid-eaters. In fact, there are some barfed-up squid remains known from ichthyosaurs. Some Jurassic ichthyosaurs had cone-shaped teeth, but a few had lost their teeth and evolved swordfish-like beaks. Jurassic ichthyosaurs differed from their Triassic ancestors by being even better built for life at sea. Some features, such as their long snouts, humongous eyes, and paddle-shaped flippers, were retained from the earlier forms.

But the body shape of Jurassic ichthyosaurs was different from that of the earlier ones. Jurassic ichthyosaurs had a profile much more like that of modern tuna and dolphins. Their tails had evolved into a half-moon-shaped fin, and on their backs was a triangular-shaped dorsal fin. These features are found in tuna, dolphins, predatory sharks, and swordfish. All these sea creatures share a couple of things in common. They are all hunters, and they are all very, *very* fast. In fact, these are the fastest creatures in the modern seas, swimming between 20 and 30 miles per hour (32.2 to 48.3 kilometers per hour), and leaping up to 60 miles per hour (96.6 kilometers per hour). Jurassic ichthyosaurs were probably capable of reaching the same speed.

While not as swift as ichthyosaurs, the other Jurassic euryapsids were also formidable sea creatures. These were the plesiosaurs. Plesiosaurs first appeared at the very end of the Triassic, but did not become common until the Jurassic. While the ichthyosaurs had a fish-shaped body, the closest comparison for plesiosaurs would be a shell-less sea-turtle body. They had short tails, wide, flat bodies, and four enormous flippers that propelled them through the water. This much is common to all plesiosaurs.

The front end, however, showed more variation. Some plesiosaurs had tiny heads and enormously long necks; others had small heads and moderately long necks; and still others had gigantic heads and fairly short necks. In all cases, the teeth were cone-shaped. The long-necked ones probably snatched small fish from schools; the moderately long-necked ones probably hunted larger fish, squid, and ammonoids; and the big-headed ones probably ate other marine reptiles and giant fish like *Leedsichthys.* Jurassic plesiosaurs ranged from just under 10 feet (3 meters) long to 46-foot (14-meter) and possibly even larger goliaths.

The most extremely long-necked plesiosaurs had up to seventy-six neck vertebrae, far more than any dinosaur (which had, at most, nineteen). The largest of the big-headed plesiosaurs had skulls 10 feet (3 meters) long or bigger, larger than those of any theropod dinosaur.

Also swimming the Jurassic seas were marine crocodiles. These were descendants of land-dwelling crocodilians, but they had become fully adapted for sea life. Their tails had evolved into paddles, and their hands and feet into flippers. It may be that they were able to come up onto land to lay eggs, however. Like many marine reptiles, they were fish- and squid-eaters.

We know a lot about marine animals in the Jurassic because water began to cover the continents as the fragments of Pangaea—Laurasia in the north and Gondwana in the south—continued to move apart. As sea levels rose, areas that were once low-lying ground became flooded. The area we now call Europe, for example, which had been a series of mountain ranges separated by valleys and low plains during the Triassic and Early Jurassic, became an archipelago (like modern Indonesia) during the Middle Jurassic. The interior of modern North America was partially flooded in the Middle and Late Jurassic. Similar events happened in other parts of the world. Marine sediment and fossils settled in these shallow seas, even-

tually turning into rock. Later, geologic changes drained these seas and lifted up those rocks, so now we can go into the mountains to look for Jurassic oceans.

THE REAL "JURASSIC PARK"

Mountain building during the Jurassic is important to our understanding of American dinosaurs. Starting in the Middle Jurassic, the Rocky Mountains began to be lifted up . . . again. (There had been early episodes of mountain building there in the late Paleozoic and in the Triassic.) As these young mountains were pushing upward, weather eroded their sides, and the sediments produced washed down toward the shallow seas in the center of the continent. Part of that big wedge of sediment would eventually solidify into the Morrison Formation, the *real* "Jurassic Park."

The Morrison Formation is a record of lakes, streams, swamps, and other environments from the Late Jurassic Epoch of western North America. It contains one of the densest and most diverse assortments of dinosaur fossils known. Theropods included the carnosaurs *Allosaurus* and *Saurophaganax,* the megalosaurids *Torvosaurus* and *Edmarka,* the ceratosaurs *Elaphrosaurus* and *Ceratosaurus,* and various smaller theropods such as the tyrannosauroid *Stokesosaurus,* the primitive coelurosaurs *Tanycolagreus, Ornitholestes,* and *Coelurus,* and three different possible maniraptorans. Ornithischians included the ornithopods *Camptosaurus, Dryosaurus, Drinker, Othnielia,* and *Echinodon,* the ankylosaurs *Mymoorapelta* and *Gargoyleosaurus,* and the stegosaurs *Hesperosaurus, Hypsirophus,* and *Stegosaurus.* Both major types of sauropods were also wonderfully diverse. Morrison whip-tailed diplodocoids included *Suuwassea, Apatosaurus, Diplodocus, Barosaurus,* and *Supersaurus,* while their contemporaries among the big-nosed macronarians were *Haplocanthosaurus, Camarasaurus,* and *Brachiosaurus.* That was an awfully big menu for the many Morrison predators! And the Morrison isn't just loaded with dinosaur fossils, either. There are lots of crocodilians, lizards, turtles, mammals, and other animals and plants.

Apatosaurus at the watering hole.

What is really important to remember, though, is that there is no reason to suspect that western North America had any more dinosaur species than other parts of the world. What is more likely is that the geological conditions there—lots of new sediment and a place to dump it—made it conducive to forming fossils. In addition, these rocks have been explored more intensely than just about any dinosaur-bearing place on the planet. In other words, although it might seem that the Morrison fossil record is exceptional, that diversity of dinosaurs may actually be typical of what lived everywhere in the Late Jurassic Epoch.

That is not to say that *all* these species happened to live at exactly the same place and time. Some were found in only the earliest parts of the Morrison, others in only the later parts. It might be that some lived in different areas of the environment, too. Even so, if you were going on a Jurassic safari in western North America, I suspect you would have a good chance of seeing nearly all those types of dinosaurs over a short period of time.

Other spots on Earth almost certainly had this kind of diversity. In fact, most places where lots of Late Jurassic dinosaurs have been found—

341

Torvosaurus contemplates an *Apatosaurus* dinner.

Portugal, Tanzania, and especially China—show a similar batch of big theropods, stegosaurs, and sauropods. One place with very different dinosaur fossils is central Europe (especially what is now France and Germany). In this region were tropical islands separated by warm, shallow seas. The limestone that formed from the mud in those seas contains the fossils of many pterosaurs and other forms of sea life. It also contains the fossils of little coelurosaurs that washed out to sea from the islands. These include *Compsognathus* and *Archaeopteryx,* the latter one of the oldest known feathered maniraptorans.

The Jurassic Period ended with an extinction, but it was not as severe as the one at the beginning. Nearly all the major types of dinosaurs that lived in the Late Jurassic are also found in the Cretaceous (although not always the same species). In the sea, all but one type of ichthyosaur died out, and there were die-offs among primitive pterosaurs and some marine reptiles. But in general, the golden age of the dinosaurs continued into the beginning of the Cretaceous Period. During that time, though, there would be great changes in the dinosaurs' world.

Jurassic Detective

Dr. Robert T. Bakker
Wyoming Dinosaur International
Society

Photo courtesy of HMNS

I'm a dinosaur detective. A homicide detective. My crew goes up to Como Bluff, Wyoming, to dig up murder victims from 144 million years ago. Then we figure out who killed them.

We want to know the gory details of who ate whom. Not because we're fascinated by blood and guts but because we can't understand the Jurassic world until we have a good picture of how these animals affected one another.

Como Bluff is full of meat-eaters—36-foot (11-meter) allosaurs, 20-foot (6.1-meters) ceratosaurs with horns on their snouts, thick-boned megalosaurs that grew to 44 feet (13.4 meter) and were almost as heavy as a T. rex. Plus there were a dozen kinds of mini-predators as small as 3 feet (0.9 meters) long.

That's a lot of hungry carnivores prowling around a spot that is only about 8 miles long and 2 miles wide. How can we tell where each Como dinosaur hunted? Dinosaur "bullets" and "bullet wounds," that's how.

Most dinosaur skeletons we dig have chew marks on the bones. We call this tooth damage "bullet wounds." We also find some of the "bullets" that did the damage mixed in with the victims' bones. The "bullets" are meat-eater teeth that were shed when the predators were chewing up their prey.

People shed teeth just once—when we lose our baby teeth and our adult crowns grow in. Dinosaurs never had permanent teeth. As new teeth grew in each socket, the old teeth were pushed out. This went on throughout a dinosaur's life. We call shed teeth "bullets" because we use them the way detectives use slugs found at a murder scene. Just as a bullet can tell us which kind of gun fired it, so, too,

can a shed tooth identify the kind of dinosaur that lost it. Of the meat-eaters found at Como Bluff, ceratosaurs had the sharpest teeth and allosaurs had blunter, thicker, and slightly twisted teeth.

The rock in which meat-eater teeth are found can tell us about the crime scene. Red and green blotchy rock comes from soil that was dry most of the year. Black rock was formed in a swamp. Sandstone with pebbles was once in a stream or river.

So where did the Jurassic meat-eaters hunt? Nearly all of the teeth found where the soil was once dry came from allosaurs. They were feeding on gigantic, long-necked herbivorous dinosaurs: Apatosaurus, Diplodocus, Brachiosaurus.

Since megalosaurs were heavier and had stronger teeth, we thought these carnivores would have fed on giant prey, too. But we were wrong. Megalosaurs left their teeth at sites that were once swampy. Their teeth are found with the fossils of chewed-up turtles and crocodiles.

Ceratosaurs shed their teeth in spots jammed with the remains of giant fish and crocodiles. This not only tells us what they might have eaten but also suggests something about the hunting habits of these carnivores. Ceratosaurs have a tail that is almost unbelievably strong and flexible. Why? "Bullets" solved the mystery. Ceratosaurs must have used their tails to swim after prey in the Jurassic waters.

What about the smaller predatory dinosaurs— what did they kill? We have some Jurassic raptors— the earliest Velociraptor-like fossils known anywhere (all other raptors are from the next period, the Cretaceous). Our Como raptors were only as heavy as coyotes, and shed teeth show that they preferred to hang around the swampy sites where there was lots of small prey. We find raptor teeth next to chewed-up little lizard bones and skeletons of turkey-size plant-eating dinosaurs. These raptors also ate our own ancestors. We find raptor-nibbled bones that came from little, furry, shrew-like critters, whose descendants eventually evolved into monkeys and apes and people.

Being a dinosaur detective is the best way I know to make dinosaur fossils come alive.

41

LIFE IN THE CRETACEOUS PERIOD

The Cretaceous Period (145.5–65.5 MYA) was the last part of the Mesozoic Era (251–65.5 MYA). This long period saw great changes in the world of dinosaurs. When it began, life on Earth was very similar to the preceding Jurassic Period, but by its end, the planet was populated by many types of animals and plants that we would recognize today. During the Cretaceous, each of the major groups of dinosaurs—ornithischians, sauropodomorphs, and theropods—evolved their largest species. The continued moving of the continents and the rise and fall of sea levels isolated different parts of the Earth, so that dinosaurs in one region began to evolve very differently from those in other regions.

Dinosaurs remained the dominant group of land vertebrates throughout the Cretaceous, even though other types of animals also diversified. But the Cretaceous Period—and the Age of Dinosaurs—eventually came to an end with a great mass extinction.

BLOSSOMING OF THE FIRST FLOWERS

When we consider the prehistoric world, we tend to overlook the plants. Compared to fossil animals, which often look bizarre, fossil plants look pretty normal. In fact, if you look just at Mesozoic Era plants, they don't look much different from what you'd see at a botanical garden. But they were important nonetheless. And one of the greatest events in the history of plants happened near

the beginning of the Cretaceous Period.

Most plant groups from the Triassic and Jurassic periods are still with us today. These include ferns, cycads, ginkgoes, and conifers (pines, cypresses, redwoods, and their relatives). There were some groups in the Mesozoic Era that are now extinct, like the *bennettitaleans,* but mostly the Triassic and Jurassic plants belong to familiar living types. These early Mesozoic floras—communities of plants that grew at the same place and time—differed from modern ones by what they lacked rather than what they had. There were no angiosperms, or flowering plants.

As you might guess from their name, flowering plants normally have flowers at least part of the year. We think of flowers as something nice to look at and smell. But really, flowers are a plant's way of reproducing. The appearance and smell of flowers attract insects—and occasionally other types of animals—who go into the flower to drink the

Opposite: The Late Cretaceous gang's all here! *Tyrannosaurus* chases an oviraptorosaur, ankylosaur, and ornithomimid while the giant pterosaur *Quetzalcoatlus* flies above.

The Cretaceous Period saw the first snakes, flowering plants, and modern-type mammals.

sweet nectar that the plant makes. This nectar is a kind of bribe to make an insect land on and crawl into the flower. While the insect is drinking the nectar, it brushes against structures in the flower that dust it with pollen. The insect then flies off and lands on another flower. If that second flower is the same species as the first, the pollen from the first one fertilizes the second, and that second plant starts to make seeds.

Cycads, ginkgoes, conifers, and cycadeoids also make seeds, but these seeds normally lack much of a covering. Angiosperms, on the other hand, wrap their seeds in fruit. Some fruit is of the soft, succulent variety, like cherries and peaches and oranges. But nuts are also a type of fruit. And so is grain, like corn, wheat, and rice. Why would a plant want to wrap its seeds in fruit? To get animals to eat them!

That sounds a bit strange at first. What benefit does a plant get if its seeds are eaten? The main benefit is that its seeds get spread around. When an animal eats a fruit (soft, nutty, or grainy), it nor-

mally swallows the hard, indigestible seed as well. The animal then goes about its business, eventually depositing the seed, plus fertilizer (poop), some distance from the "mother" plant. And so plants with tasty fruit are spread over a wider distance than those without fruit. Plants protect their seeds from being eaten too soon by having fruit that is bitter and unappealing until the seeds are ready and then having the fruit ripen.

As you can probably guess (otherwise I wouldn't be talking about them), the first angiosperms appeared in the Cretaceous Period. It is true that there are some earlier plant fossils that might be ancestors of the angiosperms, but the oldest *definite* flowering plants are from near the beginning of the Cretaceous. Just as now, their flowers would have attracted insects for pollination. But who was the intended target of their fruit?

There were some Cretaceous herbivorous

Early Cretaceous European dinosaurs: young (left) and adult *Iguanodon* in the foreground; a pair of long-snouted *Baryonyx* charging directly behind them; and a herd of brachiosaurids in the background. Overhead is the pterodactyloid *Ornithocheirus*.

mammals, turtles, pterosaurs, and even crocodilians that might have eaten the occasional fruit and deposited its seeds. But the biggest and most common herbivores that could spread seeds over long distances were the plant-eating dinosaurs. It is very likely that fruit first evolved to attract dinosaurs. So next time you eat an apple or a walnut, thank the ornithischians and sauropodomorphs!

Early Cretaceous angiosperms were generally small weedy plants. During the Late Cretaceous, however, big flowering trees appeared. Early representatives of the palms, laurels, magnolias, sycamores, and walnuts formed parts of the Late Cretaceous forests, with early roses as bushes and water lilies in the ponds. (That is not to say that the other plant groups had disappeared. In fact, conifers and ginkgoes were still major forest trees during that time.)

One major type of angiosperm evolved toward the very end of the Cretaceous. Grasses are known from a few traces in the Late Cretaceous. But as far as we can tell, they did not yet form big prairies or savannahs. So despite some pictures you might see, no tyrannosaurid ever hunted a ceratopsian through the tall grass.

AN ODDLY FAMILIAR FAUNA

Just as Late Cretaceous flora would be familiar to us, so, too, would the fauna—the community of animals that lived at the same place and time. At least the smaller members of the fauna, that is. Obviously ceratopsids and saltasaurids and tyrannosaurids aren't the sort of animals you encounter today. But among the little animals, the Cretaceous saw a great diversity of salamanders, turtles, and lizards, for instance. One group of Cretaceous lizards, in fact, evolved into their familiar legless descendants—the first snakes appeared.

Mammals of the Cretaceous continued to evolve. Some reached giant size, at least by Mesozoic standards. While most were the size of mice and rats, some of the Cretaceous mammals were as big as cats, badgers, and small dogs. A few were threats to dinosaurs—dinosaur *babies,* that is! In 2004, a specimen of the dog-size *Repenomamus* was found with a belly full of the bones of baby *Psittacosauruses.* Among the diversity of Cretaceous mammals were various primitive egg-laying varieties, as well as early representatives of the pouched mammals (marsupials) and placental mammals (placentals). Some were tree climbers, others ground dwellers. Most would not seem out of place in the small-mammal house at a modern zoo. But in fact their internal structure would show them to be more primitive than living mammals.

In many ways, the Cretaceous was the heyday of the crocodilians. Triassic crocs were mostly small, land-dwelling varieties. Some were slow-moving sprawlers, others more upright runners. Both types survived into the Jurassic, and during that period the sprawlers that invaded the ponds and streams evolved into types that would look like modern crocodilians. In fact, they were still more primitive than modern-style alligators, crocodiles, and gavials, which did not appear until the Cretaceous Period. Some of these Cretaceous freshwater crocodilians reached tremendous sizes, such as 33-foot (10.1-meter) *Deinosuchus* of Late Cretaceous North America and 39-foot (11.9-meter) *Sarcosuchus* of Early Cretaceous North Africa. These could have taken down adult dinosaurs, although studies suggest *Deinosuchus* ate mostly big turtles, and *Sarcosuchus* mostly big fish.

But there were many other types of Cretaceous crocs besides the lake lurkers. Marine crocodilians continued to swim in the seas. And on land, a wide variety of crocodilians roamed. Some seem to have had mammal-like teeth and may have been omnivores. Some—like *Simosuchus* of Madagascar—had teeth that looked like those of ornithischians and were herbivores! In fact, short-faced, armor-backed *Simosuchus* seems to be a crocodilian doing a good ankylosaur impression!

AIRPLANE-SIZE PTERODACTYLS AND GIANT SEA LIZARDS

The Cretaceous was also the heyday of the pterodactyls. A few of the long-tailed pterosaurs survived into the beginning of the period, but the short-tailed, long-necked species of Pterodactyloidea dominated the skies. Some were small, but during this period a few reached sizes unsurpassed by any other flying group. The biggest, such as *Ornithocheirus* of the Early Cretaceous and *Quetzalcoatlus* of the Late Cretaceous, had wingspans of nearly 40 feet (12.2 meters) or more. Some of the pterodactyls sported bizarre crests of spectacular size. The diversity of Cretaceous pterosaur diets included fish, insects, fruit and other plant parts, and even plankton.

The seas of the Cretaceous, and especially the Late Cretaceous, were very warm. Throughout this period, the sea levels rose and fell, but at their highest, the seas flooded more of the continents than at almost any point in Earth's history. During those times, shallow seas separated many parts of the continents from each other. For example, a seaway—a shallow sea crossing a continent from one end to another—ran north to south in North America from the Arctic Ocean to the Gulf of Mexico, separating the western Rocky Mountain region from the eastern highlands of the Appalachians. At the bottom of these shallow seas, thick layers of limy mud settled. This limy mud, composed of the skeletons of a type of single-celled algae, eventually became the type of rock we

Enormous *Quetzalcoatlus* was one of the last pterosaurs.

call chalk. In fact, the name Cretaceous comes from the Latin *creta,* or "chalk." Nearly all of the world's chalk was deposited during the Late Cretaceous Epoch. So when someone is drawing with chalk, they are drawing with millions of microscopic fossils from the Age of Dinosaurs!

The shellfish of the Cretaceous included many species of ammonoids (armored relatives of the modern squid and octopuses) and belemnoids, extinct squid relatives with a solid core. Coral was still present, but in the warm Late Cretaceous seas the main reef makers were the rudists, a type of giant clam. Another group of giant clams, the inoceramids, were huge scallop-like forms.

Cretaceous sharks included an increasing number of rays and the first representatives of the mod-

Underneath the waves swam new types of marine reptiles, like the giant sea turtle *Archelon* . . .

ern fast-swimming shark groups. Rivaling these sharks were swift, powerful, toothy ray-finned fish, including 20-foot (6.1-meter) *Xiphactinus.*

But the top predators of the oceans remained the marine reptiles. Marine crocodiles continued to thrive, as did the plesiosaurs. Some of the Cretaceous plesiosaurs, both the extremely long-necked variety and the extremely large-skulled forms, reached lengths of more than 46 feet (14 meters). A few species of ichthyosaurs were present in the Early Cretaceous, but these had died out entirely by the beginning of the Late Cretaceous.

Three new forms of marine reptiles entered the seas during the Cretaceous. The first were the earliest sea turtles. Then, as now, these were lightly armored, paddle-finned descendants of

. . . and mosasaur sea lizards like *Globidens.*

349

Feathered dinosaurs galore in the Early Cretaceous of China.

hard-shelled land turtles. Their diet included fish, squid, jellyfish, and sea plants. As today, they almost certainly dragged themselves onto beaches to lay their eggs but otherwise spent their whole lives at sea. Some Cretaceous sea turtles, notably *Archelon* of Late Cretaceous North America, grew up to perhaps 15 feet (4.6 meters) long. Even at this size, however, the sea turtles had predators, as the first-discovered *Archelon* specimen had a hind leg that had been bitten off.

The culprit behind that bite was most likely *not* a giant large-headed plesiosaur, as none of those species are known from the chalk in which *Archelon* was found. Instead, the attacker was probably one of the second major group of new marine reptiles, the mosasaurs. These were honest-to-goodness lizards—close kin to today's monitor lizards and Gila monsters—that had evolved into seagoing hunters. Like the euryapsids, mosasaurs retained their young inside their bodies until they were developed enough to swim on their own, and so they spent their entire lives in the water. Their limbs had become webbed flippers, and their tails

strong and tall, to propel them through the seas. Mosasaur diets included clams, ammonoids, fish, squid, and other marine reptiles, depending on the size of the mosasaur and the shape of its teeth. Some species were only 6 feet (1.8 meters) long, but others grew up to nearly 55 feet (16.8 meters), longer than the largest theropods! (The biggest plesiosaurs were shorter than the biggest mosasaurs but a lot heavier, having massive rather than slender bodies.)

The final group of reptiles to enter the oceans during the Cretaceous was the hesperornithines, or flightless toothed birds. Of all the many Mesozoic marine reptiles, *only* hesperornithines were actually a type of seagoing dinosaur.

DINOSAURS DIVERSIFY IN DISTANT LANDS

On land, however, dinosaurs were very diverse. Nearly all the groups of dinosaurs found in the Late Jurassic Epoch were still around in the Early

Cretaceous Epoch. The most obvious difference between these epochs is that some groups that had been rare before became common, and vice versa. While the sauropods and stegosaurs were generally more common than ornithopods and ankylosaurs during the Late Jurassic, the latter two groups became increasingly abundant in the Early Cretaceous (at least in the northern supercontinent of Laurasia). Some paleontologists have suggested that there is a link between the success of these groups and the rise of the angiosperms. For example, there are paleontologists who think that the latter two groups (ornithopods and ankylosaurs) preferred the flowering plants, and so their numbers "bloomed" with the new flora. Others reverse this pattern, suggesting that the low-browsing ornithopods and ankylosaurs cleared ground more effectively than sauropods and stegosaurs, and that the newly evolved flowering plants took advantage of this. Either scenario is just speculation.

The next major difference between the Late Jurassic and Early Cretaceous was due to the effects of plate tectonics. As Laurasia moved away from the southern continent of Gondwana, each of these regions began to evolve its own distinctive community of dinosaurs. For example, *Iguanodon* was the main herbivore in North America, Europe, and Asia, and very similar small ornithopods and ankylosaurs are also known from all these regions. Some sauropods—especially brachiosaurids and early titanosaurs—were present. The last of the stegosaurs lived in Early Cretaceous Laurasia and were extinct by the end of this epoch. It was also in Early Cretaceous Laurasia that the first definite marginocephalians, or ridge-headed ornithischians, evolved. Curiously, while they were present in Asia (such as the ubiquitous little ceratopsian *Psittacosaurus*), they were very rare in Europe and North America. Carnosaurs and spinosauroids were rivals as the top predators, while diverse coelurosaurs made up the medium-

Giants of Late Cretaceous Asia (left to right): the long-necked titanosaur *Nemegtosaurus*, the hadrosaurines *Saurolophus* and *Shantungosaurus*, and the arm, belly, and leg of the theropod *Deinocheirus*.

Not all disasters in the Late Cretaceous were extinction events! Here ash clouds from an erupting volcano threaten a pair of *Corythosaurus* (rear) and a baby and two adult *Parasaurolophus* (center and foreground).

to-small-size hunters. Among these were the various feathered dinosaurs known from the Yixian Formation of China. Similar dinosaur species have been found in Europe and North America, but those fossils are generally much less well preserved, having been buried in moving streams rather than in quiet lakes or under volcanic ashfalls. The Yixian discoveries indicate that the Laurasian coelurosaurs had diversified into many forms—predatory tyrannosauroids and dromaeosaurids, tiny compsognathid and troodontid hunters, and plant-eating ornithomimosaurs, oviraptorosaurs, and therizinosauroids.

Things were different in the southern continent of Gondwana. Sauropods such as dicraeosaurids, rebbachisaurids, and early titanosaurs were the most common large herbivores. In Australia, at least, ornithopods were diverse, from little *Leaellynasaura* to big *Muttaburrasaurus.* Iguanodontians and ankylosaurs were present, but never as common as they were in northern lands. Spinosauroids, carnosaurs, and ceratosaurs were the main theropods, and in contrast to Laurasia, coelurosaurs were very rare, if not absent. So unlike the Triassic and Jurassic periods, the Cretaceous saw different dinosaur communities in different parts of the world.

By the middle of the Cretaceous, around the time that the Early Cretaceous Epoch ended and the Late Cretaceous Epoch began, the various parts that made up the southern supercontinent began to break away from each other as the South Atlantic and Indian oceans formed. South America, Africa, Madagascar, India, and the combined landmass of modern-day Australia and Antarctica became separate continents. Similarities in the flora and fauna suggest that there was some kind of land connecting Australia and Antarctica—perhaps similar to the Isthmus of Panama between North America and South America today. But overall the world became more and more divided.

During this middle part of the Cretaceous, the Earth became exceptionally hot and the seas reached their highest level. Plants were probably producing more oxygen and nutrients than at any time since long before the Mesozoic Era began (or since). It is probably not a coincidence that the largest dinosaurs—gigantic titanosaurs like *Argentinosaurus* and *Paralititan* and huge brachiosaurids like *Sauroposeidon* among the sauropods, and *Giganotosaurus, Carcharodon-*

tosaurus, and *Spinosaurus* among the theropods—lived at this time of plenty. The world began to cool somewhat during the Late Cretaceous, however, and these forms died out.

In Late Cretaceous South America, India, and Madagascar, the saltasaurid titanosaurs were the main herbivores, although there were small ornithopods present, too. Ankylosaurs lived there, but were fairly rare. Toward the end of this time, hadrosaurids arrived in South America, possibly from North America. Among the predators, the abelisaurid ceratosaurs were the dominant group, with noasaurids, *Megaraptor,* and unenlagiine dromaeosaurids as the smaller predators. Alvarezsaurids are also known from South America.

At present, we don't know what Late Cretaceous dinosaurs of continental Africa were like. Few Late Cretaceous fossils have been found there. What little is known of Australian and Antarctic Late Cretaceous dinosaurs shows that they were similar to Early Cretaceous forms, with many small ornithopods and ankylosaurs. (A hadrosaurid fossil has been found in Antarctica, however.)

Europe remained an archipelago during the Cretaceous Period, similar to modern Indonesia. On at least some of the larger islands—what is now Transylvania and France—there were rhabdodontid ornithopods, ankylosaurs, hadrosaurids, titanosaurids, primitive dromaeosaurids, and abelisaurids (these abelisaurids are probably immigrants from Gondwana, as they are not known from earlier in any Laurasian region).

Asian dinosaurs of the Late Cretaceous are mostly descendants of forms known from the Yixian Formation. For example, club-tailed ankylosaurids and frill-necked neoceratopsians both had ancestors in the Early Cretaceous there. Also present were the first definite pachycephalosaurs. In the wetter regions of Late Cretaceous Asia lived big titanosaurs, hadrosaurids (both lambeosaurines and hadrosaurines), therizinosauroids, and ornithomimosaurs, all keeping a watchful eye on tyrannosaurid predators. The deserts of central Asia, however, could not support a community of these giant dinosaurs, and so

instead we find only smaller dinosaurs there: ankylosaurids and small ceratopsians like *Udanoceratops* and *Protoceratops.* The largest hunters in those desert sands were dromaeosaurids like *Achillobator* and *Velociraptor.* Smaller coelurosaurs, such as troodontids and alvarezsaurids, were also present.

In the mid-Cretaceous of North America, the main dinosaurs had been sauropods, iguanodontians, small ornithopods, therizinosauroids, and nodosaurid ankylosaurs among the plant-eaters, and carnosaurs, dromaeosaurids such as *Deinonychus,* and oviraptorosaurs among the meat-eaters. During the Late Cretaceous, however, dinosaurs from Asia replaced these forms. Within this new world, the Asian immigrants evolved into the many species that gave North America at the end of the Age of Dinosaurs its distinctive appearance. It was here, and nowhere else, that the true horned dinosaurs—Ceratopsidae—were found. These herds lived alongside equally vast herds of diverse duckbills, both hadrosaurines and lambeosaurines. Nodosaurids—which had survived the arrival of the new dinosaurs—lived with their Asian-descended relatives, the ankylosaurids. At the very end of the Cretaceous, a saltasaurid titanosaur—*Alamosaurus*—arrived on the scene, probably from South America. Oviraptorosaurs and ornithomimosaurs were present, too, as were rare alvarezsaurids and therizinosauroids. Small dromaeosaurids and troodontids may have been threats to tiny dinosaurs, but the large hunters were all tyrannosaurids.

As you can see, the world at the end of the Cretaceous Period had many types of dinosaurs. Like today, if you traveled from land to land, you would see distinctive groups of animals in each region. More are being found as fossils every year.

If the dinosaurs could have thought deep thoughts, they might have imagined that this was how things were going to be until the end of time. But that wasn't how it turned out—65.5 million years ago, disaster struck and the Age of Dinosaurs came to an end. How that happened, and what caused it, are the subjects of the next (and last) chapter.

South American Dinosaurs

Dr. Rodolfo Coria
Museo Carmen Funes,
Plaza Huincul, Argentina

The dinosaurs of South America are remarkable in many ways. Some were extraordinarily huge. Some were among the strangest-looking dinosaurs in all the world. Perhaps even more important is that South America was the cradle of dinosaur evolution. The earliest of all dinosaurs have been discovered on this continent. Herrerasaurus, Eoraptor, and Pisanosaurus are their names. But that was just the beginning.

During the first half of the Mesozoic Era—the Age of Dinosaurs—South America was part of a giant landmass that connected the Northern and Southern hemispheres. Many kinds of early dinosaurs were able to spread to any part of the Earth. This included early dinosaurs from what is now South America. By the end of the Mesozoic Era, however, South America became separated from the landmass of the Northern Hemisphere. It became a continent of its own surrounded by both the Pacific and Atlantic oceans. For 80 to 90 million years, during the Cretaceous Period, dinosaurs could no longer migrate by land from South America to the Northern Hemisphere. During this time, the dinosaurs of South America became isolated from the rest of the world and evolved in their own unique ways. That's why South American dinosaurs look so odd when compared to dinosaurs from other parts of the world—as odd as kangaroos, koalas, and many other weird Australian animals look to those who live elsewhere.

The story of dinosaurs in South America is also one of survival. By the end of the Jurassic Period, the world was widely populated with a variety of long-necked sauropods, small herbivorous iguanodontians, and meat-eaters. By the beginning of the Cretaceous Period, many of these became extinct in the Northern Hemisphere. However, these same kinds of dinosaurs continued to thrive in South America, where they evolved for many more millions of years. Titanosaurs, abelisaurs, and gasparinisaurs are all "modern" Cretaceous versions of "old" Jurassic dinosaur forms that once lived in North America and Asia.

Among these dinosaurs, we have found the biggest dinosaur ever known, Argentinosaurus. It is the biggest known land animal that ever lived. This dinosaur was so big that its largest back bones were the size of refrigerators. It may have been almost 130 feet (39.6 meters) long and weighed more than 70 tons. It must have been a unique spectacle when this slow, herbivorous, four-legged behemoth walked the arid South American plains, shaking the earth with every step.

Some of the meat-eaters of South America also reached impressive sizes. These included the 45-foot (13.7-meter) Giganotosaurus and its relatives, some of which are thought to have hunted in packs. Their skulls were over 6 feet (1.8 meters) long and were armed with threatening rows of banana-size teeth, sharp as steak knives. Giganotosaurus was not related to Tyrannosaurus from North America, but they rivaled each other in size.

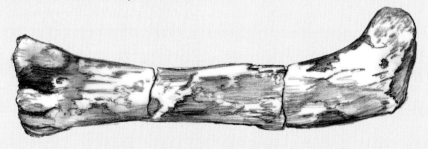

South America has produced many bones of gigantic sauropods.

354

Dinosaurs of Europe

Dr. Darren Naish
University of Portsmouth, England

If asked to name places where new kinds of dinosaurs are discovered, many people might answer Montana or Mongolia. They would be correct, but would they also think of France, Spain, England, or Germany? Everyone interested in dinosaurs knows that Europe was once home to such famous dinosaurs as Iguanodon *and* Megalosaurus. *But did you know that Europe also continues to be one of the most important places to find new kinds of dinosaurs?*

Some of Europe's most recently discovered dinosaurs are fascinating creatures that have taught paleontologists many new things about dinosaur evolution. Pelecanimimus, *named in 1994, is a primitive ostrich dinosaur from Spain with more than 200 teeth.* Scipionyx *(Italy, 1998) is remarkable for having its internal organs preserved. The English dinosaur* Eotyrannus *(2001) is one of the oldest tyrannosaurs.*

Although North America is famous for many dinosaur discoveries, Europe was actually the place where dinosaur science began. The concept of dinosaurs originated in Europe. It was the British scientist Richard Owen who, in 1842, recognized dinosaurs as a distinct group of animals. Owen based this idea on scrappy fossils of Iguanodon, Megalosaurus, *and the ankylosaur* Hylaeosaurus. *During the 1860s and 1870s, Europe was home to many spectacular dinosaur discoveries. Among these were the first well-preserved theropod (tiny* Compsognathus *from Germany), the first complete armored dinosaur (*Scelidosaurus *from England), and numerous complete skeletons of* Iguanodon *from Belgium. The famous first bird,* Archaeopteryx, *discovered in Germany in 1860, is one of the most important fossils in the world.*

The last thirty years have seen greatly renewed interest in European dinosaurs. Europe's dinosaurs have been found to be more diverse than once thought. Stegosaurs and ankylosaurs were found to be important in the European Jurassic and Early Cretaceous. Theropods including spinosaurs, abelisaurs, and dromaeosaurs were reported from Europe in the 1980s, and recent reinterpretations have shown that pachycephalosaurs, camptosaurs, heterodontosaurs, and oviraptorosaurs occur in the European fossil record as well.

There are several current hot spots for dinosaur research in Europe. Lourinhã in Portugal has proven to be home to Late Jurassic dinosaurs otherwise known only from North America. There are Late Cretaceous rocks in Romania that produce puzzling sauropods, ornithopods, and theropods. New theropods, giant sauropods, and other dinosaurs continue to be discovered on the Isle of Wight in England.

New discoveries every year continue to prove that the dinosaurs of Europe are some of the most interesting and important ever found.

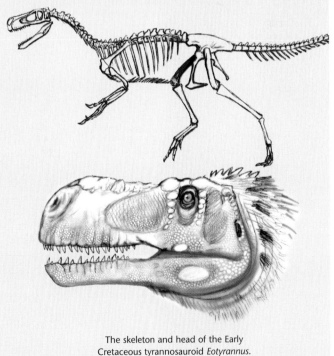

The skeleton and head of the Early Cretaceous tyrannosauroid *Eotyrannus.*

42

EXTINCTIONS:
The World of the Dinosaurs Ends

There's an old saying: "All good things must come to an end." And it's true of the Age of Dinosaurs at least. Dinosaurs first appeared about 235 million years ago, and between 200 million and 65.5 million years ago, they were the dominant group of land animals. But then their rule was over. With the dawn of the Cenozoic Era (65.5 MYA–present), the Age of Mammals had begun.

But the events of 65.5 million years ago are both less and more than the *extinction of the dinosaurs.* *Less,* because the dinosaurs are not extinct. And *more,* because land-dwelling dinosaurs were far from the only victims! As birds are descendants of the most recent common ancestor of *Iguanodon* and *Megalosaurus,* the Dinosauria lives on in them. So in a strict sense, dinosaurs aren't extinct. (To be fair, however, it *was* the end of the great diversity of nonflying dinosaurs—or what I would call the interesting ones.) However, a great number of animal and plant species—perhaps 65 percent of all species both on land and in the sea—died out at this time. In other words, it was a true mass extinction. It wasn't the greatest one—that "honor" goes to the Permo-Triassic mass extinction, which separates the Permian Period of the Paleozoic Era from the Triassic Period of the Mesozoic Era. It wasn't even the second greatest, since there were ones within the Paleozoic Era that saw more than 65 percent of species die off. But it *was* one of the most important mass extinctions, for it was the end of one era and the beginning of the modern one.

Opposite: The "Last Supper." *Tyrannosaurus* sees the asteroid blast its way toward impact in Mexico.

THE END OF AN ERA, LITERALLY!

Even before the discovery of the dinosaurs, geologists and paleontologists had noticed great changes in the types of fossils found from this time. These changes were easy to recognize, and they occurred in rocks all over the world.

The most obvious change was the disappearance of chalk, the type of limestone after which the Cretaceous Period was named. Also, the characteristic shellfish of the Cretaceous Period—the various species of ammonoids, belemnoids, inoceramids, and rudists—had vanished.

The disappearance of all these once-common fossils was such a dramatic change, geologists decided it made a good marker for a boundary between eras. This is the moment in time when the Mesozoic Era ended and the Cenozoic Era began, the change between "middle life" and "recent life." But era boundaries are also boundaries between periods. The last period of the Mesozoic Era, the Cretaceous, has the geological symbol of *K.* The first period of the Cenozoic, the Tertiary Period (65.5–1.8 MYA), has the geological symbol of *T.* So this event is called the Cretaceous-Tertiary mass extinction, or the K/T extinction or K/T

357

boundary, for short.

Strictly speaking, geologists don't formally use the name Tertiary anymore. Instead of dividing the Cenozoic Era up into the extremely unequal Tertiary and Quaternary (1.8 MYA–present) periods, modern geologists use the more balanced Paleogene (65.5–23 MYA) and Neogene (23 MYA–present). But few people call the events of 65.5 million years ago the Cretaceous-Paleogene mass extinction or the K/Pg boundary. I guess we're just used to the older names.

Survivors! The multituberculate mammal (in tree), avian bird, and champsosaur (in water) all made it through the disaster. (Multituberculates and champsosaurs, though, have since died out.)

VICTIMS AND SURVIVORS

So what died out at the K/T boundary? What survived? The algae whose skeletons became chalk did not become entirely extinct, but most of the species within that group did. The survivors were not common after the extinction. Because of that, chalk never again accumulated in thick layers in the shallow seas of the world. Other types of plankton suffered, too. The shelled ammonoids and solid-centered belemnoids disappeared from the seas, as did the reef-making rudist clams and their giant, flat inoceramid relatives. The paddling plesiosaurs, sea lizard mosasaurs, and flightless hesperornithines made it all the way to the end of

the Cretaceous, then disappeared. Sea turtles survived, of course. So did a few species of marine crocodiles, although these disappeared early in the Paleogene. (Today's so-called saltwater crocodiles are fine swimmers, but they are only recently evolved and are not really adapted for life at sea. The marine crocs of the Mesozoic Era and early Paleogene Period were fully seagoing creatures, with finned tails and reduced armor to help them swim very quickly.)

The last of the pterosaurs vanished from the skies. Except for stingrays, the freshwater sharks died out. (Freshwater sharks? Other than stingrays and the occasional stray bull shark, we don't have sharks in freshwater today. In Cretaceous rivers and streams, though, there were many species of sharks.) Many types of Cretaceous mammals vanished. Various forms of crocodilians, including the plant-eating ones, went extinct at that time. And, of course, all the dinosaurs other than the avian birds died out, from little enantiornithine birds through medium-size ankylosaurids to mighty saltasaurid sauropods.

But there are some things we should note. Not everything that died out during the Cretaceous did so at 65.5 million years ago. Many types of dinosaurs and other animals had died out long before. The last of the ichthyosaurs, for example, vanished from the seas around 100 million years ago, at the dawn of the Late Cretaceous Epoch. At about the same time, the stegosaurs disappeared from the land. The herds of the centrosaurine ceratopsids died out around 70 million years ago or so. None of these, therefore, were really victims of the K/T extinction. Something can't be killed if it is *already* dead!

And there *were* many survivors. Remember: *every* living thing on Earth today has an ancestor that survived the K/T extinction. No exceptions! And there are several types of animals that survived the K/T event to die at later, lesser mass extinctions. On land, the insects survived in vast numbers. The amphibians also made it through, as did turtles, lizards, snakes, and modern-style crocodilians. The champsosaurs, a group of aquatic archosaur relatives that looked like long-snouted

crocodilians, survived to flourish in the Paleogene, only to die out toward its end. The same pattern is seen in the multituberculate, a group of mammals that were common from the Jurassic Period until the late Paleogene Period. The ancestors of each of the major groups of living mammals—the egg-laying monotremes, the pouched marsupials, and (our own group) the placentals—were present at the K/T boundary and made it through.

SEARCHING FOR SOLUTIONS

Let's take this information and see if we can find any patterns in the survivors and victims. This might give us a better idea of what the K/T extinction was like and, therefore, a better idea of what caused it.

Nearly all the survivors on land were small animals—but many victims, like enantiornithine birds and various mammal groups, were also small. Most freshwater animals survived, but freshwater sharks did not. In the sea, more surface-dwelling plants and animals died out than did bottom-dwelling plants and feeders. Why?

Finding the answer to that question is complicated. In fact, there are still many disagreements about the details of this event. But one thing is clear: there was *a lot* more to the K/T extinction than the loss of the dinosaurs. So we can forget about ideas that "explain" just the dinosaurs' disappearance. Plenty of these have been suggested—like the idea that mammals ate all the dinosaurs' eggs or that the dinosaurs died of allergies to the newly evolved angiosperms. These types of events *couldn't* have affected ammonoids and chalk-making algae *and* various extinct mammal groups, yet they were all victims of the K/T extinction, too.

There are other reasons to reject these hypotheses, anyway. There is no evidence suggesting the sudden appearance of egg-eating mammals, and why would such creatures eat the eggs of most dinosaurs but not the eggs of the species in Aves? Or the eggs of plant-eating crocodilians but not the eggs of meat-eating ones? And angiosperms were hardly "newly evolved." Sure, they first appeared in the Cretaceous Period, but at its beginning, not its end. The Cretaceous Period lasted a *long* time, 14.5 million years longer than the entire Cenozoic Era (so far)!

If we are looking for some agent that caused the extinction, we should try to find evidence for it apart from the extinction itself. That is to say, we should be able to demonstrate that some change occurred by looking for *independent evidence* of the cause of the extinction in the rock record and not just observing the extinction itself.

It turns out that there were three major environmental changes that happened around the time of the K/T extinction. We know that all three things really happened because we have independent geological evidence for each. Two of these— changing sea levels and a huge period of volcanism—we'll look at later. The third was one of the great geological discoveries in the twentieth century, and was the biggest change, so we'll examine it first. That was the recognition that 65.5 million years ago, an enormous chunk of rock clobbered the Earth!

DEATH FROM ABOVE

The discovery that a space rock—an asteroid— collided with the Earth at the end of the Cretaceous began with a simple question about a layer of mud. There are limestones near the town of Gubbio, Italy, that record the end of the Cretaceous and the beginning of the Paleogene. Right at the boundary between the two, the limestones change into a thin layer of clay. How much time does that layer of clay represent? A few years? A few centuries? A few million years . . . or more?

In the late 1970s, University of California, Berkeley, geologist Walter Alvarez wanted to find the answer to this question, but he could not use the normal techniques for dating rocks. There were no fossils in the clay, so he couldn't compare them to the succession of fossils in better-dated rocks. Since this was clay and not igneous rock, he couldn't use radiometric dating. So like a lot of people, he went to his dad to help him with his "homework." (Of course, it helps when your father is the Nobel Prize–winning nuclear physicist Luis Alvarez!) Together the Alvarezes and a

pair of chemists, Frank Asaro and Helen Michel, worked out a way they *thought* might give them an answer.

They knew that meteors—chunks of space ice, rock, and metal—are constantly falling into Earth's atmosphere and burning up. (That's what we call a shooting star.) The ash from meteors eventually falls down to the surface of the Earth and settles on the land and on the seafloor. So these scientists figured that by looking for iridium—an element that is similar to gold and platinum but is much more common in meteors than on the Earth's surface— they could find the traces of ancient space ash. And if you knew how much space ash would fall on the Earth in a given year, you could look at the iridium in the Gubbio clay and calculate how many years it took to make it.

So they took chunks of the rocks, tested the samples, and found something very unexpected. Instead of tiny amounts of iridium throughout the clay—what you would expect from a constant shower of meteors over years—they found an incredibly high abundance of this metal at the base of the clay. What had happened? They thought of many different scenarios, but the only one that matched the pattern and the amount of iridium

The extinction asteroid burns its way through Earth's atmosphere.

was if a giant piece of space rock and metal—an asteroid 6.2 to 9.3 miles (10 to 15 kilometers) in diameter—had slammed into the Earth. It would have caused a tremendous explosion, and scattered ash and dust around the world.

Further calculations showed that this impact would have been truly tremendous. The force would be like 183 trillion tons of TNT! (By comparison, the biggest nuclear blast ever made was only as powerful as 50 million tons of TNT.) The explosion would produce an earthquake of magnitude 10.1, far more powerful than any known in human history, and blasted out a crater more than 100 miles (160 kilometers) across. A tremendous fireball would vaporize anything nearby, and shock waves in the air and tsunamis in the oceans would radiate away from it and spread around the world.

But the worst thing would be the ash. Immense amounts of rock—including the asteroid itself—would be pulverized and sent high into the atmosphere. Some of this powdered rock would rain down right away, but a lot of it would hang in the air. All over the world, it would turn dark for weeks, possibly months. Plants and algae would die from lack of sunlight. The herbivores that lived on the vegetation would starve, and after a period of feasting on the carcasses of herbivores and other dead animals, the carnivores, too, would run out of food. All over the world, on land and sea, many creatures would perish in the darkness.

That's a lot of speculating from one layer of clay! But that was just the start of the search. The Alvarez team, and many other scientists, began to examine rocks at the K/T boundary all over the world. They found many additional places that showed this giant increase in iridium. They found melted glass and shocked-quartz grains that were the remains of the blasted rock that had rained down out of the sky.

And most importantly, they found the crater. Underneath the Yucatán Peninsula of Mexico were the remains of the impact. It was buried underneath 990 to 3,300 feet (302 to 1,006 meters) of Cenozoic rock, so it couldn't be seen directly. But by drilling cores through the ground and later

using more sophisticated scanning techniques, they revealed a crater 112 miles (180 kilometers) in diameter, right in the proper range for the Alvarez team's prediction! This is now called the Chicxulub crater, after the name of a town near where the first core with evidence for the impact was drilled.

So, many people thought the K/T extinction was solved. The impact of this tremendous blast had brought the Mesozoic Era, and the Age of Dinosaurs, to an end.

FIRE AND WATER

It turns out, however, that the story is a bit more complicated. The Chicxulub impact was almost certainly the most important event in the extinction, but it wasn't the only one. There were definitely changes that were already going on that would have helped bring the reign of the dinosaurs to its conclusion.

One event was a peak in volcanic activity around that time. At about 70 million years ago, the style of the uplift of the Rocky Mountains of the American West changed. It shifted from pushing pieces of crust buckling upward into a series of powerful volcanic eruptions. Much more significant, however, were events on the other side of the world. Starting about 500,000 years before the Chicxulub impact, a gigantic series of lava flows started in what is now western India. These were the Deccan Traps. In pulse after pulse of eruptions, 123,000 cubic miles (512,000 cubic kilometers) of lava spread out over India and the nearby ocean over the span of a million years. This is an amazing amount of lava. If you spread it evenly over the whole of present-day North America, it would form a layer 79 feet (24 meters) deep. This might be small compared to the Siberian Traps lava flows at the end of the Permian Period, but it was still one of the largest in Earth's history.

The Siberian Traps are the likely cause for the Permo-Triassic mass extinction, the largest known. So it seems reasonable that the Deccan Traps might have had *some* role in the K/T extinction. Like the Chicxulub impact, the Deccan Traps would have produced ash and dust that would reduce sunlight around the world. This might not have entirely darkened the world, but it would have made conditions very harsh for Cretaceous animals and plants.

Another environmental change had to do with water rather than fire. The sea level, which had risen so high that large sections of the continents were flooded for most of the Cretaceous, began to drain back around 69 million years ago. The same plate-tectonic activity that started the change in Rocky Mountain volcanism allowed for this sea-level drop. More land was exposed, so that regions that were once near the sea were now far away. Climates would change, creating harsher winters and hotter summers. Also, those warm, shallow seas were full of plankton, the base of the food chain in the oceans. As the inland seas drained away, there was much less surface of the world covered by water. With less surface, there was less plankton,

and with less plankton, there was less food for other sea creatures to eat.

It may be that neither the volcanoes nor the sea-level changes (alone or combined) would have brought about the end of the Age of Dinosaurs. But we *do* know that these events took place, and they must have made life difficult for many animals and plants on the land and in the sea. And these living things, already living in stressful environments, faced oblivion when the asteroid finally hit.

UP FROM THE ASHES

Whether the Chicxulub impact alone would have been sufficient to end the Mesozoic Era, we'll never know for certain. In any case, the combina-

A pair of the saltasaurid *Isisaurus* watch eruptions of the Deccan Traps volcanoes in latest Cretaceous India.

tion of sea-level drop, volcanoes, and asteroid blast left a devastated world in its wake.

Some of the patterns of extinction make sense. In the seas, for example, the loss of many types of algae—especially the chalk-formers—would lead to starvation of big, active animals, like mosasaurs, plesiosaurs, and hesperornithines. Many paleontologists think that ammonoids ate plankton, so their disappearance makes sense, too. And like today's giant clams, rudists and inoceramids may have needed algae living in their tissues to grow and survive, so a world plunged into darkness might have done them in.

There are aspects of the extinctions on land that fit the impact theory, too. Dinosaurs and pterosaurs were reasonably large animals with active metabolisms, so they needed a lot of food. In a world of darkness, the herbivores would starve as the plants died, and the carnivores after that. But small warm-blooded animals—like mammals—would need less food because of their size. Small- and medium-size cold-blooded animals—like turtles, lizards, and crocodiles— would also need less food because their metabolisms were slow.

But other patterns are harder to explain. In the modern world, frogs are notoriously sensitive to changes in their environment, but they survived. And why should birds of the group Aves survive, but not *Ichthyornis* or the enantiornithines? In some cases, it may have been no more than blind luck—members of one group happened to find just enough food to make it through the hard times, while none of the others did.

Whatever the exact circumstances, eventually the disaster was over. Although many plants had died, their seeds and spores were still present, and they began to grow back. Surviving animals found a world where the big animals had almost all vanished, much like the beginning of the Triassic, when the main potential rivals were the amphibians, the protomammals, and the reptiles.

This time it would be different. The amphibians once again survived, but they were still stuck in the ponds when they had to reproduce. Champsosaurs and crocodilians were the largest animals outside of the seas, but the extinction had eliminated nearly all the land-dwelling forms, so most were only freshwater hunters. Turtles, lizards, and snakes were diverse, but they were all cold-blooded. So it was down to the warm-blooded animals, the birds—the only surviving dinosaurs— and the mammals.

The birds gave it a good try at first. Some of the largest predators of the Paleogene were 6-foot (1.8-meter) flightless birds, like *Diatryma.* But for the most part, it was the mammals that inherited the world. In the space of a few million years, the mammals developed many different ecological habits—what is called an adaptive radiation. Flying mammals (bats) appeared, as did various seagoing mammals—sea cows, whales, seals, and other, extinct groups. And on land a host of groups diversified—little gnawers, grazing hoofed herd animals, elephants, stalking predators, and many more. In the trees, a group of very brainy placental mammals with clutching hands and fingernails instead of claws evolved. Descendants of shrewlike placentals from the very end of the Cretaceous Period, this new group of tree dwellers was the primates. Eventually, over the course of tens of millions of years, the primates would diversify into lemurs, monkeys, apes, and ape-men. About only 200,000 years ago, a very smart and successful species of primate had evolved. This was *Homo sapiens*—in other words, us.

And for less than a thousandth of that time, we've looked into the rocks of the Mesozoic Era to discover that the world was once populated by that amazing group of reptiles, the dinosaurs.

DINOSAURS ALIVE?

Those "fearfully great lizards" haven't walked the Earth for over 65.5 million years. To be fair, birds outnumber mammal species 9,000 to 4,500 (2 to 1), so in a sense the dinosaurs are still doing very nicely. But most of the important animals—the top carnivores, omnivores, and herbivores—in most Cenozoic environments are mammals. The great dinosaurs are no longer with us, never to return.

Or perhaps not? Every so often, someone reports that dinosaurs and other Mesozoic reptiles

Some Cenozoic mammals—like the saber-toothed cat *Smilodon* (left) and the giant ground sloth *Megatherium* (right)—were as strange and wonderful as the dinosaurs!

on the book) used this idea. Crichton suggests that by finding dinosaur DNA, we could piece together the complete genetic instructions, or genome, to clone a dinosaur. But this idea is just science fiction. So far, no one has found fossilized dinosaur DNA. There has been some broken-down soft tissue found, but no evidence that strands of DNA are still in it.

And even if we were to find fragments of DNA—like the bits and pieces found from much more recent fossils, like woolly mammoths and Neanderthal men—that still wouldn't be good enough. To make a *real* dinosaur, you would have to have 100 percent of that species's genome. Filling in the gaps from other species wouldn't do. For comparison, the DNA of humans and chimps is about 98.5 percent identical. That little 1.5 percent makes all the difference between every human and every chimp there has *ever* been! Those little differences in DNA are all it takes for you to be able to read this book—if you're a human—or to hold it with your feet while you hang from a branch, on the off chance that you're a chimpanzee. I would love it if someone found dinosaur DNA fragments, because it would be spectacular to study. But cloning dinosaurs is almost certain to never happen.

are still lurking in some distant land. You may have heard claims that explorers in Africa have reported seeing living sauropods. Or you may have read that rotting plesiosaur carcasses have been fished from the sea. But, sadly, these were hoaxes or mistakes. The "plesiosaur" carcasses turned out to be rotting basking sharks. And the reports of living sauropods are never backed up by good physical evidence. Just because someone claims something, even something we want to be true, doesn't make it so. After all, to this day, people claim to see the singer Elvis Presley alive and shopping at supermarkets, even though he died back in 1977!

Maybe instead of finding a living sauropod or tyrannosaurid or other non-avian dinosaur, we could bring one back to life? The book *Jurassic Park* by Michael Crichton (and the movies based

But there *is* another way to bring dinosaurs back to life. It's a better way, which improves with each year and each discovery. It is the science of paleontology. By looking at the evidence from fossils and rocks, by making comparisons with modern animals, by studying old bones with our eyes and computers, we can make the "interesting" dinosaurs live again in our minds. As we combine the wonder of our imagination and the power of our reason, the Age of Dinosaurs lives on.

Will *Jurassic Park* Ever Happen?

Dr. Mary Higby Schweitzer
Montana State University

The *Jurassic Park* movies brought a lot of attention to dinosaur science and made people think about dinosaurs in a whole new way. The movies were based on the idea that DNA, the molecule that carries genetic information that makes all living things unique, could be recovered from fossils and used to "grow" new dinosaurs. Could that ever really happen?

Well, if I had my way, it would. I would like nothing better than to have a dinosaur farm in my backyard. But, sadly, there are too many obstacles to bringing the dinosaurs back to life—even the nice ones.

My job as a dinosaur scientist is to study the bones and teeth, and sometimes skin and muscle, for remnants of molecules that were part of the animals when they were alive. This requires a lot of chemistry, as well as techniques other scientists use to study cells and processes in living organisms. While we haven't been able to prove that DNA is still around in old dinosaur bones, we can show that bits and pieces of proteins and other molecules persist. By studying chemical traces of molecules that are part of dinosaur fossils, we can learn much about how they lived and about organisms that lived with them, such as plants and microbes.

The study of dinosaur molecules can also give us a better picture of how dinosaurs are related to animals that are alive today. Using methods developed to study proteins and DNA in living animals, we compare bits and pieces of dinosaur molecules to those of living animals and see how similar they are. This can help us understand how the molecules changed during evolution, as well as how similar they are to molecules from living animals that are related.

My job in the lab is not what people usually picture when they think of dinosaur science and digging for bones in the wonderful badlands. However, this kind of information is important, too, and can tell us a lot about the dinosaurs and the environments they inhabited.

Dinosaurs from a beaker? Not likely! But the future will bring entirely new ways of understanding the world of dinosaurs.

365

DINOSAUR GENUS LIST

In this list, I've attempted to arrange all the known genera of Mesozoic dinosaurs according to the groups to which they belong. A genus, as you may recall, is the one-word name that we typically use when talking about dinosaurs. *Tyrannosaurus, Triceratops,* and *Anatotitan* are all examples of a genus. Each genus is a group of one or more species. Most dinosaur genera are known from only a single species, but a few (such as *Psittacosaurus, Apatosaurus,* and *Edmontosaurus*) are known from several different species.

Some things to note: I have not included Cenozoic bird genera in this list—there are simply too many of them! And since dinosaurs are being discovered and named at a rate of about two new genera per month, this list will lack a few recent names. (In an illustrated book such as this, there is a minimum time of approximately three months between when the text is released to print and when finished books are available in bookstores and libraries.) Also, in some cases, the placement of a particular genus in a group is very uncertain. This can happen when a genus is known only from a very incomplete fossil, or when it has a confusing mixture of features. I've excluded dinosaur genus names that are based only on material so fragmentary that it is very difficult to say what groups they belong to.

Some dinosaurs are currently without proper names. For example, there are dinosaurs that were once called *"Syntarsus," "Diceratops,"* and *"Ingenia."* Unfortunately, there are also insects called *Syntarsus, Diceratops,* and *Ingenia,* and these got those names first! So by the rules of naming, the bugs keep the names and the dinosaurs need new ones. Also, there are dinosaur fossils that were once considered species in a named genus but that new studies now show belong in their own genus. These will eventually get their own genus name when newer studies are completed. Because some of these species are interesting, I've put them in the appendix, too.

(If you want to take a look at the most up-to-date version of this list, check out my Web site at www.geol.umd.edu/~tholtz/dinoappendix/.)

For each genus, I list the name and what it means.

I also give the dinosaur's age: both the geologic epoch it comes from and approximately when (in millions of years ago—MYA) it lived. Unfortunately, our understanding of how old a dinosaur was is only as good as our understanding of the age of the rocks it was found in. The ages of some rocks are pretty well known: for these dinosaurs, we have very narrow time ranges. For others, the ages are much less certain.

I give the length for these dinosaurs, based on the largest specimens. (Of course, for dinosaurs that are known only from babies, those "largest specimens" are a lot smaller than the adult would be!) Since most dinosaurs are known from incomplete fossils, these measurements are often just guesses. Particularly wild guesses are marked with a question mark.

Weights are even tougher to determine. A baby dinosaur of just a few pounds could grow up to be a dinosaur weighing dozens of tons. So where I can, I give the weight of the biggest individuals. But instead of giving exact numbers (which sound pretty accurate but are really just guesses), I list a modern animal of around the same size. As with length, though, there are plenty of genera of dinosaurs that are known only from very fragmentary fossils. For ones where I could guess the weight even approximately, I indicate that with a question mark next to the weight; for those that are simply too hard to figure out, I just put a question mark.

I also list where the dinosaurs have been discovered. Of course they lived in other places, too. In fact, you can pretty much guarantee that if a dinosaur species is known from fossils in (for example) Montana and New Mexico, it almost certainly lived in the states in between. We just haven't found them yet.

Primitive Dinosauromorphs—the Dinosaurs' Closest Relatives (Chapter 11)

These animals are not true dinosaurs, but they are the closest relatives to the dinosaurs that we know of.

Name	Meaning	Age	Length	Weight	Where found	Comments
Agnosphitys [ag-noh-SFY-tis]	unknown begetter	Late Triassic (216.5–203.6 MYA)	2.3 ft (70 cm)	Chicken	England	Not certain if this is a dinosaur or just a very close relative.
Camposaurus [kam-poh-SAW-rus]	[American paleontologist Charles Lewis] Camp's reptile	Late Triassic (228–216.5 MYA)	9.8 ft (3 m)?	Beaver	Arizona, U.S.A.	Previously considered a herrerasaurid or a coelophysoid. Poorly known.
Eucoelophysis [yoo-SEE-loh-FY-sis]	true *Coelophysis*	Late Triassic (228–216.5 MYA)	9.8 ft (3 m)	Beaver	New Mexico, U.S.A.	Once thought to be a coelophysoid theropod.
Lagerpeton [la-GUR-puh-ton]	rabbit reptile	Middle Triassic (237–228 MYA)	2.6 ft (80 cm)	Chicken	Argentina	May have hopped like a rabbit.
Lagosuchus [LA-guh-SOOK-us]	rabbit crocodile	Middle Triassic (237–228 MYA)	1.7 ft (51 cm)	Pigeon	Argentina	*Marasuchus* may be the same species.
Lewisuchus [LOO-wuh-SOOK-us]	[American fossil preparator Arnold] Lewis's crocodile	Middle Triassic (237–228 MYA)	3.8 ft (1.2 m)	Chicken	Argentina	Some consider it the same creature as *Pseudolagosuchus;* others think it is a primitive relative of crocodiles.
Marasuchus [MA-ruh-SOOK-us]	*mara* [South American rodent that looks and acts like a rabbit] crocodile	Middle Triassic (237–228 MYA)	1.7 ft (51 cm)	Pigeon	Argentina	Originally considered a type of *Lagosuchus.*
Pseudolagosuchus [SOO-doh-LAH-guh-SOOK-us]	false *Lagosuchus*	Middle Triassic (237–228 MYA)	4.3 ft (1.3 m)	Chicken	Argentina	Possibly the same species as *Lewisuchus.*
Saltopus [SAWL-toh-pus]	jumping foot	Late Triassic (216.5–203.6 MYA)	2 ft (60 cm)	Pigeon	Scotland	*Saltopus* is known only from the spaces left in the rock where its bones had dissolved away: a sort of "negative fossil."
Scleromochlus [SKLAIR-oh-MOCK-lus]	hard fulcrum	Late Triassic (216.5–203.6 MYA)	8 in (20 cm)	Sparrow	Scotland	Thought by some to be the ancestor of the pterosaurs (flying reptiles).
Silesaurus [SIH-leh-SAW-rus]	Silesia [Poland] reptile	Late Triassic (228–216.5 MYA)	7.5 ft (2.3 m)	Turkey	Poland	Known from many individuals. Among the closest relatives of the dinosaurs currently known.
Spondylosoma [SPAWN-duh-loh-SO-muh]	vertebral body	Middle Triassic (237–228 MYA)	?	?	Brazil	May actually be a mixture of primitive dinosauromorph, early dinosaur, and other archosaur bones.
Technosaurus [TEK-noh-SAW-rus]	Texas Tech University reptile	Late Triassic (228–216.5 MYA)	3.3 ft (1 m)?	Beaver	Texas, U.S.A.	Only a jawbone is known. Once thought to be a primitive ornithischian.
Teyuwasu [TEY-yoo-WAH-soo]	big lizard	Late Triassic (228–216.5 MYA)	?	Beaver	Brazil	Known only from the thigh and shin of its right leg!
Trialestes [TRY-uh-LESS-teez]	thief of the Triassic Period	Late Triassic (228–216.5 MYA)	?	Turkey	Argentina	The arm of this skeleton may actually belong to a primitive crocodile relative.

Primitive Saurischians—Early Lizard-Hipped Dinosaurs (Chapter 12)

These dinosaurs are members of the group Saurischia, but it is debatable whether they are the oldest and most primitive members of the group Theropoda or if they instead branched off from the family tree before the common ancestor of theropods and sauropodomorphs first evolved.

Name	Meaning	Age	Length	Weight	Where found	Comments
Alwalkeria [al-wuh-KEE-ree-uh]	for [British paleontologist] Alick Walker	Late Triassic (228–203.6 MYA)	1.6 ft (50 cm)?	Turkey	Lesotho	Only known from a single partial specimen, and possibly not even a dinosaur.
Eoraptor [EE-oh-RAP-tur]	dawn thief	Late Triassic (228–216.5 MYA)	3.3 ft (1 m)	Beaver	Argentina	Known from many skeletons, this is our best view of what early dinosaurs looked like.
Guaibasaurus [GWY-buh-SAW-rus]	Rio Guaiba [Brazil] reptile	Late Triassic (228–216.5 MYA)	6.6 ft (2 m)	Beaver	Brazil	A slender early saurischian.
Sinosaurus [SY-noh-SAW-rus]	Chinese reptile	Early Jurassic (199.6–183 MYA)	?	?	China	Only known from a chunk of jaw with some teeth. May be a primitive carnivorous saurischian, true theropod, or non-dinosaur carnivore.

Herrerasaurids—Primitive Saurischians (Chapter 12)

These dinosaurs are all members of Herrerasauridae, a group of primitive saurischians. Some paleontologists consider them to be extremely primitive theropods.

Name	Meaning	Age	Length	Weight	Where found	Comments
Caseosaurus [KAY-see-oh-SAW-rus]	[American paleontologist E. C.] Case's reptile	Late Triassic (228–216.5 MYA)	6.6 ft (2 m)?	Wolf?	Pennsylvania, U.S.A.	May be the same species as *Chindesaurus.*
Chindesaurus [CHIN-dee-SAW-rus]	Chinde Point [Arizona] reptile	Late Triassic (228–216.5 MYA)	6.6 ft (2 m)?	Wolf?	Arizona and New Mexico, U.S.A.	The first specimen found was nicknamed "Gertie," after an early cartoon dinosaur.
Herrerasaurus [huh-REAH-ruh-SAW-rus]	[Argentine farmer Victorino] Herrera's reptile	Late Triassic (228–216.5 MYA)	13.1 ft (4 m)	Grizzly bear	Argentina	A powerful hunter, but was probably eaten by the much larger rauisuchian predator *Saurosuchus.*
Staurikosaurus [STAW-ree-koh-SAW-rus]	Southern Cross reptile	Late Triassic (228–216.5 MYA)	6.6 ft (2 m)	Wolf	Brazil	For many years, this was the oldest and most primitive known dinosaur.

Coelophysoids—Kink-Snouted Dinosaurs (Chapter 13)

Coelophysoidea was a very successful group of early primitive theropods.

Name	Meaning	Age	Length	Weight	Where found	Comments
Coelophysis [see-loh-FY-sis]	hollow form	Late Triassic (228–203.6 MYA)	8.9 ft (2.7 m)	Beaver	Arizona and New Mexico, U.S.A.	The most completely known coelophysoid. At "Ghost Ranch" quarry dozens of individual skeletons—many of them complete—have been uncovered.
Dilophosaurus [dy-LOAF-oh-SAW-rus]	double-crested reptile	Early Jurassic (199.6–189.6 MYA)	23 ft (7 m)	Grizzly bear	Arizona, U.S.A.	Despite some movie portrayals, this dinosaur did not have a frill, nor is there any evidence that it could shoot poison.
Gojirasaurus [go-JEE-ruh-SAW-rus]	Godzilla reptile	Late Triassic (216.5–203.6 MYA)	18 ft (5.5 m)	Lion	New Mexico, U.S.A.	Did not get its name because it was particularly gigantic, nor did it look like the Japanese movie monster Godzilla that much. However, its discoverer (American paleontologist Ken Carpenter) is a big Godzilla fan, so he wanted to name a dinosaur after his "hero."
Liliensternus [LIH-lee-un-STERN-us]	for [German paleontologist Hugo Ruele von] Lilienstern	Late Triassic (216.5–203.6 MYA)	16.9 ft (5.2 m)	Lion	Germany	Although known for many decades, this dinosaur has yet to be completely described.
Megapnosaurus [muh-GAP-noh-SAW-rus]	big dead reptile	Early Jurassic (199.6–189.6 MYA)	7.2 ft (2.2 m)	Beaver	South Africa; Zimbabwe; England?	Better known by the name *"Syntarsus,"* but that is properly the name of a beetle! Considered by some paleontologists to be a late-surviving species of *Coelophysis.*
Podokesaurus [puh-DOAK-uh-SAW-rus]	swift-footed reptile	Early Jurassic (189.6–175.6 MYA)	4.9 ft (1.5 m)	Turkey	Massachusetts, U.S.A.	The original, and so far only definite, specimen of this dinosaur was unfortunately destroyed in a museum fire.
Procompsognathus [proh-komp-soh-NAY-thus]	before *Compsognathus*	Late Triassic (216.5–203.6 MYA)	3.6 ft (1.1 m)	Chicken	Germany	A tiny coelophysoid, possibly closely related to *Segisaurus* and *Podokesaurus.*
Sarcosaurus [SAR-koh-SAW-rus]	flesh reptile	Early Jurassic (199.6–196.5 MYA)	?	Sheep	England	Various bones are known, but not enough to determine exactly what it looked like.
Segisaurus [SEH-gee-SAW-rus]	Segi Canyon [Arizona] reptile	Early Jurassic (189.6–175.6 MYA)	4.9 ft (1.5 m)	Turkey	Arizona, U.S.A.	Known from a nearly complete skeleton lacking a skull. Once mistakenly thought to have solid bones; further examination shows that they are hollow, just like those of other theropods.
Zupaysaurus [zoo-PAY-SAW-rus]	devil reptile	Late Triassic (216.5–199.6 MYA)	16.9 ft (5.2 m)	Lion	Argentina	A medium-size crested coelophysoid once thought to be the oldest known tetanurine.
No official genus name; formerly *"Liliensternus" airelensis*		Early Jurassic (199.6–196.5 MYA)	9.8 ft (3 m)	Lion	France	Originally considered to be an early species of *Liliensternus.*
No official genus name; formerly *"Syntarsus" kayentakatae*		Early Jurassic (199.6–189.6 MYA)	7.1 ft (2.2 m)	Beaver	Arizona, U.S.A.	Originally thought to be a species of *"Syntarsus"* (now *Megapnosaurus*). Had a pair of small crests.

Name	Meaning	Age	Length	Weight	Where found	Comments
No official genus name; formerly *"Zanclodon" cambrensis*		Late Triassic (203.6–199.6 MYA)	?	?	England	Known only from a jawbone.
Not yet officially named		Early Jurassic (199.6–189.6 MYA)	3.6 ft (1.1 m)?	Chicken?	Arizona, U.S.A.	Not yet described; a small coelophysoid.

Primitive Ceratosaurs—Early Ceratosaurs (Chapter 13)

These dinosaurs are members of Ceratosauria, but they are not part of the more specialized ceratosaur groups Noasauridae or Abelisauridae.

Name	Meaning	Age	Length	Weight	Where found	Comments
Betasuchus [BAY-tuh-SOOK-us]	"B" crocodile	Late Cretaceous (70.6–65.5 MYA)	?	?	Netherlands	Originally thought to be an ornithomimosaur.
Ceratosaurus [suh-RAT-oh-SAW-rus]	horned reptile	Late Jurassic (155.7–150.8 MYA)	20 ft (6.1 m)	Horse	Colorado and Utah, U.S.A.; Tanzania?	The most completely known ceratosaur. Had a distinctive narrow horn on its nose and smaller crests in front of each eye. The first large theropod known from a complete skeleton.
Chuandongocoelurus [CHWAN-dun-goh-suh-LOOR-us]	Chuandong [China] *Coelurus*	Middle Jurassic (167.7–161.2 MYA)	?	?	China	Possibly a close relative of *Elaphrosaurus*.
Coeluroides [see-loor-OY-deez]	like *Coelurus*	Late Cretaceous (70.6–65.5 MYA)	?	?	India	Tail vertebrae similar to, but larger than, those of *Jubbulpuria* (which is possibly a juvenile of this species).
Elaphrosaurus [el-AFF-roh-SAW-rus]	fleet reptile	Late Jurassic (155.7–150.8 MYA)	20.3 ft (6.2 m)	Lion	Tanzania; possibly Colorado, U.S.A.	Long thought to be the most primitive ornithomimosaur, and still thought by some to be the last of the coelophysoids. Unfortunately, its skull is not known.
Genusaurus [GEN-oo-SAW-rus]	knee reptile	Early Cretaceous (112–99.6 MYA)	9.8 ft (3 m)?	?	France	May be a true abelisaurid.
Genyodectes [JEN-ee-oh-DEK-teez]	jaw biter	Early Cretaceous (125–99.6 MYA)	?	Rhino?	Argentina	One of the first dinosaurs discovered in South America. It seems to be a close relative of *Ceratosaurus*, but it is known only from partial jaws.
Ilokelesia [ee-loh-kay-LAY-see-uh]	flesh-eating reptile	Late Cretaceous (97–93.5 MYA)	?	?	Argentina	Some consider this to be a true abelisaurid.
Jubbulpuria [jub-ul-PYOOR-ee-uh]	from Jabalpur [India]	Late Cretaceous (70.6–65.5 MYA)	?	?	India	Known from two small vertebrae.
Lukousaurus [LOO-kuh-SAW-rus]	Lukou Bridge [China] reptile	Early Jurassic (199.6–183 MYA)	?	?	China	Known only from a small front end of a skull. Not necessarily even a dinosaur!
Piveteausaurus [peev-eh-toh-SAW-rus]	[French paleontologist Jean] Piveteau's reptile	Middle Jurassic (164.7–161.2 MYA)	36 ft (11 m)?	Rhino?	France	A braincase with similarities to that of *Ceratosaurus*. Some consider this a megalosaurid.
Spinostropheus [SPY-noh-STROH-fee-us]	spine vertebra	Early Cretaceous (136.4–125 MYA)	20.3 ft (6.2 m)	Lion	Niger	Originally considered a late species of *Elaphrosaurus*.

Noasaurids—Slender Ceratosaurs (Chapter 13)

The dinosaurs in Noasauridae were a diverse group of slim-legged, fast-running ceratosaurs.

Name	Meaning	Age	Length	Weight	Where found	Comments
Bahariasaurus [bah-huh-REE-yuh-SAW-rus]	Bahariya [Egypt] reptile	Early to Late Cretaceous (112–93.5 MYA)	39.4 ft (12 m)?	Rhino	Egypt; Niger?	May be the same dinosaur as *Deltadromeus*.
Compsosuchus [KOMP-soh-SOOK-us]	delicate crocodile	Late Cretaceous (70.6–65.5 MYA)	?	?	India	Known only from a neck vertebra.
Deltadromeus [DEL-tuh-DROH-mee-us]	delta runner	Early to Late Cretaceous (112–93.5 MYA)	26.2 ft (8 m)	Rhino	Morocco; Egypt?	Its skull is not known. "*Deltadromeus* teeth" are sold in rock shops, but we have no idea if those are actually *Deltadromeus* teeth!
Laevisuchus [LEE-vuh-SOOK-us]	light crocodile	Late Cretaceous (70.6–65.5 MYA)	?	?	India	Little is known of this small theropod.

Name	Meaning	Age	Length	Weight	Where found	Comments
Ligabueino [LEE-guh-BOO-uh-EE-noh]	[Italian dinosaur hunter Giancarlo] Ligabue's reptile	Early Cretaceous (130–120 MYA)	2.3 ft (70 cm)	?	Argentina	One of the oldest noasaurids.
Masiakasaurus [mah-SHEEK-uh-SAW-rus]	vicious reptile	Late Cretaceous (70.6–65.5 MYA)	4.9 ft (1.5 m)	Beaver	Madagascar	The most completely known noasaurid, with very unusual teeth.
Noasaurus [NOH-uh-SAW-rus]	northwest Argentina reptile	Late Cretaceous (70.6–65.5 MYA)	7.9 ft (2.4 m)	Beaver	Argentina	A large claw on this dinosaur was once thought to be a deinonychosaur-like foot claw, but it is actually a hand claw.
Velocisaurus [vuh-LAH-see-SAW-rus]	swift reptile	Late Cretaceous (86–83 MYA)	?	Chicken	Argentina	Not much is known beyond its feet.

Abelisaurids—Stump-Armed Ceratosaurs (Chapter 13)

Abelisauridae consists of the top predators of the Late Cretaceous Epoch in the southern continents. They were characterized by short snouts, relatively small teeth, and very stumpy arms.

Name	Meaning	Age	Length	Weight	Where found	Comments
Abelisaurus [uh-BEL-ee-SAW-rus]	[Argentine museum director Roberto] Abel's reptile	Late Cretaceous (83–78 MYA)	21.3 ft (6.5 m)?	Rhino	Argentina	The first abelisaurid recognized as belonging to a distinct group. Known only from a large, nearly complete skull.
Aucasaurus [OW-kuh-SAW-rus]	Auca Mahuevo [site in Argentina] reptile	Late Cretaceous (83–78 MYA)	13.8 ft (4.2 m)	Grizzly bear	Argentina	Known from a very complete, but not yet fully described, skeleton.
Carnotaurus [KAR-noh-TAW-rus]	meat[-eating] bull	Late Cretaceous (83.5–65.5 MYA)	26.2 ft (8 m)	Rhino	Argentina	The first abelisaurid known from a relatively complete skeleton (with skin impressions); it showed the highly reduced nature of the forelimbs of these dinosaurs.
Dryptosauroides [DRIP-toh-saw-ROY-deez]	like *Dryptosaurus*	Late Cretaceous (70.6–65.5 MYA)	?	Elephant?	India	Known from tail vertebrae of an abelisaurid larger than *Carnotaurus*.
Ekrixinatosaurus [uhk-RIX-uh-nah-toh-SAW-rus]	explosion-born reptile	Late Cretaceous (99.6–97 MYA)	20 ft (6.1 m)	Rhino	Argentina	Discovered when people were blasting rocks with dynamite: hence the name!
Indosaurus [IN-doh-SAW-rus]	Indian reptile	Late Cretaceous (70.6–65.5 MYA)	?	Grizzly bear?	India	Originally known only from a partial skull; a new, more complete skull and skeleton have been discovered but not fully described. Similar to *Abelisaurus*.
Indosuchus [IN-doh-SOOK-us]	Indian crocodile	Late Cretaceous (70.6–65.5 MYA)	?	Horse?	India	Like *Indosaurus*, it was known for a long time, but was thought to be either a carnosaur or a tyrannosauroid until the discovery of *Abelisaurus* and *Carnotaurus* showed that there was a distinct group of southern giant theropods.
Lametasaurus [luh-MAY-tuh-SAW-rus]	Lameta Formation reptile	Late Cretaceous (70.6–65.5 MYA)	?	Horse?	India	Named for a mixture of crocodilian and titanosaur armor found with some abelisaurid bones.
Majungasaurus [mah-JUNG-uh-SAW-rus]	Majunga District [Madagascar] reptile	Late Cretaceous (70.6–65.5 MYA)	29.5 ft (9 m)	Rhino	Madagascar	Sometimes called *"Majungatholus."* Originally thought to be a pachycephalosaur when the thick dome on its head was discovered. Nearly the entire skeleton is known from individuals of different sizes.
Ornithomimoides [or-NIH-thoh-my-MOY-deez]	like *Ornithomimus*	Late Cretaceous (70.6–65.5 MYA)	?	?	India	Known from tail vertebrae of an abelisaurid.
Pycnonemosaurus [PIKE-non-ee-moh-SAW-rus]	dense-forest reptile	Late Cretaceous (70.6–65.5 MYA)	19.7 ft (6 m)	Rhino	Brazil	The fossil was collected in the 1950s but was not described until 2002.
Quilmesaurus [keel-may-SAW-rus]	Quilmes [an ancient native people of Argentina] reptile	Late Cretaceous (72.8–66.8 MYA)	19.7 ft (6 m)	Rhino	Argentina	Known only from a partial leg.

Name	Meaning	Age	Length	Weight	Where found	Comments
Rajasaurus [RAH-jah-SAW-rus]	regal reptile	Late Cretaceous (70.6–65.5 MYA)	19.7 ft (6 m)	Rhino	India	Possibly the same dinosaur as *Lametasaurus,* but known from much better fossils.
Rugops [ROO-gopz]	rough face	Late Cretaceous (99.6–93.5 MYA)	19.7 ft (6 m)	Rhino	Niger	An early abelisaurid. Holes for blood vessels on its face suggest its head was covered by horny masses.
Tarascosaurus [tuh-RAS-koh-SAW-rus]	Tarasque [legendary medieval French monster] reptile	Late Cretaceous (83.5–80 MYA)	19.7 ft (6 m)	Rhino	France	Only some vertebrae and a femur are known, which might not all belong to the same species.
Xenotarsosaurus [zee-no-TAR-soh-SAW-rus]	strange-ankle reptile	Late Cretaceous (99.6–93.5 MYA)	19.7 ft (6 m)?	Rhino?	Argentina	Some vertebrae and a nearly complete leg are known. Despite the name, its ankle is actually similar to those of other ceratosaurs.

Primitive Tetanurines—Early Stiff-Tailed Dinosaurs (Chapter 14)

These dinosaurs are members of Tetanurae, but they are not clearly members of the more advanced tetanurine groups Spinosauroidea, Carnosauria, or Coelurosauria.

Name	Meaning	Age	Length	Weight	Where found	Comments
Becklespinax [BEK-ul-SPINE-aks]	[British fossil collector Samuel Husband] Beckles's spine	Early Cretaceous (130–125 MYA)	26.2 ft (8 m)?	Rhino?	England	Known only from some tall-spined vertebrae; once thought to come from *Megalosaurus.*
Chilantaisaurus [chy-LAN-ty-SAW-rus]	Jilantai [Inner Mongolia] reptile	Early Cretaceous (125–99.6 MYA)	42.7 ft (13 m)?	Elephant	China	A giant theropod with enormous curved claws; possibly a spinosauroid (maybe even a close relative of *Megaraptor*).
Cryolophosaurus [kry-oh-LOAF-oh-SAW-rus]	frozen-crested reptile	Early Jurassic (189.6–183 MYA)	20 ft (6.1 m)	Horse	Antarctica	Had an unusual flared crest on its head.
Iliosuchus [IL-lee-oh-SOOK-us]	ilium crocodile	Middle Jurassic (167.7–164.7 MYA)	4.9 ft (1.5 m)?	Beaver	England	Known only from a pair of ilia (upper hip bones).
Kaijiangosaurus [ky-JYANG-oh-SAW-rus]	Kai River [China] reptile	Middle Jurassic (167.7–161.2 MYA)	19.7 ft (6 m)?	Horse?	China	It could be a primitive carnosaur.
Kelmayisaurus [kul-MAH-yee-SAW-rus]	Karamay City [China] reptile	Early Cretaceous (time very uncertain)	?	?	China	Known from some poorly described jaws. May actually be a ceratosaur rather than a tetanurine.
Marshosaurus [MARSH-oh-SAW-rus]	[American paleontologist Othniel Charles] Marsh's reptile	Late Jurassic (155.7–150.8 MYA)	16.4 ft (5 m)	Lion	Utah, U.S.A.	Incompletely known, it has some traits like those of spinosauroids, some like those of carnosaurs, and some like those of primitive coelurosaurs.
Megaraptor [MEG-uh-RAP-tur]	big thief	Late Cretaceous (91–88 MYA)	29.5 ft (9 m)	Rhino	Argentina	Originally thought to have a dromaeosaurid-like sickle foot claw, but it turns out that it was a carnosaur or spinosauroid with enormous hand claws.
Ozraptor [OZ-rap-tur]	thief of Oz [nickname of Australia]	Middle Jurassic (171.6–167.7 MYA)	6.6 ft (2 m)	?	Australia	Known only from an ankle; possibly a ceratosaur.
Razanandrongobe [ruh-ZAHN-an-DRON-goh-bee]	ancestor of the large lizards	Middle Jurassic (167.7–164.7 MYA)	?	?	Madagascar	Known from a very fragmentary specimen with extremely thick teeth. Probably a crocodile relative rather than a dinosaur!
Valdoraptor [VAL-doh-RAP-tur]	thief of the Wealden Group	Early Cretaceous (130–125 MYA)	16.4 ft (5 m)?	Lion?	England	Known only from an incomplete foot.
Xuanhanosaurus [SHWAN-han-oh-SAW-rus]	Xuanhan County [China] reptile	Middle Jurassic (167.7–161.2 MYA)	19.7 ft (6 m)	Grizzly bear	China	Known from some good forelimbs and some other bones.
No official genus name; formerly *"Dilophosaurus" sinensis*		Early Jurassic (199.6–183 MYA)	19.7 ft (6 m)	Grizzly bear	China	Originally thought to be a new species of the coelophysoid *Dilophosaurus* because it, too, has a pair of crests on its head.

Name	Meaning	Age	Length	Weight	Where found	Comments
Not yet officially named		Early Jurassic (199.6–189.6 MYA)	?	Beaver	Arizona, U.S.A.	The oldest known tetanurine.
Not yet officially named		Middle Jurassic (167.7–161.2 MYA)	26.2 ft (8 m)	Horse	China	Known from a good skeleton and other material, it is traditionally called "*Szechuanosaurus.*" Unfortunately, that name properly belongs to a set of teeth that isn't definitely related to this particular primitive tetanurine.

Megalosaurids—Primitive, Large Carnivorous Dinosaurs (Chapter 14)

Megalosauridae includes many of the large meat-eaters of the Middle Jurassic Epoch.

Name	Meaning	Age	Length	Weight	Where found	Comments
Afrovenator [AF-roh-veh-NAY-tor]	African hunter	Early Cretaceous (136.4–125 MYA)	24.9 ft (7.6 m)	Horse	Niger	A rather primitive-looking theropod for its time. Lived at the same time as the giant sauropod *Jobaria,* and may have hunted young *Jobaria* for food.
Dubreuillosaurus [doo-BRAY-loh-SAW-rus]	Dubreuil [family that discovered the dinosaur] reptile	Middle Jurassic (167.7–164.7 MYA)	24.9 ft (7.6 m)	Horse	France	Originally thought to be a new species of the much more heavily built *Poekilopleuron.*
Edmarka [ed-MAR-kuh]	for [University of Colorado scientist Bill] Edmark	Late Jurassic (155.7–150.8 MYA)	36 ft (11 m)	Rhino	Wyoming, U.S.A.	Many paleontologists consider this to be the same dinosaur as *Torvosaurus,* but others think that some *Edmarka* fossils should be regarded as a third megalosaurid, called "*Brontoraptor.*"
Eustreptospondylus [yoo-STREP-toh-SPON-duh-lus]	well-curved vertebrae	Middle Jurassic (164.7–161.2 MYA)	23 ft (7 m)	Lion	England	Known from the nearly complete skeleton of a young individual. Considered by some to be a species of *Magnosaurus.*
Magnosaurus [MAG-noh-SAW-rus]	great reptile	Middle Jurassic (175.6–167.7 MYA)	?	Lion	England	Some consider it to be the same dinosaur as *Eustreptospondylus.*
Megalosaurus [MEG-uh-loh-SAW-rus]	big reptile	Middle Jurassic (175.6–155.7 MYA)	29.5 ft (9 m)	Rhino	England	Despite its being the first Mesozoic dinosaur named, we don't know that much about it. Many fossils that have been labeled "*Megalosaurus*" have since turned out to be from totally different types of theropods.
Metriacanthosaurus [MEH-tree-uh-KAN-thoh-SAW-rus]	medium-spined reptile	Late Jurassic (161.2–155.7 MYA)	26.2 ft (8 m)?	Rhino	England	May actually be a sinraptorid.
Piatnitzkysaurus [pee-aht-NITZ-kee-SAW-rus]	[Argentine geologist Alejandro Mateievich] Piatnitzky's reptile	Middle Jurassic (164.7–161.2 MYA)	19.7 ft (6 m)	Grizzly bear	Argentina	One of the most completely known megalosaurids.
Poekilopleuron [POE-ee-kill-oh-PLOOR-on]	varied ribs	Middle Jurassic (167.7–164.7 MYA)	29.5 ft (9 m)	Rhino	France	One of the first dinosaurs discovered; the original fossil was destroyed during World War II.
Streptospondylus [STREP-tuh-SPON-duh-lus]	reversed vertebrae	Middle to Late Jurassic (164.7–155.7 MYA)	?	?	France	Originally thought to be fossils of a crocodilian.
Torvosaurus [TOR-voh-SAW-rus]	savage reptile	Late Jurassic (155.7–150.8 MYA)	39.4 ft (12 m)	Elephant	Colorado and Utah, U.S.A.; Portugal?	A large, heavily built megalosaurid with very powerful arms.
No official genus name; formerly "*Megalosaurus*" *hesperis*		Middle Jurassic (175.6–167.7 MYA)	?	?	England	Known only from jawbones similar to those of true *Megalosaurus;* may be the jaws of *Magnosaurus.*

Spinosaurids—Crocodile-Mimic Dinosaurs (Chapter 14)

These dinosaurs, members of Spinosauridae, are characterized by long crocodile-like snouts with huge cone-shaped teeth. As with modern crocodiles, their diet probably included both fish and land animals.

Name	Meaning	Age	Length	Weight	Where found	Comments
Angaturama [AN-guh-too-RAH-muh]	noble one	Early Cretaceous (112–99.6 MYA)	26.2 ft (8 m)?	Rhino?	Brazil	Known only from a partial skull. May be the same dinosaur as *Irritator.*
Baryonyx [BARE-ee-ON-icks]	heavy claw	Early Cretaceous (140.2–112 MYA)	32.8 ft (10 m)	Rhino	England; Spain	The original specimen was nicknamed "Claws."
Cristatusaurus [kris-TAH-too-SAW-rus]	crested reptile	Early Cretaceous (125–112 MYA)	32.8 ft (10 m)?	Rhino?	Niger	Known from only a few bones. Possibly the same dinosaur as *Suchomimus* and/or *Baryonyx.*
Irritator [IHR-uh-TAY-tur]	irritator	Early Cretaceous (112–99.6 MYA)	26.2 ft (8 m)?	Rhino?	Brazil	Known only from a partial skull. It got its name because the paleontologists who studied it were irritated that the collectors had added fake bones to the skull!
Siamosaurus [sy-AM-oh-SAW-rus]	Siam [old name for Thailand] reptile	Early Cretaceous (145.5–125 MYA)	?	?	Thailand	Known only from teeth, which might actually be from a fish rather than a dinosaur!
Spinosaurus [SPY-noh-SAW-rus]	spine reptile	Early to Late Cretaceous (112–93.5 MYA)	52.5 ft (16 m)	Elephant	Egypt; Morocco; Kenya?; Tunisia?	One of the largest of all theropods. The original specimen was destroyed during World War II, but more recently several specimens have been discovered (although none are complete).
Suchomimus [SOOK-oh-MY-mus]	crocodile mimic	Early Cretaceous (125–112 MYA)	36 ft (11 m)	Rhino	Niger	Some consider this simply an African species of *Baryonyx.*
Suchosaurus [SOOK-oh-SAW-rus]	crocodile reptile	Early Cretaceous (140.2–125 MYA)	32.8 ft (10 m)?	Rhino?	England	Originally considered a crocodile. May be the same dinosaur as *Baryonyx.*

Primitive Carnosaurs—Early Giant Meat-Eating Dinosaurs (Chapter 15)

The top predators of the Late Jurassic and Early Cretaceous epochs were the members of Carnosauria.

Name	Meaning	Age	Length	Weight	Where found	Comments
Erectopus [ee-REK-toh-pus]	erect foot	Early Cretaceous (112–99.6 MYA)	?	Lion	France	The original specimens were destroyed in World War II, but casts remain for study.
Fukuiraptor [foo-KOO-ee-RAP-tur]	thief of Fukui Prefecture [Japan]	Early Cretaceous (136.4–125 MYA)	16.4 ft (5 m)	Lion	Japan	When only a few bones, including a giant claw, were found, this was thought to be an enormous dromaeosaurid raptor. But as additional specimens were discovered, that "foot claw" turned out to be a hand claw.
Lourinhanosaurus [LOOR-in-hah-noh-SAW-rus]	Lourinha [Portugal] reptile	Late Jurassic (150.8–145.5 MYA)	16.4 ft (5 m)	Lion	Portugal	Many eggs and embryos of this dinosaur are known because a nest site of *Lourinhanosaurus* was discovered.
Monolophosaurus [MON-uh-LOAF-oh-SAW-rus]	single-crested reptile	Middle Jurassic (167.7–161.2 MYA)	16.4 ft (5 m)	Grizzly bear	China	Had a large, hollow crest along the top of its skull.
Siamotyrannus [sy-AM-oh-ty-RAN-us]	tyrant of Siam [old name for Thailand]	Early Cretaceous (145.5–125 MYA)	19.7 ft (6 m)?	Horse?	Thailand	Originally thought to be a tyrannosauroid.
Sigilmassasaurus [sih-GIL-mah-suh-SAW-rus]	Sijilmassa [Morocco] reptile	Late Cretaceous (99.6–93.5 MYA)	?	Rhino	Morocco; Egypt?	Considered to be the same dinosaur as *Carcharodontosaurus* by some. Originally thought to be a species of *Spinosaurus.*

Sinraptorids—Chinese Giant Meat-Eating Dinosaurs (Chapter 15)

The dinosaurs of Sinraptoridae are currently known only from the Middle and Late Jurassic epochs of China.

Name	Meaning	Age	Length	Weight	Where found	Comments
Gasosaurus [GAS-oh-SAW-rus]	gas reptile	Middle Jurassic (167.7–161.2 MYA)	11.5 ft (3.5 m)	Lion	China	A primitive sinraptorid.
Sinraptor [sine-RAP-tur]	Chinese thief	Middle to Late Jurassic (167.7–155.7 MYA)	29 ft (8.8 m)	Rhino	China	Known from some very complete skeletons.
Yangchuanosaurus [yang-CHUAN-oh-SAW-rus]	Yangchuan County [China] reptile	Late Jurassic (161.2–155.7 MYA)	34.4 ft (10.5 m)	Rhino	China	The largest sinraptorid, and one of the largest Jurassic theropods.

Allosaurids—American and European Giant Meat-Eating Dinosaurs (Chapter 15)

Allosaurus, the best known of all carnosaurs, is a member of the group Allosauridae.

Name	Meaning	Age	Length	Weight	Where found	Comments
Allosaurus [AL-oh-SAW-rus]	strange [vertebra] reptile	Late Jurassic (155.7–150.8 MYA)	39.4 ft (12 m)	Rhino	Portugal; Colorado, New Mexico, Utah, and Wyoming, U.S.A.	The best-known Jurassic theropod, and one of the most studied of all dinosaurs. Known from dozens of skeletons, from embryos to adults.
Saurophaganax [SAW-roh-FAG-uh-naks]	king of the reptile-eaters	Late Jurassic (155.7–150.8 MYA)	42.7 ft (13 m)	Elephant	Oklahoma, U.S.A.	Thought by some to be a giant species of *Allosaurus.*

Carcharodontosaurids—Gigantic Meat-Eating Dinosaurs (Chapter 15)

Last, and largest, among the carnosaurs, the members of Carcharodontosauridae lived during the Cretaceous Period.

Name	Meaning	Age	Length	Weight	Where found	Comments
Acrocanthosaurus [ACK-roh-KAN-thoh-SAW-rus]	high-spined reptile	Early Cretaceous (125–99.6 MYA)	39.4 ft (12 m)	Rhino	Oklahoma, Texas, Utah, and possibly Maryland, U.S.A.	The largest North American theropod before the evolution of the tyrannosaurids. Footprint trackways show that it hunted sauropods.
Carcharodontosaurus [kar-KAR-oh-don-toh-SAW-rus]	*Carcharodon* [scientific name for great white shark] reptile	Early to Late Cretaceous (112–93.5 MYA)	39.4 ft (12 m)	Rhino	Algeria; Egypt; Morocco; Niger	Although no good single skeleton is known, a nearly complete skull and various other isolated bones have been found.
Giganotosaurus [jig-uh-NOTE-oh-SAW-rus]	giant southern reptile	Late Cretaceous (99.6–97 MYA)	43.3 ft (13.2 m)	Elephant	Argentina	One of the largest of all theropods. A partial jawbone is known that is 8 percent bigger than that of the original *Giganotosaurus* skeleton.
Mapusaurus [MAH-poo-SAW-rus]	earth reptile	Late Cretaceous (97–93.5 MYA)	41.3 ft (12.6 m)	Elephant	Argentina	Before it was described, *Mapusaurus* was thought by some to be a new species of *Giganotosaurus.* Known from a series of skeletons of different-size individuals, suggesting that they lived in packs.
Neovenator [NEE-oh-veh-NAY-tor]	new hunter	Early Cretaceous (130–125 MYA)	24.6 ft (7.5 m)	Horse	England	First thought to be an allosaurid, it has small crests on its snout.
Tyrannotitan [ty-RAN-oh-TY-tun]	giant tyrant	Early Cretaceous (125–112 MYA)	40 ft (12.2 m)	Elephant	Argentina	A very large carcharodontosaurid.
Not yet officially named		Late Cretaceous (83–78 MYA)	37.7 ft (11.5 m)	Rhino	Argentina	Last known carcharodontosaurid. Its bones are very hollow.

Primitive Coelurosaurs—Early Fuzzy Dinosaurs (Chapter 16)

These small dinosaurs are early members of Coelurosauria.

Name	Meaning	Age	Length	Weight	Where found	Comments
Bagaraatan [BAH-guh-RAH-tahn]	little predator	Late Cretaceous (70.6–68.5 MYA)	11.2 ft (3.4 m)	Sheep	Mongolia	Possibly a tyrannosauroid.
Coelurus [suh-LOOR-us]	hollow tail	Late Jurassic (155.7–150.8 MYA)	6.6 ft (2 m)	Beaver	Utah and Wyoming, U.S.A.	A long-legged, fast-running theropod. Possibly an early tyrannosauroid.
Condorraptor [KON-door-RAP-tur]	thief of Cerro Condor [locality where found]	Middle Jurassic (164.7–161.2 MYA)	?	Beaver	Argentina	Many isolated bones, probably from just one individual, are known.
Juravenator [JOO-ruh-veh-NAY-tor]	Jurassic hunter	Late Jurassic (155.7–150.8 MYA)	2.6 ft (80 cm)	Chicken	Germany	Originally thought to be a compsognathid. Impressions of patches of scaly skin are preserved, but no protofeathers impressions.
Nedcolbertia [ned-kohl-BER-tee-uh]	for [American paleontologist Edwin] "Ned" Colbert	Early Cretaceous (130–125 MYA)	?	Beaver	Utah, U.S.A.	A long-legged theropod, still not completely known.
Nqwebasaurus [nn-KWEY-buh-SAW-rus]	Nqweba [South Africa] reptile	Early Cretaceous (145.5–136.4 MYA)	12 in (30 cm)	Chicken	South Africa	Possibly an early relative of the ornithomimosaurs.
Ornitholestes [or-NIH-thoh-LES-teez]	bird thief	Late Jurassic (155.7–150.8 MYA)	6.6 ft (2 m)	Beaver	Wyoming and Utah, U.S.A.	Possibly a primitive tyrannosauroid. Shorter and stockier legs than those of Coelurus.
Phaedrolosaurus [FEE-droh-loh-SAW-rus]	nimble reptile	Early Cretaceous (time very uncertain)	23 ft (7 m)?	Rhino?	China	Known only from a single tooth. Bones that were once considered to belong to Phaedrolosaurus have now been given their own name: Xinjiangovenator.
Proceratosaurus [proh-seh-RAH-toh-SAW-rus]	before Ceratosaurus	Middle Jurassic (167.7–164.7 MYA)	9.8 ft (3 m)?	Wolf	England	Known from a single incomplete skull. Possibly an early tyrannosauroid.
Richardoestesia [rih-KAR-doh-es-TAY-zee-uh]	for [American paleontologist] Richard Estes	Late Cretaceous (83.5–65.5 MYA)	?	?	Throughout the American and Canadian West	The original specimen is known only from a pair of lower jaws, but teeth from this dinosaur are found in nearly every Rocky Mountain state and province. A real mystery dinosaur because we don't yet know what the rest of its body looks like!
Scipionyx [skih-pee-ON-ix]	Scipio's [both Italian geologist Scipione Breislak and Roman general Publius Cornelius Scipio Africanus] claw	Early Cretaceous (112–99.6 MYA)	12 in (30 cm) long as a baby	Pigeon	Italy	Known only from a hatchling, so no one knows how big this dinosaur would grow. The only known specimen had fossilized soft tissues.
Tanycolagreus [tah-NEE-koh-LOG-ree-us]	long-limbed hunter	Late Jurassic (155.7–150.8 MYA)	10.8 ft (3.3 m)	Wolf	Colorado, Utah, and Wyoming, U.S.A.	Probably a very primitive tyrannosauroid. First thought to be a new species of Coelurus.
Teinurosaurus [ty-NOO-roh-SAW-rus]	stretched-tail reptile	Late Jurassic (155.7–150.8 MYA)	?	?	France	Known only from a single vertebra, which was destroyed in World War II.
Timimus [tih-MIME-us]	Tim [Rich]'s mimic	Early Cretaceous (112–99.6 MYA)	9.8 ft (3 m)?	Wolf?	Australia	Known from a single femur. Possibly an ornithomimosaur.
Tugulusaurus [too-GOO-loo-SAW-rus]	Tugulu Group reptile	Early Cretaceous (time very uncertain)	?	Wolf	China	Once thought to be an ornithomimosaur, it seems to be a coelurosaur with a mixture of traits of different groups.
Xinjiangovenator [SHIN-jyang-oh-veh-NAY-tor]	hunter of Xinjiang [China]	Early Cretaceous (time very uncertain)	13.1 ft (4 m)	Wolf	China	Known from an incomplete fossil with some traits like those of Bagaraatan and others like those of maniraptorans.

Compsognathids—Small Early Coelurosaurs (Chapter 16)

One common group of primitive coelurosaurs is the short-armed Compsognathidae.

Name	Meaning	Age	Length	Weight	Where found	Comments
Aristosuchus [uh-RIS-toh-SOOK-us]	superior crocodile	Early Cretaceous (130–125 MYA)	6.6 ft (2 m)	Beaver	England	One of the larger compsognathids.
Compsognathus [KOMP-soh-NAY-thus]	delicate jaw	Late Jurassic (155.7–145.5 MYA)	4.1 ft (1.3 m)	Turkey	France; Germany	One of the first small Mesozoic dinosaurs known from a nearly complete skeleton.
Huaxiagnathus [HWAH-shah-NAY-thus]	Chinese jaw	Early Cretaceous (125–121.6 MYA)	5.9 ft (1.8 m)	Beaver	China	When it was discovered, some thought it was a large *Sinosauropteryx*.
Mirischia [muh-RISH-ee-ah]	wonderful pelvis	Early Cretaceous (112–99.6 MYA)	6.9 ft (2.1 m)	Beaver	Brazil	The left and right side of this dinosaur's hips are asymmetrical.
Sinosauropteryx [SINE-oh-saw-ROP-tur-icks]	Chinese feathered reptile	Early Cretaceous (125–121.6 MYA)	4.3 ft (1.3 m)	Turkey	China	The first dinosaur other than avialians for which feathers (or at least protofeathers) were discovered.

Primitive Tyrannosauroids—Early Tyrant Dinosaurs (Chapter 17)

These coelurosaurs are members of Tyrannosauroidea but not the more advanced Tyrannosauridae.

Name	Meaning	Age	Length	Weight	Where found	Comments
Aviatyrannis [AY-vee-uh-ty-RAN-us]	grandfather of the tyrants	Late Jurassic (155.7–150.8 MYA)	13.1 ft (4 m)?	Lion	Portugal; South Dakota, U.S.A.?	Known only from a few bones and teeth.
Calamosaurus [KAH-luh-moh-SAW-rus]	reed reptile	Early Cretaceous (130–125 MYA)	?	?	England	Often confused with *Calamospondylus* and *Aristosuchus,* this seems to be an *Eotyrannus*-like early tyrannosauroid.
Dilong [dee-LONG]	emperor dragon	Early Cretaceous (128.2–125 MYA)	4.9 ft (1.5 m)	Beaver	China	One of the most complete skeletons of a primitive tyrant dinosaur, and the first to show that they had protofeathers.
Dryptosaurus [DRIP-toh-SAW-rus]	tearing reptile	Late Cretaceous (71–68 MYA)	19.7 ft (6 m)	Rhino	New Jersey, U.S.A.	When discovered, its skeleton showed that theropods were bipedal.
Eotyrannus [EE-oh-ty-RAN-us]	dawn tyrant	Early Cretaceous (130–125 MYA)	14.8 ft (4.5 m), possibly larger	Lion, maybe grizzly bear	England	A long-legged, long-armed early tyrant dinosaur.
Guanlong [gwan-LONG]	crowned dragon	Late Jurassic (161.2–155.7 MYA)	9.8 ft (3 m)	Sheep	China; U.S.A.	The most complete skeleton of an early tyrannosauroid, with a spectacular skull crest.
Itemirus [ee-tee-MEER-us]	after the Itemir site [Uzbekistan]	Late Cretaceous (93.5–89.3 MYA)	?	?	Mongolia	Known only from a braincase.
Labocania [lah-boh-KAN-ee-uh]	after the La Boca Rioja Formation	Late Cretaceous (83.5–70.6 MYA)	24.6 ft (7.5 m)?	Rhino	Mexico	First theropod named from Mexico.
Santanaraptor [san-TAN-uh-RAP-tur]	thief of the Santana Formation	Early Cretaceous (112–99.6 MYA)	4.1 ft (1.3 m)	Beaver	Brazil	Known only from a partial skeleton, but one that has fossilized muscle tissue!
Stokesosaurus [STOKE-soh-SAW-rus]	[American paleontologist William Lee] Stokes's reptile	Late Jurassic (155.7–150.8 MYA)	13.1 ft (4 m)?	Lion?	Utah, U.S.A.	One of the oldest known tyrannosauroids.
Not yet officially named		Early Cretaceous (125–99.6 MYA)	19.7 ft (6 m)?	Horse	China	Previously considered a species of the primitive tetanurine *Chilantaisaurus.*

Primitive Tyrannosaurids—Early, Giant Tyrant Dinosaurs (Chapter 17)

These are members of Tyrannosauridae, but they do not belong to either the slender species in Albertosaurinae or the massive ones in Tyrannosaurinae.

Name	Meaning	Age	Length	Weight	Where found	Comments
Alectrosaurus [ah-LEK-troh-SAW-rus]	mateless reptile	Late Cretaceous (95–80 MYA)	16.4 ft (5 m)?	Horse	China; Mongolia	Only known from partial skeletons; a primitive fast-running tyrant dinosaur.
Appalachiosaurus [ah-puh-LAY-chee-oh-SAW-rus]	Appalachian Mountain reptile	Late Cretaceous (83.5–76 MYA)	21.3 ft (6.5 m)	Horse	Alabama, U.S.A.	One of the most complete dinosaurs ever found in the American South.

Albertosaurines—Slender Giant Tyrant Dinosaurs (Chapter 17)

Albertosaurines are currently known only from western North America.

Name	Meaning	Age	Length	Weight	Where found	Comments
Albertosaurus [al-BUR-toh-SAW-rus]	Alberta [Canada] reptile	Late Cretaceous (72.8–66.8 MYA)	28.2 ft (8.6 m)	Rhino	Alberta, Canada; Montana, U.S.A.	Fossils show that they probably lived in family groups and may have even hunted in packs.
Gorgosaurus [GORE-goh-SAW-rus]	fierce reptile	Late Cretaceous (80–72.8 MYA)	28.2 ft (8.6 m)	Rhino	Alberta, Canada; Montana, U.S.A.	Sometimes considered a second species of the genus *Albertosaurus;* known from many skeletons.

Tyrannosaurines—Massive, Giant Tyrant Dinosaurs (Chapter 17)

These were the top predators of western North America and eastern and central Asia at the end of the Age of Dinosaurs.

Name	Meaning	Age	Length	Weight	Where found	Comments
Alioramus [AL-ee-oh-RAY-mus]	other branch	Late Cretaceous (70.6–68.5 MYA)	19.7 ft (6 m)?	Horse	Mongolia	Known from a couple of very nice skulls and very scrappy other bones; had a row of small bumps on its nose. Some think it might be a juvenile *Tarbosaurus.*
Daspletosaurus [das-PLEE-toh-SAW-rus]	frightful reptile	Late Cretaceous (80–72.8 MYA)	29.5 ft (9 m)	Rhino	Alberta, Canada; Montana and New Mexico, U.S.A.	The Montana and New Mexico specimens might represent new species of *Daspletosaurus.*
Nanotyrannus [NAN-oh-ty-RAN-us]	dwarf tyrant	Late Cretaceous (66.8–65.5 MYA)	19.7 ft (6 m)	Horse	Montana, U.S.A.	Many paleontologists consider this nothing more than a juvenile *Tyrannosaurus.*
Tarbosaurus [TAR-boh-SAW-rus]	dreadful reptile	Late Cretaceous (70.6–68.5 MYA)	32.8 ft (10 m)	Rhino	China; Mongolia	The largest theropod known from China; sometimes considered a species of *Tyrannosaurus.*
Tyrannosaurus [ty-RAN-oh-SAW-rus]	tyrant reptile	Late Cretaceous (66.8–65.5 MYA)	40.7 ft (12.4 m)	Elephant	Saskatchewan and Alberta, Canada; Colorado, Montana, Wyoming, South Dakota, Utah, New Mexico, and possibly Texas, U.S.A.	The largest tyrannosauroid, the largest coelurosaur, and the largest known theropod in North America.

Primitive Ornithomimosaurs—Early Ostrich Dinosaurs (Chapter 18)

Ornithomimosauria—the ostrich dinosaurs—were slender, small-headed, omnivorous or herbivorous theropods. The following were members of Ornithomimosauria but not part of the advanced group Ornithomimidae.

Name	Meaning	Age	Length	Weight	Where found	Comments
Deinocheirus [DY-noh-KY-rus]	terrible hands	Late Cretaceous (70.6–68.5 MYA)	39.4 ft (12 m)?	Elephant	Mongolia	Known only from its enormous 8-foot arms and a few vertebrae, this seems to be a *Tyrannosaurus*-size ornithomimosaur.
Garudimimus [guh-ROO-dee-MY-mus]	Garuda [mythological Indian bird] mimic	Late Cretaceous (99.6–89.3 MYA)	13.1 ft (4 m)	Sheep	Mongolia	A nearly complete skull and partial skeleton are known.
Harpymimus [HAR-pee-MY-mus]	Harpy [mythological Greek bird] mimic	Early Cretaceous (136.4–125 MYA)	16.4 ft (5 m)	Sheep	Mongolia	Known from a crushed, but nearly complete, skeleton, *Harpymimus* was the first toothed ornithomimosaur discovered.
Pelecanimimus [peh-luh-KAN-ee-MY-mus]	pelican mimic	Early Cretaceous (130–125 MYA)	5.9 ft (1.8 m)	Wolf	Spain	With 220 tiny teeth, *Pelecanimimus* has more teeth than any other known theropod.
Shenzhousaurus [SHEN-zhoh-SAW-rus]	China reptile	Early Cretaceous (125–121.6 MYA)	6.6 ft (2 m)	Sheep	China	Known from the front end of an individual.
Sinornithomimus [SINE-or-NIH-thoh-MY-mus]	Chinese *Ornithomimus*	Late Cretaceous (85.8–83.5 MYA)	8.2 ft (2.5 m)	Sheep	China	Many individuals, including nearly complete skeletons, were found together, suggesting that *Sinornithomimus* lived in herds.

Ornithomimids—Advanced Ostrich Dinosaurs (Chapter 18)

These were among the fastest dinosaurs of the Mesozoic Era.

Name	Meaning	Age	Length	Weight	Where found	Comments
Anserimimus [AN-ser-ee-MY-mus]	goose mimic	Late Cretaceous (70.6–68.5 MYA)	9.8 ft (3 m)	Sheep	Mongolia	Little is known of this straight-clawed ornithomimid.
Archaeornithomimus [AR-kee-or-NIH-thoh-MY-mus]	ancient *Ornithomimus*	Late Cretaceous (99.6–85.8 MYA)	11.2 ft (3.4 m)	Sheep	China	One of the more poorly known ornithomimids.
Gallimimus [GAL-ee-MY-mus]	chicken mimic	Late Cretaceous (70.6–68.5 MYA)	19.7 ft (6 m)	Horse	Mongolia	The most completely known ostrich dinosaurs, with skeletons of babies, half-grown individuals, and large adults.
Ornithomimus [or-NIH-thoh-MY-mus]	bird mimic	Late Cretaceous (80–65.5 MYA)	11.5 ft (3.5 m)	Lion	Alberta and Saskatchewan, Canada; Montana, Wyoming, Utah, Colorado, and South Dakota, U.S.A.	First known from very incomplete fossils, but nearly complete skulls and skeletons have been discovered. The dinosaur once called *"Dromiceiomimus"* is now considered a species of *Ornithomimus*.
Struthiomimus [STROO-thee-oh-MY-mus]	ostrich mimic	Late Cretaceous (80–72.8 MYA)	13.1 ft (4 m)	Lion	Alberta, Canada	The first ornithomimid known from nearly complete skeletons, and the one that showed how ostrich-like they really were.

Primitive Alvarezsaurids—Early Thumb-Clawed Dinosaurs (Chapter 18)

Alvarezsauridae is a group of bizarre, small coelurosaurs of the Cretaceous Period.

Name	Meaning	Age	Length	Weight	Where found	Comments
Alvarezsaurus [AL-vuh-rez-SAW-rus]	[historian Don Gregorio] Alvarez's reptile	Late Cretaceous (86–83 MYA)	4.6 ft (1.4 m)?	Turkey	Argentina	Known from only a partial skeleton.
Bradycneme [BRAD-ee-NEE-mee]	heavy shin	Late Cretaceous (70.6–65.5 MYA)	?	Turkey	Romania	This specimen has also been considered a fossil owl and a troodontid.
Heptasteornis [hep-TAS-tee-ORN-is]	seven-towns bird	Late Cretaceous (70.6–65.5 MYA)	?	Turkey	Romania	Like *Bradycneme*, it was once considered a fossil owl or a troodontid.

Name	Meaning	Age	Length	Weight	Where found	Comments
Patagonykus [pat-uh-GON-ih-kus]	claw of Patagonia [Argentina]	Late Cretaceous (91–88 MYA)	5.6 ft (1.7 m)	Beaver	Argentina	This dinosaur was the link that let paleontologists connect Alvarezsaurus with the mononykines (previously thought to be only distantly related).
Rapator [rah-PAY-tur]	plunderer	Early Cretaceous (112–99.6 MYA)	?	Grizzly bear	Australia	Known only from a hand bone, this seems to be an early, and very large, alvarezsaurid.

Mononykines—Advanced Thumb-Clawed Dinosaurs (Chapter 18)

The alvarezsaurids with a specialized pinched foot are grouped into Mononykinae.

Name	Meaning	Age	Length	Weight	Where found	Comments
Mononykus [muh-NON-ee-kus]	one claw	Late Cretaceous (85.8–70.6 MYA)	3 ft (90 cm)	Turkey	Mongolia	The first alvarezsaurid known from relatively complete skeletons, it was once considered an early bird or a bizarre ornithomimosaur.
Parvicursor [PAIR-vee-KOOR-sur]	small runner	Late Cretaceous (85.8–70.6 MYA)	12 in (30 cm)	Pigeon	Mongolia	Known from a partial skeleton, this is a small relative of Shuvuuia and Mononykus.
Shuvuuia [shuh-VOO-ee-uh]	bird	Late Cretaceous (85.8–70.6 MYA)	2 ft (60 cm)	Chicken	Mongolia	Known from excellent fossils, including the best-preserved alvarezsaurid skull.
No official genus name; formerly "Ornithomimus" minutus		Late Cretaceous (66.8–65.5 MYA)	12 in (30 cm)	Pigeon	Colorado, U.S.A.	Isolated bones of a North American mononykine were once thought to belong to a tiny species of Ornithomimus.

Primitive Maniraptorans—Early Feathered Dinosaurs (Chapters 19 and 20)

Maniraptora is the group of dinosaurs that includes the most advanced coelurosaurs. The following genera are maniraptorans but not alvarezsaurids, oviraptorosaurs, therizinosauroids, deinonychosaurs, or avialians.

Name	Meaning	Age	Length	Weight	Where found	Comments
Archaeornithoides [AR-kay-OR-nih-THOY-deez]	similar to Archaeornis [former name for Archaeopteryx]	Late Cretaceous (85.8–70.6 MYA)	?	?	Mongolia	Known only from an incomplete skull, once thought to be from a hatchling Tarbosaurus.
Epidendrosaurus [eh-pee-DEN-droh-SAW-rus]	upon-a-branch reptile	Middle Jurassic (171.6–164.7 MYA?)	12 in (30 cm)	Pigeon	China	The original Epidendrosaurus was a hatchling. A second specimen was given a separate name ("Scansoriopteryx"), but it is probably just an adult Epidendrosaurus. The age of this dinosaur is uncertain: it may actually be from the Early Cretaceous.
Euronychodon [yoor-oh-NIKE-uh-don]	European claw tooth	Late Cretaceous (83.5–65.5 MYA)	?	?	Portugal	Known only from teeth. Similar teeth have been found from the Late Cretaceous of Uzbekistan.
Kakuru [KAK-oo-roo]	ancestral serpent	Early Cretaceous (125–112 MYA)	4.9 ft (1.5 m)?	Turkey	Australia	Known only from a lower tibia and a toe bone, which may actually be from an oviraptorosaur or an abelisauroid.
Nuthetes [noo-THEE-teez]	monitor	Early Cretaceous (145.5–140.2 MYA)	5.9 ft (1.8 m)?	Turkey	England	Possibly a dromaeosaurid.
Palaeopteryx [PAY-lee-OP-tur-icks]	ancient wing	Late Jurassic (155.7–150.8 MYA)	12 in (30 cm)?	Pigeon?	Colorado, U.S.A.	Known only from hip bones and a femur. May be an early bird or an early deinonychosaur.
Paronychodon [par-oh-NIKE-uh-don]	near-claw tooth	Late Cretaceous (83.5–65.5 MYA)	?	?	Montana, New Mexico, and Wyoming, U.S.A.	Known only from teeth.
Pedopenna [PED-oh-PEN-uh]	feather foot	Middle Jurassic (171.6–164.7 MYA?)	2 ft (60 cm)?	Chicken?	China	Known from a partial arm and leg with feathers. The age of the rocks that this dinosaur was found in is very uncertain; it may be from the Early Cretaceous.

Name	Meaning	Age	Length	Weight	Where found	Comments
Yaverlandia [yah-ver-LAN-dee-uh]	from Yaverland Battery [Isle of Wight]	Early Cretaceous (130–125 MYA)	?	Beaver	England	Known only from a top of a skull, originally thought to be from a pachycephalosaur!
Yixianosaurus [yee-SHYEN-oh-SAW-rus]	Yixian Formation reptile	Early Cretaceous (125–121.6 MYA)	?	Turkey	China	Known from an incomplete skeleton with very long hands.

Primitive Oviraptorosaurs—Early Egg-Thief Dinosaurs (Chapter 19)

Oviraptorosauria was a diverse group of short-beaked omnivorous theropods.

Name	Meaning	Age	Length	Weight	Where found	Comments
Avimimus [AY-vee-MY-mus]	bird mimic	Late Cretaceous (99.6–70.6 MYA)	4.9 ft (1.5 m)	Turkey	China; Mongolia	A weird, fat-bodied, long-necked, short-tailed, long-legged early oviraptorosaur. Trackways suggest that it lived in big herds.
Calamospondylus [KAL-uh-moh-SPON-duh-lus]	reed vertebrae	Early Cretaceous (130–125 MYA)	?	?	England	Isolated vertebrae suggest it is either an early oviraptorosaur or a relative of both oviraptorosaurs and therizinosauroids.
Caudipteryx [kaw-DIP-tur-icks]	tail wing	Early Cretaceous (125–110.6 MYA)	3 ft (90 cm)	Turkey	China	One of the most common dinosaurs from the Yixian Formation of China.
Incisivosaurus [in-size-EE-voh-SAW-rus]	incisor reptile	Early Cretaceous (128.2–125 MYA)	3 ft (90 cm)?	Turkey	China	Known only from a skull, which may be the head of *Protarchaeopteryx* or a close relative.
Microvenator [MIKE-roh-veh-NAY-tor]	small hunter	Early Cretaceous (118–110 MYA)	4.3 ft (1.3 m)	Turkey	Montana, U.S.A.	Known from a fragmentary skeleton. Was going to be called "*Megadontosaurus*" (big-tooth reptile) because it was once thought that the teeth of the much larger *Deinonychus* belonged to it!
Protarchaeopteryx [PROH-tar-kee-OP-tur-icks]	first *Archaeopteryx*	Early Cretaceous (125–121.6 MYA)	2.3 ft (70 cm)	Turkey	China	Known from an incomplete skeleton, which may actually be the body of *Incisivosaurus* or a close relative.
Shanyangosaurus [shan-YANG-oh-SAW-rus]	Shanyang Formation reptile	Late Cretaceous (70.6–65.5 MYA)	5.6 ft (1.7 m)	Beaver	China	Known from an incomplete skeleton. May be some other kind of maniraptoran.
Thecocoelurus [THEE-koh-see-LOOR-us]	sheathed *Coelurus*	Early Cretaceous (130–125 MYA)	23 ft (7 m)?	Grizzly bear	England	Known only from an incomplete vertebra. Possibly a therizinosauroid rather than an oviraptorosaur.

Caenagnathids—Pinch-Footed Egg-Thief Dinosaurs (Chapter 19)

Caenagnathidae was a group of fast-running oviraptorosaurs.

Name	Meaning	Age	Length	Weight	Where found	Comments
Caenagnathasia [see-nah-nath-AY-zhee-uh]	*Caenagnathus* from Asia	Late Cretaceous (93.5–89.3 MYA)	3.3 ft (1 m)?	Turkey	Uzbekistan	Known from toothless jaws.
Caenagnathus [see-nah-NAY-thus]	recent jaws	Late Cretaceous (80–72.8 MYA)	6.6 ft (2 m)?	Wolf	Alberta, Canada	Known only from jaws. May be the same dinosaur as *Chirostenotes*.
Chirostenotes [KY-roh-sten-OH-teez]	narrow-handed one	Late Cretaceous (80–66.8 MYA)	6.6 ft (2 m)?	Wolf	Alberta, Canada	The first oviraptorosaur known from North America.
Elmisaurus [EL-mih-SAW-rus]	hind-foot reptile	Late Cretaceous (80–68.5 MYA)	6.6 ft (2 m)?	Wolf	Mongolia; Alberta, Canada; Montana, U.S.A.	First known from hand and feet.
Hagryphus [hah-GRY-fus]	claws of the western desert	Late Cretaceous (80–72.8 MYA)	9.8 ft (3 m)?	Sheep	Utah, U.S.A.	A newly discovered large North American oviraptorosaur.
Not yet officially named		Late Cretaceous (66.8–65.5 MYA)	16.4 ft (5 m)	Lion	Montana, U.S.A.	The largest known oviraptorosaur.

Oviraptorids—Advanced Egg-Thief Dinosaurs (Chapter 19)

The dinosaurs of Oviraptoridae, the most advanced of the oviraptorosaurs, are currently known only from Late Cretaceous Asia.

Name	Meaning	Age	Length	Weight	Where found	Comments
Citipati [CHEE-tee-pah-tee]	Citipati [Tantric Buddhist lord of the cemeteries]	Late Cretaceous (85.8–70.6 MYA)	8.9 ft (2.7 m)	Wolf	Mongolia	Known from several nearly complete skulls and skeletons. One of the skulls of this crested dinosaur was often labeled *"Oviraptor"* in older drawings, before it was recognized as a distinct genus. Several individuals have been found lying on their nests.
Conchoraptor [KON-koh-RAP-tur]	shellfish thief	Late Cretaceous (85.8–70.6 MYA)	4.9 ft (1.5 m)	Turkey	Mongolia	Had only a small crest. Its name was given based on the idea that it was a shellfish-eater (small clams are known from the deposits in which it was found).
Heyuannia [hee-YUAN-nee-uh]	for Heyuan City [China]	Late Cretaceous (time very uncertain)	4.9 ft (1.5 m)	Turkey	China	Known from some very good skeletons.
Khaan [KHAN]	ruler	Late Cretaceous (85.8–70.6 MYA)	4.9 ft (1.5 m)	Turkey	Mongolia	Known from several nearly complete skulls and skeletons. Similar to *Conchoraptor* and *"Ingenia."*
Nemegtomaia [NEH-meg-toh-MY-uh]	good mother of the Nemegt Formation	Late Cretaceous (70.6–68.5 MYA)	4.9 ft (1.5 m)	Turkey	Mongolia	First known as *"Nemegtia,"* but that name was already used for a crustacean.
Nomingia [noh-MIN-jee-uh]	from the Nomingiin region [Gobi Desert]	Late Cretaceous (70.6–68.5 MYA)	4.9 ft (1.5 m)	Turkey	Mongolia	Only the hind end of this dinosaur is known, showing that it had a stump tail (pygostyle) like advanced avialians.
Oviraptor [OH-vih-RAP-tur]	egg thief	Late Cretaceous (85.8–70.6 MYA)	4.9 ft (1.5 m)	Turkey	Mongolia	Had a somewhat longer skull than other oviraptorids. The original specimen was found associated with a nest of eggs, which were mistakenly thought to be *Protoceratops* eggs.
Rinchenia [rin-CHEN-ee-uh]	for Rinchen [Barsbold, Mongolian paleontologist]	Late Cretaceous (70.6–68.5 MYA)	4.9 ft (1.5 m)	Turkey	Mongolia	A very tall, crested oviraptorid.
Shixinggia [SHEE-shing-GEE-uh]	for Shixing County [China]	Late Cretaceous (70.6–65.5 MYA)	4.9 ft (1.5 m)?	Turkey?	China	Only a partial skeleton is known.
No official genus name; formerly *"Ingenia"* yanshini		Late Cretaceous (85.8–68.5 MYA)	5.9 ft (1.8 m)	Turkey	Mongolia	Originally called *"Ingenia,"* but that name actually belongs to an insect.

Primitive Therizinosauroids—Early Sloth Dinosaurs (Chapter 19)

These are the early members of Therizinosauroidea.

Name	Meaning	Age	Length	Weight	Where found	Comments
Alxasaurus [ALK-sah-SAW-rus]	Alxa Desert [Inner Mongolia] reptile	Early Cretaceous (125–112 MYA)	12.4 ft (3.8 m)	Grizzly bear	China	The first primitive therizinosauroid known, showing that these weird dinosaurs were in fact maniraptoran theropods.
Beipiaosaurus [BAY-pyow-SAW-rus]	Beipiao City [China] reptile	Early Cretaceous (125–121.6 MYA)	6.1 ft (1.9 m)	Sheep	China	The first therizinosauroid found with feather impressions.
Falcarius [fal-KAR-ee-us]	sickle blade	Early Cretaceous (130–125 MYA)	13.1 ft (4 m)	Grizzly bear	Utah, U.S.A.	Known from a mass accumulation of dozens, possibly hundreds, of individuals.

Therizinosaurids—Advanced Sloth Dinosaurs (Chapter 19)

The dinosaurs of Therizinosauridae were the more specialized therizinosaurids of the Late Cretaceous Epoch.

Name	Meaning	Age	Length	Weight	Where found	Comments
Enigmosaurus [ee-NIG-moh-SAW-rus]	enigmatic reptile	Late Cretaceous (99.6–85.8 MYA)	16.4 ft (5 m)	Horse	Mongolia	Known only from a pelvis, and quite possibly the same dinosaur as *Erlikosaurus*.
Erlianosaurus [er-LYEN-oh-SAW-rus]	Erlian [China] reptile	Late Cretaceous (99.6–85.8 MYA)	8.4 ft (2.6 m)	Lion	China	A link between the more primitive therizinosauroids and the advanced therizinosaurids.
Erlikosaurus [ER-lick-oh-SAW-rus]	Erlik [Mongolian death god] reptile	Late Cretaceous (99.6–85.8 MYA)	11.2 ft (3.4 m)	Grizzly bear	China; Mongolia	The original specimen includes a very well-preserved skull.
Nanshiungosaurus [NAN-shee-un-goh-SAW-rus]	Nanxiong Formation reptile	Late Cretaceous (70.6–68.5 MYA)	14.4 ft (4.4 m)	Horse	China	First thought to be a very weird small sauropod.
Neimongosaurus [NEE-mon-goh-SAW-rus]	Inner Mongolia reptile	Late Cretaceous (99.6–85.8 MYA)	7.6 ft (2.3 m)	Lion	China	A long-necked therizinosauroid with a deep lower jaw.
Nothronychus [noh-throh-NIKE-us]	sloth claws	Late Cretaceous (93.5–89.3 MYA)	17.3 ft (5.3 m)	Rhino	New Mexico and Utah, U.S.A.	The first-discovered North American therizinosauroid, it has an oddly flared-out pelvis.
Segnosaurus [SEG-noh-SAW-rus]	slow reptile	Late Cretaceous (99.6–85.8 MYA)	23 ft (7 m)	Rhino	China; Mongolia	The first therizinosaurid known from more than its arms. First considered a fish-eating theropod.
Therizinosaurus [THER-ee-ZEE-noh-SAW-rus]	scythe reptile	Late Cretaceous (70.6–68.5 MYA)	31.5 ft (9.6 m)	Elephant	Mongolia	The largest known therizinosauroid, known from its enormous, powerful arms. Partial hind limbs from the same rocks probably belong to this species.

Primitive Dromaeosaurids—Early Raptor Dinosaurs (Chapter 20)

The group of raptor dinosaurs—Deinonychosauria—contains two major divisions. One of these, the Dromaeosauridae, has heavier, shorter legs and longer arms.

Name	Meaning	Age	Length	Weight	Where found	Comments
Dromaeosauroides [droh-MAY-oh-saw-ROY-deez]	like *Dromaeosaurus*	Early Cretaceous (145.5–136.4 MYA)	?	?	Denmark	Known only from teeth.
Ornithodesmus [or-NIH-thoh-DES-mus]	bird link	Early Cretaceous (130–125 MYA)	?	Turkey	England	Known only from hip vertebrae.
Pyroraptor [PY-roh-RAP-tur]	fire thief	Late Cretaceous (72.8–66.8 MYA)	?	Wolf?	France	Very fragmentary. Possibly the same as *Variraptor*.
Variraptor [VAH-ree-RAP-tur]	thief of Var Department [France]	Late Cretaceous (72.8–66.8 MYA)	8.9 ft (2.7 m)	Wolf?	France	Very fragmentary. Possibly the same as *Pyroraptor*.

Unenlagiines—Long-Snouted Southern Raptor Dinosaurs (Chapter 20)

Unenlagiinae is a recently discovered group of long-snouted dromaeosaurids from the southern continents.

Name	Meaning	Age	Length	Weight	Where found	Comments
Buitreraptor [BWEE-tree-RAP-tur]	vulture roost [location where discovered] hunter	Late Cretaceous (99.6–97 MYA)	4.3 ft (1.3 m)	Turkey	Argentina	The most completely known unenlagiine.
Neuquenraptor [NAY-oo-ken-RAP-tur]	Neuquén Province [Argentina] thief	Late Cretaceous (91–88 MYA)	5.9 ft (1.8 m)	Turkey	Argentina	Incompletely known, and possibly the same dinosaur as *Unenlagia*.
Rahonavis [rah-hoo-NAY-vis]	menace-from-the-cloud bird	Late Cretaceous (70.6–65.5 MYA)	2.3 ft (70 cm)	Chicken	Madagascar	Bumps on its forearms show that powerful flight feathers were attached there.
Unenlagia [oon-en-LOG-ee-uh]	half bird	Late Cretaceous (91–88 MYA)	7.5 ft (2.3 m)	Beaver	Argentina	Originally thought to be an early bird (or at least more closely related to birds than to dromaeosaurids).

Name	Meaning	Age	Length	Weight	Where found	Comments
Unquillosaurus [oon-KEE-oh-SAW-rus]	Unquillo River [Argentina] reptile	Late Cretaceous (83.5–70.6 MYA)	9.8 ft (3 m)?	Wolf	Argentina	Once thought to be a carnosaur or other large theropod. Many books and Web sites have mistakenly stated that this was a 36-ft (11-m) giant! Known only from the pelvis and a few other bones.
Not yet officially named		Late Cretaceous (78–65.5 MYA)	19.7 ft (6 m)	Lion	Argentina	A giant unenlagiine, nearly as big as *Utahraptor.*

Microraptorines—Small Raptor Dinosaurs (Chapter 20)

Microraptorinae is a group of small, tree-climbing raptors best known from the Early Cretaceous Epoch of China.

Name	Meaning	Age	Length	Weight	Where found	Comments
Graciliraptor [GRAH-sil-ee-RAP-tur]	slender thief	Early Cretaceous (128.2–125 MYA)	3 ft (90 cm)	Turkey	China	Known from a skeleton that is less complete than those of the other microraptorines but of the same general form.
Microraptor [MIKE-roh-RAP-tur]	small thief	Early Cretaceous (121.6–110.6 MYA)	3 ft (90 cm)	Turkey	China	Known from many skeletons. Includes the specimen formerly called *"Cryptovolans."*
Sinornithosaurus [SINE-or-nih-thoh-SAW-rus]	Chinese bird reptile	Early Cretaceous (125–110.6 MYA)	3 ft (90 cm)	Turkey	China	The first deinonychosaur found with feathers. Had odd wrinkles on its facial bones.

Velociraptorines—Slender Raptor Dinosaurs (Chapter 20)

Velociraptor, Deinonychus, and their kin form the group Velociraptorinae within the dromaeosaurids.

Name	Meaning	Age	Length	Weight	Where found	Comments
Bambiraptor [BAM-bee-RAP-tur]	thief the size of Bambi [fictional baby deer]	Late Cretaceous (80–72.8 MYA)	3 ft (90 cm)	Turkey	Montana, U.S.A.	Considered by some to be a late-surviving microraptorine. Originally thought to be a North American fossil of *Velociraptor.*
Deinonychus [dy-NON-ih-kus]	terrible claws	Early Cretaceous (118–110 MYA)	13.1 ft (4 m)	Wolf	Montana, Oklahoma, Wyoming, and possibly Maryland, U.S.A.	The first dromaeosaurid known from relatively complete skeletons. One of the most important dinosaur discoveries of all because it got paleontologists thinking about dinosaur warm-bloodedness and about the relationship between dinosaurs and birds.
Tsaagan [tsah-GON]	white	Late Cretaceous (85.8–70.6 MYA)	5.9 ft (1.8 m)?	Beaver	Mongolia	Known from a good skull and some vertebrae. Had a more powerful snout than most velociraptorines.
Velociraptor [vuh-LAH-suh-RAP-tur]	swift thief	Late Cretaceous (85.8–70.6 MYA)	5.9 ft (1.8 m)	Beaver	China; Mongolia	The most famous dromaeosaurid (thanks to *Jurassic Park*), and known from many good skulls and skeletons.

Dromaeosaurines—Heavy Raptor Dinosaurs (Chapter 20)

Dromaeosaurinae includes the most heavily built raptor dinosaurs.

Name	Meaning	Age	Length	Weight	Where found	Comments
Achillobator [ah-KHEE-loh-bah-TOR]	Achilles [tendon] hero	Late Cretaceous (99.6–85.8 MYA)	19.7 ft (6 m)	Lion	Mongolia	Only incompletely known, this is one of the largest and most heavily built dromaeosaurids.
Adasaurus [AH-duh-SAW-rus]	Ada [Mongolian evil spirit] reptile	Late Cretaceous (70.6–68.5 MYA)	5.9 ft (1.8 m)	Beaver	Mongolia	Very little is known in detail of this Mongolian dinosaur.
Atrociraptor [ah-TROH-shee-RAP-tur]	atrocious hunter	Late Cretaceous (72.8–66.8 MYA)	5.9 ft (1.8 m)	Beaver	Alberta, Canada	A deep-snouted dromaeosaurid, still only partially known.
Dromaeosaurus [DROH-may-oh-SAW-rus]	swift reptile	Late Cretaceous (80–72.8 MYA)	5.9 ft (1.8 m)?	Beaver	Alberta, Canada; Montana, U.S.A.	When it was discovered, it was thought to be a small tyrannosauroid. Only the discovery of Deinonychus revealed how distinctive dromaeosaurids were from other theropods.
Saurornitholestes [sawr-ORN-ih-thoh-LES-teez]	birdlike reptile thief	Late Cretaceous (80–72.8 MYA)	5.9 ft (1.8 m)?	Turkey	Alberta, Canada; New Mexico, U.S.A.	Possibly a velociraptorine.
Utahraptor [YOO-tah-RAP-tur]	Utah thief	Early Cretaceous (130–125 MYA)	23 ft (7 m)	Grizzly bear	Utah	At present, the largest known dromaeosaurid.

Troodontids—Long-Legged Raptor Dinosaurs (Chapter 20)

Close relatives of the dromaeosaurids, the dinosaurs in Troodontidae make up the other group of deinonychosaurs.

Name	Meaning	Age	Length	Weight	Where found	Comments
Borogovia [BORE-oh-GOH-vee-uh]	borogove [fictional creature from Lewis Carroll's "Jabberwocky"]	Late Cretaceous (85.8–70.6 MYA)	6.6 ft (2 m)?	Beaver	Mongolia	Known from hind-limb material, and thought by some to be a species of Saurornithoides.
Byronosaurus [BY-rah-noh-SAW-rus]	Byron's reptile [for Byron Jaffe, who helped support the expedition]	Late Cretaceous (85.8–70.6 MYA)	4.9 ft (1.5 m)?	Turkey	Mongolia	Known from a snout and several other bones.
Elopteryx [eh-LOP-tur-icks]	marsh wing	Late Cretaceous (70.6–65.5 MYA)	?	?	Romania	Once thought to be a bird, and later to be a dromaeosaurid.
Jinfengopteryx [JIN-fen-GOP-tur-icks]	golden phoenix feather	Late Jurassic or Early Cretaceous (exact age uncertain)	2.3 ft (70 cm)	Chicken	China	Originally called a primitive bird but is more likely a primitive troodontid.
Koparion [koh-PAIR-ee-un]	scalpel	Late Jurassic (155.7–150.8 MYA)	?	?	Utah, U.S.A.	Known only from teeth. A newly discovered Wyoming skeleton may turn out to be from Koparion.
Mei [MAY]	sleeping [dragon]	Early Cretaceous (128.2–125 MYA)	2.3 ft (70 cm)	Chicken	China	Known from a nearly complete skeleton, curled up as if sleeping (although it was more likely protecting itself from volcanic ash!).
Saurornithoides [SAWR-orn-ih-THOY-deez]	birdlike reptile	Late Cretaceous (85.8–68.5 MYA)	6.6 ft (2 m)?	Wolf	Mongolia; China	Known from several partial skulls and skeletons.
Sinornithoides [sine-OR-nih-THOY-deez]	Chinese and birdlike	Early Cretaceous (130–125 MYA)	3.9 ft (1.2 m)	Chicken	China	Like Mei, known from a fossil in "sleeping" position.
Sinovenator [SINE-oh-veh-NAY-tor]	Chinese hunter	Early Cretaceous (128.2–121.6 MYA)	3.9 ft (1.2 m)	Chicken	China	A primitive troodontid with some dromaeosaurid-like features.
Sinusonasus [SINE-us-oh-NAY-sus]	curved nose	Early Cretaceous (128.2–125 MYA)	3.9 ft (1.2 m)	Chicken	China	The nose bones were found to be curved, hence the name.
Tochisaurus [TOK-ih-SAW-rus]	ostrich [foot] reptile	Late Cretaceous (70.6–68.5 MYA)	?	?	Mongolia	Known only from a foot.

Name	Meaning	Age	Length	Weight	Where found	Comments
Troodon [TROO-uh-don]	wounding tooth	Late Cretaceous (80–65.5 MYA)	7.9 ft (2.4 m)	Sheep	Alberta, Canada; Montana and Wyoming, U.S.A.	All Late Cretaceous troodontid fossils from North America get called "*Troodon,*" but when more skeletons are discovered, it may turn out that there were several different troodontids in that region. If so, the old names "*Stenonychosaurus*" and "*Pectinodon*" may be revived.
Not yet officially named		Late Jurassic (155.7–150.8 MYA)	?	?	Wyoming, U.S.A.	Known from an incomplete skeleton. The oldest troodontid known from bones.

Long-Tailed Avialians—Earliest Birds (Chapter 21)

Avialae includes modern birds and their ancient relatives. The ones listed here are the most primitive birds, retaining the long, bony tail typical of other dinosaurs.

Name	Meaning	Age	Length	Weight	Where found	Comments
Archaeopteryx [AR-kee-OP-tur-icks]	ancient wing	Late Jurassic (150.8–145.5 MYA)	1.3 ft (40 cm)	Chicken	Germany; Portugal?	For many decades the best-known primitive bird. May actually be less closely related to modern birds than are deinonychosaurs.
Dalianraptor [DAH-lyen-RAP-tur]	Dalian City [China] thief	Early Cretaceous (121.6–110.6 MYA)	2.6 ft (80 cm)	Turkey	China	A short-armed (and therefore flightless) dinosaur. Some similarities to *Jeholornis,* but others to *Confuciusornis.* However, it might not even be a bird but a more primitive maniraptoran.
Jeholornis [JUH-hoh-LORE-nis]	Jehol Group [China] bird	Early Cretaceous (121.6–110.6 MYA)	2.5 ft (75 cm)	Turkey	China	One of the most completely known long-tailed birds of the Cretaceous. Known to eat both seeds and fish.
Jixiangornis [JEE-shyeng-OR-nis]	[Chinese geologist Yin] Jixiang's bird	Early Cretaceous (121.6–110.6 MYA)	2.6 ft (80 cm)	Turkey	China	Very likely the same as *Jeholornis.*
Shenzhouraptor [SHEN-zhoh-RAP-tur]	China thief	Early Cretaceous (121.6–110.6 MYA)	2.6 ft (80 cm)	Turkey	China	Very likely the same as *Jeholornis.*
Wellnhoferia [WEL-en-hof-AIR-ee-uh]	for [German paleontologist Peter] Wellnhofer	Late Jurassic (150.8–145.5 MYA)	1.5 ft (45 cm)	Chicken	Germany	Very similar to, and possibly the same as, *Archaeopteryx.*
Yandangornis [YAN-dang-OR-nis]	Yandang [China] bird	Late Cretaceous (85.8–83.5 MYA)	2.6 ft (80 cm)	Turkey	China	A toothless, long-tailed bird or close relative.

Primitive Short-Tailed Avialians—Handy Short-Tailed Birds (Chapter 21)

These birds—and all more advanced ones—have a stubby pygostyle instead of a long, bony tail. But like their primitive relatives (and unlike more advanced birds), these had fully developed hands and claws.

Name	Meaning	Age	Length	Weight	Where found	Comments
Changchengornis [CHANG-cheng-OR-nis]	Great Wall [China] bird	Early Cretaceous (125–121.6 MYA)	8 in (20 cm)	Pigeon	China	A close relative of *Confuciusornis.*
Chaoyangia [chow-YANG-ee-uh]	from Chaoyang [China]	Early Cretaceous (121.6–110.6 MYA)	6 in (15 cm)	Pigeon	China	Only the torso, hips, and legs are known. Some skeletons that were once thought to be from *Chaoyangia* are now considered to be from a different bird, *Songlingornis.*
Confuciusornis [kun-FYU-shus-OR-nis]	[Chinese philosopher] Confucius's bird	Early Cretaceous (125–121.6 MYA)	1.6 ft (50 cm)	Chicken	China	Probably the most common Mesozoic dinosaur fossil. Known from thousands of specimens.
Jinzhouornis [JIN-zhoh-OR-nis]	Jinzhou [China] bird	Early Cretaceous (125–121.6 MYA)	6 in (15 cm)	Pigeon	China	A close relative of *Confuciusornis.*
Liaoningornis [LYOW-ning-OR-nis]	Liaoning Province [China] bird	Early Cretaceous (125–121.6 MYA)	8 in (20 cm)	Pigeon	China	One of the most primitive birds to have a large breastbone.
Omnivoropteryx [OM-nee-voh-ROP-tur-icks]	winged omnivore	Early Cretaceous (121.6–110.6 MYA)	12 in (30 cm)	Turkey	China	Very similar to, and possibly the same as, *Sapeornis.*

Name	Meaning	Age	Length	Weight	Where found	Comments
Proornis [proh-OR-nis]	preceding bird	Early Cretaceous (130–125 MYA)	?	Pigeon	North Korea	Not yet studied in detail. The shape of its hand suggests that it is a close relative of *Confuciusornis*.
Sapeornis [SAP-ee-OR-nis]	Society for Avian Paleontology and Evolution bird	Early Cretaceous (121.6–110.6 MYA)	3.9 ft (1.2 m)	Turkey	China	A fairly large early bird.

Enantiornithines—Cretaceous Birds (Chapter 21)

The most diverse group of avialians in the Cretaceous Period is Enantiornithes.

Name	Meaning	Age	Length	Weight	Where found	Comments
Abavornis [AB-uh-VOOR-nis]	great-great-grandfather bird	Late Cretaceous (93.5–89.3 MYA)	?	Pigeon	Uzbekistan	Known only from isolated shoulder bones.
Aberratiodontus [AB-air-at-ee-oh-DON-tus]	unusual teeth	Early Cretaceous (121.6–110.6 MYA)	12 in (30 cm)	Chicken	China	One of the "toothiest" early birds.
Alexornis [AL-ex-OR-nis]	[American paleontologist] Alex [Wetmore]'s bird	Late Cretaceous (83.5–70.6 MYA)	?	?	Mexico	Very little is known of this bird.
Avisaurus [AY-vee-SAW-rus]	bird reptile	Late Cretaceous (80–65.5 MYA)	3.9-ft (1.2-m) wingspan	Turkey	Argentina; Montana, U.S.A.	Possibly a hunting bird, sort of an enantiornithine equivalent of a hawk.
Boluochia [BOW-loo-oh-CHEE-uh]	from Boluochi [China]	Early Cretaceous (121.6–110.6 MYA)	?	Pigeon	China	A toothless member of Enantiornithes.
Catenoleimus [KAT-en-oh-lee-I-mus]	remainder of a lineage	Late Cretaceous (93.5–89.3 MYA)	?	Pigeon	Uzbekistan	Based on a particularly badly preserved fossil.
Concornis [kon-KORE-nis]	Cuenca Province [Spain] bird	Early Cretaceous (130–125 MYA)	6 in (15 cm)	Pigeon	Spain	One of the first enantiornithines known from a good skeleton.
Cuspirostrisornis [KUS-pee-rah-strih-SOR-nis]	pointed-snout bird	Early Cretaceous (121.6–110.6 MYA)	?	Chicken	China	Possibly a close relative of *Avisaurus*.
Dapingfangornis [DAH-ping-fan-OR-nis]	Dapingfang [site in China] reptile	Early Cretaceous (121.6–110.6 MYA)	?	Chicken	China	Known (like most Cretaceous birds) from a crushed specimen. It has some similarities to *Vescornis* and others to *Aberratiodontus*.
Enantiornis [ee-NAN-tee-OR-nis]	opposite bird	Late Cretaceous (93.5–65.5 MYA)	3.3-ft (1-m) wingspan	Turkey	Argentina; Uzbekistan	Discovery of the South American *Enantiornis* species revealed the existence of this important group of Cretaceous birds. The Uzbekistan species may eventually be recognized as belonging to a new genus.
Eoalulavis [EE-oh-ah-loo-LAY-vis]	dawn alula [thumb-feather] bird	Early Cretaceous (130–125 MYA)	?	Pigeon	Spain	At the time it was discovered, it was the oldest bird known to have the alula, a special feather on the thumb that helps birds steer.
Eocathayornis [EE-oh-KAH-thay-OR-nis]	dawn *Cathayornis*	Early Cretaceous (121.6–110.6 MYA)	?	Pigeon	China	Despite its name, it does not seem to be particularly closely related to "*Cathayornis*" (now *Sinornis*).
Eoenantiornis [EE-oh-ee-NAN-tee-OR-nis]	dawn *Enantiornis*	Early Cretaceous (125–121.6 MYA)	4 in (10 cm)	Sparrow	China	Had a relatively short, blunt snout.
Explorornis [EX-ploh-ROOR-nis]	discoverer bird	Late Cretaceous (93.5–89.3 MYA)	?	Pigeon	Uzbekistan	Known from several parts of the skeleton, but not yet fully described.
Gobipteryx [goh-BEEP-tur-icks]	Gobi Desert wing	Late Cretaceous (85.8–70.6 MYA)	?	Pigeon	Mongolia	Known from a pair of toothless skulls.
Gurilynia [GUR-uh-LINE-ee-uh]	from Gurilyn Tsav [Mongolia]	Late Cretaceous (70.6–68.5 MYA)	?	Chicken	Mongolia	A relatively large enantiornithine.
Halimornis [HAL-eh-MOR-nis]	marine bird	Late Cretaceous (83.5–80 MYA)	?	Pigeon	Alabama, U.S.A.	Found in rocks that were deposited about 50 km off what was then the shoreline, showing that at least some enantiornithines were seabirds.
Iberomesornis [I-bare-oh-meh-SOOR-nis]	Spanish Mesozoic bird	Early Cretaceous (130–125 MYA)	8-in (20-cm) wingspan	Sparrow	Spain	One of the most primitive enantiornithines.

Name	Meaning	Age	Length	Weight	Where found	Comments
Incolornis [IN-koh-LOOR-nis]	inhabitant bird	Late Cretaceous (93.5–89.3 MYA)	?	Pigeon	Uzbekistan	Known only from some shoulder bones.
Jibeinia [JEE-bay-NEE-uh]	from Jibei [China]	Early Cretaceous (125–121.6 MYA)	?	Pigeon	China	Although sometimes described as similar to *Confuciusornis*, this seems to be a more typical toothed enantiornithine.
Kuszholia [KUZ-oh-LEE-uh]	Milky Way	Late Cretaceous (93.5–89.3 MYA)	?	Pigeon	Uzbekistan	Several possible parts of the skeleton from this bird have been found, but it is uncertain if they really belong together.
Kyzylkumavis [KIH-zool-koo-MAH-vis]	Kyzylkum [Kazakhstan] bird	Late Cretaceous (93.5–89.3 MYA)	?	Pigeon	Uzbekistan	As with most of the bird fossils discovered in the Bissetky Formation, only fragments of bones are known (in this case, a humerus).
Largirostrornis [LAR-jee-roh-STROR-nis]	large-snout bird	Early Cretaceous (121.6–110.6 MYA)	?	Chicken	China	One of several long-snouted enantiornithines.
Lectavis [lek-TAY-vis]	Lecho Formation bird	Late Cretaceous (70.6–65.5 MYA)	?	Pigeon	Argentina	Only partial hind limbs are known.
Lenesornis [LEH-neh-SOOR-nis]	[Russian paleontologist] Lev Nessov's bird	Late Cretaceous (93.5–89.3 MYA)	?	Pigeon	Uzbekistan	Known only from some hip vertebrae.
Liaoxiornis [LYOW-shee-OR-nis]	Liaoxi [China] bird	Early Cretaceous (125–121.6 MYA)	3 in (7 cm)	Sparrow	China	One of the smallest known Mesozoic birds, but possibly only a juvenile of a larger species.
Longchengornis [LONG-cheng-OR-nis]	Longcheng [China] bird	Early Cretaceous (121.6–110.6 MYA)	?	Pigeon	China	Not much is yet known about this bird.
Longipteryx [lon-GIP-tur-icks]	long wing	Early Cretaceous (121.6–110.6 MYA)	5.7 in (14.5 cm)	Pigeon	China	A long-snouted enantiornithine that may have caught fish.
Longirostravis [LON-jee-roh-STRAY-vis]	long-snout bird	Early Cretaceous (125–121.6 MYA)	5.7 in (14.5 cm)	Pigeon	China	Another long-snouted enantiornithine. May have probed in the mud to find worms and crustaceans to eat.
Nanantius [nah-NAN-tee-us]	dwarf *Enantiornis*	Early to Late Cretaceous (112–70.6 MYA)	?	Pigeon	Australia; possibly Mongolia	The Mongolian fossils show that it was toothless, but it likely belongs to a new genus.
Neuquenornis [NAY-oo-ken-OR-nis]	Neuquén Province [Argentina] bird	Late Cretaceous (86–83 MYA)	?	Pigeon	Argentina	Known from a partial skeleton and eggs with embryos.
Noguerornis [NOH-geer-OR-nis]	Noguera River [Spain] bird	Early Cretaceous (145.5–128 MYA)	?	Pigeon	Spain	One of several species of enantiornithine known from the Cretaceous of Spain.
Otogornis [OH-toh-GOR-nis]	Otog-qi [Inner Mongolia] bird	Early Cretaceous (121.6–110.6 MYA)	?	Pigeon	China	Known only from the forelimb and shoulder.
Protopteryx [proh-TOP-tur-icks]	first wing	Early Cretaceous (132–128 MYA)	5.1 in (13 cm)	Pigeon	China	One of the oldest, and most primitive, enantiornithines.
Sazavis [sah-ZAY-vis]	clay bird	Late Cretaceous (93.5–89.3 MYA)	?	Pigeon	Uzbekistan	Like many of the Bissetky Formation bird species, it is known from only fragments of bones (in this case, a lower shin).
Sinornis [sine-OR-nis]	Chinese bird	Early Cretaceous (121.6–110.6 MYA)	5.5 in (14 cm)	Pigeon	China	The first enantiornithine known from a nearly complete skeleton. Specimens once called "*Cathayornis*" have turned out to be fossils of *Sinornis*.
Soroavisaurus [SOH-roh-AH-vee-SAW-rus]	sister to *Avisaurus*	Late Cretaceous (70.6–65.5 MYA)	?	Chicken	Argentina	Known only from a foot. Named because it seems to be the "sister group" (that is, the closest relative) to true *Avisaurus*.
Vescornis [vez-KOR-nis]	thin[-fingered] bird	Early Cretaceous (125–121.6 MYA)	4.7 in (12 cm)	Pigeon	China	Like many enantiornithines, it still had small claws on its wings.
Yungavolucris [YOON-gah-voh-LOO-kris]	Yunga [Argentina] bird	Late Cretaceous (70.6–65.5 MYA)	?	Pigeon	Argentina	Known from a series of feet.
Zhyraornis [ZHY-rah-OR-nis]	Dzhyrakuduk [Uzbekistan] bird	Late Cretaceous (93.5–89.3 MYA)	?	Pigeon	Uzbekistan	Known only from two sets of hip vertebrae.

Advanced Short-Tailed Avialians—Close Relatives of Modern Birds (Chapter 21)

These birds are close relatives of Aves (the modern birds) but lack a few of the specializations found in true avians.

Name	Meaning	Age	Length	Weight	Where found	Comments
Ambiortus [AM-bee-OR-tus]	uncertain origin	Early Cretaceous (136.4–125 MYA)	?	Chicken	Mongolia	Its name refers to the fact that it has a mixture of advanced and primitive features.
Apsaravis [AP-sah-RAY-vis]	Apsara [Buddhist and Hindu female cloud spirits] bird	Late Cretaceous (85.8–70.6 MYA)	?	Chicken	Mongolia	One of the most complete bird fossils of the Late Cretaceous—sadly, lacking a skull. Very close to true avians.
Archaeorhynchus [AR-kee-or-INK-us]	ancient beak	Early Cretaceous (125–121.6 MYA)	?	Pigeon	China	Has a broad bill somewhat similar to a duck's.
Eurolimnornis [YOO-roh-lim-NOR-nis]	European *Limnornis*	Early Cretaceous (142–128 MYA)	?	Pigeon	Romania	Only a few parts are known. Thought by some to be an avian; possibly an early relative of *Ichthyornis* or some other type of now-extinct bird.
Gansus [GAN-soos]	from Gansu Province [China]	Early Cretaceous (115–105 MYA)	?	Chicken	China	Known from many skeletons (but not yet a head!). Webbed feet and heavier wings suggest it was a foot-propelled diver, like modern loons and grebes.
Gargantuavis [gar-GAN-choo-AY-vis]	Gargantua [mythological French giant] bird	Late Cretaceous (70.6–65.5 MYA)	?	Beaver	France	Possibly the largest bird of the Mesozoic.
Guildavis [gil-DAY-vis]	[American fossil collector E. W.] Guild's bird	Late Cretaceous (87–82 MYA)	?	Chicken	Kansas, U.S.A.	Once considered a species of *Ichthyornis.*
Holbotia [hol-BOH-tee-uh]	from Kholbotu [Mongolia]	Early Cretaceous (136.4–125 MYA)	?	Chicken	Mongolia	Possibly the same as *Ambiortus.*
Hongshanornis [HONG-shan-OR-nis]	Hongshan [ancient Chinese culture] bird	Early Cretaceous (125–121.6 MYA)	5.5 in (14 cm)	Pigeon	China	Known from a complete skeleton with feather impressions. Had a predatory bone that evolved convergently with that of ornithischians.
Horezmavis [HOR-ez-MAY-vis]	Khorezm [Uzbekistan] bird	Late Cretaceous (93.5–89.3 MYA)	?	Pigeon	Uzbekistan	Known only from a foot.
Hulsanpes [hool-SAN-pes]	Khulsan [Mongolia] foot	Late Cretaceous (70.6–68.5 MYA)	?	Chicken	Mongolia	Known only from a foot. Originally considered a dromaeosaurid (which it might actually be).
Iaceornis [ee-ah-see-OR-nis]	neglected bird	Late Cretaceous (87–82 MYA)	9.8 in (25 cm)	Chicken	Kansas, U.S.A.	Once considered a species of *Ichthyornis.*
Ichthyornis [ICK-thee-OR-nis]	fish bird	Late Cretaceous (87–82 MYA)	9.8 in (25 cm)	Chicken	Alabama and Kansas, U.S.A.	One of the first fossil birds discovered in North America, and one of the first fossil birds that showed that many Cretaceous birds still had teeth.
Limenavis [lim-eh-NAY-vis]	threshold bird	Late Cretaceous (72.8–66.8 MYA)	?	Pigeon	Argentina	Known only from a partial wing.
Palaeocursornis [PAY-lee-oh-kur-SOR-nis]	ancient running bird	Early Cretaceous (142–128 MYA)	?	Turkey	Romania	Known only from a poorly preserved thighbone. Thought by some to be an early representative of the group containing modern ostriches and tinamous, but more likely from some other group of extinct birds.
Patagopteryx [pat-uh-GOP-tur-icks]	Patagonia [Argentina] wing	Late Cretaceous (86–83 MYA)	1.6 ft (50 cm)	Turkey	Argentina	Known from much of a skeleton (although not a complete skull). An early flightless bird.
Piksi [PICK-see]	big bird	Late Cretaceous (80–72.8 MYA)	?	Chicken	Montana, U.S.A.	From what is known, it seems to be a heavy-bodied ground bird, something like a modern chicken or turkey.
Platanavis [PLAT-uh-NAY-vis]	sycamore bird	Late Cretaceous (93.5–89.3 MYA)	?	Chicken	Uzbekistan	Known from a set of hip vertebrae.
Songlingornis [SONG-ling-OR-nis]	Songling [Mountains] bird	Early Cretaceous (121.6–110.6 MYA)	?	Sparrow	China	A close relative of *Yanornis* and *Yixianornis.*
Vorona [vuh-RONE-uh]	bird	Late Cretaceous (70.6–65.5 MYA)	?	Pigeon	Madagascar	Known only from its legs.
Wyleyia [wy-LEE-uh]	for [British fossil collector J. F.] Wyley	Early Cretaceous (130–125 MYA)	?	Pigeon	England	May actually be a non-avian maniraptoran.

Name	Meaning	Age	Length	Weight	Where found	Comments
Yanornis [yan-OR-nis]	Yan Dynasty bird	Early Cretaceous (121.6–110.6 MYA)	11 in (27.5 cm)	Chicken	China	Ate fish and possibly plants, too. A famous hoax claimed the existence of *"Archaeoraptor,"* whose "skeleton" combined the front end of a specimen of *Yanornis* with the back end of a specimen of the dromaeosaurid *Microraptor*.
Yixianornis [YEE-shyen-OR-nis]	Yixian Formation bird	Early Cretaceous (121.6–110.6 MYA)	8 in (20 cm)	Chicken	China	A close relative of *Yanornis*.

Hesperornithines—Flightless, Toothed Swimming Birds (Chapter 21)

Hesperornithes is the group of toothed swimming birds of the Late Cretaceous.

Name	Meaning	Age	Length	Weight	Where found	Comments
Asiahesperornis [AY-zhah-heh-speh-ROR-nis]	Asian *Hesperornis*	Late Cretaceous (85.8–80 MYA)	?	Turkey	Kazakhstan	Only some vertebrae and partial legs are known.
Baptornis [bap-TOR-nis]	diving bird	Late Cretaceous (87–82 MYA)	3.9 ft (1.2 m)	Turkey	Kansas, U.S.A.	A nearly complete skeleton is known.
Canadaga [KAN-uh-DAH-guh]	Canadian bird	Late Cretaceous (70.6–65.5 MYA)	4.9 ft (1.5 m)	Beaver	Northwest Territories, Canada	The last, and largest known, hesperornithine.
Coniornis [KONE-ee-OR-nis]	Cretaceous bird	Late Cretaceous (80–72.8 MYA)	?	Turkey	Montana, U.S.A.	Known from vertebrae and shinbones.
Enaliornis [EH-nah-lee-OR-nis]	seabird	Late Cretaceous (99.6–93.5 MYA)	?	Chicken	England	Known from fragmentary skeletons. One of the oldest known enantiornithines, and possibly capable of flying.
Hesperornis [HEH-speh-ROR-nis]	Western bird	Late Cretaceous (87–82 MYA)	4.6 ft (1.4 m)	Beaver	Alberta, Manitoba, and Northwest Territories, Canada; Kansas and Nebraska, U.S.A.	The best-studied and most commonly discovered hesperornithine, known from dozens of skulls and skeletons.
Judinornis [JOO-din-OR-nis]	Yudin's bird	Late Cretaceous (70.6–68.5 MYA)	?	Turkey?	Mongolia	Incompletely known. Apparently lived in freshwater.
Parahesperornis [PAH-rah-HEH-speh-ROR-nis]	near *Hesperornis*	Late Cretaceous (87–82 MYA)	3.9 ft (1.2 m)	Turkey	Kansas, U.S.A.	A nearly complete skeleton is known.
Pasquiaornis [pas-KWY-uh-OR-nis]	Pasquia Hills bird	Late Cretaceous (99.6–93.5 MYA)	?	Turkey	Saskatchewan, Canada	Known from leg bones and one skull bone.
Potamornis [POH-tam-OR-nis]	river bird	Late Cretaceous (66.8–65.5 MYA)	?	Turkey	Wyoming, U.S.A.	Known from very few bones; apparently lived in freshwater.

Avians—Modern-Style Birds (Chapter 21)

The genera listed below are members of the group of modern-style birds—Aves—which was present in the Cretaceous Period. All birds alive today are avians.

Name	Meaning	Age	Length	Weight	Where found	Comments
Anatalavis [AN-uh-tah-LAY-vis]	duck-winged bird	Late Cretaceous to Paleogene (66.8–48.6 MYA)	?	Chicken	England; New Jersey, U.S.A.	A primitive member of the duck and goose group. The best fossils are from the Paleogene Period of the Cenozoic Era, but fragmentary fossils from the very end of the Cretaceous Period in New Jersey seem to belong to an old species of this genus.
Apatornis [AH-pah-TOR-nis]	deceptive [vertebra] bird	Late Cretaceous (87–82 MYA)	?	Chicken	Kansas, U.S.A.	Once thought to be a species of *Ichthyornis*.
Austinornis [AW-stin-OR-nis]	Austin [Texas] bird	Late Cretaceous (87–82 MYA)	?	Chicken	Texas, U.S.A.	A primitive member of the chicken and pheasant group.

Name	Meaning	Age	Length	Weight	Where found	Comments
Ceramornis [SEH-ruh-MOR-nis]	Cretaceous bird	Late Cretaceous (66.8–65.5 MYA)	?	Chicken	Wyoming, U.S.A.	Known only from a shoulder bone, which resembles those of modern shorebirds.
Cimolopteryx [SY-muh-LOP-tur-icks]	Cretaceous wing	Late Cretaceous (80–65.5 MYA)	?	Chicken	Alberta and Saskatchewan, Canada; Wyoming, U.S.A.	Possibly an early representative of the modern shorebirds.
Gallornis [gal-OR-nis]	French bird [also, chicken bird]	Early Cretaceous (145.5–130 MYA)	?	Chicken	France	Known only from fragments of the arm and leg.
Graculavus [GRAK-oo-LAY-vus]	cormorant ancestor	Late Cretaceous (66.8–65.5 MYA)	?	Turkey	New Jersey and Wyoming, U.S.A.	A relatively large bird.
Laornis [lah-OR-nis]	stone bird	Late Cretaceous to Paleogene (66.8–64 MYA)	?	Chicken	New Jersey, U.S.A.	One of the last birds of the Age of Dinosaurs.
Lonchodytes [lon-koh-DY-teez]	Lance Formation diver	Late Cretaceous (66.8–65.5 MYA)	?	Chicken	Wyoming, U.S.A.	A single partial foot is the only known specimen; perhaps an early relative of the modern petrels.
Neogaeornis [NEE-oh-gay-OR-nis]	New World bird	Late Cretaceous (70.6–65.5 MYA)	?	Chicken	Chile	One of the first Cretaceous birds discovered in South America. A possible close relative of modern loons.
Novacaesareala [NOH-vuh-SAY-sah-ree-AL-uh]	from New Jersey	Late Cretaceous to Paleogene (66.8–64 MYA)	?	Chicken	New Jersey, U.S.A.	A relative of *Torotix*, and therefore an early representative of the group containing pelicans, frigate birds, and cormorants.
Palaeotringa [PAY-lee-oh-TRING-uh]	ancient shore bird	Late Cretaceous to Paleogene (66.8–64 MYA)	?	Chicken	New Jersey, U.S.A.	Several isolated bones are known, but it is uncertain to which group of modern birds it is most closely related.
Palintropus [PAL-in-TROH-pus]	backward bender	Late Cretaceous (80–65.5 MYA)	?	Chicken	Alberta, Canada; Wyoming, U.S.A.	A Cretaceous member of the chicken and pheasant group.
Telmatornis [TEL-mah-TOR-nis]	marsh bird	Late Cretaceous to Paleogene (66.8–64 MYA)	?	Chicken	New Jersey, U.S.A.	Possibly the same as *Cimolopteryx*.
Teviornis [TEH-vee-OR-nis]	[Russian paleontologist Victor] Tereschenko's bird	Late Cretaceous (70.6–68.5 MYA)	?	Chicken	Mongolia	Possibly a relative of the ancestors of ducks and geese.
Torotix [tor-OH-tix]	flamingo	Late Cretaceous (66.8–65.5 MYA)	?	Chicken	Wyoming, U.S.A.	Despite its name, it seems to be an early representative of the modern group of seabirds that contains pelicans, frigate birds, and cormorants.
Tytthostonyx [TYT-thoh-STON-icks]	little spur	Late Cretaceous to Paleogene (66.8–64 MYA)	?	Chicken	New Jersey, U.S.A.	Considered by some to be an early member of the major seabird group that contains albatrosses, petrels, and shearwaters.
Vegavis [veh-GAY-vis]	Vega Island [Antarctica] bird	Late Cretaceous (70.6–65.5 MYA)	?	Chicken	Antarctica	A Cretaceous duck.
Volgavis [vol-GAY-vis]	Volga River bird	Late Cretaceous to Paleogene (66.8–64 MYA)	?	Chicken	Russia	Possibly an early relative of the modern pelican and frigate bird group.
Not yet officially named		Late Cretaceous (85.8–70.6 MYA)	?	Pigeon	Mongolia	Known only from embryos found in eggs.

Prosauropods—Early Long-Necked Plant-Eating Dinosaurs (Chapter 22)

Sauropodomorpha is the group of long-necked plant-eating dinosaurs. Many of the Triassic Period and Early Jurassic Epoch genera—the prosauropods—could walk on either two or four legs.

Name	Meaning	Age	Length	Weight	Where found	Comments
Ammosaurus [AM-oh-SAW-rus]	sandstone reptile	Early Jurassic (189.6–175.6 MYA)	14.1 ft (4.3 m)	Lion	Arizona and Connecticut, U.S.A.	One of the first prosauropods found in North America (along with *Anchisaurus*). Some consider this to be the same genus as *Anchisaurus*.
Anchisaurus [AN-kee-SAW-rus]	near reptile	Early Jurassic (189.6–175.6 MYA)	7.9 ft (2.4 m)	Wolf	Connecticut and Massachusetts, U.S.A.	Possibly the smallest and most primitive sauropod.
Camelotia [KAM-uh-LOH-tee-uh]	for Camelot [King Arthur's legendary castle]	Late Triassic (203.6–199.6 MYA)	29.5 ft (9 m)	Horse	England	Possibly an early sauropod rather than a giant prosauropod.
Coloradisaurus [KOH-loh-RAH-dee-SAW-rus]	Los Colorados Formation [Argentina] reptile	Late Triassic (216.5–203.6 MYA)	13.1 ft (4 m)	Lion	Argentina	Known from a good adult skull.
Efraasia [eh-FRAH-zhee-uh]	for [German paleontologist] Eberhard Fraas	Late Triassic (216.5–203.6 MYA)	3.3 ft (1 m)	Turkey	Germany	Sometimes considered a species of *Sellosaurus,* but new studies show that it is a distinct, primitive sauropodomorph.
Eshanesaurus [ee-SHAH-noh-SAW-rus]	Eshan County [China] reptile	Early Jurassic (199.6–196.5 MYA)	?	?	China	Some paleontologists consider this fossil—known only from a lower jaw—to be from an incredibly early therizinosauroid.
Eucnemesaurus [yoo-NEE-moh-SAW-rus]	good-shinned reptile	Late Triassic (216.5–203.6 MYA)	?	Rhino?	South Africa	A *Riojasaurus*-like prosauropod. Includes a femur once thought to be from a carnivorous dinosaur and given the name *"Aliwalia."*
Euskelosaurus [YOOS-kel-oh-SAW-rus]	good-legged reptile	Late Triassic (220–210 MYA)	26.2 ft (8 m)	Horse	South Africa; Zimbabwe	Actual *Euskelosaurus* fossils are rare and not well described. Better fossils once called *"Euskelosaurus"* are now regarded as coming from distinct types of dinosaurs: the prosauropod *Plateosauravus* and the early sauropod *Antetonitrus.*
Fulengia [foo-LEN-jee-uh]	anagram for Lufeng [region in Yunnan Province, China, where discovered]	Early Jurassic (199.6–183 MYA)	3.3 ft (1 m)	Turkey	China	May simply be a baby *Lufengosaurus.*
Jingshanosaurus [JING-shan-oh-SAW-rus]	Jingshan [China] reptile	Early Jurassic (199.6–183 MYA)	32.8 ft (10 m)	Rhino	China	Don't confuse it with *Jiangshanosaurus,* a Cretaceous titanosaur!
Lessemsaurus [LEH-sum-SAW-rus]	[American dinosaur writer Donald] Lessem's reptile	Late Triassic (216.5–203.6 MYA)	32.8 ft (10 m)	Rhino	Argentina	Possibly an early sauropod rather than a giant prosauropod.
Lufengosaurus [loo-FUNG-oh-SAW-rus]	Lufeng Basin [China] reptile	Early Jurassic (199.6–183 MYA)	20.3 ft (6.2 m)	Horse	China	Closely related to *Plateosaurus* and *Yunnanosaurus.* Known from over thirty individuals.
Massospondylus [mas-oh-SPON-duh-lus]	elongated vertebrae	Early Jurassic (199.6–183 MYA)	13.1 ft (4 m)	Lion	Lesotho; South Africa; Zimbabwe; possibly Arizona, U.S.A.	The best-studied prosauropod after *Plateosaurus.* Known from many good skulls and skeletons, and now from nests with embryos.
Melanorosaurus [meh-lah-NOR-oh-SAW-rus]	Black Mountain [South Africa] reptile	Late Triassic to Early Jurassic (216.5–189.6 MYA)	32.8 ft (10 m)	Rhino	Lesotho; South Africa	Possibly an early sauropod rather than a giant prosauropod.
Mussaurus [moo-SAW-rus]	mouse reptile	Late Triassic (216.5–203.6 MYA)	8 in (20 cm) long as a baby	Chicken	Argentina	The original specimen was a tiny hatchling; however, larger adult fossils are known but have not yet been described.
Plateosauravus [PLAH-tee-oh-SAW-rah-vus]	*Plateosaurus* ancestor	Late Triassic (228–216.5 MYA)	26.2 ft (8 m)	Horse	South Africa	The dinosaur fossils that most books call *"Euskelosaurus"* actually belong to this genus.
Plateosaurus [PLAH-tee-oh-SAW-rus]	broad reptile	Late Triassic (216.5–203.6 MYA)	26.2 ft (8 m)	Horse	France; Germany; Greenland; Switzerland	The best-studied prosauropod. Known from dozens of individuals, including complete skulls and skeletons.

Name	Meaning	Age	Length	Weight	Where found	Comments
Riojasaurus [ree-OH-hah-SAW-rus]	La Rioja Province [Argentina] reptile	Late Triassic (216.5–203.6 MYA)	32.8 ft (10 m)	Elephant	Argentina	Known from more than twenty individuals. Once considered a close relative of *Melanorosaurus* and sauropods; new research suggests that it is more closely related to *Plateosaurus, Massospondylus,* and "typical" prosauropods.
Ruehleia [ROO-lay-EE-uh]	for [German paleontologist Hugo] Ruehle [von Lilienstern]	Late Triassic (216.5–203.6 MYA)	26.2 ft (8 m)	Horse	Germany	Once considered a species of *Plateosaurus.*
Saturnalia [SAT-ur-NAH-lee-uh]	Saturnalia [Roman festival]	Middle to Late Triassic (235–220 MYA)	3.3 ft (1 m)	Turkey	Brazil	One of the most primitive sauropodomorphs. It was discovered during the festival of Carnival (celebrated in Brazil), so the describers decided to name it after a similar ancient festival.
Sellosaurus [SEL-oh-SAW-rus]	saddle [vertebra] reptile	Late Triassic (216.5–203.6 MYA)	21.3 ft (6.5 m)	Grizzly bear	Germany	Often considered a species of *Plateosaurus,* but seems to be a more primitive dinosaur.
Tawasaurus [DAH-wah-SAW-rus]	Dawa Village [China] reptile	Early Jurassic (199.6–183 MYA)	3.3 ft (1 m)	Turkey	China	May simply be a baby *Lufengosaurus.*
Thecodontosaurus [THEEK-oh-DON-toh-SAW-rus]	socket-toothed reptile	Late Triassic (216.5–199.6 MYA)	6.9 ft (2.1 m)	Wolf	England; Wales	A very primitive sauropodomorph. The best specimen is a juvenile.
Unaysaurus [OO-nay-SAW-rus]	black-water reptile	Late Triassic (228–203.6 MYA)	8.2 ft (2.5 m)	Lion	Brazil	Recently discovered, it appears to be similar to but smaller than *Plateosaurus.*
Yimenosaurus [yee-MUN-oh-SAW-rus]	Yimen County [China] reptile	Early Jurassic (189.6–175.6 MYA)	23 ft (7 m)	Horse	China	Its skull is short and deep, more like those of sauropods than those of prosauropods. Known from several skeletons.
Yunnanosaurus [YOO-nan-oh-SAW-rus]	Yunnan Province [China] reptile	Late Triassic to Early Jurassic (216.5–183 MYA)	23 ft (7 m)	Horse	China	Over twenty skeletons are known. Unlike most prosauropods, it had teeth that were not leaf-shaped but instead more spoon-shaped (as in macronarian sauropods).
No official genus name; formerly *"Gyposaurus" sinensis*		Early Jurassic (199.6–183 MYA)	26.2 ft (8 m)	Horse	China	Several skeletons from China are known. It was originally considered a Chinese species of *"Gyposaurus"* (an invalid name for the dinosaur now called *Massospondylus*).
Not yet officially named		Late Triassic (228–216.5 MYA)	32.8 ft (10 m)	Elephant	Lesotho	A large African sauropodomorph, not yet described in the scientific literature.
Not yet officially named		Early Jurassic (189.6–175.6 MYA)	6.9 ft (2.1 m)	Wolf	Connecticut, U.S.A.	Once considered specimens of *Anchisaurus* (under the now-invalid name *"Yaleosaurus"*); these fossils seem to be different from *Anchisaurus* and *Ammosaurus,* and so will need a new name.

Primitive Sauropods—Early Giant Long-Necked Plant-Eating Dinosaurs (Chapter 23)

Sauropoda is the group of giant, long-necked, four-legged sauropodomorphs. The following genera are sauropods but not members of either the whip-tailed Diplodocoidea or the big-nosed Macronaria.

Name	Meaning	Age	Length	Weight	Where found	Comments
Aepisaurus [AY-pee-SAW-rus]	high reptile	Early Cretaceous (125–112 MYA)	49.2 ft (15 m)	Two elephants	France	Possibly a macronarian.
Algoasaurus [al-GOH-uh-SAW-rus]	Algoa Bay [South Africa] reptile	Late Jurassic to Early Cretaceous (148–138 MYA)	29.5 ft (9 m)?	Rhino	South Africa	Known only from very poorly preserved fossils. Significant because they were among the first sauropod fossils found in Africa.
Amygdalodon [ah-mig-DAL-uh-don]	almond tooth	Middle Jurassic (171.6–167.7 MYA)	39.4 ft (12 m)?	Elephant?	Argentina	Three different individuals, although none complete, are known.
Antetonitrus [an-tay-toh-NY-trus]	before the thunder	Late Triassic (220–210 MYA)	40 ft (12.2 m)	Elephant	South Africa	One of the most primitive known sauropods. Its bones were originally cataloged as belonging to the prosauropod *Euskelosaurus.*

Name	Meaning	Age	Length	Weight	Where found	Comments
Archaeodontosaurus [AR-kee-oh-DON-toh-SAW-rus]	ancient-tooth reptile	Middle Jurassic (167.7–164.7 MYA)	?	?	Madagascar	Named because its teeth resemble those of more primitive prosauropods rather than typical sauropods.
Asiatosaurus [ay-zhee-AT-oh-SAW-rus]	Asian reptile	Early Cretaceous (time very uncertain)	?	?	China; Mongolia	Possibly the same dinosaur as *Euhelopus.*
Barapasaurus [buh-RAH-puh-SAW-rus]	big-leg reptile	Early Jurassic (199.6–175.6 MYA)	60 ft (18.3 m)	Two elephants	India	The most completely known Early Jurassic sauropod, but, sadly, no one has yet found the skull.
Blikanasaurus [blee-KAN-uh-SAW-rus]	Mount Blikana [South Africa] reptile	Late Triassic (220–210 MYA)	16.4 ft (5 m)	Lion	South Africa	For a long time, thought to be a giant prosauropod, but this form (known from a partial hind limb) seems to be one of the oldest sauropods.
Campylodoniscus [kam-PIL-oh-don-NIS-kus]	bent tooth	Late Cretaceous (72.8–66.8 MYA)	?	?	Argentina	Only an upper jaw is known. Has more primitive teeth than the typical sauropods (titanosaurs) with which it lived.
Cardiodon [kar-DY-oh-don]	heart tooth	Middle Jurassic (167.7–164.7 MYA)	?	?	England	Known from a single tooth, sometimes considered as coming from *Cetiosaurus.* A new study of *Cetiosaurus* showed it was distinct from *Cardiodon.*
Cetiosaurus [SEE-tee-oh-SAW-rus]	whale reptile	Middle Jurassic (171.6–164.7 MYA)	45.9 ft (14 m)	Two elephants	England	The first named sauropod, once thought to be a giant seagoing crocodile.
Chebsaurus [cheb-SAW-rus]	teenager dinosaur	Middle Jurassic (time very uncertain)	29.5 ft (9 m)	Rhino	Algeria	Named because the specimen was not fully grown. A fair amount of the skeleton is known.
Chinshakiangosaurus [CHIN-shah-KYANG-oh-SAW-rus]	Chinshakiang [China] reptile	Early Jurassic (time very uncertain)	29.5 ft (9 m)	Rhino	China	Possibly a large prosauropod rather than a true sauropod.
Chuanjiesaurus [CHWAN-jeh-SAW-rus]	Chuanjie Village [China] reptile	Middle Jurassic (171.6–164.7 MYA)	82 ft (25 m)	Four elephants	China	One of the largest early sauropods.
Datousaurus [DAH-toh-SAW-rus]	chieftain reptile	Middle Jurassic (167.7–161.2 MYA)	45.9 ft (14 m)	Two elephants	China	Possibly a primitive diplodocoid.
Euhelopus [yoo-HEE-loh-pus]	true marsh foot	Late Jurassic (155.7–148 MYA)	39.4 ft (12 m)	Elephant	China	A very long-necked sauropod thought by some to be closely related to *Mamenchisaurus* or *Omeisaurus* and by others to the titanosaurs.
Ferganasaurus [fur-GAN-uh-SAW-rus]	Fergana Valley [Kyrgyzstan] reptile	Middle Jurassic (164.7–161.2 MYA)	45.9 ft (14 m)	Two elephants	Kyrgyzstan	Similar to *Jobaria,* and therefore possibly a primitive macronarian.
Galveosaurus [gal-VEE-oh-rus]	Galve [Spain] reptile	Late Jurassic to Early Cretaceous (148–142 MYA)	45.9 ft (14 m)	Two elephants	Spain	A *Cetiosaurus*-like dinosaur. Two teams of paleontologists wound up describing these fossils with slightly different names at just about the same time, so there is a debate whether this should be called "*Galveosaurus*" or "*Galvesaurus.*"
Gongxianosaurus [GOONG-shyen-oh-SAW-rus]	Gongxian County [China] reptile	Early Jurassic (199.6–175.6 MYA)	45.9 ft (14 m)	Two elephants	China	One of the most primitive known sauropods.
Hudiesaurus [HOO-dee-eh-SAW-rus]	butterfly [vertebrae] reptile	Late Jurassic (150.8–145.5 MYA)	65.6 ft (20 m)?	Two elephants	China	Known from a complete forelimb, a vertebra, and four teeth.
Isanosaurus [EE-san-oh-SAW-rus]	Isan [Thailand] reptile	Late Triassic (210–199.6 MYA)	55.8 ft (17 m)	Two elephants	Thailand	A very primitive sauropod.
Jiutaisaurus [jyoo-tai-SAW-rus]	Jiutai Village [China] reptile	Early Cretaceous (125–112 MYA)	?	?	China	Known only from a series of tail vertebrae.
Klamelisaurus [klah-MEH-lee-SAW-rus]	Klameli [China] reptile	Late Jurassic (161.2–155.7 MYA)	55.8 ft (17 m)	Two elephants	China	May be an adult *Bellusaurus.*
Kotasaurus [KOH-tuh-SAW-rus]	Kota Formation reptile	Early Jurassic (183–175.6 MYA)	29.5 ft (9 m)	Rhino	India	Known from a nearly complete skeleton, which unfortunately has no skull.
Lourinhasaurus [loh-REEN-yuh-SAW-rus]	Lourinha [Portugal] reptile	Late Jurassic (153–148 MYA)	55.8 ft (17 m)	Two elephants	Portugal	First thought to be a species of *Apatosaurus,* then *Camarasaurus.*
Mamenchisaurus [mah-MUN-chee-SAW-rus]	Mamenchi Ferry [China] reptile	Late Jurassic (161.2–155.7 MYA)	85.3 ft (26 m)	Three elephants	China	Possessed one of the longest necks known among dinosaurs.
Ohmdenosaurus [OM-den-oh-SAW-rus]	Ohmden [Germany] reptile	Early Jurassic (183–175.6 MYA)	13.1 ft (4 m)?	Horse?	Germany	First mistakenly thought to be a plesiosaur!

Name	Meaning	Age	Length	Weight	Where found	Comments
Omeisaurus [OH-may-SAW-rus]	Mount Emei [China] reptile	Middle to Late Jurassic (167.7–155.7 MYA)	49.2 ft (15 m)	Two elephants	China	A long-necked sauropod, possibly a close relative of *Mamenchisaurus*.
Oplosaurus [OP-loh-SAW-rus]	armored reptile	Early Cretaceous (130–125 MYA)	?	?	England	Known from a tooth, originally thought to be from an ankylosaur.
Patagosaurus [pah-TAG-oh-SAW-rus]	Patagonia [Argentina] reptile	Middle Jurassic (164.7–161.2 MYA)	49.2 ft (15 m)	Two elephants	Argentina	Over a dozen specimens of different ages (from juveniles to adults) are known.
Protognathosaurus [proh-toh-NAY-thoh-SAW-rus]	first-jaw reptile	Middle Jurassic (167.7–161.2 MYA)	?	?	China	Only a jaw is known.
Pukyongosaurus [puk-YONG-oh-SAW-rus]	Pukyong National University [South Korea] reptile	Early Cretaceous (136.4–120 MYA)	?	?	South Korea	A tall-spined form, not yet fully described.
Qinlingosaurus [CHIN-ling-oh-SAW-rus]	Qin Ling Mountains [China] reptile	Late Cretaceous (66.8–65.5 MYA)	?	?	China	One of the last sauropods of Asia.
Rhoetosaurus [REE-toh-SAW-rus]	Rhoetus [mythological Greek giant] reptile	Middle Jurassic (171.6–167.7 MYA)	39.4 ft (12 m)	Two elephants	Australia	Known only from the rear half of a skeleton.
Shunosaurus [SHOO-noh-SAW-rus]	Sichuan [China] reptile	Middle Jurassic (167.7–161.2 MYA)	28.5 ft (8.7 m)	Elephant	China	The best-studied and most completely known early sauropod, and one of the few with a tail club.
Tazoudasaurus [tah-ZOO-duh-SAW-rus]	Tazouda [Morocco] reptile	Early Jurassic (183–175.6 MYA)	29.5 ft (9 m)	Elephant	Morocco	Both an adult and a juvenile are known; very similar to *Vulcanodon* of Zimbabwe.
Tehuelchesaurus [tay-WAY-el-chay-SAW-rus]	Tehuelche [Native Argentine people] reptile	Late Jurassic (155.7–145.5 MYA)	39.4 ft (12 m)	Two elephants	Argentina	An *Omeisaurus*-like sauropod, found with hexagonal (six-sided) scale impressions.
Tendaguria [TEN-dah-GOO-ree-uh]	from Tendaguru Hill [Tanzania]	Late Jurassic (155.7–150.8 MYA)	?	Two elephants	Tanzania	A heavily built dinosaur known only from vertebrae. May be the same dinosaur as the titanosaur *Janenschia*.
Tienshanosaurus [TYEN-SHAN-oh-SAW-rus]	Heavenly Mountains [China] reptile	Late Jurassic (161.2–155.7 MYA)	39.4 ft (12 m)	Elephant	China	A *Euhelopus*-like dinosaur.
Volkheimeria [VOL-ky-MEER-ee-uh]	for [Argentine paleontologist Wolfgang] Volkheimer	Middle Jurassic (164.7–161.2 MYA)	29.5 ft (9 m)	Rhino	Argentina	Possibly an early macronarian.
Vulcanodon [vul-KAN-oh-don]	volcano tooth	Early Jurassic (199.6–196.5 MYA)	21.3 ft (6.5 m)	Horse	Zimbabwe	One of the oldest sauropods. Originally, some theropod teeth were thought to come from this plant-eater!
Yuanmousaurus [YWAN-moh-SAW-rus]	Yuanmou [China] reptile	Middle Jurassic (time very uncertain)	49.2–65.6 ft (15–20 m)	?	China	A large early sauropod, with traits of *Omeisaurus, Euhelopus,* and *Patagosaurus.*
Zigongosaurus [tzuh-GONG-oh-SAW-rus]	Zigong City [China] reptile	Middle Jurassic (167.7–161.2 MYA)	?	?	China	Shares some traits with *Omeisaurus* and *Mamenchisaurus.*
Zizhongosaurus [tzuh-JUNG-oh-SAW-rus]	Zizhong County [China] reptile	Early Jurassic (183–175.6 MYA)	29.5 ft (9 m)	Rhino	China	An early Chinese sauropod. Not to be confused with *Zigongosaurus.*
Not yet officially named		Middle to Late Jurassic (time very uncertain)	?	?	China	Not yet fully described; said to have a *Camarasaurus*-like skull.
Not yet officially named		Early Jurassic (196.5–189.6 MYA)	36 ft (11 m)	Elephant	China	Not yet fully described, but known from relatively complete material.

Primitive Diplodocoids—Early Whip-Tailed Dinosaurs (Chapter 24)

The following dinosaurs are diplodocoids, but they are not members of the gigantic Diplodocidae, the tall-spined Dicraeosauridae, or the wide-snouted Rebbachisauridae.

Name	Meaning	Age	Length	Weight	Where found	Comments
Amazonsaurus [AH-muh-zon-SAW-rus]	Amazon River reptile	Early Cretaceous (118–110 MYA)	?	?	Brazil	Possibly a dicraeosaurid, possibly a rebbachisaurid.
Amphicoelias [AM-fee-SEE-lee-as]	biconcave [vertebra]	Late Jurassic (155.7–150.8 MYA)	147.6 ft (45 m)?	Eighteen elephants?	Colorado and Montana, U.S.A.	A primitive diplodocoid, and (if measurements from a specimen now lost are correct) one of the largest dinosaurs known.
Cetiosauriscus [see-tee-oh-saw-RIS-kus]	like *Cetiosaurus*	Middle Jurassic (164.7–161.2 MYA)	49.2 ft (15 m)	Two elephants	England	May actually be a close relative of long-necked *Omeisaurus* and *Mamenchisaurus.*
Dinheirosaurus [din-AIR-oh-SAW-rus]	Porto Dinheiro [Portugal] reptile	Late Jurassic (153–148 MYA)	?	Elephant	Portugal	May actually be a diplodocid.
Dyslocosaurus [dis-LOKE-oh-SAW-rus]	hard-to-place reptile	Late Jurassic (155.7–150.8 MYA)	59 ft (18 m)?	Elephant	Wyoming, U.S.A.	Originally recorded as coming from the end of the Late Cretaceous.
Dystrophaeus [dis-TROH-fee-us]	coarse joint	Late Jurassic (155.7–150.8 MYA)	?	Elephant	Utah, U.S.A.	The first sauropod named from North America, but very poorly known.
Losillasaurus [loh-SIL-yah-SAW-rus]	Losilla [Spain] reptile	Early Cretaceous (145.5–140.2 MYA)	?	?	Spain	May be a primitive macronarian instead.
Zapalasaurus [zah-PAH-lah-SAW-rus]	Zapala City [Argentina] reptile	Early Cretaceous (130–120 MYA)	?	?	Argentina	Just named in 2006, and known from vertebrae.
No official genus name; formerly *"Cetiosaurus" glymptonensis*		Middle Jurassic (167.7–164.7 MYA)	?	?	England	Possibly the oldest diplodocoid.

Diplodocids—Giant Whip-Tailed Dinosaurs (Chapter 24)

Diplodocids include the longest of all dinosaurs.

Name	Meaning	Age	Length	Weight	Where found	Comments
Apatosaurus [uh-PAT-oh-SAW-rus]	deceptive [chevron] reptile	Late Jurassic (155.7–150.8 MYA)	85.3 ft (26 m)	Four elephants	Colorado, Wyoming, Utah, and Oklahoma, U.S.A.	Includes the species formerly called *"Brontosaurus."* The most heavily built diplodocid. Some isolated vertebrae hint that it may be even bigger than stated here: in fact, it might regain its place as one of the largest dinosaurs!
Barosaurus [BAR-oh-SAW-rus]	heavy reptile	Late Jurassic (155.7–150.8 MYA)	85.3 ft (26 m)	Two elephants	Utah and South Dakota, U.S.A.	The longest-necked Jurassic dinosaur of North America.
Diplodocus [dih-PLOH-dok-us]	double beam [chevron]	Late Jurassic (155.7–150.8 MYA)	88.6 ft (27 m)	Two elephants	Colorado, Wyoming, Utah, and Montana, U.S.A.	One of the best-known, best-studied dinosaurs. Some paleontologists consider *Seismosaurus* and *Supersaurus* to be very old grown-up *Diplodocus;* if this is true, then *Diplodocus* is one of the longest of all dinosaurs.
Eobrontosaurus [EE-oh-BRON-toh-SAW-rus]	dawn thunder reptile	Late Jurassic (155.7–150.8 MYA)	68.9 ft (21 m)	Three elephants	Wyoming, U.S.A.	Once considered a species of *Apatosaurus* (and also *Camarasaurus*).
Seismosaurus [SIZE-moh-SAW-rus]	earthquake reptile	Late Jurassic (155.7–150.8 MYA)	121.4 ft (37 m)	Six elephants	New Mexico, U.S.A.	Possibly just a very old individual *Diplodocus.*
Supersaurus [SOO-pur-SAW-rus]	super reptile	Late Jurassic (155.7–150.8 MYA)	131.2 ft (40 m)?	Six elephants	Colorado, U.S.A.	Possibly just a very old individual *Barosaurus* or *Diplodocus,* but possibly its own species.
Suuwassea [SOO-oo-WAH-see-uh]	first thunder heard in spring	Late Jurassic (155.7–150.8 MYA)	68.9 ft (21 m)	Two elephants	Montana, U.S.A.	Has some features that are more like those of dicraeosaurids.
Tornieria [tor-nee-AIR-ee-uh]	for [German paleontologist Gustav] Tornier	Late Jurassic (155.7–150.8 MYA)	85.3 ft (26 m)?	Two elephants?	Tanzania	Considered by some to be an African species of *Barosaurus.*

Dicraeosaurids—Tall-Spined Whip-Tailed Dinosaurs (Chapter 24)

These dinosaurs had extremely short necks for sauropods and very tall spines on their backs.

Name	Meaning	Age	Length	Weight	Where found	Comments
Amargasaurus [ah-MAR-guh-SAW-rus]	La Amarga Creek [Argentina] reptile	Early Cretaceous (130–120 MYA)	39.4 ft (12 m)	Rhino	Argentina	Has very tall neural spines on the neck, back, and hips.
Brachytrachelopan [BRACK-ee-tray-KEL-oh-pan]	short-necked shepherd god	Late Jurassic (155.7–150.8 MYA)	32.8 ft (10 m)	Rhino	Argentina	One of the smallest, and shortest-necked, sauropods.
Dicraeosaurus [dy-KREE-oh-SAW-rus]	bifurcated [neural spine] reptile	Late Jurassic (155.7–150.8 MYA)	45.9 ft (14 m)	Elephant	Tanzania	The most completely known dicraeosaurid.

Rebbachisaurids—Wide-Snouted Whip-Tailed Dinosaurs (Chapter 24)

The recently discovered dinosaurs in Rebbachisauridae were the most specialized diplodocoids.

Name	Meaning	Age	Length	Weight	Where found	Comments
Cathartesaura [kah-THAR-tay-SAW-ruh]	vulture roost [locality where discovered] reptile	Late Cretaceous (99.6–93.5 MYA)	?	?	Argentina	Only a few parts have been described at present.
Histriasaurus [HIS-tree-uh-SAW-rus]	Istria [Croatia] reptile	Early Cretaceous (136.4–125 MYA)	?	?	Croatia	The first dinosaur named from the little central European nation of Croatia.
Limaysaurus [lih-MAY-SAW-rus]	Rio Limay Group reptile	Late Cretaceous (99.6–97 MYA)	?	?	Argentina	Known from several individuals, including one 80 percent complete.
Nigersaurus [NIH-jeer-SAW-rus]	Niger reptile	Early Cretaceous (118–110 MYA)	49.2 ft (15 m)	Elephant	Niger	Several specimens are known, including the best skull material of a rebbachisaurid. With 600 teeth, it had the most teeth known in any saurischian.
Rayososaurus [ray-OH-soh-SAW-rus]	Rayoso Formation reptile	Early Cretaceous (117–100 MYA)	?	?	Argentina	A relatively primitive rebbachisaurid.
Rebbachisaurus [ruh-BAH-chih-SAW-rus]	Ait Rebbach [Berber tribe of Morocco] reptile	Early Cretaceous (112–99.6 MYA)	65.6 ft (20 m)	Two elephants	Morocco	The largest known rebbachisaurid, with tall neural spines (1.5 m tall).

Primitive Macronarians—Early Big-Nosed Dinosaurs (Chapter 25)

Macronaria is a group of sauropods with extremely large nasal regions. These genera are macronarians but not members of the advanced groups Brachiosauridae or Titanosauria.

Name	Meaning	Age	Length	Weight	Where found	Comments
Abrosaurus [AB-roh-SAW-rus]	delicate [skull] reptile	Middle Jurassic (167.7–161.2 MYA)	?	?	China	Very similar to *Jobaria*.
Aragosaurus [ah-RAG-oh-SAW-rus]	Aragon [Spain] reptile	Early Cretaceous (130–125 MYA)	59 ft (18 m)	Two elephants	Spain	A *Camarasaurus*-like species.
Atlasaurus [AT-luh-SAW-rus]	Atlas Mountains reptile	Middle Jurassic (167.7–164.7 MYA)	59 ft (18 m)	Two elephants	Morocco	Known from a nearly complete skeleton; possibly an early brachiosaurid.
Bellusaurus [BEL-oo-SAW-rus]	fine reptile	Late Jurassic (161.2–155.7 MYA)	16.4 ft (5 m)	Horse	China	Known from parts of at least seventeen juvenile sauropods.
Camarasaurus [KAM-uh-ruh-SAW-rus]	chambered [vertebrae] reptile	Late Jurassic (155.7–150.8 MYA)	59 ft (18 m)	Two elephants	Colorado, Wyoming, Utah, Montana, and New Mexico, U.S.A.	The most common dinosaur of the Late Jurassic of North America.
Chondrosteosaurus [kon-DROS-tee-oh-SAW-rus]	cartilage-boned reptile	Early Cretaceous (130–125 MYA)	59 ft (18 m)?	Two elephants?	England	Known only from vertebrae.
Dinodocus [dy-noh-DOH-kus]	terrible beam	Early Cretaceous (125–99.6 MYA)	?	?	England	Known only from teeth.
Erketu [er-KEH-too]	Erketu [Mongolian creator-god]	Later Early Cretaceous (time very uncertain)	?	?	Mongolia	A long-necked sauropod, possibly a relative of *Euhelopus*.

Name	Meaning	Age	Length	Weight	Where found	Comments
Europasaurus [yoo-ROH-puh-SAW-rus]	Europe reptile	Late Jurassic (155.7–150.8 MYA)	20.3 ft (6.2 m)	Horse	Germany	One of the smallest sauropods. Lived on an island in what is now Germany.
Haplocanthosaurus [hap-loh-KAN-thoh-SAW-rus]	simple-spined reptile	Late Jurassic (155.7–150.8 MYA)	70.5 ft (21.5 m)	Three elephants	Colorado and Wyoming, U.S.A.	Has been considered a primitive diplodocoid, a *Cetiosaurus* relative, or a primitive macronarian.
Jobaria [joh-BAH-ree-uh]	after Jobar [mythical Nigerian monster]	Early Cretaceous (136.4–125 MYA)	78.7 ft (24 m)	Four elephants	Niger	Known from an excellent skeleton.
Marmarospondylus [MAR-mar-oh-SPON-duh-lus]	marble vertebrae	Middle Jurassic (171.6–164.7 MYA)	?	?	England	Often included in the (younger) genus *Bothriospondylus*.
Ornithopsis [or-nih-THOP-sis]	bird-looking [vertebrae]	Early Cretaceous (130–125 MYA)	?	?	England	Known only from two back vertebrae.
Not yet officially named		Late Jurassic (155.7–150.8 MYA)	?	?	France	Known from fragmentary remains since 1885. May be similar to *Camarasaurus*.
Not yet officially named		Early Cretaceous (time very uncertain)	?	?	China	A very large sauropod.

Brachiosaurids—Long-Armed Big-Nosed Dinosaurs (Chapter 25)

Macronarians with very long necks and long arms, Brachiosauridae includes some of the largest dinosaurs.

Name	Meaning	Age	Length	Weight	Where found	Comments
Astrodon [AS-troh-don]	star tooth	Early Cretaceous (118–110 MYA)	49.2 ft (15 m)	Three elephants	Maryland, U.S.A.	Known from teeth, the skeleton of a juvenile, and some bones of a large adult. Includes fossils originally called "*Pleurocoelus*."
Bothriospondylus [BOTH-ree-oh-SPON-duh-lus]	furrowed vertebrae	Late Jurassic (161.2–150.8 MYA)	65.9 ft (20.1 m)?	Three elephants?	England; France	Known from various bones and teeth. A good skeleton from France has been discovered, but has not yet been fully studied.
Brachiosaurus [BRACK-ee-oh-SAW-rus]	arm reptile	Late Jurassic (155.7–150.8 MYA)	85.3 ft (26 m)	Six elephants	Colorado and Utah, U.S.A.; Tanzania?	For many decades, this was the largest known dinosaur.
Cedarosaurus [SEE-duh-roh-SAW-rus]	Cedar Mountain Formation reptile	Early Cretaceous (130–125 MYA)	?	?	Utah, U.S.A.	Probably a close relative of *Astrodon*.
Daanosaurus [DAH-an-oh-SAW-rus]	Da'an [China] reptile	Late Jurassic (time very uncertain)	?	?	China	Known from the remains of a juvenile dinosaur.
Giraffatitan [jih-RAF-uh-TY-tun]	giant giraffe	Late Jurassic (155.7–150.8 MYA)	85.3 ft (26 m)	Six elephants	Tanzania; Argentina?	Considered a species of *Brachiosaurus* by most paleontologists.
Lapparentosaurus [lah-puh-REN-toh-SAW-rus]	[French paleontologist Albert de] Lapparent's reptile	Middle Jurassic (167.7–164.7 MYA)	?	?	Madagascar	Closely related, if not ancestral, to *Brachiosaurus*.
Lusotitan [LOO-soh-TY-tun]	Portuguese giant	Late Jurassic (150.8–145.5 MYA)	?	?	Portugal	Originally thought to be a Portuguese species of *Brachiosaurus*.
Pelorosaurus [puh-LOH-roh-SAW-rus]	gigantic reptile	Early Cretaceous (140.2–125 MYA)	78.7 ft (24 m)	Five elephants	England	Similar to the larger *Brachiosaurus*.
Sauroposeidon [SAW-roh-puh-SY-dun]	reptile of Poseidon [Greek god of seas and earthquakes]	Early Cretaceous (118–110 MYA)	98.4 ft (30 m)	Eight elephants	Oklahoma, U.S.A.	A gigantic sauropod. When its neck is fully known, it will probably surpass that of *Mamenchisaurus*.
Sonorasaurus [suh-NOR-uh-SAW-rus]	Sonora Desert [Arizona] reptile	Early Cretaceous (105–99.6 MYA)	49.2 ft (15 m)	Three elephants	Arizona, U.S.A.	A small, poorly preserved sauropod.
No official genus name; formerly "*Cetiosaurus*" *humerocristatus*		Late Jurassic (155.7–150.8 MYA)	82 ft (25 m)?	Four elephants?	England	Known from a large (1.5 m), slender humerus.
No official genus name; formerly "*Ornithopsis*" *leedsii*		Middle Jurassic (164.7–161.2 MYA)	?	?	England	Known from vertebrae and fragments of rib and hip bones.
No official genus name; formerly "*Pleurocoelus*" *valdensis*		Early Cretaceous (130–125 MYA)	?	?	England	Known from teeth and vertebrae.

Name	Meaning	Age	Length	Weight	Where found	Comments
Not yet officially named		Early Cretaceous (125–112 MYA)	60 ft (18.3 m)	Two elephants	Texas, U.S.A.	Not yet fully described, and possibly closely related to *Cedarosaurus*. Once considered to be *Astrodon*.
Not yet officially named	English Poseidon [Greek god of seas and earthquakes]	Early Cretaceous (130–125 MYA)	78.7 ft (24 m)	Five elephants	England	A giant brachiosaurid from the Isle of Wight.

Primitive Titanosaurs—Early Wide-Bodied Big-Nosed Dinosaurs (Chapter 25)

Titanosaurs were characterized by wide bodies. At least some also had armor. The following titanosaurs are not part of the advanced group Saltasauridae.

Name	Meaning	Age	Length	Weight	Where found	Comments
Aegyptosaurus [ee-JIP-toh-SAW-rus]	Egypt reptile	Late Cretaceous (99.6–93.5 MYA)	52.5 ft (16 m)	Two elephants	Egypt	Once known from a good, if incomplete, skeleton, which was unfortunately destroyed during World War II.
Agustinia [ah-goo-STEE-nee-uh]	for Agustin [Martinelli, a young Argentine student who helped discover the dinosaur]	Early Cretaceous (117–100 MYA)	?	Elephant	Argentina	A titanosaur with spiky armor (which was once thought to come from a stegosaur).
Ampelosaurus [AM-peh-loh-SAW-rus]	vineyard reptile	Late Cretaceous (70.6–68.5 MYA)	49.2 ft (15 m)	Two elephants	France	Known from the bones of many individuals, found in a vineyard.
Andesaurus [AN-dee-SAW-rus]	Andes Mountains reptile	Late Cretaceous (99.6–97 MYA)	59 ft (18 m)	Two elephants	Argentina	A primitive titanosaur with similarities to the (much larger) *Argentinosaurus*.
Argentinosaurus [AR-jun-TEE-noh-SAW-rus]	Argentina reptile	Late Cretaceous (97–93.5 MYA)	120 ft (36.6 m)?	Thirteen elephants	Argentina	Perhaps the largest dinosaur known.
Austrosaurus [AW-stroh-SAW-rus]	southern reptile	Early Cretaceous (112–99.6 MYA)	65.6 ft (20 m)?	Two elephants?	Australia	The largest dinosaur from Australia. A good skeleton is known, but is not yet described in detail.
Borealosaurus [bore-ee-AL-oh-SAW-rus]	northern reptile	Late Cretaceous (99.6–89.3 MYA)	?	?	China	Its tail vertebrae show similarities to those of *Opisthocoelicaudia*.
Chubutisaurus [choo-BOO-tee-SAW-rus]	Chubut Province [Argentina] reptile	Late Cretaceous (89.3–65.5 MYA)	75.5 ft (23 m)	Four elephants	Argentina	One of the most primitive titanosaurs.
Epachthosaurus [eh-PAK-thoh-SAW-rus]	heavy reptile	Late Cretaceous (99.6–93.5 MYA)	59 ft (18 m)	Three elephants	Argentina	Previously known from incomplete material, but a newly discovered skeleton will show us many more details of this titanosaur.
Gobititan [GOH-bee-TY-tun]	Gobi Desert giant	Early to Late Cretaceous (112–93.5 MYA)	?	?	China	Known from tail and leg bones similar to those of *Tangvayosaurus*.
Gondwanatitan [gon-DWAN-uh-TY-tun]	giant of Gondwana [southern supercontinent]	Late Cretaceous (85.8–83.5 MYA)	?	?	Brazil	Similar to *Aeolosaurus*.
Hypselosaurus [HIP-seh-loh-SAW-rus]	high reptile	Late Cretaceous (70.6–65.5 MYA)	39.4 ft (12 m)	Two elephants	France	One of the last sauropods of Europe. Eggs and nests of a titanosaur from France are thought to come from *Hypselosaurus*.
Isisaurus [ISS-ee-SAW-rus]	Indian Statistical Institute reptile	Late Cretaceous (70.6–65.5 MYA)	59 ft (18 m)	Three elephants	India	Previously considered a species of *Titanosaurus*.
Iuticosaurus [YOO-tih-koh-SAW-rus]	Jutes [ancient people of the Isle of Wight] reptile	Early Cretaceous (130–125 MYA)	49.2 ft (15 m)	Two elephants?	England	Poorly known but definitely titanosaurian.
Jainosaurus [JANE-oh-SAW-rus]	[Indian paleontologist Sohan Lal] Jain's reptile	Late Cretaceous (70.6–65.5 MYA)	70.5 ft (21.5 m)	Three elephants?	India	A giant sauropod from the end of the Age of Dinosaurs in India, once thought to be a species of *Antarctosaurus*.
Janenschia [yah-NEN-shee-uh]	for [German paleontologist Werner] Janensch	Late Jurassic (155.7–150.8 MYA)	?	Two elephants	Tanzania	A heavily built sauropod known only from limb bones. May be the same dinosaur as *Tendaguria*. The oldest known titanosaur.
Jiangshanosaurus [JYANG-shan-oh-SAW-rus]	Jiangshan [China] reptile	Early Cretaceous (112–99.6 MYA)	?	?	China	Features of its shoulder girdle show it to be a titanosaur. Don't confuse it with the older prosauropod *Jingshanosaurus*.

Name	Meaning	Age	Length	Weight	Where found	Comments
Karongasaurus [kuh-RON-guh-SAW-rus]	Karonga District [Malawi] reptile	Early Cretaceous (time very uncertain)	?	Elephant	Malawi	Known only from jaws and teeth.
Ligabuesaurus [LEE-guh-BOO-ay-SAW-rus]	[Italian dinosaur hunter Giancarlo] Ligabue's reptile	Early Cretaceous (117–100 MYA)	?	?	Argentina	Its long forelimbs are like those of *Brachiosaurus*.
Macrurosaurus [mah-KROO-roh-SAW-rus]	long-tailed reptile	Late Cretaceous (99.6–93.5 MYA)	39.4 ft (12 m)	Elephant	England	Known from various parts of the skeleton. At least some of the bones are from a titanosaur, but others might be from a different type of sauropod.
Magyarosaurus [MAG-yar-oh-SAW-rus]	Magyar [Hungarian people] reptile	Late Cretaceous (70.6–68.5 MYA)	17.4 ft (5.3 m)	Horse	Romania	One of the smallest sauropods. Lived on an island in what is now Transylvania.
Malawisaurus [mah-LAH-wee-SAW-rus]	Malawi reptile	Early Cretaceous (time very uncertain)	39.4 ft (12 m)	Elephant	Malawi	Had a short face and armor.
Mendozasaurus [men-DOH-zuh-SAW-rus]	Mendoza City [Argentina] reptile	Late Cretaceous (90–85.8 MYA)	?	?	Argentina	Shows some similarities to India's *Isisaurus*.
Paralititan [pah-RAL-uh-TY-tun]	shoreline giant	Late Cretaceous (99.6–93.5 MYA)	105 ft (32 m)	Ten elephants	Egypt	A giant swamp-dwelling sauropod.
Phuwiangosaurus [PHOO-wee-AN-goh-SAW-rus]	Phu Wiang [Thailand] reptile	Early Cretaceous (140.2–130 MYA)	82 ft (25 m)	Four elephants	Thailand	Similar to *Tangvayosaurus*.
Puertasaurus [PWER-tuh-SAW-rus]	[Argentine fossil hunter Pablo] Puerta's reptile	Late Cretaceous (70.6–68.5 MYA)	98.4 ft (30 m)?	Eleven elephants	Argentina	Known only from some vertebrae, but of gigantic size.
Tangvayosaurus [tang-VAY-oh-SAW-rus]	Tang Vay Village [Laos] reptile	Early Cretaceous (125–99.6 MYA)	?	?	Laos	Several individuals are known.
Venenosaurus [veh-NEE-noh-SAW-rus]	Poison Strip Member [area of Cedar Mountain Formation] reptile	Early Cretaceous (118–110 MYA)	?	?	Utah, U.S.A.	Known from both juveniles and adults.
No official genus name; formerly *"Pelorosaurus" becklesii*		Early Cretaceous (130–125 MYA)	?	?	England	Known from a forelimb with skin impressions.
Not yet officially named		Late Cretaceous (91–88 MYA)	98.4 ft (30 m)?	Eight elephants?	Argentina	A very large sauropod that lived at the same time and place as *Megaraptor*.

Saltasaurids—Advanced Wide-Bodied Big-Nosed Dinosaurs (Chapter 25)

Saltasauridae includes the specialized group of Late Cretaceous wide-mouthed titanosaurs.

Name	Meaning	Age	Length	Weight	Where found	Comments
Adamantisaurus [AH-duh-MAN-tee-SAW-rus]	Adamantina Formation reptile	Late Cretaceous (70.6–65.5 MYA)	?	?	Brazil	Based on tail bones.
Aeolosaurus [EE-oh-loh-SAW-rus]	Aeolus [Greek wind god] reptile	Late Cretaceous (72.8–66.8 MYA)	49.2 ft (15 m)	Two elephants	Argentina	Shows some similarities to *Gondwanatitan*.
Alamosaurus [AL-uh-moh-SAW-rus]	Ojo Alamo [New Mexico] reptile	Late Cretaceous (66.8–65.5 MYA)	68.9 ft (21 m)	Four elephants	Texas, Utah, and possibly New Mexico, U.S.A.	North America's youngest sauropod.
Antarctosaurus [ant-ARK-toh-SAW-rus]	southern reptile	Late Cretaceous (83–78 MYA)	59 ft (18 m)	Three elephants	Argentina; Brazil; Chile; Uruguay	Shows the same blunt snout as *Bonitasaura*.
Argyrosaurus [ar-JY-roh-SAW-rus]	silver reptile	Late Cretaceous (99.6–93.5 MYA)	91.9 ft (28 m)?	Seven elephants	Argentina	One of several tremendously large sauropods from this time.
Baurutitan [BAH-roo-TY-tun]	Bauru Group [Brazil] giant	Late Cretaceous (83.5–65.5 MYA)	?	?	Brazil	Known from hip and tail vertebrae.
Bonatitan [BONE-uh-TY-tun]	[Argentine paleontologist José] Bonaparte's giant	Late Cretaceous (72.8–66.8 MYA)	?	?	Argentina	Parts of the skull and tail are known.
Bonitasaura [bone-EE-tuh-SAW-ruh]	La Bonita Hill [Argentina] reptile	Late Cretaceous (85.8–83.5 MYA)	23 ft (7 m) as a juvenile	?	Argentina	The only known specimen so far is a juvenile, so adults would be bigger than this. Known from a very complete skull.
Huabeisaurus [HWAH-bay-SAW-rus]	North China reptile	Late Cretaceous (83.5–70.6 MYA)	?	?	China	A large sauropod with similarities to *Opisthocoelicaudia* and *Nemegtosaurus*.

Name	Meaning	Age	Length	Weight	Where found	Comments
Laplatasaurus [lah-PLAY-tuh-SAW-rus]	La Plata [Argentina] reptile	Late Cretaceous (72.8–66.8 MYA)	59 ft (18 m)	Three elephants	Argentina	Once considered a species of *Titanosaurus.*
Lirainosaurus [lee-RINE-oh-SAW-rus]	slender reptile	Late Cretaceous (72.8–66.8 MYA)	?	?	Spain	Several individuals are known.
Loricosaurus [LOH-rik-oh-SAW-rus]	cuirass reptile	Late Cretaceous (72.8–66.8 MYA)	?	?	Argentina	Known from armor once thought to be ankylosaurian.
Nemegtosaurus [NEH-meg-toh-SAW-rus]	Nemegt Formation reptile	Late Cretaceous (70.6–68.5 MYA)	39.4 ft (12 m)?	Elephant	Mongolia	Known only from its skull. Possibly the same dinosaur as *Opisthocoelicaudia.*
Neuquensaurus [NAY-oo-ken-SAW-rus]	Neuquén Province [Argentina] reptile	Late Cretaceous (85.8–83.5 MYA)	49.2 ft (15 m)	Two elephants	Argentina; Uruguay	Related to *Saltasaurus,* but much larger.
Opisthocoelicaudia [aw-PIS-thoh-SEH-luh-KAW-dee-uh]	hollow-backed tail [vertebrae]	Late Cretaceous (70.6–68.5 MYA)	37.4 ft (11.4 m)	Two elephants	Mongolia	Known only from a headless skeleton. Possibly the same dinosaur as *Nemegtosaurus.*
Pellegrinisaurus [pel-uh-GREE-nee-SAW-rus]	Lake Pellegrini [Argentina] reptile	Late Cretaceous (72.8–66.8 MYA)	72.2 ft (22 m)	Three elephants	Argentina	Known from back and tail vertebrae and a femur.
Quaesitosaurus [kwee-SY-toh-SAW-rus]	extraordinary reptile	Late Cretaceous (85.8–70.6 MYA)	39.4 ft (12 m)?	Elephant	Mongolia	Very similar to, and possibly an ancestor of, *Nemegtosaurus.* Known only from its skull.
Rapetosaurus [rah-PAY-too-SAW-rus]	Rapeto [mischievous giant in Malagasy legend] reptile	Late Cretaceous (70.6–65.5 MYA)	49.2 ft (15 m)	Two elephants	Madagascar	Known from nearly complete skeletons.
Rinconsaurus [RIN-kon-SAW-rus]	Rincón de los Sauces [site in Argentina] reptile	Late Cretaceous (89.3–85.8 MYA)	49.2 ft (15 m)	Two elephants	Argentina	Some similarities to *Aeolosaurus.*
Rocasaurus [ROH-kuh-SAW-rus]	General Roca City [Argentina] reptile	Late Cretaceous (72.8–66.8 MYA)	?	?	Argentina	Many bones are known.
Saltasaurus [SAL-tuh-SAW-rus]	Salta Province [Argentina] reptile	Late Cretaceous (72.8–66.8 MYA)	39.4 ft (12 m)	Elephant	Argentina	A small sauropod. Its discovery showed that titanosaurs had armor.
Sonidosaurus [son-IH-doh-SAW-rus]	Sonid Region [China] reptile	Late Cretaceous (95–80 MYA)	29.5 ft (9 m)	Rhino	China	Shows some similarities to *Opisthocoelicaudia.*
Titanosaurus [ty-TAN-oh-SAW-rus]	Titan [race of mythological Greek giants] reptile	Late Cretaceous (70.6–65.5 MYA)	39.4 ft (12 m)?	Elephant?	India	Despite giving its name to a large group of dinosaurs, true *Titanosaurus* is known from only a few tail bones and a femur.
Trigonosaurus [try-GON-oh-SAW-rus]	Triangulo Mineiro [region in Brazil] reptile	Late Cretaceous (83.5–65.5 MYA)	?	?	Brazil	Known from some connected tail bones and many isolated bones.
No official genus name; formerly "*Antarctosaurus*" *giganteus*		Late Cretaceous (88–86 MYA)	108.2 ft (33 m)?	Nine elephants	Argentina	Once considered a species of *Antarctosaurus;* one of the largest dinosaurs known.
Not yet officially named		Late Cretaceous (70.6–65.5 MYA)	?	Three elephants	Madagascar	Not yet described, but distinct from *Rapetosaurus.*

Primitive Ornithischians—Early Bird-Hipped Dinosaurs (Chapter 26)

Ornithischia—or bird-hipped dinosaurs—was a major group of plant-eating dinosaurs. The following genera are ornithischians that do not belong to any of the advanced ornithischian groups—armored Thyreophora, beaked Ornithopoda, or ridge-headed Marginocephalia.

Name	Meaning	Age	Length	Weight	Where found	Comments
Agilisaurus [AH-jil-uh-SAW-rus]	agile reptile	Middle Jurassic (167.7–161.2 MYA)	5.6 ft (1.7 m)	Turkey	China	Long considered a primitive ornithopod; known from a nearly complete skeleton.
Alocodon [ah-LOH-koh-don]	furrowed tooth	Middle Jurassic (164.7–161.2 MYA)	?	Turkey?	Portugal	Known only from teeth.
Crosbysaurus [KROZ-bee-SAW-rus]	Crosby County [Texas] reptile	Late Triassic (228–216.5 MYA)	?	Chicken?	Arizona and Texas, U.S.A.	Known only from teeth.
Fabrosaurus [FAB-roh-SAW-rus]	[French geologist Jean] Fabre's reptile	Early Jurassic (196.5–183 MYA)	3.3 ft (1 m)?	Turkey	Lesotho	Known only from a partial jawbone with teeth.
Ferganocephale [fur-GAN-oh-SEH-fuh-lay]	Fergana Valley [Kyrgyzstan] head	Middle Jurassic (164.7–161.2 MYA)	?	Chicken?	Kyrgyzstan	Known only from teeth, originally considered to be from a pachycephalosaur.

Name	Meaning	Age	Length	Weight	Where found	Comments
Galtonia [gal-TOH-nee-uh]	for [American paleontologist Peter] Galton	Late Triassic (228–216.5 MYA)	?	Turkey?	Pennsylvania, U.S.A.	Known only from teeth first thought to be from a prosauropod.
Gongbusaurus [GONG-boo-SAW-rus]	Ministry of Public Works reptile	Late Jurassic (165.7–161.2 MYA)	4.9 ft (1.5 m)	Beaver	China	May actually be a primitive ornithopod, but some *"Gongbusaurus"* teeth might be from a primitive stegosaurian.
Hexinlusaurus [heh-SHIN-loo-SAW-rus]	[Chinese paleontologist] He Xin Lu's reptile	Middle Jurassic (167.7–161.2 MYA)	5.9 ft (1.8 m)	Beaver	China	Known from nearly complete skeletons. Long thought to be a primitive ornithopod.
Jeholosaurus [juh-HOH-loh-SAW-rus]	Jehol Group reptile	Early Cretaceous (128.2–125 MYA)	2.6 ft (80 cm)	Turkey	China	May only be a baby of a large ornithopod.
Krzyzanowskisaurus [kur-zuh-zan-OW-skee-SAW-rus]	[American fossil collector Stan] Krzyzanowski's reptile	Late Triassic (228–216.5 MYA)	?	?	Arizona and New Mexico, U.S.A.	Known only from teeth, very likely from a plant-eating crocodile relative rather than a dinosaur.
Lesothosaurus [leh-SOH-thoh-SAW-rus]	Lesotho reptile	Early Jurassic (196.5–183 MYA)	3.3 ft (1 m)	Turkey	Lesotho	Possibly the same species as *Fabrosaurus*.
Lucianosaurus [loo-see-AN-oh-SAW-rus]	Luciano Mesa [New Mexico] reptile	Late Triassic (216.5–203.6 MYA)	?	Turkey?	New Mexico, U.S.A.	Known only from teeth.
Pekinosaurus [peh-KIN-oh-SAW-rus]	Pekin Formation reptile	Late Triassic (228–216.5 MYA)	?	Chicken?	North Carolina, U.S.A.	Known only from teeth.
Pisanosaurus [pee-SAN-oh-SAW-rus]	[Argentine paleontologist Juan A.] Pisano's reptile	Late Triassic (228–216.5 MYA)	3.3 ft (1 m)?	Turkey?	Argentina	The only ornithischian known that probably had a forward-pointing pubis.
Protecovasaurus [PROH-tuh-KOH-vuh-SAW-rus]	before *Tecovasaurus*	Late Triassic (228–216.5 MYA)	?	Chicken?	Texas, U.S.A.	Known from teeth, possibly from an omnivorous ornithischian.
Strombergia [strom-BERG-ee-uh]	for the Stromberg Group	Early Jurassic (196.5–183 MYA)	6.6 ft (2 m)	Wolf	Lesotho; South Africa	Named in 2005; a bigger relative of *Lesothosaurus*.
Taveirosaurus [tah-VAY-roo-SAW-rus]	Taveiro Village [Portugal] reptile	Late Cretaceous (78–68 MYA)	?	Beaver?	Portugal	Known only from teeth.
Tecovasaurus [tuh-KOH-vuh-SAW-rus]	Tecovas Formation reptile	Late Triassic (228–216.5 MYA)	?	Beaver?	France; Arizona and Texas, U.S.A.	Known only from teeth.
Trimucrodon [try-MOO-kruh-don]	triple-point tooth	Late Jurassic (155.7–150.8 MYA)	?	Turkey?	Portugal	Known only from teeth.
Xiaosaurus [shyow-SAW-rus]	dawn reptile	Middle Jurassic (167.7–161.2 MYA)	3.3 ft (1 m)	Turkey	China	May be a very primitive ornithopod.

Heterodontosaurids—Strong-Snouted Early Bird-Hipped Dinosaurs (Chapter 26)

Heterodontosauridae was a group of early specialized ornithischians, once considered to be ornithopods.

Name	Meaning	Age	Length	Weight	Where found	Comments
Abrictosaurus [ah-BRICK-toh-SAW-rus]	awake reptile	Early Jurassic (199.6–189.6 MYA)	3.9 ft (1.2 m)	Turkey	South Africa; Lesotho	Possibly just the juvenile or female form of *Heterodontosaurus*.
Echinodon [eh-KINE-oh-don]	prickly tooth	Early Cretaceous (145.5–140.2 MYA) (and maybe Late Jurassic [155.7–150.8 MYA])	2 ft (60 cm)	Chicken	England; possibly Colorado, U.S.A.	Known from jawbones and teeth found in England. Supposed *Echinodon* fossils have been found in the Late Jurassic of Colorado.
Geranosaurus [juh-RAN-oh-SAW-rus]	crane reptile	Early Jurassic (196.5–189.6 MYA)	?	Turkey	South Africa	Known only from jawbones.
Heterodontosaurus [HEH-tur-oh-DON-toh-SAW-rus]	different-toothed reptile	Early Jurassic (199.6–189.6 MYA)	3.6 ft (1.1 m)	Turkey	South Africa	The most completely known heterodontosaurid.
Lanasaurus [LAH-nuh-SAW-rus]	wool reptile	Early Jurassic (199.6–189.6 MYA)	3.9 ft (1.2 m)?	Turkey?	South Africa	Known only from jawbones; possibly the same dinosaur as *Lycorhinus*.
Lycorhinus [LIKE-oh-RINE-us]	wolf snout	Early Jurassic (199.6–189.6 MYA)	3.9 ft (1.2 m)?	Turkey?	South Africa	Known only from jawbones.

Primitive Thyreophorans—Early Armored Dinosaurs (Chapter 27)

The following genera are early members of Thyreophora and not part of either Stegosauria or Ankylosauria.

Name	Meaning	Age	Length	Weight	Where found	Comments
Bienosaurus [BYEN-oh-SAW-rus]	[Chinese paleontologist Mei Nien] Bien's reptile	Early Jurassic (196.5–189.6 MYA)	13.1 ft (4 m)?	Grizzly bear?	China	Known from a Scelidosaurus-like jaw.
Emausaurus [em-ow-SAW-rus]	Ernst Moritz Arndt University reptile	Early Jurassic (183–175.6 MYA)	6.6 ft (2 m)	Sheep	Germany	May be the oldest and most primitive stegosaurian.
Lusitanosaurus [LOO-suh-TAY-noh-SAW-rus]	Portuguese reptile	Early Jurassic (196.5–189.6 MYA)	?	?	Portugal	Known only from the top of a skull; possibly the same dinosaur as Scelidosaurus.
Scelidosaurus [skeh-LIH-doh-SAW-rus]	shin reptile	Early Jurassic (196.5–183 MYA)	13.1 ft (4 m)	Grizzly bear	England; Arizona, U.S.A.	Known from a couple of good skeletons; thought by some to be the most primitive ankylosaurian.
Scutellosaurus [skoo-TEL-oh-SAW-rus]	small-shield reptile	Early Jurassic (199.6–189.6 MYA)	3.9 ft (1.2 m)	Beaver	Arizona, U.S.A.	The most primitive thyreophoran known from a good fossil.
Tatisaurus [DAH-dee-SAW-rus]	Dadi Village [China] reptile	Early Jurassic (196.5–189.6 MYA)	3.9 ft (1.2 m)?	Beaver?	China	Known from skull material that resembles the skulls of stegosaurians and Scelidosaurus.

Stegosaurs—Plated Dinosaurs (Chapter 28)

These are thyreophorans with a series of spikes and armor plates along their backs.

Name	Meaning	Age	Length	Weight	Where found	Comments
Chialingosaurus [jyah-LING-oh-SAW-rus]	Jialing River [China] reptile	Late Jurassic (161.2–155.7 MYA)	13.1 ft (4 m)	Grizzly bear	China	Known from a partial skeleton of a not-fully-grown individual.
Chungkingosaurus [chung-CHIN-goh-SAW-rus]	Chongqing [China] reptile	Late Jurassic (161.2–155.7 MYA)	11.5 ft (3.5 m)	Grizzly bear	China	Known from several skeletons. A fairly small stegosaurian.
Craterosaurus [krah-TEER-oh-SAW-rus]	cup [skull] reptile	Early Cretaceous (145.5–136.4 MYA)	13.1 ft (4 m)	Grizzly bear	England	Known only from a vertebra.
Dacentrurus [dah-sen-TROOR-us]	very spiky tail	Late Jurassic (161.2–145.5 MYA)	26.2 ft (8 m)	Rhino	England; Portugal; France	One of the biggest stegosaurs, known from many fossils (most not yet fully described).
Hesperosaurus [HEH-spuh-roh-SAW-rus]	western reptile	Late Jurassic (155.7–150.8 MYA)	16.4 ft (5 m)	Horse	Wyoming, U.S.A.	A Dacentrurus-like stegosaurian from America.
Huayangosaurus [hwah-YAN-goh-SAW-rus]	Sichuan reptile	Middle Jurassic (167.7–161.2 MYA)	14.8 ft (4.5 m)	Horse	China	Known from several skeletons. The best-known primitive stegosaurian.
Hypsirophus [hip-sur-OH-fus]	high-roofed [vertebrae]	Late Jurassic (155.7–150.8 MYA)	23 ft (7 m)?	Rhino?	Colorado, U.S.A.	Known from only a few vertebrae. Possibly just a species of Stegosaurus.
Kentrosaurus [KEN-troh-SAW-rus]	sharp-point reptile	Late Jurassic (155.7–150.8 MYA)	16.4 ft (5 m)	Horse	Tanzania	Over thirty partial skeletons were found, but most were destroyed when the German museum they were in was bombed during World War II.
Lexovisaurus [lek-SOH-vih-SAW-rus]	Lexovii [ancient people of France] reptile	Middle to Late Jurassic (164.7–150.8 MYA)	16.4 ft (5 m)	Horse	England; France	Similar in many ways to Kentrosaurus.
Paranthodon [puh-RAN-thoh-don]	near Anthodon [fossil reptile]	Early Cretaceous (145.5–136.4 MYA)	16.4 ft (5 m)?	Horse?	South Africa	Known from a partial skull.
Regnosaurus [REG-noh-SAW-rus]	Regni [ancient tribe of Britain] reptile	Early Cretaceous (145.5–136.4 MYA)	13.1 ft (4 m)?	Grizzly bear	England	A partial lower jaw, similar to the jaw of Huayangosaurus, is all that is known of this dinosaur.
Stegosaurus [STEG-oh-SAW-rus]	covered reptile	Late Jurassic (155.7–150.8 MYA)	29.5 ft (9 m)	Rhino	Utah, Colorado, and Wyoming, U.S.A.; Portugal	The best-known stegosaurian. Some paleontologists think that this genus should be broken up into two genera: true Stegosaurus and smaller Diracodon.
Tuojiangosaurus [twaw-JYANG-oh-SAW-rus]	Tuo River [China] reptile	Late Jurassic (161.2–155.7 MYA)	23 ft (7 m)	Rhino	China	The largest known Chinese stegosaurian.

Name	Meaning	Age	Length	Weight	Where found	Comments
Wuerhosaurus [woo-AIR-hoh-SAW-rus]	Wuerho [China] reptile	Early Cretaceous (time very uncertain)	20 ft (6.1 m)	Rhino	China	One of the last stegosaurs. Had long and low plates rather than tall plates or spikes.
Not yet officially named		Late Jurassic (155.7–150.8 MYA)	16.4 ft (5 m)	Horse	Tibet; China	Not yet fully described. The first Mesozoic dinosaur found in Tibet.

Primitive Ankylosaurs—Early Tank Dinosaurs (Chapter 29)

Ankylosaurs had heavy armor plates over their bodies. The interrelationships among the ankylosaurs are still uncertain. The following dinosaurs are definitely ankylosaurs, but they may not be in either of the advanced groups Nodosauridae or Ankylosauridae.

Name	Meaning	Age	Length	Weight	Where found	Comments
Acanthopholis [ah-kan-THOH-fuh-lis]	spine scutes	Early to Late Cretaceous (105–93.5 MYA)	18 ft (5.5 m)	Horse	England	Although long known, still not fully studied.
Anoplosaurus [ah-NOH-ploh-SAW-rus]	unarmored reptile	Early Cretaceous (105–99.6 MYA)	?	?	England	Probably a juvenile skeleton of a primitive nodosaurid.
Antarctopelta [ant-ARK-toh-PEL-tuh]	Antarctic shield	Late Cretaceous (75–70.6 MYA)	13.1 ft (4 m)	?	Antarctica	The first ornithischian named from Antarctica.
Crichtonsaurus [KRY-tun-SAW-rus]	[*Jurassic Park* author Michael] Crichton's reptile	Late Cretaceous (99.6–89.3 MYA)	?	?	China	Not yet well described. Very likely an ankylosaurid.
Cryptosaurus [KRIP-toh-SAW-rus]	hidden reptile	Late Jurassic (161.2–155.7 MYA)	?	?	England	Known only from a femur. Once also called *"Cryptodraco."*
Dracopelta [DRAK-oh-PEL-tuh]	dragon shield	Late Jurassic (155.7–150.8 MYA)	6.6 ft (2 m)	Sheep	Portugal	A medium-size ankylosaur.
Gargoyleosaurus [gar-GOY-loh-SAW-rus]	gargoyle reptile	Late Jurassic (155.7–150.8 MYA)	9.8 ft (3 m)	Lion	Wyoming, U.S.A.	Known from many good specimens.
Gastonia [gas-TONE-ee-uh]	for [discoverer Robert] Gaston	Early Cretaceous (130–125 MYA)	19.7 ft (6 m)	Rhino	Utah, U.S.A.	Very similar to *Polacanthus*.
Heishansaurus [hay-shan-SAW-rus]	Black Mountain [China] reptile	Late Cretaceous (83.5–80 MYA)	?	?	China	Known only from a partial skull. Might actually be from a pachycephalosaur.
Hoplitosaurus [hoh-PLY-toh-SAW-rus]	shield-carrier reptile	Early Cretaceous (130–125 MYA)	13.1 ft (4 m)	Grizzly bear	South Dakota, U.S.A.	Similar to *Gastonia* and *Polacanthus*.
Hylaeosaurus [hy-LEE-oh-SAW-rus]	Wealden [region of southern England] reptile	Early Cretaceous (140.2–136.4 MYA)	16.4 ft (5 m)	Horse	England	One of the original members of Owen's Dinosauria.
Liaoningosaurus [LYOW-ning-oh-SAW-rus]	Liaoning Province [China] reptile	Early Cretaceous (125–121.6 MYA)	1.1 ft (34 cm) as juvenile	Turkey	China	Known only from a nearly complete juvenile skeleton.
Minmi [MIN-mee]	from Minmi Crossing [Australia]	Early Cretaceous (125–99.6 MYA)	6.6 ft (2 m)	Sheep	Australia	Known from a couple of skeletons. Has unique structures in its vertebrae.
Mymoorapelta [my-MOR-uh-PEL-tuh]	Mygatt-Moore Quarry [Colorado] shield	Late Jurassic (155.7–150.8 MYA)	8.8 ft (2.7 m)	Lion	Colorado, U.S.A.	The first Jurassic ankylosaur named in North America.
Polacanthus [pol-uh-KAN-thus]	many spines	Early Cretaceous (130–125 MYA)	13.1 ft (4 m)	Grizzly bear	England; Spain?	The most common thyreophoran of Early Cretaceous England.
Priconodon [pry-KOH-noh-don]	saw-cone tooth	Early Cretaceous (118–110 MYA)	?	?	Maryland, U.S.A.	Known only from a tooth. Possibly the same dinosaur as *Sauropelta*.
Priodontognathus [PRY-uh-DON-to-NAY-thus]	saw-toothed jaw	Late Jurassic to Early Cretaceous (exact age uncertain)	?	?	England	Known from an upper jaw. Loss of the appropriate paperwork means that no one is certain which rocks this fossil was found in!
Sarcolestes [SAR-koh-LES-teez]	flesh thief	Middle Jurassic (164.7–161.2 MYA)	9.8 ft (3 m)	Lion	England	Originally thought to be a carnivorous dinosaur.
Tianchiasaurus [TYEN-choo-uh-SAW-rus]	Heavenly Pool Lake [China] reptile	Middle Jurassic (167.7–164.7 MYA)	9.8 ft (3 m)	Lion	China	Was going to be called *"Jurassosaurus."* One of the most primitive ankylosaurs.

Nodosaurids—Spike-Shouldered Tank Dinosaurs (Chapter 29)

These ankylosaurs are characterized by huge spines on their shoulders.

Name	Meaning	Age	Length	Weight	Where found	Comments
Aletopelta [ah-lee-toh-PEL-tuh]	wandering shield	Late Cretaceous (80–72.8 MYA)	?	?	California, U.S.A.	Known from a partial skeleton. California's first named Mesozoic dinosaur.
Animantarx [an-ee-MAN-tarks]	living fortress	Early to Late Cretaceous (102–98 MYA)	?	?	Utah, U.S.A.	A small nodosaurid, discovered by detecting the radioactivity of the bones while they were still completely buried.
Cedarpelta [SEE-dur-PEL-tuh]	Cedar Mountain Formation shield	Early to Late Cretaceous (102–98 MYA)	29.5 ft (9 m)	Rhino	Utah, U.S.A.	One of the largest ankylosaurs, rivaling Ankylosaurus. Considered by some to be an ankylosaurid.
Danubiosaurus [day-NOO-bee-oh-SAW-rus]	Danube River reptile	Late Cretaceous (83.5–80 MYA)	13.1 ft (4 m)	Grizzly bear	Austria	Possibly the same dinosaur as Struthiosaurus.
Edmontonia [ED-mon-TONE-ee-uh]	from the Edmonton Formation	Late Cretaceous (80–65.5 MYA)	23 ft (7 m)	Rhino	Alberta, Canada; Montana, Wyoming, South Dakota, New Mexico, and Texas, U.S.A.	A common nodosaurid from the Late Cretaceous of North America. Some paleontologists consider the youngest species of Edmontonia (66.8–65.5 MYA) to be a distinct form called "Denversaurus."
Hierosaurus [hy-UR-oh-SAW-rus]	sacred reptile	Late Cretaceous (87–82 MYA)	13.1 ft (4 m)	Grizzly bear	Kansas, U.S.A.	Sometimes considered the same dinosaur as Nodosaurus.
Hungarosaurus [HUN-gur-oh-SAW-rus]	Hungary reptile	Late Cretaceous (85.8–83.5 MYA)	13.1 ft (4 m)	Grizzly bear	Hungary	One of Hungary's first named dinosaurs.
Niobrarasaurus [NEE-uh-BRAH-ruh-SAW-rus]	Niobrara Chalk reptile	Late Cretaceous (87–82 MYA)	16.4 ft (5 m)	Grizzly bear	Kansas, U.S.A.	Known from partial remains of a dinosaur that had floated out into the middle of the inland seas of Kansas.
Nodosaurus [NOH-doh-SAW-rus]	lumpy reptile	Late Cretaceous (99.6–93.5 MYA)	20 ft (6.1 m)	Horse	Wyoming, U.S.A.	One of the first ankylosaurs discovered, but known only from one partial specimen.
Panoplosaurus [pan-OH-ploh-SAW-rus]	completely armored reptile	Late Cretaceous (80–72.8 MYA)	23 ft (7 m)	Rhino	Alberta, Canada	Known from good skulls and skeletons.
Pawpawsaurus [PAW-paw-SAW-rus]	Paw Paw Formation reptile	Early Cretaceous (105–99.6 MYA)	14.8 ft (4.5 m)	Grizzly bear	Texas and possibly Utah, U.S.A.	Possibly the same dinosaur as Texasetes.
Sauropelta [SAW-roh-PEL-tuh]	reptile shield	Early Cretaceous (118–110 MYA)	24.9 ft (7.6 m)	Rhino	Wyoming, Montana, and Utah, U.S.A.	One of the most common dinosaurs of Early Cretaceous North America. Known from many good skeletons.
Silvisaurus [SIL-vee-SAW-rus]	woodland reptile	Late Cretaceous (96–93.5 MYA)	13.1 ft (4 m)	Grizzly bear	Kansas, U.S.A.	A distinctive ankylosaur known from a skull and the front end of the body.
Stegopelta [STEG-oh-PEL-tuh]	covered shield	Early to Late Cretaceous (102–98 MYA)	13.1 ft (4 m)	Grizzly bear	Wyoming, U.S.A.	May be related to Texasetes, or may actually be a primitive ankylosaurid.
Struthiosaurus [STROO-thee-oh-SAW-rus]	ostrich reptile	Late Cretaceous (83.5–65.5 MYA)	13.1 ft (4 m)	Grizzly bear	Austria; France; Romania; Spain	One of the most common dinosaurs of Late Cretaceous Europe.
Texasetes [tek-sus-EE-teez]	Texas dweller	Early Cretaceous (105–99.6 MYA)	9.8 ft (3 m)	Lion	Texas, U.S.A.	May be the same dinosaur as Pawpawsaurus.

Ankylosaurids—Club-Tailed Tank Dinosaurs (Chapter 29)

The dinosaurs of Ankylosauridae had tails ending in heavy armored clubs.

Name	Meaning	Age	Length	Weight	Where found	Comments
Ankylosaurus [an-KEE-loh-SAW-rus]	fused reptile	Late Cretaceous (66.8–65.5 MYA)	29.5 ft (9 m)	Rhino	Montana and Wyoming, U.S.A.; Alberta, Canada	The last, and largest, ankylosaurid.
Bissektipelta [bih-SEK-tih-PEL-tuh]	Bissekty Formation shield	Late Cretaceous (93.5–89.3 MYA)	?	?	Uzbekistan	Known only from a braincase.

Name	Meaning	Age	Length	Weight	Where found	Comments
Euoplocephalus [YOO-oh-ploh-SEF-uh-lus]	well-armored head	Late Cretaceous (80–66.8 MYA)	23 ft (7 m)	Rhino	Montana, U.S.A.; Alberta, Canada	The best-studied ankylosaurid, known from many excellent specimens.
Glyptodontopelta [GLYP-toh-don-toh-PEL-tuh]	Glyptodon [extinct armored mammal] shield	Late Cretaceous (66.8–65.5 MYA)	16.4 ft (5 m)	Horse	New Mexico, U.S.A.	Known only from some armor.
Gobisaurus [GOH-bee-SAW-rus]	Gobi Desert reptile	Early Cretaceous (125–99.6 MYA)	16.4 ft (5 m)	Horse	China	Similar to Shamosaurus.
Maleevus [mal-YAY-yev-us]	for [Russian paleontologist Evgenii Aleksandrovich] Maleev	Late Cretaceous (99.6–85.8 MYA)	?	?	Mongolia	Probably the same dinosaur as Talarurus.
Nodocephalosaurus [NOH-doh-SEH-fuh-loh-SAW-rus]	lumpy-headed reptile	Late Cretaceous (72.8–66.8 MYA)	?	?	New Mexico, U.S.A.	Similar to Asian Saichania and Tarchia.
Pinacosaurus [pih-NAK-oh-SAW-rus]	plank reptile	Late Cretaceous (85.8–70.6 MYA)	16.4 ft (5 m)	Horse	Mongolia	Many specimens are known, including very small babies.
Saichania [sy-KAN-ee-uh]	beautiful one	Late Cretaceous (85.8–70.6 MYA)	23 ft (7 m)	Rhino	Mongolia	One of the few ankylosaurs found with belly armor.
Shamosaurus [SHAH-moh-SAW-rus]	desert reptile	Early Cretaceous (120–112 MYA)	23 ft (7 m)	Rhino	Mongolia	A primitive narrow-snouted ankylosaurid.
Talarurus [TAH-luh-ROOR-us]	wicker tail	Late Cretaceous (99.6–85.8 MYA)	16.4 ft (5 m)	Horse	Mongolia	Had a relatively small tail club and was rounder (less wide) than most ankylosaurids.
Tarchia [TAR-kee-uh]	brainy one	Late Cretaceous (70.6–68.5 MYA)	26.2 ft (8 m)	Rhino	Mongolia	The largest Asian ankylosaurid.
Tianzhenosaurus [TYEN-jen-oh SAW-rus]	Tianzhen County [China] reptile	Late Cretaceous (83.5–70.6 MYA)	13.1 ft (4 m)	Grizzly bear	China	A second specimen of this dinosaur was named "Shanxia" at almost the same time.
Tsagantegia [tzah-gan-TAYG-ee-uh]	for Tsagan Teg [Mongolia]	Late Cretaceous (99.6–85.8 MYA)	23 ft (7 m)	Rhino	Mongolia	A long-snouted ankylosaurid.

Primitive Ornithopods—Early Beaked Dinosaurs (Chapter 30)

Ornithopoda was a very diverse group of ornithischians. Early ornithopods were all two-legged. The following dinosaurs are not members of either Heterodontosauridae or Iguanodontia. These were once called "hypsilophodonts."

Name	Meaning	Age	Length	Weight	Where found	Comments
Anabisetia [AN-uh-BIH-set-ee-uh]	for [Argentine archaeologist] Ana Biset	Late Cretaceous (94–91 MYA)	?	?	Argentina	May actually be a primitive iguanodontian.
Atlascopcosaurus [AT-lus-KOP-koh-SAW-rus]	Atlas Copco [company that makes drilling tools] reptile	Early Cretaceous (118–110 MYA)	6.6 ft (2 m)	Beaver	Australia	Similar in some ways to Zephyrosaurus, but in other features to the much larger Muttaburrasaurus.
Bugenasaura [boo-gen-uh-SAW-ruh]	large-cheek reptile	Late Cretaceous (66.8–65.5 MYA)	9.8 ft (3 m)	Wolf	South Dakota and Montana, U.S.A.	A short-snouted relative of Thescelosaurus.
Changchunsaurus [CHANG-chun-SAW-rus]	Changchun City [China] reptile	Early Cretaceous (125–112 MYA)	13.1 ft (4 m)?	Sheep?	China	Very similar to Thescelosaurus.
Drinker [DRIN-kur]	for [American paleontologist Edward] Drinker [Cope]	Late Jurassic (155.7–150.8 MYA)	6.6 ft (2 m)	Beaver	Wyoming, U.S.A.	Similar to Othnielia.
Eucercosaurus [yoo-SUR-koh-SAW-rus]	good-tailed reptile	Early Cretaceous (112–99.6 MYA)	?	?	England	Once thought to be an ankylosaur.
Fulgurotherium [FOOL-goo-roh-THEER-ee-um]	Lightning Ridge [Australia] beast	Early Cretaceous (118–110 MYA)	6.6 ft (2 m)	Beaver	Australia	Many bones have been lumped under this name; difficult to sort out how many species are really represented by these fossils.
Gasparinisaura [gas-pah-REE-nee-SAW-ruh]	[Argentine paleontologist Zulma B.] Gasparini's reptile	Late Cretaceous (83–78 MYA)	2.1 ft (65 cm)	Chicken	Argentina	Over fifteen individuals are known, including nearly complete skeletons.

Name	Meaning	Age	Length	Weight	Where found	Comments
Hypsilophodon [hip-sih-LOAF-oh-don]	*Hypsilophus* [old scientific name for a modern iguana] tooth	Early Cretaceous (130–125 MYA)	5.9 ft (1.8 m)	Beaver	England	Known from many skeletons, including juveniles.
Kangnasaurus [KANG-nuh-SAW-rus]	Kangna [South Africa] reptile	Early Cretaceous (time very uncertain)	?	?	South Africa	Possibly a *Dryosaurus* relative.
Leaellynasaura [LAY-uh-LIN-uh-SAW-ruh]	Leaellyn [Rich]'s reptile	Early Cretaceous (118–110 MYA)	3 ft (90 cm)	Turkey	Australia	Large-eyed *Hypsilophodon*-like dinosaur.
Notohypsilophodon [NOT-oh-hip-sih-LOAF-oh-don]	southern *Hypsilophodon*	Late Cretaceous (99.6–93.5 MYA)	?	?	Argentina	One of relatively few South American ornithopods.
Orodromeus [OR-oh-DROH-mee-us]	mountain runner	Late Cretaceous (80–72.8 MYA)	8.2 ft (2.5 m)	Wolf	Montana, U.S.A.	Several individuals are known, although what were once thought to be *Orodromeus* nests and eggs are really from troodontids.
Othnielia [oth-NEE-lee-uh]	for [American paleontologist] Othniel [Charles Marsh]	Late Jurassic (155.7–150.8 MYA)	4.6 ft (1.4 m)	Turkey	Colorado, Utah, and Wyoming, U.S.A.	The most common small dinosaur from the Late Jurassic of North America.
Parksosaurus [PARK-soh-SAW-rus]	[Canadian paleontologist William Arthur] Park's reptile	Late Cretaceous (72.8–66.8 MYA)	8.2 ft (2.5 m)	Wolf	Alberta, Canada	A close relative of *Thescelosaurus*.
Phyllodon [FIL-oh-don]	leaf tooth	Late Jurassic (155.7–150.8 MYA)	4.6 ft (1.4 m)?	Turkey	Portugal	Known only from a partial jaw and teeth. Similar to *Drinker*.
Qantassaurus [KWAN-tuh-SAW-rus]	Qantas [Airways] reptile	Early Cretaceous (112–99.6 MYA)	4.6 ft (1.4 m)?	Turkey	Australia	Jawbones and teeth show some similarities to the rhabdodontids.
Siluosaurus [see-LOO-oh-SAW-rus]	Silk Road reptile	Early Cretaceous (130–125 MYA)	4.6 ft (1.4 m)?	Turkey	China	Known only from teeth.
Thescelosaurus [THES-kel-oh-SAW-rus]	wonder reptile	Late Cretaceous (66.8–65.5 MYA)	13.1 ft (4 m)?	Sheep	Colorado, Montana, South Dakota, and Wyoming, U.S.A.; Alberta and Saskatchewan, Canada	Known from some very complete skeletons, including one (nicknamed "Willo") that preserves soft tissues.
Yandusaurus [YAN-doo-SAW-rus]	Salt Capital reptile	Late Jurassic (161.2–155.7 MYA)	4.9 ft (1.5 m)	Turkey	China	Known from relatively complete, but not yet fully described, fossils.
Zephyrosaurus [ZEF-ih-roh-SAW-rus]	Zephyr [Greek god of the west wind] reptile	Early Cretaceous (118–110 MYA)	5.9 ft (1.8 m)	Beaver	Wyoming, U.S.A.	Known from a few partial skeletons and skulls.
No official genus name; formerly "*Hypsilophodon*" *wielandi*		Early Cretaceous (130–125 MYA)	5.9 ft (1.8 m)?	Beaver	South Dakota, U.S.A.	Fossils originally considered as being from a U.S. species of *Hypsilophodon*.

Primitive Iguanodontians—Early Advanced Beaked Dinosaurs (Chapter 31)

The iguanodontians were generally larger and more heavily built than more primitive ornithopods. They were among the most common plant-eating dinosaurs of the Early Cretaceous Epoch. The following genera are iguanodontians, but not members of Rhabdodontidae or Hadrosauroidea.

Name	Meaning	Age	Length	Weight	Where found	Comments
Altirhinus [AL-tih-RINE-us]	high nose	Early Cretaceous (120–112 MYA)	26.2 ft (8 m)	Rhino	Mongolia	A large, big-nosed iguanodontian, once considered as belonging to *Iguanodon* itself.
Bihariosaurus [bee-HAH-ree-oh-SAW-rus]	Bihor [Romania] reptile	Early Cretaceous (145.5–130 MYA)	9.8 ft (3 m)?	Sheep?	Romania	A *Camptosaurus*-like dinosaur.
Callovosaurus [kah-LOH-voh-SAW-rus]	Callovian [Age] reptile	Middle Jurassic (164.7–161.2 MYA)	?	Lion?	England	Known from an incomplete femur. At present, the oldest known iguanodontian.

Name	Meaning	Age	Length	Weight	Where found	Comments
Camptosaurus [KAMP-toh-SAW-rus]	flexible [back] reptile	Late Jurassic (155.7–150.8 MYA)	23 ft (7 m)	Rhino	Colorado, Oklahoma, Utah, and Wyoming, U.S.A.	Known from several good skeletons, from babies to large adults.
Craspedodon [kras-PEED-oh-don]	bordered tooth	Late Cretaceous (85.8–83.5 MYA)	?	?	Belgium	Known only from an *Iguanodon*-like tooth.
Cumnoria [kum-NOR-ee-uh]	from Cumnor [England]	Late Jurassic (150.8–145.5 MYA)	16.4 ft (5 m)	Lion	England	Sometimes considered a species of *Camptosaurus*.
Draconyx [drah-KON-icks]	dragon claw	Late Jurassic (152–148 MYA)	19.7 ft (6 m)	Horse	Portugal	Known from only a partial skeleton. Similar to *Camptosaurus*.
Dryosaurus [DRY-oh-SAW-rus]	tree reptile	Late Jurassic (155.7–150.8 MYA)	9.8 ft (3 m)	Sheep	Wyoming, Colorado, and Utah, U.S.A.; Tanzania	Some paleontologists consider the African species to be its own genus, "*Dysalotosaurus*."
Fukuisaurus [foo-KOO-ee-SAW-rus]	Fukui Prefecture [Japan] reptile	Early Cretaceous (136.4–125 MYA)	19.7 ft (6 m)	Rhino	Japan	An iguanodon with a relatively solid skull.
Iguanodon [ih-GWON-oh-don]	iguana tooth	Early Cretaceous (140.2–112 MYA)	42.7 ft (13 m)	Elephant	England; Belgium; France; Spain; Germany; possibly Portugal, Mongolia, and South Dakota, U.S.A.	One of the best-studied dinosaurs! Some of its various species may eventually be split into several other genera (possibly under the names "*Vectisaurus*" or "*Sphenospondylus*").
Jinzhousaurus [JIN-joh-SAW-rus]	Jinzhou [China] reptile	Early Cretaceous (125–121.6 MYA)	32.8 ft (10 m)	Rhino	China	Close to the ancestors of the hadrosauroids.
Lanzhousaurus [LAN-joh-SAW-rus]	Lanzhou [China] reptile	Early Cretaceous (130–100 MYA)	32.8 ft (10 m)	Rhino	China	Unlike most iguanodontians, had only a few enormous teeth (the biggest of any herbivorous dinosaur) rather than many small teeth.
Lurdusaurus [LOOR-doo-SAW-rus]	heavy reptile	Early Cretaceous (125–112 MYA)	29.5 ft (9 m)	Rhino	Niger	A squat, heavily built iguanodontian.
Muttaburrasaurus [muh-tuh-BUR-uh-SAW-rus]	Muttaburra [Australia] reptile	Early Cretaceous (112–99.6 MYA)	29.5 ft (9 m)	Rhino	Australia	A big-nosed iguanodontian with rather powerful jaws.
Ouranosaurus [oo-RAN-oh-SAW-rus]	brave reptile [also, monitor reptile]	Early Cretaceous (125–112 MYA)	19.7 ft (6 m)	Rhino	Niger	A fin-backed, slender iguanodontian.
Planicoxa [plan-ih-KOK-suh]	flat hip bone	Early Cretaceous (118–110 MYA)	?	?	Utah, U.S.A.	A wide-hipped iguanodontian.
Talenkauen [TAL-en-ka-OO-en]	small skull	Late Cretaceous (70.6–65.5 MYA)	13.1 ft (4 m)	Sheep	Argentina	Has some similarities with *Thescelosaurus,* but seems to be a primitive iguanodontian.
Tenontosaurus [teh-NON-toh-SAW-rus]	tendon reptile	Early Cretaceous (118–110 MYA)	23 ft (7 m)	Horse	Montana, Oklahoma, Texas, Utah, Wyoming, and possibly Maryland, U.S.A.	A well-known primitive iguanodontian with a particularly long and deep tail.
Valdosaurus [VAL-doh-SAW-rus]	reptile of the Wealden Group	Early Cretaceous (145.5–112 MYA)	9.8 ft (3 m)	Sheep	England; Romania; Niger	Very similar to *Dryosaurus*.
No official genus name; formerly "*Iguanodon*" *hoggi*		Early Cretaceous (145.5–140.2 MYA)	23 ft (7 m)?	Horse	England	Originally thought to be a new species of *Iguanodon,* but is more similar to (and possibly the same as) *Cumnoria* and/or *Camptosaurus*.
No official genus name; formerly "*Iguanodon*" *ottigeri*		Early Cretaceous (130–125 MYA)	23 ft (7 m)?	Horse	Utah	Not yet fully described. A tall-spined iguanodontian.

407

Rhabdodontids—Advanced European Beaked Dinosaurs (Chapter 31)

These were some of the more important medium-size plant-eaters of the end of the Age of Dinosaurs in Europe.

Name	Meaning	Age	Length	Weight	Where found	Comments
Mochlodon [MOK-loh-don]	barred tooth	Late Cretaceous (83.5–80 MYA)	14.8 ft (4.5 m)?	Lion?	Austria	Known from very incomplete material. May be the same dinosaur as *Rhabdodon* or *Zalmoxes*.
Rhabdodon [RAB-doh-don]	fluted tooth	Late Cretaceous (70.6–65.5 MYA)	14.8 ft (4.5 m)	Lion	France; Spain	One of the more common ornithopods of Late Cretaceous Europe.
Zalmoxes [zal-MOX-eez]	Zalmoxes [slave of Greek philosopher Pythagoras]	Late Cretaceous (70.6–68.5 MYA)	14.8 ft (4.5 m)	Lion	Romania	A deep-snouted ornithopod, originally thought to be some kind of ceratopsian.

Primitive Hadrosauroids—Early Duckbilled Dinosaurs (Chapter 32)

Hadrosauroidea—duckbilled dinosaurs—was one of the most successful of all plant-eating dinosaur groups. The following are hadrosauroids that are not part of the more specialized Hadrosauridae.

Name	Meaning	Age	Length	Weight	Where found	Comments
Bactrosaurus [BAK-troh-SAW-rus]	club[-spined] reptile	Late Cretaceous (99.6–85.8 MYA)	20 ft (6.1 m)	Rhino	Mongolia	Once considered a primitive lambeosaurine.
Eolambia [EE-oh-LAM-bee-uh]	dawn lambeosaurine	Early to Late Cretaceous (102–98 MYA)	20 ft (6.1 m)	Rhino	Utah, U.S.A.	Once thought to be the oldest lambeosaurine. May actually be a more primitive iguanodontian. Several skeletons are known.
Equijubus [EH-kwee-JOO-bus]	horse mane	Early to Late Cretaceous (102–98 MYA)	20 ft (6.1 m)	Rhino	China	Similar to *Altirhinus* (except without as deep a nose) and *Jinzhousaurus*.
Nanyangosaurus [nan-YAN-goh-SAW-rus]	Nanyang City [China] reptile	Early Cretaceous (112–99.6 MYA)	20 ft (6.1 m)	Rhino	China	Known from a skeleton lacking a skull. Very close to the ancestors of the true hadrosaurids.
Penelopognathus [peh-NEH-loh-poh-NAY-thus]	wild-duck jaws	Early Cretaceous (112–99.6 MYA)	20 ft (6.1 m)	Rhino	Mongolia	Known from long, slender jaws.
Probactrosaurus [proh-BAK-troh-SAW-rus]	before *Bactrosaurus*	Early Cretaceous (136.4–125 MYA)	11.5 ft (3.5 m)	Lion	China	A rather unspecialized early member of the hadrosauroid group.
Protohadros [PROH-toh-HAD-ros]	first hadrosaurid	Late Cretaceous (99.6–93.5 MYA)	23 ft (7 m)	Rhino	Texas, U.S.A.	A deep-chinned primitive hadrosauroid, nicknamed the "Jay Leno dinosaur" (after that TV host's big chin).
Shuangmiaosaurus [SHWANG-myow-SAW-rus]	Shuangmiao Village [China] reptile	Late Cretaceous (99.6–89.3 MYA)	?	?	China	Known from a skull. Very close to true hadrosaurids.
No official genus name; formerly *"Iguanodon" hilli*		Late Cretaceous (99.6–93.5 MYA)	?	?	England	Known only from an incomplete tooth.
No official genus name; formerly *"Trachodon" cantabrigiensis*		Early Cretaceous (112–99.6 MYA)	?	?	England	Known only from a tooth.

Primitive Hadrosaurids—Early Specialized Duckbilled Dinosaurs (Chapter 32)

These duckbills are part of the specialized group Hadrosauridae but are not members of the crested Lambeosaurinae or the broad-billed Hadrosaurinae.

Name	Meaning	Age	Length	Weight	Where found	Comments
Amtosaurus [AM-toh-SAW-rus]	Amtgay [Mongolia] reptile	Late Cretaceous (99.6–85.8 MYA)	?	?	Mongolia	Known only from part of a braincase. First thought to be an ankylosaurid!
Claosaurus [KLAY-oh-SAW-rus]	broken reptile	Late Cretaceous (87–82 MYA)	12.1 ft (3.7 m)	Lion	Kansas, U.S.A.	A primitive hadrosaurid known from a nearly complete skeleton. Unfortunately, the skull was missing when it was collected.

Name	Meaning	Age	Length	Weight	Where found	Comments
Gilmoreosaurus [GIL-mor-oh-SAW-rus]	[American paleontologist Charles Whitney] Gilmore's reptile	Late Cretaceous (99.6–85.8 MYA)	26.2 ft (8 m)	Rhino	China	An early slender hadrosaurid.
Hypsibema [HIP-suh-BEEM-uh]	high step	Late Cretaceous (83.5–70.6 MYA)	49.2 ft (15 m)?	Two elephant?	North Carolina, U.S.A.	A gigantic hadrosaurid; sadly, known only from a few isolated bones.
Mandschurosaurus [man-CHUR-oh-SAW-rus]	Manchuria [China] reptile	Late Cretaceous (70.6–68.5 MYA)	?	?	China; Russia	A large hadrosaurid from Asia; unfortunately, the skull is not yet known.
Parrosaurus [PAR-oh-SAW-rus]	[American zoologist Albert Eide] Parr's reptile	Late Cretaceous (70.6–68.5 MYA)	49.2 ft (15 m)?	Two elephant?	Missouri, U.S.A.	A gigantic hadrosaurid, known from tail bones and a partial jaw so big that they were originally thought to come from a sauropod.
Secernosaurus [see-SER-noh-SAW-rus]	separated reptile	Late Cretaceous (70.6–65.5 MYA)	9.8 ft (3 m)	Lion	Argentina	One of the few South American hadrosaurids.
Telmatosaurus [tel-MAT-oh-SAW-rus]	marsh reptile	Late Cretaceous (70.6–65.5 MYA)	16.4 ft (5 m)	Grizzly bear	Romania; France; Spain	A primitive hadrosaurid known from across Late Cretaceous Europe.

Lambeosaurines—Hollow-Crested Duckbilled Dinosaurs (Chapter 32)

Most of the species in Lambeosaurinae—one of the two major groups of Hadrosauridae—had a hollow crest formed by the nasal passages.

Name	Meaning	Age	Length	Weight	Where found	Comments
Amurosaurus [ah-MUR-oh-SAW-rus]	Amur River [Siberia] reptile	Late Cretaceous (66.8–65.5 MYA)	?	?	Russia	A late but primitive lambeosaurine. The shape of its crest isn't known.
Aralosaurus [ah-RAL-oh-SAW-rus]	Aral Sea reptile	Late Cretaceous (93.5–85.8 MYA)	26.2 ft (8 m)	Rhino	Kazakhstan	Once considered a Gryposaurus-like hadrosaurine, but now seems to be the most primitive lambeosaurine. Lacks a crest.
Barsboldia [bars-BOL-dee-uh]	for [Mongolian paleontologist Rinchen] Barsbold	Late Cretaceous (70.6–68.5 MYA)	32.8 ft (10 m)?	Rhino	Mongolia	Known only from the rear half of a skeleton.
Charonosaurus [kah-RON-oh-SAW-rus]	Charon's [Greek boatman of the River Styx] reptile	Late Cretaceous (66.8–65.5 MYA)	32.8 ft (10 m)	Rhino	Russia	A Parasaurolophus-like form (although the complete crest is not actually known).
Corythosaurus [koh-REETH-oh-SAW-rus]	helmet reptile	Late Cretaceous (80–72.8 MYA)	29.5 ft (9 m)	Rhino	Alberta, Canada	Known from many individual skeletons and skulls, including some with skin impressions.
Hypacrosaurus [hih-PAK-roh-SAW-rus]	near-topmost reptile	Late Cretaceous (80–66.8 MYA)	32.8 ft (10 m)	Rhino	Alberta, Canada; Montana, U.S.A.	Known from eggs and nests, juveniles through adults, and whole herds.
Jaxartosaurus [jak-SAR-toh-SAW-rus]	Jaxartes River [Kazakhstan] reptile	Late Cretaceous (93.5–83.5 MYA)	29.5 ft (9 m)	Rhino	Kazakhstan	Known from juvenile material.
Lambeosaurus [LAM-bee-oh-SAW-rus]	[Canadian paleontologist Lawrence Morris] Lambe's reptile	Late Cretaceous (80–72.8 MYA)	49.2 ft (15 m)	Two elephants	Alberta, Canada; Mexico?	The Mexican material (which has no skull, so we aren't certain if it is really from Lambeosaurus) is one of the largest ornithischian fossils.
Lophorhothon [LOAF-oh-ROH-thon]	crested nose	Late Cretaceous (83.5–70.6 MYA)	26.2 ft (8 m)	Rhino	Alabama and North Carolina, U.S.A.	Sometimes considered a Saurolophus-like hadrosaurine, but may even be a non-hadrosaurid hadrosauroid.
Nipponosaurus [NIP-on-oh-SAW-rus]	Japan reptile	Late Cretaceous (85.8–80 MYA)	26.2 ft (8 m)	Rhino	Russia (specifically Sakhalin Island, which was owned by Japan when Nipponosaurus was discovered and named)	A not-fully-grown specimen, very similar to North America's Hypacrosaurus.
Olorotitan [oh-LOR-oh-TY-tun]	giant swan	Late Cretaceous (66.8–65.5 MYA)	39.4 ft (12 m)	?	Russia	A giant Siberian lambeosaurian with a tube crest that flares out at the end.
Pararhabdodon [PAR-uh-RAB-doh-don]	near Rhabdodon	Late Cretaceous (70.6–65.5 MYA)	16.4 ft (5 m)	Horse	Spain; France?	Originally thought to be a rhabdodontid.

Name	Meaning	Age	Length	Weight	Where found	Comments
Parasaurolophus [PAR-uh-sawr-OH-loaf-us]	near *Saurolophus*	Late Cretaceous (80–72.8 MYA)	32.8 ft (10 m)	Rhino	New Mexico and Utah, U.S.A.; Alberta, Canada	Had a tube-shaped crest.
Tsintaosaurus [CHING-dow-SAW-rus]	Qingdao City [China] reptile	Late Cretaceous (70.6–68.5 MYA)	29.5 ft (9 m)	Rhino	China	Appears to have a narrow vertical crest; the rest of the skeleton is similar to *Parasaurolophus.*

Hadrosaurines—Broad-Snouted Duckbilled Dinosaurs (Chapter 32)

The Hadrosaurinae is one of the two major groups of hadrosaurids, or true duckbilled dinosaurs.

Name	Meaning	Age	Length	Weight	Where found	Comments
Anasazisaurus [an-uh-SAH-zee-SAW-rus]	Anasazi [Native American tribe] reptile	Late Cretaceous (80–72.8 MYA)	?	Rhino	New Mexico, U.S.A.	Known only from a partial skull. May be the same as *Kritosaurus.*
Anatotitan [ah-NAT-oh-TY-tun]	giant duck	Late Cretaceous (66.8–65.5 MYA)	39.4 ft (12 m)	Elephant	Montana, South Dakota, and Wyoming, U.S.A.	The most "duckbilled" of the duckbills. Considered by some to be the most advanced species of *Edmontosaurus.*
Brachylophosaurus [BRAK-ee-LOAF-oh-SAW-rus]	short-crested reptile	Late Cretaceous (80–72.8 MYA)	27.9 ft (8.5 m)	Rhino	Alberta, Canada; Montana, U.S.A.	Has a tall snout, but not as arched as that of *Gryposaurus.* A specimen called "Leonardo" is among the best preserved of all dinosaur fossils.
Edmontosaurus [ed-MON-toh-SAW-rus]	Edmonton [Formation] reptile	Late Cretaceous (70.6–65.5 MYA)	39.4 ft (12 m)	Elephant	Alberta and Saskatchewan, Canada; Montana, North Dakota, South Dakota, Colorado, and Wyoming, U.S.A.	Known from many good skulls and skeletons. Contains the species formerly called *"Anatosaurus."*
Gryposaurus [GRIP-oh-SAW-rus]	hook-nosed reptile	Late Cretaceous (83.5–72.8 MYA)	21.3 ft (6.5 m)	Rhino	Alberta, Canada; Montana, U.S.A.	A large-nosed hadrosaurine, similar to *Kritosaurus.*
Hadrosaurus [HAD-roh-SAW-rus]	heavy reptile	Late Cretaceous (83.5–80 MYA)	26.2 ft (8 m)?	Rhino	New Jersey, U.S.A.	The first-discovered duckbill, and the dinosaur skeleton that showed at least some dinosaurs walked on their hind legs. Not enough is known to actually show that it belongs in Hadrosaurinae!
Kerberosaurus [kur-BUR-oh-SAW-rus]	Cerberus [Greek three-headed watchdog of the underworld] reptile	Late Cretaceous (66.8–65.5 MYA)	26.2 ft (8 m)?	Rhino	Russia	Not much is known about it, but it seems to be a flat-nosed form.
Kritosaurus [KRIT-oh-SAW-rus]	separated reptile	Late Cretaceous (80–72.8 MYA)	29.5 ft (9 m)	Rhino	New Mexico, U.S.A.	Some paleontologists regard it as the same dinosaur as *Gryposaurus.*
Maiasaura [MY-uh-SAW-ruh]	good-mother reptile	Late Cretaceous (80–72.8 MYA)	29.5 ft (9 m)	Rhino	Montana, U.S.A.	Known from eggs, nests, embryos, hatchlings, and entire herds.
Naashoibitosaurus [nah-SHOY-bee-toh-SAW-rus]	Naashoibito Member [of the Kirtland Formation] reptile	Late Cretaceous (80–72.8 MYA)	29.5 ft (9 m)	Rhino	New Mexico, U.S.A.	Known only from a partial skull. May be the same as *Kritosaurus.*
Prosaurolophus [proh-SAW-roh-LOAF-us]	before *Saurolophus*	Late Cretaceous (80–72.8 MYA)	26.2 ft (8 m)	Rhino	Alberta, Canada; Montana, U.S.A.	Known from many skeletons of varying ages.
Saurolophus [SAW-roh-LOAF-us]	crested reptile	Late Cretaceous (72.8–66.8 MYA)	39.4 ft (12 m)	Elephant	Alberta, Canada; Mongolia	Known from many skeletons, including some with skin impressions. Common in both Mongolia and Canada. Has a broad snout and a solid spike pointing backward from its head.
Shantungosaurus [SHAN-dung-oh-SAW-rus]	Shandong Province [China] reptile	Late Cretaceous (70.6–68.5 MYA)	49.2 ft (15 m)?	Two elephants	China	The largest known ornithischian. (*Hypsibema* and *Parrosaurus,* both known only from a few bones, may rival it.)
Tanius [TAN-ee-us]	for [Chinese geologist Xi Zhou] Tan	Late Cretaceous (70.6–68.5 MYA)	26.2 ft (8 m)?	Rhino	China	Known only from fragmentary specimens; may actually be a lambeosaurine.

410

Name	Meaning	Age	Length	Weight	Where found	Comments
No official genus name; formerly *"Kritosaurus" australis*		Late Cretaceous (72.8–66.8 MYA)	26.2 ft (8 m)?	Rhino	Argentina	A *Kritosaurus*- or *Gryposaurus*-like hadrosaurine.
Not yet officially named		Late Cretaceous (72–70.6 MYA)	36 ft (11 m)	Elephant	Mexico	A large *Kritosaurus*-like hadrosaurine (possibly just a new species of *Kritosaurus*).

Pachycephalosaurs—Domeheaded Dinosaurs (Chapter 33)

The dinosaurs of Pachycephalosauria, one of the two main branches of the ridge-headed Marginocephalia, had thickened skulls.

Name	Meaning	Age	Length	Weight	Where found	Comments
Alaskacephale [uh-LAS-kuh-SEF-uh-lee]	Alaska head	Late Cretaceous (72–70.6 MYA)	?	?	Alaska, U.S.A.	Known only from a dome.
Colepiocephale [KOH-leh-pee-oh-SEF-uh-lee]	knuckle head	Late Cretaceous (80–72.8 MYA)	5.9 ft (1.8 m)	Wolf	Alberta, Canada	Once considered a species of *Stegoceras*.
Dracorex [DRAK-oh-rex]	dragon king	Late Cretaceous (66.8–65.5 MYA)	7.9 ft (2.4 m)	Wolf	South Dakota, U.S.A.	Possibly just a juvenile *Pachycephalosaurus* or *Stygimoloch*. Its full name, *D. hogwartsia,* honors the fictional Hogwarts Academy.
Goyocephale [GOH-yoh-SEF-uh-lee]	decorated head	Late Cretaceous (85.8–70.6 MYA)	5.9 ft (1.8 m)	Beaver	Mongolia	Known from a relatively complete skull and skeleton.
Gravitholus [GRAV-ih-THOL-us]	heavy dome	Late Cretaceous (80–72.8 MYA)	9.8 ft (3 m)?	Wolf?	Alberta, Canada	Known only from a dome.
Hanssuesia [han-SOO-see-uh]	for [Austrian-Canadian-American paleontologist] Hans-Dieter Sues	Late Cretaceous (80–72.8 MYA)	7.9 ft (2.4 m)	Wolf	Alberta, Canada; Montana, U.S.A.	Once considered a species of *Stegoceras*. Known from several skulls.
Homalocephale [HOM-uh-loh-SEF-uh-lee]	level head	Late Cretaceous (70.6–68.5 MYA)	5.9 ft (1.8 m)	Wolf	Mongolia	A flat-topped pachycephalosaur, known from a very good skeleton.
Micropachycephalosaurus [MIKE-roh-PAK-ee-SEF-uh-loh-SAW-rus]	small *Pachycephalosaurus*	Late Cretaceous (70.6–68.5 MYA)	1.6 ft (50 cm)	Turkey	China	Known only from an incomplete skull and pelvis, it may be a juvenile of some other Asian pachycephalosaur.
Ornatotholus [or-nay-toh-THOL-us]	decorated dome	Late Cretaceous (80–72.8 MYA)	6.6 ft (2 m)?	Wolf?	Alberta, Canada	Quite likely just a juvenile *Stegoceras*.
Pachycephalosaurus [PAK-ee-SEF-uh-loh-SAW-rus]	thickheaded reptile	Late Cretaceous (66.8–65.5 MYA)	23 ft (7 m)	Grizzly bear	Wyoming, Montana, and South Dakota, U.S.A.	The largest, and one of the last, pachycephalosaurs, with a very large dome and a long snout.
Peishansaurus [BAY-shan-SAW-rus]	North Mountain [China] reptile	Late Cretaceous (83.5–80 MYA)	?	?	China	Known only from a partial skull. Might actually be from a juvenile ankylosaur.
Prenocephale [PREN-oh-SEF-uh-lee]	sloping head	Late Cretaceous (70.6–68.5 MYA)	7.9 ft (2.4 m)	Wolf	Mongolia	Known from an excellent skull. Some paleontologists think that *Sphaerotholus* and *Tylocephale* are just species of *Prenocephale*.
Sphaerotholus [SFAY-roh-THOL-us]	sphere dome	Late Cretaceous (80–65.5 MYA)	7.9 ft (2.4 m)	Wolf	Montana and New Mexico, U.S.A.	A round-domed pachycephalosaur very similar to *Prenocephale*.
Stegoceras [steg-AH-ser-as]	roof horn	Late Cretaceous (80–72.8 MYA)	6.6 ft (2 m)	Wolf	Alberta, Canada	A relatively primitive round-domed pachycephalosaur.
Stenopelix [steh-NOP-eh-licks]	narrow pelvis	Early Cretaceous (130–125 MYA)	4.9 ft (1.5 m)	Beaver	Germany	Known from a skeleton lacking a skull. It is either an early European pachycephalosaur or some other kind of marginocephalian.
Stygimoloch [STIG-ee-MOH-lock]	demon of the Styx [river of the underworld in Greek mythology]	Late Cretaceous (66.8–65.5 MYA)	9.8 ft (3 m)	Lion	Montana and Wyoming, U.S.A.	A large, long-snouted pachycephalosaur, with large spikes at the rear of its head. A close relative of *Pachycephalosaurus*.
Tylocephale [TY-loh-SEF-uh-lee]	swelled head	Late Cretaceous (85.8–70.6 MYA)	7.9 ft (2.4 m)	Wolf	Mongolia	Known only from a partial skull, intermediate in form between the skulls of flat-tops like *Homalocephale* and those of round-tops like *Prenocephale*.

Name	Meaning	Age	Length	Weight	Where found	Comments
Wannanosaurus [WAN-an-oh-SAW-rus]	southern Anhui [China] reptile	Late Cretaceous (70.6–68.5 MYA)	2 ft (60 cm)	Turkey	China	Known only from an incomplete juvenile specimen.
No official genus name; formerly "*Troodon*" *bexelli*		Late Cretaceous (75–70.6 MYA)	?	?	China	An advanced pachycephalosaur from China.
Not yet officially named		Late Cretaceous (66.8–65.5 MYA)	7.9 ft (2.4 m)	Wolf	Montana and South Dakota, U.S.A.	Nearly complete skulls and skeletons of what might be two new close relatives of *Stygimoloch* and *Pachycephalosaurus,* or just juveniles of the same, have been found.
Not yet officially named		Late Cretaceous (80–72.8 MYA)	?	Chicken	Alberta, Canada	Not yet described. Known from small domes.

Psittacosaurids and Other Primitive Ceratopsians—Parrot Dinosaurs and Relatives (Chapter 34)

The earliest and most primitive members of Ceratopsia—the horned dinosaur group—including the parrot-faced Psittacosauridae.

Name	Meaning	Age	Length	Weight	Where found	Comments
Chaoyangsaurus [CHOW-yang-SAW-rus]	Chaoyang [China] reptile	Late Jurassic (150.8–145.5 MYA)	?	Turkey	China	Known from the skull and other parts of the front end of a dinosaur.
Hongshanosaurus [HONG-shan-oh-SAW-rus]	Hongshan [ancient Chinese culture] reptile	Early Cretaceous (128.2–125 MYA)	3.9 ft (1.2 m)?	Turkey	China	Known from juvenile and adult skulls. May actually be a species of *Psittacosaurus.*
Psittacosaurus [sih-TAK-oh-SAW-rus]	parrot reptile	Early Cretaceous (140.2–99.6 MYA)	5.9 ft (1.8 m)	Beaver	China; Mongolia; Thailand?	Several species are known, some of which may eventually get their own genera. Known from hatchlings to adults. One of the best-studied dinosaurs.
Yinlong [YIN-long]	hidden dragon	Late Jurassic (161.2–155.7 MYA)	9.8 ft (3 m)	Wolf	China	Known from many excellent skulls and skeletons.
No official genus name; formerly "*Psittacosaurus*" *sibiricus*		Early Cretaceous (136.4–99.6 MYA)	4.9 ft (1.5 m)?	Beaver	Russia	Not yet well described. Similar to *Psittacosaurus,* but apparently with small horns.

Primitive Neoceratopsians—Early Frilled Dinosaurs (Chapter 34)

The following are frilled dinosaurs, but they are not members of Leptoceratopsidae, Protoceratopsidae, or Ceratopsidae.

Name	Meaning	Age	Length	Weight	Where found	Comments
Archaeoceratops [AR-kee-oh-SER-uh-tops]	ancient horned face	Early Cretaceous (130–125 MYA)	4.9 ft (1.5 m)	Beaver	China	A bipedal, slender neoceratopsian.
Asiaceratops [AY-zhuh-SER-uh-tops]	Asia horned face	Early to Late Cretaceous (102–98 MYA)	5.9 ft (1.8 m)	Beaver	Uzbekistan	Uncertain if this is a primitive neoceratopsian or a true leptoceratopsid.
Auroraceratops [uh-ROH-ruh-SER-uh-tops]	dawn horned face	Early Cretaceous (140.2–99.6 MYA)	?	Wolf	China	A rather lumpy-faced primitive neoceratopsian.
Kulceratops [kool-SER-uh-tops]	lake horned face	Early Cretaceous (112–99.6 MYA)	?	?	Central Asia	Poorly described, and known only from jaw fragments. The describer didn't even clarify where in central Asia it was found!
Liaoceratops [lee-ow-SER-uh-tops]	Liaoning Province [China] horned face	Early Cretaceous (128.2–125 MYA)	?	Beaver	China	A small, frilled ceratopsian known from both adult and juvenile skulls.
Notoceratops [not-oh-SER-uh-tops]	southern ceratopsian	Late Cretaceous (70.6–68.5 MYA)	?	?	Argentina	Known from a jaw fragment that might actually be from a hadrosaurid.
Serendipaceratops [suh-ren-DIP-uh-SER-uh-tops]	Serendip [legendary name for Sri Lanka] horned face	Early Cretaceous (118–110 MYA)	?	Turkey?	Australia	Known only from a forearm bone; may not even be a ceratopsian.
Turanoceratops [too-RAN-oh-SER-uh-tops]	Turan [Persian for region of central Asia] horned face	Late Cretaceous (70.6–65.5 MYA)	?	?	Kazakhstan	Known from horn cores and double-rooted teeth, suggesting that it was a *Zuniceratops*-like dinosaur or even a true ceratopsid.
Zuniceratops [ZOO-nee-SER-uh-tops]	Zuni [Native American people] horned face	Late Cretaceous (93.5–89.3 MYA)	11.5 ft (3.5 m)	Grizzly bear	New Mexico, U.S.A.	Had brow horns but no nose horn.

Leptoceratopsids—Small-Frilled Dinosaurs (Chapter 34)

This is a group of neoceratopsians with relatively short frills.

Name	Meaning	Age	Length	Weight	Where found	Comments
Bainoceratops [BANE-oh-SER-uh-tops]	Bayn Dzak [site in Mongolia] horned face	Late Cretaceous (75–70.6 MYA)	?	Beaver	Mongolia	Its vertebrae show that it is more like *Udanoceratops* and *Leptoceratops* than like *Protoceratops*.
Graciliceratops [GRAS-il-ih-SER-uh-tops]	slender horned face	Late Cretaceous (99.6–83.5 MYA)	2 ft (60 cm)	Turkey	Mongolia	A slender, possibly bipedal dinosaur. Probably a juvenile.
Leptoceratops [LEP-toh-SER-uh-tops]	small horned face	Late Cretaceous (66.8–65.5 MYA)	5.9 ft (1.8 m)	Sheep	Alberta, Canada; Montana, U.S.A.	The last small ceratopsian in North America.
Montanoceratops [mon-TAN-oh-SER-uh-tops]	Montana horned face	Late Cretaceous (72.8–66.8 MYA)	9.8 ft (3 m)	Lion	Montana, U.S.A.	Once thought to have a horn on its nose, but that was a misplaced cheek horn.
Prenoceratops [PREN-oh-SER-uh-tops]	sloping horned face	Late Cretaceous (80–72.8 MYA)	9.8 ft (3 m)	Lion	Montana, U.S.A.	Known from a herd of mostly juveniles.
Udanoceratops [oo-DAN-oh-SER-uh-tops]	Udan Sayr [Mongolia] horned face	Late Cretaceous (85.8–70.6 MYA)	14.8 ft (4.5 m)	Grizzly bear	Mongolia	A large, possibly bipedal ceratopsian.

Protoceratopsids—Deep-Tailed Frilled Dinosaurs (Chapter 34)

Protoceratopsidae contains the four-legged Asian frilled dinosaurs with deep tails.

Name	Meaning	Age	Length	Weight	Where found	Comments
Bagaceratops [BAH-guh-SER-uh-tops]	little horned face	Late Cretaceous (85.8–70.6 MYA)	3 ft (90 cm)	Turkey	Mongolia	Many specimens, including embryos, are known. Had a small nose horn.
Breviceratops [BREH-vee-SER-uh-tops]	short horned face	Late Cretaceous (85.8–70.6 MYA)	6.6 ft (2 m)	Wolf	Mongolia	May be the same as *Bagaceratops*.
Lamaceratops [LAH-muh-SER-uh-tops]	monk horned face	Late Cretaceous (85.8–70.6 MYA)	?	Wolf	Mongolia	Similar to *Bagaceratops*, it had a small nose horn.
Magnirostris [MAG-nih-ROS-tris]	big snout	Late Cretaceous (75–70.6 MYA)	?	Wolf	China	Had a large beak and small horns.
Platyceratops [PLAH-tee-SER-uh-tops]	flat horned face	Late Cretaceous (85.8–70.6 MYA)	?	Wolf	Mongolia	Based on a single poorly preserved skull, quite likely just a specimen of *Bagaceratops*.
Protoceratops [PROH-toh-SER-uh-tops]	first horned face	Late Cretaceous (85.8–70.6 MYA)	6.6 ft (2 m)	Lion	Mongolia; China	Probably the most common dinosaur found in the Late Cretaceous of Asia. Known from eggs, embryos, hatchlings, juveniles, and adults.

Centrosaurines—Nose-Horned True Horned Dinosaurs (Chapter 35)

Ceratopsidae—true horned dinosaurs—contains two major branches. Centrosaurinae includes species with deep snouts and large nose horns.

Name	Meaning	Age	Length	Weight	Where found	Comments
Achelousaurus [ah-KAY-loo-uh-SAW-rus]	Achelous [Greek river god] reptile	Late Cretaceous (80–72.8 MYA)	19.7 ft (6 m)	Rhino	Montana, U.S.A.	A close relative of *Pachyrhinosaurus*, it also has a lumpy nose and brow.
Albertaceratops (al-BUR-tuh-SER-uh-tops)	Alberta [Canada] horned face	Late Cretaceous (80–72.8 MYA)	19.7 ft (6 m)	Rhino	Alberta, Canada; Montana, U.S.A.	Named in 2007, it is the first centrosaurine known with longer brow horns than nose horn.
Avaceratops [AY-vuh-SER-uh-tops]	[American fossil hunter] Ava [Cole]'s horned face	Late Cretaceous (80–72.8 MYA)	8.2 ft (2.5 m)	Grizzly bear	Montana, U.S.A.	First known from a juvenile specimen, but other fossils are now known. Some consider the fossils to be just from the juveniles of other centrosaurines. Others consider *Avaceratops* a unique species of centrosaurine. Still others think it might actually be the same dinosaur as *Ceratops*, and therefore a ceratopsine!

Name	Meaning	Age	Length	Weight	Where found	Comments
Centrosaurus [SEN-troh-SAW-rus]	spur [frill] reptile	Late Cretaceous (80–72.8 MYA)	18.7 ft (5.7 m)	Rhino	Alberta, Canada	Known from entire herds that died together, as well as nearly complete skeletons with skin impressions.
Einiosaurus [i-NEE-oh-SAW-rus]	bison reptile	Late Cretaceous (80–72.8 MYA)	19.7 ft (6 m)	Rhino	Montana, U.S.A.	A hook-horned centrosaurine.
Pachyrhinosaurus [PAK-ee-RINE-oh-SAW-rus]	thick-nosed reptile	Late Cretaceous (80–66.8 MYA)	26.2 ft (8 m)	Rhino	Alaska, U.S.A.; Alberta, Canada	Last, and largest, of the centrosaurines. Known from herds.
Styracosaurus [sty-RAK-oh-SAW-rus]	spike [frill] reptile	Late Cretaceous (80–72.8 MYA)	18 ft (5.5 m)	Rhino	Alberta, Canada; Montana, U.S.A.	Known from several good specimens. Distinctive because of the big spikes on its frill.

Ceratopsines—Brow-Horned True Horned Dinosaurs (Chapter 35)

One of the two branches of Ceratopsidae—true horned dinosaurs—Ceratopsinae contains species with typically large brow horns and shallow, long snouts.

Name	Meaning	Age	Length	Weight	Where found	Comments
Agujaceratops [ah-GOO-huh-SER-uh-tops]	Aguja [Formation] horned face	Late Cretaceous (80–72.8 MYA)	23 ft (7 m)	Rhino	Texas, U.S.A.	Once considered its own species of Chasmosaurus. Known from a herd.
Anchiceratops [AN-kee-SER-uh-tops]	intermediate [frill] horned face	Late Cretaceous (80–72.8 MYA)	19.7 ft (6 m)	Rhino	Alberta, Canada	A relatively unspecialized ceratopsine.
Arrhinoceratops [ah-RINE-oh-SER-uh-tops]	no-nose horned face	Late Cretaceous (72.8–66.8 MYA)	23 ft (7 m)	Rhino	Alberta, Canada	It actually does have a nose horn, despite its name.
Ceratops [SER-uh-tops]	horned face	Late Cretaceous (80–72.8 MYA)	8.2 ft (2.5 m)?	Grizzly bear?	Montana, U.S.A.	Poorly known, it apparently had relatively small brow horns.
Chasmosaurus [KAS-moh-SAW-rus]	wide-opening [frill] reptile	Late Cretaceous (80–72.8 MYA)	23 ft (7 m)	Rhino	Alberta, Canada	At least three species are known, with different patterns of size and orientation of horns.
Pentaceratops [PEN-tuh-SER-uh-tops]	five-horned face	Late Cretaceous (80–72.8 MYA)	26.2 ft (8 m)	Elephant	New Mexico, U.S.A.	A very large ceratopsine. The five horns are the brow horns, the nose horn, and two hornlike projections from the cheek. In fact, all ceratopsids (and many other ceratopsians) have these cheek horns!
Torosaurus [TOR-oh-SAW-rus]	perforated [frill] reptile [not bull reptile!]	Late Cretaceous (66.8–65.5 MYA)	24.9 ft (7.6 m)	Elephant	Wyoming, Montana, South Dakota, Utah, New Mexico, and Texas, U.S.A.; Saskatchewan, Canada	A large, and enormously frilled, ceratopsine.
Triceratops [try-SER-uh-tops]	three-horned face	Late Cretaceous (66.8–65.5 MYA)	29.5 ft (9 m)	Elephant	Colorado, Wyoming, Montana, North Dakota, and South Dakota, U.S.A.; Alberta and Saskatchewan, Canada	Probably the most common dinosaur at the end of the Cretaceous in western North America.
No official genus name; formerly "Diceratops" hatcheri		Late Cretaceous (66.8–65.5 MYA)	24.9 ft (7.6 m)?	Elephant	Wyoming, U.S.A.	Originally called "Diceratops," but an insect already had that name. Thought by some to be its own genus, by others to be a species of Triceratops, and by others to be just a not-fully-grown Triceratops.

GLOSSARY

This glossary gives definitions for many of the technical words in this book. Names of groups of living things are listed in the formal, Latin-based form; the version of these names in English form is shown in parentheses.

Abelisauridae [uh-BEL-uh-SAW-ruh-day] (**abelisaurid**): A group of short-armed ceratosaurs common in Gondwana during the Cretaceous Period.

adaptive radiation: That which occurs when a common ancestor produces many surviving descendant lineages with diverse adaptations in a geologically short period of time.

aetosaur [ay-EE-tuh-sawr]: Any of a group of armored herbivorous archosaurs common in the Triassic Period.

air sac: A part of the respiratory system of archosaurs used to move air, cool the body, and retain moisture.

Albertosaurinae [al-BUR-tuh-SAW-ruh-nay] (**albertosaurine**): The group of slender tyrannosaurids from the Late Cretaceous Epoch of western North America.

Allosauridae [AL-uh-SAW-ruh-day] (**allosaurid**): A group of large allosauroid carnosaurs common in the Late Jurassic Epoch.

Allosauroidea [AL-uh-suh-ROY-dee-uh] (**allosauroid**): A group of large carnosaurs characterized by a pair of ridges running along the edges of the skull. Allosauroidea is composed of Allosauridae, Carcharodontosauridae, and Sinraptoridae.

Alvarezsauridae [AL-vuh-rez-SAW-ruh-day] (**alvarezsaurid**): A group of bizarre-looking, large-thumbed coelurosaurs of the Cretaceous Period.

Amniota [AM-nee-OH-tuh] (**amniote**): A group of tetrapods capable of laying shelled eggs on land and their descendants. Amniotes include mammals, reptiles (including dinosaurs), and their closest extinct relatives.

Ankylosauria [AN-kuh-luh-SAW-ree-uh] (**ankylosaur**): A group of thyreophorans with heavy plate armor on the skull.

Ankylosauridae [AN-kuh-luh-SAW-ruh-day] (**ankylosaurid**): A group of club-tailed ankylosaurs of the Cretaceous Period.

Archosauria [AR-koh-SAW-ree-uh] (**archosaur**): A group of diapsids with an antorbital fenestra, including the dinosaurs. Crocodiles and birds are living archosaurs.

Aves [AY-veez] (**avian**): The group of avialians composed of modern-style birds. The only surviving members of Dinosauria.

Avialae [AY-vee-uh-lay] (**avialian**): The group of maniraptorans containing modern birds and their closest relatives.

body fossil: The remains of a living thing preserved in the rock record. Bones, teeth, shells, pollen, leaves, and wood are common types of body fossils.

Brachiosauridae [BRAA-kee-uh-SAW-ruh-day] (**brachiosaurid**): A group of long-armed macronarians common in the Late Jurassic and Early Cretaceous epochs.

Caenagnathidae [SUH-nag-NAY-thuh-day] (**caenagnathid**): A group of oviraptorosaurs possessing an arctometatarsus.

Carcharodontosauridae [kar-KAR-uh-don-tuh-SAW-ruh-day] (**carcharodontosaurid**): A group of extremely large allosauroid carnosaurs of the Cretaceous Period.

carnivore: An animal that eats meat.

Carnosauria [KAR-nuh-SAW-ree-uh] (**carnosaur**): A group of tetanurine theropods, often with large heads and short but powerful arms.

Cenozoic Era [SEN-uh-ZOH-ick EHR-uh]: The current era of the Phanerozoic Eon, from 65.5 million years ago to the present. Traditionally divided into the Tertiary and Quaternary periods, but now officially divided into the Paleogene and Neogene periods. Often called the "Age of Mammals."

Centrosaurinae [SEN-truh-SAW-ruh-nay] (**centrosaurine**): A group of ceratopsids characterized by short, deep snouts and a large nose horn.

Ceratopsia [SEH-ruh-TOP-see-uh] (**ceratopsian**): A group of marginocephalians possessing a rostral bone. Often called the "horned dinosaurs," although only the most advanced forms actually had horns.

Ceratopsidae [SEH-ruh-TOP-suh-day] (**ceratopsid**): A group of large neoceratopsians with horns over their eyes and nose and a dental battery. The true horned dinosaurs. Known only from the Late Cretaceous Epoch of western North America.

Ceratopsinae [SEH-ruh-TOP-suh-nay] (**ceratopsine**): The group of ceratopsids characterized by long, shallow snouts and large brow horns. Sometimes called "Chasmosaurinae."

Ceratosauria [SEH-ruh-tuh-SAW-ree-uh] (**ceratosaur**): The group of theropod dinosaurs with short fingers and specialized hip bones.

clade: A group composed of an ancestor and all of its

descendants, no matter how much they might differ in form from the ancestral condition.

cladistics: The system of classification developed by Willi Hennig. Cladistics uses the shared presence of specialized features to infer the pattern of common ancestry between living things.

cladogram: A branching diagram connecting groups of living things based on the shared presence of specialized features.

Coelophysoidea [SEE-luh-fy-SOY-dee-uh] (**coelophysoid**): A group of slender theropods with a kinked snout common in the early Mesozoic Era.

Coelurosauria [suh-LOOR-uh-SAW-ree-uh] (**coelurosaur**): A group of tetanurine theropods possessing a narrow hand, slender tail, and (at least in most groups) protofeathers. Coelurosaurs include compsognathids, tyrannosauroids, ornithomimosaurs, alvarezsaurids, and maniraptorans.

cold-blooded: Describing animals that get most of their heat from outside their bodies. Modern fish, amphibians, and reptiles (other than birds) are typically cold-blooded.

Compsognathidae [COMP-sog-NAY-thuh-day] (**compsognathid**): A group of small, primitive coelurosaurs of the Late Jurassic and Early Cretaceous epochs.

convergent evolution: That which occurs when two or more different groups independently evolve the same adaptations.

coprolite: A mass of fossilized dung.

Cretaceous Period [krih-TAY-shus PIR-ee-ud]: The third, and last, period of the Mesozoic Era, from 145.5 to 65.5 million years ago. The Cretaceous Period is divided into the Early Cretaceous and Late Cretaceous epochs.

Deinonychosauria [dy-NON-ih-kuh-SAW-ree-uh] (**deinonychosaur**): The group of maniraptoran coelurosaurs characterized by a sickle-shaped claw on the second toe. Nicknamed the "raptor dinosaurs."

dental battery: Many rows of teeth closely interlocked to form a single grinding, slicing, or gnawing surface, with new teeth ready to replace old ones that get worn away. Hadrosaurid ornithopods, ceratopsid marginocephalians, and rebbachisaurid sauropods all had dental batteries.

Diapsida [dy-AP-sih-duh] (**diapsid**): A group of reptiles characterized by a pair of jaw-muscle openings on each side of the skull. Diapsids include lizards, snakes, and their extinct relatives as well as archosauromorphs.

Dicraeosauridae [dy-KREE-uh-SAW-ruh-day] (**dicraeosaurid**): A group of short-necked diplodocoids from the Late Jurassic and Early Cretaceous epochs of Gondwana.

dicynodont [dy-SIN-uh-dont]: Any of a group of omnivorous and herbivorous synapsids from the Permian and Triassic periods.

Dinosauria [dy-nuh-SAW-ree-uh] (**dinosaur**): The group of dinosauromorph ornithodirans characterized by upright limbs, an open hip socket, and grasping hands. Dinosauria is composed of the most recent common ancestor of *Iguanodon* and *Megalosaurus* and all of its descendants.

Dinosauromorpha [dy-NUH-saw-ruh-MOR-fuh] (**dinosauromorph**): A group of ornithodirans with a fully upright stance and long legs. Comprises Dinosauria and its closest relatives.

Diplodocidae [DIP-luh-DAH-suh-day] (**diplodocid**): A group of giant diplodocoids with very long necks.

Diplodocoidea [dih-PLOD-uh-KOY-dee-uh] (**diplodocoid**): A group of neosauropods with pencil-shaped teeth, long skulls, and whip tails.

display: A structure or behavior animals use to "show off" to other animals. Might be used to attract mates or scare off predators, among many other things.

Dromaeosauridae [DROH-mee-uh-SAW-ruh-day] (**dromaeosaurid**): A group of long-armed predatory deinonychosaurs of the Cretaceous Period.

Dromaeosaurinae [DROH-mee-uh-SAW-ruh-nay] (**dromaeosaurine**): The group of heavily built dromaeosaurids of the Cretaceous Period of Laurasia.

Enantiornithes [uh-NAN-tee-OR-nuh-theez] (**enantiornithine**): A group of Cretaceous avialians.

eon: The largest division of the geologic time scale, composed of multiple eras. We and the dinosaurs are in the Phanerozoic Eon.

epoch: A smaller interval on the geologic time scale. Periods are divided into two or more epochs.

era: The second-largest division of the geologic time scale. Eras are divided into two or more periods.

evolution: Descent with modification, the observation that the lineages of living things change through time.

extinct: Describing a species or clade that has entirely died out.

fossil: The remains of a living thing or traces of its behavior preserved in the rock record.

gap: In geology, a section of geologic time that is not represented by rocks in a certain location because of erosion or because no rocks formed there during that time.

gastrolith: Gizzard stone, or rock swallowed by animals as ballast or to help with digestion.

genetic: Relating to information passed on by DNA from parent to offspring.

genus (genera): In taxonomy, a category of living things composed of one or more species. Genera have one-word names that are capitalized and italicized. *Triceratops, Tyrannosaurus,* and *Mei* are examples of dinosaur genera.

geologic time: The long span of Earth history.

geologic time scale: The formal division of geologic time into eons, eras, periods, epochs, and other units.

geology: The study of the Earth, its structure, and its history.

Gondwana: A supercontinent composed of modern-day South America, Africa, Madagascar, India, Antarctica, Australia, and various smaller landmasses. Gondwana began to break up during the Cretaceous Period.

Hadrosauridae [HAD-ruh-SAW-ruh-day] **(hadrosaurid):** A group of hadrosauroids with a dental battery and lacking a thumb. One of the most common groups of Late Cretaceous dinosaurs, especially in Laurasia.

Hadrosaurinae [HAD-ruh-SAW-ruh-nay] **(hadrosaurine):** The group of broad-billed hadrosaurids.

Hadrosauroidea [HAD-ruh-saw-ROY-dee-uh] **(hadrosauroid):** A group of iguanodontian ornithopods with an expanded front of the snout that were common in the Cretaceous Period. Nicknamed the "duckbilled dinosaurs."

herbivore: An animal that eats plants.

Herrerasauridae [huh-REAH-ruh-SAW-ruh-day] **(herrerasaurid):** A group of primitive carnivorous saurischians of the Triassic Period. Some paleontologists consider herrerasaurids to be theropods.

Hesperornithes [heh-spuh-ROR-nuh-theez] **(hesperornithine):** A group of swimming toothed avialians of the Cretaceous Period. At least some hesperornithines were flightless.

Heterodontosauridae [HEH-tuh-ruh-DON-tuh-SAW-ruh-day] **(heterodontosaurid):** A group of primitive ornithischians with strong, thick skulls. Once thought to be primitive ornithopods or close relatives to the marginocephalians.

hypothesis (hypotheses): A possible answer to a question about a pattern observed in nature. Science is the process of testing hypotheses.

Hypsilophodontia [hip-sih-LOF-uh-DON-chuh]: A name formerly used for ornithopods other than heterodontosaurids and iguanodontians. However, "hypsilophodonts" are probably not a clade, and so this name isn't used anymore under the rules of cladistics.

Iguanodontia [ih-GWAH-nuh-DON-chuh] **(iguanodontian):** A group of advanced ornithopod dinosaurs characterized by a toothless premaxilla.

index fossil: The fossil of a particular species used to determine if two strata at different locations are from the same age.

Jurassic Period [juh-RASS-ick PIR-ee-ud]: The second, and middle, period of the Mesozoic Era, from 199.6 to 145.5 million years ago. The Jurassic Period is divided into the Early Jurassic, Middle Jurassic, and Late Jurassic epochs.

keratin: The naturally occurring hard material of which fingernails, hair, claws, horn coverings, and so forth are made.

K/T boundary: The time boundary 65.5 million years ago between the Cretaceous Period (the symbol *K* in geology) of the Mesozoic Era and the Paleogene Period of the Cenozoic Era. Older geologic time scales used the Tertiary Period (the symbol *T* in geology) rather than the Paleogene. Marked by the K/T mass extinction.

K/T mass extinction: The event 65.5 million years ago that saw the end of the Age of Dinosaurs and the disappearance of many types of other animals and plants.

Lambeosaurinae [LAM-bee-uh-SAW-ruh-nay] **(lambeosaurine):** The group of hollow-crested hadrosaurids.

Laurasia: A supercontinent composed of present-day North America, Europe, and most of modern Asia (but not India).

Leptoceratopsidae [LEP-tuh-SEH-ruh-TOP-suh-day] **(leptoceratopsid):** A group of small neoceratopsians of the Late Cretaceous of Asia and western North America.

lumper: A scientist who thinks there is a wide range of variation found in any given species or genus. The opposite of a "splitter."

Macronaria [MAK-ruh-NEAR-ee-uh] **(macronarian):** A group of neosauropods characterized by greatly enlarged nares.

Mammalia [muh-MAYL-ee-uh] **(mammal):** A group of advanced synapsids that have a body covering of fur or hair and produce milk. Living mammals include the placentals, marsupials, and monotremes. Multituberculates are one example of the various extinct mammal groups.

Maniraptora [man-uh-RAP-tor-uh] **(maniraptoran):** A group of coelurosaurs characterized by long arms with a semilunate carpal and true feathers on at least the arms and tail.

Marginocephalia [mar-JIN-uh-suh-FAA-lee-uh] **(marginocephalian):** A group of ornithischian dinosaurs characterized by an extension of the back of the skull.

Marginocephalia includes Ceratopsia and Pachy-cephalosauria.

mass extinction: Events in Earth history when many distantly related groups disappear in a geologically short period of time.

Megalosauridae [MEG-uh-luh-SAW-ruh-day] (**megalosaurid**): A group of primitive spinosauroid theropods from the Middle Jurassic to Early Cretaceous epochs.

Mesozoic Era [MES-uh-ZOH-ick EHR-uh]: The middle era of the Phanerozoic Eon, from 251 to 65.5 million years ago. Divided into the Triassic, Jurassic, and Cretaceous periods. Often called the "Age of Reptiles" or "Age of Dinosaurs."

Microraptorinae [MY-kroh-rap-TOR-uh-nay] (**microraptorine**): The group of small-bodied dromaeosaurids known best from the Early Cretaceous of China. Microraptorines (and possibly other dromaeosaurids) had long feathers on both their arms and their legs.

mitochondrion [MY-toh-KON-dree-un] (**mitochondria**): A tiny structure within the cells of living things, which combines nutrients and oxygen to release heat.

Mononykinae [muh-NON-uh-KIH-nay] (**mononykine**): The group of alvarezsaurids characterized by an arctometatarsus.

multituberculate [MUL-tee-too-BUR-kyoo-lit]: Any of a group of extinct primitive mammals with highly specialized teeth. Multituberculates were common in the later Mesozoic Era, survived the K/T extinction event, but died out in the early Cenozoic Era.

natural selection: The primary way that evolution works whereby differences in individuals mean that some have a better chance of surviving and passing on those differences to the next generation.

Neoceratopsia [NEE-uh-SEH-ruh-TOP-see-uh] (**neoceratopsian**): A group of ceratopsians characterized by a frill.

Neogene Period [NEE-uh-jeen PIR-ee-ud]: The second, and current, period of the Cenozoic Era, from 23 million years ago to today.

Neosauropoda [NEE-uh-saw-RAH-puh-duh] (**neosauropod**) [NEE-uh-SAW-ruh-POD]: The group of advanced sauropods characterized by nares placed high on the skull and teeth concentrated at the front of their mouths.

Noasauridae [NOH-uh-SAW-ruh-day] (**noasaurid**): A group of slender-legged ceratosaurs.

Nodosauridae [NOH-duh-SAW-ruh-day] (**nodosaurid**): A group of ankylosaurs characterized by large shoulder spines.

omnivore: An animal that eats both meat and plants, such as humans and bears.

Ornithischia [or-nuh-THIS-kee-uh] (**ornithischian**): The group of "bird-hipped" dinosaurs, characterized by a predentary bone. *Iguanodon* and all dinosaurs more closely related to it than to *Megalosaurus*. Major groups of ornithischians include thyreophorans, marginocephalians, and ornithopods. (Note: birds are *not* ornithischians, but are instead saurischians.)

Ornithodira [or-nuh-THAH-duh-ruh] (**ornithodiran**): A group of archosaurs characterized by a birdlike neck and simple ankle joint. Ornithodirans include dinosaurs, pterosaurs (probably), and their closest relatives.

Ornithomimidae [or-NIH-thuh-MY-muh-day] (**ornithomimid**): A group of advanced toothless ornithomimosaurs.

Ornithomimosauria [or-NIH-thuh-MY-muh-SAW-ree-uh] (**ornithomimosaur**): The "ostrich dinosaurs," a group of long-limbed coelurosaurs.

Ornithopoda [or-nuh-THAH-puh-duh] (**ornithopod**) [or-NIH-thuh-POD]: A group of beaked ornithischians.

osteoderm: An armor plate made of bone.

Oviraptoridae [OH-vuh-rap-TOR-uh-day] (**oviraptorid**): A group of advanced toothless oviraptorosaurs. Many had elaborate crests.

Oviraptorosauria [OH-vuh-RAP-tor-uh-SAW-ree-uh] (**oviraptorosaur**): The "egg-thief" dinosaurs. A group of omnivorous and herbivorous maniraptorans with short skulls.

Pachycephalosauria [PAK-ee-SEF-uh-luh-SAW-ree-uh] (**pachycephalosaur**): A group of marginocephalians characterized by thickened skulls. Known only from the Cretaceous Period. The "boneheaded," "domeheaded," or "head-banger" dinosaurs.

paleoenvironment: The conditions that existed in a given location when a particular rock was being formed. The paleoenvironment might have been very different from the modern environment at that same spot.

Paleogene Period [PAY-lee-uh-jeen PIR-ee-ud]: The first period of the Cenozoic Era, from 65.5 to 23 million years ago.

paleontology: The study of ancient living things preserved as fossils.

Paleozoic Era [PAY-lee-uh-ZOH-ick EHR-uh]: The oldest era of the Phanerozoic Eon, from 542 to 251 million years ago. The last period of the Paleozoic Era is the Permian Period.

period: The third-largest division of the geologic time scale. Periods are divided into two or more epochs.

Permian Period [PER-mee-un PIR-ee-ud]: The last

period of the Paleozoic Era, from 299 to 251 million years ago.

Permo-Triassic mass extinction: The event 251 million years ago, between the Permian Period of the Paleozoic Era and the Triassic Period of the Mesozoic Era, that saw the largest loss of species in Earth history.

Phanerozoic Eon [FAN-uh-ruh-ZOH-ick EE-on]: The current eon of Earth history, composed of the Paleozoic, Mesozoic, and Cenozoic eras.

phylogeny: A family tree of organisms.

physiology: The functioning of living things and their various parts.

plate: In geology, any of the dozens of enormous upper sections of the Earth, including the crust. In dinosaur paleontology, any of the broad osteoderms on the back of a stegosaur.

Polacanthidae [POLE-uh-KAN-thuh-day] (**polacanthid**): A group of primitive ankylosaurs. Some cladistic studies suggest that "polacanthids" are simply the early members of Ankylosauridae and Nodosauridae and not their own group at all.

primitive: Similar to the ancestral state.

prosauropod [proh-SAW-ruh-POD]: Any sauropodomorph that is not a true sauropod.

Prosauropoda [proh-saw-RAH-puh-duh]: According to some cladistic studies, the group of primitive sauropodomorphs. However, other studies suggest that the prosauropods do not form their own clade, and therefore there wouldn't be a distinct group called "Prosauropoda."

Protoceratopsidae [PROH-toh-SEH-ruh-TOP-suh-day] (**protoceratopsid**): A group of large-frilled neoceratopsians.

protofeather: A fluffy structure in the integument of many types of coelurosaurs. The ancestral structure that evolved into true feathers among the maniraptorans.

protomammal: Any synapsid that is not a mammal.

Psittacosauridae [sih-TAK-uh-SAW-ruh-day] (**psittacosaurid**): A group of primitive ceratopsians. The "parrot dinosaurs."

pterodactyl: Another name for a pterodactyloid.

Pterodactyloidea [TEHR-uh-dak-tih-LOYD-ee-uh] (**pterodactyloid**): A group of advanced pterosaurs, often with short tails and crests on their heads.

Pterosauria [TEHR-uh-SAW-ree-uh] (**pterosaur**): A group of diapsid reptiles (probably ornithodirans) characterized by a forelimb that evolved into a wing. The "flying reptiles" of the Mesozoic Era. Pterosaurs are *not* birds, nor are they any other sort of dinosaur.

Quaternary Period [kwah-TUR-nuh-ree PIR-ee-ud]: In older geologic time scales, the second, and current,

period of the Cenozoic Era, from 1.806 million years ago to the present.

raptor: An informal term used both for deinonychosaurian maniraptorans and for birds of prey.

Rebbachisauridae [ruh-BASH-ih-SAW-ruh-day] (**rebbachisaurid**): A group of wide-mouthed, short-necked diplodocoids with a dental battery at the front of the mouth.

Reptilia [rep-TIL-ee-uh] (**reptile**): A group of amniotes characterized by specialized color vision, water-conserving kidneys, and various other features. Reptiles include Anapsida and Diapsida. Living reptiles include turtles, lizards, snakes, the tuatara, crocodilians, and birds.

Rhabdodontidae [RAB-duh-DON-tuh-day] (**rhabdodontid**): A group of primitive iguanodontians from the Late Cretaceous Epoch of Europe.

Saltasauridae [SAWL-tuh-SAW-ruh-day] (**saltasaurid**): A group of advanced wide-mouthed titanosaurs from the Late Cretaceous Epoch.

Saurischia [saw-RIS-kee-uh] (**saurischian**): The group of "lizard-hipped" dinosaurs, characterized by a long neck and hollow vertebrae. *Megalosaurus* and all dinosaurs more closely related to it than to *Iguanodon*. Major groups of saurischians include herrerasaurids, sauropodomorphs, and theropods (including birds).

Sauropoda [saw-RAH-puh-duh] (**sauropod**) [SAW-ruh-POD]: The group of enormous, quadrupedal, advanced sauropodomorphs.

Sauropodomorpha [saw-RAH-puh-duh-MOR-fuh] (**sauropodomorph**): The group of long-necked, small-headed, plant-eating saurischians.

sexual selection: Evolution by the favoring of those variations that members of the opposite sex find the most attractive.

Sinraptoridae [sine-RAP-tor-uh-day] (**sinraptorid**): A group of primitive allosauroids of the Jurassic Period of Asia.

specialization: A structure or behavior modified from the ancestral condition so that it works better for some particular function or set of functions.

species: In taxonomy, the smallest category of living things normally recognized. Each species belongs to one, but only one, genus. Species have two-word names, the first part of which is the capitalized generic name, and the second of which is the lowercase specific name. Species names are italicized. *Triceratops horridus, Tyrannosaurus rex,* and *Mei long* are examples of dinosaur species.

Spinosauridae [SPY-nuh-SAW-ruh-day] (**spinosaurid**): A group of giant, advanced, long-snouted, conical-toothed spinosauroids of the Cretaceous Period.

Spinosauroidea [SPY-nuh-suh-ROY-dee-uh] (**spinosauroid**): A group of long-snouted tetanurines. Spinosauroidea includes Megalosauridae and Spinosauridae.

splitter: A scientist who thinks there is only a narrow range of variation found in any given species or genus. The opposite of a "lumper."

Stegosauria [STEG-uh-SAW-ree-uh] (**stegosaur**): The group of plated dinosaurs, characterized by paired plates and spikes on their backs and a thagomizer at the end of their tails.

Synapsida [sih-NAP-sih-duh] (**synapsid**): A group of amniotes characterized by a large jaw-muscle opening in the back of the skull.

taxonomy: The rules and procedures for giving names to groups of living things.

Tertiary Period [TUR-shee-eh-ree PIR-ee-ud]: In old-fashioned geologic time scales, the first period of the Cenozoic Era, from 65.5 to 1.806 million years ago.

Tetanurae [TET-uh-NOR-ee] (**tetanurine**): A group of theropod dinosaurs characterized by large hands and a stiff tail. Spinosauroidea, Carnosauria, and Coelurosauria are the major groups in Tetanurae.

thagomizer: The pairs of sideways-facing tail spikes of stegosaurs.

Therizinosauridae [THER-uh-ZEE-nuh-SAW-ruh-day] (**therizinosaurid**): A group of advanced therizinosauroids.

Therizinosauroidea [THER-uh-ZEE-nuh-suh-ROY-dee-uh] (**therizinosauroid**): The "sloth dinosaurs," a group of herbivorous, small-headed, large-clawed maniraptorans.

Theropoda [thuh-RAH-puh-duh] (**theropod**) [THER-uh-POD]: The bipedal saurischians characterized by a three-toed foot and a furcula. Commonly called the "carnivorous dinosaurs," Coelophysoidea, Ceratosauria, and Tetanurae are the major groups of Theropoda.

Thyreophora [THY-ree-OH-foor-uh] (**thyreophoran**): The armored dinosaurs, a group of ornithischians characterized by osteoderms. Thyreophora includes Ankylosauria, Stegosauria, and their primitive relatives.

Titanosauria [ty-TAN-uh-SAW-ree-uh] (**titanosaur**): The group of macronarian sauropods characterized by wide hips. Includes the largest known dinosaurs.

trace fossil: Evidence of the behavior of an animal—such as trackways, nests, coprolites, or burrows—preserved in the rock record.

trackway: A series of fossil footprints.

Triassic Period [try-ASS-ick PIR-ee-ud]: The first period of the Mesozoic Era, from 251 to 199.6 million years ago. The Triassic Period is divided into the Early Triassic, Middle Triassic, and Late Triassic epochs.

type specimen: The individual fossil or modern organism to which a particular species name was first given.

Tyrannosauridae [ty-RAN-uh-SAW-ruh-day] (**tyrannosaurid**): A group of advanced two-fingered tyrannosauroids, also characterized by thick teeth and the arctometatarsus. Known only from the Late Cretaceous of Asia and North America. Tyrannosauridae includes Albertosaurinae and Tyrannosaurinae. My favorite dinosaurs!

Tyrannosaurinae [ty-RAN-uh-SAW-ruh-nay] (**tyrannosaurine**): The group of heavily built tyrannosaurids from the Late Cretaceous of Asia and western North America.

Tyrannosauroidea [ty-RAN-uh-suh-ROY-dee-uh] (**tyrannosauroid**): The "tyrant dinosaurs," a group of coelurosaurs characterized by scraping front teeth. Includes the Tyrannosauridae and its primitive relatives.

Unenlagiinae [oon-en-LOG-uh-nay] (**unenlagiine**): The group of long-snouted dromaeosaurids from the Cretaceous Period of Gondwana.

Velociraptorinae [vuh-LAH-suh-rap-TOR-uh-nay] (**velociraptorine**): The group of slender dromaeosaurids of the Cretaceous Period of Laurasia.

Vertebrata [VUR-tuh-BRAH-tuh] (**vertebrate**) [VUR-tuh-BRATE]: The group of animals with individual back bones.

warm-blooded: Describing animals that get most of their heat from inside their bodies. Modern mammals and birds, and also some fish, are typically warm-blooded.

Italic page numbers refer to illustrations.

abelisaurids, 83–85, *83, 84, 85,* 87, 105, 263, 353, 370–71
Achelousaurus, 287, 288
Acrocanthosaurus, 102, 104, 207
adaptive radiation, 328, 363
aetosaurs, *63,* 64, 178, 223, 332
Agilisaurus, 215, 246
Agustinia, 209, *209*
Alamosaurus, 207, 210
Albertaceratops, 287
albertosaurines, 377
Albertosaurus, 106, 124, 125, 128, *310*
Alectrosaurus, 124
allosaurids, 374
allosauroids, 3, 100–1, 103–4
Allosaurus
    ankylosaurs and, 240
    as carnosaur, 99
    characteristics of, 100, 101
    Diplodocus and, 193
    discovery of, 9
    eating habits of, 107
    hands of, 79
    illustrations of, *98, 101, 104, 107, 334*
    scaly skin of, 115
    size of, 81
    skeletons of, *100,* 103
    specimens of, 103–4
    Stegosaurus and, 231
Altirhinus, 252, 257
Alvarez, Luis, 360–61
Alvarez, Walter, 360–61
alvarezsaurids
    in Cretaceous Period, 353
    discovery of, 2
    features of, 131, 137–38, *138*
    genus list, 378–79
    as maniraptorans, 153
    mononykines, 136–37
Alvarezsaurus, 137
Amargasaurus, 93, *190, 196,* 197, 198
Amazonsaurus, 195, 199
ammonoids, 337, 349, 357, 358, 363
Anatotitan, 47, *47, 121,* 261
Anchiceratops, 287, 288
Andrews, Roy Chapman, 10, *10,* 142
angiosperms, 345–47, 359–60
animal cell, *313*
ankylosaurids
    in Cretaceous Period, 353
    features of, 237–38
    genus list, 404–5
    noses of, 239
    tail of, 187, 237, 241
ankylosaurs
    ankylosaurids, 187, 237–38, 239, 241, 353, 404–5
    armor of, 231, 235, 240–41
    cladograms of, 239
    in Cretaceous Period, 351, 353
    eating habits of, 232, 236, 253
    features of, 235–36

genus list, 403
habitat of, 240
illustration of, *344*
in Jurassic Period, 340
nodosaurids, 237, 238, 239
pachycephalosaurs
    compared to, 273
as prey of tyrannosaurids, 214, 241
Ankylosaurus, 235, 237, 238, *241*
Antarctosaurus, 104, 203, 210
Antetonitrus, 186, 187
Apatosaurus
    "Brontosaurus" as type of, *44,* 195–96
    discovery of, 185
    growth and development of, 2, 298, 301
    illustrations of, *190, 334, 341, 342*
    size of, 196–97, 205
    species of, 42
Appalachiosaurus, 124
Archaeoceratops, 279, 280
Archaeopteryx
    as avialian, 164, 167
    brain of, *319,* 320
    comparative anatomy and, 47
    Deinonychus compared to, 11, 152
    discovery of, 10
    in Europe, 355
    evolution and, *48,* 49
    feathers and, *164,* 167
    features of, 167–68, 172
    illustration of, *162*
    nesting behavior of, 296
    Rahonavis compared to, 156, 161
    skeleton of, 11, *164,* 167, 168
Archelon, 349, 350
archosaurs
    breathing of, 317
    of Jurassic Period, 335
    of Triassic Period, 326–28, 329, 330–31, 333
    types of, 64, 307
Argentinosaurus, 104, *105,* 106, 195, 203, 207, 209–10, 354
Aristosuchus, 111
Asaro, Frank, 360
asteroid impact, 11, 126, 229, 247, 360–61, *360,* 363
Astrodon, 211
Atlantic Ocean, 332
Aucasaurus, 83, 87
avialians
    avians, 166–67, 170, 389–90
    birds as, 163–64
    early avialians, 167–68
    enantiornithines, 168–69
    feathers and, 115
    genus list, 385–86, 388–89
    as maniraptorans, 153
    seabirds of Cretaceous, 169–70
avians. *See also* birds
    features of, 166–67, 170
    genus list, 389–90
    illustrations of, *358*
Avimimus, 143, 147, 148

Bactrosaurus, 260, 261
Bakker, Robert T., 11, 62, 113–14, 192, 314, *314,* 317, 343, *343*
Bambiraptor, 156, 158
Barrett, Paul, 92, 191, 236
Baryonyx, 93, 94, 95, 97, 122, *347*
Baryonyx walkeri, 94, 97
behavior of dinosaurs. *See also* nesting behavior
    comparison with modern animals, 305–7
    dinosaur science and, 11, 12
    models of, 307
    physical evidence of, 304–5
    study of, 303
    walking and running, 308
Beipiaosaurus, 148, *165*
belemnoids, 337, 349, 357, 358
bennettitaleans, 345
Benton, Michael J., 176
bird-hipped dinosaurs. *See* ornithischians
birds. *See also* avians
    air sacs of, 79–80, 186, 317
    as avialians, 163–64
    behavior and, 306–7
    brain of, 320
    circulatory system of, 318
    cladistics and, 55
    coelurosaurs and, 7, 166
    deinonychosaurs as close relatives of, 144, 149, 152, 161, 166
    dinosaurs as ancestors of, 11, 36, 37, 79–80, 86, 152
    eggs of, 293
    feathers and, 157, 165, 173
    origin of flight in, 173
    oviraptorosaurs and, 143–44
    specialized traits of, 164–66
    survival of extinction, 363
    as type of dinosaur, 163, 170, 213, 306, 311, 313, 357
    and wing-assisted incline running, 153
Bonaparte, José, 62, 137, 176, 215
bone beds, 259, 289
bone slices, microscopic study of, 129, 300, *300,* 301, 321, *321*
Bonitasaura, 207
brachiosaurids
    in Cretaceous Period, 351, 352
    genus list, 397–98
    illustration of, *347*
    as macronarians, 203, 205–7
    titanosaurs and, 210
Brachiosaurus
    illustration of, *202, 206*
    as macronarian, 197
    neck of, 205–6
    nose of, 16, 203

size of, 189, 205
skeleton of, 205, *205,* 207
Brachylophosaurus, 261
Brachytrachelopan, 197, *197*
bradymetabolic, 312
Brainerd, Elizabeth, 317
Breislak, Scipione, 112
Brett-Surman, Michael, 144, 267, *267*
"Brontosaurus," as type of *Apatosaurus, 44,* 195
brooding. *See also* nesting behavior
    of deinonychosaurs, 153, 161
    of maniraptorans, 115, 141, 148, 153, 295
Brown, Barnum, 106, 118, 119
Buchholtz, Emily, 228
Buckland, William, 7, 92, 304
Buitreraptor, 155, *155*

caenagnathids, 143, 380
Calvo, Jorge, 191
Camarasaurus
    illustrations of, *193, 339*
    in Jurassic Period, 197
    nose of, 203
    skeleton of, 185, *204,* 205
Camptosaurus, 250, 253, 254–55, 256
carcharodontosaurids, 101, 104, 374
Carcharodontosaurus, 92, *103,* 104, 106
carnosaurs
    allosauroids, 100–101, 103–4
    carcharodontosaurids, 101, 104
    coelurosaurs compared to, 99–100
    in Cretaceous Period, 351, 352
    genus list, 373
    in Jurassic Period, 336, 340
    primitive carnosaurs, 100
    sauropods as prey of, 102, 104–5, 107
    scaly skin of, 115
    young of, 297
Carnotaurus, 83, *83,* 84, *84,* 87, 115
Carpenter, Ken, 125, 193, 230
Carr, Thomas D., 128, *128*
Carrano, Matthew T., 208, 308, *308*
Carrier, Richard, 317
caruncle (egg tooth), 296
CAT scans, 11, *11,* 12
Caudipteryx
    feathers of, 37, 115, *143,* 148
    features of, 143, 147
    illustration of, *140, 297*
    size of, 154
cementation, 15
Cenozoic Era, 25, 357, *364*
centrosaurines, *286,* 287, 413–14
Centrosaurus, 286, *286,* 287, 288
ceratopsians
    cladogram of, 55, *55*
    discovery of, 214
    frills and, 277, 280–81, 285

habitat of, 281
leptoceratopsids, 280
as marginocephalians, 273
neoceratopsians, 279–82,
285, 286, 353, 412
primitive ceratopsians,
277–83
protoceratopsids, 280, 413
psittacosaurids, 278–79,
285, 412
teeth of, 253, 267
ceratopsids
centrosaurines, 287, 288
in Cretaceous Period, 353
dental batteries of, 199,
286–87
frills and, 286, 287
herds of, 288–90
horns and, 277, 285–86,
287
as prey of tyrannosaurids,
123, 124, 289
sauropods compared to,
183
young of, 288, 289, 297
ceratopsines, 287, 287, 414
ceratosaurs
abelisaurids, 83–85, 83, 84,
85, 87
in Cretaceous Period, 352
early ceratosaurs, 81–82, 81
genus list, 369
in Jurassic Period, 340
noasaurids, 82–83, 82
scaly skin of, 115
tails of, 88
teeth of, 342
trace fossils of, 84–85
Ceratosaurus, 76, 81–82, 81, 87,
339
Cetiosauriscus, 195
Cetiosaurus, 184, 187, 201
chalk, 348–49, 357, 358, 363
champsosaurs, 258, 359, 363
Chaoyangsaurus, 280
Chapman, Ralph E., 270, 275,
275
Charig, Alan, 224
Chasmosaurus, 286, 288
Chialingosaurus, 231
Chiappe, Luis, 172, 172
Chicxulub crater, 361, 362
Chin, Karen, 22, 22
Chindesaurus, 331
Chinsamy-Turan, Anusuya, 319,
321, 321
Chungkingosaurus, 231
Citipati, 140, 145, 147, 148, 296
cladistics
advantages of, 53 54
evolutionary relationships
and, 11, 52, 55
and family tree, 51–53
Linnaean taxonomy
distinguished from,
54–55
cladograms
of ankylosaurs, 239
of ceratopsians, 55, 55
cladistics and, 52–55, 52,
54, 55
of ornithischians, 218–19
of saurischians, 74–75
of stegocephalians, 57

of tyrannosauroids, 54, 54
Claessens, Leon, 317
Cleveland-Lloyd Quarry, Utah,
103–4
Coelophysis
as ceratosaurs, 87
as coelophysoid, 80
and evolution of theropods,
86
illustrations of, 1, 76, 86,
324, 333
in Late Triassic, 332
as predator, 186
size of, 81
skeleton of, 79
trace fossils of, 84–85
coelophysoids
early coelophysoids, 80–81,
80
genus list, 368–69
illustration of, 181
in Jurassic Period, 335, 336
size of, 86
tails of, 88
trace fossils of, 84
coelurosauravids, 330
coelurosaurs
birds and, 7, 166
brain of, 320
carnosaurs compared to,
99–100
compsognathids, 111–14,
119, 131
in Cretaceous Period, 351,
352
feathers of, 20, 109, 113–15
features of, 109, 153
genus list, 375
in Jurassic Period, 336, 340
ornithomimosaurs as, 131
size of, 109–10
tyrannosaurids as, 109, 113,
118, 119, 131
Coelurus, 109–10
Colbert, Edwin, 275
cold-blooded animals, 311–14,
312, 318–20, 322, 363
comparative anatomy, 7, 46–47,
47
compsognathids, 111–14, 119,
131, 376
Compsognathus, 10, 86, 111, 112,
355
computers
cladistic analysis and, 53, 54
dinosaur science and, 11, 11
mounted skeletons and, 32
Conchoraptor, 144
Confuciusornis
as avialian, 164
illustrations of, 39, 162,
165, 167
nesting behavior of, 296
size of, 172
skeleton of, 166, 168
convergent evolution, 53, 62,
253, 306
Cope, Edward Drinker, 9–10, 9,
11, 185, 195
coprolites, 19, 22, 22, 124, 210,
304
Coria, Rodolfo, 104, 354, 354
Corythosaurus, 258, 262, 352
Crassigyrinus, 56

Craterosaurus, 232
Creisler, Ben, 45, 45
Cretaceous Period
diversification of dinosaurs,
350–53
fauna of, 347–48
feathered dinosaurs of, 350
geologic time and, 26
illustrations of, 344, 346,
352
marine life of, 348–50
plants of, 345–47
pterodactyls and, 348
seabirds of, 169–70
Crichton, Michael, 364
crocodilians, 306–7, 311–13, 318,
319, 331, 335, 348,
359, 363
Crocodylus, 319
Cryolophosaurus, 90–91, 90
Cryptoclidus, 337
Currie, Philip, 104, 106, 106,
114, 118, 193, 288
Cuvier, Georges, 7, 46

Dacentrurus, 231
Dal Sasso, Cristiano, 112
Darwin, Charles, 44, 46, 46, 47,
49–52, 54
Day, Julia, 92
de Camp, L. Sprague, 269
Deccan Traps, 361
Decherd, Sara, 315
Deinocheirus, 12, 130, 135–36,
351
deinonychosaurs
behavior of, 161
birds as close relatives of,
144, 149, 152, 161,
166
as coelurosaurs, 131
dromaeosaurids, 10, 151,
154–59, 161
feathers and, 37, 114, 115,
153
troodontids, 151, 159–61
Deinonychus
ankylosaurs and, 241
Archaeopteryx compared to,
11, 152
discovery of, 10, 151
iguanodontians and, 252
illustrations of, 4, 150, 156,
161
ornithopods and, 246
as pack-hunting dinosaur,
159
size of, 157
specializations and, 47, 47
specimens of, 86
speed of, 151–52
dental batteries
of ceratopsids, 199, 286–87
of hadrosaurids, 199, 261,
286, 314
of hadrosauroids, 260–61,
260, 266, 267
Dial, Ken, 149, 153
dicraeosaurids, 195, 197–99, 203,
396
Dicraeosaurus, 197, 198
dicynodonts, 63, 64, 178
Dilong, 37, 38, 113–15, 116, 119,
120–21

Dilophosaurus, 78, 81, 91, 92,
186, 223, 335
dinosaur, definition of term, 7–8,
11, 163
dinosaur art
changes in, 2, 5, 5
color and, 38, 39, 40, 40
dinosaur science and,
34–40
muscles and guts, 35, 36
in nineteenth century, 7, 8,
34
outsides, 36–38, 36, 37
skeleton and, 34–36, 34, 38
speculations and, 4
dinosaur biology
bone growth, 318–19, 321
bone pathology, 323
brains, 319–20
circulatory system, 317–18
metabolism, 311–12, 317,
318–19, 322, 363
microscopic study of bone
slices, 300, 300, 301,
321, 321
physiology and, 311–15,
317, 319
Dinosauria, as natural group, 62,
62, 66, 70, 331
dinosaur science
computer and technology
in, 11
dinosaur art and, 34–40
disagreement and, 4–5
DNA and, 365
fossils and, 2–3
frontiers of, 12
hypotheses and, 3
research and, 3, 4
speculations and, 3–4
diplodocids, 195–97, 203, 395
diplodocoids
dicraeosaurids, 195,
197–99, 203
diplodocids, 195–97, 203
features of, 191–92
genus list, 395
in Jurassic Period, 195–97,
340
necks of, 193–95, 193, 197
nostrils of, 191–92
rebbachisaurids, 2, 195,
199, 203, 210
tails of, 192–93, 192, 197
teeth of, 191, 210
Diplodocus
Amphicoelias compared to,
195
as diplodocid, 195, 196
discovery of, 185
double-beamed chevron
bones and, 191
illustrations of, 194
neck of, 193
size of, 205, 207
skeleton of, 195
skull of, 192
tail of, 193
discoveries
in American West, 6, 9–10
Dinosaur Renaissance and,
10–11
of eggs, 293, 299
in England, 6, 7–8, 9

in Europe, 9, 10, 355
history of, 6–12
in New England, 9
new species and, 2, 5, 12, 31–32
DNA, 364, 365
Dodson, Peter, 322, *322*
domeheaded dinosaurs. *See* pachycephalosaurs
Drepanosaurus, 330
Drinker, 242, 246
dromaeosaurids, 10, 151, 154–59, 161, 237, 271, 353, 382
dromaeosaurines, 155, 156, 157, 158, 384
droppings. *See* coprolites
Dryosaurus, 251, 252
Dryptosaurus, 9, 122
duckbilled dinosaurs. *See* hadrosauroids

Earth
age of, 7, 23, 28, 49
geologic time and, 23
ectothermic, 312
Edmontonia, 236, 237, 239, 270
Edmontosaurus, 124, 129, 261, *266,* 310
Efraasia, 175, 177
eggs. *See also* brooding; nesting behavior
discoveries of, 293, 299
of pterosaurs, 330
size of, 294
surface differences, 293–94
as trace fossils, 19, 21
Einiosaurus, 284, 286, 287, 288
Elaphrosaurus, 82, 87, 135
Emausaurus, 220, 223, 224, 225
Enantiornis, 164, 169, 172
enantiornithines, 168–69, 172, 386–87
endothermic, 312
Engelhardt, Johann Friedrich, 176
eons, 25
Eoraptor, 68, 71–72, 71, 73, 80, 177, 332
Eotyrannus, 116, 120, 122, 247, 355, 355
Epidendrosaurus, 152, 154, 296
epochs, 26
Equijubus, 257, 260, 261
eras, 25
Erickson, Gregory M., 129, *129,* 298
Eshanosaurus, 147
Estesia, 148
Eubrontes, 84
Eudimorphodon, 329
Euhelopus, 187
Euoplocephalus, 234, 237, 237
euryapsids, 329, 330, 339
Euskelosaurus, 180
evolution
adaptations and, 47
cladistics and, 11, 52, 55
comparative anatomy and, 46–47
convergent evolution, 53, 62, 253, 306
descent with modification, 46, 49

of feathers, 173
geologic time scale and, 26, 27, 28
independent evolution, 53
natural selection and, 10, 47, 49–50
of sauropods, 201
taxonomy and, 51
Tree of Life and, 50, *50,* 51–53
of vertebrates, 56, *57,* 58–59
extinction. *See also* mass extinctions
evolution and, 50
fossils and, 6, 7, 24

Fabrosaurus, 215
facultative bipeds, 278
Falcarius, 144–45, 144, 145, 146, 147, 148
Farmer, Colleen, 317
fauna, 347–48
feathers
Archaeopteryx and, *164, 167*
of coelurosaurs, 20, 109, 113–15
evolution of, 173
fossil evidence of, 12, 37
function of, 115, 149
maniraptorans and, 37–38, 115, 119, 149, *149,* 153
oviraptorosaurs and, 37, 115, 141, 148, 149
protofeathers, 37, 115, 119, 120, 123–24, 148, 153
of *Sinosauropteryx,* 20, 37, 38, 114, 115, 119, *165*
Velociraptor and, 2, 38
Fiorillo, Anthony, 191
fish, in Jurassic Period, 338
flight stroke, 173
footprints
behavior and, 308
of brachiosaurids, 207
fossilized imprints of tracks, *303*
of iguanodontians, 256
locomotion and, 305
pack-hunting dinosaurs and, 106
of prosauropods, 178, 181
of sauropods, 186, 201, 210
of titanosaurs, 210
as trace fossils, 21, *21,* 102
fossilization, *18–21,* 19
fossilized feces. *See* coprolites
fossil jackets, 31, 33
fossils
as bits and pieces, 19–20, 21
body fossils, 18–19, 21, 303
collections of, 31–32, 33
coprolites, 19, 22, *22,* 124, 210, 304
discoveries of, 6–8, 12
exposure of, 29–30
finding, 11, 12, 29–33
formation of, 18–19, *18–21*
geologic time and, 24–25
index fossils, 24–25, *25*
mounted skeletons, 10, 32, *32, 33, 33*

observations about, 3
paleontology and, 2
protection of, *30*
scraping, 30–31
strata and, 24
technology for finding, 11, 12
trace fossils, 18, 19, 20, 21, 84–85, 102, 210, 303
types of rock and, 13–16, 29
fruit, 346–47
furcula, 79, 80, 165

Gallimimus, 130, 132, 133, 135, 139
Galton, Peter M., 62, 176, 216–17, 275
ganglia, 228
Garcia, Mariano, 309
Gargoyleosaurus, 238, 240
Garudimimus, 133
Gasosaurus, 100
Gasparinisaura, 246
Gastonia, 238, 239
gastralia, 317
gastroliths, 278
Gauthier, Jacques, 163
genetic variations, 49
genomes, 364
genus, 42
geologic time
geologic time scale, 25, 26, 27, *27,* 28
index fossils and, 24–25, *25*
layers of time, 23–24
names for, 25–26
radioactive dates and, 26
geologists and geology, 13, 30
Giganotosaurus, 98, 101, *102,* 104, 106, *106,* 354
Gilmoreosaurus, 261
Globidens, 349
Gobisaurus, 237
Gojirasaurus, 81
Gondwana, 82, 83, 87, 155, 332, 340, 351, 352
Gongbusaurus, 216
Gongxianosaurus, 187
Gorgosaurus, 116, 124, *125*
Goyocephale, 271
GPS (Global Positioning System), 17
Grand Canyon, 23, 24
grasses, 347
ground-penetrating radar, 12
growth of dinosaurs, 11, 297–98, 301, 322
Gryposaurus, 262, 266
Guanlong, 118, 122, *122*
Gyposaurus, 180

hadrosaurids
in Cretaceous Period, 353
dental batteries of, 199, 261, 286, 314
genus list, 408–9
hadrosaurines, 260, 261–65, 267, 410–11
hands of, 261, *261*
lambeosaurines, 260, 261, 262–65, 267, 409–10
hadrosaurines
genus list, 410–11

heads of, *266*
illustration of, *351*
noses of, 263
size of, 262
teeth of, 267
young of, 264–65
hadrosauroids
dental batteries of, 260–61, *260,* 266, 267
genus list, 408
habitat of, 265–66
hands of, 260
jaws of, 254, 260, 267
nests of, 264–65
noses of, 263
origin of, 259–60
as ornithopods, 243, 259
primitive hadrosauroids, 260, 261
scales of, 265
size of, 259, 267
skeletons of, 259
teeth of, 257, 260–61
young of, 264
hadrosaurs, as prey of tyrannosaurids, 123, 124, 129
Hadrosaurus, 9, 30, 261
Haeckel, Ernst, Tree of Life, *50*
half-life, of radioactive element, 26
Hammer, William, 90
Haplocanthosaurus, 197, 204
Harpymimus, 135
Hawkins, Benjamin Waterhouse, 8, *8*
Henderson, Donald, 307
Hennig, Willi, 44, 51, 52, 53, 54
herrerasaurids, 71–72, 80, 368
Herrerasaurus, 67, 68, 71–72, *71, 72,* 331, 332
Hesperornis, 170, 171, 172
hesperornithines, 170, 350, 358–59, 389
Hesperosaurus, 229, *230,* 231
heterodontosaurids, 216, 244, 401
Heterodontosaurus, 66, 216, *216, 217*
Heyuannia, 145
Hickerson, William, 90
Histriasaurus, 199
Hitchcock, Edward, 9, 84
Holmes, Thom, 22
Holtz, Thomas, 4, *29,* 118, 120, 123, 134, 144
Homalocephale, 268, 269, 271
homeothermic, 312
Homo sapiens, 363
Hongshanosaurus, 278
Horner, John R. "Jack," 11, 293, 298, 300, *300,* 319
Huaxiagnathus, 111
Huayangosaurus, 226, 228, 229, *230,* 231
Hutchinson, John R., 307, 309, *309*
Hylaeosaurus, 7, 8, 9, 235, 239, 355
Hypacrosaurus, 262, 294
hypotheses, 3, 38, 304
Hypsilophodon
beak of, *245*
brain of, 317

brooding and, 295
iguanodontians and, 252
illustrations of, *242, 244,
247*
jaws of, 254
pachycephalosaurs
compared to, 272,
273
as primitive ornithopod, 51
skulls of, 244–45
speed of, 122
young of, 246
hypsilophodontids, 249, 300
"hypsilophodonts," 244, 273
Hypsirophus, 231

Iaceornis, 170
Ichthyornis, 170, 172, *173*
ichthyosaurs, 170, *328,* 329–30,
338, 339, 342, 349
igneous rocks, 13, *14,* 17, 24, 26
Iguanodon
ancestors of, 66, 163
Baryonyx as predator of, 94,
95
in Cretaceous Period, 351
discovery of, 7
in Europe, 355
feeding behavior of, 304
footprints and, 9
hands of, *253,* 255–56
illustrations of, *7, 8, 250,
256, 347*
jaws of, 254
legs of, 176
models of, 8, *8*
size of, 184
skeletons of, 10, 251, *253*
spike thumb of, 35, 254–55
teeth of, 257
iguanodontians
genus list, 406–7
hadrosauroids and, 257,
259
hands of, *253,* 254–56,
259–60
mouths of, 251–52
as ornithopods, 243, 244,
251
rhabdodontids, 252–53
sails of, 257
sliding jaws of, 253–54,
256–57, 260
Incisivosaurus, 142, 143, 145, 147
independent evolution, 53
index fossils, 24–25, *25*
Indosuchus, 87
inferences, 3
integument, 36, 37, 38
intramandibular joint, 79, 80
Irritator, 94–95
Isanosaurus, 182, 184, 185, 187
Isisaurus, 207, *362*

Jaffe, Byron, 45
Janenschia, 207
Jeholornis, 168, 172, *297*
Jeholosaurus, 216, 246
Jinfengopteryx, 160
Jinzhousaurus, 257, 260
Ji Qiang, 114
Ji Shuan, 114
Jixiangornis, 168, *297*
Jobaria, 202, 203, 204, *204*

Jurassic Park (Crichton), 364
Jurassic Park (films), 365
Jurassic Period
Camarasaurus in, 197
diplodocids of, 195–97, 340
geologic time and, 26
marine life and, 337–40
Morrison Formation and,
340–42
new breeds of, 336–37
plants of, 345
pterodactyls and, 337
reign of dinosaurs and,
335–36

Keichousaurus, 328
Kentrosaurus, 231
keratin, 20, 223, 233, 282, 286
Kermack, K. A., 192
Khaan, 144
Kobayashi, Yoshitsugu, 139, *139*
Kotasaurus, 187
Kritosaurus, 261
K/T extinction, 357–65

La Brea Tar Pits, 103–4
Lagerpeton, 60, 64–65, 66
Lagosuchus, 64, *64,* 65, 66, *67*
Lamanna, Matthew C., 12, *12*
Lambe, Lawrence, 42
lambeosaurines
dental battery of, 261
genus list, 409–10
heads of, *264*
hollow crest of, 260,
262–63, *263,* 267,
306, 307
young of, 264–65
Lambeosaurus, 262, 264
Larson, Gary, 230
Late Triassic, 62
Laurasia, 332, 340, 351, 352
lava, 13
Leaellynasaura, 246, 248, 249,
352
Leedsichthys, 338–39, 340
Leidy, Joseph, 9
Leptoceratops, 280, 281–82
leptoceratopsids, 280, 413
Lesothosaurus
features of, 215–16
illustration of, *212*
pubis bone of, *69*
Scutellosaurus compared to,
221, 225
skeleton of, *214,* 215
teeth of, 243
Lessemsaurus, 180
Lexovisaurus, 231
Liaoceratops, 280
Liaoningosaurus, 238
Limaysaurus, 104, 199
Linnaean system of taxonomy,
42, 44, 54–55, 244
Linnaeus, Carolus, 41, *41,* 42, 43,
44, 51, 54
Linster, Wes, 45
lizard-hipped dinosaurs. *See*
saurischians
Longipteryx, 162
Losillasaurus, 195
Lurdusaurus, 254, 257

macronarians

brachiosaurids, 203, 205–7
genus list, 396–97
in Jurassic Period, 340
noses of, 203–5
primitive macronarians,
204–5
saltasaurids, 210
as sauropods, 184, 188
species of, 197, 203
titanosaurs, 203, 205,
207–10
trace fossils of, 210
magma, 13, 14, 17, 24
Magyarosaurus, 203, 207, 209
Mahajangasuchus, 208
Maiasaura, 261, 296, 298
Majungasaurus, 11, 84, *85,* 87, 92
Makovicky, Peter, 155
Mamenchisaurus, 187–88, *187,
188,* 195
mammals, 332, 333, 335, 347–48,
357, 359, 363, *364*
maniraptorans
birds and, 166
brain of, 320
brooding and, 115, 141,
148, 153, 295
deinonychosaurs as, 153
feathers and, 37–38, 115,
119, 149, *149,* 153
features of, 113, 131, 141,
148
genus list, 379–80
in Jurassic Period, 340, 342
in trees, *152,* 153–54, *153*
Mantell, Gideon, 7, 235, 304
Mantell, Mary Ann, 7
Mapusaurus, 104, 105
Marasuchus, 60, 64, 65, 66
marginocephalians, 277, 351
Markgraf, Richard, 93
Marsh, O. C., 9–10, *9, 11,* 69,
124, 132, 137, 139,
185, 195, 213, 214,
227–30, 243, 277
marsupials, 348, 359
Maryaska, Teresa, 238
Masiakasaurus, 76, 82, *82,* 87
mass extinctions
causes of, 359–63
Cretaceous-Tertiary mass
extinction, 325,
357–65
of Mesozoic Era, 11, 25, 26,
27, 357
of Triassic Period, 80,
325–26, *327,* 332–33,
357
Massospondylus, 174, 178, 180,
180
McKenna, Malcolm, 136
megalosaurids, 92–93, 96, 340,
372
Megalosaurus
ancestors of, 66, 163
classification of, 8
discovery of, 7, 92
in Europe, 355
feeding behavior, 304
footprints of, 9
illustrations of, *7, 88*
legs of, 176
as predator, 186
restorations of, 34–35

size of, 184
teeth of, 78
Megapnosaurus, 66, 69, 81
Megaraptor, 95–96, 95, 353
Megatherium, 364
Mei, 160, *161,* 168
Melanorosaurus, 180
Mesozoic Era
climate of, 10
extinction in, 11, 25, 26, 27,
357
geologic time scale and, 25
rocks from, 29
metabolism, 311–12, 317,
318–19, 322, 363
metamorphic rocks, 14, *14,* 17
Michel, Helen, 360
Microraptor
Archaeopteryx compared to,
168
evolution and, 49
feathers and scales of, 37,
37, 115, 119
features of, 167
illustrations of, *150, 152,
165, 297*
as microraptorine, 156
mudstones found in, 154
nesting behavior, 296
size of, 161
microraptorines, 155, 156–57,
160, 383
microstructure, of bones, 129,
300, *300,* 301, 321,
321
Microvenator, 143
Middle Triassic, origin of
dinosaurs and, 62,
63–64, *63*
migration, 322
Milner, Angela C., 97, *97*
mineralized soft tissues, 20
Minmi, 236, 237, 238, *238*
Mirischia, 111
mitochondria, 312–13, 317
Monolophosaurus, 98, 100, 186
mononykines, 136–37, 138, 379
Mononykus, 136–37
monotremes, 359
Montanoceratops, 280
Morrison Formation, 340–42
mosasaurs, 350, 358–59
mud cracks, 16
multituberculates, *358,* 359
Mussaurus, 180
Muttaburrasaurus, 252, 252, 315,
352
Myhrvold, Nathan, 193
Mymoorapelta, 239

Naish, Darren, 355, *355*
Nanyangosaurus, 260
Nemegtomaia, 145
Nemegtosaurus, 351
neoceratopsians, 279–82, 285,
286, 353, 412
neosauropods, 188
Neovenator, 101, 122
nesting behavior. *See also*
brooding
discoveries of, 11, 12
location of nests, 295–96
of maniraptorans, 141
mound nests, 294–95

of oviraptorids, 142
of oviraptorosaurs, 142, 148, 295
protofeathers and, 115
of titanosaurs, 210
of tyrannosaurids, 126
of tyrannosauroids, 125–26
Neuquenraptor, 155
Neuquensaurus, 104
Nigersaurus, 198, 199
noasaurids, 82–83, *82,* 369–70, 404
Noasaurus, 82, 87
Nodocephalosaurus, 237
nodosaurids, 237, 238, 239, 353
Nodosaurus, 237, 238
Nopsca, Ferenc, 221
Norell, Mark A., 136, 137, 283
Norman, Dave, 224, 253–54, 256
nothosaurs, 329
Notohypsilophodon, 246
Novas, Fernando E., 87, *87,* 118, 137, 156
Nqwebasaurus, 112
numerical time, 23, 26, 27

observations, 3
Ohmdenosaurus, 187
Olorotitan, 263, *265*
Olsen, Paul, 84
Omeisaurus, 182, 185, 187, 203
origin of dinosaurs
ancestors of dinosaurs and, 64–66
existence of dinosaurs, 61–62
features of dinosaurs, 66–67, *66, 67*
Middle Triassic and, 63–64, 331
ornithischians
air sacs of, 317
bird-hipped dinosaurs, 67, 70, 213–14
cheeks of, 216–17
cladogram of, *218–19*
in Cretaceous Period, 345
early ornithischians, 215–16
genus list, 400
hand shape of, 71
in Jurassic Period, 335, 336, 340
in Late Triassic, 331–32
pachycephalosaurs as, 269
predentary bone, *214*
prosauropods and, 180
pubis of, 214–15
sauropods compared to, 183
teeth of, 214, 253
Ornithocheirus, 347, 348
ornithodirans, 64–65, 66
Ornitholestes, 108, 110, *110,* 111, *111,* 113
ornithomimids, 134, *134,* 135–36, *344,* 378
Ornithomimosauria, 113
ornithomimosaurs
as bird mimics, 131–32
eating habits of, 134, *134,* 139, *139*
genus list, 378
as ostrich mimics, 132–33
primitive

ornithomimosaurs, 133, 135, 139
troodontids and, 160
Ornithomimus, 132, 133, 139
ornithopods
beaks and, 243
brain of, 320
in Cretaceous Period, 351, 352, 353
defenses of, 243–44
features of, 69–70, 180, 213, 214
genus list, 405–6
heterodontosaurids and, 216
in Jurassic Period, 335
primitive ornithopods, 243–49, 254
Ornithopsis, 184
Orodromeus, 245, 246, 251, 300
Osborn, Henry Fairfield, 117, 118, 309
osteoderms, 221, 223, 227, 229, 230, 233, 235
Ostrom, John, 10, *10,* 11, 151–52, 266, 317
Ouranosaurus
illustrations of, *250, 255, 302*
sails of, 93, 198, 257
skeleton of, *255*
Oviraptor, 142, *142,* 143, *145, 148,* 294, 296
oviraptorids, 143, 283, 381
oviraptorosaurs
birds and, 143–44
as coelurosaurs, 141
eating habits of, 147–48
feathers and, 37, 115, 141, 148, 149
features of, 141, 143, 148
genus list, 380
heads of, *144, 145*
illustration of, *344*
as maniraptorans, 153
nesting behavior of, 142, 148, 295
primitive oviraptorosaurs, 142–43
young of, 296
Owen, Richard, 7–8, 11, 184, 224, 235, 312, 313, 355

pachycephalosaurs
in Cretaceous Period, 353
discovery of, 214
genus list, 411–12
as marginocephalians, 273, 277
skulls of, 269–71, 273, 275
teeth of, 159, 243, 271–72
Pachycephalosaurus
head of, 269, *272, 274*
illustrations of, *268, 275*
skeleton of, *273*
Pachydermata, 61, *61*
pachypleurosaurs, 329
Pachyrhinosaurus, 286, 287, 288
pack-hunting dinosaurs, 106, 125, 159
Padian, Kevin, 173, *173,* 319
paleoartists, 34–40. *See also*
dinosaur art

paleoenvironment, 16
paleontology, 2, 3–5, 12
paleopathology, 323
Paleozoic Era, 25
Pangaea, 328, 332, 340
Panoplosaurus, 237
Paralititan, 104, 210
Paranthodon, 232
Parasaurolophus
crest of, 262, *264, 306,* 307
illustrations of, *258, 352*
skeleton of, *262*
parasuchians, *63,* 64, 223
Parrish, Michael, 194
Patagopteryx, 169, *169*
Patagosaurus, 187
Paul, Greg, 113–14
Pedopenna, 154
Pelecanimimus, 133, 134, 135, 355
Pentaceratops, 285, 287, *287, 304*
periods, 26
Perle, Altangerel, 136, 137
Permo-Triassic mass extinction, 325–28, *327,* 357
Phanerozoic Eon, 25
phylogenies, 50, 51, 54
physiology, 311–15, 317, 319
Piatnitzkysaurus, 92
Pinacosaurus, 236, 237, 239, 240, 283
Pisanosaurus, 212, 215, 216, 332
placentals, 348, 359
placodonts, 329
Placodus, 328
plated dinosaurs. *See* stegosaurs
Plateosaurus
discovery of, 176
hands of, *66,* 176, *177*
head of, *178*
illustrations of, *174, 181*
skeleton of, 176, *177,* 180
specialization and, 47, *47*
plate tectonics, 17, *17,* 332, 351
plesiosaurs, 170, 232, 330, 339–40, 358–59
Poekilopleuron, 92
poikilothermic, 312
polacanthids, 239
Poole, Jason "Chewie," 33, *33*
Poposaurus, 331
predator traps, 103–4
predentary bone, 214, *214,* 277, 278
Prenocephale, 269, *270*
preparators, 31, 32, 33
primates, 363
Principle of Priority, 44
Probactrosaurus, 257, 260, 261, *261*
Proceratosaurus, 110
Procompsognathus, 81, 295
Prosaurolophus, 261
prosauropods
as bipedal and quadrupedal, 177, 178–79, *179,* 180
discoveries of, 175–76
early prosauropods, 179–80
features of, 177–79, 185
genus list, 391–92
in Late Triassic, 331
predators of, 180–81
as primitive

sauropodomorphs, 175
sauropods compared to, 177, 183, 185
thumb claws of, 177–78, *178*
Protarchaeopteryx, 37, 143, 147, 148
Protoceratops
eggs, 142, 279, 294
growth cycle, *279*
illustration of, *276*
male/female differences, 291
skeleton of, *280*
Velociraptor and, 159, 281, *282,* 283
protoceratopsids, 280, 413
protofeathers, 37, 115, 119, 120, 123–24, 148, 153
Protohadros, 260
protomammals, 326, 328, 330–31, 332, 333, 335
Pseudolagosuchus, 65
psittacosaurids, 278–79, 285, 412
Psittacosaurus
brooding and, 295
in Cretaceous Period, 351
illustrations of, *158, 165, 276,* 297
predators of, 121
scales of, 38, 278–79
skeleton of, 278, *278,* 279
tail of, 20, *278,* 279
young of, 297, 348
pterodactyloids, 337, 348
pterodactyls, 330, 337, 348
Pterodactylus, 319, *336*
pterosaurs, 64, 168, 184, 330, 333, 335, 337, 342, 347, 348, 359
pygostyle, 143, 166, 168

Qantassaurus, 246
Quetzalcoatlus, 344, 348, *348*

radioactive dates, 26
Rahonavis, 155, *155,* 156, 161, 167
raindrop marks, 16, *16*
Rapetosaurus, 208, 210
rauisuchians, *63,* 64
Rayfield, Emily, 102, 107, *107,* 307
Rayososaurus, 199
rebbachisaurids, 2, 195, 199, 203, 210, 286, 396
Rebbachisaurus, 93, 199
Rega, Elizabeth, 323, *323*
Regnosaurus, 232
Reid, R.E.H., 319
relative time, 23, 26, 27
Repenomamus, 348
reptiles
of Cretaceous Period, 349–50
of Jurassic Period, 335, 339, 342
recovery from Permo-Triassic mass extinction, 326–28
of Triassic Period, 329–30, 332, 333
research, 3, 4, 10, 31

reworking, 318, 319
Rey, Luis V., 5, *34*, 217
rhabdodontids, 252–53, 408
Rhamphorhynchus, 336
Rich, Leaellyn, 45, 249
Ricqlès, Armand de, 319
Riley, Henry, 175
Rinchenia, 144
Riojasaurus, 174, 180
ripple marks, 16, *16*
rock cycle, 17
rocks
    age of Earth and, 7
    formation of, 6, 13–16, 17, 23
    igneous rocks, 13, *14*, 17, 24, 26
    metamorphic rocks, 14, *14*, 17
    sedimentary rocks, 14–16, *15*, 17
Rogers, Kristina Curry, 301, *301*, 319
Rogers, Raymond R., 28, *28*
Romer, Alfred Sherwood, 64
rostral bone, 277–78, 285
rudists, 349, 357, 358, 363
Rugops, 76
Rybczynski, Natalia, 236

saltasaurids, 104, 210, 399–400
Saltasaurus
    armor of, 209
    illustrations of, *95*, *202*, *292*, *295*
    as saltasaurid, 104
    skeleton of, *207*
Sampson, Scott D., 291, *291*
Sapeornis, 172
Sarcosuchus, 348
Saturnalia, 175, *179*, 180
saurischians
    air sacs of, 317
    birds as, 166
    cladogram of, *74–75*
    genus list, 367
    growth and development of, 301
    hand shape, 71, 186–87, 216
    hollow bones of, 80
    lizard-hipped dinosaurs, 67, 69–75, 213
    long necks of, 70
    problem saurischians, 71–72
    prosauropods and, 177
    pubis of, *69*, 70
    vertebrae of, 70, *70*, 186
Saurolophus, 262, 266, *351*
Sauropelta, 159, *234*, 237, 241
Saurophaganax, 101, 104
sauropodomorphs
    common ancestor of, 71
    in Cretaceous Period, 345
    long necks of, 70–71
    prosauropods and, 175
    as quadrupeds, 215
    sauropods and, 183
    theropods and, 80
sauropods
    adaptations of, 189
    brain of, 320
    carnosaurs as predators,

102, 104–5, 107
    in Cretaceous Period, 351, 352, 353
    diplodocoids, 184, 188, 191–99
    eggs and, 293
    evolution of, 201
    features of, 183–84, 185, 201, 213
    genus list, 392–94
    hind legs of, *200, 201*
    in Jurassic Period, 335, 336–37, 340, 342
    life cycle of, 298, 300
    long necks of, 186, 187–88, 189, 193–94, 201
    macronarians, 184, 188, 197, 203–11
    neosauropods, 188
    primitive sauropods, 183–89, 203
    prosauropods compared to, 177, 183, 185
    pubis bone of, 70, 213
    as quadrupeds, 179, 183
    size of, 185–87, 189
    speed of, 308
Sauroposeidon, 102, 104, 189, 195, 207
Saurornithoides, 160
Saurornitholestes, 157
scales, 20, 36, 37–38, *37*, 265
Scelidosaurus
    as ankylosaur, 239
    armor of, 223–24, *224*, *225*, 227, 229, 231, 235
    in England, 355
    illustration of, *220*
    as quadruped, 224, 225
    skeleton of, *223*
    tail of, 224
Schweitzer, Mary Higby, 365, *365*
Scipionyx, *108*, *111*, 112–13, *112*, 355
Scutellosaurus, 220, 221–22, *222*, 223, *224*, 225, 227
scutes, 221, 222, 235
sea levels, 360, 362, 363
Secernosaurus, 261
sedimentary rocks, 14–16, *15*, 17, 24, 26, 29
sedimentary structures, 16, *16*, 21
Seeley, Harry G., 69–70, 184, 213–14
Segisaurus, 81
Sellosaurus, 180
Sereno, Paul, 273
sex differences, 291
sexual selection, 49–50
Shamosaurus, 237
Shantungosaurus, 258, 262, 266, *351*
sharks, 104, 338, 359
Sharovipteryx, 330
Shell, Wyoming, *29*
Shenzhouraptor, 168, 172
Shenzhousaurus, 133, 135
Shuangmiaosaurus, 257
Shunosaurus, *182*, 187, *189*
Shuvuuia, 130, 136, 137, *137*
Siberian Traps, 325–26, 361
Signore, Marco, 112
Silesaurus, 60, 65–66, *65*, 215
Silvisaurus, 237

Simosuchus, 232, 348
Sinornis, 166
Sinornithoides, 160, 161
Sinornithosaurus, 37, *39*, 115, 154, 156
Sinosauropteryx
    brooding and, 295
    feathers of, 20, 37, 38, 114, 115, 119, *165*
    features of, 111, 112
    illustrations of, *108*, *113*, *114*, *297*
Sinovenator, 157, *158*, 160
sinraptorids, 100, 374
Sinusonasus, *159*, 304
skeletochronology, 321
skeletons
    dinosaur art and, 34–36, *34*, 38
    evolution of vertebrates and, 56
    mounted skeletons, 10, 32, *32*, 33, *33*
    postcranial skeletal anatomy, 59
    reconstruction of, 35–36, 38
    skull anatomy, 58
Smilosuchus, 331
Smith, William "Strata," 24
snake, skeleton of, *56*
Snively, Eric, 134
source rock, 26
South America, 354
Spaerotholus, 269
specializations, 47, 49, 52, 53, 54, 55
species
    discovery of, 2, 5, 12, 31–32
    evolution and, 50
    taxonomy and, 42
speculations, 3–4
spinosauroids
    in Cretaceous Period, 351, 352
    features of, 89, 93, 94, 97
    as fish-eating dinosaurs, 94–95, 97
    genus list, 373
    habitat of, 95–96, 97
    primitive species of, 89–90, 92
Spinosaurus, 88, 89, 93–95, *96*, *97*, 198, 257
Spinostropheus, 82
stegocephalians, 56, *57*
Stegoceras, 269, *274*
stegosaurs
    armor of, 209, 229–33
    brain of, 320
    as common type, 187, 231–32
    in Cretaceous Period, 351
    distribution of, 231–32
    features of, 69–70, 213, 214, 229
    genus list, 402–3
    heads of, *230*
    in Jurassic Period, 336, 340, 342
    life habits of, 232–33
    tails of, 230
Stegosaurus
    armor of, 227, *229*, 230
    defenses of, 102

    discovery of, 9
    geologic time scale and, 27
    illustrations of, *18*, *226*, *334*
    myths of, 227–31, 232
    sexual selection and, *49*, 50
    skeleton of, *228*
    specializations and, 47, *47*
    thagomizer of, *229*, 230–31, *232*, *233*
Stenopelix, 272
Stevens, Kent, 194
Stokesosaurus, 121
strata, 15, *15*, 16, 23–25
Struthiomimus, 132–33
Struthiosaurus, 237
Stutchbury, Samuel, 175
Stygimoloch, 268, 269, *270*, 275
Styracosaurus, 286, 287, 288, *288*
Suchomimus, 88, *92*, 94
Sues, Hans, 275
Supersaurus, 200
Suuwassea, 195
Syntarsus, 223

tachymetabolic, 312
Talarurus, 237
Talenkauen, 251, 253
Tanke, Darren, 288
Tanycolagreus, 110
Tanystropheus, *328*, 329, 330
Tarbosaurus, 124, 241
Tarchia, 237, *240*, 241
taxonomy
    beyond genus, 44
    choosing names, 45
    evolution and, 51
    lumping and splitting, 42–43
    scientific system of names, 41–42
    types and priority, 43–44
technology, 11, *11*, 12
Telmatosaurus, 261
Tenontosaurus, 156, 159, 241, 252
Teratosaurus, 176, 178
tetanurines, 89, 90–92, 99, 109, 166, 335, 336, 371–72
thagomizer. See *Stegosaurus*, thagomizer of
Thecocoelurus, 143
Thecodontosaurus, 175–76, 180, 295
therizinosauroids
    advanced therizinosauroids, 145–47
    as coelurosaurs, 131, 141
    eating habits of, 147, 148
    embryo of, *294*
    feathers and, 141, 148, 149
    features of, 141, 143
    genus list, 381–82
    as maniraptorans, 153
    primitive therizinosauroids, 144–45
Therizinosaurus, 140, 145, *146*, 147, *147*, 149
theropods
    big brains of, 77–78
    birds and, 166
    crests of, 91
    in Cretaceous Period, 345
    hands of, 79
    hollow vertebrae of, 79–80, 213

in Jurassic Period, 340, 341
long necks of, 70, 71
as meat-eating dinosaurs, 77
naming of, 213
pubis bone of, 70, 213
size of, 86
speed and agility of, 78, 221–22
tails of, 89
teeth of, 78–79, 95
Thescelosaurus, 245–46, *246,* 247, *247,* 251, 318
thighbone, *6*
thyreophorans
  ankylosaurs as, 235
  armor of, 180, 208
  genus list, 402
  in Jurassic Period, 335
  primitive thyreophorans, 221–25
  stegosaurs as, 229
  teeth of, 243
titanosaurs
  armor of, 208–9, 223
  carnosaurs and, 104–5
  in Cretaceous Period, 351, 352, 353
  eggs of, 294
  features of, 208
  genus list, 398–99
  as macronarians, 203, 205, 207–10
  nests of, 210
  as prey of tyrannosaurids, 123
Torosaurus, 284, 285, 287, *287*
Torvosaurus, 81, *91,* 92, *200,* 240, *342*
toys, 2
trace fossils
  of carnosaurs, 102
  of coelophysoids and ceratosaurs, 84–85
  dinosaur behavior and, 303
  formation of, 18, 19, 21
  of macronarians, 210
trackways. *See* footprints
Tree of Life, 50, *50,* 51–53, 56
Triassic Period
  geologic time and, 26
  Late Triassic mass extinction, 332–33
  map of world, 17, *17*
  Permo-Triassic mass

extinction, 325–26, *327,* 357
plants of, 345
recovery from mass extinction, 326–28
reptiles of, 329–30
Triceratops
  from baby to adult, *318*
  behavior of, 305
  brain of, *319*
  discovery of, 9
  frills of, 286
  herds and, 288
  illustrations of, *284, 308*
  male/female differences, 291
  nasal chambers of, *316*
  as prey of *Tyrannosaurus,* 121, 124, 129
  sexual selection and, *49*
  size of, 285, 287
  skeleton of, *289*
  Tyrannosaurus and, *290*
trilobites, 326, *326*
Troodon, 150, *157,* 160, 161, 245, 271, 296, 320
troodontids, 151, 159–61, 295, 384–85
Tsagantegia, 237
Tsintaosaurus, 262
Tuojiangosaurus, 230, 231, *231*
Tykoski, Ron, 86, *86*
type specimens, 43–44
tyrannosaurids
  albertosaurines, 124
  arms of, 123, *123,* 125
  carnosaurs and, 105
  as coelurosaurs, 109, 113, 118, 119, 131
  in Cretaceous Period, 353
  features of, 122–23
  genus list, 377
  habits of, 125–26
  origins of, 117–19
  ornithomimids' legs compared to, 134–35
  as pack-hunting dinosaurs, 106, 125
  prey of, 124–25, 289
  primitive species of, 124
  protofeathers of, 123–24
  scaly skin of, 115
  teeth of, 124
  young of, 126, 297, 298
tyrannosaurines, 377

tyrannosauroids
  cladogram for, 54, *54*
  early tyrannosauroids, 117, 120–22, 124, 125–26
  genus list, 376
  hadrosauroids and, 263, 267
Tyrannosaurus
  ankylosaurids and, 237
  brain of, 320
  coprolite of, 124
  dinosaur art and, 35
  discoveries about, 2
  eyes of, 122
  femur of, *300*
  habits of, 125
  hands of, 79
  illustrations of, *121, 127, 241, 299, 309, 344, 356*
  life cycle of, 298
  myths of *Stegosaurus* and, 229
  Ornithomimus compared to, 132, 134
  running capabilities of, 123
  as sauropod predators, 189
  size of, 124
  skeleton of, *120*
  speed of, 308, *309*
  Triceratops and, *290*
  young of, *128*
Tyrannosaurus rex
  coprolite of, 22, *22*
  fossils of, 30
  geologic time scale and, 27
  life cycle of, 300
  as scavenger, 124
  speed of, 309
  teeth of, 129
  young of, 126, 128
Tyrannotitan, 104

Unaysaurus, 180
Unenlagia, 155
unenlagiines, 155–56, 160, 382–83
Unquillosaurus, 155
Upchurch, Paul, 189, *189,* 191
Utahraptor, 158, *211, 238*

Valdosaurus, 251
variations, 42, 47
Velociraptor
  brain of, 317, *319*

feathers and, 2, 38
hands of, 79
hunting techniques of, 159
Protoceratops and, 159, 281, *282,* 283
size of, 151, 157, 158
skeleton of, *154*
specimens of, 10
speed of, 160–61
velociraptorines, 154, 156, 157–58, 383
vertebrates, evolution of, 56, *57,* 58–59
Vickaryous, Matthew, 236, 238
Vickers-Rich, Patricia, 249, *249*
volcanism, 325, 360, 361–62, 363
von Huene, Friedrich, 99, 109, 118, 119
von Meyer, Christian Erich Hermann, 176
von Reichenbach, Ernst Freiherr Stromer, 93
Vulcanodon, 187, 189

Walker, William, 94
Wallace, Alfred Russel, 47, 50, 51
Wannanosaurus, 269, 271
warm-blooded animals, 311–14, *312,* 318–20, 322, 363
Weishampel, David, 238, 254, 307
Wilson, Jeffrey A., 201, *201,* 208
wing-assisted incline running (WAIR), 149, 153, 154, 168
Witmer, Larry, 38, 191, 203, 217, 239
Wuerhosaurus, 232

Xiaosaurus, 216, 246, 273
Xiphactinus, 349

Yandusaurus, 221, 246, 273
Yangchuanosaurus, 100, *100,* 231
Yimenosaurus, 180
Yinlong, 122, 273

Zalmoxes, 252, 253
Zephyrosaurus, 246
Zuniceratops, 276, 277, 280, 281, *281,* 282, 285, 287
Zupaysaurus, 80, 81

Photo credits: page 2: photo by Michael Meskin, plastic dinosaurs courtesy of Mike Fredericks; page 4: courtesy of Thomas Holtz; page 5: courtesy of Luis Rey; page 6 (top): image #18103-f, photo by Thomson, American Museum of Natural History Library; page 6 (bottom): "Plot's Unrecognized Dinosaur Bone," 1676, Linda Hall Library of Science, Engineering & Technology; page 7: "Figuier's World Before the Deluge," 1867, Linda Hall Library of Science, Engineering & Technology; page 8: image #1265, "Dinner in the Iguanodon Model" © Natural History Museum, London; page 9 (top): from the Collections of the University of Pennsylvania Archives; page 9 (bottom): courtesy of Peabody Museum of Natural History, Yale University, New Haven, CT; page 10 (left): image #338695, photo by Schackelford, American Museum of Natural History Library; page 10 (right): © Peabody Museum of Natural History, Yale University, New Haven, CT; page 11: image courtesy of L. M. Witmer and Ohio University; page 13: Ingram Publishing/SuperStock; page 14 (top left): photo by D. W. Peterson, U.S. Geological Survey; pages 14 (top right), 15, 16 (bottom), 21, and 22 (bottom): courtesy of Thomas Holtz; page 14 (bottom): photo by J. P. Lockwood, U.S. Geological Survey; page 16 (top): *U.S. Geological Survey Bulletin* 1309; page 23: photo by W. B. Hamilton, U.S. Geological Survey; page 28 (bottom): "The Blue Marble," NASA: Visible Earth (http://visibleearth.nasa.gov); pages 29 (top and bottom) and 30: courtesy of Thomas Holtz; pages 31 and 33 (bottom): courtesy of Jason C. Poole; page 32: photo by J. S. Lucas, courtesy of Carnegie Museum of Natural History; page 37 (left and right): courtesy of Thomas Holtz; page 41 (top): courtesy of Hunt Institute for Botanical Documentation, Carnegie Mellon University, Pittsburgh, PA; page 41 (bottom left): The Metropolitan Museum of Art, purchase, Lila Acheson Wallace Gift, 1990 (1990.59.1), photo © 1990 The Metropolitan Museum of Art; page 41 (bottom middle): The Metropolitan Museum of Art, gift of Katherine Keyes, in memory of her father, Homer Eaton Keyes, 1938 (38.157), photo © The Metropolitan Museum of Art; page 41 (bottom right): The Metropolitan Museum of Art, gift of Florene M. Schoenborn, 1994 (1994.486), photo © The Metropolitan Museum of Art; page 43 (left and right): Corel Photos; page 46: Library of Congress, Prints and Photographs Division, reproduction #LC-DIG-ggbain-03485; page 50: "Haeckel's Tree of Life" (1866); page 51: PhotoDisc; page 56: IT Stock Free; page 300 (right): courtesy of Museum of the Rockies; page 312 (left and right): PhotoDisc; page 321: photo by Dr. Anusuya Chinsamy-Turan; page 365: photo by Michael Meskin.

Dr. Thomas R. Holtz, Jr.'s passion for paleo began when he was three years old and received two plastic dinosaurs—a *Tyrannosaurus rex* and a *"Brontosaurus"* (*Apatosaurus* these days)—as gifts. Tiny Tom was dumbfounded that the two wildly different-looking creatures could possibly be related, and thus began his lifelong obsession with phylogenetic taxonomy—and with *T. rex*.

Today, Dr. Holtz (self-proclaimed "King of the Dino Geeks") is recognized as one of the world's leading dinosaur phylogeneticists and experts on tyrannosaurs. In addition to his many scientific papers, he has been involved in the making of several documentaries, including the award-winning *Walking with Dinosaurs* and *When Dinosaurs Roamed America*. Dr. Holtz is the director of the Earth, Life, and Time program at the University of Maryland in College Park. To learn more about him, visit www.geol.umd.edu/~tholtz.

Luis V. Rey is a Spanish artist who resides in London. He received his MA in visual arts from the San Carlos Academy in Mexico.

A painter, sculptor, journalist, and author, Mr. Rey wrote and illustrated his first dinosaur book when he was twelve. His attention then turned to surrealism, fantasy, and science fiction. He returned to real science with a vengeance after becoming inspired by the Dinosaur Renaissance during the 1970s. Since then, he has become a full-time paleoartist, authoring books and collaborating on publications with some of the top paleontologists in the world. He recently swapped his brushes, acrylics, inks, canvases, and cardboards for the computer screen and digital painting techniques, where he has found a complete new world to discover. To learn more about him and to see much of his work, visit www.ndirect.co.uk/~luisrey.